ACCOUNT ROLLS
OF
UNIVERSITY COLLEGE, OXFORD

VOLUME I
1381/2–1470/1

Oxford Historical Society
NEW SERIES, VOL. XXXIX

ACCOUNT ROLLS OF UNIVERSITY COLLEGE, OXFORD

VOLUME I
1381/2–1470/1

Transcribed by
A. D. M. COX
Former Fellow and Archivist of University College
Edited by
R. H. DARWALL-SMITH
Archivist of University College

This volume commemorates
the 750th anniversary of the benefaction of
William of Durham, Founder of University College, Oxford

OXFORD HISTORICAL SOCIETY
MCMXCIX (*for* MCMXCVIII–MCMXCIX)

ISBN 0 904107 17 5

Typeset by Joshua Associates Ltd, Oxford
Printed in Great Britain by
Print Wright Ltd., Ipswich

PREFACE

This book constitutes the fulfilment of a promise made over forty years ago by David Cox, when the minutes of the General Purposes Committee of University College for 9 June 1954 note that 'Permission be given to Mr. Cox to publish some of the Bursars' Accounts'. Unfortunately, although he had transcribed all the accounts from 1381/2 to 1596/7 in his characteristically clear hand into four exercise books, he was never able to complete the project. In the intervening years his transcripts have been used in various works, such as A. B. Emden's great register of medieval members of the University and the *Victoria County History of Oxfordshire*, but that was all until in July 1993 I examined the exercise books in the archives. The books showed just how much Cox had done, and I therefore decided to complete the project. By then David Cox was very ill, and he died in 1994 unaware that work had begun afresh. At last, however, this first of two volumes will make his work available to a wider public in a year that marks the 750th anniversary of the benefaction of William of Durham, the founder of University College.

In the following pages the transcriptions of the accounts are largely Cox's; I have checked them all off against the originals, making a few small corrections and tidying up their presentation, which Cox would have done himself. The footnotes are partly mine and partly Cox's, the latter prefixed by [ADMC]. The Introduction is entirely my work, as are the glossary, appendices, and indexes.

I have received help from many different sources. First I am grateful to David Cox's widow, Geraldine, for agreeing to the project, which is in part intended to honour the memory of a much-respected Tutor and Fellow of University College. At University College I have been encouraged in my work by Gwynne Ovenstone and Alexander Murray. The College generously agreed to contribute towards the Oxford Historical Society's publication costs. Dr. L. G. Mitchell kindly allowed me to quote from his address at David Cox's memorial service. Dr. A. B. Cobban, Prof. P. D. A. Harvey, and Dr. C. M. Woolgar gave me much helpful advice on the wider university and college context for these accounts and advised on secondary literature. For passing on information about the accounts of other Oxford colleges I am very grateful to

Elizabeth Boardman, Christine Butler, Judith Curthoys, Caroline Dalton, Dr. V. H. H. Green, Prof. J. R. L. Highfield, Dr. John Jones and Mr. J. M. Kaye. Julian Munby helped unravel the topographical mysteries surrounding some of University College's Oxford estates. The Introduction, and the volume as a whole, have benefited greatly from the careful reading and generous advice of Alan Crossley, General Editor of the Oxford Historical Society. Finally I owe much to Peter Gilliver for tolerating my desertion of modern Oxford during much of my spare time in favour of medieval University College.

CONTENTS

A. D. M. COX (1913–1994)

This appreciation of David Cox is based, with permission, on an address given at his Memorial Service by Dr. L. G. Mitchell, Fellow and Tutor in Modern History of University College.

David became a Fellow of Univ. in 1939, beginning a tutorial association with the College of some forty-one years. Univ. was the centre of his working life, particularly the Radcliffe Quad, and very particularly the few yards from his rooms in Staircase 9 to the College Office. He felt deeply about Univ., more deeply perhaps than he publicly showed. Senior Tutor, Domestic Bursar, Recorder, Tutor for Admissions, Archivist, Vice-Master; this represents a record of dutiful service to the College. But so, too, do less well-publicised aspects of his life. His contributions to the *University College Record* are well known. What is less known is the amount of work that went into it. He gave me the folder of notes on which an article on William of Durham was written. Re-reading them, one can only be struck by a painstaking scholarship that made the finished product merely the tip of an iceberg of knowledge and information. David also compiled a personal index of all the medieval Fellows of Univ. So meticulous is this work that articles could be written about a number of them. Careful in scholarship and careful in administration, David handsomely repaid whatever benefits the College conferred on him.

It seemed to me that David represented the very best of pre-war Oxford. No quality assessments, no appraisals; and undergraduates were friends, not customers waving charters of rights. Above all, it was a world in which the tutorial was everything, and a Fellow of an Oxford College was a teacher or he was nothing. Many people have tried to describe a tutorial with David. All of them gave the impression of a kind of therapy; soothing to the spirit and very good for morale. He literally flattered people into learning. The worst he could say about an essay was that it was 'quite good'. 'Pretty good' and 'very good' were also known. A relaxed style should not, however, be taken as lack of care. David was no pushover. On one occasion, he was very struck by a passage in an undergraduate essay; so struck in fact that he got up, went to his bookshelves, took down the volume from which the passage had been copied, and went on reading until the undergraduate asked him to stop. David the double first, David the Prize Fellow of All Souls, could be short with the academic phoney.

Admittedly there were aspects of academic life that he never much cared for. Full of practical good sense, David had a deep distrust of the visionary. Academe probably needs both sorts of men. But if the visionary points to the horizon, David would probably be checking the compass. He spoke frequently in College Meetings, merely executing honestly what the College had decided to do. Feeling as many historians come to do, that man's capacity for creating mess is so well developed, that, if any institution is working reasonably well, the only thing to do is to leave it alone, David was of a conservative disposition. But when change came, as it did with a rush in the 60s and 70s, he uncomplainingly accepted it. It's hard to think of an occasion when a decision left him raw. When a meeting was over, it was over. It was, if you like, already in the archives. David liked gossip, but not the *odium theologicum* that seems to sustain so many academics. He was also not impressed by academic power brokers, bullies or those who find an emotional resource in committees. Like Ko-Ko in *The Mikado*, he would have had no trouble in compiling a little list of people who never would be missed. He was a modest man. Asking for early demobilization in 1945, he gave as his reason the idea that his services were 'not likely to have much bearing on the overthrow of Japan'.

Touching everything he did as tutor or administrator was a profound calm. David never lost his temper, never banged a table, never raised his voice. Calm in tutorials, with the tapping of a pipe, and then its filling and emptying, making the counterpoint to wise remarks. Calm in counsel, when problems were dealt with in terms of a one gin problem, a two gin problem, or, sometimes, a three gin problem. Calm in defusing a difficult situation with a remark of masterful irony or understatement. Calm, above all, in conquering a crippling illness that he made light of.

Where this sense of calm came from is hard to say, but it clearly sprang, to a large extent, from a profound self-knowledge. Perhaps all great mountaineers have this capacity. David learnt his craft while still an undergraduate at Hertford, climbing to the top of the Indian Institute to return a weathervane, or climbing the Radcliffe Camera to retrieve a flag that had appeared there to celebrate the accession of Edward VIII. And then the serious stuff. Towering peaks like Machupachare and terrible rock climbs like Craig yr Ysfa in Wales.

David was a natural choice for the editorship of the Alpine Journal and the Presidency of the Alpine Club. Perhaps the real image of David is to see him lighting his pipe near the summit of and in the silence of a great mountain. As he looked down on the world, everything must have acquired a sense of proportion that more earth-bound people cannot see. In those mountain silences, David acquired that strength and self-knowledge which allowed him to give a just weight to whatever he might find when he came down into the low country again. With his passing we have lost a trustee of Oxford's very best values. Warden Adams of All Souls, writing a reference for David's Fellowship application, referred to a man 'with no show but with a great deal of substance'. Everyone here will know what he meant.

INTRODUCTION

I UNIVERSITY COLLEGE IN THE MIDDLE AGES

University College, one of Oxford's three 13th century foundations, owes its origins to William of Durham, who had been a Regency Master at the University of Paris and Rector of Monkwearmouth, Co. Durham. He had also been elected Archbishop of Rouen, but the election had been challenged and never took effect.[1] In 1249, William died, leaving 310 marks (£206 13s 4d) to the University of Oxford to buy rents to support up to ten or eleven Masters of Arts to study Theology.[2] After some delay, during which the University did purchase some properties but unfortunately lent half of William's money to 'certain magnates of the realm',[3] it finally drew up statutes in 1280/1 to use what was left of William's money to set up a society of four Masters.

Compared with the magnificent foundation created by Walter de Merton the new College was very poorly endowed. Even the site of its first home remains uncertain: it was not until in 1332 that the College purchased Spicer Hall on the High Street (now the site of the central part of the Front Quadrangle). Before that date the most likely home for the College was either Brasenose Hall or Little University Hall next door to it (see pp. xx–xxi below).

The slow growth of the College over the next three centuries is well documented,[4] and needs no recapitulation here. However, to help understand the working of the rolls certain topics need to be

[1] The best modern accounts of William are A. D. M. Cox, 'William of Durham and the Archbishopric of Rouen', in *University College Record* (henceforth *UCR*), 1948/9, pp. 11–20, and 'Who was William of Durham?', in *UCR*, 1981, pp. 115–123.

[2] William's will is lost; the main evidence for his bequest comes from the first Statutes of the College, of 1280/1 (ref. **UC:GB1/L1/1**; all references are to the archives of University College unless otherwise indicated).

[3] *Quibusdam magnatibus terre* (from **UC:GB1/L1/1**). These magnates have tentatively been identified with some of Simon de Montfort's party, who were in Oxford several times between 1258 and 1263, and most notably for the Parliament of 1258 (see *VCH Oxon.* IV, pp. 13–14).

[4] The only major histories of University College are William Smith's magnificent, if chaotic, *Annals of University College,* of 1728, and W. Carr's *University College*, of 1902. Two more recent, but brief, accounts are A. Oswald, in *VCH Oxon.* III (1954), pp. 61–81 and Peter Bayley, *University College: A Guide and Brief History* (Oxford, 1992). From the *History of the University of Oxford*, *HUO* I, pp. 225–310, *HUO* II, pp. 485–539 and 581–708, and *HUO* III, pp. 1–69, 521–558, and 645–732 are especially relevant for this Introduction.

considered. First the name University College requires explanation. Early documents refer to 'The Master and Scholars of the Hall of the University of Oxford'.[5] By 1367/8, however, a deed (ref. **UC:E/B5/D/7**) refers to 'The Hall of Master William of Durham, usually called the Hall of the University of Oxford', and indeed the Bursars' Accounts, until 1547/8, call the College 'The College of Master William of Durham, commonly called the Great Hall of the University of Oxford'. Sometimes the latter part is given in its English version of 'Mickel Universitehall'. In 1560/1, however, the English version is given for the first time as 'University College', and its Charter of Incorporation in 1573 (ref. **UC:GB2/L3/1**) gives the College an official name of the 'College of the Great Hall of the University', with 'University College' being the name in common use. This style has remained unchanged to this day.

The greatest difference between medieval and modern University College was that, like many of the older Oxford Colleges, membership was open to Fellows only. Their number was never very large: the original four fellowships were increased by later endowments, but even by the 1590s numbers had scarcely reached double figures.[6] University was unusual in that many of the Fellows came from the north of England;[7] partly this reflected the northern connections of its founder, but also several Fellowships, such as those endowed by Walter Skirlaw, Bishop of Durham, or Henry Percy, Earl of Northumberland, were restricted to applicants from that region. The College's patron saint was that great Northern monk, St. Cuthbert.

The statutes of 1292 allowed the Fellows to admit others to the College, who would pay dues and observe its customs but were not actually members.[8] The Fellows took up this provision with alacrity, and throughout most of the period covered by the Account Rolls

[5] This form of words was used, for example, in **UC:E1/2D/1** or **UC:E/B5/D/6** (two deeds of 1317/8 and 1343). In 1320, a deed (ref. **UC:E1/2D/6**), refers to 'the Master and Scholars of the University of Oxford living and studying in the same or in England if it happens that the University of Oxford is moved' (*magistris et scolaribus universitatis Oxon' ibidem vel in Anglia si contigat universitatem Oxon' transferri commorantibus et studentibus*). Since there had already been migrations of the University (and there was to be one more, in the 1330s, to Stamford), this deed was clearly hedging its bets.

[6] By way of contrast, a wealthy College like Magdalen was given enough endowments to support, according to its first statutes of 1480, 40 Fellows, 30 Scholars, and a choir.

[7] See T. A. R. Evans, 'The Number, Origins and Careers of Scholars', *HUO* II, p. 518.

[8] No contemporary copy of the 1292 statutes survives, but later copies are in the University archives (ref. NED/Supra/Register A, B and C). The statutes are published in *Munimenta Academica* I, ed. H. Anstey (Rolls Ser. 1868), pp. 56–61.

several College rooms were rented to lodgers, who frequently outnumbered the Fellows themselves. Many are named in the rolls: some were Bachelors or Masters, using the College's facilities during their stay in Oxford; some were former Fellows who had resigned their posts after preferment but stayed on to study in Oxford; others were what we might today call undergraduates, preferring to reside in a College rather than an Academic Hall or private accommodation as they worked towards their first degree. One such was John Tiptoft, later Earl of Worcester, who stayed in the College with his tutor in the early 1440s.[9]

Although University College was not unique in admitting non-members it was unusual in accepting so many. For the period 1385/6–1495/6 A. B. Cobban counted at least 187, far more than any other College in Oxford or Cambridge, with the exception of King's Hall, Cambridge, a much larger foundation.[10] Large-scale renting of rooms to outsiders was evidently a deliberate policy, traceable to the 1390s. Until then Ludlow Hall, to the east of the central site of the College, was leased as a separate building, but was last mentioned in 1391. After a gap in the accounts the number of rooms rented in 1396/7 was 18, compared with only 7 in 1391, while the expected rent[11] from College rooms rose in that period to £9 8s 4d, compared with £5 13s from College rooms and Ludlow Hall together in 1391. The implication is that the College had incorporated Ludlow Hall into its main site, in order to rent out its rooms on a speculative basis and increase its annual income. Since the College was emerging at this time from a long and expensive legal battle over some of its estates[12] such a scheme makes excellent sense. By the 1470s the number of lodgers had decreased greatly, but in the early 15th century lodgers played a prominent part in the College and its finances.

Within so small a community they would have been a noticeable presence and, if not *de jure* members of the College, would have been almost *de facto* ones.[13] It is normal to call such tenants 'commoners', or

[9] See A. B. Cobban 'Colleges and Halls 1380–1500', *HUO* II, p. 620, for an analysis of the College's commoners.

[10] Cobban, *loc. cit.*; in his *Medieval English Universities* (Aldershot 1988), pp. 331–332, Cobban notes that the accounts of Oriel College for the years 1409–1415 and 1450–1482 only yielded about 30 commoners.

[11] The Latin word used here is *redditus*. See Section 4 below for discussion of the meaning.

[12] See Appendix II in Vol. II.

[13] A young nobleman like John Tiptoft, for example, lodging with his tutor, would certainly have been very conspicuous in the College.

commensales or *commorantes*; the Accounts, however, almost never use the former term,[14] although in 1430/1 eight pence received from the *socii et commorantes* was used to repair the altar vestments. Instead the section of the accounts relating to their rent payments almost always has a heading such as 'Room Rents' (e.g. *Redditus camerarum*). There is no doubt that these people were commoners in the sense most readily understood in medieval Oxford, in that they lived in the College, and, as the 1430/1 account hints, took part in its activities; it is just striking that the expected vocabulary is not used in the Accounts to record them.

It was not until the 16th century that University began to accept undergraduate commoners in the modern sense.[15] It has been suggested[16] that they first appeared in the early 1520s: much depends on the interpretation of the roll of 1519/20, which, instead of referring to rents from *camerae*, has rents from *cubicula* instead, and their rental has risen from between 13 and 20 shillings a year, from only one or two residents, to £3 17s, from twelve, six of them sharing three rooms. This could indeed be our first glimpse of undergraduates in University College, squeezed into rooms designed for one, but it could be nothing more than a change in vocabulary. However, undergraduates were certainly part of College life by the time of the University census of 1552, which assigns the College a Master, 7 Fellows and 17 *subgraduati.*[17]

In the later 16th century, the Accounts include evidence of steps taken to give undergraduates a more formal place in the life of the College: the Roll for 1563/4 includes the first mention of receipts for the admission of Commoners (*commensales*), and in the Roll for 1584/5 appear the first payments for Praelectors, or lecturers, in Greek, philosophy, logic, and theology, so that by this date University had in place a complete system for teaching and administering undergraduates.

The College had always employed servants, and the Accounts regularly record their payment. Although their functions are always given their names appear only infrequently. Throughout the period

[14] *Pace* A. Oswald in *VCH Oxon.* III, p. 63, who uses the terms *commensalis* or *commorans* without noting this anomaly.

[15] See J. McConica, 'Rise of the Undergraduate College', *HUO* III, pp. 1–68, for an account of this phenomenon in the University as a whole.

[16] By Carr, *op. cit.* p. 71, and D. Sturdy, 'Undergraduates in the Sixteenth Century', in *UCR*, 1991, pp. 63–65.

[17] See Carr, *op. cit.* pp. 82–83.

1381–1597 the College employed between four and six servants, who worked as manciple, butler, cook, subcook, barber, or laundress (the only woman who had regular dealings with the College).

In 1280 the first statutes of University College had provided for a Fellow to act as *procurator* or Bursar[18] with a stipend of 5s a year. His position was confirmed in the later statutes of 1292 and 1311,[19] and his salary doubled in 1292. Few details, however, are given on the type of accounts he was to submit: the 1292 statutes refer to a *computum rationabilem ac strictum, ut in aliis collegiis* ('a reasonable and accurate account, as in other colleges'), and the 1311 statutes to an account *de omnibus receptis et expensis* ('for all rents and expenses'). The 1292 statutes also declared that an account be made every year on Corpus Christi Day (the Thursday after Trinity Sunday), and that it be exhibited before the Chancellor. Bursars were supposed to pay up any arrears in their accounts at the end of their year in office, which was not always possible, so that in the 1478 statutes (ref. **UC:GB1/L1/4**) they were ordered to be responsible for this amount and to provide a bond as security.[20] This undoubtedly made the office all the more burdensome – a difficult problem when there were so few Fellows among whom to circulate it – and in 1567 the Vice-Chancellor had to ordain that any Fellow refusing to take up the post when elected would lose his stipends until he gave way.[21]

Normally a Fellow held the Bursarship for a year. Only a few held the post more than twice, sometimes in successive years, and only four were Bursars five times or more: John Huchenson and Ralph Cockey both five times, Robert Burton six times, and Thomas Benwell an extraordinary nine times. Yet almost every known Fellow of the College who stayed there for more than a year or two was Bursar at some stage. A notable exception was Richard Hindemersh, Fellow for most of the 1470s and 1480s, but never apparently Bursar.

The College buildings changed greatly during the 15th and 16th centuries. In 1381/2 University College comprised only Great

[18] The Accounts until 1470/1 call the Bursar the *procurator*. The Arrears Roll for that year calls him the 'Procurator or Bursar', and from 1472/3 onwards he is the Bursar.

[19] There is no contemporary copy of the 1311 statutes in the College's archives, but the University Archives' copy survives (ref. WPβ/1/10). This is edited in *Medieval Archives of the University of Oxford*, I, ed. H. E. Salter (OHS 70, 1917), pp. 84–86. On the 1292 statutes, see note 8 above.

[20] Carr *op. cit.*, pp. 70–71.

[21] Carr *op. cit.*, pp. 86–87. In the 17th century the problems of Bursarial debt grew even more serious (see A. D. M. Cox, 'The Bursar and the Beer', in *UCR*, 1977, pp. 136–141, for an account of one particular crisis), but this lies beyond our chronological scope.

University Hall, bought in 1332 when it was known as Spicer Hall. In the 1390s the adjacent Ludlow Hall was incorporated and during the first half of the 15th century a quadrangle was gradually erected to replace both this and the original Hall.[22] This first Front Quadrangle was only two-thirds the size of the present one, which was built between the 1630s and 1670s, and covers not only the site of this old quad, but also a house to the west acquired in 1559.

University College was one of the poorer foundations in Oxford. In 1420, a dispensation from Archbishop Chichele to Robert Burton, then Master, spoke of the College's dire condition: much debt, property in pledge, some tenements in ruins, and others in an irreparable state (*quid debitis quid impignoratis et quid tenementis ruinosis et quampluribus penitus subrutis irreparabilibus*).[23] In 1381/2 its expected income from rents amounted to £48 9s 7d, and by 1490/1 this had risen only to £76 5s 3½d. By contrast the expected rent of wealthy Magdalen College in 1490/1 was almost £700.[24] However, by the end of the sequence of Accounts, in 1596–7, University College's expected rental was a slightly more respectable £200 3s 9d.[25]

Much of this income came to the College from its estates in Oxford and elsewhere.[26] In Oxford itself, in theory, the Fellows could keep some sort of control on collecting their rents, although tenants accumulated bad debts with surprising frequency. Outside Oxford they appointed a tenant in each area to collect rents on their behalf, and then visited the estate themselves during the summer vacation to collect the money in person.[27] Expenses for such journeys are regularly noted in the rolls, their destinations less often. The 1420s and 1430s, however, are particularly informative. At that time, University College owned just two properties outside Oxford, namely the manor of Marks

[22] See Oswald, *op. cit.* pp. 71–73 on the first Front Quad of the College.

[23] This document is published in E. F. Jacob, *Reg. of Henry Chichele, Archbishop of Canterbury 1414–1443*, IV (Oxford, 1947), pp. 223–225.

[24] Figure taken from the list of receipts (called the *Indentura Magna*) of Magdalen College (Magd. Coll. Archives, ref. EP/187/4).

[25] Although (see Section 4) these figures do not show the exact rents which University, or Magdalen, were receiving in a given year, they do give a sense of scale both to University's slowly growing income and its comparative poverty.

[26] See Section 2 for a list of the estates of University College. On endowments in general, see T. H. Aston and R. J. Faith, 'Endowments of the University and Colleges to *circa* 1348', *HUO* I, pp. 265–311; T. A. R. Evans and R. J. Faith, 'College Estates and University Finances, 1350–1500', *HUO* II, pp. 635–708; and G. E. Aylmer, 'Economics and Finances of the College and University, c.1530–1640', *HUO* III, pp. 521–558.

[27] Two letters of attorney (of 1386 and 1432) to Fellows of the College to collect rents from their Holderness estate still survive (**UC:E1/3D/12–13**).

Hall, Essex, and land in Paull, near Hull. Visits were not made every year, but those which were made were usually to Essex, and only a handful to Paull (hardly surprising, perhaps, when the rent from Paull was only £3 12d a year).

One surviving document (ref. **UC:MA10/L2/1**) does shed light on one of these progresses and indeed on the difficulties which a solitary traveller might face. It is an affidavit signed by over a dozen inhabitants (including two priests) from the region near Marks Hall, which records that on 15 May 1426 Thomas Benwell, that most indefatigable of Bursars, appeared in the village of Good Easter (*Godestur*), Essex, with a sick horse, which he had bought in Oxford from one Thomas Smyght. An inhabitant of Good Easter, Edmund Smyght the Elder, examined the horse, and concluded (it is hard to know on what evidence) that the horse had not fallen ill due to any mistreatment on Benwell's part, but that it had been unwell for some time. The document provides food for thought regarding fifteenth century veterinary practice, and leaves us wondering whether Benwell obtained this affidavit so that he would not be out of pocket for the horse when he returned to Oxford.[28]

Nevertheless, the duty of visiting the College's most distant estates, which by 1500 included land in North Yorkshire and Northumberland, should not be seen as totally burdensome. Since many of the Fellows did have northern roots, as noted above, these journeys north would have given them a chance to see family and friends.

2 THE ESTATES OF UNIVERSITY COLLEGE

Like most older Oxford and Cambridge Colleges[29] University College largely survived on the revenue from its various estates. Much of the content of the Bursars' Accounts is concerned with this revenue, and with the administration of the College's various properties. From the later 15th century there also occur payments from obits and other cash funds.

The properties and payments fall into five groups, (a) Academic Halls in Oxford, (b) houses and gardens in Oxford, (c) properties outside Oxford, (d) quit rents on Oxford properties and (e) payments

[28] No reference was made to this incident in the Roll for 1426/7, indicating that not all events relating to the College and its affairs were recorded in its accounts.

[29] The exceptions being the monastic colleges (e.g Canterbury College, Oxford), which were sponsored by their orders, and King's Hall, Cambridge, which was funded almost entirely from the Royal Exchequer.

from obits and other sources. Only properties owned by the College between 1381/2 and 1596/7 are discussed here. In all cases, references to them in Salter's *Survey of Oxford*, and to deeds about them in the College's archives, are given.

(a) Academic Halls

University College is an unusual College in that it owned several Academic Halls, and rented them out as such,[30] and the accounts from the late 14th century and 15th show how much of its annual revenue the College expected to derive from its Halls. However, as Academic Halls began either to disappear or (as with, say, Magdalen Hall) expand into something much larger,[31] University's Halls were either rented afresh as private houses (like Drawda Hall and Stanton Hall), or their sites sold outright to other, newer, foundations (as with Maiden Hall or Brasenose Hall), until by 1511/2 it had no Halls left.[32]

University College had itself, to a degree, begun this latter process, for alongside the properties listed below were four other Halls, namely Spicer Hall (also known as Great University Hall), Rose Hall, White Hall, and Hart Hall, which, almost as soon as the College acquired them, were incorporated into its central site, and therefore never appear on the rolls. Deeds relating to these properties in the College's archives have been catalogued as **UC:E/A4** (Great University Hall; Salter Vol. I, p. 189), **UC:E/C1** (Rose Hall and White Hall; Salter Vol. I, pp. 254–255) and **UC:E/C2** (Hart Hall; Salter Vol. I, p. 254).

1 & 2. Little University Hall in Schools Street and Brasenose Hall. These two halls were acquired by Oxford University in c.1252/3 and c.1262, and thus, like Drawda Hall and 83–84 High Street below, were bought before the College's first statutes of 1280; that all four properties were transferred to the ownership of the College makes it almost certain that they were purchased with William of Durham's legacy. Little University Hall in Schools Street (so called to prevent confusion with Little University Hall in High Street) and Brasenose Hall remained in use as academic halls until 1508, when they were leased to the newly-founded Brasenose College (their sites now form part of Brasenose' Main Quadrangle). They last appear in the account of 1510/1.

[30] See A. B. Cobban, *Medieval English Universities*, p. 157.

[31] On the decline of the Academic Hall, see Cobban, *op. cit.*, pp. 158–160.

[32] Rather surprisingly it was not until 1515/16 that the section which recorded them was titled *Redditus scolarum* instead of *Redditus aularum et scolarum*.

Deeds relating to these Halls in the College's archives have been catalogued as **UC:E/A1** and **UC:E/A2** respectively (Salter Vol. I, pp. 67–69).

3. **Drawda Hall.** Drawda Hall appears to derive its unusual name (which undergoes many changes in orthography in the accounts) from William of Drogheda, who owned the property in the early 13th century, and was acquired by Oxford University in c.1255, almost certainly with William of Durham's money. 33 High Street now stands on its site. Drawda Hall was rented out as an Academic Hall at least until 1457/8,[33] by which time it may already have ceased to function as one. In 1455/6, it was leased to one John Flecher for 26s 8d, but in 1460/1, the first year in which Drawda Hall does not appear in the rolls, a rent of 26s 8d from John Flecher appears among the houses in the Oxford parish of St. Peter in the East, which suggests that the Bursar for that year had accepted that the property was never to be leased out as a Hall again. The house was finally sold to Magdalen College in 1884.

Deeds relating to this Hall in the College's archives have been catalogued as **UC:E/B1** (Salter Vol. I, pp. 136–137).

4. **St. Edward Hall (or Edward Hall).** St. Edward Hall lay to the north of what is now Oriel Square, between Oriel Street and King Edward Street. It was given to University College in 1307 and thereafter continued to function as an Academic Hall. By the 1480s, however, the site had fallen into disrepair (its appearances in the rolls are very sporadic by the 1470s), and it was sold in 1486 to Oriel College.

Deeds relating to this Hall in the College's archives have been catalogued as **UC:E/A3** (Salter Vol. I, p. 214).

5. **Maiden Hall.** Maiden Hall, like St. Edward Hall, was bought by the College in 1307. In 1389 it was sold to New College for an annual quit rent of 10 shillings. It probably lay to the south of Holywell Street.

Deeds relating to this Hall in the College's archives have been catalogued as **UC:E/B3** (Salter Vol. I, p. 149).

6. **Ludlow Hall.** Ludlow Hall was bought by the College in 1343, and used as an Academic Hall. It last appears in the Accounts in 1391,

[33] The roll of 1458/9 survives only in the extracts of William Smith (see below, pp. xxxiv–xxxvi), which do not list properties in detail; the roll of 1459/60 is lost.

after which it was incorporated into the main site of the College and its rooms rented out individually for greater profit (see p. xv above). In the 15th century it was demolished when the first Front Quad of the College was built. Ludlow Hall's site is now the eastern third of the College's present Front Quad.

Deeds relating to this Hall in the College's archives have been catalogued as **UC:E/B5** (Salter Vol. I, pp. 189–190).

7. **Stanton Hall.** Stanton Hall was bought by the College in 1357 and rented out as an Academic Hall until 1418/9. It was first rented out as a private building in 1420/1. In the 17th and 18th centuries it was the Three Tuns inn, which was demolished in the early 1840s to make way for the New Buildings.

Deeds relating to this Hall in the College's archives have been catalogued as **UC:E/A5** (Salter Vol. I, p. 188).

8. **Olifaunt Hall.** Olifaunt Hall, acquired by the College at an unknown date, was being leased by the early 1370s and appears on the early Bursars' Accounts as a Hall. Even by this date the building itself may already have been demolished, and from 1396/7 it was rented out only as a garden.

Olifaunt Hall lay on the south side of St. Mildred's Lane (now known as Brasenose Lane), to the west of Sheld Hall below. In 1463, Olifaunt Hall, along with Hampton Hall and Sekyll Hall (see below), was sold to Lincoln College and incorporated into the central site of that College.

Deeds relating to this Hall in the College's archives have been catalogued as **UC:E/D1** (Salter Vol. I, pp. 61–62; note that Salter is unsure whether it was ever an Academic Hall).

9. **Sheld Hall.**[34] Like Olifaunt Hall to its east Sheld Hall came into the College's possession at an unknown date, but was being leased in 1381/2. Likewise Sheld Hall was demolished, and, from 1436/7, was leased as a garden,[35] usually to the Principal of Brasenose Hall. It appears to have been sold to Brasenose College in 1508.

[34] This is the hall's usual English name. The accounts usually call it *aula scuti* (i.e. Shield Hall).

[35] The building may have been demolished much earlier. The expected rent from the garden in 1436/7 was 6s 8d, a rent which had been charged on the Hall since at least 1405/6 (the accounts for 1402/3–1404/5 are lost). In 1401/2 the rent was 10s and in 1400/1 20s, implying that the Hall was demolished at around this time.

Deeds relating to this Hall in the College's archives have been catalogued as **UC:E/D2** (Salter Vol. I, p. 61).

10. **St. Thomas (earlier Staple) Hall.** St. Thomas Hall was bought by University College in 1353, when it was known as Staple Hall (it had changed its name by 1381/2), and lay to the east of Sheld Hall above. It last appears in the accounts for 1481/2, after which it seems to have been leased to the Principal of Brasenose Hall and was sold to Brasenose College in 1508.

Deeds relating to this Hall in the College's archives have been catalogued as **UC:E/D3** (Salter Vol. I, pp. 60–61).

11. **Hampton Hall.** Hampton Hall was bought by University College in 1356. It was on the east side of Turl Street, to the north of Sekyll Hall below, and was sold, along with Sekyll Hall and the site of Olifaunt Hall, to Lincoln College in 1463.

Deeds relating to this Hall in the College's archives have been catalogued as **UC:E/D4** (Salter Vol. I, p. 51).

12. **Sekyll Hall.** Sekyll Hall was bought by University College in 1360, and lay to the south of Hampton Hall above. It was one of the three halls sold to Lincoln College in 1463.

Deeds relating to this Hall in the College's archives have been catalogued as **UC:E/D5** (Salter Vol. I, pp. 50–51).

13. **Little University Hall and the Cock on the Hoop.** These two adjoining properties, on the south side of the High Street, were bought by the College in 1400. The former was called 'Little University Hall on the High Street', to distinguish it from its namesake in Schools Street.

Little University Hall, the western property, was leased as an Academic Hall until 1476/7, but in 1478/9 a new rent of 26s 8d appears in the lists of houses in St. Peter in the East. In 1489/90 the *aula universitatis* is explicitly listed among the St. Peter's properties, and there it remained, the name eventually being dropped. In 1531 it was converted into lodgings for the Master of the College (on Loggan's 1675 engraving of the College it is the building to the left of the Front Quad).

The Cock on the Hoop was soon divided into two portions, which were leased out separately, the larger becoming known later as the Half Moon.

In 1716–1719 both Little University Hall and the Cock on the Hoop were replaced by the Radcliffe Quadrangle, although the function of Little University Hall was not forgotten: the eastern staircases of the new Quad were set aside for the Master's Lodgings until the late 1870s, when a separate building was erected for the Master.

Deeds relating to both buildings in the College's archives have been catalogued as **UC:E/B6** (Salter Vol. I, pp. 190–191).

(b) Houses and Gardens in Oxford

The College has owned private houses or gardens in Oxford since its foundation, and these took on an increasingly prominent role in its revenues as its Academic Halls were converted to other uses. Unfortunately their history is harder to trace in the Bursars' Accounts than that of the Academic Halls or the properties outside Oxford; very few are identified by location (the property on the north-east corner of Carfax being a notable exception), but instead by their tenant; they were not even arranged by parish until 1426/7. An appendix in Volume II will attempt to disentangle their history.

1. 83–84 **High Street (Parish: St. Peter in the East).** These, the first private houses to be owned by the College, were bought by the University in c.1269/70, almost certainly with William of Durham's money, and formally passed to the College in 1307. They were usually leased as two separate properties, but from 1825–1935 were treated as one (the lessee for some of this time being Frank Cooper, of Oxford Marmalade fame).

Deeds relating to these houses in the College's archives have been catalogued as **UC:E/B2** (Salter Vol. I, p. 193).

2. **The Goldsmith/Gonwardby Properties.** In the years 1358–1361, University College purchased various properties in Oxford from a certain John de Gonwardby. A defect in the title to those of the properties which Gonwardby had inherited from his mother, Joan Goldsmith, provoked a long legal dispute which was not resolved until 1391.[36]

The properties which came to University College in 1361 were as follows:

(i) *All Saints*: three neighbouring houses on the north side of the High Street, owned by the Goldsmith family since at least the

[36] See Appendix II in Vol. II for the College's dispute with Gonwardby's descendants.

early 13th century. The College leased the houses in several permutations, until all three properties were sold in 1772 to the City of Oxford to form part of the site of the Covered Market (Salter Vol. I, pp. 112–114).[37]

(ii) *St. Martins*: a shop on the north-east corner of Carfax. In the mid 13th century this shop was divided, and the south half was acquired by the Goldsmith family at an unknown date. In 1423 the College bought the northern half, and thenceforth leased the property as one. The shop was sold to the Paving Commissioners in 1787 and subsequently demolished (Salter Vol. I, pp. 1–3).

(iii) *Grandpont*: The Goldsmith/Gonwardby lands included several fields and small islands in the Thames, called Friars Mead, Kings Mead, Aldrichside (or Aldrish), Ireland,[38] and University Mead. At several stages in the late 14th century and early 15th all these fields were leased together with one or more of the All Saints houses. Various parts of the fields were later sold: Ireland, for example, was sold to the Commissioners building Folly Bridge in the 1824 (not in Salter).

(iv) *Fields behind Osney*. These lands bordered on the Thames, and are usually described as being 'behind Osney' in the deeds (not in Salter).

(v) *St. Peter le Bailey*: A house on the north side of Sewy Street (now Shoe Lane). Although the exact topography of this area was never completely established by Salter, the later history of this property shows that it lay on the north side of the street, and, having been a garden for many years, was leased in the 19th century to the Clarendon Hotel for use as a stable, until it was sold to the hotel in 1905.

(vi) *St. Giles*: John de Gonwardby sold various lands in the St. Giles area, mostly small pieces of field described in great detail in **UC:E2/5/2D/17**, which were all re-assigned during the enclosure of the parish in 1832. However, the lands also included what is now the north side of Little Clarendon

[37] Records concerning the sale of the houses to the City are also preserved in the Oxford City Archives (ref. D.3.10[11–12]).

[38] Not to be confused with Irish Mead below.

Street, the present Old Parsonage Hotel, and a house opposite the latter (Salter Vol. II, pp. 206–207).

(vii) *St. Thomas*: A garden (later a house) on the site of what is now the corner between Park End Street and the west side of Tidmarsh Lane. It was sold by the College to the Paving Commissioners in 1772 or 1773 (not in Salter).[39]

Of the above properties, (i)–(v) all descended to John de Gonwardby from his mother's side, and were therefore at the centre of the College's long battle with his heirs; (vi)–(vii), having descended to him via his paternal ancestors, were free of any claim from John's heirs.

Deeds of all these properties in the College's archives have been catalogued as **UC:E2**.

3. Some Schools in Schools Street (Parish: St. Mary the Virgin). These schools in Schools Street, almost opposite Brasenose Hall and Little University Hall, were given to the College in 1399, some adjoining property being added in 1439. Until 1543/4, the property was leased out as teaching rooms, sometimes to a single tenant, at other times to several. From 1545/6–1549/50 no rents were collected from them, but one of 12d is recorded in 1551/2. They were then omitted in the accounts until 1560/1, when the College's properties were listed in full again, and a rent of 12d was collected from 'a garden on Schools Street'. The garden continued to be rented until 1736, when it was sold to make way for the construction of the Radcliffe Camera.

Deeds relating to this property in the College's archives have been catalogued as **UC:E/A7** (Salter Vol. I, p. 73).

4. Wakeman's Tenement (Parish: All Saints). The reversion on this property (now 9 High Street) was sold to the College in 1401, and the College's earliest extant lease of it dates from 1417. In the late 1420s, it was the subject of a dispute between the College and Osney Abbey, which successfully claimed an annual quit rent of 6s 8d.

This property was sold in 1542 for £6; deeds relating to it in the College's archives have been catalogued as **UC:E/E1** (Salter Vol. I, pp. 107–109).[40]

[39] Information supplied by Julian Munby.

[40] Three deeds about members of the Aurifaber (or Goldsmith) family which Salter quotes here are all forgeries, probably made in the 1420s during the dispute with the Abbot of Osney (see R. H. Darwall-Smith, 'Medieval Skulduggery? Some Forged Deeds from the Archives' in *UCR*, 1996, pp. 58–69).

5. A moiety of the manor of Eastwick, normally known as Eastwick Farm (classed as 'Suburbs and Fields'). University College acquired a moiety of the manor of Eastwick in 1527/8, and rent from it seems to appear in the roll for this year.[41] The property was leased out as a whole, and became known as Eastwick Farm. It lies to the south of the city, in Grandpont, on both sides of the Abingdon Road. Some of its lands are now used by the College as playing fields.

Deeds relating to Eastwick Farm in the College's archives have been catalogued as **UC:E/H1** (not in Salter).

6. A house to the west of Great University Hall (Parish: St. Mary the Virgin). This property, which never seems to have had a name, was owned by Studley Priory and acquired at its dissolution by Richard Gunter. In 1559 Gunter gave it to University College in exchange for land in Merton, Oxfordshire (see no. 5 in the list of non-Oxford properties below). In the 17th century the house was demolished, and the west side of the present Front Quad built on the site.

Deeds relating to this house in the College's archives have been catalogued as **UC:E/A7** (Salter Vol. I, p. 189).

7. 49–51 St. Giles, including the Eagle and Child Inn (classed as 'Suburbs and Fields'). In 1565/6 Thomas Gold bequeathed these properties to his son John, on condition that, if John chose to sell them, he should do so to University College. Between 1565 and 1572/3 John Gold did indeed sell them to the College, and they first appear in the rolls in 1572/3.

Deeds relating to these houses in the College's archives have been catalogued as **UC:E/G1** (Salter Vol. II, p. 210; Salter appears not to have known the above information).

8. Irish Mead, Grandpont (classed as 'Suburbs and Fields'). Irish Mead[42] adjoins some of the lands of Eastwick Farm above. In 1571 Brasenose College, which still held the sites of Brasenose Hall and Little University Hall (see above) from University College on a lease of 92 years from 1508, leased Irish Mead to University in lieu of rent, so that University could sublet. The new field first appeared on the

[41] That year's rent for the suburbs and fields of Oxford rose from £3 13s 8d to £10 10s 4d, almost certainly because of the new property.

[42] Not to be confused with Ireland Mead above.

1574/5 account. When the 1508 lease was expiring (the copy of the relevant deed in the College archives is undated), University agreed to cede all title to the two halls in return for the outright ownership of Irish Mead.

Deeds relating to this field in the College's archives have been catalogued as **UC:E/H2** (not in Salter).

9. The Crown Inn (Parish: St. Martin) and related fields near Osney. The Crown Inn is in Cornmarket Street. In 1567 the College bought the reversion, together with that of the buildings immediately around it and some fields near Osney. The College was in possession by 1581,[43] although the first rents are not recorded in the accounts until 1586/7. The Crown Inn and surrounding buildings were sold in 1828.

Deeds relating to these properties in the College's archives have been catalogued as **UC:E/F1** (Salter Vol. II, pp. 151–154).

(c) Properties outside Oxford

Although the College owned property outside Oxford from the 1320s it took over two centuries to accumulate outlying estates to match its Oxford estates in value.

1. Lands in Paull, near Hull, in Holderness. The College's first property outside Oxford was some fields at Paull,[44] given to the College in 1320 by Philip Ingleberd (also known as Philip Beverley), Rector of the nearby parish of Keyingham. William Smith[45] rather sourly commented that all or most of this property had been swallowed up by the Humber; it nevertheless yielded an income of sorts until sold in 1528/9 to John Lambert, Vice-Chancellor of the Duchy of Lancaster for £51.[46] Lambert sold it the following year to St. John's College, Cambridge, which retained it for several centuries.

Deeds relating to the Paull estate in the College's archives have been catalogued as **UC:E1**.

2. The manor of Marks Hall, Essex. Marks Hall, north-west of Chelmsford, is the only manor which the College owned in the Middle

[43] Salter (*loc. cit.*) thought that the property was in the College's possession by 1570.
[44] Paull is almost always referred to in the accounts under its Latinised name of *Pagula*.
[45] Smith, *Annals*, p. 169.
[46] This deed is now in the archives of St. John's College, Cambridge (reference D62.104; information provided by Dr. M. Underwood).

Ages. It was given in 1403 by Walter Skirlaw, Bishop of Durham, who may once have been a Fellow, for the maintenance of three Fellows.[47] The first rent from Essex appears on the roll of 1406/7.

Deeds relating to the manor in the College's archives are to be catalogued as **UC:E3**.

3. **The rectory of Arncliffe, Yorkshire.** Arncliffe is a remote village in the north Yorkshire Dales, about 20 miles north of Skipton. Its rectory was given to the College in 1443 by Henry Percy, Earl of Northumberland, for the maintenance of three Fellows, apparently in response to an appeal from the University for his help.[48] Although the roll of 1444/5 notes a payment of 26s 8d for Master William Sharp 'for the ratification of the parish church of Arncliffe (*pro ratificatione ecclesie paroch' de Arnecliffe*), no rents from it appear until 1452/3.

Deeds relating to the rectory in the College's archives are to be catalogued as **UC:E4**.

4. **Various lands in Newcastle-upon-Tyne.** A collection of properties in Newcastle was given to the College in 1447 by Alice de Bellasys. The exact sites of these places remain uncertain. The first rent from Newcastle appears on the roll of 1450/1, but until 1473/4 the benefits of this gift were rather cancelled out by a large annuity paid to Alice during her lifetime.

Deeds relating to these lands in the College's archives are to be catalogued as **UC:E5**.

5. **Land at Merton, Oxfordshire.** Merton lies about six miles north-east of Oxford. Some land here was acquired by the College in 1505 or 1506 (rent from it first appears in the roll of 1506/7; the 1505/6 roll is lost). In 1559 the land was given to Richard Gunter in exchange for the house to the west of the old Front Quad (see no. 6 in the list of Oxford houses above).

Only two relevant deeds, of 1413 and 1498, survive in the College's archives (no doubt the others were given to Gunter); these have been catalogued as **UC:E/A7/D2/1–2**.

6. **Land at Hailey, Oxfordshire.** Hailey is on the outskirts of Witney, in the west of Oxfordshire. Some fields here called Great Norcroft, Little Norcroft and Losingrove, as well as some land in the

[47] See Carr, *op. cit.* p. 58.
[48] See Carr, *op. cit.* p. 62.

common fields of the village, were acquired by the College in 1540/1, and sold only in 1920. Hailey is named in the roll of 1542/3, but the rolls for the two previous years are lost.

Deeds relating to this land in the College's archives have been catalogued as **UC:E6**.

7. Land at Handborough, Oxfordshire. Handborough lies between Oxford and Witney. The College bought some land there in the 1520s or 1530s, when the accounts give no details of individual properties. The property is first named in the 1542/3 account, where it is described as 'our tenement near the bridge of Hanborough' (*Tenemento nostro iuxta pontem Hanborowe*), and last appears in 1566/7, after which it was almost certainly sold. The title deeds were transferred at this time, and only a bond of 1551 survives in the College's archives (catalogued as **UC:E7**).

8. Property at Headington, Oxfordshire. From 1542/3–1567/8, the Account Rolls include income from a property in Headington, on the edge of Oxford itself. The 1542/3 roll describes the property as a tenement, but no other details are given. Presumably, as with the Handborough property, it was acquired in the 1520s or 1530s, and sold in the late 1560s. No deeds on the Headington property survive in the archives, and these entries in the accounts are the only evidence that the College owned land here.

9. Lands in Waterstock and the Blandford Arms at Woodstock, Oxfordshire. Waterstock lies just north-east of Oxford, and Woodstock to the north-west. Land in Waterstock, and a house in Woodstock which later became the Blandford Arms at 3–5 Market Street,[49] were given to University College in 1584 by Sir Simon Perrot (or Parrot). Rents from these properties first appear in the roll of 1585/6.[50]

Deeds relating to these properties in the College's archives are to be catalogued as **UC:E8**.

(d) Quit Rents, mostly from Oxford

University College sold several of its Academic Halls to other Colleges in return for annual quit rents. The College had also been receiving

[49] See *VCH Oxon*. XII, pp. 347–8 for this property, now demolished.

[50] The roll for 1584/5, although not naming properties, has a noticeably larger total for 'rents from distant parts', presumably because of the rents from these new properties.

quit rents on other places. No documents about them exist in the archives, but Salter's *Survey of Oxford* identifies some of them.

1. **A quit rent of 2s 2d (or 2s 6d) from Canterbury College on Silver Hall.** This rent appears on the 1381/2 roll and until the middle of 1543/4. No deeds in the archives mention Silver Hall, nor does Salter, but it could have been part of the central site of Canterbury College.

2. **Quit rents of 20d and 14d from Godstow Abbey.** Quit rents for these amounts were paid by Godstow Abbey on properties identified respectively as 'a shop opposite the gate of St. Frideswide' and 'a garden once occupied by Thomas Maister [or Master]' from 1401/2 and 1434/5 until 1474/5, when both entries cease to appear. Thomas Maister's house cannot be identified; as for the shop opposite the gate of St. Frideswide, Salter's maps do not offer any obvious candidates, although in Vol. II, p. 77 he mentions a rent of 6d a year from a house on the west side of St. Aldates Street, south of the church.

3. **A quit rent of 8s, paid latterly by All Souls' College.** This rent was paid on a property in St. Mary the Virgin parish, Oxford, which is now part of the site of All Souls' College (Salter Vol. I, pp. 130–131). The quit rent had been paid to University by the properties' several owners for many years (although it is not specifically identified as such in the Bursars' Accounts until 1426/7). In 1438 Roger Skibbow, the then owner, sold it to All Souls' College which took over payment of the quit rent, which was still being paid in 1596/7.

4. **Quit rents of 5s and 8s 10½d, also latterly paid by All Souls' College.** These rents were paid on a property in St. Peter le Bailey parish, Oxford, on the site of 30 Queen Street (see Salter II, pp. 138–139). Salter shows that it had never been owned by University, but from at least 1396/7 a rent from it can be traced in the accounts, paid from 1399/1400 by John Sprunt. Sprunt, and later his heirs, paid rents to the College until 1433/4. In 1439/40, after a gap, quit rents were paid by All Souls' College (according to Salter, the property had been given to Humphrey, Earl of Stafford, in 1433, who gave it to Archbishop Chichele in 1438 for his new College). However, unlike the preceding quit rent, these rents cease to appear in accounts after 1484/5.[51]

[51] This was the last roll to record rents under the old system, which listed all uncollected rents in full (see Section 4 below). According to these lists this pair of quit rents had not been collected for years. Their disappearance therefore seems an acceptance of a *fait accompli.*

5. A quit rent of 4s, paid latterly by St. Bernard's College. The property on which this rent was paid was once a garden in St. Mary Magdalen parish, Oxford, just north of the church on the east side of St. Giles (see Salter Vol. II, p. 200). It appears to have been owned by University, and rented out for 20d in the early rolls (although no deeds about it survive in the archives). From 1435/6, however, it was rented to the 'White Monks' (i.e. to St. Bernard's College) for 4s, and from 1439/40 this amount was included among the quit rents. It ceased to be paid from 1543/4.

6. A quit rent of 6s 8d from Osney Abbey. A quit rent on a shop in St. Martin's parish, Oxford, can be traced back to 1428/9, and from 1439/40 it was paid by Osney Abbey. Osney Abbey owned several shops on the west side of Cornmarket Street in the parish (see Salter Vol. II, pp. 148 and 155–156), but it is not certain which one yielded this rent.

(e) Obits and annuities from other sources

From the later 15th century, the account rolls start to include records of extra payments to the Fellows, mainly in return for obits, yearly masses said for the donors. These yearly payments continued to be made even after the Reformation, when such services were banned; presumably the Fellows continued to receive the money without holding the service.

1. An obit from John Crosby, died 1477. John Crosby had rented rooms at University College in the 1440s before becoming a Fellow of Lincoln College. In 1482 his executors gave the College a sum of £40, of which £10 was to be reserved for a mass to be said yearly for Crosby for the next 20 years, when payments were to be made to the Master and any Fellows attending (**UC:BE8/L1/1**). The accounts for 1480/1 notes a payment of £20 from his will, and the first payments for obits appear in 1484/5. The payment last appears in 1507/8.

2. An obit for Anne, Countess of Warwick, died 1492. In February 1493, Henry VII gave the College £40 to say a requiem mass once a year in memory of Anne, Countess of Warwick (the widow of Warwick the Kingmaker), for the next 60 years, at which 10s was to be divided among all participants (**UC:BE9/L1/1**). Records of the payment first appear in 1493/4 and it is still recorded well into the 17th century.

3. An obit for John Barnaby, d. 1517/8. Barnaby was a Fellow and latterly a lodger in 1504/5–1509/10, and then moved to a London parish. He bequeathed £20 to University College for an annual requiem, the sum to go to Lincoln College if the conditions were not acceptable. They clearly were: payments for the obit were recorded from 1524/5 into the 17th century.

4. An obit for George Staveley, fl. 1524. In August 1524, George Staveley gave £50 to University College, in order that a requiem was said in his memory each year, at which 24s 8d was to be distributed among the Master and Fellows (**UC:BE10/L1/1**). This payment is first recorded in 1529/30 (although the rolls for the two previous years are missing or damaged), and, like the previous two obits, is still being paid in the 17th century.

5. The benefaction of William Holcot, 1573. In 1573, William Holcot left £20 each to University College and to the Queen's College, to be spent as commons for the Fellows (**UC:BE11/W1/1**), on condition that at each College daily at dinner the following response is made:

V: Lyft upp youre hartes.
R: We lift them upp unto ye lorde.
V: Lett us geve thankes to ye lord oure god for Williame Holcotte.
R: Yt is meete and right soe to doe.

It is not known if the College obeyed this injunction, but payments from Holcot's fund appear in the accounts between 1577/8 and 1587/8.

6. The benefaction of William Hearne, 1580. In 1580, William Hearne left money with the Clothworkers' Guild in London to pay £5 a year each to University College and Peterhouse College, Cambridge, no doubt as being the oldest Colleges in either University. Records of this payment first appear in the roll of 1587/8, and continue in the following century.[52]

52 However a document of 1703 in the College archives, **UC:BE12/L1/1**, suggests that the payment had been allowed to lapse by that date.

3 THE APPEARANCE OF THE ACCOUNTS, AND THE ROLE OF WILLIAM SMITH

Records of 185 Bursars' Accounts for University College for the years 1381/2–1596/7 survive. All (except for a few from the later 16th century[53] on large parchment sheets) are on parchment rolls in the Chancery style, usually comprising two membranes, written on both sides. Sometimes there is a clear distinction between a 'credit' side and a 'debit' side; more usually the break occurs merely when the writer reached the end of the membrane, and had to turn over.

The rolls are in a wide variety of hands, which suggests that they were usually written out by the Bursar himself.[54] From 1406/7 the roll is signed at the bottom by the Chancellor, his Official, or (by the end of the 16th century) the Vice-Chancellor. On the whole the accounts are set out clearly, being divided into obvious sections, usually with headings, and the handwriting is mostly fairly neat. The manner of their composition shows that they were written at the end of the year, rather than compiled piecemeal during it.[55] Section 6 shows that other Colleges (such as Magdalen) kept duplicate sets of some accounts; University appears not to have done this, although there are two years (1476/7 and 1508/9) for which two copies of the account survive.

The survival rate of the accounts is good. From the whole 215-year span of the accounts there are only 39 years for which there is no trace of any roll (a survival rate of over 80%), and ten more years for which rolls are lost, but were extant in c.1700 when notes were made from them by William Smith.[56] The longest continuous gap in the accounts is of only seven years, from 1497/8–1503/4. Of the extant rolls, although a few have been damaged by damp and are now very hard to read,[57] most remain in fair condition and for the most part legible.

No discussion of the Bursars' Accounts, however, or indeed of any of the medieval archives of University College, would be complete without noting the contribution made to their organisation and

[53] Those for 1570/1, 1575/6, 1576/7, 1577/8, 1578/9, 1580/1, 1583/4, and 1586/7.

[54] Note, however, that the rolls of 1479/80–1484/5 are all written in the same hand, although there were six different Bursars. It is not known why this happened.

[55] None of the Bursars' working papers are preserved although an account from 1436/7 might have been part of them (see p. xl below).

[56] Appendix I in Vol. II lists those years for which no roll survives, or for which we only have Smith's extracts.

[57] The worst examples are the extant rolls from 1450/1–1458/9, where over half their texts are now illegible. This suggests that, at some date since 1700, these rolls were ruined by damp.

preservation by William Smith. Smith (1651–1734) had matriculated at the College in 1668, and was a Fellow from 1675 to 1704, when he married and took up a College living at Melsonby in Yorkshire. In the late 1690s he began to organise, number and transcribe or calendar all the documents then in the archives. His work appears to have been completed before he left for Melsonby, and the results are preserved in eleven manuscript volumes.

Smith's numbering of the documents was based on his physical arrangement of individual items in bundles (*fascicula*) which were in turn stored in boxes (*Pyxides*), so that his references were along the lines of 'Pyx F fasc. 2 no. 4'.[58] He usually transcribed title deeds in full, although tending to summarise deeds of properties outside Oxford. As for letters, receipts, and other documents, he sometimes copied them out in full, sometimes summarised.

Volume VIII of Smith's transcripts is devoted to the Bursar's Accounts. He never transcribed a roll in full, but noted the date, the name of the Bursar, and the general totals on the credit and debit side. He sometimes commented on the size and condition of documents, and sometimes noted difficulties in dating, or working out where a gap in the sequence occurs.[59] Any extra information in them was included as fancy took him: for example he almost always took an interest in room rents, payments to Fellows, and repairs to the College, and frequently quotes these sections in full. Other entries, especially those concerning the Colleges' estates, tended only to be included if a particular property or tenant represented a first appearance in the series, or if there was something unusual about them. The earliest rolls are described in great detail; however, as he went through the sequence, Smith made fewer and fewer extracts, as if he was losing interest. The results, therefore, are too unsystematic to be considered proper summaries.

In spite of these omissions Smith's work remains invaluable. Ten rolls which he thus summarised (see Appendix I) are now missing, so that his extracts now provide the only evidence for their contents. In several other instances, although a roll has survived, its legibility has

[58] Since Smith's day no further listing of the College's archives took place until the 1990s; it then proved impossible to relate the 300-year backlog of records to Smith's system, so a new system was created, with new references for the older documents. A concordance table is on pp. liv–lvi below.

[59] Many of Smith's notes on the rolls are included in this edition. Whether or not ADMC or I have necessarily agreed with his conclusions, readers may appreciate a third opinion on some of the more complex questions.

deteriorated so much that Smith's evidence is crucial. Even for rolls which are largely well-preserved Smith frequently supplies an important lost word or total. Unfortunately Smith extracted this information at some cost to the documents, on occasions daubing some text with gall to bring out the letters. This method certainly worked for him, but has left the relevant portions almost illegible (see the Rents section from 1414/15, for example).

Extensive comparison of Smith's other transcripts with extant documents in the College archives confirms a very high standard of accuracy on his part, with an unusually good understanding of palaeography for his period.[60] In this edition, therefore, wherever Smith can supply missing material, his extracts are given exactly as he wrote them. The fate of the College's accounts before 1381/2 is unknown. Injunctions on the keeping of accounts in the 1280 and 1292 statutes make it likely that some kind of account was kept, presumably in roll form. Smith, however, made no note of any accounts earlier than those for 1381/2, so presumably they were not preserved even in his time.

Some other notes on the Account Rolls survive in the papers of Antony Wood in the Bodleian Library (ref. MS Wood F28). These comprise a few pages, in which Wood listed the names of Fellows, and sometimes occupiers of College rooms, usually giving the date of the relevant roll. He gave no other information, and thus there is next to nothing here which is not in Smith's fuller notes. Wood's notes suggest that he inspected the rolls himself, and may have done so before Smith began his calendaring, but they also show that the rolls missing in Smith's day were lost before Wood examined the collection.

4 THE CONTENTS OF THE BURSARS' ACCOUNTS

The Bursars' Accounts of University College cover all aspects of the College's financial transactions, both income and expenditure, both domestic and estate, for its financial year. Although the 1292 statutes stated that the College's accounts were to be ratified on Corpus Christi Day the dates given on the rolls varies greatly over the 200 years of the sequence. Until 1384 the rolls began at Michaelmas, but from 1384–1447 and again from 1472–1483 they usually start at Pentecost

[60] The few occasions when ADMC or I disagree with Smith mostly concern unusual proper names.

(although the rolls for 1448–1472 are only dated by regnal year it is assumed that these also ran from one Pentecost to the next). From 1483–1507 the starting date is Trinity or Ascensiontide, and in 1507–1527 it is St. George's Day. From 1529–1588 an exact day of the month (usually in April), without any apparent link to a festival, is chosen, and for the last few rolls only a calendar year is given. Occasionally a roll was compiled for only part of a year,[61] and there are two years (1476/7 and 1508/9) when there are two copies of the same set of accounts.

The earliest rolls are dated by regnal year only; from 1483/4 they include the calendar year as well. The dating of one roll, that of 1482/3, is of especial interest: it records the financial year as starting in Pentecost 22 Edward IV (26 May 1482), but leaves a blank where the concluding date should be. In 1483 Pentecost fell on 18 May, in the middle of the short reign of Edward V. Evidently that year's Bursar was not sure whether Edward V or Richard III was King, and therefore decided not to write anything at all.

The basic layout of the Bursars' Accounts remained strikingly constant over 200 years (indeed it remained so until 1882, when all Oxford Colleges were ordered by Parliamentary Commissioners to keep their accounts in the same way),[62] as can be seen from the following schematic guide.

CREDIT SECTION

(1) Until 1485/6 the rolls opened with arrears (*arreragia*) on College property from the previous year, listed in full. 'Unpaid rents' might be a better translation of *arreragia*, because this section records rents which had not yet been paid by the College's tenants. Until 1436/7 they were arranged by regnal year; after that date they were sorted into types of property (private houses, Halls, schools, and rooms). There was almost always a total of arrears at the end. From 1485/6 some totals of arrears are given, without naming individual properties, and they cease altogether after 1556/7.

(2) There follow lists of *Redditus* from College properties. For the first hundred or so years of the Accounts 'Rents' meant the sums expected from the College's properties and rooms rather than those

[61] Such as in 1391, 1392, 1463, and 1518–1519.

[62] For the circumstances which led to this change, see M. J. Jones, 'Accounting Revolution at Oxford in 1882', in *Accounting and Business Research*, Vol. 22 no. 86 (1992), pp. 125–132.

actually paid. The earliest rolls arranged these according to tenements, academic halls, and quit rents, each section with its own subtotal; from 1426/7, however, the tenements were divided into separate sections for each Oxford city parish, followed by one for 'the suburbs and fields of Oxford' (*de suburbiis et campis Oxon'*) and another for 'distant parts' (*de partibus remotis*), covering all properties outside Oxford city, irrespective of geography (this method of grouping properties was unchanged until 1882). There was usually a grand total of all rents.

Except for the years 1521/2–1539/40, 1547/8–1558/9, 1561/2, and 1584/5 College properties were listed individually; in the case of Oxford city properties tenants were almost always named, elsewhere only the chief tenant, if any (although the rolls for 1477/8–1484/5 named all the tenants of the manor of Marks Hall in Essex).[63]

(3) There is sometimes a section for miscellaneous income, such as one-off payments to the College.

(4) From 1450/1 there are references to money paid into, or received from, a chest (*cista*). By the mid 16th century this appears to refer to money left over in the College Treasury from previous years.

(5) The Credit section ends with a 'Total of all items charged' (*Summa omnium oneratorum*).

DEBIT SECTION

(1) Until 1485/6 this section opened with a list of Allowances (*Allocaciones*) for unpaid College income. In many cases the list of one year is identical with the *Arreragia* list of the next (this includes the change in layout in 1436/7). After 1485/6, although the *Arreragia* section disappeared, the *Allocaciones* section remained, but comprised only a list of money not yet collected from properties for that year. From 1516/17 only the total sum was given, and even this was dropped in 1556/7.

[63] In 1424/5–1441/2 there are regular sections for properties 'in hand' (*in manu Collegii*), which imply that some properties were not rented out that year (perhaps because they needed repair), and for the rolls for 1436/7–1437/8 there is a section for 'in dispute' (*in briga*), which seems to refer to instances in which the College was taking action on tenants in default of their rent.

(2) Until 1411/12 there are weekly accounts of Fellows' Commons, battels, and daily allowances, showing how many Fellows were in residence and how much they were paid. Yearly summaries only were given until 1521/2, when termly totals were provided.

(3) Repairs on College property. Until 1391/2 these were listed in full detail; from then until 1423/4 only yearly totals were given, and thereafter subtotals for work on each house (where applicable) and on each part of the College itself. More detailed accounts reappear intermittently from 1569/70.

(4) Other payments such as travelling expenses. These were listed in varying detail, similar to the repairs costs.

(5) From 1574/5 there were entries for *Billa Bursarii*, effectively an account of the previous year's surplus.

(6) Payments to Fellows and College Servants. All Fellows were named (except in 1517/18–1564/5); servants were sometimes named, but more usually listed only under the job which they did. From 1565/6, instead of listing the total stipends paid to each Fellow, the accounts listed the amounts paid out by each foundation to each Fellow. To find out, therefore, how much a particular Fellow earned, it is necessary to add up the sums mentioned in each section for him.

(7) Payments of Quitrents to other institutions. These were listed in similar detail, or lack of it, as the *Redditus* in the Credit section.

(8) The Debit Side had a total of all expenses (*Summa omnium expensarum*) and the roll usually ended with a statement of the difference between the two totals in the hand of the Chancellor of the University or his Commissary.

Alongside the main sequence of account rolls there are also two rolls, dating from 1416/17 and 1470/1, which list all the arrears to date on College properties.[64] When the list of arrears/allowances on a roll grew unwieldy the oldest debts were written on these separate rolls and no longer mentioned in the main sequence. Although this apparently acknowledged desperate debts the 1416/17 arrears roll at least has several later annotations recording payment. In addition to these two rolls there were almost certainly others which are now lost: for example, the arrears in the 1434/5 account are much smaller than the allowances in the previous year, suggesting that an arrears roll may

[64] A list of arrears attached to the end of the 1385/6 roll may be related to these.

have been drawn up. Likewise William Smith suspected that in c.1459/60 'a distinct Roll of desperate arrears' was drawn up, as some arrears were not carried over into the 1460/1 roll (his note is given in full at the end of the 1458/9 roll).

As with all medieval accounts the Bursars' Accounts do not record the College's exact income or any profit and loss in a way readily recognisable to a modern reader. The crucial task for the Bursar was to account for all the money which he had received or paid out, to avoid liability for any debts (see p. xvii above). This may help to explain the apparently eccentric recording of income from rooms and properties up to 1485/6: the Bursar needed to show why he might not have received all the expected rents, and, by including arrears and allowances alongside expected rents, he could indicate defaulters and exonerate himself. As for rents from properties and rooms, it is possible to calculate actual rent receipts by adding together all the arrears and expected rents for a property, then subtracting the allowances for it.

Two unusual rolls deserve mention. That of Richard Gysbourn, Bursar in 1383/4, includes, after the usual Arrears and expected rents, a section headed 'receipts' (*Recepta*), which lists rents from which the allowances have been deducted. This section was then crossed out (it is not clear by whom). The other unusual roll dates from 1436/7, the penultimate set of accounts compiled by Thomas Benwell. For this year two separate rolls are preserved. One is set out conventionally, with arrears, expected rents, and allowances; the second has, instead of these, a set of *Recepta*. Although Benwell's arithmetic was erratic the *Recepta* can usually be calculated by subtracting the allowances from the total of arrears and expected rents. It is certainly clear, however, that this *Recepta* roll records the rents which Benwell actually received.

Unlike the main roll the *Recepta* roll does not have a formal audit at the end. Possibly this roll, and Gysbourn's list of *recepta* in 1383/4, were not experiments in accounting but merely the Bursar's *aide-memoires* of the College's actual annual income, other Bursars perhaps keeping such *Recepta* rolls for their own use.

In addition to calculating the College's exact rents in a given year the reader can work out the profit to the College from any given property by deducting any expenses on it, such as repairs, from the rent received.[65]

[65] See A. B. Cobban, *Medieval English Universities*, p. 157, for just such an experiment on the College's Academic Halls in a few sample years.

Even after the Arrears/Allowances system ceased in 1485/6, the presence of a few Arrears and Allowances in the rolls can still be used to give an idea of the College's actual income. Nuances in vocabulary are no longer much guide, however, since by the mid 16th century the same section was headed *Redditus* or *Recepta* almost at whim.

The Account Rolls do not reveal all the College's financial affairs. One major omission is entry fines, lump sums paid to the College by tenants on admission to, or renewal of, their leases, and, until the 19th century, an important means of augmenting the Fellows' revenue. The earliest extant Fine Book for University College (**UC:EB2/F/1**) starts in 1639, but none of its entries appear in the main sequence of accounts. It is not known when entry fines began, but one should be aware that this important aspect of College life was unrecorded.[66]

The Accounts also take no heed of corn rents. These were introduced by Act of Parliament in 1576, under which, in order to improve their finances, a proportion of the rents from properties of Oxford and Cambridge Colleges, and of Eton and Winchester, should be paid in kind, or according to the price of wheat and malt barley that year.[67] University College's leases after 1576 record the proportion of rent to be paid in this way, but no trace appears in the Accounts, which only record the overall expected rent and ignore fluctuations caused by the price of corn.[68]

Another notable omission from the 14th century rolls, and most of the 15th century ones, is that they do not take account of any money remaining in the College Treasury. Furthermore the accounts might not record major 'windfall' payments, such as from sale of land. There is no record, for example, of the £6 purchase price of 9 High Street, Oxford, in 1542, or of the sale of the Handborough property in the 1560s.[69] In the case of the former property, the only indication of its sale in the accounts occurs in 1542/3, where no rent is recorded from the house, 'because it is sold' (*quia venditur*).

[66] The Fellows' stipends from 1478/9–1506/7 regularly include payments of *dividencia* or *dividenda*, which might be references to entry fines (see T. A. R. Evans and R. J. Faith, 'College Estates and University Finances, 1350–1500', *HUO* II, pp. 681–682).

[67] See G. E. Aylmer, 'Economics and Finances of the Colleges and University c.1530–1640', in *HUO* III, pp. 535–537 for a full explanation of this system.

[68] The rolls also ignore certain special conditions, such as that attached to the fields in Grandpont (bordering the Thames), whose tenant had to supply fish worth 2s to the College each year on St. Cuthbert's Day.

[69] It is not known if the sale of the Holderness property was recorded in 1528, because the account roll is missing.

Such omissions are comprehensible in the light of the limited function of these Accounts. The Bursar had to prove to the Chancellor that he could account for the moneys received or spent by him in his office, to save himself from major financial loss. Sums such as entry fines, which were given to the Fellows as a whole, were immaterial to this purpose. In short, although the Bursars' Accounts may seem eccentric to a modern reader, they are consistent with their purpose, and provide much information about the medieval College.

Since the Bursars' Accounts performed much the same function in much the same way for 200 years, it is interesting to note changes in language and orthography, not least as they were written by academics who were not trying to impress, as they might in their scholarly work. Roman numerals were the norm for the greater part of the period, but in many of the rolls for 1391–1411/12, which record Fellows' Commons in detail, Arabic numerals were used for the number of weeks or Fellows. The roll of 1509/10 was the first to give the calendar year in the opening paragraph in Arabic numerals, but it was not until 1578/9 that they were used in the body of the accounts, at first only for subtotals. In 1583/4 the Bursar used Arabic and Latin numerals in almost equal proportions, even in individual entries (such as one for 'vj s 8 d'). Roman numerals were used exclusively in 1584/5 and 1585/6, but in 1586/7 Arabic numbers appeared throughout except for the subtotals, and finally in 1589/90 Roman numerals were dropped entirely.

The text of the rolls remained in Latin until 1569/70,[70] when detailed accounts of repairs re-appeared, written in English. The headings for this section, however, remained in Latin along with the rest of the text. This hybrid of Latin and English continued in the Account Volumes from 1632 until 1828, when at last the College's Accounts were compiled exclusively in English.

The 16th century also saw changes in the language and the orthography of Latin, as the old medieval language gave way to one more responsive to traditional 'Classical' Latin. Two examples of spelling changes are the replacement of 'c' by 't' in certain words, and the reinstatement of 'ae' for 'e'. The first time that a word like *reparaciones* is spelled as *reparationes* is in the roll of 1518. However, the 'c' is then reinstated for the next few years until 1522/3, when 't' returns; also there are several instances of 't' and 'c' being used in the

[70] Except for one or two isolated entries, such as 'Item for a old masser + broken spoon', from 1515/16.

same roll. The first appearance of 'ae' for 'e' is in 1548/9, but only for some words, and 'ae' is not used fully until the later 1550s.

Changes in vocabulary are also noteworthy. The medieval Latin word for 'week' is *septimana*, and this was used continuously until 1547/8, when in mid roll the Bursar replaced it with the Classical equivalent, *ebdomada*. *Septimana* reappeared in 1548/9, but then in 1549/50 *ebdomada* took over for good. Two earlier changes were the replacement of the medieval *capella* ('chapel') by *sacellum* in 1518,[71] and of *camera* ('bedroom') by *cubiculum* in 1519/20.[72] Even the name of the roll was not immune to change. The accounts had been described as a *computus*, but in 1553/4 the roll was described as a *Liber Supputationis*. For the next few years, however, *computus* returned, and it was not until the 1570s that *Liber Supputationis* became the normal way of referring to the accounts.

5 LATER ACCOUNTS AND RELATED DOCUMENTS

The last extant Bursars' Roll dates from 1596/7. There is then a long gap in the accounts of the College until 1632, when a series of so-called General Accounts began to be kept in bound paper volumes (catalogued as **UC:BU2**). Only two sets of accounts survive from the intervening period, both preserved as drafts in the so-called Bursar's Books **UC:BU3/F1/1–2** (see below), for the years 1616 and 1629. As for the rest, not even William Smith recorded any trace of them.[73]

Despite the gap these later accounts have a layout almost identical with those of the 1590s (with the exception of that for 1596/7), even down to the order of material and the mixture of Latin and English. Indeed the only major change of layout before the reforms of 1882[74] was when in 1828, when it was at last decided to use English throughout. It is a remarkable testimony to the conservatism of accounting methods at University College that the Bursar of the

[71] The Bursar of 1572/3 went even further when he called the chapel a *templum*.

[72] But see p. xvi above for an alternative interpretation of this particular change.

[73] Were the missing accounts kept on rolls or in volume form? The earliest extant volume is labelled 'Volume A', so that when it received its present binding (in Smith's day?) no earlier volume was known. It seems likely, however, that there was an earlier volume of accounts for the years 1597/8–1631/2, perhaps lost during the Civil War. Not only is the loss of one volume more plausible than that of over thirty rolls, but also the first extant volume covers a similar time span (from 1632–1667). George Abbot, Fellow of Balliol, who became Master of University College in 1597 may have introduced to his new college the Balliol method of recording accounts in volume form (see p. xlvi below).

[74] See p. xxxvii above.

early 1880s was keeping accounts in a manner which his predecessor 500 years earlier would have understood without too much difficulty.

Unlike the Accounts Rolls the General Accounts are preserved alongside several other records of the College's finances. The most important of these are the Bursars' Books (catalogued as **UC:BU3**), the earliest of which dates from 1616. These changed greatly from the 17th to the 20th centuries. In the 17th century there were two varieties of book: one was used to record payments by Senior and Junior Members for food and drink, the other, the earliest of which dates from the 1650s, for day-to-day accounts which would have been used to draw up the final accounts for the year. Finally, from 1698/9, a single series of books recorded both type of transaction. Unfortunately, the survival rate of the Bursars' Books is the worst for any of the College's financial records: 22 books survive from the 17th century, and only 4 from the whole of the 18th, although from 1809/10 the sequence is almost continuous.

Next are the Buttery Books (catalogued as **UC:BU4**), which record College members' daily expenditure in the Buttery. A new page was started each week, and each member's daily expenditure written in against his name, often in a very abbreviated and obscure manner. One book was used for a year, usually (until 1882) starting at the end of March. In addition to learning how much each member spent on food and drink, one can also use these books to determine members' exact periods of residence in the College, according to the amount of money they spent there. The earliest extant Buttery Book dates from 1639/40, but the sequence is incomplete until 1754/5. Smith knew of books going back to 1615, now lost, and even in the Bursars' Accounts of 1569/70, 2s 8d was spent 'for iiij quear paper ryall for the butterie booke'.[75] Buttery Books were a very long-lived type of record, being maintained well into the present century, and are found in many other Colleges.[76]

Finally there are the so-called *Billae Bursarii*, or Bursar's Bill (catalogued as **UC:BU5**). As mentioned above, from the 1570s the Bursars' Accounts include entries for a *Billa Bursarii*, which was effectively the surplus of the previous year. From at least 1671 (the date of the earliest such document to survive) separate accounts were

[75] Since the 1569/70 roll was the first for many years to record College expenditure in detail, Buttery Books may have been kept even earlier.

[76] Those, for example, at Brasenose, Magdalen, Merton, Oriel, and St. John's are all strikingly similar in layout.

kept of this *Billa*, and by the 18th century they often include information not found in the General Accounts, such as money from land transactions or exceptional gifts of money. From 1676/7 the *Billa* was also used to record undergraduates' 'Caution Money' (a deposit paid at matriculation against damage to College property or unpaid buttery bills).

The chance mention of a Buttery Book in 1569/70 shows that the Bursars' Accounts were not the only types of financial record kept in University College before the 17th century. However, no other such records are preserved, or indeed mentioned in the Accounts. The only exception is that several rolls from the early 15th century refer to repairs or other expenses 'as appears on a paper' (*ut patet per papirum*), presumably referring to more detailed, itemised accounts, long lost: none survived even in Smith's day, and perhaps such supplementary material was disposed of once the main account had been approved by the Chancellor.

6 THE CONTEXT OF THE UNIVERSITY COLLEGE ACCOUNTS

How typical are the accounts of University College compared with those of other Colleges at Oxford or Cambridge? Unfortunately, although such accounts have long been exploited for other topics, very little work has been done on them as accounts *per se*. Few have been published: there are two important volumes of domestic accounts from Merton College, for the later 13th century and the late 15th century, the accounts of Canterbury College, a monastic foundation, from c.1379/80–1528/9, and a Brasenose College account for 1545/6.[77] In addition there are detailed discussions in print of accounts from Balliol, Brasenose, Corpus Christi, and Lincoln.[78] The present volume,

[77] See *Early Rolls of Merton College, Oxford*, ed. J. R. L. Highfield (OHS n.s. 18, 1964); *Domestic Accounts of Merton College, Oxford, 1482–1494*, ed. J. M. Fletcher and C. A. Upton (OHS n.s. 34, 1996); W. A. Pantin, *Canterbury College, Oxford*, II (OHS n.s. 7, 1947); and *Brasenose College Quatercentenary Monographs*, II (OHS 53, 1909), pp. 177–187.

[78] See J. H. Jones, *Archives of Balliol College, Oxford – A Guide* (Chichester, 1984), pp. 30–34 and *Balliol College – A History* (Oxford, 1989), pp. 56–73; *Brasenose College Quatercentenary Monographs* (as above), pp. 133–154; A. D. Duncan, 'Introduction to the Accounts of Corpus Christi College' in *HUO* III, pp. 574–596, and 'Tudor Corpus: The College Accounts', in *The Pelican*, 1980–1981, pp. 40–46; V. H. H. Green, *The Commonwealth of Lincoln College* (Oxford, 1979), Chapter V. For an unrivalled analysis of a Cambridge College's accounts, see A. B. Cobban, *The King's Hall within the University of Cambridge in the Later Middle Ages* (Cambridge, 1969).

therefore, comprises the first extensive edition of the accounts, both domestic and estate, of a secular Oxford or Cambridge College covering a long period of time.

The following preliminary sketch of accounting practices is based on a sample of the older Oxford foundations, namely Balliol, Brasenose, Christ Church, Corpus Christi, Lincoln, Magdalen, Merton, New College, Oriel, and Queen's (as well as Canterbury College).[79] It is concerned only with the Colleges' general accounts: Battels, Buttery Books, and other documents recording the *minutiae* of domestic expenditure are not discussed here.

Compared with other types of medieval account there are some obvious differences and similarities: while there is nothing at University College comparable with the detailed so-called diet accounts kept by households great and small,[80] nor with the accounts of manors, there are comparable institutions, particularly monasteries. The Bursars' accounts from Durham Abbey, for example, are based on a similar system of recording general expenditure and income, albeit on a much larger scale.[81]

An initial examination of the basic systems used by Colleges reveals great diversity. Balliol, Brasenose, Canterbury, Lincoln, Oriel, and Queen's are all similar to University in using just one set of accounts to cover all financial activities, although Balliol and Lincoln, for example, preferred to use volumes or booklets rather than rolls.[82] Most accounts were compiled yearly, but Balliol had a set of half-yearly ones. By contrast Christ Church, Corpus Christi, Magdalen, Merton, and New College kept several sets of accounts. Normally one set recorded receipts, often rather summarily,[83] and another recorded expenditure, usually in much more detail, which at New College, Magdalen, and

[79] The following discussion owes much to information provided by Mrs. E. A. Boardman (Oriel and Brasenose), Mrs. C. Butler (Corpus Christi), Mrs. J. Curthoys (Christ Church), Mrs. C. Dalton (New College), Dr. V. H. H. Green (Lincoln), Prof. J. R. L. Highfield (Merton), Dr. J. H. Jones (Balliol), and Mr. J. M. Kaye (Queen's).

[80] For a good published selection and full discussion of diet accounts, see *Household Accounts from Medieval England*, ed. C. M. Woolgar (Recs. of Soc. and Econ. Hist., Vols. 17–18, 1993).

[81] *Extracts from the Account Rolls of the Abbey of Durham*, II and III, ed. Canon J. T. Fowler (Surtees Soc., Vols. 100 and 105, 1898 & 1901).

[82] At Lincoln College the account was called the *Calculus*, at Oriel the Style, and at Queen's the long roll. At Brasenose the single annual account was supplemented in the early 17th century by accounts for the Senior and Junior Bursars, which covered estate and domestic expenditure respectively.

[83] At both Magdalen and Corpus Christi, where two copies of these accounts were made, one each for the President and Bursar, they were called the *Magna Indentura*.

Corpus Christi was prefaced with a summary of the year's receipts.[84] These three Colleges in particular kept several sets of accounts for individual estates and manors, or groups of them, which could be very numerous (almost three dozen sets of such accounts were produced for Magdalen alone in 1490/1, for example).[85]

New College, Magdalen, and Corpus Christi tended to have one expenditure account to cover the whole year. Merton and Christ Church divided their yearly expense accounts into three and four parts respectively; in the case of Merton, each third was administered by one of the three Bursars created that year.[86] Merton's accounts are perhaps the most complex of any College, as the basic expense account was supplemented by separate accounts for the Warden and Subwarden; in preserving several late 15th century accounts of the bursars' stewards of hall it appears to be unique among the Oxford Colleges.

It is noteworthy that many of the Colleges which managed with one set of accounts, such as University, Balliol, and Lincoln, were among the poorest, and those which needed several, such as New College, Merton, and Magdalen, were among the wealthiest.[87] It would have been hopelessly impractical for Magdalen, with its vast estates, and seventy Fellows and Demies, to record all its accounts on one roll.

Such differences in presentation mask many similarities. All the accounts have some means of recording domestic expenditure, including Fellows' stipends and commons, albeit in varying degrees of detail. All have a mechanism for recording rents (or at least expected rents) from their estates, and expenditure on them. None of the accounts supply a complete picture of their College's income and expenditure: entry fines, for example, and corn rents are very rarely, if ever, included (usually, as at University, they tend to get recorded in a separate book). Much that is in the accounts of University College can be paralleled elsewhere in Oxford, even if the method of recording was not the same.

Another common factor was extreme conservatism. Every College maintained its original accounting system until well into the 19th

[84] At Magdalen these accounts were called the *Libri Computi* and at Corpus Christi the *Libri Magni*.

[85] The close similarities between the accounts of New College, Magdalen, and Corpus Christi is probably not coincidence. William Waynflete, the founder of Magdalen, clearly modelled it on New College in many ways, and the first President and many of the first Fellows of Corpus Christi had migrated from Magdalen.

[86] Magdalen elected three Bursars a year, too, but all seem to have collaborated on a single expenditure account.

[87] In 1470/1 Lincoln's rental was £70 7½d (V. H. H. Green, *op. cit.*, p. 31) and University's was £86 17s 10½d, but in 1490/1 Magdalen's rental was almost £700 (see p. xviii above).

century, and in many cases until the Parliamentary Commissioners forced a change in 1882. New College, Christ Church, and Corpus Christi were unusual in ending their old sequences in 1855/6, 1864/5, and c.1873 respectively; Magdalen doggedly maintained its *Magna Indentura/Liber Computi* system in Latin right up to the end.[88]

The perplexity of the Parliamentary Commission in the 1870s when it tried to estimate the respective wealth of the Oxford Colleges may thus be understood: Victorian accountants, accustomed to double-entry bookkeeping, were faced with accounts which had changed little since the charge-discharge days of the Middle Ages, replete with omissions well-known to the Bursars but incomprehensible to an outsider. Sometimes these traditions could be burdensome: at Queen's, for example, the accounting system of long rolls, ordained by the original statutes, was adhered to strictly, even though obsolescent from the later 16th century. The Bursars there tended to keep other account books to record the true state of affairs, whilst keeping up the annual long roll as it withdrew ever further from reality.[89]

Not every College was as rigid as Queen's: we have seen how University was prepared to tinker with its system over the years, while still retaining the basic structure. Furthermore, Colleges could reasonably argue that there was little point in changing a system which they could understand, and which gave them the information most useful for their needs; double-entry bookkeeping may have been appropriate for businesses, but what need did they have of it?[90]

The survival rate of the University College Bursars' Accounts (over 80% between 1381/2 and 1596/7, the longest gap being seven years) compares well with other Colleges. The only extant Oriel accounts before 1583 date from 1409–1415 and 1450–1525, and Balliol has lost all its accounts before 1544.[91] At New College for the years 1379–1599 67% of receipt accounts survive and 55% of expenses,[92] whereas at

[88] M. J. Jones, 'Accounting System of Magdalen College, Oxford, in 1812', *Accounting, Business and Financial History*, Vol. I, no. 2 (1991), pp. 141–161, which shows that the basic system created in the 1480s was little changed after three centuries.

[89] Dr. J. M. Kaye pointed out that the mid-19th century long rolls recorded the Fellows' 'statutory' stipends of £4 a year, whereas their true income, mainly thanks to entry fines, was between £200 and £300.

[90] A point well made by M. J. Jones, *op. cit.*

[91] Even the accounts for 1544–1568 now survive only in the form of transcriptions made c.1910 (see J. H. Jones, *Archives of Balliol College*, p. 30).

[92] Information from Caroline Dalton. For 1379–1399 33% of receipt accounts survive and 47% of expenses; for 1400–1499 the respective figures are 67% and 39%, and for 1500–1599 76% and 63%.

Queen's, although the general survival rate is good, there are only two rolls for the years 1340–1350, and just one from the period 1494–1516. The great gap in University's accounts for 1597–1631 is thus all the more regrettable, when so much remains both before and after.

EDITING THE TEXT

The aim of this book was to provide a complete transcription of the Account Rolls, but certain compromises proved unavoidable.[1]

Although every attempt has been made to record the spelling and numeration as found on the rolls, some words have been discreetly expanded to aid comprehension. Personal names are recorded as they occur in the text, although elsewhere I have used the spelling adopted by A. B. Emden for people mentioned in his biographical register of Oxford University.

The most important editorial intervention concerns the Arrears and Allowances in accounts before 1485/6. As shown in Section 4 of the Introduction, the Arrears at the start of these accounts tend to be identical with the Allowances at the end of the previous one. In such cases, therefore, reproduction of the Arrears was considered unnecessary and they have been omitted, although small omissions or corrections are noted.

The accounts usually have initial headings, either at the top or sides of each section, frequently in larger writing than the rest of the text, with each individual entry starting on a fresh line.[2] Instead of recording each modification, it was considered most useful for readers to use the same method of indicating headings, individual entries, and totals and subtotals throughout.

In the text itself, the following conventions are used:

[. . .	Text missing to the right of this point.
. . .]	Text missing to the left of this point.
[. . .]	Text missing or illegible in the middle of a line.
[text thus]	Missing text supplied from William Smith's extracts.
[*text thus*]	Missing text supplied editorially (where there is little doubt), or editorial comment.
[*?text thus*]	Conjectural text for missing part
[*(text thus)*]	English paraphrase of missing text supplied editorially,

[1] Although ADMC never set down his own editorial principles, they were implicit enough in his transcriptions (in particular the policy on Arrears before 1485/6), and I have not added many of my own.

[2] Some sections are written in one continuous paragraph (e.g. the property repairs in 1381/2), which are set out in that way in this edition.

	where content can be deduced but not exact words or spelling.
⟨text thus⟩	Text added in a different hand.
[*sic*]	Entry in the text which may be an error by the writer.
[*blank*]	No entry in the text where one would be expected (usually in reference to sums).
\`text thus′	Text written above the line, added in later.
~~text thus~~	Text deleted in the original.
[ADMC]	Footnote written by A. D. M. Cox.

COMMONLY USED ABBREVIATIONS

A° = Anno
Abb' = Abbatissa
All' *or* Alloc' = Allocaciones
Arr' = Arreragia
Arre^{a} = Arreragia
Aul' = Aula
cam' = camera
Cant' = Cantuariensis
clav' = clavis
coll' = collegium
d = denarius
di *or* dim' *or* dimi' = dimidius
eod' = eodem
gard' = gardinum
It' = Item
ij^{bus} = duobus
iiij^{or} = quattuor
j^{us} = unius
Joh' = Johannes
li = liber
liber' = liberavi (or liberatus, -a, -um)
M = Magister
marc' = marca
Mic' *or* Mich' = Michael
Nat' = Natalis
ob = obolus
o^{to} = opposito
pasc' = pascha
pinc' = pincerna
pent' = pentecoste
prat' = pratum
prox' = proximus
q^{a} = quadrans
quad' *or* quadr' = quadrivium
quond' = quondam
redd' = redditus
reparac' = reparaciones
resol' = resoluciones
Ric' = Ricardus
rr' = regno regis
s = solidus
scol' = scola
sep' *or* sep^{a} = septimana
soc' = socius
stip' = stipendium
ten' = tenementum
ter' = terminus

CONCORDANCE WITH THE REFERENCE NUMBERS OF WILLIAM SMITH

Old Reference	New Reference
Pyx EE fasc. 1 no. 1	**UC:BU1/F/1**
Pyx EE fasc. 1 no. 2	**UC:BU1/F/2**
Pyx EE fasc. 1 no. 3	**UC:BU1/F/3**
Pyx EE fasc. 1 no. 4	**UC:BU1/F/4**
Pyx EE fasc. 1 no. 5	**UC:BU1/F/5**
Pyx EE fasc. 2 no. 1	**UC:BU1/F/6**
Pyx EE fasc. 2 no. 2	**UC:BU1/F/7**
Pyx EE fasc. 2 no. 3	**UC:BU1/F/8**
Pyx EE fasc. 2 no. 4	**UC:BU1/F/9**
Pyx EE fasc. 2 no. 5	**UC:BU1/F/10**
Pyx EE fasc. 3 no. 1	**UC:BU1/F/11**
Pyx EE fasc. 3 no. 2	**UC:BU1/F/12**
Pyx EE fasc. 3 no. 3	**UC:BU1/F/13**
Pyx EE fasc. 3 no. 4	**UC:BU1/F/14**
Pyx EE fasc. 3 no. 5	**UC:BU1/F/15**
Pyx EE fasc. 3 no. 6	**UC:BU1/F/16**
Pyx EE fasc. 3 no. 7	**UC:BU1/F/17**
Pyx EE fasc. 3 no. 8	**UC:BU1/F/18**
Pyx EE fasc. 3 no. 9	**UC:BU1/F/19**
Pyx EE fasc. 3 no. 10	**UC:BU1/F/20**
Pyx EE fasc. 3 no. 11	**UC:BU1/F/21**
Pyx EE fasc. 4 no. 1	**UC:BU1/F/22**
Pyx EE fasc. 4 no. 2	**UC:BU1/F/23**
Pyx EE fasc. 4 no. 3	**UC:BU1/F/24**
Pyx EE fasc. 4 no. 4	**UC:BU1/F/25**
Pyx EE fasc. 4 no. 5	**UC:BU1/F/26**
Pyx EE fasc. 4 no. 6a	**UC:BU1/F/27**
Pyx EE fasc. 4 no. 6b	**UC:BU1/F/28**
Pyx EE fasc. 4 no. 7	**UC:BU1/F/29**
Pyx EE fasc. 4 no. 8	**UC:BU1/F/30**
Pyx EE fasc. 4 no. 9	**UC:BU1/F/31**
Pyx EE fasc. 5 no. 1	**UC:BU1/F/32**
Pyx EE fasc. 5 no. 2	**UC:BU1/F/33**
Pyx EE fasc. 5 no. 3	**UC:BU1/F/34**
Pyx EE fasc. 5 no. 4	**UC:BU1/F/35**
Pyx EE fasc. 5 no. 5	**UC:BU1/F/36**
Pyx EE fasc. 5 no. 6	**UC:BU1/F/37**
Pyx EE fasc. 5 no. 7	**UC:BU1/F/38**
Pyx EE fasc. 5 no. 8	**UC:BU1/F/39**
Pyx EE fasc. 5 no. 9	**UC:BU1/F/40**
Pyx EE fasc. 5 no. 10	**UC:BU1/F/41**
Pyx EE fasc. 6 no. 1	**UC:BU1/F/42**
Pyx EE fasc. 6 no. 2	**UC:BU1/F/43**
Pyx EE fasc. 6 no. 3	**UC:BU1/F/44**
Pyx EE fasc. 6 no. 4	**UC:BU1/F/45**
Pyx EE fasc. 6 no. 5	**UC:BU1/F/46**
Pyx EE fasc. 6 no. 6	**UC:BU1/F/47**
Pyx EE fasc. 6 no. 7	**UC:BU1/F/48**
Pyx EE fasc. 6 no. 8	**UC:BU1/F/49**
Pyx EE fasc. 6 no. 9	**UC:BU1/F/50**
Pyx EE fasc. 6 no. 10	**UC:BU1/F/51**
Pyx EE fasc. 6 no. 11	**UC:BU1/F/52**
Pyx EE fasc. 6 no. 12	**UC:BU1/F/53**
Pyx EE fasc. 7 no. 1	**UC:BU1/F/54**
Pyx EE fasc. 7 no. 2	**UC:BU1/F/55**
Pyx EE fasc. 7 no. 3	**UC:BU1/F/56**
Pyx EE fasc. 7 no. 4	**UC:BU1/F/57**
Pyx EE fasc. 7 no. 5	**UC:BU1/F/58**
Pyx EE fasc. 7 no. 6	**UC:BU1/F/59**
Pyx EE fasc. 7 no. 7	**UC:BU1/F/60**
Pyx EE fasc. 8 no. 1	**UC:BU1/F/61**
Pyx EE fasc. 8 no. 2	**UC:BU1/F/62**
Pyx EE fasc. 8 no. 3	**UC:BU1/F/63**
Pyx EE fasc. 8 no. 4	**UC:BU1/F/64**
Pyx EE fasc. 8 no. 5	**UC:BU1/F/65**
Pyx EE fasc. 8 no. 6	**UC:BU1/F/66**
Pyx EE fasc. 8 no. 7	**UC:BU1/F/67**
Pyx EE fasc. 8 no. 8	**UC:BU1/F/68**
Pyx EE fasc. 8 no. 9	**UC:BU1/F/69**
Pyx GG fasc. 1 no. 1	**UC:BU1/F/70**
Pyx GG fasc. 1 no. 2	**UC:BU1/F/71**
Pyx GG fasc. 1 no. 3	**UC:BU1/F/72**
Pyx GG fasc. 1 no. 4	**UC:BU1/F/73**
Pyx GG fasc. 1 no. 5	**UC:BU1/F/74**
Pyx GG fasc. 1 no. 6	**UC:BU1/F/75**
Pyx GG fasc. 1 no. 7	**UC:BU1/F/76**
Pyx GG fasc. 1 no. 8	**UC:BU1/F/77**
Pyx GG fasc. 1 no. 9	**UC:BU1/F/78**
Pyx GG fasc. 1 no. 10	**UC:BU1/F/79**
Pyx GG fasc. 2 no. 1	**UC:BU1/F/80**
Pyx GG fasc. 2 no. 2	**UC:BU1/F/81**
Pyx GG fasc. 2 no. 3	**UC:BU1/F/82**
Pyx GG fasc. 2 no. 4	**UC:BU1/F/83**
Pyx GG fasc. 2 no. 5	**UC:BU1/F/84**
Pyx GG fasc. 2 no. 6	**UC:BU1/F/85**

Old Reference	New Reference
Pyx GG fasc. 2 no. 7	**UC:BU1/F/86**
Pyx GG fasc. 2 no. 8a	**UC:BU1/F/87**
Pyx GG fasc. 2 no. 8b	**UC:BU1/F/88**
Pyx GG fasc. 2 no. 9	**UC:BU1/F/89**
Pyx GG fasc. 2 no. 10	**UC:BU1/F/90**
Pyx GG fasc. 2 no. 11	**UC:BU1/F/91**
Pyx GG fasc. 3 no. 1	**UC:BU1/F/92**
Pyx GG fasc. 3 no. 2	**UC:BU1/F/93**
Pyx GG fasc. 3 no. 3	**UC:BU1/F/94**
Pyx GG fasc. 3 no. 4	**UC:BU1/F/95**
Pyx GG fasc. 3 no. 5	**UC:BU1/F/96**
Pyx GG fasc. 3 no. 6	**UC:BU1/F/97**
Pyx GG fasc. 3 no. 7	**UC:BU1/F/98**
Pyx GG fasc. 3 no. 8	**UC:BU1/F/99**
Pyx GG fasc. 3 no. 9	**UC:BU1/F/100**
Pyx GG fasc. 4 no. 1	**UC:BU1/F/101**
Pyx GG fasc. 4 no. 2	**UC:BU1/F/102**
Pyx GG fasc. 4 no. 3	**UC:BU1/F/103**
Pyx GG fasc. 4 no. 4	**UC:BU1/F/104**
Pyx GG fasc. 4 no. 5	**UC:BU1/F/105**
Pyx GG fasc. 4 no. 6	**UC:BU1/F/106**
Pyx GG fasc. 5 no. 1	**UC:BU1/F/107**
Pyx GG fasc. 5 no. 2	**UC:BU1/F/108**
Pyx GG fasc. 5 no. 3	**UC:BU1/F/109**
Pyx GG fasc. 5 no. 4a	**UC:BU1/F/110**
Pyx GG fasc. 5 no. 4b	**UC:BU1/F/111**
Pyx GG fasc. 5 no. 5	**UC:BU1/F/112**
Pyx GG fasc. 5 no. 6	**UC:BU1/F/113**
Pyx GG fasc. 6 no. 1	**UC:BU1/F/114**
Pyx GG fasc. 6 no. 2	**UC:BU1/F/115**
Pyx GG fasc. 6 no. 3	**UC:BU1/F/116**
Pyx GG fasc. 6 no. 4	**UC:BU1/F/117**
Pyx GG fasc. 6 no. 5	**UC:BU1/F/118**
Pyx GG fasc. 6 no. 6	**UC:BU1/F/119**
Pyx GG fasc. 6 no. 7	**UC:BU1/F/120**
Pyx GG fasc. 6 no. 8	**UC:BU1/F/121**
Pyx GG fasc. 6 no. 9	**UC:BU1/F/122**
Pyx GG fasc. 6 no. 10	**UC:BU1/F/123**
Pyx GG fasc. 7 no. 1	**UC:BUI/F/124**
Pyx GG fasc. 7 no. 2	**UC:BU1/F/125**
Pyx GG fasc. 7 no. 3	**UC:BU1/F/126**
Pyx GG fasc. 7 no. 4	**UC:BU1/F/127**
Pyx GG fasc. 7 no. 5	**UC:BU1/F/128**
Pyx GG fasc. 7 no. 6	**UC:BU1/F/129**
Pyx GG fasc. 7 no. 7	**UC:BU1/F/130**
Pyx GG fasc. 7 no. 8	**UC:BU1/F/131**
Pyx GG fasc. 7 no. 9	**UC:BU1/F/132**
Pyx GG fasc. 8 no. 1	**UC:BU1/F/133**
Pyx GG fasc. 8 no. 2	**UC:BU1/F/134**
Pyx GG fasc. 8 no. 3	**UC:BU1/F/135**
Pyx GG fasc. 8 no. 4	**UC:BU1/F/136**
Pyx GG fasc. 8 no. 5	**UC:BU1/F/137**
Pyx GG fasc. 8 no. 6	**UC:BU1/F/138**
Pyx GG fasc. 8 no. 7	**UC:BU1/F/139**
Pyx GG fasc. 8 no. 8	**UC:BU1/F/140**
Pyx GG fasc. 8 no. 9	**UC:BU1/F/141**
Pyx GG fasc. 8 no. 10	**UC:BU1/F/142**
Pyx HH fasc. 1 no. 1	**UC:BU1/F/143**
Pyx HH fasc. 1 no. 2	**UC:BU1/F/144**
Pyx HH fasc. 1 no. 3	**UC:BU1/F/145**
Pyx HH fasc. 1 no. 4	**UC:BU1/F/146**
Pyx HH fasc. 1 no. 5	**UC:BU1/F/147**
Pyx HH fasc. 1 no. 6	**UC:BU1/F/148**
Pyx HH fasc. 1 no. 7	**UC:BU1/F/149**
Pyx HH fasc. 1 no. 8	**UC:BU1/F/150**
Pyx HH fasc. 1 no. 9	**UC:BU1/F/151**
Pyx HH fasc. 1 no. 10	**UC:BU1/F/152**
Pyx HH fasc. 1 no. 11	**UC:BU1/F/153**
Pyx HH fasc. 1 no. 12	**UC:BU1/F/154**
Pyx HH fasc. 2 no. 1	**UC:BU1/F/155**
Pyx HH fasc. 2 no. 2	**UC:BU1/F/156**
Pyx HH fasc. 2 no. 3	**UC:BU1/F/157**
Pyx HH fasc. 2 no. 4	**UC:BU1/F/158**
Pyx HH fasc. 2 no. 5	**UC:BU1/F/159**
Pyx HH fasc. 2 no. 6	**UC:BU1/F/160**
Pyx HH fasc. 2 no. 7	**UC:BU1/F/161**
Pyx HH fasc. 2 no. 8	**UC:BU1/F/162**
Pyx HH fasc. 2 no. 9	**UC:BU1/F/163**
Pyx HH fasc. 3 no. 1	**UC:BU1/F/164**
Pyx HH fasc. 3 no. 2	**UC:BU1/F/165**
Pyx HH fasc. 3 no. 3	**UC:BU1/F/166**
Pyx HH fasc. 3 no. 4	**UC:BU1/F/167**
Pyx HH fasc. 3 no. 5	**UC:BU1/F/168**
Pyx HH fasc. 3 no. 6	**UC:BU1/F/169**
Pyx HH fasc. 3 no. 7	**UC:BU1/F/170**
Pyx HH fasc. 3 no. 8	**UC:BU1/F/171**
Pyx HH fasc. 3 no. 9	**UC:BU1/F/172**
Pyx HH fasc. 3 no. 10	**UC:BU1/F/173**
Pyx HH fasc. 3 no. 11	**UC:BU1/F/174**
Pyx HH fasc. 3 no. 12	**UC:BU1/F/175**
Pyx HH fasc. 3 no. 13	**UC:BU1/F/176**
Pyx HH fasc. 4 no. 1	**UC:BU1/F/177**
Pyx HH fasc. 4 no. 2	**UC:BU1/F/178**
Pyx HH fasc. 4 no. 3	**UC:BU1/F/179**
Pyx HH fasc. 4 no. 4	**UC:BU1/F/180**

Old Reference	New Reference	Old Reference	New Reference
Pyx HH fasc. 4 no. 5	**UC:BU1/F/181**	Pyx HH fasc. 4 no. 8	**UC:BU1/F/184**
Pyx HH fasc. 4 no. 6	**UC:BU1/F/182**	Pyx HH fasc. 4 no. 9	**UC:BU1/F/185**
Pyx HH fasc. 4 no. 7	**UC:BU1/F/183**		

MICH. 5 RICHARD II to MICH. 6 RICHARD II (ROLL UC:BU1/F/1)
(29 September 1381–29 September 1382)

BURSAR: ROBERT GOWER

Rotul' 5 Anni

Compotus Magistri Roberti Gower socij ac Procuratoris Collegii Magistri W[*illelmi de Dunelmi*] Micheluniversitehall' vulgariter nuncupat' a festo sancti Mich' Archangeli Anno [*Regni regis*] Ricardi secundi post conquestum quinto ad idem festum anno revoluto.

Arr'	Recepta per [*eundem pro arr'*][1] anno supradicto	
	In primis de [*Olyfaunt*]halle	xij d
	It' de aula S[*cuti*]	xiij s iiij d
	[*It'*] de aula sancti Thome	xxvj s viij d
	[*It' de*] aula universitatis in vico scolarum	xv s
	Item de Stauntonhall'	iij s iij d
	Item de Drowdalehall'	xxiij s iiij d
	Item de Lodelowhall'	xxx s
	Item de hamptonhalle	iij li
	Item de domo Holwey	vij s vj d
	Item de Aula Sancti Edwardi	xvi s viij d
	Item de Colleg' Cant'	ij s vj d
	Item de Johanne Baret	iiij s
	Item de Holderness'	iiij li ix s xj d
	Item de camera principali	xvj s viij d
	Item recepimus de arr' camerarum in [. . .] nostro	xxv s
	Item de orto ultra castrum	ij s vj d
	Summa xvj li xvij s iiij d	

Redditus Collegii supradicti qui debentur Collegio supradicto pro tempore predicto procuratoris

In primis de Maydenhall'	xiij s iiij d
Item de Olyfaunthall'	iiij s
Item de aula Scuti	xl s
Item de Aula Sancti Thome	xl s
Item de Aula universitatis in vico scolarum	xxxiij s iiij d

[1] The roll has a hole at this point.

Item de aula Brasenose	v marc'
Item de Hamptonhall'	iij li
Item de Aula Sancti Edwardi	xxx s
Item de Stauntonhall'	xlviij s
Item de Drowdalehall'	lj s iiij d
Item de Lodelowhall'	liij s iiij d
Item de domo Holwey	xv s
Item de orto ex opposito domui predicto	iij s
Item de Johanne Baret	viij s
Item de ten' Johannis Brasier'[2]	x s
Item de orto ultra Castrum[3]	ij s vj d
Item de Colleg' Cant'	ij s vj d
Item de ten' Ricardi Merser[4]	l s
Item de shopa pyry	xiij s iiij d
Item de ten' Willelmi Saundres	xl s
Item de ten' Roberti Westby[5]	ix marc' xvj s
Item de ten' Johannis Wyndesore	xiij s iiij d
Item de ten' Johannis vaginarij[6]	xviij s
Item de ten' Ricardi Cornewayle[7]	xxx s
Item de Holdornesse	iiij li ix s xj d
Summa xliij li xj s vij d	

Redditus Recept' de cameris in Collegio supradicto de tempore predicti procurat'

De camera principali	xx s
De sibi proxima camera	x s

[2] On 7 April 1360, a building on the site of both 83 and 84 High Street had been leased to John Brasier (**UC:E/B2/D1/7**).

[3] This garden in St. Thomas' parish, part of the Gonwardby lands (see pp. xxiv–xxvi of the Introduction), had been leased to Maurice Taloure on 27 July 1365 (**UC:E2/11/1D/1**).

[4] On 9 January 1363/4, the easternmost of the three houses on High Street bought from John de Gonwardby was leased to Richard de Garston, Mercer (**UC:E2/7/1D/1**).

[5] On 10 December 1367, the westernmost of the 'Gonwardby' houses in High Street was leased to Robert de Westby (**UC:E2/7/3D/1**). Westby may also have been the College's tenant on its fields and islands in Grandpont by 1381/2, which had been leased on 11 January 1362/3 to Robert Fyssher (**UC:E2/10/1D/1**), whose name does not appear here. It was certainly common practice in later years for the College to lease the house and the fields together.

[6] In 1366/7, the house on the north-east corner of Carfax, another of the Gonwardby properties, had been leased to John Mason at a rent of 18s a year (**UC:E2/8/1D/1**), so this *Johannes vaginarius* must be the same man.

[7] On 7 November 1364, the central 'Gonwardby' house on High Street was leased to Richard de Cornwayle (**UC:E2/7/2D/1**).

De camera sub illa xiij s iiij d ⟨r' vj s viij d⟩
De camera super erbarium iuxta aulam x s
De camera super erbarium in a° disporto vj s viij d ⟨r' vj s viij d⟩
De camera cum aula xviij s ⟨r' ix s⟩
De camera fonti opposita x s
De camera sibi proxima x s
Summa iiij li xviij s

Item recepi de communi Cista xxviij s v d ⟨Summa xxviij s v d⟩

⟨Summa omnium receptorum et oneratorum lxvj li xv s iiij d⟩

Expense

Resolucio Redditus

In primis liberavi Canonico sancte ffrideswyde pro redditu anni presentis xiij s iiij d

Item liberavi procuratori abathie de Abyndon' pro quibusdam annualibus redditibus duorum annorum proximorum preteritorum vj s

Item liberavi procuratori de Osneye pro quodam annuali redditu vj s viij d

Item liberavi procuratori Ecclesie sancti Petri in Oriente pro quibusdam annualibus redditibus duorum annorum preteritorum v s viij d

Item liberavi pro minutis redditibus pro redditu de Holdernesse xviij s vj d

Summa lvj s ij d

Communes primi termini a festo sancti Albani usque ad festum sancti Mich' exclusive

Communes Sociorum

In prima septimana in communibus trium sociorum iij s
It' in batellis ij d

In secunda septimana in communibus trium sociorum iij s
It' in batellis ij d ob

In tercia septimana in communibus trium sociorum iij s
It' in batellis ij d ob

In quarta septimana in communibus trium sociorum iij s
It' in batellis ij d

In quinta septimana in communibus trium sociorum iij s
It' in batellis ij d ob
In sexta septimana in communibus trium sociorum ij s
It' in batellis vj d
In septima septimana in communibus trium sociorum ij s
It' in batellis iij d ob
In Octava septimana in communibus trium sociorum xij d
It' in batellis ij d ob
In Nona septimana in communibus trium sociorum ij s
It' in batellis iij d ob
In decima septimana in communibus trium sociorum ij s
It' in batellis iij d ob
In undecima septimana in communibus trium sociorum ij s
It' in batellis iij d ob
In duodecima septimana in communibus trium sociorum ij s
It' in batellis iij d ob
In terciadecima septimana in communibus trium sociorum ij s
It' in batellis v d
In quartadecima septimana in communibus trium sociorum ij s
It' in batellis v d ob

Summa istius xxxvj s

Communes secundi termini a festo sancti Mich' usque ad festum Nat' domini inclusive

In prima septimana in communibus duorum sociorum ij s
In secunda septimana in communibus duorum sociorum ij s
In tercia septimana in communibus trium sociorum iij s
In batellis j d ob
In quarta septimana in communibus trium sociorum iij s
Item in batellis j d
In quinta septimana in communibus trium sociorum iij s
In sexta septimana in communibus trium sociorum iij s
In batellis v d
In septima septimana in communibus trium sociorum iij s
It' in batellis iij d ob
In Octava septimana in communibus trium sociorum iij s
It' in batellis ij d
In Nona septimana in communibus trium sociorum iij s
It' in batellis ob

In decima septimana in communibus trium sociorum iij s

It’ in batellis j d

In undecima septimana in communibus trium sociorum iij s

It’ in batellis ob

In duodecima septimana in communibus trium sociorum iij s

In terciadecima septimana in communibus trium sociorum iij s

Summa istius xxxviij s iij d

Communes tercii termini a festo Nat’ domini usque ad festum Pasche exclusive

In prima septimana in communibus duorum sociorum ij s

In secunda septimana in communibus trium sociorum ij s

In tercia septimana in communibus trium sociorum iij s

In quarta septimana in communibus trium sociorum ij s

In batellis ij d ob

In quinta septimana in communibus trium sociorum ij s

It’ in batellis v d

In sexta septimana in communibus trium sociorum iij s

Item in batellis iij d

In septima septimana in communibus trium sociorum iij s

In octava septimana in communibus trium sociorum iij s

In nona septimana in communibus trium sociorum iij s

In decima septimana in communibus trium sociorum iij s

In undecima septimana in communibus trium sociorum iij s

It’ in batellis ob

In duodecima septimana in communibus trium sociorum iij s

In terciadecima septimana in communibus trium sociorum iij s

In quartadecima septimana in communibus trium sociorum iij s

Summa istius xxxviij s xi d

[*No heading*]

In prima septimana in communibus trium sociorum iij s

In secunda septimana in communibus trium sociorum iij s

In batellis iiij d ob

In tercia septimana in communibus trium sociorum iij s

In quarta septimana in communibus trium sociorum iij s

In quinta septimana in communibus trium sociorum iij s

Item in batellis ob

In sexta septimana in communibus trium sociorum iij s

It’ in batellis iiij d ob

In septima septimana in communibus trium sociorum iij s
Item in batellis ob
Summa xxj s x d

Expense fforincese [*sic*] ffacte circa pavimentum de Stauntonhall' primo
In primis liber' Stephano Palmer pro lapidibus xiij s iiij d
Item in duobus Cenefactoribus iiij d
Item liber' uni bigario pro lapidibus ducendis per unum diem xxij d
Item liber' sex pueris laborantibus circa arenam per duos dies xix d
Item liber' uni bigario pro fimo ducend' per unum diem xvj d
Item liber' uni bigario pro lapibus ducendis per unum diem xx d
Item pro lapidibus emptis a vicario Ecclesie sancti Petri in Oriente xiij s iiij d
Item liber' pro una manuca ij d
Item liber' paviatori pro stipendio suo xx s
Summa liij s vij d

Item alie expense forinsece facte circa pavimentum hospicii proprii
In primis in lapidibus emptis de Stephano Palmer xiij s iiij d
Item liber' decem pueris laborantibus circa arenam per duos dies v s ij d
Item in cervisia data operario xij d
Item liber' uni bigario pro fimo ducendo per unum diem xx d
Item liber' quatuor pueris laborantibus circa arenam per quinque dies iiij s xj d
Item liber' paviatori pro stipendio suo xxx s viij d
Item in una tributa empta eodum tempore ij d ob
Item liber' sex pueris laborantibus circa arenam per quatuor dies iij s
Summa lix s xj d ob

Item alie expense facte circa pavimentum de drowdalehalle
In primis liber' Stephano Palmer pro lapidibus vj s viij d
Item liber' quinque pueris laborantibus circa arenam per duos dies iij s iiij d
Item liber' uni bigario pro fimo ducendo per unum diem xiij d
Item liber' tribus pueris laborantibus circa arenam per duos dies xxij d

Item liber' paviatori pro stipendio suo xxvj s x d
Item liber' uni puero laboranti circa arenam per unum diem iiij d

Summa xl s j d

Expense forincese facte per M. Johannem Midylton et M. Robertum Gower versus London' et ibi in Octav' sancti Hillarii cum famulo M. J. et Robert' Westby cum famulo suo

In primis apud Tettusworth' in potu j d ob in pane equino j d ob.
Item apud Wycumbe pernoctando in pane j d in cervis' ij d In ovis ij d In vino v d in igne ij d in candel' ob in lect j d in feno pro tribus equis iij d in Aven' vj d. In ferur[a] ob Item in crastino apud Woxobrogge in pane j d in cervisio j d in vino ij d ob in carne iiij d in pane equino iij d Item apud Lond' eodem die ante cenam in potu ij d in cena xj d in feno pro tribus equis iij d in Aven' vj d
Secunda die apud Lond' in jantaculo iiij d in cena xj d in Aven' pro iijbus equis iij d In stramine j d
Tercia die Apud Lond' in prandio v d in cena vij d in Aven' iij d in pane equino j d ob
Quarta die apud Lond' in jantaculo ij d in potu j d ob in cena ix d in Aven' iij d
Quinta die apud Lond' in prand' in pane j d in potu j d ob in carn' iij d in igne j d in cena in pane j d in potu iij d in carn' ij d in igne ij d in lectibus ij d in candel' ob in Aven' iij d
Sexta die apud Lond' in prand' xiiij d In nocte in Lectibus j d in igne j d in candel' ob in Aven' iij d
Septima die apud Lond' in prand' xij d in Lectibus ij d in potu ij d in igne j d in candel' j d in Aven' iij d
Octava die apud Lond' in prand' j d ob in carn' iiij d In igne ij d in nocte in pane j d ob in potu j d in carn' ij d in lectibus ij d in igne ij d in candel' ob in Aven' iij d
Nona die apud Londi' in pane j d ob in potu ij d in carn' iiij d in igne j d In cena in pane j d ob in potu ij d in igne j d in lectibus ij d in candel' ob in pane equino ij d
Decima die apud London' in prand' in pane j d ob in potu ij d in carn' iij d in igne j d in cena in pane j d in potu ij d in igne j d in lectibus ij d in candel' ob in Aven' iij d
Undecima die apud London' in jantaculo iiij d ob in prand' in pane j d in potu ij d in carn' v d in igne ij d in pane equino ob

item in feno pro iij^{bus} equis pro novem diebus et tot noctibus – v s Eod' die post prand' in expensis M. Roberti Gower a Lond' versus Oxon' apud Woxebregge pernoctando in pa [*sic*] ob in potu j d in carn' iij d in igne ob in lecto j d in feno j s in Aven' j d in pane equino ob Item apud Wycumbe in prand' in pane ob in potu j d in carn' ij d in pane equino j d Item apud Tettusworth' in potu ob in pane equino ob

Item solvi attorn' nostro in communi banco vj s viij d Item in vino dato Ed' Gifford et Alano Cooper x d Item in una copia placiti viij d Item In vino dato david Hammer xj d In conductione unius equi xx d

Summa xxxvij s

[*Dorse*]

[*Reparaciones*] Aularum

In primis circa Hospicium nostrum, In luto empto pro pariete Albe Aule viij d Item in feno j d In clavibus vj d ob In meremio empto xix [*d*] In latis xij d Item liber' duobus operarijs operantibus circa parietem predictum x d Item pro purgacione latrine ij s ij d Item in stramine empto pro domo supra Erbarium in a^{o} disporto vj d ob Item liber' tribus operarijs operantibus circa predictam cameram et murum inter nos et Lodelowhall' xvij d Item in luto iiij d Item in latis xij d Item in clavibus iiij d Item in tegulis ij s v d Item liber' uni bigario operanti per unum diem xij d Item in mosse iiij d Item in emendacione unius hostii in hospicio nostro ij d In emendacione unius sere cum clavibus iij d In pari g[. . .] v d ob In Cenefactorio ij d

Summa xv s ij d ob

Reparaciones Stauntonhall'

In primis in uno ligno empto ad reparacionem gurgitis viij d Item in latis xij d In clavis v d ob In meremio empto ad reparacionem unius camere ix d Item liber' duobus operarijs operantibus circa predictam cameram per unum diem ix d ob in duobus lignis emptis ad reparacionem stabuli x d Item in tegulis ij s vj d Item in mosse iiij d Item in potu j d ob In reparacione hostii orti et purgacione gurgitis xv d Item uni operario operanti circa stabulum v d In una sera et duobus clavibus viij d

Summa ix s ix d ob

Reparaciones drowdalehalle

In primis in tabulis pro una camera vij d ob item in clavibus pro eadem camera ij d In correctione unius sere cum clave j d ob in ligno empto ad composicionem introitus j d ob In findulis et clavibus pro dormalio v d In luto empto viij d In clave empto ad coquinam ij d In calce et arena x d In feno j d ob In ligno empto ad reparacionem camere iuxta coquinam iiij d ob In clave pro eadem camera et alijs v d In findulis pro eadem camera iij d In factura gradus xij d In ligno empto pro eodem gradu ij d In clave j d ob In tabula pro latrina iiij d ob In tabula pro gradu ij d ob In conductione unius operarii pro sex diebus ij s vj d In factura latrine xij d In ligno et tabulis emptis pro eadem latrina xvi d ob In clave iij d In tabula hostii et eius factura vj d In fenestris et hamis xv d ob In sera hostii aule iij d In sera et clave camere sub aula vj d In emendacione gurgitus xiiij d ob Item uni operario cum suo famulo operanti circa predictum gurgitem et diversa domus per duos dies xiij d In stramine empto pro muro ix d Item duobus operariis operantibus circa predictam cameram per tres dies ij s ij d In mosse v d ob

Summa xix s v d

Reparaciones aule Scuti

In primis luto x d In factura murorum ij d In clave pro coquina v d In Twyst' iiij d In latis j d In tabula iiij d In tribus clavibus viij d

Summa ij s x d

Reparaciones aule sancti Edwardi

In primis in tectoribus vij d ob[8] In tegulis iij d In clave hostij aule ij d In hamo ad hostium magne aule alte ij d In mosse j d ob In reparacione hostij promptuarij viij d ob In reparacione camere basse iuxta coquinam xij d Item liberavi uni carpentario pro reparacione fenestrarum aule et camerarum iiij d In tabulis et ligamentis vj d In magnis clavibus j d Item in tabulis pro refectione dictarum camerarum v d In duobus operarijs operantibus circa parietes viij d In parvis clavibus iij d In findulis ij d ob In tribus lignis emptis pro refectione parietis inter coquinam et stabulum iiij d ob Item uni bigario qui ducebat terram ad dictos parietes viij d

Summa vj s vj d ob

[8] These underlinings are on the roll itself.

Reparaciones Hamptonhalle

In primis in luto iiij d In uno ligno empto ad reparacionem unius camere viij d In potu dato operari[*js*] ij d Item liberavi uni latamo cum suo famulo operatant[*ibus*] circa fontem et murum xiiij s iiij d In cratis iij d In mosse ij d

Summa xv s xj d

Reparaciones aula Sancti Thome

In primis in tegulis xx d In luto viij d In duabus seris ix d In emendacione duarum serarum cum clave vj d In quinquedecim hamis ix d ob In quinque ligamentis ix d In plumbo ij d ob In novo hostio et clave xvij d In feno ij d Item pro labore unius operarij viij d In latis at clav[*ibus*] iij d ob In factura unius camere cum terra empta viij d ob In factura gradus xij d In gemmis vij d In sera iiij d In duabus fenestris et ligamentis vij d In clave pro promptuario iiij d In Calce vj d Item liberavi duobus operariis operantibus circa diversas domos per quatuor dies ij s x d Item uni tegulatori pro duobus diebus viij d

Summa xv s v d

Alie expense

In mutacione vasorum pro panteria et coquina vij s ix d In vino tempore quo Cancellarius audivit Compotum x d In vino tempore inpugnoracionis librorum v d In cervisijs apud T. dolle tempore quo recipimus libros j d In pergamino iij d ob In cervisiis taxatis taxantibus drowdalehalle j d In vino dato apprentic' v d In vino dato Ed' Sperswold et Johanno jackes xij d In expensis apud apyndon factis per M.J.P. xiij d ob In mosse v d In vino dato david' hammer x d ob Item liberavi Thome Sampson pro diversis laboribus x s Item liberavi uni operanti circa lapidibus reparandos per tres dies xij d

Summa xxiij s x d ob

Stipendia famulorum

In primis liberavi Mancipio et coco ad festum translacionis sancti Thome Martiris v s Item liberavi Mancipio ad festum Sancti Mich' iij s iiij d Item liberavi Pock pro labore in autumpno xij d Item liberavi Mancipio et coco ad festum Nat' domini v s Item liberavi Manicipio et coco ad festum Pasche v s Item liberavi barbitonsori et lotrici x s Item liberavi pro stipendio procuratoris x s

Summa xxxix s iiij d

liberacio denariorum

Item liberavi communi Ciste xiij s iiij d
Summa xiij s iiij d

Deffectus redditus

Item petit Allocacionem de deffectu reddituum qui sunt in manibus Ed Frauncseys[9]

De ten' Ricardi Merser	l s
Item de shopa pyry	xiij s iiij d
Item de ten' Ricardi Cornewayle	xxx s
Item de ten' Willelmi Saundres	xl s
Item de ten' Roberti Westby	vj li xvj s
Item de ten' Johannis Wyndesore	xiij s iiij d
Item de ten' Johannis vaginarii	xviij d

Summa xv li viij d

Deffectus redditus Quia non dum solvuntur

In primis de aula Scuti	xviij s iiij d
Item de Olyfaunthall'	xij d
Item de aula Sancti Thome	xj s viij d
Item de aul' universitatis in vico scolarum	vj s viij d
Item de Stauntonhall'	xxiiij s
Item de drowdalehall'	xxiiij s ij d
Item de aula sancti Edwardi	x s
Item de ten' J. Baret	iiij s
Item de ten' J. Brasier	x s
Item de Hamptonhalle	xlvj s viij d
Item de Collegio Cant'	ij s vj d
Item de orto ultra castrum	ij s vj d
Item de lodelowhall'	xxvj s viij d
Item de domo Holwey	xiiij s
Item de orto ex opposito domui predicto	xij d
Item de Brasenose xxvi s viij d qui condonatur per socios	
Item de holdirnesse	iiij li ix s xj d

Summa istius xv li xix s ix d

[9] These, and other similar entries in the rolls up to 1387/8, are connected with a dispute between the College and Edmund Francis over the ownership of these properties. Several sums in the payments sections of the 1380s rolls are also clearly linked with expenses incurred in the case. See Appendix II in Vol. II for an account of the dispute.

⟨defectus redditus arrerag'⟩

Item petit Allocari de deffectu Arr' viz. de Hamptonhalle iij li quod solvebatur M.T. ffurneys

Item de drowdalehalle – xxiij s iiij d

Item de aula universitatis in vico scolarum viij s iiij d quos retinet penes se R. Yonge pro pavimento Item de camera principali xvj s viij d

Summa v li viij s iiij d

Deffectus redditus camerarum que non dum solvuntur

In primis de camera principali	xx s
Item de camera sibi proxima	x s
De camera sub illa	vj s viij d
Item de camera supra erbarium iuxta aulam	x s
De camera cum aula in alio disporto	ix s
De camera fonti opposita	x s
Item de camera sibi proxima	vj s

Summa istius iij li xj s viij d

Summa omnium expensarum et allocatorum lxvij li iij s x d ob

Et sic in plusagio viij s vj d ob

[*A clearly written, neat roll, in a small legible hand. 2 membranes. Smith has made entries on it.*]

MICH. 6 RICHARD II to MICH. 7 RICHARD II (ROLL UC:BU1/F/2) (29 September 1382–29 September 1383)

BURSAR: JOHN TAYLOR

Rotul[*us*] 6 Anni testatur de solucione ij s

Computus Magistri Johannis Taylour socij ac procuratoris Collegij Magistri Willelmi de Dunelm' Michiluniversitehalle vulgariter nuncupati a festo sancti Mich' Archangeli Anno regni regis Ricardi secundi post conquestum sexto usque ad idem festum anno revoluto

Arr' Recepta per eundem procuratorem anno supradicto

In primis de Olyfaunthalle	xij d
Item de Aula scuti	xviij s iiij d
Item de Aula sancti Thome	xij s viij d
Item de Aula universitatis in vico scolarum	vj s viij d
Item de Stauntonhalle	xxiiij s
Item de Drowdalehalle	xxiiij s ij d
Item de Aula Sancti Edwardi	x s
Item de ten' Johannis Baret	iiij s
Item de ten' Johannis Brasier	x s
Item de Hamptonhalle pro arr' 2^{orum} annorum preteritorum	v li vj s viij d
Item de Lodelowehall	xxvj s viij d
Item de Collegio cantuar'	ij s vj d
Item de Orto ultra Castrum	ij s vj d
Item de domo Holewey	xiiij s
Item de orto ex opposito domui predicto	xij d
Item de Holdornesse	iiij li ix s xj d
Item de aula universitatis in vico scolarum pro arr' anni penultimi preteriti	viij s iiij d
Item de camera principali pro anno penultimo preterito	xvj s viij d
Item de Arr' camerarum anni ultimo preteriti	iij li ⟨xij s iij d⟩[1]

[1] [ADMC] This entry has been altered. In the previous roll it is £3 11s 8d.

Item de Drowdalehalle pro anno penultimo preterito	xxiij s iiij d
⟨Summa xxiij li xij s v d⟩	

Redditus Collegio supradicti qui debentur Collegio supradicto pro tempore predicti procuratoris

In primis de Maydenhalle	xiij s iiij d
Item de Olyfaunthalle	iiij s
Item de Aula scuti	xl s
Item de Aula sancti Thome	xl s
Item de Aula universitatis in vico scolarum	xxxiij s iiij d
Item de Aula Brasenose	v marc'
Item de Hamptonhalle	iij li
Item de Aula sancti Edwardi	xxx s
Item de Stauntonhalle	xlviij s
Item de Drowdalehalle	lj s iiij d
Item de Lodelowehall	liij s iiij d
Item de domo Holewey	xv s
Item de Orto ex opposito domui predicto	iij s
Item de ten' Johannis Baret	viij s
Item de ten' Johannis Brasyer	x s
Item de Orto ultra Castrum	ij s vj d
Item de Collegio Cant'	ij s vj d
Item de ten' Ricardi Merser	l s
Item de shopa Pyry	xiij s iiij d
Item de ten' Willelmi saundres	xl s
Item de ten' Roberti Westby	ix marc' xvj s
Item de ten' Johannis Wyndeshore	xiij s iiij d
Item de ten' Johannis vaginarij	xviij s
Item de ten' Ricardi Cornewayle	xxx s
Item de Holdornesse	iiij li ix s xj d
⟨Summa xliij li xj s vij d⟩	

Redditus De cameris recipiendi per eundem procuratorem in Collegio predicto

In primis de camera principali	xx s
Item de camera sibi proxima	xiij s iiij d
Item de camera sub illa	xij s
Item de camera supra Erbarium in alio disporto	x s
Item de camera cum Aula	xviij s
Item de camera fonti opposita	x s

Item de camera sibi proxima x s
Item de Alba Aula xij s
⟨Summa v li v s iiij d⟩

⟨Summa totalis omnium reddituum et oneratorum lxxij li ix s iiij d⟩

Expense

Resolucio redditus

In primis liberavi Canonico sancte ffrideswyde pro redditibus annorum preteriti et presentis xxiij s iiij d
Item liberavi procuratori Abbathie de Abyndon pro quodam anuali [*sic*] redditu ij s
Item liberavi procuratori Abathie de Osney pro quodam anuali redditu vj s viij d
Item liberavi procuratori Ecclesie sancti Petri in oriente pro parte solucionis anni preteriti ij s x d
Item liberavi procuratori ecclesie sancte Marie pro redditu de Stantonhalle xij d
⟨Summa xxxv s x d⟩

Communes primi termini a festo sancte Petronille usque ad festum sancti Michaelis

Communes sociorum

In prima septimana in communibus duorum sociorum ij s
In batellis ix d ob
In secunda septimana in communibus unius socij xij d
In batellis iiij d
In tercia septimana in communibus duorum sociorum ij s
In batellis [*blank*]
In quarta septimana in communibus duorum sociorum ij s
In quinta septimana in communibus duorum sociorum ij s
In sexta septimana in communibus duorum sociorum ij s
In septima septimana in communibus duorum sociorum ij s
In Octava septimana in communibus duorum sociorum ij s
In nona septimana in communibus duorum sociorum ij s
In decima septimana in communibus duorum sociorum ij s
In undecima septimana in communibus duorum sociorum ij s
In duodecima septimana in communibus duorum sociorum xviij d
In terciadecima septimana in communibus unius socij xij d

In quartadecima septimana in communibus duorum sociorum ij s In batellis iij d

In quintadecima septimana in communibus duorum sociorum ij s In batellis pro operar[*io*] iij d

In sextadecima septimana in communibus duorum sociorum ij s In batellis j d

In septimadecima septimana in communibus duorum sociorum ij s In batellis j d ob

⟨Summa xxxiij s iiij d⟩

Communes secundi termini a festo sancti mich' usque ad festum Nat' domini

In prima septimana in communibus duorum sociorum ij s

In secunda septimana in communibus duorum sociorum ij s In batellis ij d ob

In tercia septimana in communibus duorum sociorum ij s In batellis j d

In quarta septimana in communibus trium sociorum iij s In batellis ob

In quinta septimana in communibus trium sociorum iij s In batellis j d ob

In sexta septimana in communibus ~~in communibus~~ trium sociorum ij s x d In batellis j d

In septima septimana in communibus trium sociorum ij s ix d ob In batellis ij d ob

In Octava septimana in communibus trium sociorum iij s In batellis ij d

In nona septimana in communibus trium sociorum ij s ix d q[a] In batellis ij d ob

In x[ma] septimana in communibus duorum sociorum ij s Item in batellis iij d ob

In xj[ma] septimana in communibus duorum sociorum ij s In batellis j d

In xij[ma] septimana in communibus duorum sociorum ij s

⟨Summa xxx s xj d o[b] q[a]⟩

Communes tercij termini a festo Nat' domini usque ad festum Pasche

In prima septimana in communibus trium sociorum iij s

In ij[a] septimana in communibus duorum sociorum ij s

In iij[a] septimana in communibus trium sociorum iij s In batellis v d ob

In iiij^{ta} septimana in communibus trium sociorum iij s
In dict[*is*] et batellis viij d ob
In v^{ta} septimana in communibus trium sociorum iij s
In vi^{ta} septimana in communibus trium sociorum iij s
Item in batellis j d
In vij^{ma} septimana in communibus trium sociorum iij s
In viij^{ma} septimana in communibus trium sociorum iij s
In ix^{na} septimana in communibus trium sociorum iij s
In x^{ima} septimana in communibus trium sociorum ij s ix d ob
In xj^{ma} septimana in communibus duorum sociorum ij s
In batellis j d
In xij^{ma} septimana in communibus duorum sociorum ij s
Item in batellis vj d
In xiij^{ma} septimana in communibus trium sociorum iij s
⟨Summa xxxvij s vij d o[b]⟩

Communes quarti termini a festa Pasche
In prima septimana in communibus duorum sociorum ij s
In secunda septimana in communibus trium sociorum iij s
In batellis iij d
In tercia septimana in communibus trium sociorum iij s
In quarta septimana in communibus trium sociorum iij s
In quinta septimana in communibus trium sociorum iij s
Item in batellis ob
In sexta septimana in communibus trium sociorum iij s
In septima septimana in communibus trium sociorum iij s
⟨In octava septimana ij s⟩
⟨Summa xxij s iij d o[*b*]⟩

Expense forincese ffacte per eundem procuratorum anno supradicto
In primis liberavi Magistris Johanni Midilton et Johanni Taylour pro ~~eor~~ expensis Lond' in negocijs domus xx s ex quibus expenderunt viij^{to} diebus in se et uno famulo cum tribus equis et Roberto Westby cum equo suo per partem eiusdem septimane xiiij s q^{a}[2] / Et idem M. Johannes Taylour reliquit postea cum M. Johanne Mydelton de eisdem iiij s ij d et liberavit Roberto Westby pro expensis versus Oxon' viij d
⟨Item solvitur xij d per facturam istius compotus⟩

[2] These underlinings are on the original roll.

In conductione unius equi eodum tempore – ij s ij d
⟨Summa xxij s q[a]⟩

Item liberavi M Johanni Poklyngton versus Lond' in negocijs domus xxij s iiij d Et quibus idem M. J.P. reliquit cum M. Johanne Midilton – xiij s iiij d Item de eisdem cuidam attorn[*at*] iij s iiij d In expensis M. J.P. cum famulo suo et equo eodum tempore ij s ij d In conductione equi – xx d Item clerico ambulanti in itinere cum eo vj d
⟨Summa xxj s⟩

Item liberavi Magistro Roberto Gower pro expensis versus Lond' in seipso et equo suo – xiiij s iiij d In conductione unius equi eodem tempore – xij d Item Attorn[*ato*] in communi banco xl d Et idem M. J. Taylour liberavit M. Johanni Alkebarow pro rettorn' brevium xx d Item in expensis M. R' Gower in negocijs domus versus vic' v d ob/
⟨Summa xx s ix d ob⟩

Reparaciones Aularum ffacte per eundem procuratorem in anno supradicto

In primis in hospicio nostro in latis emptis xxiij d Item in tegulis vij s ij d Item liberavi duobus operantibus circa Albam Aulam per septimanam vj s Item liberavi duobus operarijs operantibus circa diversos domos per x dies in yeme vij s x d Item liberavi uni laboranti circa cameram supra Erbarium in Alio disporto per unum diem v d Item tectori eiusdem camere pro una die v d Item puero adiuvanti eum ij d In stramine pro eodem camera v d Item in stramine pro eadem camera iij d Item mulieribus trahentibus stramina v d In clav' vj d In clavis latarum ij d in cervisio pro tegulatoribus j d Item pro dimidio mill[i]/ camillarum tegularum ij d Item alia vice in clav' latarum iiij d Item in cervisijs pro tegulatoribus ij d / in reparacione parietis ~~an~~ iuxta Cudyngton x d Item pro clavis latarum iij d In musto vj d ob / Item pro camillarum tegulorum ij d Item pro clavis ad tabulam ciforum [*sic*] j d In rubea terra iiij d In emendacione sere hostij aule ij d In emendacione sere promptuarij j d Item uni bigario pro ductu later' iiij d In crist' ij d/
⟨Summa xxix s iij d ob⟩

Reparaciones de Maydenhalle

In primis in stramine iiij s x d ob in Cenefactorio ij d Item mulieribus trahentibus stramina viij d ob Item liberavi operantibus ibidem per viij^to dies – ij s x d In Calce viij d In clavis ij d In fixalis ij d

⟨Summa ix s vij d⟩

Reparaciones Drowdale Halle

In primis liberavi uni plumberio pro emendacione guttar' xij d Item in sowdur ad idem tempor' xv d In clavis iij d In reparacione unius muri [*blank*]

[*No total given*]

Reparaciones Stauntonhalle

In primis in uno puteo facto pro purgacione latrine xvj d In pane et potu vj d In mundacione latrine v s In clavis pro parietibus et coopertura latrine xvj d ob In luto iiij d In gurgis et vertinellis v d Item in Argento dato Carpentario ij s xj d In lapidibus emptis xij d In tabulis pro coopertura latrine ij s ob In reparacione muri lapidei iij s iiij d In reparacione muri promptuarij iij d Item pueris laborantibus in eodem opere et purgacione vie vj d In emendacione parietum iij d Item in reparacione parietum iij d in feno j d in latis vij d Item in tabulis et meremio xvij d In reparacione parietis stabuli x d Item in reparacione stabuli vj d In supposicione parietis vj d Item per manus procuratoris in cervisia data cloacarijs j d In cervisia data carpentarijs et alijs operarijs ij d Item puero expellenti ruder' ibidem iij d In crate pro latrina ij d Item liberavi pueris portantibus lapides ij d

⟨Summa xiiij s iiij d⟩

[*Dorse*]

Reparaciones aule sancti Thome

In primis in reparacione unius camere x d In mundacione latrine per manus T Sygruston xviij d Item pro tabulis vj d In duabus seris iiij d Item uni operario operanti circa reparaciones unius parietis per t[*re*]s dies cum dimidio xviij d Item pro reparacione Aliarum camerarum vj d Item in rubea terra xij d Item pro sera hostij Aule xij d Item pro spera facta in certis cameris viij d In argento liberato cloacario per manus procuratoris vj d

⟨Summa viij s iiij d⟩

Reparaciones Hamptonhalle

In primis in reparacione unius parietis xij d

⟨Summa xij d⟩

Alie expense

In primis in vino et sp[*eci*]ebus duabus vicibus domino Cancellario ij s viij d In vino dato domino Johanni Newnham xvj d In jantaculo eiusdem domini Johannis v s iij d ob / Item in vino dato ´ dyghton clerico ij s In vino dato Thome Sampson pro scriptura literarum iiij d Item in Argento dato clerico vic' iiij d Item pro scriptura copie ultimi panelli iiij d Item pro scriptura copie Petycopy iiij d In emendacione diversarum ollarum xij d Item pro mutacione unius olle euer iij s iiij d Item in vino dato hominibus procurantibus lateres ij d Item liberavi Thome dolle pro Thoma super quartum sentenciarum xiij s iiij d In argento dato Thome dolle pro servicio suo ij s In cervisia data duabus vicibus ij d In papiro j d ob In pergamino iij d Item pro tegulis emptis de Holway vij s Item liberavi Willelmo quondam mancipio pro debitis Collegij a retro vj s viij d In cervisia data carpentario operanti apud Lodelowhalle vj d Item liberavi M. Henrico ffowler pro labore suo xx d In securi v d In acucione securis ob In pane equino dato equis M. Johannis Midilton iiij d

⟨Summa xlix s vij d ob⟩

Stipendia famulorum

In primis liberavi mancipio et coco pro termino sancti Thome Martiris v s Item liberavi mancipio et coco pro termino sancti Mich' v s Item liberavi mancipio et coco pro termino Nat' domini v s Item liberavi mancipio et coco pro termino Pasche v s Item liberavi lotrici pro stipendio anni preteriti v s Item liberavi Roberto Barbour pro anno preterito v s Item liberavi lotrici pro parte solucionis stipendij [*sic*] anni presentis ij s

⟨Summa xxxij s⟩

Liberacio denariorum

In primis liberavi commune ciste xxxviiij s ⟨Item xij s iij d
Summa l s iii d⟩

Defectus redditus Quia non in manu Collegij

In primis de ten' Ricardi Merser l s
Item de shopa Pyry xiij s iiij d

Item de ten' Willelmi Saundres	xl s
Item de ten' Ricardi Westby	ix marc' xvj s
Item de ten' Johannis Wyndsore	xiij s iiij d
Item de ten' Johannis vaginarij	xviij s
Item de ten' Ricardi Cornewayle	xxx s
⟨Summa xv li viij d⟩	

Defectus redditus Quia non dum solvuntur[3]

In primis de Lodelowhalle	xl s
Item de drowdalehalle	xxxviij s
Item de Aula sancti Edwardi	xxiij s iiij d
Item de eadem	xxvj s iiij d
Item de domo Holway	xj s
Item de Stauntonhalle	xxiiij s vij d
Item de Aula scuti	xl s
Item de ten' Johannis Brasier	v s
Item de Holdornesse	iiij li ix s xj d
Item de Collegio Cant'	ij s vj d
Item de Olyfaunthalle	xij d
Item de Aula universitatis in vico scolarum	vj s viij d
Item de Aula Brasenose	vj s viij d
⟨quia condonantur per socios⟩	
Item de Orto ex opposito domui predicto	iij s
Item de Aula santi Thome	xxxviij s
Item de ten' Johannis Baret	viij s
Item de Hamptonhalle	iij li
Item de Orto ultra Castrum	ij s vj d
⟨Summa xxj li vj s x d⟩	

defectus redditus Arr'

In primis petit allocari viz. de Aula scuti v ⟨s⟩ x d Item de Aula universitatis in vico scolarum viij s iiij d q[a] M. R. Young' pro pavimento Item de Drowdalehalle xxiij s iiij d Item de Hamphall [*sic*] v li vij s viij d q[a] solvebantur M Thome ffurneys Item de Holdornesse xvj s vij d Item de Aula sancti Edwardi v s q[a] condonantur per socios

Item petit allocari pro defectu arr' camerarum

In primis de camera principali	xxxvj s viij d

[3] These entries are set out in two columns on the roll, the second column starting with the entry for Olifaunt Hall.

Item de camera sibi proxima	xiij d
Item de camera supra Erbarium iuxta aulam	x s
Item de camera fonti opposita	xx d
Item de camera cum aula	xiiij d

⟨Summa x li xvj s iiij d⟩

defectus redditus camerarum

Item petit allocari pro defectu reddit[*us*] camerarum q^{a} non dum solvuntur

In primis de camera principali	xx s
Item de camera sibi proxima	vj s viij d
Item de camera sub illa	xj s
Item de camera supra Erbarium in Alio disporto	iij s iiij d
Item de camera cum aula	iiij s viij d
Item de camera fonti opposita	x s
Item de camera sibi proxima	x s
Item de Alba Aula	xij s

[*No total given*]

⟨Summa lxx li viij s viiij d⟩[4]

⟨Et sic debet xl s viij d

Et solvit super compotum et remisit in cista⟩

[*A neat, legible roll of 2 membranes, the hand very like that of the 1381/2 roll*]

[4] [ADMC] It looks as if this figure had been altered from lxxvij s viij d (which is the total of the last group) to lxx li viij s viij d. 'li' is inserted above the line.

MICH. 7 RICHARD II to MICH. 8 RICHARD II (ROLL UC:BU1/F/3) (29 September 1383–29 September 1384)

BURSAR: RICHARD GYSBORN

⟨Rotulu 7 Anni testatur de solucione xij d. a⟩

Compotus magistri Ricardi Gysborn Socij ac procuratoris Collegij magistri Willelmi de dunelm Micheluniversitehalle vulgariter nuncupati a festo Sancti Mich' archangeli Anno regno regis Ricardi Secundi post conquestum Septimo usque ad idem festum anno revoluto

Arr' redditus anni precedentis

In primis de Lodelowhalle xl s Item de Olyfonthalle xij d Item de drowdalehalle iij li xvj d Item de aula universitatis in vico scolarum xv s Item de Aula Sancti Edwardi xxiij s iiij d et alij quinque solidi condonantur per Socios Item de Brasenose vj s viij d et de eadem xxvj s viij d condonantur per Socios Item de domo Holleway xj s Item de orto exopposito domui predicte [*sic*] iij s Item de Stantonhalle xxiij s vij d Item de Aula Sancti Thome xxxviij s Item de Aula Scuti xlv s x d Item de ten' Benet viij s Item de ten' Johnanis Brasier v s Item de Hamptonhalle iij li etiam de eadem v li vj s viij d qui solvebantur magistro Thome ffurneys Item de Holderness' iiij li ix s xj d Item de orto ultra castrum ij s vj d Item de collegio Cantuar' ij s vj d Item de camera principali lvj s viij d Item de camera sibi proxima vij s ix d Item de camera super herbarium iuxta aulam x s Item de camera fonti opposita x s xx d Item de camera cum aula v s x d Item de camera proxima illi camera que opposita fonti x s Item de alba aula xij s Item de camera que super herbarium in alio disporto iiij s viij d Item de Holdornesse xvj s vij d Item de camera que est q [*sic*] sub illa camera que est proxima camere principali xj solid'

Summa xxxvj li ij s ij d

Redditus collegij

Qui debentur eidem collegio pro tempore predicti procuratoris

In primis de Maydenhalle	xiij s iiij d
Item de Olyfanthalle	iiij s

Item de Aula Scuti	xl s
Item de Aula Thome	xl s
Item de Aula universitatis in vico Scolarum	xxxiij s iiij d
Item de Brasenose	iij li vj s viij d
Item de Amptonhalle	iij li
Item de Aula Sancti Edwardi	xxx s
Item de Stantonhalle	xlviij s
Item de Drowdahalle	lj s iiij d
Item de lodelowhalle	liij d iiij d
Item de domo holway	xv s
Item de Orto ex opposito domui predicte	iij s
Item de ten' Johannis Baret	viij s
Item de ten' Johannis Brasier	x s
Item de orto ultra castrum	ij s vj d
Item de Collegio cantuar'	ij s vj d
Item de Ten' Ricardi merser	l s
Item de Shopa Pyry	xiij s iiij d
Item de ten' Willelmi Saundres	xl s
Item de ten' Roberti Westeby	ix marc' xvj s
Item de ten' Johannis Wyndeshore	xiij s iiij d
Item de ten' Johannis vaginarij	xviij s
Item de ten' Ricardi Cornewale	xxx s
Item de Holdornesse	iiij li ix s xj d
Summa xliij li xj s vij d	

Redditus

De cameris recipiendis per eundem procuratorem in collegio Supradicto

In primis de camera principali	xx s
Item de camera Sibi proxima	xiij s iiij d
Item de camera sub illa	xij s
Item de camera super herbarium in Alio disporto	x s
Item de camera cum aula	xviij s
Item de camera fonti opposita	x s
Item de camera Sibi proxima	x s
Item de Alba Aula	xij s
Summa v li v iiij d	

Summa totalis lxxxiiij li xix s j d

Recepta[1] Per eundem procuratorum de arr' et redditibus Collegij predicti

In primis de Olyfanthalle	iiij s
Item de Aula Scuti	xl s viij d
Item de Aula Sancti Thome	xx s
Item de Aula universitatis in vico Scolarum	xxxiij s iiij d
Item de Stantonhalle	xxxiij s iiij d
Item de Drowdahalle	xxvj s viij d
Item de Aula Sancti Edwardi	xxx s
Item de Aula Brasenose	xl s
Item de ten' Johannis Baret	iij s
Item de ten' Johannis Brasier	v s
Item de Hamptonhalle	xl s
Item de Lodelowhalle	lviij s iiij d
Item de Holdornesse	iiij li ix s xj d
Item de una camera super herbarium iuxta aulam	x s
Item de camera principalis pro anno preterito	xvj s viij d
Item de camera furnes	xij s
Item de tenemento Brasyer pro anno preterito	v s
Item de Aula scuti pro anno preterito	v s
Item de camera lavinton pro anne preterito	x s

Summa xxij li xiiij s xj d

Summa \`receptorum in hoc anno non onerata´ xxj li xxxiiij s xj d ista summa non ponitur in Summa totali [. . .] arr' et rental' et recepta de cista reponuntur in Summa totali ~~inferius~~ inferiori

Recepta de cista communi

per eundem procuratorem in predicto Collegio in toto xiij li ij d ob

~~Summa totalis oneris lxxxxvij li~~ xix s ij d ob

Summa xiij li ij d ob

Summa totalis omnium receptorum iiij^{xx}xvij li xix s iij d ob

[1] These two sections headed *Recepta* have been deleted. They are unusual in recording the actual rents received by University College this year, and are discussed in detail on p. xl of the Introduction. See too the unusual pair of rolls for 1436/7.

Expense

Resolucio redditus

In primis liberavi canonico Sancte frideswyde pro redditu anni presentis xiij s iiij d

Item liberavi procuratori abathie de Osenay pro quodam annuali redditu vj s viij d

Item liberavi de redditu palusflet pro fine Secta Wepentake ij s

Item pro firma de xx acris ~~terre~~ prati quas petrus Grumysby tenuit liberavi manorie de Bruswyll' xiij d ob

Item liberavi Senescallo de Holdornesse pro redditu de Pael vj d

Item liberavi pro firma de xx acris pro anno presenti manerie de Bruswyll' xiij d ob

Item liberavi predicto Senescallo pro secta Wepentak anno presenti vj s viij d

Item pro redditu de Pahal anno presenti vj d

Item liberavi domino Philippo de Spenser xv d

Item domino Abbrede Connstable vij d ob

Summa xxxiiij s ix d ob

Communes sociorum Primi termini a festo Sanctorum Gordiani et Epimachi

In prima septimana in communibus duorum sociorum ij s x d

In batellis j d

In vino et speciebus xij d ob

In secunda septimana in communibus duorum sociorum ij s ix d ob

In tercia septimana in communibus trium sociorum iij s

In quarta septimana in communibus trium sociorum iij s

In quinta septimana in communibus trium sociorum iij s

In sexta septimana in communibus trium sociorum iij s

In septima septimana in communibus trium sociorum iij s

In Octava septimana in communibus trium sociorum iij s

In Nona septimana in communibus trium sociorum iij s

In Decima septimana in communibus trium sociorum iij s

In undecima septimana in communibus trium sociorum iij s

In batellis j d

In duodecima septimana in communibus trium sociorum iij s

In decima tercia septimana in communibus trium sociorum iij s

In decima quarta septimana in communibus duorum sociorum ij s et pro dicte Gower vj d ob

In decima quinta septimana in communibus duorum sociorum ij s

In decima sexta septimana in communibus duorum sociorum ij s

In decima septima septimana in communibus duorum sociorum ij s

In decima ~~septima~~ octava septimana in communibus duorum sociorum ij s In batellis ob

In decima nona septimana in communibus duorum sociorum ij s In batellis ij d ob

In vicesima septimana in communibus unius socii ij s In batellis j d ob

In dictorum magistrorum Johannis Taylour et Ricardi Gysborn xix d

⟨Summa lv s iiij d⟩

Communes secundi termini a festo sancti mich' usque ad festum Nat' domini

In prima septimana in communibus trium sociorum et dimidij iij s vj d In batellis iij d ob

In secunda septimana in communibus trium sociorum iij s In batellis j d

In tercia septimana in communibus trium sociorum iij s In batellis ij d ob

In quarta septimana in communibus quatuorum [*sic*] sociorum iiij s In batellis ob

In quinta septimana in communibus quatuor sociorum v s In batellis iij d

In sexta septimana in communibus quattuorum [*sic*] sociorum v s In batellis ob

In septima septimana in communibus quattuor sociorum v s In batellis ob

In octava septimana in communibus quattuor sociorum v s In batellis j d ob

In Nona septimana in communibus quatuor sociorum v s In batellis ob

In Decima septimana in communibus quatuor sociorum v s

In undecima septimana in communibus quatuor sociorum v s

In duodecima septimana in communibus quatuor sociorum v s
⟨Summa liiij s vij d ob⟩

Communes tercij termini a festo Nat' domini usque ad festum Pasche
In prima septimana in communibus quattuor sociorum vij s vj d — In batellis ij d
In secunda septimana in communibus trium sociorum iiij s viij d ob q[a] — In batellis iiij d
In tercia septimana in communibus quattuor sociorum v s
In batellis ob
In quarta septimana in communibus quattuor sociorum v s
In batellis ob
In quinta septimana in communibus quattuor sociorum v s
In batellis ob
In sexta septimana in communibus quattuorum sociorum v s
In batellis j d ob
In septima septimana in communibus quattuor sociorum v s
In batellis ij d
In Vecco[a] j d ob
In Octava septimana in communibus quattuor sociorum v s
In batellis ob
In Nona septimana in communibus quattuorum sociorum v s
In batellis ob
In Decima septimana in communibus quattuor sociorum v s
In undecima septimana in communibus quattuor sociorum v s
In batellis vj d ob
In ostis j d
In duodecima septimana in communibus quatuor sociorum v s
I [*sic*]
In decima tercia septimana in communibus quattuor sociorum v s
In decima quarta septimana in communibus quattuor sociorum v s
⟨Summa iij li xj d ob q[a]⟩
In decima quinta septimana in communibus quattuor sociorum v s
In decima sexta septimana in communibus quattuor sociorum v s
⟨Summa iiij li iij s xj d ob q[a]⟩

Communes quarti termini a festo pasche usque [*blank*]
In prima septimana In communibus quattuor sociorum [*blank*]
In secunda septimana In communibus quattuor sociorum [*blank*]

In tercia septimana In communibus quattuor sociorum [*blank*]
Item Summa pro isto tempore xl s

Summa totalis in communibus xij li viij s viij d q^a ob

Expensa forinsece facte per eundem procuratorem anno supradicto

In primis liberavi pro expensis apud Abundon' et in uno equo versus Mylton xiij d ob
Item usque Northampton pro expensis in negocijs domus iij s iiij d
Item una vice versus London' in negocijs domus ix s viij d ob
Item alia vice versus London' liberavi in proprijs expensis pro ij septimanis in negocijs domus et multis alijs sumptibus scilicet in donis pro consilio habendo in vino et iantaculo et in uno brevi et pluribus alijs xxxij s xj d ob
Item tercia vice versus London' pro expensis magistorum Johannis Taylour et Ricardi Gysborn xx s j d
Item apud Abyndon In vino dato Samforth at alijs de duodena xij d
Item Apud Gybbes bina vice circa negocia domus in vino xvj d
Item in vino samforth' et in donis sibi et socijs suis pro favore domus iij s x d
Item in camera Gower bina vice hominibus de Abyndon in vino xij d
Item Boklok et Alijs de duodena in vino pro consilio viij d
Item in dono Daggawylle circa negocia domus in vino viij d
Item liberavi pro expensis magistri Johannis Taylour apud Abyndon xij d
Item in aula Sanforth in vino iij d

[*Dorse*]

Item cognato belknap viij d
Item liberavi magistro Roberto Gower pro expensis iij s iiij d
Item Ampton in vino iiij d
Item liberavi pro expensis dicti magistri Ricardi procur' pro expensis versus Holdornesse xvij s iij d
Item Clerico Willelmi haneslay Et atornato xl d
Item Clerico de castro et morton vj d
Item pro prandijs clerici de Haneslay et in quis Myndylton iij s v d
Item in vino iiij d

Item expensis magistri Robert Gower versus London' die lune proxima post festum sancti dionisij xxix s

Item in expensis eiusdem Roberti versus Holdornesse in crastino beate virginis in assumpcionis x s viij d ob

Item in expensis eiusdem Roberti versus London' in octavo sancti Hillarij xx s j d ob

Item in expensis eiusdem Roberti in secunda septimana quadrasima xvij s j d

Item liberavi Willelmo Scryne et Roberto Hampton cum eorum famulis xxxvij s ij d

Summa xj li ij d ob

Stipendia famulorum

In primis mancipio et coco pro termino Sancti Thome v s Item pro termino Mich' v s Item pro termino Nat' domini v s Item pro termino pasche v s

Item barbitonsori domus v s

Item lotrici ij s vj d

Item pro servicio procuratoris x s

Summa xxxvij s vj d

Reparacio aularum[2]

In primi in reparacione Aula Santi Thome

In meremio ad latrinam v s

In carpentario iij s iiij d

In clav' et in coopertura domus iiij d

In asseribus xiiij d

Summa ix s x d

Reparacio aula Scuti

In clav' et seris x d

In factore murorum sex diebus ij s

In uno operario viij d

In tabulis pro fenestris ij s ij d

In operario xx d

Summa vij s iiij d

[2] The accounts for repairs to the academic halls were originally arranged in two columns, the left hand one containing St. Thomas Hall, St. Edward Hall, and Drowda Hall, the right hand one Shield Hall, Little University Hall (in School Street) and Stanton Hall.

Aule [*sic*] Edwardi

In primis pro lignis videlicet stawres	xiij d
In lathomis	xij d
In clavis et in feno circa murum	iij d
Item Hugoni cok et alij [*sic*] famulo	xiij d
Item Holway pro servicio	vij s
et preter hec Gower et Poklynton comput' sibi de redditu pro quarterio Mich'	iij s ix d
Item tegulatori	ix s ij d
In clav' in cuneis et in una crate	xx d ob
In ij laborantibus per dimidium diem	iij d ob
In cervisia lathomis	iiij d
In cervisia petro carpentario	iij d
In domo holway bina vice	ij d
Item in cervisia lathomis certis vicibus	iiij d
In plumbatore aquaductuli	ij s x d
In cervisia sibi et alijs operarijs	ij d ob
In ligno ponendo super aulam	iij d
In tribus carectis tegularum	ix s
In latt'	xxj d
In potu lathomis et alijs operarijs	iij d
In carect' et in lapidibus	ix d
Item pro una carecta	iiij d
Item in operarijs pro latrina	vj d
Item in omnibus operarijs pro cervisia quattuor diebus	xiij d
Item hugoni pro servicio	xx d
Item holway et servienti eius pro una septimana	vj s viij d
Item in uno serviente	iij d
Item lathomo et uni servienti	ij s iiij d
Item petro carpentario	vj s viij d
Item holway pro quattuor septimanis	xxx s
Item in servientibus eius eodem tempore	xx s iij d
Et ipse Holway retinet pro servicio de redditu	vj s viij d
Item in uno serviente	xviij d
Item in tribus hominibus servientibus per septimanam ij diebus ex'	xxij d
In tabulis emptis pro fenestris	x d
In ferr' et clav' et uno stapilo	xx d
Item in uno operario	vj d
Item in clave et emendacione sere	iij d

Item in nova cera et emendactione sere	viij d
Item in emendacione sere et pro clav' ad coquinam	iij d
In cariag' lapidum et pro crate	iiij d ob
In potu lathomis	j d
Item pro cariagio argill'	xx d
Item latere et tegulatoribus	ij s iij d
In expensis in die veneris	ix d
Summa vj li x s v d	

Reparacio Drowdalehall'

In primis in ij laborantibus	vj d
In magnis clavis	ij d
In potu laborantibus	ij d
In Asseribus	v d ob
In lathomo	iiij d
In uno operario	viij d
In potu holway quinque diebus	viij d ob
In sera	j d
In factum parietis	xx d
Summa iiij s ix d	

Aule [*sic*] universitatis

In primis in emptis et expensis ibi et in alijs locis	
In tegulis	vij s
In cavillis	iiij d
In tegugulatoribus [*sic*]	iiij s vj d
In calce in asseribus et in clav'	xij d ob
Item in diversis potibus	iiij d
In c^c^stp [*sic*] in musco et in clav'	xiij d
In tabulis et in ligno	viij d
In coopertore domorum pro j septimana	ij s
In muliere aptante stramina	ix d
In uno plumbatore	ij s
Item holway	x d
In serviente holway pro j septimana	ij s vj d
Item in potu	ij d
Item plumbatori	ij s iiij d
Item cooptori [*sic*] domorum	iiij d
Item holway	iij s iiij d
Item scalis	v s
In asseribus	xv d

In operario	xx d
In plumbatore	ij s vj d
In Soudour	v d
In tectore	viij d
In tribus carectis straminis	ij s ix d ob
In pinnis	iiij d
Item in stramine	xij d ob
In mossa	v s ij d
In clav'	ij d
In operario	iiij d ob
Item tegulatori	ij s vj d
Item in tripode	xiij d
In vanga et sera	x d ob

Summa lv s ob

Aula Stontonhall'

In primis in uno operario pro uno die	v d
In calca	ij d
In operarijs	v s
In potibus eorum	vj d
In operario	xvj d
In igne	vj d
In sera	iij d

Summa viij s ij d

Summa totalis reparacionibus domorum x li xv s vj d ob

Allocacio arr' Idem procurator petit allocari de Arreragijs – q non dum solvitur [*sic*]

\+ In primis Drowdalhall' iij li xvj d

Item de aula in vico scolarum universitatis quorum magister Rogerus Young' solvit pro pavimento viij s iiij d

\+ Item de Aula Sancti Edwardi v s q'condonantur per socios

\+ Item de domo Holway xj s Item de Brasenose xxvij s viij d

Item de orto ex opposito domui predicte iij s

\+ Item de Stantonhall'

xxiij s vij d q' concordatum inter socios et principalem

\+ Item de aula Sancti Thome xxxviij s

\+ Item de Aula Scuti xl s x d

\+ Item de ten' Baret viij s

+	Item de ten' Brasier	[*blank*]
+	Item de hamptonhall' viij li vj s viij d q' concordatum inter socios et principalem	
	Item de orto ultra castrum	ij s vj d
	Item de collegio cantuar'	ij s vj d
+	Item de camera principali	xl s
+	Item sibi proxima vij s ix d Et de camera sub illa	xj s
+	Item de camera fonti opposita	xx d
+	Item de camera cum aula	v s x d
+	Item de camera que dicitur Alba Aula	xij s
+	Item de camera super herbarium in alio disporto	iiij s viij d
	Item de Holdornesse	xvj s viij d
	Summa xxiiij li xvij s xj d	

Allocacio reddituum Quia non sunt in manu collegij

In primis de ten' Ricardii Merser	l s
Item de Schopa pyry	xiij s iiij d
Item de ten' Willelmi Saundres	xl s
Item de ten' Roberti Westeby	vj li xvj s
Item de ten' Joh' Wyndeshore	xiij s iiij d
Item de ten' Joh' vaginarij	xviij s
Item de ten' Ricardi Cornewale	xxx s
Summa xv li viij d	

Allocacio reddituum Quia non dum solvuntur

In primis de Maydenhall'	xiij s iiij d
Item de olyfanthalle	xij d
Item de aula scuti	xxviij s iiij d
Item de aula sancti thome	xx s
Item de Brasenose	xxxiij s iiij d
Item de hamptonhall'	xx s
Item de Aula Edwardi	xx s iij s iiij d
Item de Stantonhall' xiiij s viij d q^{a} condonantur per socios	
Item de Drowdalehall'	xxiiij s viij d
Item de lodlowhall'	xxxv s
Item de domo holway	xv s
Item de orto ex opposito domui predicte	iij s
Item de ten' Joh' Baret	iiij s
Item de orto ultra castrum	ij s vj d
Item de collegio cantuar'	ij s vj d
Item de Holdornesse	iiij li ix s xj d

Item de Aula universitatis in vico scolarum	vj s viij d
Item de ten' Joh' Brasier	v s
Summa xvij li ij s iij d	

Allocacio redditus camerarum Quia non dum solvuntur

In primis de camera principali	xx s
Item de camera sibi proxima	xvj d
Item de camera sub illa q' fuit occupata per socium domus	xij s
Item de camera super herbarium in alio disporto	x s
Item de camera cum aula	xviij s
Item de camera fonti opposita	x s
Item de camera sibi proxima	x s
Item de Alba Aula	xij s
Summa iiij li xiij s iiij d	

Summa totalis allocacionis lxj li xiiij s iij d

[*Remainder of the text has been heavily galled, & is difficult to make out*]

Summa totalis Oneracionis lxxxxvij li xvj s ij d ob q^{a}[3]

⟨Summa totalis omnium expensarum et allocatorum iiij^{xx}xviij li xvj s j d ob q^{a}
in quibus continentur xl s positi interim in fine communarum Nota pro proximo compoto
Et sic solvuntur [. . .] supradicto xvj s x d q^{a}. Et sic solvuntur super compotum predicto magistro et sic eque⟩[4]

[*Another clear, tidy roll; 2 membranes*]

[3] [ADMC] This entry has probably been deleted.

[4] [ADMC] Smith (Vol. VIII 20) reads: 'Summa total' omn' expensarum et allocationum iiij^{xx}xviij li xvj s j d ob q^{a}. in quibus continentur xl s positi in terminis in fina Comm'. Nota pro proximo compoto et sic solvunter anna're pro Ric'o supradicto xvj s x d q^{a}. Et sic solventur sup' computu' predicto M^{ro} et sic eque'.

WHITSUN 8 RICHARD II to WHITSUN 9 RICHARD II (ROLL UC:BU1/F/4)[1]

29 May 1384–21 May 1385

BURSAR: JOHN POKLYNGTON

⟨Rotulus 8 Anni testatur de solucione ij s⟩

Compotus Magistri Johannis pokelyngton socij Ac procuratoris Collegij Magistri Willelmi de Dunelm' Micheluniversitehall' vulgariter nuncupati a festo pentecostes anno regno regis Ricardi secundi post conquestum Octavo usque ad idem festum anno revoluto

Arr' arr' [*sic*]

In primis de Drowdalh[*all'*]	iij li xvj d
Item de aula universitatis in vico scolarum pro tempore Magistri Rogeri Yonge	viij s iiij d
Item de Aula sancti Edwardi	v s
Item de domo holway	xj s
Item de orto ex opposito domui predicte	iij s
Item de brasenose	xxvj s viij d
Item de stantonhall'	xxiiij s vij d
Item de aula Sancti Thome	xxxviij s
Item de aula scuti	xl s x d
Item de ten' baret	viij s
Item de ten' brasier	[*blank*]
Item de hamptonhall'	viij li vj s viij d
Item de orto ultra castrum	ij s vj d
Item de collegio cantuar'	ij s vj d
Item de Holdornesse	xvj s vij d
⟨Summa xx li xv s⟩	

Arr' arr' de c[*sic*]
cameris

In primis de camera principali	xl s
Item de camera sibi proxima	vij s ix d
Item de camera sub illa	xj s
Item de camera fonti opposita	xx d

[1] There is nothing to explain why the period May-September 1384 seems to be covered in both this, and the preceding roll.

Item de camera cum aula	v s x d
Item de camera que dicitur alba aula	xij s
Item de camera super herbarium in alio disporto	iiij s viij d

⟨Summa iiij li ij s xj d⟩

Arr' redituum qui non sunt in manu dicti collegij

[*These Arrears are identical with the Allowances in **F/3** above.*]

⟨Summa xv li viij d⟩

Arr' redituum qui sunt in manu collegij

[*These Arrears are also identical with the Allowances in **F/3** above.*]

⟨Summa xvij li ij s iij d⟩

Arr' redituum de cameris Qui [*sic*] sunt infra idem collegium

In primis de camera principali	xx s
Item de camera sibi proxima	xvj d
Item de camera super herbarium in Alio disporto	x s
Item de camera cum aula	xviij s
Item de camera fonti opposita	x s
Item de camera sibi proxima	x s
Item de alba aula	xij s
Item de camera iuxta coquinam	xij s

⟨Summa iiij li xiij s iiij d⟩

Redditus collegij Qui debentur eidem collegio pro tempore predicti procuratoris

In primis de Maydenhalle	xiij s iiij d
Item de Olyfanthalle	iiij s
Item de Aula Scuti	xl s
Item de Aula Sancti Thome	xl s
Item de Aula universitatis in vico Scolarum	xxxiij s iiij d
Item de Brasenose	iij li vj s viij d
Item de Hamptonhalle	iij li
Item de aula Sancti Edwardi	xxx s
Item de Ṣtantonhalle	xlviij s
Item de Drowdalhalle	lj s iiij d
Item de lodelowhalle	liij d iiij d
Item de domo holway	xv s
Item de orto ex opposito domui predicte	iij s
Item de ten' Johannis Baret	viij s
Item de ten' Johannis Brasier	x s
Item de orto ultra castrum	ij s vj d

Item de Collegio cantuar'	ij s vj d
Item de Holdernesse	iiij li ix s xj d
⟨Summa xxvij li x s xj d⟩	

Redditus collegij qui non sunt in manu collegij

Item de Ten' Ricardi merser	l s
Item de Shopa Pyry	xiij s iiij d
Item de ten' Willelmi Saundres	xl s
Item de ten' Roberti Westby	ix marc' xvj s
Item de ten' Johannis Wyndesore	xiij s iiij d
Item de ten' Johannis waginarij	xviij s
Item de ten' Ricardi Cornewale	xxx s
⟨Summa xv li viij d⟩	

Redditus camerarum idem collegium

In primis de camera principali	xx s
Item de camera sibi proxima	xvj s
Item de camera inferiori iuxta herbarium aule	x s
Item de camera super herbarium in Alio disporto	x s
Item de camera cum aula	xviij s
Item de camera fonti opposita	x s
Item de camera sibi proxima	x s
Item de alba aula	xij s
⟨Summa v li vj s⟩	

Item recepi de testamento Magistri Ricardi Gisborn' iij marcas Item pro uno missale xx s Item ab Henrico clerico nostro vj s ij d Item pro uno ligno vj d Item a Willelmo Ware ij s iiij d Item a Johanne mancipio nostro iiij s ij d ob Item a Magistro Willelmo Balyndem ij s viij d Item a relicto rotule xvj s x d q^{a} Item a commendato una vice ij marcas et alia vice vj s et tercia vice ij marcas et viginti denarios

⟨Summa vij li xiij s viij d ob q^{a}⟩

⟨Summa omnium receptorum et oneratorum cxviij li v s v d ob q^{a}⟩

Communes sociorum primi termini a festo Pasce

In prima septimana in communibus quatuor sociorum vij s vj d — In batellis j d

In secunda septimana in communibus quatuor sociorum v s

In Tercia septimana in communibus trium sociorum cum dimidio iiij s vj d q^{a} — In batellis iij d

In quarta septimana in communibus trium sociorum iii s ix d

In quinta septimana in communibus trium sociorum iij s ix d
In sexta septimana in communibus duorum sociorum ij s vj d
In septima septimana in communibus unius socij xv d
In Octava septimana et pentecostes in communibus trium sociorum v s iij d
In Nona septimana in communibus duorum sociorum cum dimidio ij s xj d In batellis ob
In decima septimana in communibus duorum sociorum cum dimidio iij s j d ob q[a] In batellis ob
In undecima septimana in communibus trium sociorum iij s ix d
In duodecima septimana in communibus trium sociorum iij s ix d
In terciadecima septimana in communibus trium sociorum iij s ix d

⟨Summa lj s iij d⟩

Communes termini Autumpnalis

In prima septimana in communibus trium sociorum iij s ix d
In batellis j d ob q[a]
In secunda septimana in communibus duorum sociorum ij s vj d In batellis ob
In tercia septimana in communibus duorum sociorum ij s vj d
In iurnallis pro Alkbarowe iij d
In batellis j d ob
In quarta septimana in communibus duorum sociorum ij s vj d
In batellis ob
In quinta septimana in communibus trium sociorum iij s ix d
In vino cancellario viij d
In sexta septimana in communibus trium sociorum iij s ix d
In batellis ob
In septima septimana in communibus trium sociorum iij s ix d
In Octava septimana in communibus trium sociorum iij s ix d
In batellis xviij d
In Nona septimana in communibus trium sociorum iij s ix d
In batellis ix d ob
In decima septimana in communibus trium sociorum iij s ix d
In batellis iij d ob q[a]
In Undecima septimana in communibus trium sociorum iij s ix d In batellis j d

In Duodecima septimana in communibus trium sociorum iij s ix s
In batellis vij d

⟨Summa xlv s x d⟩

Communes termini yemalis

In prima septimana in communibus trium sociorum iij s ix d
In batellis iij d
In secunda septimana in communibus trium sociorum iij s ix d
In tercia septimana in communibus trium sociorum iij s ix d
In quarta septimana in communibus trium sociorum iij s ix d
In quinta septimana in communibus trium sociorum iij s ix d
In batellis j d ob
In sexta septimana in communibus trium sociorum iij s ix d
In batellis ob
In septima septimana in communibus duorum sociorum ij s vj d
In iurnallis xj d ob
In octava septimana in communibus unius socij xv d
In Nona septimana in communibus unius socij xv d
In Decima septimana in communibus duorum sociorum ij s vj d
In batellis j d ob q^a
In Undecima septimana in communibus unius socij cum dimidio xxij s ob
In duodecima septimana in communibus unius socij xv d
In iurnallis pro alio v d

⟨Summa xxxv s ob q^a⟩

Communes termini quadregesimalis

In prima septimana in communibus trium sociorum vj s iij d
In secunda septimana in communibus trium sociorum iij s ix d
In tercia septimana in communibus trium sociorum iij s ix d
In quarta septimana in communibus trium sociorum iij s ix d
In quinta septimana in communibus unius socij xv d
In batellis q^a
In sexta septimana in communibus unius socij cum dimidio ij s ob
In iurnallis iij d
In septima septimana in communibus duorum sociorum ij s vj d
In Octava septimana in communibus unius socij xv d
In iurnallis viij d ob
In Nona septimana in communibus duorum sociorum ij s vj d
In decima septimana in communibus trium sociorum iij s ix d
In Undecima septimana in communibus trium sociorum iij s ix d

In Duodecima septimana in communibus trium sociorum iij s ix d
In terciadecima septimana in communibus trium sociorum iij s ix d In batellis ob q[a]
In quartadecima septimana in communibus trium sociorum iij s ix d In batellis ob
⟨Summa xlvj s x d ob⟩

Communes A festo pasche usque ad festum pentecostes
In prima septimana in communibus trium sociorum v s vij d ob
In secunda septimana in communibus duorum sociorum cum dimidio iij s iiij d In batellis j d
In tercia septimana in communibus duorum sociorum ij s vj d
In quarta septimana in communibus unius socij xv d
pro alio xiij d q[a]
In quinta septimana in communibus duorum sociorum ij s vj d
In batellis j d
In sexta septimana in communibus duorum sociorum ij s vj d
In batellis ob
In septima septimana in communibus duorum sociorum ij s vj d
⟨Summa xxj s vj d q[a]⟩

Resolucio redditus
In primis liberavi canonico sancte frideswyde iiij s viij d
Item alia vice eidem xiij s iiij d
Item liberavi canonico de osonay vj s viij d
Item procuratori sancti petri liberavi ij s x d
Item liberavi procuratori abendon' ij s
⟨Summa xxix s vj d⟩

Expense forinsece facte per eundem procuratorem anno supradicto
In primis liberavi Magistro Johanni Taylour versus sarum xx s
Item liberavi Magistro Roberto Gower versus london' circa habendum[2] supersedias xx s
Item liberavi Pulford pro equis versus sarum iiij s v d
Item liberavi Henrico versus sarum iiij s
Item Cancellario versus sarum ij s
Item bedello versus london' iij s

[2] [ADMC] *Circa habendum* is written over an erasure.

Item Magistro Jo Taylour et Gower versus radinge iij s ij d
Item pro equis eisdem ij s
Item Taylour et Gower versus consilium regis post festum sancti Michaelis xiij s iiij d
Item Taylour et Gower versus parliamentum ultimum london' xxx s
Item liberavi Magistro Ro. Gower qui expendit de proprio iij s iiij d
Item liberavi pro equis versus parliamentum ultimum vj s
Item Taylour qui expendit de proprio ij s
Item Henrico versus london' post festum nativitatis iiij s viij d
Item taylour versus london' post idem festum xx s
Item Gower versus london' in festo carniprivij xiij s iiij d
Item pro equo versus london' post natale ij s
Item liberavi Mancipio pro seipso et equo versus london' ij s x d
Item pro equis versus london' post pasca [*sic*] iiij s
Item Taylour versus london' post idem festum xx s
Item suthram pro equis iij s iiij d
Item in vino chorlton' et uxori eiusdem ij s iiij d
in speciebus xj d
Item in vino Magistro Willelmo aston' in eundo versus sarum xvj d
Item in vino david Hanmer' et alijs necessarijs xij d
Item in vino etc. dagvile diversis temporibus xij d
Item in vino pro burley et alijs necessarijs xix d
Item pro emendacione calicis iiij d
Item pro pergameneo ad registrum iiij d
Item pro pergameneo rotule iiij d
Item pro servicio procuratoris x s
⟨Summa x li iij s vij d⟩

[*Dorse*]

Stipendia famulorum

In primis liberavi Mancipio et coco pro termino translacionis sancti thome v s
Item pro termino sancti Michaelis Mancipio et coco v s
Item pro termino Nativitatis Mancipio et coco v s
Item pro termino Pasce Mancipio et coco v s
Item pro barbitonsori domus v s

Item lotrici	iij s vj d
⟨Summa xxviij s vj d⟩	

Reparaciones aularum In primis pro reparacione aule nostre

In stramine	xv d
Item pro labore operarij	x d
Item pro tractacione straminis	ij d
Item pro servisio puerorum	iiij d
Item pro virgis	j d ob
Item pro senovectorio	ij d
Item pro una tabula	v d
Item in stramine pro primo muro	xij d ob
Item pro labore operarij eiusdem muri	ij s x d ob
Item alio muro pro stramine et labore et potu etc.	x s v d ob
Item pro porticu	x s
Item bigatori pro portacione lapidum	ij d
Item pro calce diversis aulis	xx d
Item in latis	xiiij d
Item pro emendacione unius tabule	j d
Item pro potu dadynton	j d
⟨Summa xxx s x d⟩	

Reparacio aule scuti

In primo [*sic*] carpentario pro supportacione unius muri	xij d
Item pro potu diversis temporibus	vij d
Item in clavis	j d
Item pro rubea terra	iiij d
Item pro latis	xxij d
Item pro carpentario	xv d
Item pro alio carpentario	xxj d
Item in clavis	viij d
Item pro [*blank*] carpentario	xx d
Item carpentario	x d
Item in clavis	vij d ob
Item pro calce	iiij d
Item carpentario pro me^{ta} [*sic*] unius diei	ij d
Item pro stoddes	xj d
Item in clavis	v d ob
Item pro labore unius puero	j d
Item pro terra rubea	iiij d
Item pro tegulis	iij s vj d

Item pro portacione earundem	ij d
Item in feno	j d ob
Item famulo Holway pro labore diversarum aularum	xv s
Item pro tractacione straminis	j d
Item duobus laborantibus in una die	vij d
Item pro terra	iiij d
Item pro clavis	j d ob
Item pro stramine	vj d
Item pro clavis et emendacione sere hostij aule	ij d ob
Item pro clavis aule	iiij d
Item pro tabulis ad gradum	ix d
Item pro carpentario	ix d
Item pro clavis et gradum	iiij d
Item pro virgis ad coquinam	ij d
Item pro stramina	vij d
Item pro uno operario super coquinam	iij d et in potu j d
Item in clavis	vij d
Item pro emendacione parietis in fine aule	iiij d
Item carpentario	viij d
Item in clavis ad cameram principalem	iij d ob
Item in stapillis	j d
Item in tabulis et leggis	xix s ob
Item in tabulis et leggis duorum hostiorum	viij d ob
Item pro seris eṭ clavis	xiij d ob
Item carpentario	ij s
Item pro emendacione aquaductus	ij d
Item pro frattura unius corde	x d
⟨Summa xlv s ij d ob⟩	

[3]Reparacio Aule sancti Thome

In primis pro emendacione unius aqueductus	iiij d
Item in calce ambabus aulis	vij d
Item pro labore hominis circa fenesṭras et gradus	viij d
Item clavis	ij d
Item pro lagnis	~~iiij d~~ vj d
Item pro terra rubea	ix d
Item pro potu et in pane	vj d ob
Item pro labore puerorum	iij d

[3] The original sets out the entries for St. Thomas Hall and Drowda Hall in parallel columns.

Item pro calce	ij d
Item pro clavis	v d ob
Item pro calce	viij d
Item pro feno	ij d
Item pro terra	x d
Item in latis et clavis	viij d
Item in calce ad dealbandum [*sic*] aulam	iij d
Item Johannis [*blank*] pro labore	ij s j d
Item in potu	ij d ob
Item pro factura hostij	vj d
Item pro una sera	v d
Item pro tegulatore	vj d
⟨Summa x s viij d ob⟩	

Reparacio drowdalehall'

In primis pro soudir	v d qa
Item pro labore et in alijs	xvj d qa
Item pro factura unius muri	xx d
Item pro mundacione latrine	iij s iiij d
Item operarijs coadiuvantibus	ix d
Item pro tabulis et clavis	ij s
Item pro factura alterius muri et in calce	ij s
Item pro fenestra et ferro	x d
Item pro alijs duabus fenestris	xij d
Item pro alijs fenestris	ix d & xij d
Item uni operario	xiiij d
Item operarijs	ij s
⟨Summa xviij s iij d ob⟩	

Reparacio stantonhall'

In primis pro clavis	ij d ob
Item pro calce	iij d ob
Item in latis	j d
Item pro tabulis	iiij d ob
Item pro soudir	ix d
Item plumbatori	x d
Item potu	ob
Item pro clavo [*sic*] hostij aule	iiij d
Item pro emendacione sere et plumbo	v d
Item pro emendacione fenestrarum	v d
et unius poste et sere	ij d

Item alijs parvis emendacionibus in coquina et promptuario x d
⟨Item pro diversis reparacionibus eiusdem aule iij s iiij d⟩
⟨Summa x s ix d⟩

Reparacio Hamptonhall'
In primo pro operarijs circa Magnum murum vj s j d
Item pro terra rubea viij d
Item uno puero pro labore ij d
Item pro factura unius sere iiij d
Item pro emendacione diversorum hostiorum xiiij d
⟨Summa viij s v d⟩

Reparacio aule Edwardi
In primis pro tegulis et labore hominis vj d
⟨Summa vj d⟩

[*A gap of about 5 inches on the roll*]

Allocacio arr' Item procurator petit Allocari de arreragijs

In primis de aula universitatis in vico scolarum viij s iiij d pro tempore Magistri Rogeri Young
\+ Item de drowdalhall' iij li xvj d
\+ Item de aula sancti Edwardi v s q' condonantur per socios
Item de domo Holway xj s
\+ Item de brasenose xxvj s viij d q' condonantur per socios
\+ Item de stantonhall' xxiij s vij d q' condonantur per socios
\+ Item de aula sancti Thome xxxviij s
\+ Item de aula scuti xl s x d
\+ Item de ten' baret viij s
\+ Item de Hamptonhall' viij li vj s viij d q' condonantur per socios
Item de orto ultra castrum xv d
Item de collegio cantuar' ij s vj d
\+ Item de Holdornesse xvj s vij d
⟨Summa xx li x s ix d⟩

[*No heading*]
\+ In primis de camera principali xl s
\+ Item de camera sibi proxima vij s ix d
\+ Item de camera sub illa xj s
\+ Item de camera fonti opposita xx d
\+ Item de camera cum aula v s x d

+	Item de camera qui dicitur alba aula	ij s
+	Item de camera super herbarium in alio disporto	iiij s viij d
	⟨Summa iij li xij s xj d⟩	

[*No heading*]

	In primis de ten' Ricardi Merser	l s
	Item de schopa pyry	xiij s iiij d
	Item de ten' Willelmi saundres	xl s
	Item de ten' Roberti Westby	vj li xvj s
	Item de ten' Johannis Wyndesore	xiij s iiij d
	Item de ten' Joh' Waginarij	xviij s
	Item de ten' Ricardi Cornnwayle	xxx s
	⟨xv li viij d⟩	

Allocacio arr' pro Anno Magistri Ricardi Gysborne

+	Item de aula scuti	xxij s iiij d q' condonantur per socios
+	Item de aula sancti Thome	xx s
+	Item de brasenose	xxvj s viij d q' condonantur per socios
+	Item de Hamptonhall'	xx s q' condonantur
+	Item de aula sancti Edwardi	vj s viij d
	Item de domo holway	viij s
	Item de orto ultra castrum	ij s vj d
	~~Item de collegio cantuar'~~	~~ij s vj d~~
	Item de Holdernes	iij li iiij s j d
+	Item de stantonhall'	xiiij s viij d
	⟨Summa ix li iiij s xj d⟩	

[*No heading*]

+	In primis de camera principali	vj s viij d
+	Item de camera super herbarium in alio disporto	iij s iiij d
+	Item de camera cum aula	xviij s
+	Item de camera fonti opposita	x s
+	Item de camera sibi proxima	x s
+	Item de alba aula	v s iiij d
	⟨Summa liij s iiij d⟩	

Allocaciones reditᵘᵘm Quia non dum solvuntur

	In primis de Maydenhall'	xiij s iiij d
	Item de olyfanthall'	iij s
	Item de aula scuti	xiiij s viij d
+	Item de aula sancti Thome	xiiij s x d ob
	Item de brasenose	xx s

Item de Hamptonhall'	ij Marc'
Item de aula sancti Edwardi	xvj s iiij d
Item de stantonhall'	xiij s ij d
Item de Drowdalhall'	xxxj s ij d
Item de lodlowhall'	iij Marc' vj s viij d
Item de domo holway	xv s
Item de orto ex opposito domui predicte	xviij d
~~Item de ten' baret~~	~~iiij s~~
Item de orto ultra castrum	ij s vj d
Item de collegio cantuar'	ij s vj d
Item de Holdornesse	iiij li ix s xj d
Item de Aula universitatis in vico scolarum	xxiij s iiij d
Item de ten' Johannis Brasier	v s
Item de ten' baret	viij s
⟨Item pro quadam concordia inter clericos et laycos	ij Marc'⟩[4]
⟨Summa xviij li xiiij s vij d ob⟩	

Allocacio redd [*sic*] Quia non sunt in Manu collegij

In primo de ten' Ricardi Merser	l s
Item de schopa pyry	xiij s iiij d
Item de ten' Willelmi saundres	xl s
Item de ten' Roberti Westby	ix Marc' xvj s
Item de ten' Johannis Wyndesore	xiij s iiij d
Item de ten' Johannis Waginarij	xviij s
Item de ten' Ricardi Cornewayle	xxx s
⟨Summa xv li viij d⟩	

[*No heading*]

	In primis de camera principali	x s
	Item de camera sibi proxima	viij s viij d
	Item de camera inferiori iuxta herbarium aule	x s
	Item de camera super herbarium in alio disporto	x s
+	Item de camera cum aula	xviij s
+	Item de camera fonti opposita	vj s viij d
	Item sibi proxima	x s

[4] [ADMC] The words of this entry, which is written in the same hand as the rest of the rolls but in a different ink, appear to be deleted; but the amount (2 marks) is not.

Item de alba aula xij s

⟨Summa iiij li iiij s⟩

⟨Summa omnium expens' et allocatorum cxviij li x s ob Et [*debentur*] M. Johanni Poclynton' iiij s vj d ob q[a]⟩

[*A wide roll (10 inches), well written & well preserved. Unusual in that all the figures in it add up correctly. 2 membranes.*]

[WHITSUN 9 RICHARD II-WHITSUN 10 RICHARD II?] (ROLL UC:BU1/F/5)[1]

[21 May 1385–10 June 1386?]

BURSAR: UNKNOWN

a]nni testatur de sol' ij s a[. . .
. . .] Willelmi de Dunelm' Micheluniversite Hall' [. . .] festum anno revoluto videlicet anno regno regis [. . .[2]

Arr' annorum quorum [. . .

In primis de par [. . . *pro te*]mpore Magistri Rogeri Yonge

Item de domo Holw[*ay*]	viij s [*ii*]ij d
Item de orto ultra cas[*trum*]	xj s
Item de Collegio cantuarie	xv d
Item de domo Holway pro tempore Magistri Ricardi Gysborne	viij s
Item de orto ultra castrum pro tempor[*e eius*]dem	ij s vj d
Item de Holdernesse pro tempore eiusdem	iij li iiij s j d
Summa iiij li xvij s viij d	

Arr' redituum [. . . *pro tempore Ma*]gistri johannis poklyngton

In p[*rimis de Ma*]ydenhall'	xiij s iiij d
Item [*de Olyfant*]hall'	iij s
Item de Aula scuti	xiiij s viij d
Item de [*several words erased*]	~~xiiij s x d ob~~
Item de Brasenose	xx s
Item de Hamptonhall'	ij Marc'
Item de aula sancti Edwardi	xvj s viij d
Item de stauntonhall'	xiij s ij d
Item de Drowdalhall'	xxxj s ij d
Item de lodlowhall'	xl s vj s [*sic*] viij d
Item de Domo Holway	xv s
Item de orto ex opposito domui predicte	xviij d
Item de orto ultra castrum	ij s vj d

[1] Although this roll is undated, since the preceding and succeeding rolls each begin at Whitsun, it is highly likely that this one did as well.

[2] Smith's summary of this roll (Vol. VIII p. 25) shows that the top of the roll was aready damaged, and the name of the Bursar thus lost, even in his day.

Item de Collegio cantuarie	ij s vj d
Item de Holdornesse	iiij li ix s xj d
Item de parva aula universitatis in vico scolarum	xxiij s iiij d
Item de tenemento Johannis Brasier	v s
Item de ten' Johannis baret	viij s
⟨Summa xvj li xiij s j d⟩	

Arr' camerarum pro tempore eiusdem Johannis – infra mansum proprium

In primis de camera principali	x s
Item de camera sibi proxima	viij s viij d
Item de camera inferiori iuxta herbarium aule	x s
Item de camera super herbarium in disporto	x s
Item de camera Magistri Ricardi pester	x s
Item de alba aula	xij s
Item de camera fonti opposita	ij s vj d
⟨Summa lxiij s ij d⟩	

Redditus Collegij qui debentur eidem Collegio anno supradicto

In primis de Maydynhall'	xiij s iiij d
Item de olyfantehall'	iiij s
Item de aula scuti	xl s
Item de aula sancti Thome alias stapulhall	ij marc' et vj s viij d
Item de parva aula universitatis in vico scolarum	xxxiij s iiij d
Item de brasenose	iij li vj s viij d
Item de Hamptonhall'	iij li
Item de aula sancti Edwardi	xxx s
Item de stauntonhall'	xlviij s
Item de Drowdalhall'	lj s iiij d
Item de lodlowhall'	liij s iiij d
Item de domo Holway	xv s
Item de orto ex opposito domui predicte	iij s
Item de ten' Johannis baret'	viij s
Item de ten' Johannis brasyer	x s
Item de collegio cantuar'	ij s vj d
Item de orto ultra castrum	ij s vj d
Item de redditu de de Holdornesse	iiij li ix s xj d
Summa xxviij li iiij s iij d	

Redditus collegij qui non sunt in manu collegij

Item de Ten' Ricardi merser	l s

Item de Shopa Pyry xiij s iiij d
Item de ten' Willelmi Saundres xl s
Item de ten' Roberti Westby ix marc' xvj s
Item de ten' Johannis Wyndesore xiij s iiij d
Item de ten' Johannis Mason xviij s
Item de ten' Ricardi Cornewaile xxx s
Summa xv li viij d

Redditus camerarum infra dictum collegium
In primis de camera principali xx s
Item de camera sibi proxima viij s
Item de camera sub illa xij s
Item de camera cum aula in disporto xiij s iiij d
Item de camera fonti opposita x s
Item de camera sibi proxima x s
Item de alba aula vj s viij d
Summa iiij li

Item memorandum quod recepi de communi cista xxxiij s iiij d
Item a Magistro Thoma Barllell' xx s
Summa liij s iiij d

Summa totalis omnium Receptorum et Oneratorum lxxiiij li xij s ij d

Communes sociorum a Festo pentecostes inclusive usque Ad ffestum sancti Thome inclusive
In prima septimana in communibus trium sociorum v s j d ob
In secunda septimana in communibus duorum sociorum ij s vj d
In tercia septimana in communibus trium sociorum iij s ix d
In quarta septimana in communibus duorum sociorum cum dietis tercij socij iij s ij d
In quinta septimana in communibus duorum sociorum ij s vj d
In batellis j d q[a]
In sexta septimana in communibus duorum sociorum ij s vj d
cum dietis tercij viij d
In septima septimana in communibus trium sociorum iij s ix d
Item pro stipendijs famulorum pro termino sancti Thome scilicet Mancipij et cocj v s
Item pro lotrice ij s vj d
Summa xxxj s vj d ob q[a]

Communes sociorum A festo sancti Thome exclusive usque Ad festum sancti Michaelis inclusive

In prima septimana in communibus trium sociorum iij s ix d

In batellis pro burley et ~~alijs~~ operarijs vj d ob

In secunda septimana in communibus trium sociorum iij s ix d

In tercia septimana in communibus trium sociorum iij s ix d

In batellis ij d

In quarta septimana in communibus trium sociorum iij s ix d

In batellis iiij d

In quinta septimana in communibus trium sociorum iij s ix d

In batellis iiij d

In sexta septimana in communibus trium sociorum iij s ix d

In batellis iij d

In septima septimana in communibus trium sociorum iij s ix d

In batellis ij d ob

In octava septimana in communibus trium sociorum iij s ix d

In batellis ij d

In nona septimana in communibus trium sociorum iij s ix d

In batellis iij d ob

et in dietis pro daniel vij d

In decima septimana in communibus trium sociorum iij s ix d

In dietis pro tegulatoribus iiij d

In batellis iiij d ob q[a]

In undecima septimana in communibus trium sociorum iij s ix d

In batellis ij d ob

In duodecima septimana in communibus trium sociorum iij s ix d

In batellis ix d

Item stipendia Mancipij et coci pro termino sancti Michael' v s

Item barbitonsori v s

Item lotrici ij s vj d

Summa lxij s ob q[a]

Communes sociorum a festo sancti Michaelis exclusive usque ad festum Natalis domini exclusive

In prima septimana in communibus duorum sociorum cum dimidio iij s iij d

In batellis iiij d

In secunda septimana in communibus trium sociorum iij s ix d

In batellis iiij d

In tercia septimana in communibus duorum cum dimidio iij s iij d

In iurnallis pro alkebarowe iij d

In batellis ij d

In quarta septimana in communibus duorum sociorum ij s vj d

In batellis j d

In quinta septimana in communibus duorum sociorum iij s ix d

et in dietis tercij iiij d

In batellis ij d

In sexta septimana in communibus duorum sociorum ij s vj d

In batellis iij d ob

In septima septimana in communibus duorum sociorum ij s vj d In batellis iij d q[a]

In octava septimana in communibus duorum sociorum ij s vj d

In batellis j d ob

In nona septimana in communibus duorum sociorum ij s vj d

In decima septimana in communibus duorum sociorum ij s vj d

In undecima septimana in communibus duorum sociorum ij s vj d

In duodecima septimana in communibus duorum sociorum ij s vj d

Item in cena pro famulo Horlton' ix d

Item in dietis pro Magistro Johanni Taylour iiij d ob

Item stipendia Mancipij et coci pro termino natalis domini v s

Item lotrici ij s

Summa xliiij s vj d ob q[a]

Communes sociorum a festo nativitatis domini nostri inclusive usque at festum Pasche exclusive

In prima septimana in communibus duorum sociorum cum dimidio v s vij d

In secunda septimana in communibus duorum sociorum cum dietis tercij iij s vij d

In tercia septimana in communibus duorum sociorum cum dietis tercij iij s iiij d

In quarta septimana in communibus duorum sociorum ij s vj d

In quinta septimana in communibus duorum sociorum ij s vj d

In sexta septimana in communibus duorum sociorum ij s vj d

In septima septimana in communibus duorum sociorum ij s vj d

In octava septimana in communibus duorum sociorum ij s vj d

In nona septimana in communibus duorum sociorum ij s vj d

In decima septimana in communibus duorum sociorum ij s vj d

In undecima septimana in communibus duorum sociorum ij s vj d

In duodecima septimana in communibus duorum sociorum ij s vj d

In terciadecima septimana in communibus duorum sociorum ij s vj d In batellis j d

In quartadecima septimana in communibus duorum sociorum ij s vj d Item pro toma Myddylton et operarijs v d

In quintadecima septimana in communibus trium sociorum iij s ix d pro vasis ij d

In sextadecima septimana in communibus trium sociorum iij s ix d In batellis pro famulo chorlton iij d

In septimadecima septimana in communibus trium sociorum iij s ix d In vino pro chorlton viij d

Item stipendia Mancipij et coci pro termino pasche v s

Item lotrici ij s

Summa lx s j d

Communes sociorum a festo pasche inclusive usque at festum pentecostes exclusive etc.

In prima septimana in communibus duorum sociorum iiij s iiij d

In secunda septimana in communibus duorum sociorum cum dietis tercij iij s vij d ob in batellis q[a]

In tercia septimana in communibus duorum sociorum cum dietis tercij iij s ij d

In quarta septimana in communibus duorum sociorum ij s vj d in batellis ob

In quinta septimana in communibus duorum sociorum ij s vj d in batellis v d

In sexta septimana in communibus duorum sociorum ij s vj d in batellis j d

In septima septimana in communibus duorum sociorum ij s vj d

Summa xxj s viij d q[a]

Resolucio redditus

In primis liberavi canonico sancte ffrideswyde pro anno precedente – v s iiij d / Item pro anno isto – xviij s viij d

Item liberavi abbathie abendon' – ij s / Item liberavi canonico de osney – vj s viij d[3] pro anno isto

[3] [ADMC] Written over an erasure.

Item liberavi procuratoribus ecclesie sancti petri in oriente pro anno precedente et anno isto – v s viij d. Item procuratoribus ecclesie beate Marie pro anno isto – xij d

Summa xxxix s iiij d

Alie expense facte per eundem procuratorem in negocijs domus

In primis in vino dato cancellario tempore compot [*sic*] – viij d. Item in pir' – ij d. in s' – ij d

Item liberavi Magistro Johanni banbury pro pavimento vj s xj d

Item liberavi Holwey pro tegulis iij s

Item liberavi Roberto Heywey pro cariacione[4] iij s viij d

Item liberavi pro una tabula empta pro nostra coquina xiij d ob

Item pro calce iiij s ix d

Item pro uno cribro ~~et in~~ uno hamo unius hostij et pynnys tegularum xij d ob

Item pro moos et lapidibus xij d

Item Ricardo Morton' pro rege xxj d

Item in vino pro intitulacione iiij d

Item pro expensis Magistro Roberti Gower a london' versus oxoniam xij d

Item pro conductione equorum eodem tempore v s

Item pro copijs brevium regis xij d

Item liberavi Willelmo Casson' vj d

Item alicie Ware pro tegulis iiij d

Item liberavi alia vice pro tegulis iij s

Item liberavi Holwey pro libris nostris ij s

Item clerico castri pro reformacione brevium iij s iiij d

Item Johanni leper iij s iiij d

Item pro panno Henrico Charere v s ix d

Item Edmundo Keynyan iij s iiij d

Item pro vino dato chorlton et suo cognato iij s viij d

Item in speciebus pro eodem vij d

Item pro conductione unius equi versus london' pro Willelmo Mirfelde xx d

Item pro mosse et emendacione unius tabule v d ob

Item pro latis et pynnys iij s vj d

Item pro mose [*sic*] alia vice xxij d ob

Item pro clavis ij s viij d ob

[4] [ADMC] The first 'i' is possibly deleted.

Item pro rubia terra xij d
Item pro soudir iij d
Item pro meremio et uno lapide ij s viij d ob
Item uno plumbario v d
Item Johanni Glasyer pro factura fenestrarum capelle nostre et alijs operacionibus viij s v d
Item Johanno Chade pro emendacione camera cum aula vj d
Item liberavi ij^{bus} tegulatoribus circa eandem cameram una septimana v s
Item liberavi ij^{bus} tegulatoribus circa cameram pester et Gysborne alia septimana v s
Item pro uno tegulatori alia septimana ij s vj d
Item liberavi uni lathomo ij s iiij d
Item liberavi uni tegulatori pro quarta septimana ij s vj d
Item liberavi Johanni hamon pro iiij^{or} diebus xx d
Item ij^{bus} tegulatoribus pro quinta septimana v s
Item uni carpectario [*sic*] pro uno die vj d
Item ij^{bus} tegulatoribus pro sexta septimana v s
Item eisdem pro septima septimana v s
Item pro latis xx d
Item pro mortario et pila eiusdem iiij s iiij d
Item pro emendacione unius fenestre camere Multon ij d
Item pro moss viij d ob
Item pro conductione equorum Suthram et Hamon viij s viij d
Item pro cariagio lapidum roberto Heiway ij s x d
Item pro calce et cariagio eiusdem vj s viij d
Item pro uno coenophetorio et pro emendacione unius schaphe ij d ob
Item pro una clave capelle et emendacione alterius hostij et pro uno hyrdyl et pro s' vij d ob
Item pro meremio viij d
Item lathomis liberavi laborantibus circa murum camere principalis et alibi v s v d
Item uni operario circa promptuarium viij d
Item Willelmo casson vj d
Item pro tegulis xj s x d
Item Thome Sampson pro diversis laboribus vj s viij d
Item Holway pro libris ———— ij s Item liberavi Thomas sykryston' vj s viij d
Item pro rubia terra et uni operario videlicet carpentario vij d

Item liberavi pro Magistro Johanni Myddylton xviij s x d ob
Item liberavi pro pergameno et papiro et pro factura unius indenture vij d
⟨Summa ix li xv s x d⟩

[*Holes on the left edge of the bottom of the roll show that a slip of parchment 2½ inches wide was once attached here*]

[*Dorse*]

Reparaciones Aularum In primo pro reparacione Aula sancti Thome sive stapulhall'
In primis liberavi pro stramine viij d
Item liberavi operario laboranti super murum inter nos et Iuliañam garland' xvj d ob
Item in virgis et rubia terra xix d Item in feno ij d
Item liberavi pro meremio et latis et clavis circa cameram in disporto viij d ob
Item tribus operarijs circa eundam cameram viij d ob
⟨Summa v s ij d ob⟩

Reparaciones Aule scuti
In primis pro terra rubia xij d
Item pro clavis latis et studdes xx d ob In feno ij d
Item uni operario circa muros aule et camerarum xx d ob
⟨Summa iiij s vij d⟩

Reparaciones drowdalhall'
In primis pro terra rubia viij d
Item pro mosse xv d in potu j d
Item pro duobus operarijs pro duabus septimanis x s
Item pro clavis xij d
Item uni carpentario ix d
Item uni tegulatori pro una septimana ij s vj d
Item pro una tabula gurgitis ij d ob
Item pro soudyr et pro artifice eiusdem xx d
Item pro rubia terra viij d
Item pro duobus lathomis uno die xij d
⟨Summa xix s ix d ob⟩

Reparaciones Stauntonhall'
In primis uni operario operanti circa gradum camere iiij d
Item pro meremio et clavis v d

Item pro rubia terra iiij d
Item duobus tegulatoribus v s vj d ob
⟨Summa vj s vij d ob⟩

Reparaciones Aule sancti Edwardi
In primis liberavi uni lathomo pro factura unius muri lapide xviij s in potu ij d
Item uni carpentario circa eundem cameram viij s
Item pro meremio et clavis xxiij d
Item pro emendacione aree unius camere iij d
Item pro ferro empto pro fenestris xij d
Item uni tegulatori pro duabus septimanis v s
⟨Summa xxxiiij s iiij d⟩

Reparaciones Hamptonhall'
In primis pro stramine liberavi ix s xj d
Item pro virgis v d ob
Item pro iiij^{or} diebus uni puero viij d
Item alia vice eidem puero pro quinque diebus viij d
Item liberavi uno operario pro ix diebus iij s
Item pro rubia terra xij d
Item uni tegulatori pro una septimana ij s vj d
⟨Summa iiij s ix d⟩

Reparaciones Maydynhall'
In primis liberavi pro stramine xxiij d
Item pro factura unius muri lapidei ij s x d
⟨Summa iiij s ix d⟩

Allocacio arr' Annorum quorundem precedencium
In primis de domo Holwey pro tempore Magistri Johnanis Taylour xj s
Item de orto ultra castrum xv d q' condonantur per socios
Item de collegio cantuar' ij s vj d
Item de Holdornesse iij li iiij s j d
⟨Summa lxxviij s x d⟩

Allocacio arr' redituum pro tempore Magistri Johannis poklyngton'
In primis de aula scuti viij s
Item de Hamptonhall' x s
Item de stauntonhall' viij s q' etc.
~~Item de domo Holway xiiij d~~

Item de orto ultra castrum	ij s j d
Item de Holdornesse	iiij li ix s xj d
Item de ten' Johannis baret	iiij s quia etc.
⟨Summa vj li iij s ij d⟩	

Allocacio arr' camerarum pro tempore Magistri Johannis poklyngton' infra mansum proprium

In primis de camera inferiori iuxta herbarium aule	iij s iiij d
Item de camera super herbarium in alio disporto	iij s iiij d
Item de camera Ricardi pester	iij s iiij d
Item de alba aula	v s iiij d quia etc.
⟨Summa xv s iiij d⟩	

Allocacio reddituum quia non dum solvuntur

In primis de Maydynhall'	xiij s iiij d
Item de olyfantehall'	iiij s
Item de aula scuti	xxiij s x d ob
Item de aula sancti Thome	ix s iiij d
Item de aula universitatis in vico scolarum	xx s
Item de brasenose	xl s
Item de Hamptonhall'	ij marc' vj s viij d
Item de aula sancti Edwardi	xv s
Item de stauntonhall'	xiij s viij d
Item de Drowdalhall'	xlvj s x d
Item de lodlowhall'	xxx s
Item de domo Holway	xiij s ij d[5]
Item de orto ex opposito domui predicte	iij s
Item de ten' Johannis baret'	iiij s
Item de ten' Johannis brasyer	v s
Item de orto ultra castrum	ij s vj d
Item de redditu de de Holdornesse	iiij li ix s xj d
⟨Summa xviij li ix s ix d ob⟩	

Item petit allocari xv li et viij d de redditu qui non est in manu collegij ut pro parte superiori

Allocacio redditus camerarum infra dictum collegium

In primis de camera principali	x s

[5] [ADMC] This figure has been altered – probably from 'xv s', the figure which appears on the credit side of the roll as the rent due from Holway's property. This would give the correct total of £18 9s 9½d.

Item de camera Willelmi Multon'	v s iiij d
Item de camera cum aula in alio disporto	xiij s iiij d
Item de camera Magistri Ricardi pester[6]	x s
Item de alba aula	vj s viij d
⟨Summa xlv s iiij d⟩	

Item pro salario procuratoris	x s
⟨Summa x s⟩	

⟨Summa Totalis omnium expensarum et allocatorum lxxiiij li xij s iij d et solvitur sibi j d et sic eque⟩

[*On a Membrane attached to the roll*]

Arr' annorum precedencium

Item de Drowdalhall'	iij li xvj d
Item de aula sancti Edwardi	v s quia c'
Item de brasenose	xxvj s viij d
Item de stantonhall'	xxiij s vij d
Item de aula sancti Thome	xxxviij s
Item de aula scuti	xl s x d
Item de ten' baret'	viij s
Item de Hamptonhall'	viij li vj s viij d
Item de Holdornesse	xvj s vij d
⟨Summa xxviij li iiij s iij d⟩	

Arr' camerarum annorum precedencium

In primis de camera principali	xl s
Item de camera sibi proxima	vij s ix d
Item de camera sub illa	xj s
Item de camera fonti opposita	xx d
Item de camera cum aula	v s v d
Item de alba aula	ij s
Item de camera super herbarium in alio etc'	iiij s iiij d

Arr' qui non sunt in manu collegij

In primis de ten' Ricardi Merser	[*l s*]
Item de schpa [*sic*] pyry	xiij s [*iiij d*]
Item de ten' Willelmi saundres	xl s
Item de ten' Roberti Westby	vj li xvj s
Item de ten' Johannis Wyndesore	xiij s iiij d

6 [ADMC] These three words have been written over an erasure.

Item de ten' Johannis Waginarij xviij s
Item de ten' Ricardi Cornewayle xxx s

Arr' pro anno Magistri Gysborne
In primis de aula scuti xxij s iiij d
Item de aula sancti Thome xx s
Item de brasenose xxvj s viij d
Item de Hamptonhall' xx s
Item de aula sancti Edwardi vj s viij d
Item de stauntonhall' xiij s viij d
Item de aula sancti Thome pro tempore poklyngton' xiiij s x d ob

Arr' camerarum pro tempore eidem [*sic*] Ricardi
In primis de camera principali vj s viij d
Item de camera super herbarium in alio disporto iij s iiij d
Item de camera cum aula xviij s
Item de camera fonti opposita x s
Item de camera sibi proxima x s
Item de alba aula v s iiij d

Arr' camerarum pro tempore Magistri Johannis Poklyngton
In primis de camera cum aula xviij s
Item de camera fonti opposita vj s viij d

[*The next part heavily galled*][7]

⟨Memorandum quod ista summa contenta in ista cedula non currit in rotulo et causa est quia ut [creditur] non potest levari ideo extrahitur de rotulo anni precedentis sed non [instituetur nec oportet quot patet] in alijs rotulis [sed queratur si] possit [in futurum] levari in cedula [ista] annexa rotulo de anno r'r' Ricardi secundi post conquestum nono⟩

[*A well-written roll; 10 inches wide; 2 membranes. The beginning of the roll is slightly damaged. The membrance of arrears attached to the head of the roll is 20 inches long and 3 inches wide. This attached membrane consists of a schedule of all outstanding debts (down to and including 1384/5) which do not appear in the 1385/6 roll; i.e. presumably the ones to be written off as irrecoverable*]

The Roll for 1386/7 was missing even in Smith's day.

[7] [ADMC] Words in square brackets are taken from Smith Vol. VIII 28.

WHITSUN 10 RICHARD II to WHITSUN 11 RICHARD II (ROLL UC:BU1/F/6)

10 June 1387–17 May 1388

BURSAR: ROBERT GOWER

Compotus Magistri Robert Gower socij ac procuratoris Collegij Magistri Willelmi de dunelm' mukyluniversitehall vulgariter nuncupate A ffesto pentecostes inclusive usque ad idem festum exclusive anno revoluto videlicet anno regni regis Ricardi secundi post conquestum undecimo.

1[1] Arr' reddituum septimi anni de domo holwey	xj s
2 Arr' reddituum anni octavi regis predicti de Aula scuti	viij s
3 Arr' reddituum anno nono regis etc'	
In primis [*de*] Maydinhall'	vj s viij d
Item de aula sancti Thome	viij d
Item de Hamptonhall'	xxx s
Item de aula edwardi	x d
Item de drowdalhall'	iij s viij d ob
Item de orto ultra castrum	xviij d
Item de holdornesse	xlj s ix d ob
⟨Summa ciiij s ij d⟩[2]	
4 Arr' camerarum infra idem collegium	
In prima de camera principali	iij s iiij d
Item de camera Multon	ij s
Item de camera pester	vj s viij d
Item de alba aula	iiij d
⟨Summa xij s iiij d⟩	
5 Arr' reddituum de anno x° etc.	
In primis de Maydynhall'	xiij s iiij d
Item de olyfantehall'	iiij s

[1] These Arabic numerals written alongside each section of the roll are unique for this period. Although the formation of the figures suggests an early date, it is not known if they are contemporary with the roll, or were added later.

[2] All the totals on this roll are written in a different hand from the rest of the text, in an ink which has now faded considerably.

Item de aula scuti	xxv s vj d
Item de aula sancti Thome	xiij s v d ob
Item de aula universitatis in vico scolarum	x s
Item de brasenose	xxvj s viij d
Item de Hamptonhall'	xlvj s viij d
Item de aula sancti edwardi	xviij s v d ob
Item de stantonhall'	xxj s
Item de drowdalhall'	lj s iiij d
Item de lodlowhall'	xxxvj s viij d
Item de domo Holway	xj s ix d
Item de orto ex opposito	iij s
Item de domo buteler	viij s
Item de domo brasier	v s
Item de collegio cantuar'	ij s vj d
Item de orto ultra castrum	ij s
Item de holdornesse	v marc' x s x d
⟨Summa xviij li xvj s x d⟩	

6 Arr' camerarum

In primis principali	xx s
Item de camera sibi proxima	xvj s
Item de camera sub illa	xij s
Item de camera pester	x s
Item de camera Wynterton	vj s viij d
⟨Summa lxiij s viij d⟩	

7 Arr' reddituum qui non sunt in manu collegij. Summa omnis xv li viij d

⟨Summa patet⟩

8 Redditus eiusdem collegij

In primis de Maydinhall'	xj s viij d
Item de olyfanthall'	iiij s
Item de aula sancti Thome	xxxiij s iiij d
Item de aula scuti	xl s
Item de aula universitatis in vico scolarum	xxxiij s iiij d
Item de brasenose	iij li vj s viij d
Item de Hamptonhall'	iij li
Item de aula Edwardi	xxx s
Item de stauntonhall'	xlviij s
Item de drowdalhall'	lj s iiij d

Item de lodelowhall'	liij s iiij d
Item de domo Holwey	xv s
Item de orto ex opposito	iij s
Item de ten' Jo' brasyer	x s
Item de ten' butteler	viij s
Item de orto ultra castrum	ij s
Item de Holdornesse	v marc' x s x d
Item de collegio cantuar'	ij s vj d
⟨Summa xxvij li ix s viij d⟩	

9 Redditus camera [*sic*] infra dictum collegium

In [*sic*] de camera principali	xx s
Item de camera sibi proxima	xvj s
Item de camera sub illa	x s
Item de camera plymton	viij s
Item de camera Stapylton	xv s
Item de camera pester	x s
⟨Summa lxxix s⟩	

10 Redditus qui non sunt in manu collegij

In primis de ten' Ricardi Mercer	l s
Item de schopa pyry	xiij s iiij d
Item de ten' Willelmi Saundres	xv s[3]
Item de ten' Roberti Westby	ix marc' xvj s
Item de ten' Johannis Wyndesore	xiij s iiij s
Item de ten' Johannis Mason	xviij s
Item de ten' Ricardi Cornnwayle	xxx s
⟨Summa xv li viij d⟩[4]	

⟨Summa totalis omnium receptorum et oneratorum iiij^{xx} ix li viij s⟩

1 Communes sociorum a ffesto pentecostes inclusive usque ad ffestum sancti Thome exclusive

In prima duorum sociorum iij s viij d in batellis j d ob

In secunda septimana in communibus duorum sociorum cum iurnellis T. myddylton ij s viij d

In tercia septimana in communibus unius socij cum dimidio xxij d ob in batellis pro Myddilton x d

In quarta septimana in communibus duorum sociorum ij s vj d

3 [ADMC] 'xv s' clearly an error for 'xl s' on previous rolls.

4 [ADMC] Actually £13 15s (see preceding note).

In quinta septimana in communibus duorum sociorum ij s vj d
In sexta septimana in communibus duorum sociorum ij s vj d
⟨Summa xvj s viij d⟩

2 Communes sociorum a ffesto sancti Thome inclusive usque ad ffestum Sancti Michaelis exclusive

In prima septimana in communibus duorum sociorum ij s vj d
In secunda septimana in communibus duorum sociorum cum dietis tercij ij s xj d
In tercia septimana in communibus trium sociorum iij s ix d
In quarta septimana in communibus trium sociorum iij s ix d
in batellis j d
In quinta septimana in communibus trium sociorum iij s ix d
In sexta septimana in communibus trium sociorum iij s ix d
In septima septimana in communibus trium sociorum iij s ix d
in batellis j d ob
In octava septimana in communibus trium sociorum iij s ix d
in batellis ij d
In nona septimana in communibus trium sociorum iij s ix d
in batellis iiij d ob q[a]
In decima septimana in communibus trium sociorum iij s ix d
in batellis vj d
In xj[a] septimana in communibus trium sociorum iij s ix d
in batellis iiij d q[a]
In duodecima septimana in communibus trium sociorum iij s ix d
in batellis viij d ob q[a]
Item pro communibus Magistro Johanni Myddilton xiij s iij d ob
⟨Summa lviij s vij d ob q[a]⟩

3 Communes sociorum a festo sancti Michael' inclusive usque ad festum nativitatis domini inclusive

In prima septimana in communibus trium sociorum iij s ix d
in batellis ix d
In secunda septimana in communibus trium sociorum iij s ix d
in batellis iiij d
In tercia septimana in communibus trium sociorum iij s ix d
in batellis iij d ob
In quarta septimana in communibus unius socij xv d
in batellis et iurnallis ij s ob
In quinta septimana in communibus unius socij xv d
in batellis iij d ob q[a]

nota de omnibus sanctis
In sexta septimana in communibus unius socij xv d
in batellis vij d ob
In septima septimana in communibus unius socij xv d
in batellis v d ob
In octava septimana in communibus unius socij xv d
in batellis ob
In ix^{a} septimana in communibus trium sociorum iij s ix d
in batellis j d
In x^{a} septimana in communibus trium sociorum iij s ix d ~~in ba~~
In xj^{a} septimana in communibus iiij^{or} sociorum v s
In xij^{a} septimana in communibus quatuor sociorum v s
In xiij^{a} septimana in communibus iij sociorum vij s
⟨Summa xlvij s xj d q^{a}⟩

4 Communes sociorum a ffesto nativitatis exclusive usque at ffestum pasche exclusive
In prima septimana in communibus trium sociorum iij s ix d
In secunda septimana in communibus trium sociorum iij s ix d
In tercia septimana in communibus ~~t~~ quatuor sociorum v s
in batellis ij d
In quarta septimana in communibus iiij sociorum v s
in batellis j d
In quinta septimana in communibus iiij sociorum v s
In sexta septimana in communibus duorum sociorum ij s vj d
in iurnallis et batellis xviij d ob
In septima septimana in communibus duorum sociorum ij s vj d
In octava septimana in communibus trium sociorum iij s ix d
In nona septimana in communibus trium sociorum iij s ix d
in batellis x d
In decima septimana in communibus trium sociorum iij s ix d
In xj^{a} septimana in communibus trium sociorum iij s ix d
in batellis ij d ob
In xij^{a} septimana in communibus iiij sociorum v s
In xiij^{a} septimana in communibus trium sociorum iij s ix d
in batellis iij d ob
⟨Summa liiij s iiij d ob⟩

5 Communes sociorum a ffesto pasche ~~ex~~ inclusive usque at festum pentecostes exclusive
In prima septimana in communibus trium sociorum vj s

In secunda septimana in communibus trium sociorum iij s ix s
In tercia septimana in communibus trium sociorum cum dietis iiij s viij d ob
In quarta septimana in communibus duorum sociorum ij s vj d
In quinta septimana in communibus duorum sociorum ij s vj d
In sexta septimana in communibus duorum sociorum ij s vj d
In septima septimana in communibus duorum sociorum ij s vj d
⟨Summa xxiij s v d ob⟩

6 Stipendia ffamulorum

In primo Mancipio et coco pro termino pasche	v s
Item liberavi eisdem pro termino autumpnali	v s
Item liberavi eisdem pro termino yemali	v s
Item liberavi eisdem pro termino quadragesimali	v s
Item barbitonsori	v s
Item lotrici	v s
⟨Item in stipendio procuratoris computandis	x s⟩

⟨Summa xl s⟩

7 Resolucio redditus

In primis procuratoris ecclesie beate Marie	xij d
Item abathie de abendon	xij d
Item canonico ffrideswyde	xviij s viij d

⟨Summa xx s viij d⟩

8 Expense facte per eundem procuratorem eodem anno

In primis pro una sera hostij aule – xij d Item balton pro equis – xx d Item lapidibus emptis – x s x d ob Item in potu – iij d Item pro uno candelabro – iij s iij d Item in vino et piris cancellario – vij d Item in lapidibus – iij s iiij d Item pro equis famulo cherlton' – iij d ob Item in pergameno – iiij d Item scriptori – ij s Item plumbario – ij s iiij d Item pro pergameno – xxj d Item pro ligatura quaternorum – v d Item pro conductione unius equi – xx d Item lathomo circa cameram pester tribus diebus – xv d Item in clavis – iiij d Item carpentario – iiij d Item liberavi Thome sampson – ij s Item liberavi Mancipio et coco pro rebus emptis – xvj d Item liberavi Willelmo suthram pro equis – iiij s viij d Item in lignis emptis de Jo. forster – xvj d Item pro uno senofectorio – j d Item pro uno rasto pro orto – vj d Item pro uno verticulo castoste – ij d Item suthram pro equis – vj s viij d Item liberavi Willelmo palmer – viij s xj d Item uni carpentario circa domum galinarum – xij d Item in clavis et latis – v d Item uni tegulatori – viij s ix d ob Item alia vice liberavi Willelmo palmour – v s iiij d Item liberavi Johanni Hammund – ij s iij d ob ⟨Item liberavi pro Midilton' xxj d ob In focali xvj d Item in mappis xvj d Item in conductione equi xx d⟩

⟨Summa iiij li iij d ob⟩

9 Reparaciones aularum sancti Thome et scuti

In primis in meremio et latis	xj s vj d
Item pro terra rubia et potu	ix d
Item in lathomis et potu eisdem	xvj d
Item in clavis	vj s xj d
Item uni operario pro 3^{bus} diebus dum dimidio	xiiij d
Item lathomo pro 3^{bus} diebus	xviij d
Item in terra rubea	ij s
Item uni carpentario pro x diebus	iiij s ix d
Item uni carpentario pro 3^{bus} diebus	xviij d
Item in meremio et latis	xij s ~~iij d~~ ix d
Item operarijs	ij s v d
Item duobus tegulatoribus una septimana	v s
Item uni carpentario 3^{bus} diebus	xviij d
Item in meremio	vj s iiij d
Item uni carpentario 2^{bus} diebus	x d

[*Dorse*]

Item in mose	x d
Item in stramine	iij s v d
Item in meremio	xv d
Item 2^{bus} tegulatoribus una septimana	v s
Item in virgis et potu	v d
Item 3^{bus} operarijs uno die	xv d
Item in hurdellis	xij d
Item in meremio et twystis	v s xj d
Item duobus lathomis iiij diebus cum dimidio	iiij s j d ob
Item pro tractione straminis	vj d
Item uni operario	viij d
Item uni operario quatuor diebus cum dimidio	xvj d
Item in terra rubia	xx d
Item in meremio	iiij s ij d
Item 2^{bus} tegulatoribus una septimana et in potu	v s ij d

Item uni tegulatori iiij^{or} diebus et uni operario 3^{bus} diebus ij s vj d
Item uni carpentario pro una septimana et 3^{bus} operarijs duobus diebus et in potu v s v d
Item uni lathomo uno die et in latis iij s iiij d
Item uni tegulatori una septimana ij s vj d
Item ij^{bus} carpentarijs pro factura coquine aule scuti xv s
Item uni operario pro una septimana xx d
Item in terra rubia iiij d
Item duobus bigarijs iiij d ob
Item serrareis iiij d
Item uno carpentario pro una septimana ij s vj d
Item in seris clavibus et potu ij s v d
Item uni operario pro iiij^{or} diebus xiij d
Item in twystis et hokis viij d
Item liberavi Holway xij s
Item uni carpentario una septimana ij s vj d
Item uni operario uno die v d
Item pro rubia terra et feno et ij^{bus} operarijs xviij d
Item in meremio et latis xiij d
Item liberatus erat pro diversus operarijs et alijs necessarijs ut patet in cedula pro manus Magistri J. p[*oklyngton*] xliiij s iiij d
⟨Summa ix li xvj s xj d⟩

10 Reparaciones drowdehall
In primis uni plumbario xij d
⟨Summa patet⟩

11 Reparaciones Hamptonhall'
In primis in tabulis vj d
Item uni carpentario duobus diebus viij d
Item in hannis et twystis xij d
Item duobus operarijs pro duobus diebus xvj d
Item in una cera et clavis et twystis xiiij d
Item pro 3^{bus} operarijs certis diebus xvj d
⟨Summa vj s⟩

12 Reparaciones aule edwardi
In primis pro terra rubia et feno et duobus operarijs uno die ~~xiiij d~~ xvij d
Item uni lathomo uno die cum dimidio ix d

Item pro una sera et una twysta vj d
In potu j d ob
⟨Summa ij s ix d[5]⟩

13 Allocaciones arr' anni septimi
In primis petit allocari de domo Holway xj s
⟨Summa patet⟩

14 Item allocaciones arr' anni octavi ~~in~~ In primis petit allocari de aula scuti viij s
⟨Summa patet⟩

15 Item de anno nono petit allocari In primis de Maydenhall' – vj s viij d Item de aula sancti Thome – viij d Item de Hamptonhall' – xxx s Item de aula edwardi – x d Item de drowdahall' – iij s viij d ob Item de orto ultra castrum – xviij d Item de Holdornesse – xlj s ix d ob Item [*blank*] Item petit allocacionem camerarum – ix s
⟨Summa iiij li xiiij s ij d⟩

16 [*No heading*]
Item petit allocari de Hamptonhall' de anno x° xx s
~~Item de orto ultra castrum xij d~~
Item de drowdahall' xxviij s
Item de domo buteler ij s
Item dest [*sic*] stauntonhall' xiiij s iiij d quia etc'
Item de aula scuti v s vj d
Item de holdornesse xlvj s vj d
Item de orto Willelmi War iij s
Item de collegio cantuar' ij s vj d
⟨Summa vj li xxij d⟩

17 Item petit allocari de camera Multon' ij s quia etc'
⟨Summmma patet⟩

18 Item petit allocari de arr' reddituum qui non sunt in manu collegij xv li viij d
⟨Summa patet⟩

19 [6]Allocaciones anni presentis
In primis petit allocari de Maydenhall' v s x d
De Olyfanthall' iij s

5 [ADMC] The correct total is 2s 9½d.
6 [ADMC] The remainder of this roll is written in an ink which is much faded.

De Aula sancti Thome	xiij s iiij d
De Aula Scuti	xxvj s viij d
De Aula universitatis in vico scolarum	xx s
De Brasenose	xxj s viij d
De Hamptonhall'	xlvj s
De Aula sancti Edwardi	x s
De Stauntonhall'	xxxiiij s viij d
De Drowdalehall'	lj s iiij d
De Lodelowhall'	xl s
De Domo Holwey	xv s
De Orto ex opposito domui predicte	iij s
De ten' Johannis Brasier	vj s
De ten' Johannis Butteler	vj s
De Orto ultra ultra [*sic*] castrum	xij d
De Holdornesse	xlvj s vj d
De Collegio Cantuar'	ij s vj d

⟨Summa xvij li xj s vj d[7]⟩

20 Allocaciones camerarum infra collegium predictum de anno iam instante

Idem procurator petit allocario de iij li xix s ut patet infra in suo onere in redditu camerarum

⟨Summa iij li xix s⟩

21 Alloc' Reddituum qui non sunt in manu domus

Idem procurator petit allocari de xv li viij d prout patet infra in onere eiusdem redditus

⟨Summa xv li viij d⟩

[Summa] totalis omnium expensarum [et liberat' iiij^{xx}x li xvj]s vj d. Et sic [in plusagio xxviij s vj] d[8]

[*A neatly-written roll, & very clear except for the last part of the dorse. With two exceptions (one of them trivial), all figures add up correctly. 2 membranes*]

[7] [ADMC] This total is almost illegible, but can almost certainly be made out as given. The actual total should be £15 2s 6d.

[8] This final entry is heavily galled & practically illegible. Gaps in the text are supplied from Smith (MSS VIII, 31).

WHITSUN 11 RICHARD II to WHITSUN 12 RICHARD II (ROLL UC:BU1/F/7)
17 May 1388–6 Jun 1389

BURSAR: JOHN ALKEBAROW

[*The original roll for this year is missing. What follows is Smith's condensed transcript of it (Vol. VIII pp.32–35)*]

Rot 12 anni

a° 1388 Compotus Magistri Johannis Albarow Socij et procuratoris etc. a festo pentecostes inclusive ad idem festum . . . . . .[1] anno rr' Ricardi secundi 12mo.

Arr' a 7° anno R ad anno x° de orto Willelmi Ware annum xj inclusive — iij s

Redditus ejusdem Collegij ubi habentur (ab recupanda ten' ab Edm. franceys)[2]

De aula scuti (ante xl s)	xxvj s viij d integre exscript' infra
De Aula Universitatis in vico Scolarum ante 33s 4d	jam xlvj s
De Hamptonhall prius iij li	jam xlvj s viij d
De Aula Sancti Edwardi ante 30s	jam etiam 30s
De Staunton Hall ante xlviij s	jam xxx s
De Drowdall Hall ante xlj s iiij d	jam xxx s

Redditus ejusdem Collegij

In primis de Maydynhall'	xj s viij d
Item de Olyfanthall'	iiij s
Item de Aula Sancti Thome	xxxiij s iiij d
Item de Aula Scuti	xxvj s
Item de Aula Universitatis in vico Scolarum	xlvj s viij d
Item de Brasenose	iij li vj s viij d
Item de Hamptonhall'	xlvj s viij d
Item de Aula Sancti Edwardi	xxx s

[1] These dotted lines are Smith's own, a sign (to judge from his transcripts of extant documents) that the text was defective when he examined it.

[2] Smith seems to have deleted the whole of this paragraph. When compared with the following one, it looks as if he first intended to record the year's rents compared alongside the previous one's, but then tired of this, and just recorded the rents in the usual way.

Item de Stauntonhall'	xxx s
Item de Drowdalhall'	xxx s
Item de Lodelowhall'	liij s iiij d
Item de domo Holwey	xv s
Item de orto ex opposito	iij s
Item de ten' Johannis Brasier	x s
Item de ten' Johannis Butteler	viij s
Item de orto ultra castrum	ij s
Item de Collegio Cantuar'	ij s vj d
Item de Holdornesse	lix s vj d
Item de ten' Thome Glover	iiij li alias Masters
Item de ten' Ricardi Mercer[3]	l s
Item de schopa Jo. Walden	xxxv s
Item de schopa Rogeri Glover	xx s
Item de schopa Ricardi Glover	xx s
Item de schopa super angulum quadrivij	xx s
Item de uno Gardino	viij s
Item de prato retro osney	xx s
Item de uno orto juxta ecclesiam Sancti Egidij	viij d
Summa xxxiij li xviij s v d	

Redditus unius messuagij quia non est in manu Collegij	xxx s
Summa patet	

Item recepi de communi cista	xxxv s
Summa patet	

Redditus Camerarum infra dictum collegium

In primis de camera principali	xxiij s iiij d
Item de camera sibi proxima	xvj s
Item de camera sub illa	x s
Item de camera Wytton	x s
Item de camera Bruton	vj s viij d
Item de camera Wynterton	x s
Item de camera pester	x s
Item de camera Stapulton	xiij s iiij d

[3] On 24 August 1388 Richard de Garston (now described as a Draper rather than a Mercer) renewed his lease on the easternmost 'Gonwardby' house in High Street (UC:E2/7/1D/2).

Item de camera magistri Johannis Taylour x s

Summa v li ix s iiij d

Summa totalis omnium receptorum et oneratorum cvj li xix d

Communes Sociorum

a festo pentecostes inclusive ad festum Sancti Thome

In prima Septimana in communis trium Sociorum v s ix d

in jurnallis iij d

In 7^{a} Septimana in communis trium Sociorum iij s ix d

Summa xxvj s

a festo Sancti Thome: Summa xlv s iij d ob q^{a}

a festo Sancti Mich' Summa xl s viij d ob q^{a}

a festo nativitatis domini ad festum Pasche Summa iij li ix d

a festo pasche ad festum pentecost'

Inter septimanam 5^{am} et 6^{tam} in communis Myddylton iiij s ij d ob

Summa xxx s vij d ob

Summa 10. 03. 5

Stipendia famulorum et procuratoris Summa xl s

Resoluciones redditus

In primis Abathie de Osney pro annis preterito et presenti xiij s iiij d

Canonico Sancte frideswyde pro anno presenti xviij s

Abathie de Eynsham pro schopa super angulum quadrivij iiij s

Item Abathie de Godstow pro ten' Thome Master vij s

~~Item~~ Abathie de Abendon pro anno preterito xij d et pro anno presenti ij s

Item procuratori Ecclesie Sancti petri pro anno preterito ij s x d

Item procuratori Ecclesie beate Marie pro anno preterito xij d

Summa xlix s ij d

Expense forinsece et extrinsece facte per eundem procuratorem eodem anno

In primis pro pannis mense Aule xij d Item pro emendatione unius siphi [*sic*] ix d Item pro 2^{bus} ollis eneis et ij pro ijs iij d[4] Item pro una craticula ij s Item pro securi ad coquinam xiij d ob Item in bidente xxj d ob Item in duobus vangis ix d Item pro

[4] [ADMC] Underlined in Smith.

cenefectorio xij d Item pro uno . . .[5] iij d Item in vino et speciebus cancellario tempore compotus xvj d Item pro virgis coruli ix d Item pro sicpopris [*sic*] ad Aulam et cameras x d Item pro tabula capelle xj d Item in coreis capelle xij d Item pro storio capelle iiij d Item pro amputatione vitium vj d Item pro sortagine coquine xx d

Item pro vino uxori Chorlton xvj d Item liberavi Magistro Johanni Taylour London xlvj s viij d Item in communis Newnam et Scharte tempore consilij xxix s viij d Item in vino eisdem vj s viij d Item in vino tempore seisine recepte ij s viij d Item clavigero Regis vj s viij d Item in vino Cancellario Anglie vj s viij d Item pro Litteris Regijs ij s vj d Item clerico Scharle iij s iiij d Item in vino in die quo vocavimus xij in pretorio Oxon' vij d ob Item in secundo die viij d Item Godestow in vino iiij d Item in vino monachis de Eynsham viij d ob Item pro informatione a^corp [*sic*] duodene ij d ob Item falcatori ij d Item clerico ville pro copia unius brevis xij d Item Henrico clerico capelle xiiij d

Item Magistro Roberto Gower versus Cantebrigg' xxj s iiij d Item pro equis eundo versus Cantebrigg' et rediundo vj s viij d Item pro expensis Willelmi mancipij cum equis versus Cant' ij s j d Item liberavi Magistro Roberto Gower in xv^a Sancti Michaelis xij s et Henrico cherere xvj d Item in vino Roberto Chorlton ij s Item Willelmo Sutham xxvj s iiij d Item Henrico pro scriptura unius Rotule xv d et pro pergameno iiij d Item Magistro Roberto in octav' sancti Hilarii versus London' xxj s iiij d Item Magistri Roberto versus London in xv^a pasche xvj s Item eidem cum Henrico x s Item pro expensis Magistri Johannis Alkbarow versus London eundo et redeundo xx s Item Magistro Roberto pro debito compotus anni precendentis xxviij s ij d[6] Item pro una toga Henrico Charere vj s viij d Item liberavi Magistro Gower pro expensis iiij s viij d ob

Summa xvj li xij s xj d ob

In dorso Rotuli

Reparationes Collegij

Inprimis 2^bus tegulatoribus pro 2^bus septimanis x s

[5] Dots as in Smith, which again probably indicates a gap in the text.

[6] [ADMC] But at the foot of the last roll, Smith had read 28s 6d as the amount owing to the Bursar.

pro 2^{bus} bigis arene	x d
pro reparatione stillisdij camere Bruton	xxj d
pro uno clave camere magistri Johannis Taylour	ij d
pro una situla fontis	vj d etc.

Summa xxxv s v d ob

Lodelowhall'

Inprimis pro mundatione Camerarum	iiij d
Item pro reparatione Camere Canonici	xvj d etc.

Summa xxxij s x d ob

Hamptonhall Summa xvj s x d ob

Drowdalhall'

Inprimis pro rubea terra	v s
Tegulatori et famulo ejusdem vij septimanis xxix	xxix s ij d
Item lathomis et famulo illius [*sic*]	xiij s x d

etc.

Summa v li vij d

Aule [*sic*] Scuti Summa v s ij d ob

Shope Walden Summa xiij s iiij d

Alloc' arr' anni noni et x^{mi} et xj^{mi}
Alloc' anni presentis ten'
camerarum

Summa omnium expensorum et liberatorum cxiiij li xx d
Et sic in plusagio viij li j d

[*The roll for June-December 1389 was missing even in Smith's day.*]

CHRISTMAS 13 RICHARD II to WHITSUN 14 RICHARD II (ROLL UC:BU1/F/8)

25 Dec 1389–14 May 1391

BURSAR: RICHARD HETH

[*The original roll for this year is missing. What follows is Smith's condensed transcript of it (Vol. VIII pp.36–39)*]

a 25 Dec 1389 ad initium anni 1391 ubi comune Sociorum anno a natali domini anno 13 Ricardi 2^{di} ad initium fere 15 R 2^{di}	Computus M. Ricardi Heth socij et procuratoris etc. a festo pentecostes inclusive usque ad idem festum exclusive anno revoluto viz. anno RR Ricardi 2^{di} quartodecimo incipiente continet ergo anni 13 R 2^{di} et partem [*sic*] 14 fere desinentis et patet se seq. Rotulo.

Arr' annorum 8 9 10 xj xij xiij inclusive

Redditus ejusdem Collegij

In primis de novo Collegio pro Maydynhall'	x s
de Aula Scuti	xj s
de Aula universitatis in vico Scolarum	xxxiij s iiij d
de Aula Staunton	xl s
de Drowdalehall'	lj s iiij d
de Lodelowhall'	iij li vj s viij d
de gardino Willelmi Hampton	viij s
de tenem' Thome Glover	vj li
de ten' quod tenet Willelmus Dagville	xl s
de schopa quam tenuit Ric Waldene	xvij s vij d
de ten' Ricardi Mercer	l s
Item recepi de cistis	iij li xiij s iiij d
Item recepi pro focalibus	viij s vij d
Summa istorum etc. xliij li xix d	

Redditus Camerarum inter quos

de camera Benteley	x s
de camera magistri Jo Taylour	x s
de camera pester	x s

de camera daunport x s

Summa iiij li xiij s viij d

Summa totalis omnium receptorum et oneratorum iiij^{xx}xvj li viij s iiij d ob

Liberata anno 1389

Iste sunt comune a prima septimana natal' domini inclusive una cum medietate septimana precedentis anno RR Ricardi 2^{di} 13°

In primis pro dimidijs communis et jurnallis duorum sociorum xxj d et in jurnallis tertij socij iij d

In prima septimana natalis domini in communis 2^{orum} sociorum v s

usque ad 14 septimanam

Summa xlix s vij d

anno 1390

Comune sociorum a festo pasche inclusive ad festum pentecostes

in 3 4 5 6 et 7^{a} septimana pro communis sex sociorum singulis septimanis vij s vj d

Summa xlvij s j d ob

a festo pentecostes usque festum sancti Thome

In prima septimana in communis quinque sociorum viij s vj d ob

et in jurnallis alterius socij xv d

Summa lj s iiij d q^{a}

a festo sancti Thome inclusive usque ad festum sancti Michaelis

in prima septimana in communis trium sociorum iij s ix d

et in jurnellis 4^{ti} socij xij d

in 9^{a} septimana in communis unius socij xv d

et in communis et jurnellis 2^{di} xiij d

Summa xxvj s vj d ob

a festo sancti Michaelis Inclusive usque festum natalis dominis

ubi sepe sunt quinque socij per septimanam vj s iij d

10^{a} septimana in communis et necessarijs in aula 4^{r} sociorum viij s

In communis et Iurnellis quinti socij xij d ob

Summa iij li xvj s q^{a}

a festo natalis domini inclusive ad festum pasche

In prima septimana in communis quinque sociorum xij s j d

in Batellis j d

In 2da septimana in communis quinque sociorum x s

In 3^{a} septimana in communis 4^{r} sociorum vj s

In communis et jurnellis quinti socij xvj d

Summa v li iiij s j d ob

Anno 1391

Comune a festo pascha [*sic*] inclusive ad festum pentecostes

1^{a} In communis quinque sociorum x s

2 et 3ta tantum hic habetur

Summa xxv s iij d ob

Summa totalis 19 li 00 00d

Stipendia famulorum

quibus adjicitur Item liberavi Magistro Roberto Gower de pecunia sibi a domo debita xxj s v d

Summa iij li iiij s vj d

Resoluciones redditus

Ecclesie sancte frideswyde	xvij s viij d
Item solvi Abindon	ij s
Item Ecclesie de Eynsham	x s
Item Agneti Northen pro prato Thome Glover	iij s viij d
Item Ecclesie sancte marie	xij d
Item Edmundo fraunceys	xxvj s viij d[1]
Item Ecclesie sancte frideswide pro anno instante	vj s viij d
Item liberavi pro communis Henrico Charer'	xij s viij d

Expense facte per eundum procuratorem ubi inter alia miscellanea

pro meremio (bis) – xviij s pro calce x s pro mille teculis et dimidio x s pro octingentis latis vj s ij d pro duobus millibus clavorum xxxj d

Item pro conductione equorum vj s viiij d Item Willelmo southam iiij s Item liberavi unam marcam Lond' tempore parliamenti Item magistro Roberto Gower pro expensis suis versus oxon' vj s viij d Item pro uno storio et cereis capelle

[1] This is the first of a series of regular payments made to Edmund Francis until 1400/1 after his dispute with the College over some of its properties was resolved (see Appendix II in Vol. II for a brief account of this affair).

viij d Item pro ligatura librorum ix s Item pro pergameo iiij d Item pro vino cum famulis domini Roberti cerleton vij d ob Item pro vino cum Edm. fraunceys et alijs xj d Item pro vino cum Willelmo Dagwyle in sigillatione cartarum iij d Item pro vino misso M. Johanni Bathe in Inceptione sua ij s vj d Item in vino in compoto Cancellario xix d ob Item Henrico Charer pro expensis suis Lond' in negotijs domus iij s ij d Item liberavi pro vino in bino adventu domini Roberti cerleton xiij d Item pro arboribus crescentibus positis in gardino x d Item pro alijs iiij d Item uni adquirenti arenam in gardino viij d Item pro alijs necessarijs factis in aula circa nostrum Doser' [*sic*] circa alia xv d Item in vino dato abbati de oseney capellano M. W. Tremellus et Edm' fraunceys xij d Item pro nostro Banquer [*sic*] v s ix d Item pro pergameo ad Rotulum ij d Item in vino Willelmo Dagwile et Edm. Fraunceys xiij d ob etc.

Summa vij li vj s iiij d

Expense in reparatione (domus vel collegij ut videtur) quarum prima Summa xlvij s j d ob

Expense in camera Daumport nec non pester [*a word deleted*]

Summa xviij s ix d

Reparatio camere iuxta Capellam etc. Summa xv s v d ob

Reparationes Camere M. P pikeryng nec non super librariam et cameram Hewel vel Heswell nec non Magistri Roberti Gower

Summa xiiij s

Reparationes Aula vocate Staunton Hall

Summa xxviij s x d

In Aula Sancti Edwardi

Summa xviij s viij d ob

In dorso Rotuli

In parva aula universitatis in vico Scolarum Summa iiij s vj d ob
In aula Scuti Summa xj s iij d
In aula Sancti Thome Summa ix s ix d
In Hamptonhall Summa xiiij s ix d ob
In Drowdale hall Summa xj s iij d ob
In Lodelowe hall Summa viiij li vij d ob
ubi pro meremio 20 s et 7 s 5 d et 10 s

Allocationes arr' annorum 9 10 11 12 13
Alloc' presentis anni ideo 14

Summa totalis omnium expensarum et allocatorum cij li xviij s iij d
et sic in plusagio vj li vj s v d ob

Rotulus iste longus est sex pedes

WHITSUN 14 RICHARD II-ST. CATHERINE 15 RICHARD II (ROLL UC:BU1/F/9)
14 May 1391–24 November 1391

BURSAR: JOHN MARSHALL

⟨Rotulus 14 Anni de solucione xij d a⟩

Assit principio sancta maria meo

Compotus Magistri Johannis Marschall' Socij et procuratoris Col[legij][1] magne Aule universitatis Oxon' A festo Pentecost'[2] Anno Reg[ni regis] Ricardi secundi post conquestum quartodecimo usque ad festum sancte K[aterine vir]ginis exclusive Anno eiusdem Regis quintodecimo.

Arr' Anno noni

In primis pro Aula sancti Thome	viij d
Item de Hamptonhall'	xxx s
Item de Aula Sancti Edwardi	x d
Item de orto ultra Castrum	xviij d
Item de cameris infra mansum proprium	ix s
⟨Summa xlij s⟩	

Arr' anni decimi

In primis de Hamptonhall'	xx s
Item de domo Boteler'	ij s
Item de stantonhall'	xiiij s iiij d
Item de Aula scuti	vj d
Item de Holdernesse	xxxviij s iij d ob
Item de camera Multon	ij s
⟨Summa lxxvij s j d ob⟩	

Arr' anni undecimi

In primis de Maydenhall'	v s x d
Item de Aula sancti Thome	vij s iiij d
Item de Aula scuti	vj s viij d
Item de parva Aula universitatis in vico scolarum	xiij s iiij d
Item de Brasenos	xx d

1 [ADMC] Words in square brackets are supplied from Smith Vol. VIII p. 40.
2 This word is written over an erasure.

Item de Hamptonhall'	xxxiiij s vj d
Item de Aula sancti Edwardi	vj s viij d
Item de Stauntonhall'	xiiij s viij d
Item de Drowhdalhall'	xlix s viij d ob
Item de Gardino Willelmi Ware	ij s iij d
Item de ten' Boteler'	ij s
Item de Gardino ultra Castrum	xij d
Item de Holdernesse	xlvj s vij d
⟨Summa ix li xij s j d ob⟩	

Arr' anni duodecimi

In primis de Aula Sancti Thome	xiiij s
Item de Aula scuti	iij s iiij d
Item de Aula universitatis in vico scolarum	xiij s
Item de uno ten' quondam Ricardi Cornewayle	xxx s
Item de ten' Thome Glover'	iij s iiij d
Item de Holdernesse	lix s iij d
⟨Summa vj li ij s xj d⟩	

Item petit allocacionem camerarum infra dictum Collegium xxviij s viij d

Arr' anni tercijdecimi

In primis de Aula sancti Thome	iij s iiij d
Item de Aula scuti	xij s
Item de parva Aula universitatis in vico scolarum	xiij s iiij d
Item de Brasenose	xiij s iiij d
Item de Hamptonhall'	viij s vj d
Item de Aula sancti Edwardi	x d
Item de Droghdalhall'	x s iij d
Item de ten' Boteler'	vj d
Item de Collegij Cant'	xv d
Item de ten' Thome Glover'	v li iij s iiij d
Item de schopa super angulum quadrivij	xx s
Item de uno Gardino in parochia sancti Egidij	viij d
Item de lodlowhall'	liij s iiij d
Item de ten' quondam Ricardi Cornewayle	xxx s
Item petit allocari de arr' camerarum infra dictum Collegium	xv s viij d
⟨Summa xiiij li vj s iiij d⟩	

Arr' anni quartodecimo	
In primis de Aula sancti Thome	xvij s iiij d
Item de Aula scuti	xvj s viij d
Item de parva Aula universitatis in vico scolarum	xx s
Item de Brasenose	xvj s viij d
Item de Hamptonhall'	ix s vj d
Item de stauntonhall'	xxx s vj d
Item de Droghdalhall'	xxxviij s
Item de lodlowhall'	xlix s
Item de Collegio Cant'	ij s vj d
Item de ten' Willelmi Dagvyle	xxvj s viij d
Item petit allocari de arr' camerarum infra dictum Collegium	xlvj s vj d
⟨Summa xiiij li iij s[3]⟩	

[*A change of hand at this point*]

Redditus eiusdem Collegij	
In primis de novo Collegio pro Maydenhall'	x s
Item pro olifaunthall'	iiij s
Item pro aula sancti Thome	xx s
Item pro aula Scuti	xxiij s iiij d
Item pro aula universitatis in vico scolarum	xxxiij s iiij d
Item de Brasenose	iij li vj s viij d
Item de Hamptonhall'	xlvj s viij d
Item de Aula sancti Edwardi	xxx s
Item de Stauntonhall'	xxxiij s iiij d
Item de Drowdalhall'	lj s iiij d
Item de tenemento Holway	xv s
Item de uno gardino Willelmi Ware	iij s
Item de tenemento Johannis Brasier	x s
Item de tenemento Thome Boteler	viij s
Item de uno orto ultra castrum	ij s
Item de Collegio Cant'	ij s vj d
Item de uno gardino Willelmi Hampton	viij s
Item de uno orto in parochia sancti Egidij	viij d
Item de schopa super angulum quadrivij	xx s
Item de holdenesse	iij li xij d
Item de ten' Thome glover	vj li

[3] [ADMC] The correct total should be £14 10d.

Item de ten' quod tenet Willelmus Dagwyle xl s
Item de ten' Ricardi Merser l s
Item de lodlowhall' lviij s
⟨Summa xxxv li vj s x d⟩
⟨lj li xij s ij d[4]⟩

Redditus camerarum infra dictum collegium
In primis de camera principalis xx s
Item de camera alta sibi proxima xvj s
Item de bassa camera sub illa x s
Item de camera bentelay x s
Item de camera M. J. Taylour x s
Item de camera pester x s
Item de camera Daunport x s
⟨Summa iiij li vj s⟩

⟨Summa totalis omnium receptorum et oneratorum iiij^{xx}xj li v s⟩

Commune sociorum a tercia septimana post festum Pasche festo Pasche computato in illo numero septimanarum usque ad festum sancti Thome exclusive
In communis 5 sociorum
In 4^{a} septimana post festum pasche computando idem festum vij s vj d In batellis q^{a}
In 5ta septimana in communis 5 sociorum vij s vj d
In batellis j d q^{a}
In 6ta septimana in communis 5 sociorum vij s vj d
In 7ma septimana in communis 5 sociorum vij s vj d
In septimana pentecostes in communis 5 sociorum ix s ij d
In septimana proxima post festum pentecostes in communis 4^{or} sociorum vij s ij d
Item in batellis unius socij et domus eiusdem v d ob
In septimana 3^{a} post festum pentecostes in communis quinque sociorum vij s vj d Item in batellis q^{a}
In 4ta septimana post pent' in communis quinque sociorum vj s x d ob
In 5ta septimana in communis quinque sociorum vij s iij d ob
In 6^{a} septimana post pent' in communis quinque sociorum vij s vj d

[4] [ADMC] An informal entry, in a very small hand.

In 7^{a} septimana post pent' in communis quinque sociorum vij s vj d

In 8^{a} septimana post pent' in communis quinque sociorum vij s j d In batellis j d

⟨Summa iiij li x s id x q^{a}⟩

Commune sociorum a festo sancti Thome ⟨inclusive⟩ usque ad festum sancti Michaelis exclusive

In prima septimana in communis quinque sociorum vij s j d
In batellis ob
In 2^{a} septimana in communis $iiij^{or}$ sociorum vj s
In 3^{a} septimana in communis $iiij^{or}$ sociorum vj s
In 4^{a} septimana in communis duorum sociorum iij s
In dimidijs communis et jurnellis 3^{cij} socij xiiij d
Item in batellis $iiij^{ti}$ socij vij d ob
In 5^{a} septimana in communis trium sociorum iiij s vj d
In 6^{a} septimana in communis trium sociorum iiij s j d ob
In 7^{a} septimana in communis trium sociorum iiij s
In 8^{a} septimana in communis trium sociorum iiij s
In 9^{a} septimana in communis trium sociorum iij s x d ob
Item in iurnallis 4^{ti} socij iij d
In 10^{a} septimana in communis 4^{or} sociorum v s ij d
In batellis ij d q^{a}
In 11^{a} septimana in communis trium sociorum iij s ix d
In batellis vj d ob
In 12^{a} septimana in communis trium sociorum iij s x d ob
In batellis j d q^{a}

⟨Summa lviij s iij d ob⟩

Commune sociorum a festo sancti Michaelis ⟨inclusive⟩ usque ad festum apostolorum Symonis et Jude exclusive

In prima septimana in communis trium sociorum iiij s
In batellis q^{a}
In 2^{a} septimana in communis quinque sociorum vj s ob
In batellis iij d
In 3^{a} septimana in communis quinque septimana in communis vj s iij d In batellis j d ob
In 4ta septimana in communis quinque sociorum v s v d
In batellis vij d q^{a}

⟨Summa xxij s viij d ob⟩

Stipendia famulorum

In primis liberavi Willelmo pincerne pro termino estivali iij s iiij s

Item eidem pro termino autumpnali iij s iiij d

Item in stipendio procuratoris computantis v s

Item deliberavi Henrico Cherrer xx d

Item lotrici iiij d

Item solvi cuidam fratri pro quodam libro reportando Collegio xviij d

⟨Summa xv s ij d⟩

Resolucio reddituum

In primis liberavi Edmundo ffraunses pro duobus terminis scilicet sancti Michaelis et pasche Anno regni Regis Ricardi secundi post conquestum xiiij^{o} liij s iiij d

Item Collectori reddituum de abindon pro termino annunciacionis beate marie eodem anno xij d

Item Collectori reddituum de Aynsham vj s

Item Johanni otworth' pro quodam annuo redditu iij s viij d

Item Collectori reddituum priorisse de Godystow pro anno Regis xij^{o} vij s

Item Collectori reddituum sancte fridiswyde pro anno Regis xiiij^{o} xij s iiij d

Item procuratori ecclesie sancte marie pro stauntonhall' pro anno xv Regis antedicti xij d

Item Collectori reddituum de Abindon pro termino sancti Michaelis eodem anno xv^{o} xij d

Item Edmundo ffraunses pro termino sancti Michaelis eodem anno xv^{o} xxvj s viiij d

⟨Summa c s iij s⟩

Expense facte per eundem procuratorum In primis pro calce – v s Item pro senevecterio ij d Item in alio senevecterio – xiij d Item in meremio empto vj s iiij d Item in cccc lattis iij s Item in mosse – xxx d Item in mille tegulis – vj s Item in ferro pro uno vanga – iij d Item in vino Cancellario tempore computacionis – x d Item in vino et jantaculo factis domino Roberto Charlton – xxx d Item in sirotecis datis suis hominibus – ij d v d Item in vino Johannis otworth pro relaxacione cuiusdam interesse facti pro feno Thome Glover – vj d Item in vino quando M Robertus Gower intravit Sentencias – ij s iiij d Item in emendacione duorum bankqwers – iiij d Item uni puero pro mundacione fontis – ij d Item pro coopertorio fontis – iij d ob Item in D cuneis pro tegulis – xv d Item in uno herdyll' – iij d Item in duobus bollis – v d Item in una pinsa – xij d Item in taketis pro scabell' in capella – j d Item in terra rubea pro camera ffoston' – iiij d Item pro focario in eadem camera – x d Item pro una clave j d ob Item uni latomo facienti introitum iuxta capellam – xv d Item pueris mundantibus spaciatorium – iiij d Item in scabello pro Aula – iij d Item in vij tabulis – xvii d Item in cc lattis – x d Item Item [*sic*] in D latnayle et C sprignayle – xj d Item pro sarracione tabularum – x d Item in ceris clavibus et in twystis – xix d Item ffoston pro labore suo in holdernesse pro redditu adquirendo – xij d Item in twystis et hukys emptis pro diversis cameris – xij d Item in tabulis emptis pro fenestris camerarum – viij d Item in expensis factis Magistro Johanni Midelton et suis hominibus diversis vicibus in Collegio – xx d ⟨Item in arapis emptis pro domo et capella – vij d ob⟩

⟨Summa l s iiij d ob⟩

Iste sunt expense facte in reparacione camere Benton

In primis pro tabulis	x d
Item mille latnayle	xviij d
Item D sprignayle	vij d
Item in Bordnayle	j d
Item in evysbord'	ij d ob
Item duobus carpentarijs pro primo die	x d
Item duobus carpentarijs pro 2ª die	x d
Item uni carpentario pro vj diebus	ij s j d
Item in merenda	j d
Item uni alteri carpentario pro 2bus diebus	x d
Item duobus carpentarijs pro uno die	x d
Item duobus tegulatoribus pro tribus diebus et dimidio	ij s xj d
Item alteri tegulatori pro uno die et dimidio	viij d
Item in merenda	j d
Item in prandio illorum pro uno die	iij d
Item duobus latomis facientibus gradus pro uno die et dimidio	xvij d
Item uni alteri laboranti cum ipsis	iiij d ob

Item in Bordnayle j d
Item uni laboranti emendanti aream camere et focarium iiij d ob
Item in crestos emptos vj d
⟨Summa xv s v d ob⟩

Iste sunt expense facte in reparacione camere Pestour
In primis in asseribus emptis iij d
Item in clavis emptis iij d
Item in feno pro mortario j d
Item in terra rubea iiij d
Item uni operario pro duobus diebus xj d
Item in merenda sua j d
⟨Summa xxiij d⟩

Iste sunt expense facte in reparacione camere Dale
In primis in uno camino iij s
Item pro uno lapide magno ad cooperiendum caminum vj d
Item uni tegulatori pro uno die iiij d ob
Item in merendis tam latomorum quam tegulatorum j d ob
Item in bordnayls emptis una vice pro emendacione facta iuxta caminum j d
Item in uno evysbord' empto pro portion Dale j d ob
Item in uno stode empto j d ob
Item duobus tegulatoribus pro uno die x d
⟨Summa v s ij d⟩

Iste sunt expense facte in reparacione camere Cromp'
In primis uni laboranti anglice Dawber emendanti cameram pro duobus diebus ix d
Item eidum pro duobus diebus in communi servicio domus infra Collegium nostrum ix d
Item in tabulis emptis pro hostio cum legg' xvj d
Item Bordnayle v d
Item in legg' emptis xij d
Item in latnayle vj d
Item in bordnayle iiij d
⟨Summa v s j d⟩

Iste sunt expense facte in reparacione camere Mixbery
In primis uni latomo pro factura focarij iiij d ob.
Item uni carpentario facienti gradus ij d ob

Item in clavis	j d
Item in tabulis pro ceptura [. . .] gradus	x d
⟨Summa xviij d⟩	

Iste sunt expense facte in reparacione camere Johannis Marschall

In primis duobus latomis pro duobus diebus	x d
Item in merendis	j d
Item in clavis	iij d
⟨Summa xiij d⟩	

Reparaciones Droghdalhall'

In primis uni operario pro emendacione unius ductil'	iij s iiij d
Item in clavis emptis	viij d
Item in sowdour empto	vj d
Item in stanno	iij d
Item in factura unius cloace uni operario pro tribus diebus	xv d
Item uni puero laboranti ibidem tribus diebus	vij d
Item in merendis ipsorum	ij d
Item in terra rubea	viij d
Item in asseribus emptis	v d
Item in latnayle	iij d
Item in stramine empto	ix d ob
Item uni mulieri trahenti stramen	ij d ob
Item uni feno empto pro mortario	j d ob
Item uni puero mundanti cameras	ij d
Item uni operario pro sex[5] diebus [*a deletion*] anglice Dawber	ij s[6]
⟨Summa xj s iiij d ob⟩	

Reparaciones Stawntonhall'

In primis in terra rubea	xij d
Item uni operario facienti murum iuxta latrinam eiusdem Aule	v d
Item in merenda sua	ob
Item in C asseribus pro emendacione unius basse camere	v d
Item in feno	j d
Item uni operatori pro uno die et dimidio	vij d
Item in stodys emptis pro camera bassa	iij d ob

[5] [ADMC] Written over an erasure.
[6] [ADMC] The figure has been altered.

Item uni latomo ibidem pro uno die et dimidio vj d ob
⟨Summa iij s iiij d ob⟩

Reparaciones Aule universitatis in vico scolarum

In primis in reparacione unius muri in quadam alta camera ij s viij d
Item duobus pueris diversis vicibus ibidem operantibus vj d
Item in latnayle pro emendacione eiusdem camere xvij d
Item in alijs clavis iiij d
Item in Crestes ix d
Item tegulatoribus emendantibus illam cameram xiij s iiij d
Item in merendis xij d
Item in terra rubea xij d
Item duobus tegulatoribus emendantibus defectus Aule et aliarum camerarum pro duobus diebus et dimidio ij s iiij d
Item in merendis j d
Item in terra rubea empta per principalem ut dicit ij s
Item pro emendacione hostij j d
Item pro mundacione terre antique rubee ibidem derelicte et litura x d ob
Item pro reparacione serarum et unius stapyll' ad seram iiij d
Item pro una nova sera iij d
⟨Summa xxvj s xj d ob⟩

Reparaciones Hamptonhall'

In primis in arena iiij d
Item in terra rubea viij d
Item uni latomo facienti caminum iiij s
Item in alijs reparacionibus xvij d
⟨Summa vj s v d⟩

[*Dorse*]

⟨Anno regis ricardi 14°⟩[7]

Reparaciones Aule Sancti Edwardi[8]

In primis tribus hominibus [. . .] unius clave iiij d

[7] [ADMC] Written on what was the outside of the roll when rolled up.

[8] [ADMC] The first part of the dorse is almost faded out, and a small part of the right hand edge of the roll is missing.

Item pro emendacione [. . .] iuxta coquinam ubi est cloaca uni operario una [*sic*] die iiij [*d*]
Item secundo die eidem [. . .
Item tercio die eidem [. . .
Item quarto die in [. . . [. . .
Item quinto die uni homini iiij d [. . .
Item sexto die uni [. . .] iiij s ob
Item septimo die eidem iiij s [. . .
Item 8vo die eidem iiij s ob
[. . .] die [. . .] iiij d
Item in merend[. . .] dierum iij d
Item [. . .] una vice viij d
Item [. . .] pro duobus diebus et dimidio xj d
Item in duobus tabulis infra latrinam vj d
[. . .] empt' ad latrinam xv d
Item in clavis emptis v d
Item in legges et [. . .]ibus ad eundem latrinam xix s
Item in semento et feno vj d
Item in evacuacione putei v d
Item in latomis conductis ad idem opus emendendum vij d ob
Item in salario puerorum portancium tabulas legges et sementum ad artifices iiij d
Item carpentarijs facientibus latrinam xiij d ob
Item in merendis suis ij d ob
Item in tabulis novis legges pro hostio faciendo ad unam cameram vij d ob
Item in clavis pro eodem et reparacione fenestrarum iij d ob
Item in twystes et hokes pro eisdem vj d ob
Item in tabulis pro magno hostio Aule et camere ij s iij d ob
Item in hokes et twystes ad trie hostia vj d ob
Item carpentario pro tribus diebus et merendis suis xvij d
Item latomo propter gradus camerarum et hostij reparandos v d ob
Item in semento ad cameras et latrinam et feno miscendo sement' vj d
Item in clavis ad latinam et ad cameras iij d
Item in emendacione trestelli et tabulis ad unum gradum faciendum et plumbo ad firmandum unum viaculum[*?*] in lapide ix d ob
Item in emendacione cuiusdam sere et clavis ad cameram v d

Item in semento empto	iij d
⟨Summa xxj s v d⟩	

[*The rest of the roll is written in the original hand*]

Allociones eiusdem procuratoris de arr' anni noni

In primis pro Aula Sancti Thome	viij d
Item de Hamptonhall'	xxx s
Item de Aula sancti Edwardi	x d
Item de orto ultra castrum	xviij d
Item de cameris infra mansum proprium	ix d
⟨Summa xlij s⟩	

Allocaciones arr' de anno decimo

In primis de Hamptonhall'	xx s
Item de domo Boteler	ij s
Item de stawntonhall'	xiiij s iiij d
Item de Aula scuti	vj d
Item de Holdernesse	xxxviij s iij d ob
Item de camera Multon	ij s
⟨Summa lxxvij s j d ob⟩	

Allocaciones arr' anni undecimi

In primis de Maydenhall'	v s x d
Item de Aula sancti Thome	vij s iiij d
Item de Aula scuti	vj s viij d
Item de parva Aula universitatis in vico scolarum	xiij s iiij d
Item de Brasenos	xx d
Item de Hamptonhall'	xxxiiij s vj d
Item de Aula sancti Edwardi	vj s viij d
Item de Stawntonhall'	xiiij s viij d
Item de Drowghdalhall'	xlix s viij d ob
Item de Gardino Willelmi Ware	ij s iij d
Item de ten' Boteler'	ij s
Item de gardino ultra castrum	xij d
Item de Holdernesse	xlivj s vij d
⟨Summa ix li xij s j d ob⟩	

All' anni duodecimi

In primis de Aula Sancti Thome	xiiij s
Item de Aula scuti	iij s iiij d
Item de Aula universitatis in vico scolarum	xiij s

Item de uno ten' quondam Ricardi Cornewayle	xxx s
Item de ten' Thome Glover'	iij s iiij d
Item de Holdernesse	lix s iij d

⟨Summa vj li ij s xj d⟩

Item petit allocacionem camerarum infra dictum Collegium xxviij s viij d

⟨Summa xxviij s viij d⟩

All' anni tercijdecimi

In primis de Aula sancti Thome	iij s iiij d
Item de Aula scuti	xij s
Item de parva Aula universitatis in vico scolarum	xiij s iiij d
Item de Brasenos	xiij s iiij d
Item de Hamptonhall'	viij s vj d
Item de Aula sancti Edwardi	x d
Item de Droghdalhall'	x s iij d
Item de ten' Boteler'	vj d
Item de Collegij Cantuar'	xv d
Item de ten' Thome Glover'	v li iij s iiij d
Item de schopa super angulum quadrivij	xx s
Item de uno gardino un parochia sancti Egidij	viij d
Item de lodlowhall'	liij s iiij d
Item de ten' quondam Ricardi Cornewayle	xxx s
Item petit allocari de arr' camerarum infra dictum Collegium	ix s

⟨Summa xiij li xix s viij d⟩

All' anni quartodecimi

In primis de Aula sancti Thome	xvij s iiij d
Item de Aula scuti	xvj s viij d
Item de parva Aula universitatis in vico scolarum	vj s viij d
Item de Brasenose	xiij s iiij d
Item de stawntonhall'	xv s vj d
Item de Droghdalhall'	xxxviij s
Item de lodlowhall'	xij d
Item de Collegio Cant'	ij s vj d
Item de ten' Willelmi Dagvyle	vj s viij d

⟨Summa cx s viij d⟩

Item petit allocari de arr' camerarum infra dictum Collegium xxv s viij d

⟨Summa xxv s viij d⟩

Allocaciones anni quintidecimi

In primis de aula sancti Thome	xvj s
Item pro Olyfaunthall'	ij s
Item pro Aula scuti	xxiij s iiij d
Item pro Aula universitatis in vico scolarum	xxiij s j d ob
Item de Brasenose	xlvj s viiij d
Item de Hamptonhall'	xlvj s viij d
Item de Aula sancti Edwardi	xv s[9]
Item de Stauntonhall'	xxiij s iiij d
Item de Droghdalhall'	xlviij s iiij d
Item de tenemento holway	vij s vj d
Item de uno gardino Willelmi Ware	xviij d
Item de ten' Johannis Brasier	v s
Item de ten' Thome Boteler	vj s v d
Item de uno orto ultra castrum	xij d
Item de Collegio Cantuar'	ij s vj d
Item de uno gardino Willelmi Hampton	iiij s
Item de uno orto in parochia sancti Egidij	viij d
Item de schopa super angulum quadrivij	xv s
Item de ten' Thome glover	iiij li x s
Item de ten' quod tenet Willelmus Dagwyle	xl s
Item de ten' Ricardi Merser	xxv s
Item de lodlowhall'	xlj s iiij d

⟨Summa xxiiij li iiij s iiij d ob⟩

Item petit allocari de arr' camerarum infra Collegium iij li ix d ob[10]

⟨Summa totalis omnium receptorum et oneratorum iiij^{xx}xj li v s

Summa totalis omnium expensarum et liberatorum iiij^{xx}xiij li ix s iiij d q^{a}

et sic debentur computanti xliiij s iiij d q^{a}. unde solvuntur sibi xiij s et sic debentur computanti xxxj s iiij d q^{a}⟩

9 [ADMC] The figure has been altered.
10 [ADMC] The figure has been altered.

[A narrow roll (7½ inches) of 4 membranes; mostly very clear, with one bad patch at the beginning of the dorse]

ST. CATHERINE'S 15 RICHARD II to WHITSUN 15 RICHARD II (ROLL UC:BU1/F/10)

24 November 1391–2 June 1392

BURSAR: THOMAS FOSTON

⟨Rotulus 15 Anni testatur de solucione xij d a.⟩

Compotus magistri Thome ffoston socij et procuratoris Collegij magne Aule universitatis Oxon' a festo Sancte Katerine virginis inclusive usque ad festum Pentecostes exclusive Anno Regni Regis Ricardi secundi post conquestum quintodecimo

[*The Arrears are the same as the Allowances in* ***F/9***]

⟨Summa totalis xliij li xviij s x d⟩

Redditus eiusdem collegij qui remanent de anno quintodecimo ut patet per compotum M. Joh' Marschal cum quibus ego sum oneratus

In primis de Aula sancti Thome	xvj s
Item pro Olifaunthall'	ij s
Item pro Aula scuti	xxiij s iiij d
Item pro Aula universitatis in vico scolarum	xxiij s j d ob
Item pro Hamptonhall'	xlvj s viij d
Item pro Aula sancti Edwardi	xv s[1]
Item pro Drodalhall'	xlviij s iiij d
Item pro ten' holway	vij s vj d
Item pro uno Gardino Willelmi Ware	xviij d
Item pro ten' Joh' Brasier	v s
Item pro ten' joh' Boteler	vj s v d
Item pro orto ultra castrum	xij d
Item pro Collegio Cantuar'	ij s vj d
Item pro uno Gardino W. Hampton	iiij s
Item pro uno orto in parochia sancti Egidij	viij d
Item pro schopa super angulum quadrivij	xv s
Item pro ten' Thome Mayster	iiij li x s
Item pro ten' Dagvyl	xl s
Item pro ten' Ricardi Merser	xxv s
Item pro lodlowhall'	xlj s iiij d

[1] [ADMC] The figure has been altered.

Item pro Stauntonhall' xxiij s iiij d
⟨Summa xxiiij li iiij s iiij d ob⟩

Item sum oneratus cum tribus libris et x d ob que debentur infra Collegium pro cameris
Summa patet ⟨iij li ix d⟩

⟨Summa Totalis oneratorum lx li xj li iiij d⟩

Commune sociorum a festo apostolorum Simonis et Jude inclusive usque et festum Natal' domini exclusive
In prima septimana in communis quinque sociorum vij s j d
In batellis iij d ob
In candelis vij d in salario iij d
In 2ᵃ septimana in communis quinque sociorum vj s iij d
In batellis ij d qᵃ
In 3ᵃ septimana in communis quinque sociorum v s
In jurnallis unius socij v d
In 4ᵃ septimana in communis quatuor sociorum et dimidio v s vij d ob In batellis et jurnallis vj d ob qᵃ
In 5ᵃ septimana in communis quatuor sociorum vj s iij d
In batellis qᵃ
In 6ᵃ septimana in communis quatuor sociorum vj s iiij d
In batellis vij d ob pro Scharelton
In 7ᵃ septimana in communis quatuor sociorum v s iiij d
In 8ᵃ septimana in communis quatuor sociorum v s
⟨Summa xlix s ix d ob qᵃ⟩

Commune sociorum a festo Natal' domini inclusive usque ad festum Pasche exclusive
In prima septimana in communis sociorum [*sic*] viij s x d
In batellis qᵃ
In 2ᵃ septimana in communis quatuor sociorum v s viij d
In 3ᵃ septimana in communis quatuor sociorum vj s
In batellis ob
In 4ᵃ septimana in communis quatuor sociorum v s iiij d
In batellis ob qᵃ
In 5ᵃ septimana in communis quatuor sociorum v s iiij d
In batellis x d ob
In 6ᵃ septimana in communis quatuor sociorum v s viij d
In batellis iij d ob

In 7[a] septimana in communis quatuor sociorum v s vj d
In batellis iij s viij d
In 8[a] septimana in communis quatuor sociorum v s x d
In batellis iij d ob
In 9[a] septimana in communis quatuor sociorum v s viij d
In batellis iij d ob q[a]
In 10 septimana in communis quatuor septimana vj s
In batellis iiij d
In 11 septimana in communis quatuor septimana v s viij d
In batellis ob
In 12 septimana in communis quatuor sociorum v s x d
In batellis iij d q[a]
In 13 septimana in communis quatuor sociorum v s vj d
In batellis j d ob
In 14 septimana in communis quatuor sociorum v s x d
In 15 septimana in communis quatuor sociorum v s x d
In 16 septimana in communis quatuor sociorum v s viij d
In batellis iiij d ob q[a]
⟨Summa v li x d ob q[a]⟩

Communes sociorum a festo Pasche inclusive usque ad festum Pentecostes exclusive

In prima septimana in communis quattuor sociorum vij s vj d
In 2[a] septimana in communis quatuor sociorum vj s
In batellis ij d ob
In 3[a] septimana in communis duorum sociorum et dimidio iij s iiij d In batellis et jurnallis v d ob
In 4[a] septimana in communis trium sociorum sociorum iiij s iij d In batellis ij d ob
In 5[a] septimana in communis trium sociorum et dimidio iiij s ix d ob In batellis et iurnallis viij s ob
In 6[a] septimana in communis quatuor sociorum vj s ij d
In batellis j d
In 7[a] septimana in communis quatuor sociorum v s x d
In batellis iij d ob q[a]
⟨Summa xxxix s x d ob[2]⟩

Stipendia famulorum

In primis liberavi Willelmo pincerne pro termino sancti Mich' iij s iiij d

[2] [ADMC] The correct total is 39s 10¼d.

Item eidem pro termino natal' domini iij s iiij d
Item eidem pro termino estivali iij s iiij d
Item lotrici vij s vj d
Item liberavi coco pro tribus terminis primo termino incipiente in festo Natal' domini anno domini Millesimo CCC^{mo} nonagesimo viij s vj d
Item in stipendio procuratoris computantis v s
Item uni homini pro informacione annui redditus de Osnay xij d

Summa ⟨xxxj s x d⟩

Resolucio reddituum

In primis Edmundo frances pro termino Pasche xxvj s viij d
Item Collectori de Abindon' xij d
Item Johanni Otworth' iij s viij d
Item Collectori de Godstow xiiij s
Collectori sancte ffrideswide xvij s iiij d
Item Collectori de Aynsham vj s

Summa iij li viij s viij d

Expense facte per eundem procuratorem In primis pro calce – v s Item in CCC lattis – ij s Item pro senevectorio ij d Item pro mose xvj d Item pro duobus latneyllis pro camera M. Thome Rumsey viij d Item pro stramine muri inter Collegium nostrum et parvum Aulam universitatis xviij d Item pro una tabla [*sic*] coquine iij s Item Johanni fforester pro viridi cera – x s Item liberavi M' Roberto Gower pro expensis versus london' vj s viij d Item pro duobus equis sibi et famulo suo ij s viij d Item pro uno securi iiij d Item pro vino qu[*ando*] famulus domini Roberti Scharelton cenavit cum M. Johanne Taylyor – iiij d Item in vino in festo Pasche viij d Item in arboribus pro disporto xij d Item pro emendacione vestium capelle – xxj d Item pro calce iiij s vj d Item Willelmo Hersand' x s pro suo labore a festo sancti Martini in yeme usque ad festum sancti Joh' Baptiste Item in adventu domini Roberti Scharelton in vino – iij d Item in emendacione pincerne j d Item pro emendacione senettorij ij d Item pro emendacione muri ~~eo~~ Aule nostre uni latamo vj d Item uni operario qui dealbavit aulam nostram pro quatuor diebus xx d Item pro okyr' et coll' vj d Item illi qui posuit tabula in aula vj d

Summa lvj s iij d

Expense facte pro novo muro inter Collegium nostram et parvam Aulam universitatis In primis uni operario pro portacione terre pro viij d[3] xvj d Item duobus operarijs pro duobus diebus xx d Item alijs duobus pro duobus diebus – xx d Item in potu illorum iiij d Item duobus uno die x d Item illi qui operuit xij d Item uni tegulatori v d

Summa vij s xj d

Expense facte in camera bassa sub Buren In primis Bloxsam pro sex diebus ij s vj d Item duobus carpentarijs uno die x d Item in potu j d ob Item pro tribus diebus in emendacione infra quadratum exterium xv d Item pro quatuor diebus uni in fode[*und'*] arenam viij d Item in potu ipsius laborantis ij d ob Item pro portacione arene ad diversa loca viij d Item pro portacione antiqui muri inter disportum nostrum et disportum de lodlowhall' vj d Item liberavi Borbryg' pro hokis nayles et twestis iij s vj d Item pro una veste altare nostrum in capella – xxij d Item pro candellis in capella xij d Item pro Torchyss' xvj d

Summa ⟨xiiij s v d⟩

Expense facte circa cameram M' Henrici Crownp' in primis uni latamo uno die vj d Item uni tegulatori v d Item plumbatori v d

Summa ⟨xvj d⟩

Expense facte in Drowdalhall' in primis pro quinque fenestris vij d ob Item in twestis iiij d Item pro emendacione aqueductilis xij d Item pro emendacione porticus ij s Item pro iij Crestis iiij d Item pro iij stodis iij d Item pro terra rubea iiij d Item pro arena iiij d.

Summa ⟨v s ij d ob⟩

Expense facte in Hamptonhall' In primis pro uno stod' – ij d Item in clavis j d Item tegulatori pro duobus diebus viij d In potu j d Item pro duobus Crestis iij d Item jacobo Schaytchar' pro vij diebus ij s iiij d Item uxori eius pro tot diebus xiiij d Item in stramine pro coopertura latrine de Drothdalhall' et latrine Hamptonhall' et unius domus eiusdem ij s vj d Item duobus carpentarijs pro duobus diebus xx d Item uni latamo pro tribus diebus xv d Item pro terra rubea xij d Item pro ostio camere magistri Ricardi Tone ij s

Summa ⟨xiij s ij d⟩

[3] [ADMC] *Sic*: presumably an abbreviation for *diebus*.

Expense facte in Stantonhall' In primis pro fenestris quatuor [*sic*] viij d Item pro terra rubia viij d Item uni operario pro duobus diebus x d Item in clavis ij d Item solvi pro tempore Marschall' viij d ob

Summa iij s ob

Expense facte in Aula sancti Thome In primis pro fenestris et twestis et hokis xxij d Item uni operario pro uno die v d

Summa ij s iij d

Expense facte circa cameram heth In primis uni operario pro iij diebus xv d Item in lattis j d Item circa cameram Gower uni tegulatori pro vj diebus – ij s vj d in potu ij d Item Henrico Charer' pro con[. . .] suis xvj s viij d

Summa xx s viij d

[*Dorse*]

Allocaciones arr' anni noni

In primis pro Aula Sancti Thome	viij d[4]
Item de Hamptonhall'	[*xxx*] s
Item de Aula [*sancti*] Edwardi	x d
Item de Orto ultra castrum	xviij d
Item de cameris infra mansum proprium	ix d
[*Summa xlij s*][5]	

Allocaciones arr' de anno decimo

In primis de Hamptonhall'	[*xx s*]
Item de domo butteler	[*ij s*]
Item de Stantonhall'	xiiij s iiij d
Item de Aula Scuti	vj [*d*]
Item de Holdernesse	xxxviij s iij d ob
Item de camera Multon	ij s
[*Summa lxxvij s j d ob*[6]]	

Allocaciones arr' anni undecimi

In primis de Maydynhall'	v s x d
Item de Aula sancti Thome	vij s iiij d
Item de Aula scuti	vj s viij d
Item de parva Aula universitatis in vico scolarum	xiij s iiij d

4 [ADMC] Several of these figures are very faint; several have been taken from the Arrears above.

5 [ADMC] Totally illegible.

6 [ADMC] Almost illegible.

Item de Brasenos	xx d
Item de Hamptonhall'	xxxiiij s vj d
Item de Aula sancti Edwardi	vj s viij d
Item de Stawntonhall'	xiiij s viij d
Item de Drodalhall'	xlix s viij d ob
Item de Gardino Willelmi Ware	ij s iij d
Item de ten' boteler'	[*ij s*]
Item de Gardino ultra castrum	xij d
Item de Holdernesse	xlvj s vij d
⟨ix li xij s j d ob⟩	

All' anni duodecimi

In primis de Aula Sancti Thome	xiiij s
Item de Aula scuti	iij s iiij d
Item de Aula universitatis in vico scolarum	xiij s
Item de uno ten' quondam Ricardi Cornewayll'	xxx s
Item de ten' Thome Glover'	iij s iiij d
Item de Holdernesse	lix s iij d
Item petit allocacionem infra dictum Collegium	xxviij s viij d
⟨Summa vij li xj s vij d⟩	

All' anni tercijdecimi

In primis de Aula sancti Thome	iij s iiij d
Item de Aula scuti	xij s
Item de parva Aula universitatis in vico scolarum	xiij s iiij d
Item de brasenos	xiij s iiij d
Item de Hamptonhall'	xxij d
Item de Aula sancti Edwardi	x d
Item de Drodalhall'	x s iij d
Item de ten' boteler'	vj d
Item de ten' Thome Mayster	v li iij s iiij d
Item de schopa super angulum quadrivij	xx s
Item de uno Gardino un parochia sancti Egidij	viij d
Item de lodlowhall'	[*liij s*] iiij d
Item de ten' quondam Ricardi Cornewayll'	xxx s
Item petit allocari de arr' camerarum infra dictum Collegium	ix s
⟨xiij li xj s ix d⟩	

All' anni quartodecimi

In primis de Aula sancti Thome	xvij s [*iiij d*]

Item de Aula scuti	xiiij s viij d
Item de Aula universitatis in vico scolarum	vj s viij d
Item de Stantonhall'	xv s vj d
Item de Drodalhall'	xxxviij s
Item de lodlowhall'	xij d
Item de ten' Willelmi Dagvyle	xx d
Item petit allocari de arr' camerarum infra dictum Collegium	xxv s viij d

⟨v li xv s vj d⟩

Allocaciones anni quintidecimi

Item pro Aula universitatis in vico scolarum	xxiij s j d ob
Item de Aula sancti Edwardi	vij s x d
Item de Drodalhall'	xxxv s
Item de ten' Holway	vij s vj d
Item de ten' Brasier	v s
Item de Collegio Cant'	ij s vj d
Item de ten' W Dagwyle	xx s
Item de Lodlowhall'	ij s
Item de ten' butteler'	vj s v d
Item de Hamptonhall'	ij s xj d
Item de Stantonhall'	viij d
Item petit allocacionem de cameris infra mansum proprium	xxxvj s viij d

⟨Summa vij li ix s vij d ob⟩

⟨Summa Totalis xlix li ~~viij~~ xix s viij d ob⟩

⟨Summa Totalis omnium Expensarum et Allocacionum lxx li xv s ob

Et [*sic*] Remanet in surr' ultra summam predictam viij s xj d ob⟩

[*A roll written in a markedly different hand from all earlier ones; much less neat. Slightly damaged in places, but mostly very clear. 2 membranes*]

[*The Rolls for 1392/3, 1393/4, 1394/5 and 1395/6 were all missing even in Smith's day.*]

20 RICHARD II (ROLL UC:BU1/F/11)

1396–1397

BURSAR: EDMUND LACY

[The original roll for this year is missing. What follows is Smith's condensed transcript of it (Vol. VIII pp.45–50). His comments suggest that it was already in poor condition when he examined it.]

Ex Rotulo lacero in fronte ejusdem
a^{o} 1396 a^{o} ut videtur 20 Ricardi 2^{di}

Rot Edm. Lacy procuratoris ut patent [*sic*] ex stipendijs famulorum 21 R 2^{di} ad pag. 52 [*of Smith's transcript*]

1393 Arr' camerarum infra mansum nostrum pro eodem anno 16 Ricardi 2^{di}

De camera Gryslay	vij d
de camera Bruton	ij d
Daunport	x s
pester	v s
Runsay	xx d
Crompe	vj s viij d
Taylor	v s iiij d

1394 arr' anni 17 Ricardi 2^{di}

camera Daunport	xiij s iiij d
Crompe	iij s iiij d
Taylour	xij s
Walton	ij s
Borne	xij d
Campedene et Brugge	ij s
Burbach	ij s x d
Merston	x s
Pykeryng	xxx s

Summa iij li xvj s vj d

1395 arr' 18 Ricardi 2^{di}

camera Heswel	xiij s iiij d
Heyword	xij s
Taylor	xij s

Pykeryng	xl d
Brugge	xij d
Campeden	xij d
Ledus	vij s iiij d
camera Canonici Len'	vj d
Byngham	ij s iiij d
Marston	x s
Summa xxxv s ij d	

arr' 19 Ricardi 2^{di}

de camera Haseley	vj s viij d
Derfeld	vj s viij d
Plumpton	viij s
Pyckeryng	x s
Walter	xij s
Ledys	iij s
Chylnorck	vj s viij d
Brygge	iiij s
Canon' Leicest'	v s iiij d
Dunham	ix s
Crompe	xj s viij d
Summa iiij li xix s viij d[1]	

1396 (20 Ricardi 2^{di})
Redditus eiusdem Collegij

De ten' Dagvyle	xl s
De ten' Ricardi Merser	l s
De ten' Chydesley	xvj s
De ten' Tho Glover	vj li
De ten' Alicie Ware	iiij s
De Gardino Willelmi Ware	iij s
De Novo Collegio	x s
De Alano Lekenfield	ij s
De Gardino Willelmi Hampton	viij s
De ten' Boteler viij s a° 21 Ricardi ten' Roberti Leicester	viij s viij d
De Gardino petri Dauber	viij d
De Gardino Terry ij s 21 R. 2 Willelmi Harper [...] Terry	iij s
De ten' Holwe	xv s
De Monachis Cantuar'	ij s vj d

[1] [ADMC] The correct total is £4 3s.

De Holderness iij li xij d
De Gardino Dadyngton[2] xvj d
21° de Johanni Spronte pro gardino quod tenuit quondam Jo Dadington 16d[3]
De prato Irland' xxvj s viij d 21° de Johanne Shaw pro prate Irland
Summa xix li xj s ij d[4]

Redditus Aularum
In primis de Brasenose iij li vj s viij d
Item de Aula Universitatis in vico Scolarum xxxiij s iiij d
Item de Aula Scuti xx s
Item de Aula Sancti Thome xxvj s viij d
Item de Hampton Hall xlvj s viij d
Item de Aula Edwardi xviij s
Item de Droudehall l s
Item de Stauntonhall xxxiij s iiij d
Summa xiiij li xiiij s viij d

Redditus infra manson' [*sic*]
In primis de magna Camera Rech Haseley xx s
Item de Camera Derfeld xvj s viij d
Item de Camera Saunderton x s
Item de Camera Gardiner xij s
Item de Camera Bamfeld x s
Item de Camera Plumpton fyling interlin' sine summa
Item de Camera sub Camera Bamfeld vj s viij d
Item de Camera sub Camera Gardiner x s
Item de Camera pykeryng xvj s viij d
Item de Camera portyngale xiij s iiij d
Item de Camera Walter xiij s iiij d
Item de Camera Taylour xij s
Item de Camera sub J. Walter —
Item de Camera Brugge viij s
Item de Camera Marston ix s
Item de Camera M. Edwardi in disporto x s
Item de Camera Willelmi Donham ix s

[2] A bond dated 4 May 1393 notes that John Dadyngton agrees to perform the covenants in a (lost) lease of this land on the same day (**UC:E2/12/1D/1**).
[3] It is unclear if this entry occurred in the lost original, or is a comment added by William Smith; probably the latter.
[4] [ADMC] The correct total is £18 11s 2d.

Item de Camera Crompe xj s viij d

Summa ix li viij s iiij d

Item recepi pro ligno xxix s

Item a magistro Duffeld xxvj s viij d

Commune Sociorum a festo pasche 4 septimanis exceptis usque ad festum Sancti Thome becket ut videtur 7[tii] Julij vel transl. Tho. Apostoli 3 July

In prima septimana in communis septem sociorum ix s ob

In Batellis ij d

In 2[da] septimana in communis septem sociorum x s xj d

In Batellis ij d

In 3[a] septimana in communis septem sociorum ix s iiij d

In Batellis j d ob

In 4[ta] septimana in communis septem sociorum xj s j d

In Batellis xxiij d ob

In 5 septimana in communis sex sociorum et dimidio x s iij d ob

In Batellis iij d ob etc.

In X[a] septimana in communis septem sociorum viij s ij d

In Batellis xvij d ob q[a] Contribuciones xvij d ob etc.

Summa v li x s vij d q[a]

A Crastino Sancti Thome usque ad festum Sancti Michaelis

In prima septimana in communis 2[orum] sociorum ij s ix s

In Batellis ij s j d q[a]

In 6[ta] septimana in communis 1[us] socij cum Jurnallis alterius ij s j d

etc.

Summa liij s ij d ob q[a]

A festo S. Mich usque ad festum Nat'

in Communis sex sociorum vij s ix d

in contributionibus ij s

Summa v li xxiij d

Summa totalis communarum 21 li 14 s 4 d

Summa Dorsi desideratur septimana una vel altera

in 15[ta] septimana 16[ta] et 17 Summa totalis (istius quart') viij li viij s vj d

Inter Stipendia Famulorum

Item Willelmi Slatter cum xl d a magistro Tho Duffeld xx s

Summa lvj s iiij d

Item liberavi M' Ricardo Heth pro capella v s

Item eidem xl d

Item alias xx d

Item liberavi Henrico Charer pro anno preterito ij s pro hoc anno xx s

Item Magistro Ric' de T.G. x s

Summa xlij s

Resolutiones Imprimis Edm. fraunceys xxvj s viij d

Summa iij li

Expense facte in necessarijs in grosse necnon in diversis Aulis etc. ubi inter alias expensas intra Collegium circa capellam et alia necessaria v li v s iij d ob

Summa x li xj s iij d ob

Sequuntur allocationes que alias precedere solent

Summa totalis omnium oneratorum lxxvij li v s x d

Summa totalis omnium expensarum et allocationum lxxviij li viij s x d ob

Computatis computandis et allocatis allocandis sic debet Domus computanti xxiij s ob

(ultimus annus in quo arreragia ante annum 20 Ricardi 2 computantur)

21 RICHARD II (ROLL UC:BU1/F/12)
1397–1398

BURSAR: THOMAS HETHE

[*The original roll for this year is missing. What follows is Smith's condensed transcript of it (Vol. VIII pp.50–53)*]

1397 Rotulus in capite laceratus 21 Ricardi 2^{di}

Compotus Magistri Tho Heth ut mihi innotuit ex compotu ejus pro anno 3° II4 in allocat' ad calcem expensarum ante alias allocationes

Redditus ten' Collegii

Item ten' Robertu Leicester – viij s – nuper butler omittitur	
Item de Willelmo Harper pro gardino iuxta terry	iij s
Item de Johanne Spronte pro Gardino quod tenuit quondam Joh' Dedyngton	xvj d
Item de Johanne Shause pro ponte vocato Irland	xxvj s viij d

Redditus Aularum post Brasenose adicitur

pro usu latrine Aule Sancti Thome	v s
pro aula Sancti Thome	xl s
pro Aula Edwardi	xx s
Summa xv li xv s	

Redditus Camerarum infra Mansum proprium

In primis de camera Heswell	xx s
Item de camera Derfelde	xvj s viij d
sub illa	x s
Whytehede	xij s
sub illa	x s
Barnefelde	x s
sub illa	xiij s iiij d
Pykeryng	xvj s viij d
sub illa	xiij s iiij d
Foston	v s
sub illa	vj s viij d
Taylour	xij s
Brystowe	viij s
Magistri Edwardi	vj s viij d

sub illa x s
fylyng ix s
Crompe xj s viij d
W. Worschype xiij s iiij [*sic*]
worschope or -ype [*sic*]

Summa xj li iiij s iiij d

Item Idem respondet de xliiij s vj d quos recepit de focalibus ut patet per papirum

Item Idem repondet de xxxij s viij d quos recepit de preteritis redditibus domus ut patet per papirum

Summa iij li xvij s d[*sic*] ij d

Summa oneratorum iij^{xx} li vij li xvj s j d

Item recep' de antiquis arr' vij s x d

Summa totalis omnium oneratorum iij^{xx} li vij li iij s xj d

Allocationes etc. pro communis sociorum a festo pasche ad festum sancti Thome exclusive
ubi 4 5 6 sept' pro 7 sociis ix s et x s ij d etc.

Summa v li xviij s ob

A festo Sancti Thome ad festum Sancti Mich'

Summa iij li iiij s ix d ob q^{a}

a festo Sancti Mich. ad festum nativitatis domini

Summa iiij li xv s xj d ob q^{a}

a festo natal' domini ad festum pasche exclusive

Summa vj li x s ij d

a fest pasche inclusive etc.

pro ij septimanis pro 4 socijs 1^{a} sept' vij s viij d Batel iij d ob q^{a}
2 sept' vij s j d ob iij d ob

Summa xv s iij d ob q^{a}

21 li 04 4 ob q^{a} Summa totalis omnium Communarum et Batellorum xxj li iiij s iiij d ob q^{a}

[1]Et memorandum quod Batelli non fuerunt Batelli sociorum sed diversorum operariorum tempore edificacionis capelle

[1] Smith drew a pointing hand here.

Stipendia famulorum	
In primis liberavi Tho: Spenser pro servitio suo	xiij s iiij d
Item Tho: coquo	xiij s iij d
Item Barbitonsori	v s
Item lotrici Megote	xvj d
	de debito antiquo
Item liberavi lotrici pro annis E. Lacy et meo	vj s viij d
2 Item liberavi eidem pro sua liberata ~~solatr'~~ viij d iiij d	viij s iiij d [*sic*]
1 Item Willelmo solatr'	v s
Item liberavi Willelmo Southam certori pro debito antiquo	iij s iiij d
Item procuratori domus pro suo labore	x s
Summa iij li vj s iiij d	
Item liberavi Henrico Charer	xxvj s viij d
Resoluciones redditus	
Item Edmundo fraunceys	liij s iiij d pro anno presente
procuratori mon' sancte frideswude	xvij s
procuratori ecclesie sancti petri orient'	ij s ix d
———————— sancte marie	xij d
Abbatie de Eynsham pro anno presenti	viij s
abbate de Godstow	xxvij s et sic eq' magne ad festum Michaelis
Johanni otterworth	iij s iiij d pro anno meo
Summa v li xiiij s ix d	
Expense circa Reparaciones aularum	
circa sancti Thome [*sic*] in vico scolarum	xxxiiij s iiij d
Drowdalhall	ix s viij d
sancti Edwardi	iij s viij d
universitatis in vico scolarum	xj s v d ob
Stauntonhall	xvij s iij d
Scuti	ij s xj d
Hampton hall	vij s j d
Summa iiij li vj s iiij d ob	
Expense facte infra Collegium	vij li xj s xj d q^{a}
Item ante festum pasche	vj s iij d ob
post festum pasche	xiiij s viij d
Item tradidi Magistro Collegii diversis vicibus	v li v s j d

post festum pentecost' viij s vij d

Summa xiiij li vj s vj d ob q[a]

Summa totalis omnium expensarum l li v s j d di

Allocationes arr' a° 20[mi] [*sic*]

Allocat' anni presentis

ubi de gardino quod tenet Adam Ryver iij s

non supra nominatur

Q. an Willelmi Ware ~~vel Willelmi Hooper~~

All' Camerarum loco ultimo camera Magistri Walteri Borde

v s non nominatur supra

Item petit allocari de meremio empto capell' xx s

de xiij s iiij d deimissis in manu pincerne

de xxvj s viij d datis pincerne pro focalibus

Summa iij li

Summa omnium oneratorum iij[xx]viij li iij s ij d

Summa totalis omnium expensarum et allocatorum iij[xx]viij li vij s ix d

Computatis ergo computandis et allocatis allocandis sic debet domus computanti iij s x d

[*The Roll for 1398/9 was missing even in Smith's day.*]

WHITSUN 22 RICHARD II to WHITSUN 1 HENRY IV (ROLL UC:BU1/F/13)

18 May 1399–6 June 1400

BURSAR: JOHN FAYT

dat ⟨Henrici quarti anno primo⟩

Compotus Magistri Johannis ffayt[1]: socij et procuratoris Collegij Magistri Willelmi de Dunelmia Magne Aule universitatis Oxon' vulgariter nuncupati A festo Pentecost' inclusive usque ad idem festum exclusive Anno Henrici quarti primo

Arr' anni vicesimi Regis `Ricardi secundi´	
In primis de tenemento Boteler	xvj d
Item de Gardino quod Johannes Dadynton' tenuit	xvj d
Arr' Camerarum infra mansum proprium eiusdem anni de camera principali	x s
	quos solveret Pester
Item de Camera Dunham	ix s
Summa xxj s viij d	
Arr' anni vicesimi primi `Regis Ricardi secundi´	
In primis de Gardino quod tenent Adam Ryver	iij s
Item de Gardino quod tenet Petrus Dawber	viij d
Item de Gardino quod tenet Johannes Sprunt	xvj d
Item de Holderness	xij d
Arr' aularum eiusdem anni	
In primis de aula sancti Thome sive stapulhalle	vj s viij d
Item de Hamptonhall'	ij s
Item de Stauntonhall'	iij s iiij d
Summa xviij s	
Arr' Camerarum eiusdem anni infra mansum proprium	
In primi Wythehed'	v s iiij d
Item de camera ffoston' d [*sic*]	iij s iiij d
Item de camera ffylyng'	ij s iiij d
Summa xj s	

[1] [ADMC] 'ffayt' is written in red ink over an erasure.

Arr' anni vicesimi secundi `Ricardi secundi´

In primis de Willelmo Dagwyle	xxiij s iiij d
Item de Ric' Mersere	xij s vj d
Item de Rogero Chyddesley	viij d
Item de Shopa super angulum quadrivij	xj s
Item de Thoma Glover	liij s vij d
Item de Alicia Ware	ij s
Item de Gardino quod tenet Adam Ryver	iij s
Item de novo Collegio	v s
Item de Alano Lechynfeld'	xij d
Item de Roberto Leycester	iiij s
Item de Petro Daweber	viij d
Item de Willelmo Harper de Gardino iuxta terry	iij s
Item de tenemento quod tenet Holway	viij s xj d
Item de Collegio Cantuarie	xv d
Item de Gardino quod tenet Sprunt	xvj d
Summa ⟨vj li xviij s vij d⟩	

Arr' Aularum eiusdem anni

In primis de Aula de Brasenos	xlv s viij d
Item de aula universitatis in vico scolarum	xxij s ij d
Item de Aula Sancti Thome	xxvj s viij d
Item de Aula Scuti	x s
Item de Hamptonhall'	xxxvj s viij d
Item de Aula sancti Edwardi	xvj s viij d
Item de Droudalhall'	xxx s
Item de Stauntonhall'	xxiij s iiij d
Summa ⟨x li xj s ij d⟩	

Arr' Camerarum

In primis de camera principali	xx s
Item de Camera Darfeld'	xvj s viij d
Item de camera sub illa	vj s viij d
Item de camera Parker	xij s
Item de camera sub illa	x s
Item de camera Bamfelde	xvj d
Item de camera sub illa	xj s viij d
Item de camera Pykeryng	xvj s viij d
Item de camera sub illa	iij s iiij d
Item de camera foston'	iij s iiij d
Item de camera sub illa	vj s iiij d

Item de camera Taylour	x[*ij s*][2]
Item de camera Brystowe	viij s
Item de camera Edwardi	vj s viij d
Item de camera sub illa	x s
Item de camera Bruton'	ix s
Item de camera Crumpe	xj s viij d
Item de camera Johannis Monachi de ff'	xiij s iiij d
Summa ⟨viij li xviij s x d⟩[3]	

Redditus tenementorum eiusdem Collegij

In primis de Willelmo Dagvyle	xl s
Item de Ric' Merser	l s
Item de Rogero Cheddesley	xvj s
Item de Schopa super angulum quadrivij	xx s
Item de Thoma Glover	vj li
Item de Alicia Ware pro gardino	iiij s
Item de Adam River	iij s
Item de novo Collegio pro Maydenhall'	x s
Item de Thoma Hampton' pro gardino ultra castrum	iij s
Item pro Gardino quod tenuit Willelmus Hampton'	viij s
Item de tenemento Roberti leycester	viij s
Item de Petro Dauber pro gardino	viij d
Item de gradino [*sic*] iuxta terri	iij s
Item de tenemento quod tenuit Holeway	xxj s viij d
Item de Collegio Cantuarie	ij s vj d
Item de Holderness	iij li xij d
Item de Johanne Sprunt pro gardino	xvj d
Item de Johanne Shawe pro prato yrelond'	xxvj s viij d
Summa ⟨xix li xviij s x d⟩	

Redditus aularum

In primis de Aula Brasonose	iij li vj s viij d
Item pro usu latrine Aula sancti Thome	iiij s
Item de aula universitatis in vico scolarum	xxxiij s iiij d
Item de Aula Sancti Thome sive stapulhall'	xxx s
Item de Aula Scuti	xx s
Item de HamptonHall'	xlvj s viij d
Item de Aula sancti Edwardi	xx s

2 [ADMC] Only 'x' is visible; but see the Allowances here.
3 There is no total of arrears on this roll. It would have been £28 18s 3d.

Item de Droudalhall'	l s
Item de Stauntonhall'	xxxiij s iiij d
Summa ⟨xv li iiij s⟩	

Redditus camerarum infra mansum proprium

In primis de camera principali	xx s
Item de camera Darfeld	xvj s viij d
Item de camera Parker	xij s
Item de camera sub illa horum	x s
Item de camera Thome circester	x s
Item de camera sub illa	xiij s iiij d
Item de camera Pykeryng	xvj s viij d
Item de camera sub illa	xiij s iiij d
Item de camera foston'	iij s iiij d
Item de camera sub illa	vj s viij d
Item de camera Wythehead'	xiij s viij d
Item de camera Johannis Taylour	xij s
Item de camera Brystowe	viij s
Item de camera Edwardi	vj s viij d
Item de camera sub illa	x s
Item de camera Bruton'	ix s
Item de camera Gardener	xiij s iiij d
Item de camera Monac' de furness	xiij s iiij d
Summa ⟨x li vij s viij d⟩	

Allocaciones predicti procuratoris pro communis sociorum A septimana sancti Johannis ante Portam exclusive latinam [*sic*] usque ad festum sancti Thome exclusive

In solucione pro debito antiquo pro communis vj s

In prima septimana in communis 4^{or} sociorum vj s viij d

In batellis vj d ob

In 2^{a} septimana in communis 4^{or} sociorum vij s

In batellis xiij s ob q^{a}

In 3^{a} septimana in communis 4^{or} sociorum vj s v d

In batellis ij d q^{a}
et iurnellis unius

In 4 septimana in communis 5 sociorum vij s j d

In batellis xiij d q^{a}

In 5 septimana in communis 5 sociorum et iurnellis vj s ix d

In batellis xiiij d

In 6 septimana in communis 5 sociorum vij s iij d ob
In batellis xxj d ob
Item in contribucionibus xv d
Item 7 septimana in communis 3um sociorum iiij s
In batellis vij d ob
Item 8 septimana in communis 5^{ue} sociorum vij s j d
In batellis xj d ob q^{a}
Summa iij li ~~xiiij d~~ vij s ij d

Item a festo sancti Thome inclusive usque ad festum Michaelis exclusive
In prima septimana in communis unius socij xvij d
In batellis xiij d ob
In 2^{a} septimana in communis unius socij xvj d ob
In batellis x d ob
In 3^{a} septimana in iurnellis viij d In batelis xiiij d ob
In 4 septimana in iurnellis vij d In batellis xij d
In 5 septimana in communis unius socij xvj d In batellis v d
In 6 septimana in communis unius socij xvij d In batellis xj d q^{a}
In 7 septimana in communis unius socij xvij d ob In batellis vij d
In 8 septimana in communis unius socij xvij d In batellis x d ob
In 9 septimana in communis 2^{orum} sociorum et iurnellis ij s ij d ob In batellis xv d ob q^{a}
In 10^{a} septimana in iurnellis 2^{orum} sociorum ix d In batellis x d
In 11^{a} septimana in communis 3um sociorum iiij s
In batellis xvj d
Summa xxvij s ij d ob

Item A festo sancti Michaelis inclusive usque ad festum Natal' domini exclusive
In prima septimana in communis 4 sociorum v s iiij d
In batellis vj d
In 2^{a} septimana in communis 3um sociorum cum dimidio iiij s xj d ob In batellis xij d ob
In 3^{a} septimana in communis 5 sociorum vj s x d ob
In batellis x d [[4]] q^{a}
In 4 septimana in communis 5 sociorum vj s viij d
In batellis xiiij d q^{a}

[4] [ADMC] x d ob q^{a}, but 'ob' apparently erased.

In 5^{a} septimana in communis 6 sociorum viij s vj d
In batellis x d ob

In 6 septimana in communis 5 sociorum vj s x d ob
In batellis iij s vj d

In 7 septimana in communis 6 sociorum vij s ix [*sic*]
In batellis ij s ij d

In 8 septimana in communis 5 sociorum cum dimidio vij s iiij d
In batellis iiij d ob

In 9 septimana in communis 5 sociorum cum dimidio ij s ix d ob
In batellis v d

In 10 septimana in communis 6 sociorum viij s vj d
In batellis vij d ob

In 11^{a} septimana in communis 6 sociorum viij s vj d
In batellis ij d

In 12 septimana in communis 6 sociorum vij s vj d ob q^{a}
In batellis iiij d

In contribucionibus ij s iij d

Summa v li xj d q^{a}

Item A festo Natal' domini inclusive usque ad festum Pasche exclusive

In prima septimana in communis 3um sociorum et dimidio cum iurnellis viij s xj d q^{a}
In batellis iij d q^{a}

In 2^{a} septimana in communis 4 sociorum viij s viij d
In batellis ij s viij d

In 3^{a} septimana in communis 4 sociorum et dimidio vij s viij d q^{a}
In batellis vij d ob

In 4 septimana in communis 6 sociorum ix s
In batellis ij d

In 5 septimana in communis 5 sociorum et dimidio viij s q^{a}
In batellis j d

In 6 septimana in communis 6 sociorum viij s vj d
In batellis ob

In 7 septimana in communis 5 sociorum cum iurnellis viij s ij d ob
In batellis iij d

In 8 septimana in communis 6 sociorum et dimidio vij s ix d ob
In batellis j d

In 9 septimana in communis 5 sociorum vij s iij d ob
In batellis v d

In 10 septimana in communis 5 sociorum vij s iij d ob
In batellis viij d

In 11^{a} septimana in communis 6 sociorum x s
In batellis xv d ob q^{a}

In 12 septimana in communis 5 sociorum vij s xj d
In batellis iiij d
In 13 septimana in communis 5 sociorum viij s iiij d
In batellis v d
In 14 septimana in communis 5 sociorum vij s xj d
In batellis ij s ij d
In 15 septimana in communis 5 sociorum vij s xj d
In batellis xiij d ob
In 16 septimana in communis 5 sociorum viij s j d ob
In batellis iij d
In 17 septimana in communis 5 sociorum viij s j d ob
In batellis j d ob
Summa vij li x s viij d ob q[a]

[*Dorse*]

Item a festo Pasche inclusive ad festum [*blank*]
In prima septimana in communis 5 sociorum et dimidio x s j d
In batellis iij d
In 2[a] septimana in communis 5 sociorum vij s v d ob q[a]
In batellis ij d ob
In 3[a] septimana in communis 4 sociorum cum dimidio vij s iij d q[a] In batellis ij d
In 4[a] septimana in communis 4 sociorum et iurnellis v s j d
In batellis ij d ob
In 5[a] septimana in communis 4 sociorum cum dimidio vj s vj d ob q[a] In batellis iiij d ob
Summa xxxvij s ix d q[a][5]

Summa totalis communarum xix li iij s viij d ob q[a][6]

Expense facte in capella iiij s ij d
Expense facte in reparacionibus infra Collegium et extra sicut patet per papirum x li iij s ij d ob
Item pro meremio empto bord' latt' et studuo xlvj s viij d
Summa xij li xv s ob

[5] [ADMC] The correct total is 37s 8d.
[6] [ADMC] The correct total is apparently £19 3s 9d.

Resoluciones

In primis liberavi Edmundo ffraunceys pro pensione duorum annorum iiij li xiij s iiij d

Item domui Sancte ffrideswide pro duobus annis cum dimidio xxxv s iiij d

Item procuratoribus ecclesie sancti petri in oriente v s viij d

Item procuratoribus ecclesie beate Marie xij d

Item Abbathie Eynesham pro duobus annis xvj s

Item Abbathie de Goddestowe xiiij s

Item Utterworthe pro duobus annis vj s iiij d

Item Ballivo Wilcot' ix d

Summa viij li xiiij s v d

Stipendia famulorum

In primis pincerne xxxiij s iiij d

Item Coco iij s iiij d

Item Barbitonsori pro anno preterito iij s iiij d et pro anno isto iij s iiij d

Item lotrici pro anno preterito et pro anno isto vij s viij d

Item pro Herico [*sic*] Charrer iiij s

Item Johanni ffoxe xij d

Item procuratori Domus x s

Summa iij li vj s

Allocaciones Anni \`vicesimi´ rr' regis Ricardi secundi

In primis de camera principali xx s quos solveret Pester

Item de Camera Dunham ix s pro quibus responderet Duffeld'

Allocaciones anni vicesimi primi eiusdem regis

\+ In primis de Gardino Ade River iij s

Item de Gardino quod tenet petrus Dauber viij d

\+ Item de Holderness xij d

Summa xxiij s viij d

Allocaciones Aularum eiusdem anni

\+ In primis de Aula sancti Tho~~me vj s viij d~~

Item de Hampton' Hall' ij s

\+ Item de Stauntonhall' iij s iiij d

Allocaciones camerarum eiusdem anni infra mansum

In primis de camera Wythehed v s iiij d

\+ Item de camera ffoston' iij s iiij d

+	Item de camera ffylyng'	ij s iiij d
	Summa xxiij s[7]	

Allocaciones Reddituum anni vicesimi secundi eiusdem regis

+	In primis de W. Dagvyle	~~iij s iiij d~~
	Item de Thoma Glover	xxij s xj d
+	Item de Gardino Alicie Ware	xij d
	Item de Gardino quod tenet Adam River	~~iij s~~
	Item de Gardino quod tenet petrus dauber	viij d
+	Item de Gardino iuxta terre	~~iij s~~
+	Item de Collegio Cantuarie	xv d
	Summa xxxv s ij d	

Allocaciones Aularum eiusdem Anni

	In primis de Aula scuti	iij s iiij d
	Item de Aula sancti Thome	iij s iiij d
+	Item de Drowdalehall'	~~iij s iiij d~~
+	Item de Stauntonhall'	x s
	Summa xx s	

Allocaciones camerarum infra mansum proprium

+	In primis de camera principali	~~xx s~~
	Item de camera Darfeld'	xvj s viij d
+	Item de camera Parker	v s iiij d
	Item de camera sub illa	x s
	[8]Item de camera Pykeryng	x s
+	Item de camera ffoston'	x s
+	Item de camera Taylour	~~xij s~~
	Item de camera Brystowe	xvj d
+	Item de camera Edwardi	~~vj s viij d~~
	Item de camera Walteri Borde	x s
	I [*sic*]	
	Summa v li ij s	

Allocaciones Reddituum Anni presentis

	In primis de Thoma Glover	xxvj s
	Item de Gardino quod tenet adam river	~~iij s~~
	Item de Roberto leycester	ij s viij d

[7] [ADMC] This, and all the following totals, are correct if the amounts which have been deleted are included.

[8] 'iij s iiij d' is written in the left-hand margin of this entry.

	Item de Petro Dauyber	viij d
+	Item de Gardino iuxta Terry	~~iiij d~~
	Item de tenemento quod tenuit Holoway	vj s ix d
	Item de Holderness	xij d
	Item de Johanne Sprunt	xvj d
	Summa xliiij s v d	

Allocaciones Aularum

	In primis de parva aula universitatis in vico scolarum	xvj s viij d
	Item de Aula scuti	xiij s iiij d
	Item de Aula sancti Thome	xiij s
	Item de Aula Edwardi	iij s iiij d
	Item de HamptonHall'	xxiij s iiij d
	[9]Item de DrowdaleHall'	xxiij s iiij d
	Item de Stauntonhall'	vj s viij d
	Summa iiij li xix s viij d	

Allocaciones camerarum

	In primis de camera principali	vj s viij d
	[10]Item de camera Derfeld'	xvj s viij d
	Item de camera Parker	xij s
	Item de camera Orum	x s
+	Item de camera Cyrcester	~~xvj d~~
	Item de camera sub illa	xiij s iiij d
	Item de camera Pykeryng	xvj s viij d
	Item de camera Andree	x s
	[11]~~Item de~~ camera ffoston'	x s
+	Item de camera Taylour	v s iij d
+	Item de camera Brystowe	xvj d
	Item de camera Eland'	x s
	Item de camera Bruton'	iiij s viij d
	Item de camera Gardener	vj s viij d

[9] The sum 'xiij s iiij d' has been written in the left margin of this entry; another sum, 'xiij s iiij d', in the left margin of the following one.
[10] 'iij s iij d' has been written in the left margin against this entry.
[11] 'vj s viij d' was written in the left margin against this entry, and then deleted.

Item de camera ffourness xiij s iiij d

Summa vj li xviij s

Summa totalis omnium oneratorum lxxiiij li ix s ix d

~~Summa omnium Allocatorum istius anni~~

Item respondet dictus procurator pro vj s viij d receptis a M T Duffeld'

Item pro tribus solidis de lignis collectis

Item pro iij s iiij d receptis de M. T Saunderton

Item pro ij s receptis ad usum capelle

Item pro xx d receptis de M Henrico Crumpe

Summa xiij s viij d[12]

Item dictus procurator petit Allocari de iij s vj d q[a] dimissis in manibus pincerne

Item de xvj s solutis Nafferton' pro arr' anni ~~sui~~ officij procuracionis sui

Summa v s iij d

Summa totalis oneratorum lxxv li iij s v d

Summa omnium Allocatorum istius anni lxviij li xiij s j d q[a]

et Allocat' computanti pro anno preterito ut patet per rotulum apprensum vij li xvj s viiij d q[a]

⟨Et sic computatis computandis et allocatis allocandis domus debet compuntanti xxvj s iiij d ob⟩

[*Clearly written roll, rather large hand; 2 membranes*]

12 [ADMC] The correct sum is 16s 8d.

WHITSUN 1 HENRY IV to WHITSUN 2 HENRY IV (ROLL UC:BU1/F/14)

6 June 1400–22 May 1401

BURSAR: JOHN FAYT

⟨non dat'⟩

Computus magistri Johannis ffayt socij et procuratoris Collegij magistri Willelmi de Dunelmia magne Aule universitatis oxon, vul[*gariter*] nuncupati A festo Pentecost' inclusive usque ad idem [*festum exclusive*] Anno rr' Henrici quarti secundo

Arr' anni vicesimi regis Ricardi secundi	
In primis de camera principali	x s quos solveret Pester
Item de Camera Dunham	ix s pro quibus respondebat M T Duffeld
Arr' anni vicesimi primi eiusdem regis	
In primis de Gardino Ade Ryver'	iij s
Item de gardino quod tenet Patrus Dawber'	viij d
Arr' Aularum eiusdem Anni	
In primis de Hampton' Hale	ij [*s*]
Arr' Camerarum eiusdem Anni infra mansum proprium	
In primis de Camera Qwythede	v s iiij d
Arr' Reddituum Anni vicesimi secundi eiusdem regis	
In primis de Thoma Glover	xxij s [*xj d*]
Item de Gardino quod tenet Adam Ryver	iij s
Item de gardino quod tenet Petrus Dauber	viij d
Arr' Aularum eiusdem Anni	
In primis de Aula scuti	iij s iiij d
Item de Aula sancti Thome	iij s iiij d
Arr' Camerarum infra mansum proprium	
De Camera Darfeld	xvj s viij d
Item de Camera sub illa	x s
Item de Camera Pikrynge	iij s iiij d
Item de Camera Birstow	ij s iiij d

Item de Camera M Waltery Borde	x s
Arr' Reddituum Anni preteriti	
in primis de Thoma Glover	xvj s
Item de Gardino quod tenet Adam Ryver	iij s
Item de Roberto laycester	ij s viij d
Item de Petro Dauber'	viij d
Item de tenemento quod tenuit Holway	vj s ix d
Item de Johanne Spront	xvj d
Arr' Aularum	
In primis de parva Aula universitatis in vico scolarum	xvj s viij d
Item de Aula scuti	xiij s iiij d
Item de Aula sancti Thome	xiij s
Item de Aula Edwardi	iij s iiij d
Item de Hampton Hale	xxiij s iiij d
Item de Drowdalhale	xiij s ij d
Item de stauntonhal	xiij s iiij d
Arr' Camerarum infra mansum	
In primis de camera principali	vj s viij d
Item de Camera darfelde	iij s iiij d
Item de Camera Parker'	xij s
Item de Camera Orum	x s
Item de Camera ffylyng et canonici de Taunton'	xiij s iiij d
Item de camera Pikryng	xvj s viij d
Item de camera Andree	x s
Item de camera ffoston'	vj s viij d
Item de Camera Elande	x s
Item de Camera Broyton'	iiij s viij d
Item de Camera Gardiner'	vj s viij d
Item de Camera furneyse	xiij s iiij d
Summa omnium arr' xvij li vj s	
Redditus Tenementorum eiusdem collegij	
In primis de Willelmo Dagvile	xl s
Item de Ricardo Merser	l s
Item de Robert Lamberth	xij s
Item de Johanne Caumberay	xvj s
Item de Johanne Barber'	iij s iiij d
Item de schopa sup [*sic*] Anglum quadrivij	xx s

Item de Thoma Glover'	vj li
Item de Alicia Ware pro gardino	iij s
Item de Adam Ryver pro gardino	iij s
Item de Novo collegio pro Maydenahale	x s
Item de Thoma Hampton' pro gardino ultra castrum	iiij s
Item pro gardino quod tenuit Willelmus Hampton	viij s
Item de tenemento Roberti laycester	viij s
Item de Petro Dauber pro gardino	viij d
Item de gardino iuxta Terry de ffouk barber'	iij s
Item de tenemento quod tenuit Holway	xv s
Item de Collegio cantuar'	ij s vj d
Item de Holderness	iij li xij d
Item de Johanne Sprount pro gardino	xvj d
Item de Johanne Schaw pro prato yrelond	xxvj s viij d

Summa reddituum tenementorum xx li vij s vj d

Redditus Aularum

In primis de Aula Brasynnos	iij li vj s viij d
Item pro usu latrine Aula sancti Thome	iiij s
Item de Aula universitatis in vico scolarum	xxxiij s iiij d
Item de Aula sancti Thome	xxx s
Item de Aula scuti	xx s
Item de Hampton Hale	xlvj s viij d
Item de Aula sancti Edwardy	xx s
Item de Drowdalhale	xl s
+ ~~Item de stauntonhale~~	~~xxxiij s iiij d~~

Summa reddituum Aularum xiij li viij d

Redditus Camerarum infra mansum proprium

inprimis de Camera principali	xx s
Item de Camera Darfelde	xvj s viij d
Item de Camera Parker	xij s
Item de Camera sub illa `M J Bergisse´	x s
Item de Camera monachi	x s
Item de Camera Baumfelde	xiij s iiij d
Item de Camera Pikrynge	xvj s viij d
Item de camera ffylyng	xiij s iiij d
Item de camera ffoston	x s
Item de camera sub illa	iij s iiij d
Item de Camera M Edmundi lacy	xiij s iiij d
Item de Camera magistri Johannis Orum	xij s

Item de Camera Thome ston viij s
Item de Camera M Edwardi vj s viij d
Item de Camere [*sic*] Thome sorcester x s
Item de Camera in quo [*sic*] inhabitavit Broyton' ix s
Item de Camera broyton' xiij s iiij d
Item de Camera in fine sporti xiij s iiij d
Summa reddituum camerarum x li xj s

Et dictus procurator recepit que non ffuerant de sorte Collegij
In primis de M Edmundo lacy xx s
Item de M Thoma heth vj s viij d
Item pro scolis inferioribus iiij s
Item pro una scola superiore ij s vj d
Item pro alia scola xx d
Et adhuc debet Petyngton' pro scolis suis x d
Summa receptorum preter sortem domum xxxiiij s x d[1]

Allocaciones Dicti procuratoris pro communis sociorum a quinta septimana post festum Pasche exclusive usque ad festum Thome Inclusive
In sexta septimana in communis 5 sociorum vij s xj d
In batellis vj d ob
In 7 septimana in communis 5 sociorum vij s j d
In batellis et sonio vij d
In 8ª septimana in communis 5 sociorum viij s j d ob
In batellis ij d ob
Item in 9ª septimana in communis sex sociorum ix s vj d
In batellis ix d ob
Item in 10 septimana in communis sex sociorum ix s iij d
In batellis v d ob
Item in 11ª septimana in communis 5 sociorum vij s j d
In batellis j d
Item in 12 septimana in communis 5 sociorum vj s ij d ob
In batellis j d
In contribucionibus xxj d
Summa communarum lix s viij d

[1] [ADMC] This is correct, if the money from Petyngton is excluded. [RHDS] Note that there is no full total for the debit side of this account. It would be £62 19s 10d.

Commune sociorum a festo sancti Thome inclusive [*sic*] usque ad festum sancti Michaelis inclusive

In 1ª septimana in communis duorum sociorum ij s ix d
In batellis xij d ob
In 2ª septimana in communis duorum sociorum iij s
In batellis ij s
In 3ª septimana in communis unius socij xvj d ob
In batellis xviij d qª
Item 4 septimana in communis duorum sociorum ij s xj d
In batellis xxj d
In 5 septimana in communis duorum sociorum iij s j d
In batellis vij d ob
In 6ª septimana in communis unius socij et dimidium [*sic*] ij s ix d
In batellis vj d
In 7ª septimana in communis duorum[2] iij s j d In batellis iiij d ob
In 8ª septimana in communis duorum sociorum iij s j d
In batellis iij d ob
In 9 septimana in communis duorum sociorum iij s j d
In batellis ij d ob
In 10ª septimana in communis duorum sociorum iij s iiij d
In batellis viij d ob qª
In 11 septimana in communis duorum sociorum iij s ij d
In batellis vj d ob
In 12ª septimana in communis duorum sociorum iij s ij d
In batellis in presencia roberti Botterwick et famulorum suorum xx d
Summa communarum xlvj s j d[3]

Commune sociorum a festo Michaelis exclusive usque ad festum Nativitatis domino exclusive

In 1ª septimana in communis 4 sociorum vj s ij d
In batellis ix d qª
In 2ª septimana in communis 4 sociorum v s x d In batellis iij d
In 3ª septimana in communis 5 sociorum vij s iij d ob
In batellis xiij d ob qª
In 4 septimana in communis 5 sociorum vj s v d ob
In batellis ij d ob
In 5 septimana in communis 5 sociorum vij s viij d ob

2 [ADMC] 'sociorum' is omitted.
3 [ADMC] The correct total is 46s 1½d.

In batellis magistri Thome darfelde in equitando in negocijs domus
ij s ix d ob q[a]
In 6[a] septimana in communis 5 sociorum vij s j d
In batellis iij d q[a]
In 7 septimana in communis 5 sociorum vij s j d
In batellis viij d q[a]
In 8[a] septimana in communis 4 sociorum et dimidij vj s iiij d ob
In batellis iiij d
In 9[a] septimana in communis 4 sociorum et dimidij vj s ix d q[a]
In batellis j d ob
In 10 septimana in communis 4 sociorum vj s ob q[a]
In batellis xiiij s ob
In 11[a] septimana in communis 4 sociorum vj s iiij d
In batellis ij d ob
In 12[a] septimana in communis 4 sociorum vj s iiij d
In batellis vj d
In contribucionbus ij s vj d
Summa iiij li xj s vj d[4]

Commune sociorum a festo Nativitatis domini inclusive usque ad festum Pasche exclusive
In 1[a] septimana in communis 4 sociorum x s viij d
In batellis xv d
In 2[a] septimana in communis 4 sociorum et jurnellis vij s iiij d
In batellis iiij d ob q[a]
In 3[a] septimana in communis 5 sociorum vij s vj d
In batellis v d ob q[a]
In 4 septimana in communis 5 sociorum vj s x d ob
In batellis ij s ob
In 5 septimana in communis 3 sociorum iiij s iij d
In batellis v d q[a]
In 6[a] septimana in communis duorum et dimidij iij s j d
In batellis ob
In 7[a] septimana in communis 4 sociorum et dimidij et iurnellis iiij s j d
In batellis j d ob
In 8[a] septimana in communis 4 sociorum et jornellis vij s iiij d
In batellis j d

4 [ADMC] The correct total is £4 11s 6¼d.

In 9ª septimana in communis 5 sociorum viij s j d ob
In batellis ij d qª
In 10ª septimana in co 5 [*sic*] vij s xj d In batellis xx d
In 11ª septimana in communis 5 sociorum vij s viij d ob
In batellis ob
In 12ª septimana in communis 5 sociorum vij s xj d
In batellis ob
In 13ª septimana in communis 4 sociorum vj s
In batellis et gaudijs sancti Cuthberti et pro speciebus et vino xij s vij d
In 14ª septimana in communis 4 sociorum vj s vj d In batellis qª
Summa v li xv s v d qª

Commune sociorum a festo Pasche inclusive ad festum Pentecost' exclusive
In prima septimana in communis trium sociorum vj s
In batellis iiij d
In 2ª septimana in communis trium sociorum et dimidijs v s vj d ob
In batellis v d
In 3ª septimana in communis quinque sociorum vij s xj d
In batellis iij d ób
In 4 septimana in communis quinque sociorum vij s xj d
In batellis qu' dominus Thomas Terry fuit nobiscum ij s ob
In quinta septimana in communis quinque sociorum vij s vj d
In batellis ob
In sexta septimana in communis [*sic*] vij s vj d In batellis j d ob
In septima septimana in communis quinque sociorum vij s viij d ob
In batellis ij d ob
Summa liij s iiij d

Summa omnium communarum xviij li vj s[5]

Resoluciones reddituum

In primis procuratori de Eynsam	viij s
Item Willelmo Worsteler pro anno precedent'	ix d
Item pro Anno meo	xviij d
Item solvi Edmundo ffrauncys	xl s vj s viij d
Item Utterworth	iij s viij d
Item solvi ecclesie sancte ffridiswide	xiij s iiij d
Item procuratori sancti petri in oriente	ij s ix d

[5] [ADMC] The correct total is £18 6s ¼d.

Item procuratoribus ecclesie beate marie xij d
Summa iiij li xj s viij d[6]

Stipendia famulorum
In primis Thome Spenser x s
Item Thome Kok v s
Item lotrici v s
Item barbitonsori xl d
Item Johanni Carnaby pro reportacione pecuniarum de Holdernes xij d
Summa xxiiij s iiij d

[*Dorse*]

Hec sunt deliberata Magistro Edmundo Lacy et Magistro Johanni Appilton' ut patet per papirum pro expensis factis ad usum domus xl s j d

[*About 2 inches space left on the roll*]

~~resoluciones~~

~~H' sunt deliberata usd usum collegij pro stauro empto ut patet per papirum xxiij s~~ xj d ob
Hec sunt deliberata pro expenc' ad usum Collegij ut patet per papirum xxiij s xj d ob

[*About 2 inches space*]

Hec sunt deliberata ad usum Collegij pro stauro ut patet per papirum xx s x d

[*About 1½ inches space*]

Reparaciones Aularum et scolarum
Procurator petit Allocari pro Hampton' Hale ut patet per papirum xj s ix d
Item de stauntonhale ut patet per papirum ix s ix d q[a]
Item pro Aula sancti Edwardi ut patet per papirum iiij s x d ob
Item pro Aula sancti Thome et scuti ut patet per papirum xxvj s x d

[6] [ADMC] Individual items actually total £3 17s 8d, i.e. 14s less than this total. Probably the roll omits in error a payment of 14s to the Abbey of Godstow, which occurs in the previous roll. 'viij d' is actually written here 'viiij d'.

Item pro Aula universitatis in vico scolarum ut patet per papirum xxviij s viij d ob
Item pro Drowdalhale ut patet per papirum xiij s viij d
Item pro Brassynos ut patet per papirum x d
Item pro reparacionibus infra mansum proprium ut patet per papirum xliij s viij d ob
Item pro reparacionibus scolarum ut patet per papirum iiij li iiij s vij d q^{a}
Item in reparacionibus murorum et aliorum defectuum ut patet [*sic*] xxv s j d ob

Reparaciones tenementorum

Procurator petit Allocario pro domo Roberti lambarde ut patet per papirum x s ob
Item pro domo Johannis Caumberay ut patet per papirum vij s iiij d ob
Item pro domo Roberti Bradlay ut patet per papirum j d
Item pro uno gardino ut patet per papirum iiij d
~~Item procurator petit Allocari pro stipendio suo x~~
Summa xiij li vij s viij d ob

Item procurator petit Allocari pro stipendio suo x s

Allocaciones Anni vicesimi Regis Ricardi secundi

In primis de camera principali x s quos solveret pester
Item de camera Dunham ix s pro quibus respondebat M T Duffeld

⟨nichil⟩ ~~Allocaciones anni vicesimi primi~~ eiusdem regis In primis de gardino Ade Ryver iij s

Allocaciones reddituum Anni vicesimi secundi eiusdem regis de Thome Glover `pro Willelmo Schrope´ xvj s iij d
⟨nichil⟩ Item de gardino quod tenet Adam River' iij s

⟨nichil⟩ ~~Allocac~~iones [*sic*] Aularum eiusdem anni de Aula scuti ~~xx d~~[7]

Allocaciones camerarum infra mansum proprium de camera darfeld xvj s viij d
Item de camera sub illa x s
Item de camera Pekeryng iij s iiij d

[7] [ADMC] 'xx d' is deleted and 'vij d' written above.

	Allocaciones reddituum Anni preteriti ⟨primi regis Henrici⟩ de Thome Glover	iij s iiij d
⟨nichil⟩	Item de gardino Ade ryver	iij s
⟨nichil⟩	Item de tenemento Holway	iiij s iij d
⟨nichil⟩	Allocaciones Aularum Anni preteriti in primis de Aula universitatis in vico scolarum	xx d
⟨nichil⟩	Item de Aula sancti Thome de M Johanne fforster	iij s iiij d
	Allocaciones camerarum infra mansum	
+	In primis de Camera Darfeld	iij s iiij d
+	Item de camera Magistri Johannis Orum	x s
	Item de camera Pekeryng	iij s iiij d
	Item de Camera Andree	x s
	Item de Camera Gardiner'	vj s viij d
+	~~Item de camera foston' superiori~~	~~vj s viij d~~[8]
	Allocaciones tenementorum Anni presentis	
	In primis de tenemento dagvil	xiij s iiij d
	Item de tenemento Roberti Lambart	vj s
	Item de tenemento Caumberay	vj s
	Item de Johanne barber' pro gardino	xx d
	Item de Thoma glover	xx s
⟨nichil⟩	Item pro gardino Ade river	iij s
	Item de tenemento Botiller'	iiij s viij d
	Item de Petero Dauber pro gardino suo	viij d
	Item de ffouk barber' pro gardino iuxta terry	xviij d
+	Item de Holdernes	xij d
+	Item de tenemento Roberti Bradlay quod tenuit Holway	iij s ix d
	Allocaciones Aularum Anni presentis	
	In primis de Aula Brasynnos	xiij s iiij d
	Item pro usu latrine	iiij s
	Item de Aula universitatis in vico scolarum	xxvj s viij d
	Item de Aula sancti Thome	iij s iiij d
	Item de Aua [*sic*] Hampton'	xvj s viij d
	Item de Aula sancti Edwardi	vj d
	Item de Drowdalhal	xiiij s[9]

[8] [ADMC] Possibly this whole entry is not deleted; the line running through it may merely be a fold in the parchment.

\+ ~~Item de stauntonHale xxxiij s iiij d~~

Allocaciones camerarum infra mansum anni presentis

In primis de camera M Thome darfeld xvj s viij d
Item de Camera Magistri Johannis Parker v s
Item de Camera sub illa Magistri Johannis Berge x s
Item de Camera monachi x s
Item de Camera Bawnfeld ⟨nichil debitur pre' iij s iiij d⟩ xiij s iiij d
Item de Camera Pikryng xvj s viij d
⟨solvitur⟩ Item de M. Thome ffoston' pro camera superiori x s
Item de Magistro Thome ffoston' pro camera inferiori iij s iiij d
Item de Camera magistri edmundi lacy xiij s iiij d
Item de Camera magistri Johannis Orum xij s
Item de camera in quo [*sic*] inhabitavit canonicus de broyton ⟨vacua⟩ ix s
Item de Camera broyton x s
Item de Camera in fine sporti ⟨vacua⟩ xiij s iiij d

Summa omnium Allocactionum Aularum tenementorum et camerarum xx li ix s j d[10]

Summa omnium oneratorum lxiij li

Summa omnium alacatorum [*sic*] lxij li xiij s viij d

Et sic computatis computandis et allocatis allocandis debet computans domui vj s iiij d

[*Clearly written roll; rather similar hand to 1399/1400. 2 membranes*]

[9] [ADMC] Another figure here apparently deleted.
[10] [ADMC] Either £20 3s 6d or £20 10s 2d, if the 'camera superior' of Foston is included.

WHITSUN 2 HENRY IV to WHITSUN 3 HENRY IV (ROLL UC:BU1/F/15)

22 May 1401–14 May 1402

BURSAR: THOMAS HETHE

Compotus magistri Thome Hethe Socij et procuratoris Collegij Magistri Willelmi de Dun[*elm'*] magne Aule universitatis vulgariter nuncupati A festo Pentecost' inclusive usque idem festum ex Anno rr' Henrici quarti tercio

[1]Arr' anni vicesimi [*primi*] R[*egis Ricardi secundi. In primis de camera principali – x s quos solveret pes*]ter ac eciam pro camera iuxta N[*afferton' pro*] duo[*bus annis – xviij s*]

Item pro Camera – [*blank?*]

Arr' reddituum anni vicesimi [*secundi eiusdem Regis de Willelmo schroppe* *vj s v*]iij d

Item de Aula scuti [*vij d*]

[*Arr'*] reddituum anni primi regis Henrici quarti [*de Thoma Glover*] iij s iiij d

[*Arr'*] Camerarum eiusdem anni

In primis de Camera Pykeryng	iij s iiij d
Item de camera Andree	x s
Item de camera Gardener	vj s viij d

Arr' reddituum anni preteriti

In primis de tenemento quod tenuit dagwyle	xiij s iiij d
Item de tenemento quod tenuit Robertus lambert	vj s
Item de tenemento proximo quod tenet Johannes Caumbrey	vj s
Item de Thoma Glover	xx s
Item de tenemento Boteler quod modo tenet Robertus leycester	iiij s viij d
Item de Petro Dauber pro Gardino	viij d
Item de ffouke barbur' pro Gardino iuxta terre	xviij d
Item de Johanne Barbur	[*blank*]

[1] [ADMC] The first membrane of the roll is considerably damaged. Defective entries of arrears can be pretty accurately restored from Allowances of **UC:BU1/F/14**, or of this roll.

Arr' Aularum anni eiusdem

In primis de Aula de Brasynnose	xiij s iiij d
Item pro usu latrine	iiij s
Item de Aula universitatis in vico scolarum	xxvj s viij d
Item de Aula sancti Thome	iij [*s iiij d*]
Item de Hampton' Halle	xvj s viij d
Item de Aula sancti Edwardi	vj d
Item de Drowdalehall'	[*xiiij s . . .*]

Arr' Camerarum infra mansum proprium Anni eiusdem

In primis [*de*] camera magistri Thome derfeld'	xvj s viij d
[*Item de c*]amera magistri Johannis Parker	v s
[*Item de camera*] magistri Johannis Brigg'	iij s iiij d
[*Item de camera*] Monachi Albi	x s
[*Item de camer*]a Baumfeld'	iij s iiij d
[*Item de*] camera Pykeryng	xvj s viij d
Item de camera Magistri Thome foston'	x s
⟨Item de camera sub illa	iij s iiij d⟩
Item de camera M. Johannis Orum	xij s
Item de camera Bruton	x s

Summa totalis arr' xiij li vij s x d[2]

Redditus tenementorum eiusdem Collegij

In primis de ⟨uxore⟩ Willelmo Dagwyle quam desponsavit Cowley — xl s [*All Saints*][3]

Item de Ricardo Merser — l s [*All Saints*]

Item de Johanne Royer Mancipio — xj s [*St. Peter in the East*]

Item de Johanne Caumbrey — xv s viij d [*ditto*]

Item de Johanne Barbur — iij s iiij d [*ditto*]

Item de Schopa super angulum quadrivij — xx s [*St. Martins*]

Item de Thoma Glover
vj li [*for various lands and tenements in All Saints and elsewhere*]

Item de Alicia Ware pro Gardino [*once Oliphaunt Hall*]
iiij s [*St. Mildreds*]

Item de Adam Ryver pro Gardino
iij s [*All Saints; possibly St. Mildreds*]

Item de novo Collegio pro Maydinhall' — x s [*St. Peter in the East*]

[2] [ADMC] Apparently this should be £13 19s 7d.

[3] At this point, Smith wrote on this roll (in Latin) the parish in which he thought each property was sited. His identifications are given here in English.

Item de Thomas Hampton' pro Gardino ultra castrum
iij s [*St. Thomas*]
Item de Gardino quod tenuit Willelmus Hampton
viij s [*St. Peter le Bailey*]
Item de tenemento quod Roberti Leycester quod erat Buteler
viij s [*St. Mary the Virgin*]
Item de petro Dauber pro Gardino viij d [*St. Giles*]
Item de ffouk barbur' pro Gardino iuxta terry
iij s [*St. Mary Magdalen*]
Item de tenemento quod tenuit holway xv s [*All Saints*]
Item de Collegio cantuarie ij s vj d [*St. Edward*]
Item de Holdernes iij li [*Yorkshire*]
Item de Johanne Sprunt pro Gardino xvj d [*St. Peter le Bailey*]
Item de Johanne Schawe pro prato yreland' xxvj s viij s [*Berks.*]
Item de Abbathia de Goddestowe xx d [*St. Aldates*]
⟨Item de Abbathia de Oseney pro schopa Cudduston'
vj s viij d⟩ [*St. Martins in Sywyria, Oxon'*]
Summa xx li vj s x d[4] ⟨Hic debet M. Thomas Hethe vj s viij d⟩

Redditus Aularum

In primis de Aula Brasynnose iij li vj s viij d [*St. Mary the Virgin*]
Item pro usu latrine que erat aule sancti Thome
iiij s [*St. Mildred*]
Item de parva Aula universitatis in vico scolarum
xxxiij s iiij d[5] [*St. Mary the Virgin*]
Item de Aula sancti Thome vocata stapulhall' v s [*St. Mildred*]
Item de aula scuti x s [*ditto*]
Item de Hampton Hall' xl s [*St. Mildred; later All Saints*]
Item de aula sancti Edwardi xxiiij s [*St. Mary the Virgin*]
Item de Drowdalehall' xl s [*St. Peter in the East*]
Item de Stauntonhall' xiij s iiij d [*St. Mary the Virgin*]
⟨Summa xj li xvj s iiij d⟩

[4] [ADMC] The actual total is £20 13s 6d – i.e. 6s 8d too much. This is accounted for by the fact that the last entry was added later, which in turn explains Thomas Hethe's debt of 6s 8d.

[5] [ADMC] This figure, and those for all the following, except St. Edward Hall and Stanton Hall, have been either over-written or altered.

Redditus Camerarum infra mansum proprium	
In primis de Camera principali	[. . .[6]
Item de Camera Darfeld'	[. . .
Item de cameris rectoris de Rowesthorn	[. . .
Item de Camera magistri Johannis Heneley	x s
Item de camera bamfeld' sub illa	x s
Item de camera Pykeryng	xvj s viij d
Item de camera Sowche	xiij s iiij d
Item de camera ffoston'	x s[7]
Item de camera sub illa canonici de merton'	vj s viij d
Item de camera Magistri Edmundi Lacy	xiij s iiij d
Item de camera M. Johannis Orum	xij s
Item de camera M. Johannis Brugg	viij s
Item de camera Edwardi	vj s viij d
Item de Camera canonici de Circester	x s
Item de Camera vicarij de Multon	xiij s iiij d
Item de Camera Naferton'	x s
Item de [*blank*]	
Summa reddituum camerarum ix li viij s viij d	

Item idem procurator respondet pro pensione trium scolarum in vico scolarum	xix s viij d
Item recepit de Gilberto stone	vj s viij d
Item recepit de communi cista	xxxviij s viij d
Item recepit a Magistro Thoma Nafferton	iij s iiij d
Item de Michael' Taylour	vij s vj d
Item de ffocalibus	xxvij s iiij d
Item de Magistro Johanne ffayt	vj s iiij d[8]
Summa v li ix s vj d	

Summa omnium oneratorum ~~lxij li xiiij s ij d~~
lxij li xiiij s ij d

[6] [ADMC] The roll is damaged for these three entries.
[7] [ADMC] This figure has been overwritten or altered.
[8] [ADMC] i.e. from the last bursarship.

Allocaciones predicti procuratoris Et primo pro communis sociorum prefati Collegij A festo pentecostes inclusive usque ad festum translacionis sancti Thome Martiris inclusive:

In prima septimana pro communis 4 sociorum viij s
In batellis ij s j d

In 2ª septimana in communis 4^or sociorum vij s viij d
In batellis ij s ij d ob

In 3ª septimana in communis 4 sociorum vj s viij d
In batellis iiij d ob

In 4ª septimana in communis 4 sociorum et dimidij cum iurnellis vij s vij d ob qª In batellis x d

In 5ª septimana in communis 5 sociorum vij s j d In batellis ob

In 6ª septimana in communis 5 sociorum vj s viij d In batellis qª

In septima septimana in communis 5 sociorum vij s vj d
In batellis j d

Item pro contribucionibus xv d

Summa lviij s j d ob

Commune sociorum a festo sancti Thome Martiris exclusive ad festum sancti Michaelis inclusive

In prima septimana pro communis 4^or sociorum v s
In batellis ij d ob

In 2ª septimana in communis 4 sociorum v s In batellis v d

In 3ª septimana in communis 4 sociorum v s In batellis ix d

In 4ª septimana in communis 4 sociorum v s In batellis vj d qª

In 5ª septimana in communis 3 sociorum iij s ix d
In batellis iij s iiij d

In 6ª septimana in communis duorum sociorum cum dimidio et iurnellis iiij s j d ob In batellis xij d

In 7ª septimana in communis trium sociorum cum dimidio iiij s iiij d ob In batellis ix d ob qª

In 8ª septimana in communis 4 sociorum v s In batellis viij d

In 9ª septimana in communis 4 sociorum v s In batellis viij d

In 10ª septimana in communis 4 sociorum v s In batellis xv d qª

In 11ª septimana in communis 4 sociorum v s In batellis xj d ob

In 12ª septimana in communis 4 sociorum vj s In batellis xiij d

Summa iij li ix s xj d qª Ac xvj s x d[9]

[9] The meaning of this entry is uncertain.

Commune sociorum a festo sancti Michaelis exclusive usque ad festum Nativitatis domini ~~xe~~ exclusive

In prima septimana pro communis 4 sociorum vj s
In batellis xviij d q^{a}
In 2^{a} septimana in communis trium sociorum v s iij d
In batellis viij d q^{a}
In 3^{a} septimana in communis 4 sociorum vj s iiij d
In batellis vij d ob
In 4^{a} septimana in communis 5 sociorum vij s xj d
In batellis vj d ob
In 5^{a} septimana in communis 5 sociorum ix s vij d
In batellis ij d ob q^{a}
In 6 septimana in communis 5 sociorum vij s viij d
In batellis j d ob
In 7 septimana in communis 5 sociorum vij s vj d In batellis ij d
In 8 septimana in communis 5 sociorum vij s vj d
In batellis iiij d
In 9 septimana in communis 5 sociorum vij s viij d ob
In batellis viij d
In 10 septimana in communis 5 sociorum vij s viij d ob
In batellis vij d
In 11 septimana in communis 5 sociorum viij s j d ob
In batellis xv d ob
In 12 septimana in communis 4 sociorum vj s viij d
In batellis x d ob q^{a}
In contribucionibus ij s vj d
Summa iiij li xviij s j d ob

Commune sociorum a festo Natal' domini inclusive usque ad festum Pasche exclusive

In prima septimana pro communis 2 sociorum iiij s vj d
In batellis iiij d
In 2 septimana in communis 3um sociorum vj s
In batellis vij d pro gaudijs xij d
Item pro iantaculo facto Michaelo Taulour et Ricardo Waterman ij s vj d ob
In 3^{a} septimana in communis 3um sociorum iiij s x d ob
In batellis xj d ob
In 4 septimana in communis 3um sociorum v s
In batellis ij s iiij d pro tegulatoribus

In 5 septimana in communis 3[um] sociorum iiij s ix d
In batellis xxiij d ob
In 6 septimana in communis 3[um] sociorum v s j d ob
In batellis xv d
In 7 septimana in communis 3[um] sociorum v s iiij d ob
In batellis xiiij d ob
In 8 septimana in communis 3 sociorum v s In batellis xij d
In 9 septimana in communis 3 sociorum et duo illorum erant di' iij s vj d In batellis viij d ob q[a]
In 10 septimana in communis unius socij cum dimidio v s vij d ob In batellis viij d
In 12 [*sic*] septimana in communis unius socij xxj d
In batellis viij d ob
In 13 septimana in communis unius socij xxj d ob
In batellis v d q[a]
In Gaudijs sancti Cuthberti xiiij s
Summa iij li vij s ij d

Commune Sociorum a festo pasche inclusive usque ad festum Pentecostes exclusive

In prima septimana pro communis unius socij ij s In batellis ij d
In 2[a] septimana in communis unius socij xix d ob
In batellis iij d ob
In 3 septimana in communis unius socij cum dimidio et iurnellis ij s xj d ob In batellis vj d q[a]
In 4 septimana in communis unius socij cum iurnellis alterius ij s ij d In batellis vij d ob
In 5 septimana in communis unius socij xxij d In batellis ij d
In 6 septimana in communis 3[um] sociorum iiij s ix d
In batellis ij d
In 7 septimana in communis duorum sociorum cum dimidio et iurn' iiij s vij d In batellis iiij d ob
Summa xxij s ij d ob q[a]
⟨Summa xvj li xij s v d⟩[10]

Stipendia famulorum

In primis Thome Spenser	xiij s iiij d
Item Thome coco	viij s iiij d
Item lotrici	v s

[10] [ADMC] This entry in a very small scribble.

Item barbitonsori v s
Item Johanni de coquina xx d
Item Willelmo sclatter xiij s iiij d
a festo sancti petri in advincula [*sic*] usque ad festum sancti michaelis
Item procuratori domus v s
Summa lvj s viij d

Resoluciones reddituum
In primis Abbatie de Osneye tempore concordie pro camera in fine gardini nostri pro omnibus Arr' eiusdem camere cum gardino vj s viij d
Item pro redditu anni presentis vj s
Item Abbatie de Godstowe pro uno anno cum dimidio xxj s
Item ecclesie beate Marie xij d
Item Abbatie sancte frideswyde xiij s iiij d
Item ecclesie sancti petri in oriente ij s x d
Item Willelmo Wrasteler' pro gardino nostro in parochia sancte Marie Magdelene xviij d
Item abbatie de Eynsham viij s
Item Ottirworth iij s viij d
Summa iij li iiij s

Expense facte per Magistrum et procuratorem infra Collegium iiij li iiij d ob
ut patet per papirum et sic de summis sequentibus
Expense facte in libraria xvij s xj d
Expense facte tempore empcionis tenementi in quo habitat Michael taylour v li vj s viij d
et ix s vj d ob pro expensis
Reparaciones facte in Drowdalehall' vij s ob
Reparaciones facte in parva aula universitatis in vico scolarum ix s iij d
Reparaciones facte in HamptonHall' xij s vj d ⟨ob⟩
Reparaciones facte in aula sancti Thome xxj d
Reparaciones Aule sancti Edwardi cum summa data taxatoribus v s ij d
Reparaciones Aue [*sic*] Scuti xv s x d ob
Reparaciones facte infra mansum proprium cum cameris in gardino iij li xv d
et scolis fihu xj d
Expense facte pre M Johannem ffayt in absencia mea xxxvij s x d

Item pro stauro empto ad utilitatem Collegij iiij li xvij s ij d
Item pro expensis factis extra villam per Magistrum et procuratorem circa negocia domus v li vij s x d
Item pro expensis factis per Magistrum Thomam darfeld ad quadrivium iij s iiij d
Item pro expensis factis per dominum Robertum Bampfeld' xij d
Item pro ferrura equorum vij d ob et Bigata calcis iiij s viij d
Item pro Adam Ryver iij s
Item procurator petit allocari de – iij x d qui erant sibi debiti in suo ultimo compoto ut patet per suum rotulum

Summa xxix li vij s vij d

Summa totalis communarum et expensarum lij li viij d

⟨summa lij li viij d⟩[11]

[*Dorse*]

Allocaciones dicti procuratoris Arr' anni vicesimi primi Regis Ricardi secundi

In primis de camera principali x s quos solveret pester ac debet pro camera iuxta nafferton pro 2^{bus} annis - xviij s
Item pro camera [*blank*]
Item anni xxij eiusdem Regis de Willelmo schrope vj s viij d
Item de aula scuti eodem anno [*several words erased*] vij d
Item allocaciones anni primi Regis H 4^{ti} pro camera Gardiner vj s viij d

Allocaciones reddituum eiusdem Anni secundi

In primis de Roberto lambert xx s
~~Item de petro daweber~~ ~~viij d~~
⟨~~Item de Johanne cambrey~~ ~~ij s⟩ ij s~~

Allocaciones camerarum infra mansum proprium eiusdem anni

In primis de camera Monachi Albi iij s iiij d
\+ Item de camera ffoston ~~x s~~
\+ Item de camera Bruton ~~iiij d~~

Summa ⟨lviij s ix d⟩[12]

[11] [ADMC] This entry is in a very small scribble.
[12] [ADMC] This is the correct total if the deleted 2s 8d is included, and the 2 final items are excluded.

Allocaciones tenementorum Anni presentis

	In primis [*a long entry erased*]	
	Item de tenemento quod tenet Johannes Cambrey	viij s x d
+	~~Item de Gardino quod tenet Johannes Barbour'~~	~~xx d~~
+	~~Item de schopa super angulum quadrivij~~	[*blank or erased*]
+	~~Item de novo Collegio pro Maydinhall'~~	[*ditto*]
+	~~Item de Thome Hampton pro Gardino ultra castrum~~	[*ditto*]
	~~Item de petro Dauber~~	~~viij d~~
	Item de ffouke Barbur pro Gardino iuxta terre	ix d
+	~~Item de tenemento quod tenet J. Braddeley in parochia omnium sanctorum~~	[*erasure*]
	Item de Johanne Sprunt pro Gardino	xvj d
	Summa [*sic*] ⟨Summa xix s x d⟩[13]	

Allocaciones Aularum Anni presentis

[*probably one entry, and possibly two, erased*]	
Item de parva Aula universitatis in vico scolarum	xiij s iiij d
Item de Aula \`stapulhall' vocata´ sancti Thome	xvj s viij d
Item de Aule scuti	xv d
Item de HamptonHall'	xxj s viij d
Item de Aula sancti Edwardi	iij s viij d
Item de StauntonHall'	vj s viij d
Summa iij li iij s iij d	

Allocaciones Camerarum Anni presentis

In primis de camera principali	vj s viij d
Item de camera Rectoris de Rowesthorn	viij s iiij d
Item de camera Heneley	iij s iiij d
~~Item de camera ffoston~~	~~iij s iiij d~~
Item de camera Pykeyng [*sic*]	xvj s viij d
Item de Camera Sowche	xiij s iiij d
Item de camera canonici de cristescherche	iij s iiij d
Item de camera lacy	xiij s iiij d
Item de camera upton'	[*erasure*]

[13] [ADMC] Written over an erasure. The 'x' of 'x d' is legible, but appears to have been erased.

Item de camera Brugg ⟨xl d⟩[14]

⟨Summa iij li xiiij s⟩ ⟨ista summa est falsa et hec est vera⟩

⟨Summa iij li v s⟩

Summa totalis xj li x s vj d[15]

Summa omnium oneratorum lxij li xiiij s ij d

Summa omnium allocatorum lxiij li xj s ij d et [sic computatis computandis] et allocatis allocandis domus debet computanti [. . .xviij s][16]

[*Clearly written roll of 4 membranes, of which the first is damaged*]

[*The Rolls of 1402/3, 1403/4 and 1404/5 were lost even in Smith's day.*]

14 [ADMC] Possibly intended to be erased.

15 ADMC suggested that the real total was £9 7s.

16 [ADMC] Roll damaged; readings from Smith Vol. VIII p. 63.

WHITSUN 6 HENRY IV to WHITSUN 7 HENRY IV? (ROLL UC:BU1/F/16)

7 June 1405–30 May 1406?

BURSAR: UNKNOWN

Compotus magistri et sociorum collegij magistri Willelmi de dunelmia magne aule universitatis vulgariter nuncupate [*sic*] a festo pent' inclusive usque ad idem festum exclusive Anno rr' [*sic*] regis Henrici [*year not stated, but the context makes it clear that it was 7 Henry IV*]

Arre[a] xx[mi] primi regis ricardi	
In primis de camera principali	x s
	istam summam solveret pester
Item de camera iuxta [*naff*]yrton[1] pro ij[bus] annis	xviij s
Item de aula [*scuti*]	vij d
Item de camera [*Gard*]ener	vj s viij d
Arre[a] [*anni secundi regni regis Henrici*]	
In primis de roberto lambard	viij d
Item de petro dober'	viij d
Item de caumbray	ij s
Arre[a] aularum eiusdem anni	
In primis de aula edwardi	vj d
Item de drowdalhall'	vij s
Summa xlvj s j d	
Arr[a] ten' anno regis predicti iij[o]	
In primis de ten' cambray	ij s x d
Item de gardino quod tenet Johannes Barbour	xx d
Item de abathia de osnay pro shopa Cudston	vj s viij d
Arre[a] aularum eiusdem anni	
In primis de aula sancti Thome	x s
Item de aula scuti	iij d
Item de aula edwardi	ij d
Item de Staunton hall'	vj s viij d

[1] The roll is slightly stained here, so that a few words are lost.

Arreª camerarum eiusdem anni
In primis de camera pykeryng x s
Item de camera lacy xiij s iiij d
Summa lj s vij d

Arreª ten' Anno rr' Henrici quarto
In primis de Adam Riwer' iij s
Item de Johanne Schaw juniore xiij s iiij d
Item de Abbathia de Osenay vj s viij d

Arreª Aularum eiusdem anni
In primis de Aula sancti Thome iij s iiij d
Item de Hamptonhall' iiij s ij d
Item de Aula Edwardi viij d
Item de Staunton Hall' xiij s iiij d

Arreª Camerarum
In primis de Camera Derfeld xj s ij d
Item de Camera Magistri Johannis Henle viij s
Item de Camera ffoston xiij s iiij d
Item de camera Horum vj s
Item de Camera Magistri Edwardi vj s viij d
Item de Camera Naffirton iij s iiij d
Summa iiij li xiij s

Arreª ten' Anno rr' Henrici quinto
Item in primis de Shopa super angulum quadrivij iij s vij d
Item de gardino quod tenuit Petrus Dobar' viij d
Item de Abbathia de Osinay vj s viij d

Arreª Aularum eiusdem Anni
~~In primis de Brasynhows~~
In primis de Stantonhall' xiij s iiij d

Arreª Camerarum eiusdem Anni
In primis de Camera ffoston vj s viij d
Item de Camera Naffirton iij s iiij d
Item de Camera Horum iij s iiij d

Arreª Scolarum eiusdem Anni iiij s j d
⟨Summa xli s viij d⟩

Arreª ten' Anno rr' Henrici Sexto
In primis de Thoma Glover v li xij d

Item de Alica Ware	xij d
Item de Thoma Hampton	ix d
Item de Roberto laycester	vij s
Item de ffuke Barbour	iij s
Item de johanne Spronte pro Gardino	xvj d
Item de Abbathia de Osenay pro Schopa Cudston	vj d viij d
Item de Thoma Cowley	x s
Item de Abbathia de Godstow	xx d

Arre[a] Aularum eiusdem Anni

In primis de parva Aula universitatis in vico scolarum	xvj s viij d
Item de Hamptonhall'	xiij s iiij d
Item de Aula sancti Edwardi	x s viij d
Item de Drowthtorhall'	xx s viij d
Item de Stantonhall'	xiij s iiij d

Arre[a] Camerarum eiusdem Anni

In primis de Camera fflemmyng	iij s iiij d
Item de Camera Dorley	vj s viij d
Item de Camera Canonici de repyngton	x s
Item de Camera Canonici de laycester	v s
Item de Camera Magistri Walteri ffrene	xx d
Item de Camera Andrew Marchand	iij s iiij d
Item de Camera Magistri Thoma ffoston	x s iiij d
Item de Camera Naffirton	iij s iiij d
Item de Camera Horum	vj s viij d

Arre[a] Scolarum eiusdem Anni iij s iiij d
quos solveret Nores

⟨Summa xiij li v d[2]⟩

Redditus tenementorum eiusdem Collegij

In primis de uno tenemento quondam Dagwyll'	xl s
Item de Ricardo Mercer	l s
Item de tenemento Thome glover	vj li
Item de Schopa super angulum quadrivij	xx s
Item de tenemento quondam Hollway	xv s
Item de tenemento Cambray	xv s viij d
Item de tenemento iuxta Cambray	xj s
Item de Gardino quem [*sic*] tenet Johannes Barbour	iij s iiij d

[2] [ADMC] The correct total is £13 9d.

Item de Gardino Alicie Ware	iiij s
Item de Adam Ryver pro Gardino	iij s
Item de novo Collegio pro Maydynhall'	x s
Item de Thoma Hampton pro Gardino	iij s
Item de uxore quondam Willelmi Hampton	viij s
Item de te [*sic*] tenemento Roberti laycester	viij s
Item de Gardino quem Petrus dowbar' quondam tenuit	viij d
Item de ffoke Barbour pro Gardino iuxta terre	iij s
Item de Collegio Cantuar'	ij s vj d
⟨Item de Godstow pro quadam Schopa iuxta ffryswyth	xx d⟩
Item de Holldyrnesse	iij li xij d
Item de Johanne Sprount pro Gardino	xvj d
Item de Johanne Schaw pro prato vocato yrlande	xxvj s viij d
⟨Item de Michaele Taylour	xv s⟩
⟨Item de philippo Cordewener[3]	xx s iij s iiij d⟩
~~Summa xx li~~ Summa xxij li vj s ij d[4]	

Redditus Aularum eiusdem Collegij

In primis de Aula Brasynose	iij li vj s viij s
Item pro usu latrine Aule Sancte Thome	iiij s
Item de Aula universitatis in vico scolarum	xxxiij s iiij d
Item de Aula Scuti	vj s viij d
Item de Aula Sancti Thome	xj s[5]
Item de Hampton Hall'	xl s
Item de Aula Sancti Edwardi	xxiiij s
Item de drowhall'	xxxiiij s[6]
Item de Stanton Hall'	xiij s iiij d
Item de parva Aula ~~in Alto~~ universitatis in Alto vico	xl s
Summa xiij li xij d	

Redditus scolarum

In primis de Scola ffrowyle	viij s
Item de scola Ade Rediforde	vij s viij d
Item de schola iuxta illam	vj s viij d
Summa xxj s iiij d	

[3] On 12 March 1404/5, Little University Hall and a house known as the Cock on the Hoop (the two buildings are now the site of Radcliffe Quadrangle) were leased to Philip Forsthull, Cordwainer (**UC:E/B6/D**1/10).

[4] [ADMC] Written over an erasure.

[5] [ADMC] These figures have been changed.

[6] [ADMC] These figures have also been changed.

Redditus Camerarum infra collegium

In primis de Camera principali	xx s
Item de Camera fflemmyng	xvj s viij d
Item de Camera Magistri Johannis Henle	x s
Item de Camera Canonici de layceter	xj s viij d
Item de Camera Canonici de Notley	x s
Item de Camera Magistri Edmundi layci	xiij s iiij d
Item de Camera Naffirton	xvj s viij d
Item de Camera ffoston	xiij s iiij d
Item de Camera Horum	xiij s iiij d
Item de Camera Rogeri Morton	x s
Item de Camera Abbatis de Nottley	xiij s iiij d
Item de Camera Cleseby	xiij s iiij d
Item de Camera Andree Marchand	xiij s iiij d

Summa viij li xv s

Allocaciones predicti Magistri pro communis et batellis A ffesto pentecostes usque ad ffestum Sancti Thome ~~exclu~~ inclusive

In primis pro prima septimana in communis vj s viij d

Item in 2a septimana pro communis vj s viij d

Item pro 3a septimana pro communis vj s viij d ob

In batellis iiij d ob

Item pro 4a septimana pro communis vj s vj d In batellis vj d qa

Item in 5a septimana pro communis vj s v d ob

Summa xxxiij s x d ob qa

bat'[7]

Item commune A ffesto Sancti Thome exclusive usque ad ffestum sancto dionisij inclusive xxij s xj d qa

Novus terminus

Item commune a septimana [*sic*] sancti dionisij exclusive usque ad ffestum natal' domini inclusive

In primis in prima septimana in communis quinque sociorum vij s j d In batellis xj d qa

Item in 2a septimana in communis ~~quinque~~ sex sociorum viij s

In batellis xix d ob

[7] [ADMC] This presumably means 'commune et batelle'.

Item in 3^{a} septimana in communis sex sociorum viij s
In batellis xx d ob
Item in 4^{a} septimana in communis sex sociorum viij s
In batellis ij s iij d ob q^{a}
Item in 5^{a} septimana in communis sex sociorum viij s
In batellis iiij s ix d ob q^{a}
Item in sexta septimana in communis quinque sociorum vij s viij d
In batellis iij s v d ob q^{a}
Item in septima septimana in communis quinque sociorum vj s viij d
In batellis xxj d q^{a}
Item in octava septimana in communis quinque sociorum vj s x d ob
In batellis xiij d ob
Item in nona septimana in communis ~~sex~~ quinque sociorum vij s j d
In batellis xj d
Item in decima septimana in communis sex sociorum viij s ix d
In batellis xiiij d ob q^{a}
Item in undecima septimana in communis sex sociorum xj s
In batellis viij d ob
Item in contribucionibus ij s
Summa v li ix s v d

Novus terminus

Item commune a ffesto Natal' domini usque ad ffestum pasche exclusive

In primis in prima septimana in communis quinque sociorum et dimidij vij s j d
In batellis j d ob
Item in 2^{a} septimana in communis quatuor sociorum et jurnellis vij s viij d
In batellis iiij d q^{a}
Item in 3^{a} septimana in communis quinque sociorum et jurnellis vij s x d ob
In batellis ij d
Item in 4^{a} septimana in communis sex sociorum ix s iij d
In batellis iij d ob q^{a}
Item in 5^{a} septimana in communis sex sociorum vij s viij d
In batellis j d ob
Item in sexta septimana in communis sex sociorum vij s iij d
In batellis vj d q^{a}
Summa liij s vij d ob q^{a}[8]

[8] [ADMC] The correct total is 53s 7¼d.

Item in septima septimana in communis sex sociorum viij s ix d
In batellis xvj d ob q[a]
Item in octava septimana in communis sex sociorum ix s
In batellis x d ob q[a]
Item in nona septimana in communis sex sociorum xj s iij d
In batellis viij d
Item in decima septimana in communis sex sociorum viij s vj d
In batellis xj d
Item in undecima septimana in communis quinque sociorum viij s vj d ob In batellis xj d ob q[a]
Item in xij[a] septimana in communis quinque sociorum viij s xj d ob In batellis ij s j d
Item in xiij[a] septimana in communis quinque sociorum viij s ix d In batellis xj d
Item pro gaudijs sancti Cuthberti viij s ij d
Item in xiiij[a] septimana in communis quinque sociorum ix s ij d In batellis xiij d
Item in xv[a] septimana in communis quatuor sociorum viij s
In batellis xij d ob

Summa v li ob q[a]

Item commune a ffesto pasche Inclusive usque ad ffestum pentecostes exclusive

In primis in prima septimana in communis quatuor sociorum viij s iiij d In batellis j d
Item in 2[a] septimana in communis quatuor sociorum vj s
In batellis xj d
Item in 3[a] septimana in communis quatuor sociorum vj s
In batellis vj d
Item in 4[a] septimana in communis quatuor sociorum vj s
In batellis iij d
Item in 5[a] septimana in communis quatuor sociorum vj s
In batellis v d
Item in sexta septimana in communis quatuor sociorum vj s viij d
In batellis iij d ob q[a]
Item in septima septimana in communis quatuor sociorum vj s
In batellis ij d ob q[a]

Summa xl s vij s viij d ob

[*An entry of about 9 words erased here*]

⟨Summa omnium comunarum xviij li vij s viij d⟩

Resoluciones Reddit'

~~In primis ecclesie beate virginis xij d~~[9]
~~Item johannis Otirworth iij s viij d~~
~~Item Wilkoc' pro gardino extra portam borialem ix d~~

Reparaciones Aularum

In primis circa parvam Aulam universitatis in vico scolarum [*blank*]
Item circa ~~repar~~ parvam aulam universitatis in alto vico [*blank*]
Item circa Dorwhall' [*blank*]
⟨Item petit sibi allocari pro meremio empto a thoma mayster v li iiij s⟩

Item petit sibi allocari pro diversis expensis factis tam ad infra quam extra in diversis negocijs domus ut patet per paupirum vj li xv s iij d

Item petit sibi allocari pro diversis expensis factis per Magistrum in edificijs et in alijs negocijs quibuscumque xv li ix s iiij d ob[10]

Summa xxvij li viij s vij d ob

Summa omnium oneratorum iij^{xx} li vij s iij d

Summa omnium expensarum et allocacionum iij^{xx} li xiiij li xj s iij d ob

Et sic computatis computandis et allocatis allocandis domus est indebit' computanti in quatuor li iiij s et ob

⟨Whythede⟩[11]

[*Dorse*]

All' Anni rr' R xx primi

In primis de Camera principali x s
Item de Camera iuxta Nafferton pro ij Annis xviij s
Item de Aula Scuti vij d

[9] [ADMC] Smith Vol. VIII p. 65 takes these entries as not being deleted. The deletion is faint but definite, and if they were not deleted the otherwise correct total of the roll would be thrown out.

[10] [ADMC] The figures have been altered.

[11] [ADMC] This is the first roll to be signed by the Chancellor or his Commissary.

Item de Camera Gardener	vj s viij d
All' Redd' eiusdem Anni rr' H ij°	
In primis de Roberto lambarde	viij d
Item de P. dowber	viij d
Item de Cambray	ij s
All' Aul' eiusdem Anni	
In primis de Aula Edwardi	vj d
Item de Drowdalhall'	vij s
Summa xlvj s j d	
All' Ten' A° rr' predicti iij°	
In primis de ten' Cambray	ij s x d
Item de Gardino quod tenet Jo Barbour	xx d
Item de Abbath' de Oseny pro schopa Cudston'	vj s viij d
All' Aul' eiusdem Anni	
In primis de Aula Sancti Thome	x s
Item de Aula Scuti	iij d
Item de Aula Edwardi	ij d
Item de Stauntonhall'	vj s viij d
All' Camer' eodem Anno	
In primis de Camera Pykeryng	x s
Item de camera lacy	xiij s iiij d
Summa lj s vij d	
All' Ten' A° pred' r' iiij°	
In primis de Adam Ryver	iij s
Item de jo Schaw juniori	xiij s iiij d
Item de Abbathia de Oseny	vj s viij d
All' Aul' eiusdem Anni	
In primis de Aula sancti Thomi	iij s iiij d
Item de HamptonHall'	iiij s ij d
Item de Aula Edwardi	viij d
Item de StamptonHall'	xiij s iiij d
All' Camer' eiusdem Anni	
In primis de Camera Derfeld'	xj s ij d
Item de Camera M. Jo. Henley	viij s
Item de Camera ffoston	xiij s iiij d
Item de Camera Orum	vj s

Item de Camera M. Edwardi	vj s viij d
Item de Camera Nafferton	iij s iiij d
Summa iiij li xiij s	
All' Ten' A^{o} rr' H. v^{o}	
In primis de schopa super Angulum quadrivij	iij s vij d
Item de Gardino quod tenet P. dowber	viij d
Item de Oseny	vj s viij d
All' Aul' eiusdem Anni	
In primis de StauntonHall'	xiij s iiij d
All' Camer' eiusdem Anni	
In primis de Camera ffoston	vj s viij d
Item de Camera Nafferton	iij s iiij d
Item de Camera Orum	iij s iiij d
All' Scol' eiusdem Anni	iiij s j d
⟨Summa xlj s viij d[12]⟩	
All' Ten' Anno rr' H. vj^{o}	
In primis de Alicia Ware	xij d
Item de T Hampton	ix d
Item de R. leycester	vij s
Item de ffok barbour	iij s
Item de Abbathia de Oseny pro schopa Cudston	vj s viij d
Item de Abbathia de Godstow	xx d
All' Aul' eiusdem Anni	
In primis de HamptonHall'	xij d
Item de Aula Edwardi	iiij s
Item de Drowdalhall'	vij s iiij d
Item de stauntonhall'	xiij s iiij d
All' Camer' eiudem Anni	
In primis de Camera Dorley	vj s viij d
Item de Camera Canonici de Repyngdon	x s
Item de Camera Andree Marchaunt	iij s iiij d
Item de Camera ffoston	xvj d
⟨Summa iij li vij s j d⟩	

12 [ADMC] The figures have been altered.

All' Ten' A° rr' H. vij°

In primis de Ten' T. Glover	iij li vij s
Item de T. Cowly	xiij s iiij d
Item de schopa super Angulum quadrivij	iij s viij d
Item de Ten' Cambray	ix d
Item de Gardino quod tenet barbour	iij s iiij d
Item de Adam Ryver	iij s
Item de T. T. [*sic*] Hampton pro gardino	xviij d
Item de ten' roberti leyceter	viij s
Item de ffok barbour pro gardino iuxta terry	iij s
Item de Holdernesse	vj d
Item de Spront pro gardino	xvj d
Item de Michaele Taylour	vij s iij d
Item de Ten' Philippi Cordener	xj s viij d[13]
⟨Summa vj li xij s vij d⟩	

All' Aul' eiusdem Anni

In primis de Hamptonhall'	xx s
Item de Aula Edwardi	vij s iiij d
Item de Drowdalhall'	xvij s iiij d
Item de parva aula universitatis in alto vico	vj s viij d

All' Camer'

In primis de Camera fflemyng	vj s viij d
Item de Camera Henley	x s
Item de Camera Canonici de Notley	iij s iiij d
Item de Camera Canonici de leyceter	xx d[14]
Item de Camera M. E. lacy	xiij s iiij d
Item de Camera Murton	iij s iiij d
Item de Camera Nafferton	vj s viij d
Item de Camera Orum	~~vj s~~ vj s viij d
Item de Camera ffoston	xiij s iiij d[15]
Item de Camera Andree Marchaunt	xiij s iiij d

[13] [ADMC] This item may be deleted, but it is necessary for a correct total.

[14] [ADMC] This entry, except for the figure 'xx d', may have been meant to have been deleted.

[15] [ADMC] So entered originally, and 13s 4d is necessary for correct total. But the figure has been altered to 'x s', and appears as 'x s' in Arrears of next roll.

Item de Camera Clesby xiij s iiij d

⟨Summa vij li iij s⟩

⟨Summa totalis alloc' xxviij li xv s⟩

[*A narrow roll; 3 membranes. Written in rather a peculiar, angular hand as if with the side of a nib and with an ink slightly blurred. There are several other peculiarities, notably the addition of Allowances after the normal conclusion of the roll; the omission of servants' wages and Rents Paid; also oddities of spelling*]

WHITSUN 7 HENRY IV to WHITSUN 8 HENRY IV (ROLL UC:BU1/F/17)

30 May 1406–15 May 1407

BURSAR: ROBERT BURTON

De Tempore Burton

Compotus magistri et sociorum collegij M Wyllelmi de dunelm' Magne aula universitatis wlgariter nuncupate a festo pent' inclusive usque ad idem festum exclusive anno rr' regis Hanrici quarti post conquestum anglie octavo.

Onus eorundem anni predicti de arr' redditibus et pencionibus et primo de arr' anni septimi

Arr' tenementorum

In primis de Thome Glover	iij li vij s
De Thoma Couley	xiij s iiij d
De ten' Cambrey	ix s
De gardino quem [*sic*] tenet Johannes Barbur	iij s iiij d
De Adam Ryver	iij s
De Thoma Hamton'	xviij d
De ten' Roberti leycetur	viij s
De fouke Barbur	iij s
De Holdernes	vj d
De Sprout pro gardino	xvj d
De Michaele Taylyour	vij s iij d
Summa v li xvij s iij d	

Arr' aularum eiusdem anni

In primis de Hampton Hall'	xx s
De aula Edwardi	vij s iiij d
De droudale Hall'	xvij s iiij d
De parva aula universitatis in alto vico	vj s viij d
Summa lj s iiij d	

Arr' camerarum eiusdem anni

In primis De camera fflemyng	vj s viij d
De camera Henley	x s
De camera canonici de Notley	iij s iiij d

De M Edmundy Lacy	xiij s iiij d
De cam' Moreton'	iij s iiij d
De cam' Naffyrton'	vj s viij d
De cam' ffoston'	x s
De cam' Marchaund	xiij s iiij d
De cam' Clesby	xiij s iiij d
Summa iiij li	

Redditus ten' eiusdem collegij Anno septimo [*sic*] rr' Henrici Quarti

In primis De ten' Couley	xl s
De ten' Mercer	l s
De ten' Glover	vj li
De Schopa super angulum quadrivij	xx s
De ten' quondam Holwey	xv s
De ten' Cambrey	xv s viij d
De ten' iuxta Cambrey	xj s
De gardino quem tenet Johannes Barbur	iij s iiij d
De gardino quondam Alicie Ware modo Rycardi Caryur	iiij s
De gardino quem tenet Adam Ryver	iij s
De novo Colegio pro Maydynhall'	x s
De gardino quem tenet Thomas Hampton'	iij s
De gardino quem tenet uxor quondam Willelmi Hampton'	viij s
De ten' Roberti leycestor	viij s
De gardino quem quondam tenuit petrus dauber	viij d
De gardino quem tenet fouke barbur iuxta Terry	iij s
De collegio Cantuar'	ij s vj d
De Abbat' de Godstow pro una Schopa iuxta frydeswyd'	xx d
De Holdernes	iij li xij d
De Sprunt pro gardino	xvj d
De Johanne Schawe pro prato vocato yrelond' et alijs	ij marc'
De Mic' Taylyour	xv s
De Philippo Cordewener	xxiij s iiij d
Summa xxij li vj s ij d	

Redditus aularum eiusdem anni

In primis de Brasynnose	iij li vj s viij d
De usu latrine aula sancti Thome	iiij s
De aula scuti	vj s viij d
De aula sancti Thome	x s
De parva aula universitatis in vico scolarum	xxxiij s iiij d

De Hampton' Hall'	xl s
De aula Edwardi	xxiij s
De drowdale Hall'	xxx s
De Staunton Hall'	xiij s iiij d
De parva aula universitatis in alto vico	xl s

Summa xiij li iiij d

Penciones scolarum dicti collegij eodem anno

In primis de scol' ffrowke	viij s
De scol' Baron'	vj s viij d
De scol' fylham	vj s viij d

Summa xxj s iiij d

Penciones camerarum eiusdem anni infra dictum collegium

In primis de camera Qwythede	vj s viij d
De camera Henley	x s
De camera Canonici leicester	x s
De camera M Edmundi lacy	xiij s iiij d
De camera Naffyrton	xvj s viij d
De camera ffoston	xiij s iiij d
De camera Orum	vj s viij d
De camera Marchand	x s
De camera Beneham'	xiij s iiij d
De camera Lovell'	xxxiij s iiij d
De camera flemmyng	xxxiij s iiij d

Summa viij li vj s viij d

Summa totalis omnium onorant' [*sic*] – lvij li x s ix d

De Esexe	xvj marc' ij d

⟨Summa omnium onerat' iij^{xx}li viij li iiij s iij d⟩

All' dicti M et sociorum In primis ten' [*sic*] de anno septimo rr' Henrici

De Thome Glover ⟨quod ei perdonatum est⟩	iiij marc' ij s iiij d
De Johanne Barbur pro pencione sua a retro	xx d
De Adam Ryver	iij s
De Roberto leycetor	ij s viij d
De Holdernes	vj d
De Thoma Cowley	xiij s iiij d

Summa iij li xvj s x d

All' aularum eiusdem anni

De aula Edwardi	vij s iiij d

All' camerarum infra collegium eiusdem anni

In primis De camera Hanley	iij s iiij d
De camera canonici de Notteley	iij s iiij d
De camera Morton'	iij s iiij d
De camera Naffyrton'	vj s viij d
De camera ffoston'	iij s iiij d
De camera Clesby	xiij s iiij d
Summa xxxiij s iiij d	

All' ten' eiusdem collegij de anno octavo rr' Henrici

In primis de ten' Cowley	x s
De ten' Roberti Leycetor	viij s
De gardino quondam petri dawber	viij d
De gardino quem tenet fowke barber	xviij d
De Holdernes	iij li xij d
De schopa super angulum quadrivij	iiij d
Fui eciam oneratus de fouke barber qui ut M dixit non erant debiti cum	xviij d
Summa iiij li iij s	

All' aularum eiusdem anni

In primis de parva aula universitatis in vico scolarum	xxiij s iiij d
De Hampton' Hall	vj s viij d
De aula Edwardi	v s
De drowdale Hall'	x s
De Staunton Hall'	vj s viij d
De parva aula universitatis in alto vico	xj s viij d
De usu latrine aule sancti Thome ⟨perdonatum est⟩	iij s
Summa iij li xvij s iiij d	

All' camerarum infra dictum collegium eodem anno

In primis de camera Henley	x s
De camera Naffyrton'	x s
De camera ffoston'	xiij s iiij d
De camera lovell'	xvj s viij d
De camera fflemmyng	xiij s iiij d
De camera Benehame	vj s viij d
Summa iij li x s	

All' scolarum eiusdem anni
In primis de scol' frowyk viij s
De scol' fylham' vj s viij d
De scol' Baron' vj s viij d
Summa xxj s iiij d

All' pro resolucionibus reddituum
In primis Abbathie de Osneye pro anno septimo rr' H a retro vj s
Abbathie de Godstow pro primo termino octavi anni et omnibus arr' xxj s x d
Item Willelmo Wrysteler pro firma regis xviij d
Item procuratori Ecclesie sancti petri in oriente ij s x d
Item abbathie de Osneye pro gardino pro anno rr' H [*sic*] vj s
Item Ecclesie beate Marie virginis pro anno octavo xij d
Item Collectori xvme pro novo purchic' ij s viij d
Item abbati de Eynsham pro schopa super angulum quadrivij viij s
Item abbate de Godstow pro secundo termino octavi anni rr' H vij s
Item priori de ffryswyt' pro anno octavo et omnibus arr' xvj s viij d
Item pro ffirma utterworth' iij s viij d
Summa iij li xvij s ij d

All' pro stipendijs famulorum
In primis Thome pincerne de retro x s
Item Thome Coke de retro xiij s iiij d
Item uxori sue lotrici de retro x s
Item Thome barbur de retro iij s iiij d
Item Ade Ryver pro anno octavo rr' H iij s
Item Thome barbur pro eodem anno v s
Item Thome Spencer pro eodem anno xiij s iiij d
Item Thome Coke pro eodem anno vj s viij d
Item uxori sue lotrici pro eodem anno v s
Summa iij li ix s viij d

All' pro pencionibus sex sociorum de ordinacione domini episcopi Dunelmenc' iiij li
Item pro pencionibus trium sacercotum pro uno termino scilicet a

festo pasche usque ad festum sancti Johannis Baptiste de ordinacione eiusdem domini episcopi dunelmenc' xxx s
Item Magistro pro antiquo debito domus bina vice ij marc'

Summa vj li xvj s viij d

⟨Summa totalis xxxij li xij s viij d⟩

All' pro communis sociorum eiusdem collegij pro anno octavo rr' H' scilicet a festo pentec' inclusive usque ad idem festum anno revoluto
In primis in communis sociorum a festo pent' inclusive usque ad festum advincule sancti petri exclusive

In prima septimana in communis quatuor sociorum vij s iiij d
In batellis iiij d ob
In 2da septimana in communis iiij^or sociorum vj s vj d
In batellis ij d ob
In jurnellis iiij d
In 3^a septimana in communis 5^e sociorum vij s vj d
In batellis viij d
In 4^a septimana in communis 5^e sociorum vij s viij d ob
In batellis ij d
In 5^a septimana in communis 5^e sociorum vij s xj d In batellis j d
In 6^a septimana in communis 5^e sociorum vj s iij d In batellis ob
In contribucionibus xxv d ob
In 7^a septimana in communis 2^orum sociorum iij s j d
In batellis ob
In 8^a septimana in communis 2^orum sociorum iij s j d
In batellis iij d q^a
In 9^a septimana in communis 2^orum sociorum iij s ij d
In batellis iiij d

Summa lvij s ij d q^a

Item com et bat' a festo advincule sancti petri usque ad festum Michaelis xxvj s v d q^a

A festo Michaelis inclusive usque ad festum omnium sanctorum exclusive

In prima septimana in communis unius socij xviij d
In batellis j d ob
In 2^a septimana in communis 3um sociorum v s iij d
In batellis viij d ob
In jurnellis iiij d
In 3^a septimana in communis 4 sociorum vj s In batellis iiij d

In jurnellis vj d ob
In 4ᵃ septimana in communis 6 sociorum viij s iij d
In batellis vj d ob qᵃ
In 5ᵃ septimana in communis 6 sociorum ix s vj d
In batellis v d ob
In 6ᵃ septimana in communis 6 sociorum ix s ix d In batellis iij d
Summa xliij s vj d ob qᵃ

A festo omnium sanctorum inclusive usque ad festum natal' domini exclusive

In prima septimana in communis 6 sociorum ix s vj d
In batellis vj s ob
In 2ᵃ septimana in communis 6 sociorum viij s vj d
In batellis xix d
In 3ᵃ septimana in communis 6 sociorum viij s ix d
In batellis iij d ob
In 4ᵃ septimana in communis 6 sociorum viij s vj d
In batellis ij d ob
In 5ᵃ septimana in communis 6 sociorum viij s ix d
In batellis j d ob
In 6ᵃ septimana in communis 6 sociorum ix s In batellis iij d
In 7ᵃ septimana in communis 6 sociorum ix s vj d
In 8ᵃ septimana in communis 4 sociorum et dimidij viij s iij d
In batellis ob
In jurnellis ij d ob
In contribucionibus ij s iij d
Summa iij li xvj s ij d ob qᵃ

[*Dorse*]

A festo nat' domini inclusive usque ad festum pasche exclusive

In prima septimana in communis 4 sociorum et dimidij x s x d ob
In 2ᵃ septimana in communis 5 sociorum x s In batellis v d ob
In jurnellis ij d ob
In 3ᵃ septimana in communis 6 sociorum ix s iij d
In batellis vij d ob
In 4ᵃ septimana in communis 6 sociorum viij s vj d
In batellis xij d ob qᵃ
In 5ᵃ septimana in communis 6 sociorum ix s In batellis ob

In 6ª septimana in communis 5 sociorum vij s iij d ob
In batellis iiij d
In 7ª septimana in communis 5 sociorum ix s ij d In batellis j d
In 8ª septimana in communis 5 sociorum viij s ix d
In batellis iij d
In 9ª septimana in communis 5 sociorum viij s vj d ob
In batellis vij d ob
In 10ª septimana in communis 5 sociorum ix s ij d
In batellis j d ob
In 11ª septimana in communis 4 sociorum vij s In batellis iij d
In 12 septimana in communis 4 sociorum vij s iiij d
In batellis iiij d
In 13 septimana in communis 4 sociorum vij s In batellis vij d qª
In gaudijs sancti Cuthberti iiij s vj d ob
Summa vj li xvij d

A festo pasche inclusive usque ad festum pentecost' exclusive
In prima septimana In communis 3 sociorum vj s vj d
In batellis iiij d
Pro Roberto Tapister pro di' com pro 2^bus^ septimanis xx d
In 2ª septimana in communis 4 sociorum vij s iiij d In batellis j d
In 3ª septimana in communis 3 sociorum v s j d ob
In batellis viij d
Pro dicto Roberto Tapister alias iiij d
Pro laborantibus xij d
In 4ª septimana in communis 3 sociorum v s vj d
In batellis viij d ob
In 5ª septimana in communis 4 sociorum viij s In batellis iiij d ob
In 6ª septimana in communis 4 sociorum viij s In batellis x d ob
In 7ª septimana in communis 4 sociorum vj s x d
In batellis ij d ob
In jurnellis pro Magistro v d
In sirpis seminibus et cifis et alijs in distribuc' xij d ob
Summa lv s

Summa omnium communarum et bat' xviij li xix s x d

All' reparacionum et aliarum expensarum necessarium tam infra collegium quam extra ut patet in paupiro
In primis ante vacacionem iiij li xiiij s ob
2º xvij s ij d

3° In vacacione per Magistrum xlij s vj d ob
4° post vacacionem xxj s iij d ob
5° iij li ij s iiij d ob
6° xlvj s vij d
pro labore in officio procuracionis x s

⟨Summa totalis reparacionum et aliarum expensarum post communas xiiij li xiiij s

Summa omnium all' iij ^{xx} li vj li vj s vj d⟩

Item petit idem allocari de Thome mayster – xvj s

Et sic computatis computandis et allocatis allocandis est Magister Robertis Burton' procurator pro dicto anno acquietatus penes domum; ita tamen quod dictus M Robertus solvat Magistro Ade Redifurth procuratori eiusdem domus pro anno sequenti xxj s ix d

Ullerston Canc'

⟨Computans solvit debitum istius rotuli et acquietatus est inter socios[1]⟩

[*Neatly written roll, very clear; 4 membranes, the first and second now stuck together. All totals add up correctly*]

[1] [ADMC] Written in a semi-cursive, informal hand

WHITSUN 8 HENRY IV to WHITSUN 9 HENRY IV (ROLL UC:BU1/F/18)
15 May 1407–3 June 1408

BURSAR: ADAM RADFORD

⟨De Tempore M Ade⟩

Compotus Magistri et sociorum collegij Magistri Willelmi de dunelm' Magne aule universitatis wlgariter nuncupate [*sic*] a festo pent' inclusive usque ad idem festum exclusive anno regni regis Henrici quarti post conquestum nono.

[*The Arrears are identical with the Allowances in* **F/17**, *with the following exceptions:*

(*i*) *The arrears of tenements of 7 Hen IV do not include Thomas Glover.*

(*ii*) *The arrears of Halls of 8 Hen IV do not include the latrine from St. Thomas Hall*]

Summa totalis omnium arr' xv li viij s

Redditus ten' eiusdem collegij anno [*blank*] rr' Henrici quarti

In primis de ten' couley	xl s
de ten' Mercer	l s
de ten' Glover	vj li
de schopa super angulum quadrivij	xx s
de tenem' quondam Holway	xv s
de ten' Caumbray	xv s viij d
de ten' iuxta caumbray	xj s
de gardino quem tenet johannis barbor	iij s iiij d
de gardino quondam Alicie Warre	iiij s
de gardino quem tenet Adam Ryver	iij s
de novo collegio ⟨pro maydynhall⟩	x s
de gardino quem tenet Thomas Hampton	iij s
de gardino quem tenet uxor quondam Willelmi Hampton	viij s
de tenem' Roberti laycester	viij s
de gardino quem quondam tenuit petrus dauber	viij d
de gardino quem tenet fowk barbur iuxta tirry	iij s

de collegio cantuarie	ij s vj d
de abbatissa de godstow pro una schopa iuxta frydiswyd'	xx d
de Holdernes	iij li xij d
de sprontt pro gardino	xvj d
de johanne schaw pro prato vocato yrelond' et alijs	ij marc'
de mychel' talyour	xv s
de philippo cordewener'	xxiij s iiij d
Summa xxij li vj s ij d	

Redditus de essex Summa xxvj li vj s ij d

Item recepi a Magistro Roberto burton xxj s ix d

Redditus aularum eiusdem anni

In primis de Brasnose	iij li vj s [*viij d*][1]
de usu latrine aula sancti Thome[2]	iiij s
de aula scuti	vj s viij d
de aula sancti Thome	x s
de parva aula universitatis in vico scolarum	xxxiij s iiij d
de hampton hall'	xl s
de aula edwardi	xxiiij s
de droudalhall' que non locatur	viij d
de stauntonhall'	xiij s iiij d
de parva aula universitatis in alto vico	xl s
Summa xj li xviij s viij d[3]	

Penciones scolarum dicti collegij eodem anno

In [*sic*] scol' quondam frowyk	viij s
de alta [*sic*] scola quam tenet camell'	vj s viij d
de altera [*sic*] scola alta quam tenet more	vj s viij d
Summa xxj s iiij d	

Penciones camerarum eiusdem anni infra dictum collegium

In primis de cameris polton	xxxvj s viij d
de camera henley	xiij s iiij d
de camera canonici laycesteri	x s
de camera Naffirton	xvj s viij d
de camera Beneham	xiij s iiij d
de camera lovell'	vj s viij d

[1] [ADMC] The edge of the roll is damaged here.
[2] [ADMC] Written over an erasure.
[3] [ADMC] Shillings and pence have been altered.

de camera flemmyg	xxxiij s iiij d
Summa vj li x s	

⟨Summa omnium oneratorum anni predicti iiij^{xxxx} li iiij li xix s iij d[4]⟩

Allocaciones dicti Magistri et sociorum In primis de ten' de anno septimo rr' Henrici

de johanne Barbur pro pencione sua a retro	xx d
de Adam Ryver	iij s
de Roberto leycester	ij s viij d
de Holdermes [*sic*]	vj d
de thoma coulay	xiij s iiij d
Summa xxj s ij d	

Allocaciones Aularum eiusdem anni de aula Edwardi	vij s iiij d

Allocaciones camerarum infra dictum collegium eiusdem anni

In primis de camera heneley	iij s iiij d
de camera canonici de notley	iij s iiij d
de camera marton	iij s iiij d
de camera naffyrton	vj s viij d
de camera foston	iij s iiij d
de camera clesby	xiij s iiij d
Summa ij li viij d	

Allocaciones tene' eiusdem collegij de anno octavo rr' Henrici

In primis de tene' couley	x s
de tenemento Roberti laycester	viij s
de gardino quondam petri dauber	viij d
de holdernes	xij d
de scopa super angulum quadrivij	iiij d
Summa xx s	

Allocaciones aularum eiusdem anni

In primis de Hamptonhall'	vj s viij d
de aula Edvardi	v s
de droudalhall'	v s
de stauntonhall'	vj s viij d
Summa xxiij s iiij d – habetur cedula in fine	

[4] [ADMC] Shillings and pence have been altered.

[5]⟨Allocaciones camerarum eiusdem anni octavi `infra dictum collegium´

In primis de camera Henley	x s
de camera naffirton	xij s iiij d
de camera foston	xvj s viij d
[*an entry erased*]	
Summa xl s⟩	

Allocaciones ten' anni noni

In primis de tenemento coulay	xxx s
de ~~no~~ ten' Glover	iij li iij s
	et ultra debet iij d
de scopa super angulum quadrivij	iiij d
de tenemento caumberay	xj s
de ten' ~~iuxta caumberay~~	[*blank*]
de gardino quondam Alicie Ware modo Ricardi caryur	iiij s
de gardino quem tenet adam ryver	iij s
de ten' Roberti laycester	viij s
de gardino quem quondam tenuit petrus dauber	viij d
de gardino quem tenet fouke barbur	xviij d
de holdernes	iij li xij d
Summa ix li ij s vj d	

Allocaciones de exsex eiusdem anni	liij s iiij d

Allocaciones aularum eiusdem anni

[*about an inch left blank*]

de aula parva universitatis in vico scolarum	xxiij s iiij d
de aula hampton	xx s
de aula edvardi	xij s x d ob
de stauntonhall	vj s viij d
de aula parva universitatis in ~~vico scolarum~~ alto vico	x s

Allocaciones scolarum eiusdem anni

In primis ~~de altis scolis~~ de scolis que erant frauvit[6]	v s xj d

[5] [ADMC] This section is on a separate strip of parchment attached to the right hand side of the roll.

[6] Smith (Vol. VIII p. 69) reads 'frannet', and ADMC suggested 'frammut', with the alternatives 'frannit' or 'frauvit', which, since it is phonetically more like 'frowik' (the name given in the relevant entry in 1406/7), is the reading I give here.

de scola quem tenet camell' vj s viij d
de scola quam tenet more vj s viij d
~~de camera~~

Allocaciones camerarum eiusdem anni
[*An entry erased*]
de camera naferton x s
de camera Beneham vj s viij d
de camera flemmyg xx s[7]
Summa ix li ~~xij s j d ob~~ ij s j d ob

All' pro resolucione redituum
In primis abbathie de godstowe pro uno anno xiiij s
Willelmo Wrestiller pro gardino forke[8] xviij d
Item procuratori ecclesie beati petri in oriente ij s x d
Item abbathie de Osney pro gardino vj s
Item ecclesie beate marie virginis xij d
Item colectoribus monete regis ij s viij d
Item abbathie de heynsham pro scopa super quadrivium viij s
Summa xxxvj s

All' [*blank*]
Item thome pincerne pro anno rr' Henrici x s
Item quinque socijs quorum quatuor receperunt quilibet unam marcam et et [*sic*] quintus vj s viij d iij li
Item quinque socijs ex ordinacione domini episcopi Dunelmenc' quorum quilibit recepit unam marcam iij li vj s viij d
Item tribus sacerdotibus quorum quilibet receperunt xl s unde duo tantum totum receperunt v li iij s ij d
Item Magistro Johanni Appulton pro pencione sibi concessa a domo iiij li
Item eidem propter laborem versus partes boriales xx s
Item eidem pro se et secum laborantibus london' in negocijs domis xx s
Summa xvij li xix s x d

⟨Summa totalis xlv li v s vij d ob⟩

[7] [ADMC] The figure has been altered.
[8] [ADMC] These three words have been written over an erasure.

All' pro communis sociorum eiusdem collegij pro anno nono rr' Henrici a festo pentecostes inclusive ad festum sancto Johanni [*sic*] Baptiste eclusive [*sic*]

In prima septimana in communis 4 sociorum viij s
In batellis iij d ob
In 2^a^ septimana in communis 5 sociorum viij s v d ob
In batellis iij d
In 3^a^ septimana in communis 4^or^ sociorum vj s v d ob
In batellis x d ob
In 4^a^ septimana in communis 4^or^ sociorum vij s iiij d
In batellis xij d ob
In 5^a^ septimana in communis 5 sociorum viij s ix d
In batellis j d ob
In 6^a^ septimana in communis 5 sociorum vij s In batellis ij s ob
Summa l s vij d ob

Item a festo sancti iohannis baptiste inclusive inclusive ad festum michaelis exclusive

In prima septimana in communis trium sociorum cum dimidio vj s v d
In 2^a^ septimana in communis 2 sociorum cum dimidio v s
In 3^a^ septimana in communis 2 sociorum cum dimidio v s
In batellis vj d
In 4^a^ septimana in communis 2^orum^ sociorum iiij s
In batellis iiij d
In 5^a^ septimana in communis 2^orum^ sociorum iiij s In batellis ij d
In 6^a^ septimana in communis unius socij ij s In batellis xx d
In septima septimana in communis unius socij ij s iiij d
In octava septimana in communis unius socij ij s
pro servis [*sic*] xij d
In nona septimana in communis unius socij ij s pro servis x d
In decima septimana in communis unius socij ij s pro servis x d
In undecima septimana in communis unius socij cum dimidio iij s ij d ob pro servis vij d ob
In duodecima septimana in communis unius socij cum dimidio iij s iiij d pro servis viij d
In terciodecima septimana in communis 2^orum^ sociorum iiij s
pro servis xj d

Summa lij s x d

Item a festo santi michaelis inclusive usque ad festum omnium sanctorum exclusive

In prima septimana in communis duorum sociorum iiij s
In batellis viij d

In 2[a] septimana in communis duorum sociorum iiij s
In batellis viij d

In 3[a] septimana in communis 4[or] sociorum vj s viij d
In batellis viij d

In 4[a] septimana in communis 3[um] sociorum cum dimidio v s x d
In batellis v d ob

In 5[a] septimana in communis quinque sociorum vij s xj d
In batellis viij d

Summa xxxj s ij d ob

Item pro foston pro una septimana et dimidio ij s iij d
In batellis iij d ob

Item pro famulo suo xiij d ob

Item pro duffeld' pro una septimana xviij d In batellis j d

Item a festo omnium sanctorum inclusive ad concepcionem beate virginis exclusive

In prima septimana in communis sex sociorum x s viij d
in batellis xj d ob

In 2[a] septimana in communis sex sociorum ix s
in batellis xiij d q[a]

In 3[a] septimana in communis sex sociorum x s vj d
in batellis xvj d q[a]

In 4[a] septimana in communis sex sociorum x s in batellis xxj d q[a]

In 5[a] septimana in communis sex sociorum ix s in batellis xij d q[a]

Summa liij s iiij d

Item a festo concepcionis beate viriginis inclusive ad nativitatem domini exclusive

In prima septimana communis sex sociorum x s vj d
In batellis xij d ob

In 2[a] septimana in communis sex sociorum ix s
In batellis xv d ob q[a]

In 3[a] septimana in communis 5 sociorum cum dimidio viij s viij d ob
In batellis j d ob

In 4[a] septimana in communis 4[or] sociorum cum dimidio vij s viij d
In batellis v d

Item in contribucionibus iij s
Summa xl s iiij d q[a]

Item a nativitate domini inclusive usque ad purificationem beate virginis inclusive
In prima septimana in communibus 4[o] [*sic*] sociorum x s
In 2[a] septimana in communis 5 sociorum ix s ij d In batellis ob
In 3[a] septimana in communis 5 sociorum viij s iiij d
In batellis j d
In 4[a] septimana in communis 5 sociorum vij s viij s ob
In batellis ob
In 5[a] septimana in communis 5[e] sociorum viij s iiij d
In batellis ij d ob
In 6[a] septimana in communis 4[or] sociorum cum dimidio vij s j d ob
Item pro anno elapso pro communibus Magistri iam existentis Magistri J Revell et Ade Redyforth ij s iiij d
Summa liij s iiij d ob

Item a festo purificationis beate virginis inclusive usque ad festum sancti Ceadde inclusive
In prima septimana in communis quatuor sociorum vj s viij d
In batellis iij d ob
In 2[a] septimana in communis quatuor sociorum cum dimidio vij s vj d In batellis vij d
In 3[a] septimana in communis quinque sociorum vij s vj d
In batellis et jurnellis viij d ob
In 4[a] septimana in communis sex sociorum xij s In batellis j d
Summa xxxv s iiij d

Item in gaudijs in die sancti Cuthberti In primis in coquina xj s ij d
In vino – ij s viij d

Item a festo sancti Ceadde exclusive usque ad festum Ramispalmarum exclusive
In prima septimana in communis sex sociorum x s ix d
In batellis ob
In 2[a] septimana in communis 5 sociorum cum dimidio x s vj d ob In batellis j d
In 3[a] septimana in communis 5 sociorum ix s ij d
In batellis iij d ob q[a]

In 4[a] septimana in communis 5 sociorum ix s ij d
In batellis iij d q[a]
In quinta septimana in communis 5[e] sociorum ix s viij d
In batellis iij d ob
Summa iij li iiij s j d ob

[*Dorse*]

Item a festo Ramispalmarum inclusive ad festum pentectoste [*sic*] exclusive
In prima septimana in communis quinque sociorum et iornels [*sic*] unius socij viij s iiij d In batellis iiij d
In 2[a] septimana in communis 3[um] sociorum et iornels unius vij s viij d In batellis iij d q[a]
In 3[a] septimana in communis quatuor sociorum cum dimidio vij s viij d ob In batellis iij d
In 4[a] septimana in communis quinque sociorum vij s xj d
In batellis iiij d
In 5[a] septimana in communis quinque sociorum vij s j d
In batellis ix d ob
In 6[a] septimana in communis 3[um] sociorum v s In batellis x d ob
In septima septimana in communis quinque sociorum x s
In batellis v d ob
In octava septimana in communis quinque sociorum vij s xj d
In batellis ob
Item pro Johanne payntur iij s viij d ob
Summa iij li viij s vij d q[a]

Summa omnium expensarum in communis et batellis xxij li xv s ob

Allocaciones reparacionum et aliarum expensarum necessariarum tam infra collegium quam extra in aulis tenementis diversis ut patebit per papirum et primo reparacione hostij ad aulam parvam universitatis in vico scolarum pro meremio ad certas cameras [. . .] tegulis et tegu[bus] tabulis et liquifactione plumbi ut patet in papirio v li xj s iiij d ob
Item pro laborantibus apud Brasnose in removendo terram in clavis et clavibus diversarum camerarum v s iiij d ob

⟨All'⟩ Item pro hostio camere polton operarijs et latemis ad domum caumberary cum ceteris necessarijs xij s iij d

⟨All'⟩ Item pro carpentarijs et latamis laborantibus pro meremio et cariagio luti ad aulam ~~drowdell~~ nuncupatam Drowdalehall' vj li v d

⟨All'⟩ Item pro tegulatoribus et latamis apud brasnose pro laborantibus calce mosse et sclat pinnis et luto et cariagio luti et mil [*sic*] clavorum ij li xvj s iij s ob

⟨All'⟩ Item pro tegulatoribus latamis et cum eisdem laborantibus pro stanno et operario eiusdem et plumbi xvij s iiij d

Item pro uno carpentario in aula universitatis parva in ~~vie~~ vico scolarum et pro clavis et tegulatore xvij s iiij d

Item pro carpentarijs et meremio pertinente ad cameras aula parve universitatis in vico scolarum et clavis et ceteris multis necessarijs ut patet in papirio etc' xxxiij s xj d

Item pro reparacione facta per manus Magistri johannis lye circa coquinam et latrinam Aule de Brasynnose iiij li iij s iiij d

Memorandum est quod magna aula universitatis sive socij eiusdem debent ultra expensas nominatas Magistro johanni lye pro reparacione facta circa coquinam et latrinam aule de Brasynnos iiij li

[*About 2½ inches space left blank on the roll*]

Item petit allocari pro expensis versus essex et redeundo xxj s ob

[*A further 2½ inches space left blank*]

Item petit allocari pro reparacione facta in esex per manus johannis lygtfot videlicet pro aula camera et coquina et pro certa pecunia dimissa in manu sua ad reparacionem molendini xiiij li xij s iiij d

Summa xxxviij li xij s vij d

Item petit allocari pro labore in officio procuratoris domus x s

Summma omnium allocatorum c li vij li iij s iij d ⟨Et sic debentur computanti xxij li iiij s de quibus solvuntur sibi xx li. Et sic de claro debentur computanti xliiij s

Cancellarius Willelmus Clynt⟩

[*Very clear roll; 3 membranes. All totals correct*]

[WHITSUN 9 HENRY IV to WHITSUN 10 HENRY IV?] (ROLL UC:BU1/F/19)[1]
[3 June 1408–26 May 1409?]

BURSAR: JOHN HAMERTON

[*The original roll for this year is missing. What follows is Smith's condensed transcript of it (Vol. VIII pp.61b-62b. It may have have been damaged even in his day.*]

M^{ro} Johe Hamerton uti puto ex calce Rotuli et receptis ab eodem in in [*sic*] Rot seq:

a^{o} 1408 1409 Compotus Magistri . . .

arr' etc. a^{o} x^{o} H 4^{ti}

redd' Essex – xxvij li xiij s iiij d

Item computans respondet de ix li de Magistro Thoma powlton
Item respondit de ij s viij d receptis de inhabitantibus in Drowdalhall a^{o} rr' nono

pensiones Scolarum de Scolis Hamerton	viij s
quam tenet Mr Gilbertus	vj s viij s
" Wolton vj s viij s M^{ri} Johannis Wolton in allocat'	

pensiones Camerarum In primis de Camera M^{ri} Johannis Mydylton	xx s
powlton	xvj s viij d
canonici ecclesie x^{ti} Enseford	x s
canonici lacester	x s
M^{ri} Jo Henley	xiij s iiij d
Nafferton	xvj s viij d
Glyn	x s
M^{ri} Johannis Kexby	xiij s iiij d
M^{ri} Ricardi flemyng	xxxiij s iiij d
Hurle	xx s
(iuxta Hamerton et Johannem Tomson) Beneham	xxij s
in allocat' Makeblyth	x s

[1] Although Smith does not give exact dates, the roll almost certainly followed the usual practice at this time, and ran from Whitsun to Whitsun.

Lyclade vj s viij d

Summa x li ij s

Summa totalis omnium oneratorum vj[xx] [*li*] xviij s

Allocat' dicti Magistri et sociorum ab a[o] 7 H 4[ti]

inter red' resolut'

Item tenenti molendine domini Regis iuxta castrum pro firma quondam Utterworth iij s viij d

Collectoribus monete domini Regis xvj d

alloc' stipend' et pensionum sociorum

In primis xxvj s viij d solutis quatuor socijs cuilibet supple' vij s viij d

Item M[ro] Collegij – xiij s iiij d

Item quinque socijs iuxta ordinacionem domini nostri quondam Episcopi Dunelmenc'

iij li vj s viij d cuilibet supple xiij d iiij d

Item de iiij li x s solut' 3[bus] sacerdotibus predicti domini nostri pro tribus quaterijs anni cuilibet supple xxx s

Summa ix li xvj s viij d

In Communis Sociorum

In prima sept' pro communis 4[r] soc' et jurnell ~~alterius~~ unius socij viij s vj d

pro communis 3 sociorum et semicommunis unius cum iurnel alterius vj s ix [*d*]

Bat. x d

pro uno socio pro septem septim' a xxj d ad xxvj d per hebd.

Sepius occurrunt Jurnel' hoc a[o]

In expens' fact' die sancti Cuthberti in convivatione sociorum et extraneorum absque vino xij s ob et in vino eodem die ij s iiij d

In 2[da] sept' pro communis 4[r] soc. et Jurnell' M Ade et Revell ix [*d?*]

Bat iiij d q[a]

19 li 13 01d Summa expens' in communis et Batell' xix li xiij s j d

Expens' inter quos expens m[ri] et M Ade London et Essex etiam cum donatis M[ro] Alano Newark et suis servientibus – vij s vij s v d ob

Summa omnium allocatorum cxviij li viij s iiij d iiij d et sic debet computans Collegio xxxv s ix d ob

Cancellarius
Willelmus Clynt

WHITSUN 10 HEN IV to WHITSUN 11 HEN IV (ROLL UC:BU1/F/20)
26 May 1409–11 May 1410

BURSAR: JOHN RYVELL

[*The first few lines are damaged on the left hand side*]

. . .] Ryvell

[*Computus Magistri et sociorum*] Collegij Magistri Willelmi de Dunelm' magne aula universitatis [*vulgariter nuncupate a festo*] Pentecost' inclusive usque ad idem festum exclusive anno Regni Regis [*Henrici quarto post co*]nquestum Angl[*ie*] undecimo

. . .]et pencionibus et primo de Arr' anni vij[i] Regis Henrici	
. . .]o	xx d
[*De Adam Ryv*]er	iij s
[*De Rob'*] Leycester	ij s viij d
[*De Holder*]nes	vj d
De Thomas Cowley	xiij s iiij d
Summa xxj s ij d	
Arr' Aul' De Aula Edwardi eodem anno	vij s iiij d
[*Arr'*] cam' infra collegium eodem anno	
In primis de camera henley	iij s iiij d
De camera canonici de Notley	iij s iiij d
De camera merton	iij s iiij d
De camera Nafferton'	vj s viij d
De camera foston'	iij s iiij d
De camera Clesby	xiij s iiij d
Summa xl s viij d	
Arr' ten' eiusdem Colleg' de anno octavo rr' Hen'	
In primis de ten' Coulay	x s
De ten' Roberti laiceyster	viij s
De Holdernes	xij s[1]
De Schoppa super angulum quadrivij	iiij d
Summa xix s iiij d	

[1] [ADMC] An erratum for xij d; see the next roll.

Arr' aulorum eodem anno	
In primis de Hampton' hall'	vj s viij d
De droudalhall'	v s
De Stauntonhall'	vj s viij d
Summa xviij s iiij d	
Arr' camerarum infra collegium eodem anno	
In primis de camera Henley	x s
De camera Nafferton'	xiij s iiij d
De camera foston'	xvj s viij d
Summa xl s	
Arr' ten' eiusdem collegij de anno Nono rr' Henrici	
In primis de ten' Coulay	xxx s
De Schoppa super angulum quadrivij	iiij d
De Gardino quem tenet Adam Ryver	iij s
De ten' Roberti leycestr'	viij s
De Gardino quem tenet fouke Berbour	xviij d
De Holdernes	iij li xij d
Summa v li iij s x d	
Arr' aularum eodem anno	
In primis de aula Staunton'	vj s viij d
De parva aula universitatis in alto vico	iij s iiij d
Arr' scolarum eodem anno	
In primis de scolis quond frowyk	v s xj d
De scola quem tenuit more	vj s viij d
Summa xxij s vij d	
Arr' cam' eodem anno	
De cam' Nafferton'	x s
Arr' ten' eiusdem collegij de anno X^mo^ rr' Henr'	
In primis de ten' Mercer	ij s vj d
De ten' Thome Glover	v li xj s
De Schoppa super angulum quadrivij et de ten' quond' Holwaye	iiij d
De ten' cambrey	vij s xj d
De Gardino Ricardi Karyer	iiij s iiij d
De Gardino Ade Ryver	iij s
De ten' Robert laceyster	iij s
De Gardino quem tenet fowke Barbour	iij s

De Abbatissa de Godstow x d
De Holdernes iij li xij d
Summa ix li xvj s xj d

Arr' aularum eodem anno
In primis de aula scuti vj s viij d
De aula sancti Thome x s
De usu latrine aule sancti Thome iiij s
De parva aula universitatis in vico scolarum xxviij s iiij d
De Hampton Hall' xiij s iiij d
De aula edwardi viij s
De drouvdelhall' ix s v d ob'
De parva aula universitatis in alto vico xxvj s viij d
Summa v li vj s v d ob'

Arr' scolarum eodem anno
In primis de scola Magistri Gylberti iij s iiij d
De scolis Magistri Johannis Wotton' vj s viij d
Summa x s

Arr' cam' infra colleg' eodem anno
In primis de cam' powlton xvj s viij d
De cam' Enseford x s
De cam' canonici lacester vj s viij d
De cam' Nafferton' iij s iiij d
De cam' Glym x s
De cam' Kexby vj s viij d
De cam' hurle xiij s iiij d
De cameris Beneham iuxta Hampton' et Johannem Thomson' viij s viij d
De cam' Makeblith x s
Summa iv li v s iiij d

Summa omnium arr' lvj li xj s viij d ob'

Redditus ten' eiusdem Collegij anno Regni regis Henr' quarti post conquestum anglie undecimo
In primis de ten' Mercer l s
De ten' Cowley xl s
De ten' Glover vj li
De Scopa super angulum quadrivij xx s
De ten' quond' holwaye xv s

De ten' Cambreye	xv s ix d
De ten' iuxta Cambreye	xj s
De Gardino quem tenuit Johannes Barbour	iij s iiij d
De Gardino quem tenet Ricardus karuer	iiij s iiij d
De Gardino quem tenet Adam River	iij s
De Novo Collegij pro Maydynhalle	x s
De Gardino quem tenet uxor quondam Willelmi Hampton'	viij s
De Ten' Roberti leycester	viij s
De Gardino quem tenuit quond' petrus dauber	viij d
De Gardino quem tenet fowke barbor	iij s
De Collegio Cantuarie	ij s vj d
De Abbatissa de Godstow pro una scopa iuxta ffrydeswyd	xx d
De Holdernes	iij li xij d
De Spronte	xiij s x d ob'[2]
De Johanne Schaw pro prato vocato yr'lond et alijs	xxvj s viij d
De Mich' Tayliour	xv s
De Philippo Cordwener'	xxiij s iiij d
Summa xxij li vj s vij d[3]	

[4]⟨Item Comput rent' de x marc' mutuatis

Redditus de Essex xxvj li xiij s iiij d

Item Comput' rend' de xxxv s ix d ob' recepto a Magistro Johanne Hampton'

Item Comput' rend' de x li receptis a Magistro Alano Neuwerke

Item Comput' rend' de xl s dat' a Magistro Robert Rodushale⟩

Redditus aularum eodem anno

In primis de Brasenose	iij li vj s viij d
De usu latrine aula Sancti Thome	iiij s
De aula scuti	vj s viij d
De aula sancti Thome	x s
De parva aula universitatis in vico scolarum	xxxiij s iiij d
De Hampton' Hall'	xl s
De aula Edwardi	xxiij s

[2] [ADMC] This figure is a correction.
[3] [ADMC] This figure is 12s 6½d too much.
[4] These entries have been squashed in here very tightly as a later addition.

De droudalhall'	xl s
De Stauntonhall'	xiij s iiij d
De parva aula universitatis in alto vico	liij s iiij d
Summa xv li v s ij d ob'[5]	

Penciones scolarum eodem anno

In primis de scolis dykys	viij s
De alta scola quem tenet Magister [*blank*]	vj s viij d
De altera alta scola quem tenet pounter	v s iiij d
Summa xx s	

Penciones Camerarum eodem anno infra Colleg'

In primis de Camera Magistri Johannis Mydylton'	xx s
De Camera powlton'	xvj s viij d
De Camera Enseford	x s
De camera Canonici layceystr'	x s
De camera magistri Johannis Henley	xiij s iiij d
De camera Nafferton'	xvj s viij d
De camera Glym	x s
De camera magistri Johannis Kexby	xiij s iiij d
De camera hurle	vj s viij d
De camera fyhne	xvj s viij d
De camera Paryor	xiij s iiij d
De camera Beneham	xv s iiij d
De camera Makeblyth	xv s iiij d
Summa ix li ij s	

Summa totalis omnium oneratorum vij^{xx} li xj li vij s xj d ob'

Allocaciones dicti magistri et sociorum de ten' de anno septimo rr' Henrici

In primis de Johanne Barbour pro pensione sua a retro	xx d
De Adam Ryver	iij s
De Roberto Laceystr'	ij s viij d
De Holdernes	vj d
De Thoma Coulaye	xiij s iiij d
Summa xxj s ij d	

Alloc' Aularum eodem anno

De Aula Edwardi	vij s iiij d

[5] [ADMC] This figure is 13s 10½d too little.

Alloc' camerarum infra dictum colleg' eodem anno

In primis de camera Henley	iij s iiij d
De camera Canonici de Noteley	iij s iiij d
De camera Morton	iij s iiij d
De camera Nafferton'	vj s viij d
De camera foston'	iij s iiij d
De camera Cleseby	xiij s iiij d
Summa xl s viij d	

Alloc' ten eiusdem Colleg' de anno octavo rr' Hen'

In primis de ten' Coulay	x s
De Roberti laceystr'	viij s
De Holdernes	xij d
De Schoppa super angulum quadrivij	iiij d
Summa xix s iiij d	

Alloc' aulorum eodem anno

In primis de Hampton' Hall'	vj s viij d
De drowdalhall'	v s
De Staunton' hall'	vj s viij d
Summa xviij s iiij d	

Alloc' camerarum infra collegium eodem anno

In primis de camera Henley	x s
De camera Nafferton'	xiij s iiij d
De camera ffoston'	xvj s viij d
Summa xl s	

Arr' ten' eiusdem colleg' de anno nono rr' Henrici

In primis de ten' Coulay	xxx s
De Schoppa super angulum quadrivij	iiij d
De Gardino quem tenet Adam Ryver	iij s
De ten' Roberti laceystr'	viij s
De Gardino quem tenet fouke Berbour	xviij d
De Holdernes	xij d
Summa xliij s x d	

Alloc' aularum eodem anno

In primis de aula Staunton'	iij s iiij d
De parva aula universitatis in alto vico	iij s iiij d

Alloc' scolarum eodem anno

In primis de scolis quond' frowyk	v s xj d

De Scola quem tenuit more vj s viij d

Arr' camera eodem anno
De camera Nafferton' x s
Summa xxix s iij d

Alloc' ten' eiusdem collegij de anno X^{mo} rr' Henr'
In primis de ten' mercer ij s vj d
De ten' Glover v li xj s
De Schoppa super angulum quadrivij iiij d
De ten' Cambrey vij s xj d
De Gardino Ricardi Karier iiij d
De Gardino Ade Ryver iij s
De ten' Robert leceystr' iij s
De Holdernes xij d
Summa vj li ix s j d

De exsex xxij li xvij s j d

Alloc' aularum eodem anno
In primis de Aula Scuti vj s viij d
De aula sancti Thome x s
De usu latrine aule sancti Thome iiij s
De parva aula universitatis in alto vico ij s iiij d
De Hampton Hall' xiij s iiij d
De drouvdelhall' vj s j d ob'
Summa xliij s v d ob'

Alloc' camera infra colleg' eodem anno
In primis de camera powlton xvj s viij d
De camera Nafferton' iij s iiij d
De camera Glym x s
De cameris Beneham iuxta Hampton' et Johannem Thomson' ij s
De camera Makeblith x s
Summa xlij s

Alloc' ten' eiusdem coll' de anno xj^{o} rr' Henr'
In primis de ten' mercer vij s vj d
De Spront xiij s x d ob'[6]
De ten' Glover xv s

6 [ADMC] This figure is a correction.

De Schoppa super angulum quadrivij	iiij d
De ten' Cambrey	xv s ix d
De Gardino quem tenuit Johannes Barbur	iij s iiij d
De Gardino Ric' karier	iiij s iiij d
De Gardino quem tenet Adam River	iij s
De ten' Roberti leycestr'	viij s
De Gardino quem tenuit quond' petrus dauber	viij d
De Gardino quem tenet fowke barbor	iij s
De Holdernes	iij li xij d
De ten' Cowley	x s
De Gardino quem tenet Thomas Hampton	iij s
De Mich' Tayliour	iij s ix d
⟨Summa vij li xiij s x d ob⟩[7]	

De Exses	xxv li xiij s iiij d

Alloc' Aularum eodem anno

In primis de Brasnose	iij li vj s viij d
De usu latrine aula Sancti Thome	iiij s
De aula scuti	vj s viij d
De aula sancti Thome	x s
De parva aula universitatis in vico scolarum	xx s
De Hampton' Hall'	xl s
De aula Edwardi	xxiij s
De Droudalehall'	xl s
De Staunton' hall'	vj s viij d
De parva aula universitatis in alto vico	liij s iiij d
Summa xiij li xj s iiij d	

Alloc' scolarum eodem anno

In primis de scolis dikys	xvj d
De Scola quem tenet Odyam	vj s viij d
De Scola quem tenet pounter	iij s iiij d
Summa xj s iiij d	

Alloc' camera infra Colleg' eodem anno

In primis de camera powlton'	xvj s viij d
De camera Enseford	vj s viij d
De canonici laceyst [*sic*]	iij s iiij d

[7] This figure has been inserted later, and ADMC thought it should add up to £7 12s 6½d.

De camera Henley vj s viij d
De camera Nafferton' iij s iiij d
De camera Glym x s
De camera Kexby vj s viij d
De camera Hurle x s
De camera Beneham vj s viij d
De camera Makeblyth x s
Summa iiij li

Summa ommnium alloc' precendencium iiij^{xx} li xv li xiiij s j d

Alloc' pro communis sociorum eiusdem colleg' de anno rr' xj^{mo} A festo pentecost' inclusive usque ad idem festum anno revoluto exclusive

In primis pro communis sociorum a festo pentest' [*sic*] inclusive usque ad festum sancti Thome exclusive
In prima septimana in communis quinque sociorum x s x d
In batellis j d ob
In secunda septimana in communis quinque sociorum x s
In batellis ij d
In tercia septimana in communis quinque sociorum viij s ix d
In batellis j d ob q^{a}
In quarta septimana in communis quinque sociorum ix s ij d
In quinta septimana in communis quinque sociorum ix s ij d
In batellis ij d ob
In sexta septimana in communis quinque sociorum ix s ij d
In batellis v d
Summa lviij s j d ob q^{a}

Allocaciones communarum a festo sancti Thome inclusive usque ad festum sancti michaelis exclusive
In prima septimana pro communis quatuor et dimi' sociorum ix s
In contribucionibus xij d ob
In secunda septimana in communis quatuor sociorum vij s iiij d
In batellis xj d q^{a}
In tercia septimana in communis trium sociorum vj s ij d ob
In batellis vij d q^{a}
In quarta septimana in communis ij sociorum et dimi' v s j d ob
In batellis iij d ob
In quinta septimana in communis ij socioum iij s ij d
In batellis xiiij d ob

In sexta septimana in communis ij sociorum iij s v d
In batellis vij d q[a]
In septima septimana in communis ij sociorum iij s x d
In batellis xiiij d
In octava septimana in communis ij sociorum iij s vij d
In batellis vj d ob
In nona septimana in communis j[us] socij xxiij d
In batellis iij d ob q[a]
In decima septimana in communis j[us] socij xxiij d
In batellis ob q[a]
In undecima septimana in communis j[us] socij xxij d ob
In batellis xv d
In duodecima septimana in communis j[us] socij ij s
In batellis j d ob q[a]

Summa lvij s vj d ob

Alloc' communarum a festo sancti michaelis inclusive usque ad festum omnium sanctorum inclusive

In prima septimana pro communis j[us] socij ij s In batellis j d ob q[a]
et in jurnellis vij d
In secunda septimana in communis trium sociorum v s jx d [*sic*]
In batellis iij d
In tercia septimana in communis quatuor sociorum vj s viij d
In batellis xij d ob q[a]
In quarta septimana in communis quatuor sociorum et dimi' viij s ix d ob'
In batellis xvij d ob
In quinta septimana in communis quinque sociorum ix s vij d
In batellis v d ob

Summa xxxj s ix d[8]

Alloc' communarum a festo omnium sanctorum exclusive usque ad festum natal' domini exclusive

In prima septimana pro communis quatuor sociorum vj s viij d
In batellis x d q[a]
In secunda septimana in communis trium sociorum vj s j d ob
In batellis xj d ob

[8] [ADMC] The sum is 32s 7½d plus the 'jx d' which therefore ought to be a slip for 1½d.

In tercia septimana in communis quatuor sociorum vij s iiij d
In batellis viij d
In quarta septimana in communis quinque sociorum viij s ix d
In batellis vij d
In quinta septimana in communis quatuor sociorum et di' viij s vij s ob
In batellis ob
In sexta septimana in communis quinque sociorum viij s iiij d
In septima septimana in communis quinque sociorum jx s ij d
In batellis ob
In contribucionibus xv d
Summa lix s iiij d ob q[a]

Alloc' communarum a festo natalis domini inclusive usque ad festum Purificationis beate virginis exclusive

In prima septimana pro communis quatuor sociorum et jurnell' x s viij d
In batellis j d
In secunda septimana in communis quinque sociorum xij s j d
In batellis ij d
In tercia septimana in communis quatuor sociorum et di' x s ix d ob
In batellis ij d ob q[a]
In quarta septimana in communis quatuor sociorum et di' ix s
In batellis ij d ob
In quinta septimana in communis quinque sociorum ix s ij s
In batellis iij d
In sex[a] septimana in communis quatuor sociorum viij s viij d
In batellis j d ob
Summa iiij li xvij d ob[9]

Alloc' communarum a festo Purificacione beate virginis inclusive usque ad festum Pache exclusive

In prima septimana pro communis quatuor sociorum ix s iiij d
In secunda septimana in communis quatuor sociorum et di' ix s iiij d ob
In batellis ij d
In tercia septimana in communis quinque sociorum x s x d
In batellis iij d q[a]
In quarta septimana in communis quinque sociorum x s x d
In batellis ij s iij d q[a]
In quinta septimana in communis quatuor sociorum et di' ix s iiij d
In batellis v d ob

[9] [ADMC] Actually £3 1s 5¼d.

In Sexta septimana in communis quinque sociorum x s x d
In batellis vij d q[a]
In Septima septimana in communis quinque sociorum xj s iij d
Item pro expensis factis die sancti Cuthberti in convivacione sociorum commorantum et extra viij s viij d ob
Summa iiij li iiij s iij d q[a]

Alloc' communarum a festo pasche inclusive usque ad festum pentecost' exclusive
In prima septimana pro communis trium sociorum et di' ix s iiij d
In batellis j d ob
In secunda septimana in communis quinque sociorum x s v d
In batellis iij d q[a]
In tercia septimana in communis quinque sociorum x s x d
In batellis j d q[a]
In quarta septimana in communis quinque sociorum x s v d
In quinta septimana in communis quatuor sociorum viij s j d
In batellis viij d ob
In Sex[a] septimana in communis quinque sociorum et di' xij s v d
In batellis iij d ob
In Septima septimana in communis quinque sociorum x s x d
In batellis j d
Summa iij li xiij s xj d

Summa total' omnium communarum xxij li ij s ob q[a][10]

[*Dorse*]

All' pro resolucionibus redd' de anno x[o] rr' Henr'
In primis Abbatisse de Godstow vij s
Item priori ecclesie sancte frydeswyde partim pro anno x[o] et partim pro anno xj[o] xx s

Alloc' pro resoluc' reddituum de anno xj rr' Henr'
In primis Abbathie de Osneye vj s
Item Willelmo Wrasteler pro Gardino fowke xviij d
Item Abbathie de Enseham pro Scoppa super angulum quadrivij viij s
Item Abbathie de Abyndon' xij s
Item Abbatisse de Godstow vij s

[10] [ADMC] This total is 15s 7d too much.

Item procuratoribus sancti petri in oriente ij s x d
Item tenenti molendinam domini regis pro firma quond' Witt-worth iij s viij d
Item Ecclesie sancte marie xij d
Summa iij li ix s

Alloc' pro stipend' sacerdotum et pencionibus sociorum
In primis M' Roberto Burton' xxvj s viij d
Item M Ade Redyford' xiij s iiij d
Item M Joh' Hamyrton vj s viij d
xvlj s viij d

Alloc' pro stipend' famulorum
In primis Thome Spenser xiij s iiij d
Item Thome Coke vj s viij d
Item Thome Barbour v s
Item communis lotrici domus v s
Summa xxx s

Summa total' trium predict' summarum vij li vj d ob[11]

Item petit computans allocari pro expensis Magistri in negocijs domus xl s
Item petit allocari de xxxiij s iiij d relictis in manu tenentis de Holdernes
In reparacionibus apud Brasynnos iiij li xiiij s ij d ob
In reparacionibus apud Edwarhall' ij li xiiij d ij d
In reparacionibus apud Droudale hall' et infra mansum proprium lj s viij d ob
Item pro diversis negocijs domus ut equitacionibus et meremio et alijs necessarijs emptis cum multis alijs parvis expensis ut patet per paupirum vj li xvij s viij d ob
Summa xxj li xj s j d ob

Item pro opere procuratoris x s
Item petit allocari de xx s sibi debitis
Item petit allocari de xx s de Thoma Bruse

Summa omnium allocatorum cxlix li ij s xj d q[a]

[11] The correct total would appear to be £7 5s 8d.

Et sic computatis computandis et allocatis allocandis debet computans collegio xlv s q[a]

Willelmus Sulbury Canc'

WHITSUN 11 HENRY IV to WHITSUN 12 HENRY IV (ROLL UC:BU1/F/21)

11 May 1410–30 May 1411

BURSAR: ROBERT BURTON

De Tempore Burton'

C[*ompotus Magistri*] et soc' Coll' Willelmi de dunelm' magn' aul' universitatis vulgariter nuncupat' a festo [*pent'*] inclusive a° rr' Henr' xj° usque ad idem festum exclusive a° eiusdem xij°

[*The arrears are identical with the Allowances in **F/20** above, except that under the arrears of tenements from 11 Hen IV the second entry reads, instead of 'De Spront xiij s x d ob', 'De Sprunt pro gard' xvj d'.*]

Summa omn' arr' iiij^{xx} li xv li ij d ob

Redditus ten' eiusdem Collegij de anno xij°

In primis de ten' Mercer	l s
De ten' Cowley	xl s
De ten' Glover	vj li
De Scopa super angulum quadrivij	xx s
De ten' quond' holwaye	xv s
De ten' Cambreye	xv s ix d
De ten' Johannis Roer' iuxta Cambreye[1]	xj s jam xij s
De Gardino quem iam tenet Cambrey quem quondam ten' Johannes Barbour	iij s iiij d
De Gard' olyfant Hall' quem tenet ric' karyour	iiij s iiij d
De Gardino quem tenet Adam River	iij s
De Novo Collegij pro Maydynhalle	x s
De Gardino quem tenet uxor quondam Willelmi Hampton'	iij s
De Ten' Roberti leycester	viij s
De Gardino ex opposito ecclesie sanct egidij quond' in ten' petri dauber	viij d iam xij d
De Gardino quem tenet Fuke barbor	iij s
De Collegio Cantuarie	xxx d

[1] On 20 September 1411, the house now known as 83 High Street was leased to John Royer (**UC:E/B2/D1/8**). This implies that Cambrey was living in what is now 84 High Street.

De Abbatissa de Godstow pro una scopa iuxta ffrydeswyd	xx d
De Holdernes	iij li xij d
De Sprunt pro gard'	xvj d
De Johanne Schaw pro prato vocato yr'lond	xxvj s viij d
De Mich' Tayliour	xv s
De Philippo Cordwener'	xxiij s iiij d
Summa xxij li vj s vij d	

Redditus aularum eodem a°

De Brasenose	iij li vj s viij d
De usu latrine Aul' Sancti Thome	iiij s
De aul' scuti	vj s viij d
De aul' sancti Thome	x s
De parva Aul' universitatis in vico scol'	xxxiij s iiij d
De Hampton' Hall'	xl s
De Aul' Edwardi	xxiij s
De drowdale hall'	xl s
De parva Aul' universitatis in alto vico	xl s
De Staunton' hall'	xiij s iiij d
Summa xiiij li iij s	

Redditus Camera eodem a°

De Camera midilton'	xx s
De Camera Eynseforth	x s
De Camera Canonici leyc'	x s
De Camera fythw	xiij s iiij d
De Camera Nafferton'	xvj s viij d
De Camera Cexby	xiij s iiij d
De Camera hurle	xvj s viij d
De Camera parysch	xiij s iiij d
De Camera benham	xv s iiij d
De Camera Makblyth	x s
Summa vj li xviij s viij d	

Redditus scolarum eodem a°

De scol' bass' in ten' dykys	viij s
De scol' s[*uperiore*] in ten' felt'	vj s viij d
De scol' superior' ex opposita belstrownt in ten' schotton'	v s iiij d
Summa xxj s iiij d	

Redditus de Esex' eodem a°	
De Esex'	xxiiij li
Summa omn' redd' iij^{xx} viij li ix s vij d	
Summa omn' Onerat' viij^{xx} li iij li ix s ix d ob	
All' eiusdem magistri et sociorum	
All' de ten' de anno rr' Henr' vij°	
De Johanne Barbour pro pensione sua a retro	xx d
De Adam Ryver	iij s
De Roberto Laceystr'	ij s viij d
De Holderness	vj d
De Thoma Cowlei	xiij s iiij d
Summa xxj s ij d	
All' Aul' eodem a°	
De Aula Edwardi	vij s iiij d
All' Camera eodem a°	
De camera Henley	iij s iiij d
De camera Canonici de Notley	iij s iiij d
De camera Morton	iij s iiij d
De camera Nafferton'	vj s viij d
De camera foston'	iij s iiij d
De camera Cleseby	xiij s iiij d
Summa xl s viij d	
All' ten' de a° viij°	
In primis de ten' Cowley	x s
De Roberti leyc'	viij s
De Holderness	xij d
De Schopa super angulum quadrivij	iiij d
Summa xix s iiij d	
All' Aul' eodem a°	
De drawdale Hall'	v s
De Stanton' hall'	vj s viij d
De Hampton' Hall'	vj s viij d
Summa xviij s iiij d	
All' Camera eodem a°	
De camera Henley	x s
De camera Nafferton'	xiij s iiij d

De camera foston'	xvj s viij d
Summa xl s	
All' ten' de a° ix°	
De ten' Cowley	xxx s
De Schoppa super angulum quadrivij	iiij d
De Ada Ryver pro gardino	iij s
De ten' Roberti leyc'	viij s
De Fuke Barbour pro gardino	xviij d
De Holderness	xij d
Summa xliij s x d	
All' Aul' eodem a°	
De Staunton' halle	iij s iiij d
De parva aula universitatis in alto vico	iij s iiij d
Summa vj s viij d	
All' scol' eodem a°	
De scolis tunc froyke	v s xj d
De Scola tunc more	vj s viij d
Summa xij s viij d	
All' Camera eodem a°	
De camera Nafferton'	x s
All' ten' de a° x°	
In primis de ten' mercer	ij s vj d
De ten' Glover	v li xj s
De Schoppa super angulum quadrivij	iiij d
De ten' Cambrey	vij s xj d
De Gardino Ade Ryver	iij s
De ten' Robert leyc'	iij s
De Holderness	xij d
Summa vj li xviij s ix d	
All' Aul' eodem a°	
In primis de Aula Scuti	vj s viij d
De aula sancti Thome	x s
De usu latrine aule sancti Thome	iiij s
De parva aula universitatis in alto vico	iij s iiij d
~~De Hampton Hall'~~	~~xiij s iiij d~~
De droudelhall'	vj s j d ob'
Summa xxx s j d ob'	

All' Camera eodem a°

De Camera Nafferton' iij s iiij d
De Camera beneham iuxta Johannem Thomson' ij s
De Camera Makblyth x s
Summa xv s iiij d

Summa omn' all' precedent' xix li vj s ix d ob

[*Dorse*]

Alloc' ten' de a° xj°

De ten' mercer vij s vj d
De Sprunt pro gard' xvj d
De ten' Glover xv s
De Schoppa super angulum quadrivij iiij d
De ten' Cambreye xv s ix d
De Cambray pro gard' iij s iiij d
De Ade River iij s
De ten' Roberti leycestr' viij s
De Holdernes xij d
De ten' Cowley x s
De Gardino quem tenet Thomas Hampton iij s
De Mich' Tayliour iij s ix d
Summa iij li xij s

All' Esex pro a° x° et xj°

De Esex pro a° ix° xx li xvij s j d
De Esex de a° x° xiij li xiij s iiij d
Summa xxxiiij li x s v d

Alloc' Aul' eodem a°

De Brasenose iij li vj s viij d
De usu latrine aul' sancti Thom' iiij s
De Aul' scuti vj s viij d
De Aul' sancti Thom' x s
De parva Aul' universitatis in vico scolarum vj s viij d
De Hampton' Hall' remittebatur principali pro reparac' et alijs xiij s iiij d
De Drwdale hall' remittebatur principali viij s iiij d
De staunton' hall' vj s viij d
De parva Aul' universitatis in alto vico xliij s iiij d
Summa viij li v s viij d

All' scol' eodem a°	
De scol' tunc pounter	iij s iiij d
All' Camera eodem a°	
De Camera Eynsforth	vj s viij d
De Camera Nafferton'	iij s iiij d
De Camera hurle	x s
De Camera benham	vj s viij d
De Camera Makblyth	x s
Summa xl s	
All' ten' de a° xij°	
De ten' Glover	iij li
De ten' Caumbray	xv s ix d
De ten' Roer'	v s ix d
De Ric' Karyour pro gard'	iiij s iiij d
De gard' Ad' Ryv'	iij s
De novo Coll' pro Maydenhall'	v s
De Thom' Hampton' pro gard'	iij s
De ten' Rob' leyc'	viij s
De Coll' Cant'	ij s vj d
De Holdernes	iij li xij d
De Sprunt pro gard'	xvj d
~~De Johanne schaw pro prato vocat' yrelandes~~	~~iiij d~~
De Mic' talyour	ix s j d
Summa ix li ij d	
All' Aul' eodem a°	
De Brasenose	xl s
De usu latrine aula Sancti Thome	iiij s
De aul' scuti	vj s viij d
De aul' sancti Thom'	x s
De parva Aul' universitatis in vico scol'	xx s
De Hampton' hall'	xl s
De Aul' Edwardi	xiij s
De drwdale hall'	xviij s iiij d
De parva Aul' universitatis in alto vico	xxx s
De Staunton' hall'	xiij s viij d
Summa x li vj s ij d	
Alloc' Camera eodem a°	
De Camera Nafferton'	xvj s viij d

De Camera Hurle x s
De Camera Benham viij s viij d
De Camera Makblyth x s
Summa xlv s iiij d

All' scol' eodem a°
De scol' dykys viij s
De scol' felt' vj s viij d
De scol' schotton' vj s iiij d
Summa xxj s iiij d

De Esex eodem a°
De Esex xxiij s

Summa harum allocationum iij^{xx} xij li liij s iij d

Summa omn' all' precendent' iiij^{xx} li xj li ob

All' communarum sociorum a festo pent' a° rr' Henr' xj° usque ad diem veneris prox' post festum sancti Thome
In prima septimana communarum 28 d 4 soc' ix s iiij d
In jornellis xij d
In 2ª septimana communarum 27 d 5 soc' xj s iij d
In 3ª septimana communarum 25 d 5 soc' x s v d
In 4ª septimana communarum ij s 4 soc' et dj' [*sic*] ix s
In jornellis x d
In 5ª septimana communarum 23 d 5 soc' ix s vij d[2]
In 7ª septimana communarum 26 d 5 soc' x s x d
In 8 septimana communarum 23 d 5 soc' ix s vij d
In 9 septimana communarum ij s 4 soc' et dj' ix s
Summa iiij li xviij d

A die veneris prox' post festum sancti Thome exclusive usque ad assumpt' beate marie inclusive
In prima septimana communarum 23 d 4 soc' et dj' viij s vij d ob'
In jornellis vj d
In 2ª septimana communarum 25 d 4 soc' viij s iiij d
In 3ª septimana communarum ij s 4 soc' viij s
In 4ª septimana communarum ij s 4 soc' viij s
In 5ª septimana communarum 22 d 3 soc' et dj' vj s v d

[2] [ADMC] The commons for the sixth week have been omitted.

In jornellis viij d
Summa xl s vj d ob

Ab assumptione beate virg' que die veneris continet ad vigilium omnium sanctorum que eciam die veneris continet
In prima septimana communarum 22 d 3 soc' et dij' vj s v d
In jornellis iiij d
In 2ª septimana communarum ij s 4 soc' viij s
In 3ª septimana communarum 23 d 4 soc' vij s viij d
In 4ª septimana communarum 22 d 4 soc' vij s iiij d
In 5ª septimana communarum 22 d 4 soc' vij s iiij d
In 6ª septimana communarum 21 d 3 soc' v s iij d
In jornellis vij d ob
In 7ª septimana communarum 22 d 4 soc' vij s iiij d
In 8 septimana communarum 21 d 4 soc' vij s
In 9 septimana communarum 22 d 4 soc' vij s iiij d
In 10ª septimana communarum 20 d 5 soc' viij s iiij d
In 11ª septimana communarum 20 d 5 soc' viij s iiij d
Summa iiij li xv d ob

A vig' Omnium sanctorum exclusive usque ad diem veneris in festo Nat' domino scilicet in festum sancti stephani
In prima septimana communarum 20 d 5 soc' viij s iiij d
In 2ª septimana communarum 19 d 5 soc vij s xj d
In 3ª septimana communarum 18 d 5 soc' vij s vj d
In 4ª septimana communarum 19 d 5 soc' vij s xj d
In 5ª septimana communarum 20 d 4 soc' vj s viij d
In jornellis viij d
In 6ª septimana communarum 19 d 5 soc' vij s xj d
In 7ª septimana communarum 19 d 5 soc' vij s xj d
In 8ª septimana communarum 29 d 5 soc' xj s viij d
Summa iiij li vj s vj d

A die sancti stephani exclusive usque ad diem veneris prox' post purificacionem beate virginis
In prima septimana communarum ij s 5 soc' x s
In 2ª septimana communarum 22 d 4 soc vij s iiij d
In jornellis xvij d
In 3ª septimana communarum 20 d 4 soc' vj s viij d
In 4ª septimana communarum 21 d 4 soc' vij s
In jornellis vj d

In 5^{a} septimana communarum 20 d 4 soc' et dj' vij s vj d
In 6^{a} septimana communarum 29 d 4 soc' viij s iiij d
In jornellis vj d ob
Summa xlix s iij d ob

A die veneris prox' post purificacionem usque ad diem veneris prox' post diem cinerum inclusive
In prima septimana communarum 21 d 4 soc' vij s
In jornellis vij d
In 2^{a} septimana communarum 22 d 5 soc ix s ij d
In 3^{a} septimana communarum 28 d 4 soc' ix s iiij d
In jornellis viij d
Summa xxvj s ix d

A die veneris prox' post diem cinerum usque ad diem veneris in sep^{a} pasch' inclusive
In prima septimana communarum 23 d 5 soc' ix s vij d
In 2^{a} septimana communarum ij s 5 soc x s
In 3^{a} septimana communarum 23 d 5 soc' ix s vij d
In 4^{a} septimana communarum 22 d ob 5 soc' ix s iiij d ob
In 5^{a} septimana communarum ij s 4 soc' viij s
In semicommun' et jornellis j^{us} soc' xvj d
In 6^{a} septimana communarum ij s 4 soc' viij s
In 7^{a} septimana communarum ij s vij d 3 soc' vij s ix d
Summa iij li iij s vij d ob

In die veneris in sep^{a} pasch' exclusive usque ad diem veneris prox' ante pent' inclusive
In prima septimana communarum ij s 4 soc' viij s
In 2^{a} septimana communarum 20 d 5 soc viij s iiij d
In 3^{a} septimana communarum 21 d 5 soc' viij s ix d
In 4^{a} septimana communarum 20 d 5 soc' viij s iiij d
In 5^{a} septimana communarum 23 d 4 soc' vij s viij d
In 6^{a} septimana communarum 22 d 4 soc' vij s iiij d
Summa xlvij s v d

Summa omn' comm' xxij li xvij s xj d

All' bat'
In bat' pro extransis et [. . .] operarijs lv s iiij d q^{a}

All' stipend' soc' et penc' soc'
M Johanni Castell' liij s iiij d

M Rob' Burton' a retro	de tempore Ryvell' xxxiij s iiij d	
	de tempore Burton iij li	
	iij li xiij s iiij d	
M Ade Radeforth	xxxij s	
M Joh' Hamerton'	de tempore Ryvell' xiij s iiij d	
	de t^e Burton xx s	
	xxxiij s iiij d	
Henr' Heth' pro remiss' penc'	v li vj s viij d	
Summa xv li xviij s viij d		

All' Resol' redd'

Abb' Oseney pro gardino	vj s viij d
Abb' Abyngton pro a° xj° a retro xviij d pro a° xij°	iij s vj d
Willelmo Wryst' pro gard' in northg'	xviij d
Pro xv^a ballivis	xxxij d
Ecclesie beate mar'	xij d
Abb' de Godstow	xiij s
Abb' Eynsham pro schoppa super ang' quadrivij	viij s
Tenentis molendi regis	iij s viij d
Summa xlij s	

All' stipend' servient'

Thom' spens'	xiij s iiij d
Coco	vj s viij d
lotrici	v s
Barb'	v s
Teg'	ix s vj d
Summa xxxix s vj d	

All' staur'

In ovibus emptis Esex	vj li xiij s iiij d

All' reparacionum

In reparac' infra Coll' et extra oxon' et Esex	xix li iij d
Pro labore cursorum Lond' pro Auro Esex	xij d
In solucione procuratoris	x s
Petit autem computans allocari de drwdalehall' de Antiquis arr'	iij s viij d
Eciam de camera polton'	xvj d

Et sic computatis computandis et allocatis allocandis collegium debet computanti iij s iij d q[a]

Johannes bannard Canc'

[*In a different, fainter hand*]
⟨Et memorandum quod in tempore magistri Joh' Castell unum placitum de ferro Ric' mercer' erat arestatum in ten' dicti Ric' pro decem solidis quod dictus Ric' Collegio universit' debuit, pro ten' in quo inhabitavit. et ista arestacio fuit facta Anno undecimo regis Regni Henrici quarti per Rogerum Wyddyslay generosum Bedellum sacre theologie auctoritate Willelmi Clynt tunc cancell')
[*In a different, clear hand*]
⟨Et sciendum quod anno decimo septimo regni regis henrici sexti in tempore Willelmi Asplyon tunc procuratorem excecuta facta est concordia inter collegium et Magistri Thomas pyparde quem [*sic*] habuit predictam laminam ferream qui tho' condempnatus est in summa xxiij s iiij d dicto collegio solvendorum pro dicta lamina et alijs arreragijs per decretum et arbitrium magistrorum Johannis gervase et dicti Willelmi Asplyon' tunc procuratoris, quos quidem xxxiij s iiij d dictus Tho' pyparde fidelitur persolvit ac finaliter concordia inter ipsum et collegium facta est.⟩

[*A narrow roll of two membranes, in good condition. All totals add up correctly.*]

WHITSUN 12 HENRY IV to WHITSUN 13 HENRY IV (ROLL UC:BU1/F/22)
31 May 1411–22 May 1412

BURSAR: JOHN RYVELL

dat

De tempore Ryvell'

Computus magistri et soc' Coll' Willelmi de dunelmi mag[. . .] a festo pentecost' inclusive anni r'r' Henr' xij° usque ad[. . .

[*The Arrears are the same as the Allowances of* ***F/21****, with the following exceptions:*

Arrears of Halls, 8 Hen IV: No entry for Hampton Hall.

Arrears of Halls, 10 Hen IV: The entry for Drawda Hall has been deleted.

Arrears of Halls, 11 Hen IV: No entries for Hampton Hall and Drawda Hall.]

Summa omn' arr' iiij^{xx} li viij li xiij s vij d[1]

Redditus eiusdem Coll' de a° xiij°

In primis de ten' quond' Mercer	l s
De ten' Cowley	xl s
De ten' Glover	vj li
De Scopa super angulum quadrivij	xx s
De ten' quond' Holwaye iuxta Hampton Halle	xv s
De ten' Cambreye	xv s viij d
De Gardino Cambreye	iij s iiij d
De ten' Johannes Barbour	xij s
De Gardino quem tenet Ricardus Caruer	iiij s iiij d
De Gardino quem tenet Adam River	iij s
De Novo Collegij pro Maydynhalle	x s
De Gardino quem tenet uxor quondam Willelmi Hampton'	viij s
De Ten' Roberti leycester	viij s

[1] [ADMC] The total is 23s too little; the arrears for Essex (23s) appear to have been omitted.

De Gardino ex opposito ecclesie sancti egidij	xij d
De Gardino quond' fuk barbour	iij s
De Collegio Cantuarie	xxx d
De Abbatissa de Godstow pro una scopa iuxta ffrydeswyd	xx d
De Holdernes	iij li vj d
De Sprunt' pro gard'	xvj d
De Johanne Schaw pro prato vocato yr'lond	xxvj s viij d
De Mich' Tayliour	xv s
De Philippo Cordwener'	xxiij s iiij d
Summa xxij li vj s j d[2]	

Redditus aul' eodem a°

De Brasenose	iij li vj s viij d
De usu latrine Aul' Sancti Thome	iiij s
De aul' scuti	vj s viij d
De aul' sancti Thome	x s
De parva Aul' universitatis in vico scolarum	xxxiij s iiij d
De Hampton' Hall'	xl s
De Aul' Edwardi	xxiij s
De drowdale hall'	xlv s
De parva Aul' universitatis in alto vico	xl s
De Staunton' hall'	xiij s iiij d
Summa xiiij li iij s	

Redditus cam' eodem a°

De Cam' Midilton'	xx s
De Cam' Eynsforth	x s
De cam' Canonic' leyc'	x s
De cam' fythw	xiij s iiij d
De cam' Nafferton'	xvj s viij d
De cam' Cexby	xiij s iiij d
De cam' Hurle	xvj s viij d
De cam' Hollewell'	xvj s viij d
De cameris Edwardi	xxiij s iiij d
De cam' maxfeld'	xx s
viij li[3]	

[2] [ADMC] There are some slightly reduced rents on this roll from that of the previous year, and two slightly increased ones. This should give a total of £22 7s 4d, but the total given is 1s 3d too small. The last figure appears to have been altered, possibly from vij d.

[3] The word 'Summa' is not written in here.

Redditus scol' eodem a°

De scol' prentyce	viij s
De scol' Bannam	vj s viij d
De scol' quondam scotton'	vj s viij d
Summa xxj s iiij d	

Redditus de Esex eodem anno

De Esex	xxiiij li

Summa omn' reddit' iij^{xx} li ix li x s iiij d[4]

Summa omn' Onerat' vij^{xx} xviij li iij s xij d[5]

Alloc' eiusdem magistri et sociorum

All' ten' de an° rr' Hen' vij°

De Johanne Barbour pro pensione sua a retro	xx d
De Adam Ryver	iij s
De Roberto Laceystr'	ij s viij d
De Holdernes	vj d
De ten' Couley	xiij s iiij d
Summa xxj s ij d	

All' aul' eodem an°

De Aula Edwardi	vij s iiij d

All' cam' eodem an°

De camera Henley	iij s iiij d
De camera Canonici de Notley	iij s iiij d
De camera Morton	iij s iiij d
De camera Nafferton'	iij s iiij d
De camera foston'	iij s iiij d
De camera Clesby	xiij s iiij d
Summa xxvij s iiij d	

All' ten' de a° viij°

De ten' Coulay	x s
De Roberti laceystr'	viij s
De Holdernes	xij d

[4] [ADMC] Actually £69 10s 5d. Possibly the erasure referred to above was intended to delete all the pence.

[5] [ADMC] This is the correct total of the generalised totals of Arrears and Rents, but both these are incorrect.

De Schoppa super angulum quadrivij	iiij d
Summa xix s iiij d	
All' aul' eodem aº	
De droudale hall'	v s
De Stanton hall'	vj s viij d
Summa xj s viij d	
All' cam' eodem anº	
De cam' Henley	x s
De cam' Nafferton'	iij s iiij d
De cam' foston'	xvj s viij d
Summa xxx s	
All' ten' de aº ixº	
De Couley	xxx s
De Schoppa super angulum quadrivij	iiij d
De Ada Ryver pro gardino	iij s
De ten' Roberti laceystr'	viij s
De Holdernes	xij d
Summa xlij s iiij d	
All' aul' eodem aº	
De Staunton' hall	iij s iiij d
De parva aula universitatis in alto vico	iij s iiij d
All' scol' eodem aº	
de scolis tunc frowyk	v s xj d
De Scola tunc more	vj s viij d
All' cam' eodem aº	
De camera Nafferton'	x s
Summa xxix s iij d	
All' ten' de anº xº	
De ten' mercer	ij s vj d
De ten' Glover	v li xj s
De Schoppa super angulum quadrivij	iiij d
De ten' Cambrey	vij s xj d
De Gardino Ade Ryver	iij s
De ten' Robert leceystr'	iij s
De Holdernes	xij d
All' aul' eodem anº	
De Aula Scuti	vj s viij d

De aula sancti Thome	x s
De usu latrine aule sancti Thome	iiij s
De parva aula universitatis in alto vico	iij s iiij d
Summa xxiiij s	

All' cam' eodem an°

De Camera Nafferton'	iij s iiij d
De Camera beneham iuxta Johannem Thomson'	ij s
De Camera Makblyth	x s
Summa xv s iiij d	

All' ten' de an° xj°

De ten' mercer	vij s vj d
De Sprunt pro gard'	xvj d
De ten' Glover	xv s
De Scopa super angulum quadrivij	iiij d
De ten' Cambreye	xv s ix d
De gardino Cambray	iij s iiij d
De Adam Ryver	iij s
De ten' Roberti leyc'	viij s
De Holdernes	xij d
De ten' Coulcy	x s
De Thoma Hampton pro gardino	iij s
Summa iij li viij s iij d	

All' esex pro a° x° et xj°

De Esex de an° x°	xiij li xiij s iiij d
De Esex de an° xj°	xx li xvij s j d
Summa xxxiiij li x s v d	

All' aul' eodem a°

De Brasenose	iij li vj s viij d
De usu latrine aul' sancti Thom'	iiij s
De Aul' scuti	vj s viij d
De Aul' sancti Thom'	x s
De staunton' hall'	vj s viij d
De parva Aul' universitatis in alto vico	xliij s iiij d
Summa vj li xvij s iiij d	

All' scol' eodem a°

De scol' tunc pounter	iij s iiij d

All' cam' eodem an°

De Camera Eynsforth	vj s viij d
De Camera Nafferton'	iij s iiij d
De Camera Benham	vj s viij d
De Camera Makblyth	x s
Summa xxx s	

All' ten' de an° xij°

De ten' Glover	iij li xx d
De ten' Cambrey	xx d
De Gardino Ade ryver	iij s
De Thoma Hampton pro gardino	iij s
De ten' Roberti leyc'	viij s
De Holdernes remittebatur pro amerciementis	xix s
De Sprount pro gardino	xvj s
Summa iiij li xviij s viij d	

All' aul' eodem an°

De drowdale hall'	v s
De Brasenose	xl s
De uno latrine aule sancti Thome	iiij s
De aula scuti	vj s viij d
De aula sancti Thome	x s
De Hampton Hall'	vj s viij d
De parva aula universitatis in alto vico	xxiij s iiij d
De Staunton Hall'	x s
Summa v li v s viij d	

All' cam' eodem an°

De cam' Nafferton'	iij s iiij d
De cam' Hurle	iiij s
De cam' Benham	viij d
De cam' Makblyth	xiij s iiij d

All'scol' eodem an°

De scol' Scotton	vj s viij d
Summa xxij s viij d[6]	

All' ten' de an° xiij°

De ten' Glover	iij li v s viij d
De Scop' super angulum quadrivij	iiij d

[6] [ADMC] Actually 36s (i.e. the total was 3s 4d too little). Makblyth only owed 10s in the Arrears in this roll.

De ten' Cambrey	xv s viij d
De Johannis Roer	vj s
De Gardino Cambrey	iij s iiij d
De Gardino Ric' Cariur	xij d
De Ade Ryver	iij s
De novo Collegio pro maydynhall'	v s
De Gardino Thome Hampton'	iij s
De ten' Roberti leyc'	v s viij d
De Gardino ex o^{to} Ecclesie sancti Egidij	xij d
De Holdernes	iij li vj d
De Sprunt pro gardino	xvj d
De ten' mich' talyor	vij s j d
Summa viij li xviij s vij d	

All' aul' eodem an^{o}

De Aula sancti Thome	x s
De Aula scuti	vj s viij d
De Aula edwardi	xvij s iiij d
De usu latrine aul' sancti Thome	iiij s
De parva aula univ^{tis} in vico scol'	xx s
De Hampton' Hall'	xl s
De drowdale Hall'	xviij s iiij d
De parva aula universitatis in alto vico	xx s
De Staunton Hall'	xiij s iiij d
Summa vij li ix s viij d	

All' cam' eodem an^{o}

De cam' Henley[7]	x s
De cam' Eynsford'	x s
De cam' Naffirton'	xvj s viij d
De cam' Cexby	vj s viij d
De cam' Hurle	xvj s viij d
De cam' Hollewell'	xvj s viij d
De cam' Edwardi	x s

All' scol' eodem an^{o}

De scol' quond' Scotton'	vj s viij d
Summa iiij li xiij s iiij d	

[7] [ADMC] A puzzling entry. It does not appear under the rents for this year, and in the MS looks as though it as been inserted above the other entries as an afterthought. The entry recurs until 1415/16.

De Esex xij li

Summa all' precendent' v^{xx} li ix li ij s ix d

All' comunarum a Pentecost' inclusive a° rr' Henr' xij usque ad festum assumpcionis beate marie virginis exclusive

In prima septimana in communis duorum sociorum vij s iij d
In batellis vj d
In secunda septimana in communis trium sociorum vj s iij d
In batellis vj d
In tercia septimana in communis quattuor sociorum vij s
In batellis iij d q^a
In quarta septimana in communis quattuor sociorum vij s
In batellis iiij d q^a
In quinta septimana in communis quattuor sociorum vj s viij d
In batellis iij d ob
In sexta septimana in communis quinque sociorum ix s ij d
In batellis iij d ob
In septima septimana in communis quinque sociorum viij s iiij d In batellis iiij d
In octava septimana in communis quinque sociorum ix s ij d
In batellis ob
In nona septimana in communis quinque sociorum viij s xj d ob
In decima septimana in communis quinque sociorum viij s ix d
In batellis vij d
In undecima septimana in communis duorum sociorum et dimidij iiij d ij d In batellis vij d
In contribucionibus j s iij d
Item quum commissarij archiepiscopi erant hic iiij s ij d
Summa iiij li xij s iij d q^a[8]

All' communarum a festo assumpcionis inclusive usque ad festum omnium sanctorum exclusive

In prima septimana in communis trium sociorum v s ix d
In batellis j d
In secunda septimana in communis duorum sociorum et dimidij iiij s vij d In batellis j d
In tercia septimana in communis duorum sociorum iiij s
In batellis xij d

[8] [ADMC] The correct total is £4 12s 5¼d.

In quarta septimana in communis unius socij ij s
In batellis ix d ob
In quinta septimana in communis unius socij ij s iiij d
In batellis xiiij d
In sexta septimana in communis unius socij ij s In batellis xij d
In septima septimana in communis unius socij ij s
In batellis viij d
In octava septimana in communis trium sociorum v s vj d
In batellis j d
In nona septimana in communis duorum sociorum et dimidij iij s xj d ob In batellis xj d ob q[a]
In decima septimana in communis unius socij j s x d
In batellis iij d
In undecima septimana in communis trium sociorum iiij s vj d
In batellis xviij d ob
Summa ij li vj s ob q[a9]

All' communarum a festo omnium sanctorum inclusive usque ad festum Natalis domini inclusive
In prima septimana in communis quinque sociorum ix s ij d
In batellis iiij d ob
In secunda septimana in communis quattuor sociorum vj s
In batellis iij d q[a]
In tercia septimana in communis duorum sociorum iij s
In batellis xvj d ob
In quarta septimana in communis trium sociorum v s
In batellis xij d ob
In quinta septimana in communis quattuor sociorum et dimidij vij s j d ob In batellis v d
In sexta septimana in communis quinque sociorum viij s iiij d
In batellis ij d ob q[a]
In septima septimana in communis quinque sociorum viij s ix d In batellis ob
In octava septimana in communis trium sociorum et dimidij vij s vij d In batellis ix d
Summa ij li xix s v d q[a10]

[9] [ADMC] The correct total is £3 6s 1d.
[10] [ADMC] The correct total is £2 19s 5d.

All' communarum a festo Natal' domini usque ad festum Pasche exclusive

In prima septimana in communis trium sociorum ix s
In batellis vij d ob
In secunda septimana in communis quattuor sociorum viij s
In batellis ij d
In tercia septimana in communis quattuor sociorum vij s iiij d
In batellis v d
In quarta septimana in communis trium sociorum v s vj d
In batellis iiij d ob
In quinta septimana in communis trium sociorum v s vj d
In batellis iiij d
In sexta septimana in communis quinque sociorum vij s xj d
In batellis iiij s ij d
In septima septimana in communis quattuor sociorum et dimidij vij s j d ob In batellis vj d
In octava septimana in communis quinque sociorum x s x d
In nona septimana in communis quinque sociorum ix s vij d
In decima septimana in communis quinque sociorum ix s
In undecima septimana in communis quinque sociorum x s
In duodecima septimana in communis quinque sociorum x s x d
In terciadecima septimana in communis quinque sociorum viij s iiij d In batellis viij d
In quartadecima septimana in communis quinque sociorum x s x d In batellis iiij d
Item pro gaudijs sancti Cuthberti xj s
Summa vj li xviij s v d ob'

[*Dorse*]

Alloc' communarum a festo pasche inclusive usque ad festum pentecost exclusive

In prima septimana in communis iiij sociorum viij d viij d
In batellis ij d ob
In secunda septimana in communis v sociorum vj s viij d
In batellis iiij d
In tercia septimana in communis iiij sociorum v s iiij d
In batellis iiij d
In quarta septimana in communis iiij sociorum v s iiij d
In quinta septimana in communis v sociorum v s ij d
In sexta septimana in communis duorum sociorum iij d iiij d

In septima septimana in communis iiij sociorum v s iiij d
Summa xl s viij d ob

Summa omn' comunarum xviij li xvj s xj d q[a]

All' resol' redd de a° xij°

In primis ballivis ville pro langage	xxij d ob
Item abbathie de Godstowe	vij s
Item pro firma quond' Wyttyrworth	iij s viij d
Item Ecclesie sancti Petri	ij s x d
Item priori ecclesie sancte frideswyde partim pro anno xij° et partim an' [*sic*]	xx s

Summa xxxv s iiij d ob'

All' resol' redd' de a° xiiij°

In primis abbathie et oseneye	vj s
Item Willelmo Wrasteler	xviij d
Item Abbathie de Enseham pro schoppa super angulum quadrivij	viij s
Item Abbathie de Abyndon	xviij d
Item Abbathie de godstou	xiiij s
Item procuratoribus sancti petri in oriente	ij s x d
Item tenenti molendinas [*sic*] domini regis pro firma quondam Witterworth	iij s viij d

Summa xxxvij d vj d

All' pro stipendijs sociorum et pencionibus sociorum

In primis magistro	xxxij s
Item M° Robert' Burton'	xx s
Item M° Ade Rediford	iij li
Item M° Joh' hamerton'	vj s viij d
Item M° Joh' Ryvell'	xx s

Summa vj li xviij s viij d

All' pro stipendijs famulorum

In primis procuratori	x s
Item Thome spenser	vj s viij d
Item Thome Barbur	v s
Item communi lotrici domus	v s

Summa xxvj s viij d

In reparacionibus et expensis alijs necessarijs xxiiij li xvij s iiij d
Item solut' burton' de arrerag' iiij s iij d q[a]
Summa all' precedenc' xxxvj li xix s ix d ob q[a]

Summa omn' all' viij[xx] iiij li xix s vj d

Et sic computatis computandis et allocatis allocandis collegium debet computanti vj li xv s vij d

⟨Willelmus Sulbury⟩

[*A roll of three membranes, the last one much shorter than the others; there is some staining at the head, but the rest of is in good condition.*]

WHITSUN 13 HENRY IV to WHITSUN 1 HENRY V (ROLL UC:BU1/F/23)

22 May 1412–11 Jun 1413

BURSAR: ROBERT BURTON

De tempore Burton'

Compotus procuratoris coll' Willelmi de dunelm' Magn' aul' universitatis vulgariter nuncupat' a festo pent' inclusive a^{o} rr' Henr' quart' usque ad item festum exclusive a^{o} rr' Henr' quinti primo.

[*The Arrears are identical with the Allowances in **F/22** above, save for a few changes in spelling.*]

Summa omnium preteritorum cix li ij s ix d

Redditus eiusdem coll' de a^{o} eiusdem regis xiiij^{o}

De ten' mercer	l s
De ten' cowley	xl s
De ten' Glover	vj li
De schoppa super angulum quadrivij	xx s
De ten' quond' holway	xv s
De ten' cawmbray	xv s viij d
De gard' Cawmbray	iij s iiij d
De ten' Joh' Roer'	xij s
De gard' ric' caryour	iiij s iiij d
De gard' ad' ryver	iij s
De novo coll' pro maydenhall'	x s
De gard' Thome hampton'	iij s
De gard' quond' uxoris ~~johannis~~ hampton	viij s
De ten' rob' leyc'	viij s
De gard' ex o^{to} ecclesie sancti egidij	xij d
De gard' ric' barbour	iij s
De coll' cant'	ij s vj s
De abb' de godstow pro una schoppa iuxta sanctam frideswid'	xx d
De holdernes	iij li vj d
De sprunt	xvj d
De joh' schaw pro prato jreland'	xxvj s viij d
De ten' mic' talyour	xv s

De ten' philippi courdwaner	xxiij s iiij d
Summa xxij li vj s j d[1]	
De Esex' eodem a°	xxiiij li
Redditus aul' eodem a°	
De brasenose	iij li vj s viij d
De aul' scuti	vj s viij d
De aul' sancti Thome	x s
De parva aul' universitatis in vico scolarum	xxxiij s iiij d
De Hampton' Hall'	xl s
De aul' edwardi	xxiiij s
De drwdalehall'	xlv s
De stauntonhall'	xiij s iiij d
Summa xj li xix s	
Redditus cam' eodem a°	
De cam' mydilton	xx s
De cam' gray	xx s
De cam' Eynsforth	x s
De cam' leyc'	x s
De cam' hasu' [*sic*]	xvj s viij d
De cam' howell'	xvj s viij d
De cam' edwardi canonici	xxiij s viij d
De cam' fythw	xvj s viij d
De cam' kar'll [*sic*]	xvj s viij d
De cam' Newby	xx s
De cam' cexby	xiij s iiij d
De cam' Nafferton'	xvj s viij d
De cam' schawsby et parech'	xiij s iiij d
De cam' stirkland' et Eynsforth'	x s
Summa xj li iij s iiij d	
Redditus schol' eodem a°	
De scol' prentys	viij s
De scol' [*blank*]	vj s viij d

[1] [ADMC] The correct total is £22 7s 4d.

De scol' ex o[to] belpis de j det' ij s de scharp usque festum mic' ij s iiij s

Summa xviij s viij d

Summa omnium reddit' iij[xx] li vij s j d

Summa omnium onerat' viij[xx]xix li ix s x d

Alloc' eiusdem

All' ten' de a° vij°

De joh' barber	xx d
De ad' Ryver	iij s
De rob' leyc'	ij s viij d
De holdernes	vj d
De Cowley	xiij s iiij d

Summa xxj s ij d

All' aul' et cam' eodem a°

De aul' edwardi	vij s iiij d
De cam' henley	iij s iiij d
De cam' canonici de notley	iij s iiij d
De cam' morton	iij s iiij d
De cam' Nafferton'	iij s iiij d
De cam' Foston'	iij s iiij d
De cam' cleseby	xiij s iiij d

Summa xxxvij s iiij d

All' ten' de a° eiusdem viij°

De Cowley	x s
De Rob' leyc'	viij s
De Holdernes	xij d
De schopp' super angulum quad'	iiij d

Summa xix s iiij d

All' aul' eodem a°

De drwdalehall'	v s
De stauntonhall'	vj s viij d

Summa xj s viij d

All' cam' eodem a°

De cam' Henley	x s
De cam' nafferton'	iij s iiij d

De cam' foston'	xvj s viij d
Summa xxx s	
All' ten' de a° eiusdem ix°	
De cowley	xxx s
De schop' super angulum quad'	iiij d
De ad' ryver	iij s
De rob' leyc'	viij s
De holdernes	xij d
Summa xlij s iiij d	
All' aul' eodem a° et scol' et cam'	
De stauntonhall'	iij s iiij d
De parva aul' universitatis in alto vico	iij s iiij d
De scol' tunc Frowyk	v s xj d
De cam' Nafferton'	x s
Summa xxij s vij d	
All' ten' de a° eiusdem x°	
De mercer	ij s vj d
De Glover	v li xj s
De schop' super angulum quad'	iiij d
De ten' cawmbray	vij s xj d
De gard' ad' ryver	iij s
De rob' leyc'	iij s
De holdernes	xij d
Summa vj li viij s ix d	
All' aul eodem a° et de cam'	
De parva aul' universitatis in alto vico	iij s iiij d
De cam' nafferton'	iij s iiij d
De cam' makeblith	x s
Summa xvj s viij d	
All' ten' de a° eiusdem xj°	
De ten' mercer	vij s vj d
De sprunt	xvj d
De Glover	xv s
De schop' super angulum quad'	iiij d
De ten' cawmbray	xv s ix d
De Gard' cawmbray	iij s iiij d
De ad' ryver	iij s

De rob' leyc'	viij d
De Holdernes	xij d
De cowley	x s
Summa iij li v s iij d	

[*Dorse*]

All' Esex

De a° x°	xiij li xiij s iiij d
De a° xj°	xx li xvij s j d

All' aul' de eodem a°

De staunton' hall'	vj s viij d
De parva aula universitatis in alto vico	xliij s iiij d
Summa l s	

All' scol' et cam' eodem a°

De scol' pounter	xvj d
De cam' Eynsford	vj s viij d
De cam' Nafferton'	iij s iiij d
De cam' benham'	iij s iiij d
De cam' makeblith	x s
Summa xxiiij s viij d	

All' ten' de a° eiusdem xij°

De Glover	iij li xx d
De Cawmbray	xx d
De ad' ryver	iij s
De thoma hampton'	ij s iiij d
De Rob' leyc'	viij s
De holdernes remiss'	xix s
De sprunt	xvj d
Summa iiij li xvij s	

All' aul' eiusdem a°

De drwdalehall'	v s
De Hampton' hall'	iij s iiij d
De parva aula universitatis in alto vico	xxiij s iiij d
De staunton hall'	xiij s iiij d

All' scol' eodem a°

De scol' schotton'	vj s viij d
Summa lj s viij d[2]	
All' ten' de a° eiusdem xiij°	
De Glover	iij li v s viij d
De schop' super angulum quad'	iiij d
De ten' Cawmbray	xv s viij d
De gard' Cawmbray	iij s iiij d
De ad' ryver	iij s
De Gardino ex o^to sancti egidij	xij d
De holdernes	vij s viij d
De sprunt	xvj d
De mich' talyour	vij s j d
De Rob' Leyc	v s viij d
Summa v li x s ix d	
All' aul' eodem a°	
De parva aula universitatis in alto vico	x s
De staunton' hall'	xiij s iiij d
Summa xxiij s iiij d	
All' cam' eodem a°	
De cam' Henley	x s
De cam' Eynsforth	iij s iiij d
De cam' hurle	iij s iiij d
De cam' Holwell'	xvj s viij d
De cam' Nafferton'	iij s iiij d
Summa xxxvj s viij d	
All' ten' de a° eiusdem xiiij°	
De ten' Glover	iij li viij d
De ten' Cawmbray	viij d
De gard' ric' caryour	iiij d
De Ad' Ryver	iij s
De schop' super angulum quadrivij	iiij d
De Thom' Hampton'	iij s
De Rob' Leyc'	vj s

[2] [ADMC] The entry for the Arrears in the roll for 1413/4 below suggests that a section for the Allowances for Rooms for this year, totalling 20s 8d, has been omitted from this roll in error. A slip of parchment, containing this same entry, has been stitched onto the roll of 1420/1, where it is quite meaningless. It is clearly the omitted entry which belongs to this roll (see p. 296 below).

De abb' de godstow	x d
De Holdernes	iij li vj d
De sprunt	xvj d
De Mic' talyour	xx d
Summa vj li xviij s iiij d	

All' aul' eodem a°

De aul' edwardi	iiij s
De drwdalehall'	xj s viij d
De stauntonhall'	xiij s iiij d
De brasenose	xxvij d
De Hamptonhall'	xx s ix d
Summa iij li xvj s ix d	

All' cam' eodem a°

De cam' gray	xx s
De cam' newby	vj s viij d
De cam' skarell	xvj s viij d
De cam' Cexby	xiij s iiij d
De cam' Nafferton'	xvj s viij d
De cam' Holwell'	xvj s viij d
De cam' Edwardi canonici	xxiij s iiij d
De cam' strykland et Ensf' sol' erat per strykland v s et remanet solvend'	x s
De cam' habu'	x s
De cam' canonici leyc'	x s
Summa vij li viij s iiij d	

Esex De Esex q° abdode	xxiiij li

All' scol' eodem a°

De scol' prentys	viij s
De scol' retro prentys	vj s viij d
De scol' ex o^{to} belff a retro de scharp	ij s
Summa xvj s viij d	

Summa omn' all' preceden' cxviij li iiij d[3]

[3] [ADMC] This total is correct if the Allowances of Rooms for 11 and 12 Hen IV can be brought into line with the Arrears of the following roll.

In communis et batellis a die veneris ante fest pent' a^{o} rr' Henr' quart' xiiij^{o} usque in diem veneris prox' post festum sancti petri dicti advincula

In prima septimana com' xx d 3 soc' et di'	v s x d
In batellis	viij d
In 2^{a} septimana com' xvij d 3 soc' et di'	iiij s xj d ob
In Journellis unius socij	v d
In 3^{a} septimana com' xv d 4 soc	v s
In batellis	ix d
In 4^{a} septimana com' xvj d 4 soc	v s iiij d
In 5 septimana com' xiiij d 4 soc	iiij s iiij d
In batellis	j d
In 6 septimana com' xv d ob' 4 soc	v s ij d
In batellis	iiij d
In 7 septimana com' xv d 3 soc et di'	iiij s iiij d ob
In journellis unius socij	iiij d
In batellis	vj d
In 8^{a} septimana com' xvj d 4 soc	v s iiij d
In 9^{a} septimana com' xvj d 3 soc	iiij s
In journellis unius socij	iiij d
In 10^{a} septimana com' xvj d 3 soc	iiij s
In batellis	j d ob
In 11^{a} septimana com' xv d 2 soc	ij s vj d
In journellis unius socij	vj d
In batellis	j d

Summa liiij s xj d ob'

Solvi eodem t^{e} [*sic*] pincerne pro diversis per coll' mutuatis pro domo	ij s iij d

A die veneris post advinculam sancti petri usque ad festum sancti martini episcopi quod die veneris hoc a^{o} contigit

In p^{a} septimana com' xv d ob' 2 soc et di'	iij s ij d ob
In journellis unius soc'	iiij d
In batellis	ij d
In 2^{a} septimana com' xvj d 2 soc	ij s viij d
In journellis unius soc'	iiij d
In batellis	iiij d
In 3^{a} septimana com' xv d unius soc et di'	xxij d ob
In journellis unius soc'	iiij d ob q^{a}
In batellis	iiij d

In 4[a] septimana com' xv d 2 soc	ij s vj d
In batellis	v d ob
In 5 septimana com' xv d ob 2 soc	ij s vij d
In batellis	xj d
In 6 septimana com' xvj d 2 soc	ij s viij d
In batellis	xij d
In 7 septimana com' xv d 2 soc	ij s vj d
In batellis	xiij d
In 8 septimana com' xv d 1 soc et di'	xxij d ob
In batellis	ij d ob
In 9 septimana com' xv d 3 soc	iij s ix d
In batellis	v d ob
In 10[a] septimana com' xv d 1 soc	xv d
In journellis unius soc'	vj d
In batellis	xj d
In 11[a] septimana com' xv d 3 soc et di'	iiij s iiij d ob
In batellis	ij d
In 12[a] septimana com' xv d 4 soc	v s
In 13[a] septimana com' xvij d 3 soc	iiij s vj d
In batellis	iiij d
In 14[a] septimana com' xv d 3 soc	iij s ix d
Summa l s vij s ob[4]	

A festo sancti martini inclusive ad diem veneris ante natalem domini inclusive

In p[a] septimana com' xv d 3 soc	iij s ix d
In batellis	ij d
In 2[a] septimana com' xv d 3 soc et di'	iiij s iiij d ob
In journellis unius soc'	iiij d
In batellis	iiij d ob
In 3[a] septimana com' xv d 4 soc	v s
In batellis	ij d
In 4[a] septimana com' xvij d 4 soc	v s viij d
In 5 septimana com' xvj d 4 soc	v s iiij d
In batellis	j d ob
In 6 septimana com' xv d 4 soc	v s
In batellis	ij d
In bat' pro diversis septimanis pro tegulatoribus et latomis	ij s

[4] [ADMC] The correct total is 50s 7¼d.

In uno quelebarw	xiiij d
Pro a retro resolutis in ult' compot'	iiij d ob
Summa xxxiiij s	

A die veneris prox' ante nat' domini usque ad diem veneris prox' ante festum annunciacionis beate virg' inclusive q' dies veneris erat vigilium eiusdem festi

In p^a septimana com' ij s iiij d 3 soc	vij s
In 2^a septimana com' xxiij d 4 soc	vij s iiij d
In 3^a septimana com' xv d 4 soc	v s
In batellis	vj d
In 4^a septimana com' xvj d 4 soc	v s iiij d
In 5 septimana com' xvj d 4 soc	v s iiij d
In 6 septimana com' xvij d 4 soc	v s viij d
In 7 septimana com' xvj d 2 soc	ij s viij d
In journellis unius soc'	vj d
In 8 septimana com' xv d 3 soc	iij s ix d
In batellis	j d
In 9 septimana com' xv d 4 soc	v s
In 10^a septimana com' xvj d 4 soc	v s iiij d
In 11^a septimana com' xix d 5 soc	vij s xj d
In 12 septimana com' xix d 5 soc	vij s xj d
In 13 septimana com' xvj d 5 soc	vj s viij d
In gaudijs sancti cutberti	xiiij s ob
In contrib' 5 soc' domus cuiuslibet xxij d	ix s ij d
Summa iiij li xix s ij d ob	

A vigilio annunciacionis beate virginis vigilium [*sic*] jo ante portam latinam q' vigilium est die veneris cont'

In p^a septimana com' xviij d 5 soc	vij s vj d
In 2^a septimana com' xviij d 5 soc	vij s vj d
In 3^a septimana com' xviij d 5 soc	vij s vj d
In 4 septimana com' xix d 5 soc	vij s xj d
In 5 septimana com' ij s 3 soc	vj s
In journellis unius soc'	iiij d
In 6 septimana com' xvj d 4 soc	v s iiij d
Summa xlij s vj d	

A vigilio s jo' ante portam latinam usque ad pent' exclusive

In p^a septimana com' xvj d 4 soc	v s iiij d
In batellis	iij d

In 2[a] septimana com' xvj d 5 soc	vj s viij d
In batellis	xiij d
In 3[a] septimana com' xvj d 5 soc	vj s viij d
In batellis	j d
In 4[a] septimana com' xvij d 5 soc	vij s ij d
In 5 septimana com' xvj d 5 soc	vj s viij d
In batellis	ij d
Summa xxxiiij s	

Summa omnium com' et bat' xv li xvij s vj d ob

In reparac' infra coll' et extra et expens' alijs diversimodis
xxxviij li xvj s x d q[a]

In resol'

In primis ballivis regis extra portam borialem	xviij d
Abb' de osenay	vj s
Ecclesie beate marie	xij d
Abb' de Enesham pro schop' super angulum quad'	viij s
De firma quond' otterworth	iij s viij d
Abb' de Godstow	vij s
Summa xxvij s ij d	

In penc'

M Johi Castell	xxvj s viij d
M Ad' Redyforth	xiij s iiij d
M Johi Hamerton'	xiij s iiij d
M Johi Ryvell'	xiij s iiij d
Summa iij li vj s viij d	

Procuratori coll' x s

Summa totalis omn' all' viij[xx] li xvij li xviij s vj d ob q[a]

Et sic computatis computandis et allocatis allocandis debet procurator computans collegio xxxj s iij d q[a]

⟨Will' Sulbury Canc'⟩

[*A roll of two membranes, in fair condition, but written in a rather untidy hand.*]

WHITSUN 1 HENRY V to WHITSUN 2 HENRY V (ROLL UC:BU1/F/24)

11 June 1413–27 May 1414

BURSAR: ADAM RADFORD

de tempore Ade Radyforth Anno Henrici quinti p^{o}

Compotus procuratoris coll' Willelmi de dunelm' Magn' Aule universitatis wlgariter nuncupat' a fest pent' inclusive Anno rr' Henr' quinti primo usque ad idem festum exclusive anno rr' Henr' quinti ij^{o}

[*The Arrears are identical with the Allowances in* ***F/23*** *above, save for a few changes in spelling.*]

Summa omn' arr' precedenc' cxviij li iiij d

Redditus eiusdem coll' de an^{o} rr' Henr' quinti post conquestum primo

De ten' Alic' frenche	l s
De ten' Cowley	xl s
De ten' Glover	iij li
De Thom^{a} Coke pro prato quond' Glover	xxvj s viij d
De ten' quond' Holway	xv s
De ten' Cambrey	xv s viij d
De ten' Joh' Roer	xij d
De Gard' Cambrey	iij s iiij d
De Gard' ric' Cariour	iiij s iiij d
De Gard' Ade Revyer	iij s
De Novo Coll' pro Maydenhall'	x s
De Gard' Thome Hampton'	iij s
De Gard' quond' uxoris hamton'	viij s
De ten' Rob leyc'	viij s
De Gard' ex o^{to} sancti egidij	xij d
De Gard' ric' barbour	iij s
De coll' cant'	ij s vj d
De Abb' de Godstow pro una scopa iuxta sanctam frideswid'	xx d
De Holdernes	iij li vj d
De Sprount	xvj d
De Joh' Schaw pro prato Irelond	xxvj s viij d

De ten' Mic' Talyour xv s

De scop' super angulum quad' xx s

De ten' philippi Cordwaner xxv s x d

De Thomas Bayly Masun pro quibusdam terris quond' de tenura Mayster viij s

Summa xxj li iiij s vj d

Esex'

De Esex' xx li

Redditus Aul' eodem an°

De Brasinose iij li vj s viij d

De Aula scuti vj s viij d

De Aula sancti Thome x s

De parva aula universitatis in vico scolarum xxxiij s iiij d

De Hampton' Hall' xl s

De Aula Edwardi xxiiij s

De Drowdalehall' xlv s

De Staunton' hall' xiij s iiij d

Summa xj li xix s

Redditus cam' eodem an°

De cam' Midilton' xx s

De cam' Gray xx s

De cam' Ase x s

De cam' leyc' x s

De cam' halu' xvj s viij d

De cam' Bugwyk pro una xvj s vij d pro alia xiij s iiij d

~~De cam' canonici~~

De cam' Barton' xx s

De cam' Kekysby xiij s iiij d

De cam' Nafferton' xvj s viij d

De cam' Paryce xiij s iiij d

De cam' Eynsforth x s

Summa ix li

Redditus scolarum eodem an°

De Scol' Multon' viij s

De Scol' canaby vj s viij d

De Scol' clerk	vj s viij d
Summa xxj s iiij d	

Summa omn' Reddituum lxiij li iiij s x d

Recept' de Burton' xxxj s iij d q[a]

Summa omn' oneratorum ciiij[xx] li vj s v d[1]

All' ten' de anno rr' Henr' quarti post conquestum vij[o]

De Johanne Barbour	xx d
De Ad' Ryver	iij s
De Rob' Leyc'	ij s viij d
De Holdernes	vj d
De Cowley	xiij s iiij d
Summa xxj s ij d	

All' aularum et cam' eodem a[o]

De Aul' edwardi	vij s iiij d
De cam' henley	iij s iiij d
De cam' Canonici de Notley	iij s iiij d
De cam' moreton	iij s iiij d
De cam' Nafferton'	iij s iiij d
De cam' foston'	iij s iiij d
De cam' Cleseby	xiij s iiij d
Summa xxxvij s iiij d	

All' ten' de a[o] eiusdem viij[o]

De Cowley	x s
De Rob' leyc'	viij s
De Holdernes	xij d
De Schop' super angulum quad'	iiij d
Summa xix s iiij d	

All' aul' eodem an[o]

De drwdell' hall'	v s
De Stawntonhall'	vj s viij d
Summa xj s viij d	

All' cam' eodem an[o]

De cam' Henley	x s

[1] [ADMC] This total should be £182 16s 5¼d.

	De cam' Nafferton'	iij s iiij d
	De cam' ffoston'	xvj s viij d
	Summa xxx s	
	All' ten' de a° eiusdem ix°	
	De Cowley	xxx s
	De Scop' super angulum quad'	iiij d
	De Ad' Ryver	iij s
	De Rob' leyc'	viij s
	De Holdernes	xij d
	Summa xlij s iiij d	
	All' aul' et scol' et cam' eodem an°	
	De Staunton' Hall'	iij s iiij d
	De parva aul' universitatis in alto vico	iij s iiij d
	De Scol' ffrowyk	v s xj d
	De Cam' Nafferton'	x s
	Summa xxij s vij d	
	All' ten' de a° eiusdem x°	
	De Mercer	ij s vj d
	De Glover	v li xj s
	De Scop' super angulum quadrivij	iiij d
+	~~De ten' Cawmbray~~	~~vij s xj d~~
	De Ad' Ryver	iij s
	De Rob' leyc'	iij s
	De Holdernes	xij d
	Summa vj li x d	
	All' cam' et aul' eodem an°	
	De parva aul' universitatis in alto vico	iij s iiij d
	De cam' Naffirton'	iij s iiij d
	De cam' Makblyth	x s
	Summa xvj s viij d	
	All' \`ten'' de anno eiusdem xj°	
	De ten' mercer	vij s vj d
	De Sprunt	xvj d
	De Glover	xv s
	De Schopa super angulum quadrivij	iiij d
+	~~De ten' Cawmbray~~	~~xv s ix d~~
	De gardino cawmbray	iij s iiij d

De Adam rev'	iij s
De Holdernes	xij d
De Cowley	x s
De Roberto leycet'	viij s
Summa xlix s vj d	

All' de Esex

De anno x	xiij li xiij s iiij d
De anno xj	xx li xvij s j d per lythefot
Summa xxxiiij li x s v d	

All' aularum de eodem anno

De staunton' hall'	vj s viij d
De parva aula universitatis in alto vico	xliij s iiij d per bruns
Summa l s	

All' scolarum et camerarum eodem anno

De Scolis punter	xvj d
De camera eynsforth	vj s viij d
De camera nafferton'	iij s iiij d
De camera benham'	iij s iiij d
De camera makeblythe	x s
Summa xxiiij s viij d	

All' ten' de a° eiusdem xij°

De glover	iij li xx d
~~De Cambrey~~	
De Adam Ryver	iij s
De Thoma Hampton'	ij s iiij d
De Roberto layc'	viij s
De holdernes	xix s
De Sprunt	xvj d
Summa iiij li xv s iiij d	

All' aularum eodem anno

De droudalehall'	v s
De hampton hall ⟨remissum⟩	iij s iiij d
De parva aula universitatis in alto vico	xxiij s iiij d
De staunton hall'	xiij s iiij d
De scol' Schotton'	vj s viij d
Summa lj s viij d	

All' cam' de eodem anno

De camera naffirton'	iij s iiij d
De camera hurle	iiij s
De camera Makeblythe	xiij s iiij d
Summmma xx s viij d	

All' ten' de a° eiusdem xiij°

De ten' cambrey	xvij s viij d
De glover	iij li v s viij d
De Schop' super angulum quadrivij	iiij d
De Adam ryver	iij s
De Holdernes	vij s viij d
De Sprunt	xvj d
De mic' talyor	vij s j d
De Rob' leyc'	v s viij d
Summa v li viij s v d	

All' Aularum eodem anno

De parva aula universitatis in alto vico	x s
De Staunton' hall'	xiij s iiij d
Summa xxiij s iiij d	

All' camerarum eodem anno

De camera Henley	x s
De camera Eaynysforth	iij s iiij d
De camera horl	iij s iiij d
De camera Holvell'	xvj s viij d
De cam' naffirton'	iij s iiij d
Summa xxxvj s viij d	

Allocaciones tene' de anno eiusdem xiiij°

De ten' glover	iij li viij d
De ~~ten'~~ gardino Ric' caryour	iiij d
De gardino Ade Ryver	iij s
De schop' super angulum quad'	iiij d
De gardino Thoma Hampton'	iij s
De roberto layc'	vj s
De Abbathia de godstow	x d
De Holdernes	vj d
De Sprunt	xvj d

De Cambray	viij d
Summa iij li xvj s viij d	
Summa omn' All' precedencium lxxvij li ix s iij d[2]	

[*Dorse*]

All' aularum de eodem a° xiiij	
De aula edwardi	iiij s
De droudalehall'	xj s viij d
De Stauntonhall'	xiij s iiij d
De hampton' hall'	xx s ix d per benet
Summa xlix s ix d	
All' camerarum de eodem anno	
De camera gray	x s
De camera nuby	vj s viij d
De camera Staryll'	viij s viij d
De [*blank*]	
De camera naffirton'	iij s viij d
De camera Holwell'	xvj s viij d
De camera edwardi canonici	x s
De camera enysforth	viij s iiij d[3]
Summa iij li iij s viij d	
Essexe	
De essex quo ad bod	xxiiij li
All' scolarum de eodem anno	
De scol' prentis	viij s
De scol' supra prentis	vj s viij d
De scol' ex opposito belfront de scharp	ij s
Summa xvj s viij d	
All ten' de anno p° regis Henrici quinti	
De ten' Cowley	x s
De ten' Glover	iij li
De ten' cambrey	xv s viij d
De ten' Johannis Roer	vj s
De gardino Cambrey	iij s iiij d
De gard' Ric' carier	iiij s iiij d

2 [ADMC] This total has been written over an erasure.
3 Some notes follow here, which are now illegible.

De gardino Ade Ryver	iij s
De gardino Thome Hampton’	iij s
De gardino quond’ uxoris hampton’	viij s
De ten’ Roberti layc’	viij s
De gardino ex o^{to} sancti egidij	xij d
De gardino Ric’ barbor	iij s
De collegio cant’	ij s vj d
De abb’ de godstow pro una scop’ iuxta frideswidam	xx d
De Holdernes	iij li vj d
De Sprunt	xvj d
De ten’ Mic’ Talyur	xv s
De scop’ super anglo [*sic*] quad’	iiij d
Summa x li vj s viij d	

All’ de essex de eodem a^{o}

De Esex’	xviij li vj s viij d

All’ aularum de eodem anno

~~De Brasinose~~	
De parva aula universitatis in vico scorarum [*sic*]	vj s viij d
De aula edwardi	xiiij s
De drowdalhall’	xlv s
De Staunton’ hall’	xiij s iiij d
Summa iij li xix s	

All’ camerarum de eodem anno

De camera Midilton’	xx s
De camera gray	xx s
De camera ase	x s
De camera leyc’	x s
De camera hallum	xvj s viij d
~~De cam’ canonici~~	
De cameris Bugwith	xxx s
De camera barton’	vj s viij d
~~De camera Kexby~~	~~xiij s iiij d~~
De camera naffirton’	xvj s viij d
De camera parys	xiij s iiij d
De camera eynsforth	x s
Summa vij li xiij s iiij d	

All' aularum [4] de eodem anno
De scolis clerk vj s viij d

All' communarum de eodem anno
Solvi johanni telin in parte soluciones xiiij li v s ix d – vj li vj s viij d et deb[*entur*] telin vj li xix s j d
Item pro gaudijs sancti cuthberti
ix s ij d ob' et debentur Johanni telin x s ob'
Summa vj li xv s x d ob'

All' reparacionum de eodem anno
Item peto allocari pro reparacionibus factis infra collegium et extra ut patet per papirum xij li xvij s

All' expensarum facta [. . .] versus esex
In primis [. . .] xxviij s x d ob'
Item alias [. . .] londonias ubi recepissem aurum iij s iiij d
Item ita ultimo in expensis versus esex xxxvj s viij d
Summa totalis iij li viij s x d ob'

All' pro alijs expensis
In primis pro labore beltoft versus Hull' ij s
Item carpentario incarcerato et alijs parvis expensis iij s xj d
Summa v s xj d

All' resolucionum
In primis Willelmo vresteler balivo extra portam borealem ix d
Item colectoribus regis xvj d
Item procuratoribus eccelesie sancti petri pro tempore burton' ij s x d
Item abb' de Oseney vj s
Item procuratoribus ecclesie beate virginis xij d
Item procuratori domus beate fridisvide vj s viij d
Item lotrici pro duobus terminis ij s vj d
Item thome Coke xx s
Item abb' de Evesam viij s
Summma lj s xj d

In penc' sociorum
In primis magistro Johanni Castell magistro domus l s

[4] *Sic*; this is an error for **scolarum**.

Item magistro Johanni Revel vj s viij d
Summa lvj s viij d

Item procuratori domus x s

~~Summa totalis~~ Summa totalis istius lateris C li viij s viij d

Eciam petit computans allocari de viij s pro terris noviter ad firmam dimissis [. . .] lathomo

Et sic computatis computandis et allocatis allocandis M Adam procurator debet domui [*figure either erased or illegible – could be £4 10s 6d?*]

⟨Per cancellarium Willelmum Barowe⟩

⟨Computans solvit debitum istius rotuli et acquietatus est inter socios⟩

[*A wide roll of 2 membranes; there is a small hole near the head, but the rest of it is in fair condition.*]

WHITSUN 2 HENRY V to WHITSUN 3 HENRY V (ROLL UC:BU1/F/25)

27 May 1414–19 May 1415

BURSAR: JOHN HAMERTON

hamerton Anno Henrici quinti secundo

Compotus procuratoris Collegij Magistri Willelmi de dunelm' magne Aule Universitatis vulgariter nuncupat' a festo pentecost' inclusive Anno Regni Regis Henr' quinti secundo usque ad idem festum exclusive anno revoluto.

[*The Arrears are identical with the Allowances in* ***F/24*** above, save for a few changes in spelling.]

Summa omn' arr' precedencium vij^{xx} viij li xix s viij d

Redditus ten' eiusdem Colleg' de anno Reg' Reg' Henr' quinto secundo[1]

De ten' Alic' french	l s
De ten' quond' Cowley	xl s
De ten' Glover	iij li
De novo ten' iuxta ten' Glover	xxx s
De Thoma Coke pro prato quond' Glover	xxvj s viij d
De ten' quond' holway	xv s
De ten' Cawmbray	xv s viij d
De Gardino Cawmbray scilicet modo Johannis wykam	iij s iij d
De ten Johannis Roer	[*xij s iiij d*][2]
De Gardino Ricardi Karyer	iiij s iiij d
De Gardino Ade Ryver	iij s
De novo Collegio pro Madynhall'	x s
De Gardino Thome Hampton'	iij s
De Gardino quond' ux' Hampton' scilicet modo Thome Hampton' Sadleir	viij s

[1] This part of the roll is badly faded, and the entries very faint. It appears to have been painted with gall by William Smith in order to read the entries for himself (see Section 3 of the Introduction).

[2] The roll is illegible here; this total would make this section add up correctly. However, the Allowances for 2 Henry V below claim that Roer owed 15s 8d for this year, which would lead to an incorrect total here.

De ten' quond' Roberti lacestr'	viij s
De Gardino ex o^{to} Sancti Egidij	xij d
De Gardino Ricardi Barbour	iij s
De Colleg' Cantuar'	ij s vj d
De abb' de Godstow pro una schoppa iuxta sanctam ffrideswydam	xx d
De Holderness	iij li
De Sprunt	xvj d
De Johanne Schaw pro prato yreland'	xxvj s viij d
De ten' Mich' Talyour	xv s
De Schopa super angulum quadrivij	xx s
De ten' philippi Cordewyner	xxvj s viij d
De Bayly Mason pro quibusdam terris in tenura Thoma Maister	viij s
Summa xxij li xv s iij d	

Redditus de Esex eodem a^{o}

De Essexe	xx li per [. . .]em et John Hut
Summa patet	

Redditus Aularum eodem anno

De Brasenose	iij li vj s viij d
De Aula Scuti	vj s viij d
De Aula sancti Thome	x s
De parva Aula universitatis in vico scolarum	xxxiij s iiij d
De Hampton' Hall'	xl s
De Aula Edwardi	xxiiij s
De Drowdalhall'	xlv s
De Stauntonhall'	xiij s iiij d
Summa xj li xix s	

Redditus Camerarum eodem anno

De Camera Mydylton magna camera	xx s
De Camera Halon'	xx s
De Camera Ase	x s
De Camera lacestr'	x s
De Camera Nafferton'	xvj s viij d
De Camera Parys	xiij s iiij d
De Camera Kexby	xiij s iiij d
De Camera Enseford'	x s
De Camera Barton'	xx s

De Camera Brasebryg'	xvj s viij d
De Camera ffytzhue	xvj s viij d
De Camera Appylton	xiij s iiij d
Summa ix li	

Redditus Scolarum eodem anno

De Scol' Magistri Johannis Elys	viij s
De Scol' magistri Ric' Brodon'	vj s viij d
De Scol' magistri Joh' Eland'	vj s viij d
Summa xxj s iiij d	

Summa iij^{xx} iiij li xv s vij d

Memorandum quod computans rendit de – xviij s j d receptis pro diversis bonis et catallis arestatis in com' Esex'
Item rendit de – xij li xvj s ij d receptis pro granis arestatis in Com' predicto
Item computans rendit de – iij s iiij d receptis de Canonico Buttyllar' et de – iij s iiij d receptis de Johanne de luca. Item rendit de vj s viij d recept' de Radulph Sclatter'
[*in different ink*] Item comput' de xvj marcis recept' a magistro collegij

Summa omnium oneratorum ccxxviij li xxij d[3]

Alloc' ten' de Anno Reg' Regis Henr' quarti septimo

De Johanne Barbour	xx d
De Adam Ryver	iij s scilicet non debentur
De Roberto Lacestr'	ij s viij d
De Holdernes	vj d
De Cowley	xiij s iiij d
Summa xxj s ij d	

Alloc' Aularum et Camerarum eodem Anno

De Aula Edwardi	vij d iiij d
De Camera Canonici de Notelay	iij s iiij d
De Camera Morton'	iij s iiij d
De Camera Nafferton'	iij s iiij d
De Camera ffoston'	iij s iiij d
De Camera Clesby	xiij s iiij d
Summa xxxiiij s	

3 [ADMC] The total is correct excluding the last item of 16 marks.

Alloc' ten' de anno predicti Reg' Henr' viij^{vo}

De Cowley	x s
De Robero lacestr'	viij s
De Holdernesse	xij d
De Schopa super angulum quadr'	iiij d
Summa xix s iiij d	

Alloc' Aularum eodem anno

De Drowdelhall'	v s
De Stauntonhall'	vj s viij d
Summa xj s viij d	

Alloc' Camerarum eodem a^{o}

De Camera Nafferton'	iij s iiij d
De Camera ffoston'	xvj s viij d
Summa xx s	

Alloc' ten' de anno eiusdem Regis Henr' nono

De ten' Cowley	xxx s
De Scop' super Angulum quadr'	iiij d
De Adam Ryver	iij s scilicet non [*debentur*][4]
De Robero lacestr'	viij s
De Holderness	xij d
Summa xlij s iiij d	

[*Dorse*]

Alloc' Aularum scolarum et camerarum eodem anno

De Staunton' Hall'	iij s iiij d
De parva aul' universitatis in alto vico	iij s iiij d
De scolis frowyk	v s xj d
De Camera Nafferton'	x s
Summa xxij s vij d	

Alloc' ten' de anno eiusdem regis decimo

De Mercer	ij s vj d
De Glover	v li xij d
De Schoppa super angulum quadr'	iiij d
De Adam Ryver	iij s [*scilicet non debentur*]
De Roberto lacestr'	iij s

[4] The roll is very faint at this point. Items in square brackets have been taken from the Arrears section of roll **F/26** below.

De Holderness	[*xvj d*]
Summa v li x s [*x d*]	
Alloc' Camerarum et aularum eodem anno	
De parva aula universitatis in alto vico	iij s iiij d
De Camera Nafferton'	iij s iiij d
De Camera Makeblyth	x s
Summa xvj s viij d	
Alloc' ten' de anno eiusdem undecimo	
De ten' Mercer	vij s vj d
De Sprunt	xvj d
De Glover	xv s
De Schopa super angulum quadr'	iiij d
De ~~Gardino cawmbray~~	[*blank*]
De Adam Ryver'	iij s scilicet non [*debentur*]
De Holdernesse	xij d
De Cowley	x s
De Roberto lacestr'	viij s
Summa xlvj s ij d	
Alloc' de Esex	
De Anno decimo	xij li xiij s iiij d
De Anno undecimo	xx li xvij s j d per lygh[*tfot*]
Summa xxxiiij li x s v d	
Alloc' Aularum de eodem anno	
De Stauntonhall'	vj s viij d
De parva aula universitatis in alto vico	xliij s iiij d per Brons
Summa l s	
Alloc' Scolarum et camerarum eodem anno	
De Scol' pont'	xvj d
De Camera Ensford	vj s viij d
De Camera Nafferton'	iij s iiij d
De Camera Beneham'	iij s iiij d
De Camera Makeblyth	x s
Summa xxiiij s viij d	
Alloc' ten' de Anno eiusdem Regis duodecimo	
De Glover	iij li xx d
De Adam Ryver	iij s scilicet non debentur
~~De Thoma Hampton'~~	~~ij s iiij d~~

De Roberto lacestr'	viij s
De Holderness	xix s
De Sprunt	xvj d
Summa iiij li xiij s	
Alloc' Aularum eodem anno	
De Drowdalhall'	v s scilicet remittentur
De Hamptonhall'	iij s iiij d scilicet remittentur
De Stauntonhall'	xiij s iiij d
De Scolis Schotton'	vj s viij d
Summa xxviij s iiij d	
Alloc' Camerarum eodem Anno	
De Camera nafferton'	iij s iiij d
De Camera Hurle	iiij s
De Camera Makeblyth	xiij s iiij d
Summa xx s viij d	
Alloc' ten' de anno eiusdem Regis Henr' tercio decimo	
De Glover	iij li v s viij d
De Schoppa super angulum quadr'	iiij d
De Adam Ryver	iij s scilicet non debentur
De Holdernes	vij s viij d
De Sprunt	xvj d
De Roberto lacestr'	v s viij d
Summa iiij li iij s viij d	
Alloc' Aul' de eodem a^{o}	
De Stauntonhall'	xiij s iiij d
Summa patet	
Alloc' Camerar' eodem anno	
De Camera Enseford	iij s iiij d
De Camera Hurle	iij s iiij d
De Camera Henley	xx d
De Camera Nafferton'	iij s iiij d
Summa xj s viij d	
Alloc' ten' de anno eiusdem quarto decimo	
De Ten' Glover	iij li viij d
De Gardino Ade Ryver	iij s scilicet non debentur
De Schopa super angulum quadr'	iiij d
De Roberto lacestr'	vj s

De Holdernes	vj d
De Sprunt	xvj d
Summa iij li xj s x d	
Alloc' Aularum eodem anno	
De Aula Edwardi	iiij s
De Drowdalehall'	xj s viij d [*scilicet remittentur*]
De Stauntonhall'	xiij s iiij d
De Hamptonhall'	xx s ix d per benet
Summa xlix s ix d	
Alloc' Camerarum eodem anno	
De Camera Scarle	viij s viij d
De Camera Nafferton'	iij s viij d
De Camera Holwell	xiij s viij d
De Camera Edwardi canonici	x s
De Camera Ensford	viij s iiij d
	[*scilicet debet [. . .] iij s iiij d de isto camera*]
Summa xliij s viij d	
Alloc' de Essex' eodem a^{o}	
De Essex quo ad Bode	xxij li xiij s iiij d
Summa patet	
Alloc' Scol' de eodem a^{o}	
De scol' ex o^{to} Belfront per Scharp	ij s
Summa patet	
Alloc' ten' de Anno p^{o} Regis Henr' quinti	
De Ten' Glover	iij li
De Ten' Cawmberay	xij s v d
De Terris baylly Mayson	iiij s
De Gardino Ade Ryver	iij s [*scilicet non debentur*]
De Gardino Thome Hampton'	xx d
De Ten' Roberti lacestr'	viij s
De Holdernes	vj d
De Sprunt	xvj d
De Shopa super angulum quadr'	iiij d
Summa iiij li xj s iij d	
Alloc' de Essex eodem anno	
De Essex' per Bode	xviij li vj s viij d
Summa patet	

Alloc' aul' eodem a°

De Drowdalhall'	v s vj d q[a]
	[*scilicet remittuntur v s*]
De Staunton' hall'	xiij s iiij d
Summa xviij s x d q[a]	

Alloc' Camerarum eodem a°

De Camera Halom	vj s viij d
De Camera Bubwyth	xxx s
De Camera Nafferton'	[*iij s*] iiij d
De Camera Ensford	x s
Summa l s	

Allocac' ten' a° Regis Henr' v[i] secundo

De Ten' novo iuxta ten' Thome Glover	[*x*]v s
	[*levand' de terris Nat' sancti Johannis et Mich'*]
De Ten' Glover	iij li
De Ten' Cambery	xv s [*viij d*]
De Ten' Johannis Royer	ij s
De Gardino Cambery	ij s vj d
De Gardino Ade Ryver	iij s [*scilicet non debentur*]
De Gardino Thome Hampton'	iij s
De Ten' quond' Roberti lacestr'	viij s
De Gardino ex o[to] sancti Egidij	xij d
De Holdernese	iij li vj d
De Sprunt	xvj d
De Ten' Mich' Taylour	vij s j d
De schopa super angulum [*quadr'*]	iiij d
De Bayly Mason pro terris quond' in tenura [*Thome Glover*]	viij s
Summa ix li vij d v d	

Alloc' de Essex' eodem Anno x li pro Bode de termino sancti Mich'

Alloc' Aularum eodem Anno

De parva Aula universitatis in vico scolarum	v s ix d q[a]
De Aula Edwardi	viij s viij d
De Drowdalhall'	xviij s iiij d
	[*scilicet remittuntur v s*]
De Stauntonhall'	xiij s iiij d
Summa xlvj s j d q[a]	

Alloc' Camerar' eodem Anno

De Camera Mydylton'	xx s
De Camera Halon	xx s
De Camera Ase	vij s
De Camera lacestr'	iij s iiij d
De Camera Barton'	x s
De Camera Nafferton'	xvj s viij d
De Camera ffytzhue	xvj s viij d
De Camera Parysse	xiij s iij d
De Camera Brasebrygge	xvj s viij d
De Camera [*Ensford*]	x s
De Camera App[*ilton'*]	vj s viij d
Summa vij li iiij d	

Alloc' scolarum de eodem Anno

De M Joh' [*Holys*]	xvj d
De M Johe' [*Eland'*]	iij s iiij d
Summa iiij s viij d	

Alloc' comunarum [et gaudiorum a retro Jo. telet que fuerit [*sic*] M^ri^ Adam ult^e[5]]
ut patet in compoto eiusdem [. . .] viij li [*j d ob*[6]

Alloc' [*pro communibus*] et contribucionibus sociorum cum batellis [*Collegij a*] festo [*pent'*] inclusive [*anni regni Regis Henr' quinti*] secundo usque ad idem festum exclusive [. . .] [xij li xj s iij d ob'[7]]

Alloc' reparacionum infra collegium [*et extra ut*] patet per papirum ix li xvij s vj s ob

Alloc' expensarum infra [villam et extra] ut patet per papirum xvj li xj s ix d ob

Alloc' resolucionum

In primis Abbat' de [*Godst*]ow [*?xxj s*] a retro de temporibus quibus M. Burton et M Adam fuerunt [. . .] procuratores

Item eidem Abbatiss' xiij [*?*] in plenam solucionem omn' arr'

Item Abbat' de Osenay de termino [?] sancti Mich' iij s

[5] [ADMC] Illegible text; this is as given by Smith on Vol. VIII 72.

[6] [ADMC] This figure deduced from the last roll, **F/24**.

[7] [ADMC] This figure is from Smith. I suggest that it must actually be 'xiij li xj s iij d ob' (despite Smith); otherwise the total is wrong.

Item Priori Monasterij sancte ffrideswyde liij s iiij d
in persolucione omn' arr'
Item Thome Duke xviij d [. . .] denar' fuerunt a retro de [*tempore*] M Ade
Item Willelmo Wyr[. . .]er pro eod' Gard' iiij d ob' de termino annunciacionis beate virginis
Item procuratoribus ecclesie beate virginis xij d
Item procutoribus [*ecclesie sancti petri*] in orientis ij s x d
Summa v li v s ob'

Alloc' pensionibus socior' collegij
In primis magistro iij li xv s iiij d ob
Item M Roberto Burton' xxxiiij s iiij d
Item M Ade liij s iiij d
Item M Johanni hamerton' iij li vj s viij d
Item M Johanni Rywell' xxiij s iiij d
s[*ibi*] a retro de antiquo debita
Summa xij li xij s ob'

Alloc' pro stipendijs famulorum
In primis Johanni Telm' pro salario suo pro tribus annis xl s
Item Thome Coco in plenam solucionem sui salarij vj s viij d
Item Thome Barbitonsori vj s viij d
Item Thome Coco pro stipendio sue ix' defunct' quond' lotricis v s
Item lotrici Collegij v s
Summa iij li iij s iiij d

Item computans petit allocari pro opere suo xx s
Item computans petit allocari de xx s debitus tribus socijs ex antiquo arreragio domus

Summa totalis omn' Allocat' ccxxiiij li xvj s vj s ob'

Et sic computatis computandis et allocatis allocandis Computans debet Collegio iij li v s iij d ob

⟨Willelmus Baron Cancellarius⟩

[*A roll of 2 membranes; the ink is now very faint in many places.*]

WHITSUN 3 HENRY V to WHITSUN 4 HENRY V (ROLL UC:BU1/F/26)

19 May 1415–7 June 1416

BURSAR: JOHN HAMERTON

hamerton'

Compotus M Johannis Hamerton Procuratoris Collegij Magistri Willelmi [*de dunelm'*] Magne Aule universitatis vulgariter nuncupat' a festo Pentecost' [*inclusive*] Anno Regni Regis Henr' quint' tercio usque ad idem festum exclusive [*anno revolu*]to

[*The Arrears are identical with the Allowances in* **F/25** *above, save for a few changes in spelling. No final total of Arrears, however, is given.*]

Redditus ten' eiusdem Collegij de a° regni Regis Henr' quinti tercio

De ten' nuper Alic' ffrench	l s
De ten' Thome Mayst' Glov' [*sic*]	iij li
De novo ten' iuxta ten' Thome Maister	xxviij s iiij d
De Thoma Coke pro prat' quondam Thome Maister	xxvj s viij d
De ten' quond' Holway	xv s
De ten' Cawmbray	xv s viij d
De ten' Johannis Royer	xij s
De Gardino Johannis Wychame	iij s
De Gardino Ric' Carior'	iiij s iiij d
De Gardino Ade Riwer	iij s
De Novo Colleg' pro Maydyn' Hall'	x s
De Gardino Thome Hampton' Sadler'	iij s
De ten' quond' Roberti lacestr'	viij s
De Gardino ex opposito ecclesie Sancti Egidij	x d
De Gardino Ric' Barbour	iij s
De Colleg' Cantuar'	ij s vj d
De Abb' de Godstow pro quadam schoppa iuxta ecclesiam sancte frediswyde	xx d
De Holdernesse	iij li vj d
De Spront	xvj d
De Johanne Schawe pro prato yreland	xxvj s viij d
De Mich' Taylyour	xv s
De Schoppa super angulum quadrivij	xx s

De ten' Philippi Corwyner	xxvj s viij d
De Bayly Mason pro quibusdam terris in tenura Thoma Maister	viij s
Summa xx li x s ij d	

Redditus de Essex eodem a°

De Essexe per Rectorem de Margret Rodynges et Johannem Howtt'	xx li
Summa patet	

Redditus aularum eodem a°

De Brasenose	iij li vj s viij d
De Aula Scuti	vj s viij d
De Aula sancti Thome	x s
De parva Aula universitatis in vico scolarum	xxxiij s iiij d
De Hampton' Hall'	xl s
De Aula Edwardi	xxiiij s
De Drowdalhall'	xlv s
De Stauntonhall'	xiij s iiij d
Summa xj li xix s	

Redditus camerarum eodem a°

De camera domini Ricardi Petr'	xvj s viij d
De camera Magistri Roberto fytzhue	xx s
De [*entry erased*]	
De camera laycest'	x s
De camera Nafferton'	xvj s viij d
De camera Mich' Jamyse	xiij s iiij d
De camera Kaexby	xiij s iiij d
De camera Ensford'	x s
De camera Barton'	xx s
De camera Appilton'	xiij s iiij d
Summa vj li xiij s iiij d	

Redditus scolarum eodem a°

De scolis Magistri Johannis Elys	viij s
De scolis Magistri Thome Bernat	vj s viij d
De scolis Thome Catell' Bagillarij	ij s ij d
Summa xvj s x d	

Summa omn' reddituum lix li xix s iiij d

[*Dorse*]

Memorandum quod computans respondet de iij li iiij s ij d, recept' pro granis in Com' Essex.

Item respondet de ij s recept' de Johanne de luta Item respondet de vj s viij d recept' de Cawnbra[*y*]

Item respondet de iij s iiij d recept' de Halon' de anno presenti

Item computans respondet de iij li v s iij d ob rem' in manibus suis quando ultimo computavit

Summa vij li xvij d ob'

Summa omnium oneratorum ccxx li vij s ij d

Alloc' ten' de Anno Reg' Regis Henr' quarti vij^mo^

De Johe Barbur	xx d
De Adam Ryver	iij s scilicet non debentur
De Roberto laycestr'	ij s viij d
De Holdernesse	vj d
De Cowlay	xiij s iiij d
Summa xxj s ij d	

Alloc' Aularum et Camerarum eodem a^o^

De Aula Edwardi	vij s iiij s [*sic*]
De Camera Canonici de Noteley	iij s iiij d
De Camera Morton'	iij s iiij d
De Camera Nafferton'	iij s iiij d
De Camera ffoston'	iij s iiij d
De Camera Clesby	xiij s iiij d
Summa xxxiiij s	

Alloc' ten' de a^o^ predicti Reg' Henr' viij^vo^

De Cowlay	x s
De Roberto lacestr'	viij s
De Holdernesse	xij d
De Schoppa super Angulum quadr'	iiij d
Summa xix s iiij d	

Alloc' Aularum eodem a^o^

De Drowdellhall'	v s
De Stauntonhall'	vj s viij d
Summa xj s viij d	

Alloc' Camerarum eodem a°

De Camera Nafferton'	iij s iiij d
De Camera ffoston'	xvj s viij d
Summa xx s	

Alloc' ten' de a° eiusdem Regis Henr' nono

De Ten' Cowlay	xxx s
De Schoppa super Angulum quadr'	iiij d
De Ad' Ryver	iij s scilicet non debentur
De Roberto lacestr'	viij s
De Holdernesse	xij d
Summa xlij s iiij d	

Alloc' Aularum scolarum et camerarum eodem anno

De Staunton' Hall'	iij s iiij d
De Parva aula universitatis in alto vico	iij s iiij d
De Scolis ffrowykes	v s xj d
De Camera Nafferton'	x s
Summa xxij s vij d	

Alloc' ten' de anno eiusdem Regis decimo

De Mercer	ij s vj d
De Glover	v li xij d
De Schoppa super angulum quadr'	iiij d
De Ad' Ryver	iij s scilicet non debentur
De Roberto lacestr'	iij s
De Holdernesse	xij d
Summa v li x s x d	

Alloc' aularum et Camerarum eodem anno

De Parva Aula universitatis in alto vico	iij s iiij d
De Camera Nafferton'	iij s iiij d
De Camera Makeblyth	x s
Summa xvj s viij d	

Alloc' \`ten'' de a° eiusdem Regis undecimo

De Ten' Mercer	vij s vj d
De Spront	xvj d
De Glover	xv s
De Schoppa super Angulum quadr'	iiij d
De Adam Ryver'	iij s scilicet non debentur
De Holdernesse	xij d

De Cowlay	x s
De Roberto lacestr'	viij s
Summa xlvj s ij d	
Alloc' de Esex	
De anno decimo	xij li xiij s iiij d
De anno undecimo	xx li xvij s j d per lyghtfot
Summa xxxiiij li x s v d	
Alloc' Aularum eodem A°	
De Stantonhall'	vj s viij d
De Parva Aula universitatis in alto vico	xxiij s iiij d per Brows
Summa xxx s	
Alloc' scol' et camerarum eodem Anno	
De Scolis ponter	xvj d
De Camera Nafferton'	iij s iiij d
De Camera Beneham'	iij s iiij d
De Camera Makeblyth	x s
Summa xviij s	
Alloc' ten' de A° eiusdem Regis xij°	
De Glover	iij li xx d
De Adam Ryver	iij s scilicet non debentur
De Roberto lacestr'	viij s
De Holdernesse	xix s
De Spront	xvj d
Summa iiij li xiij s	
Alloc' Aularum eodem A°	
De Drowdalhall'	v s scilicet remittentur
De Hamptonhall'	iij s iiij d scilicet remittentur
De Stauntonhall'	xiij s iiij d
De Scolis Schotton'	vj s viij d
Summa xxviij s iiij d	
Alloc' camerarum eodem A°	
De Camera Nafferton'	iij s iiij d
De Camera Hurle	iiij s
De Camera Makeblyth	xiij s iiij d
Summa xx s viij d	

Alloc' ten' de A° eiusdem Regis terciodecimo

De Glover	iij li v s viij d
De Schoppa super Angulum quadr'	iiij d
De De [*sic*] Adam Ryver	iij s scilicet non debentur
De Holdernesse	vij s viij d
De Sprunt	xvj d
De Roberto lacest'	v s viij d
Summa iiij li iij s viij d	

Alloc' Aul' de eodem a°

De Stauntonhall'	xiij s iiij d
Summa patet	

Alloc' camerarum eodem A°

De Camera Hurle	iij s iiij d
De Camera Nafferton'	iij s iiij d
Summa vj s viij d	

Alloc' ten' de A° eiusdem Regis quartodecimo

De Ten' Glover	iij li viij d
De Gardino Ade Ryver	iij s scilicet non debentur
De Schoppa super Angulum quadr'	iiij d
De Roberto lacestr'	vj s
De Holdernesse	vj d
De Spront	xvj d
Summa iij li xj s x d	

Alloc' aularum eodem A°

De Aula Edwardi	iiij s
De Drowdelhall'	xj s viij d scilicet remittentur
De Stauntonhall'	xiij s iiij d
De Hamtonhall'	xx s ix d per bon'
Summa xlix s ix d	

Alloc' camerarum eodem a°

De Camera Scarle	viij s viij d
De Camera Nafferton'	iij s viij d
De Camera Holwell	xiij s viij d
De Camera Edwardi canonici	x s
De Camera Ensford	viij s iiij d
	scilicet debet tunc iij s iiij d de isto anno
Summa xliij s viij d	

Alloc' de Essex' eodem a°

De Johanne Bode	xxij li xiij s iiij d
Summa patet	

Alloc' scol' eodem A°

De Scol' Scharp	ij s
Summa patet	

Alloc' ten' de Anno primo Regis Henr' quinti

De Ten' Glover	iij li
De Terris Balle Mayson	iiij s
De Gardino Ade Ryver	iij s scilicet non debentur
De Gardino Thome Hampton'	xx d
De Ten' Roberti lacestr'	viij s
De Holdernesse	vj d
De Spront	xvj d
De Schoppa super Angulum quadr'	iiij d
Summa iij li xviij s x d	

Alloc' de Essex eodem anno

De Bod	xviij li vj s viij d
Summa patet	

Alloc' Aularum eodem anno

De Drowdalhall'	v s scilicet remittuntur
De Staunton' hall'	xiij s iiij d
Summa xviij s iiij d	

Alloc' camerarum eodem a°

De Camera Bowbwyth	xvj s viij d
De Camera Nafferton'	iij s iiij d
De Camera Ensford	x s
Summa xxx s	

Alloc' ten' de Anno Regis Henr' quinti secundo

De ten' Cawmbray	ij s vij d
De ten' Glover	iij li
De Gardino Ade Ryver	iij s scilicet non debentur
De Gardino Thome Hampton'	iij s
De ten' quond' Roberti lacestr'	viij s
De Holdernese	vj d
De Spront	xvj d
De Schoppa super Angulum quadr'	iiij d

De Bayli Mason pro terris quond' in ten' Thome Glover	viij s
Summa iiij li vj d ix d	

Alloc' de Essex' eodem Anno

De Bode	x li de termino sancti Mich'
Summa patet	

Alloc' Aularum eodem A°

De Drowdelhall'	v s scilicet remittuntur
De Stauntonhall'	xiij s iiij d
Summa xviij s iiij d	

Alloc' camerarum eodem anno

De Camera Asse	vij s
De Camera Nafferton'	iij s iiij d
De Camera ffytzhue	xx d
De Camera Parysse	vj s viij d
De Camera Ensford'	x s
Summa xxviij s viij d	

Alloc' ten' de Anno Regis Henr' quinti tercio

De Ten' Glover	iij li
De Ten' Galfridi Taylyour	vj s viij d
De Ten' Cawmbray	xv s viij d
De Ten' Joh' Royer	vj s
De Gardino Joh' Wycaym	ij s iij d
De Gardino Ade Riwer	iij s scilicet non debentur
De Ten' quond' Roberti lacestr'	viij s
De Gardino ex opo[to] sancti Egidij	iiij d
De Holdernesse	iij li vj d
De Spront	xvj d
De Ten' Mich' Tayliyour	viij s ix d
De Schoppa super angulum quadrivij	iiij d
De Gardino Ricardi Barbour	xviij d
Summa ix li ij s iiij d	

Alloc' Aularum eodem anno

De Parva Aula universitatis in vico scolarum	x s
De Aula Edwardi	v s viij d
De Drowdalhall'	xij s ij d q[a]
	scilicet remittuntur v s

De Stauntonhall'	xiij s iiij d
Summa xlj s ij d q[a]	

Alloc' camerarum eodem anno

De Camera Nafferton'	xvj s viij d
De Camera Appilton'	vj s viij d
De Camera domini Ricardi Petr'	xvj s viij d
De Camera Iacest'	x s
De Camera Ensford'	x s
De Camera Barton'	v s
De Camera Mich' Jamys	xiij s iiij d
Summa iij li xviij s iiij d	

Alloc' scolarum eodem anno

De Scol' Magistri Johannis Elyse	iiij s viij d
De Scol' Mich' Barnab'	iij s iiij d
Summa viij s	

Summa omn' alloc' precedenc' cliij li vj s x d q[a]

Alloc' commun' batell' et contribucionibus Collegij a festo Pent' inclusive Anno R' Regis Henr' quinti tercio usque ad idem festum exclusive xvij li vij s vj d

Summa patet

Alloc' reparacionum infra Collegium et extra xxv li vj s iiij d ob'

Summa patet

Alloc' expensarum infra villam et extra x li vj s ij d

Summa patet

Alloc' resolucionum

In primis William Wyrstylher' pro gardino extra portam Borialem	xviij d
Item Abbati de Abyngton'	vj s
Item Procuratoribus Ecclesie beate virginis	xij d
Item Abbate [*sic*] de Osnay de terminis Pasch' et sancti Mich'	vj s
Item Abbatisse de Godstow	xiiij s
Item Abbate [*sic*] de Ensham	viij s
Summa xxxvj s vj d	

Alloc' de pensionibus sociorum Collegij

In primis Magistro Collegij	iij li xvj s viij d

Item Magistro Roberto Burton'	xl s
Item Magistro Ade	iij li xvij s ix d
Item Magistro Hamerton'	xx s
Summa x li xiiij s v d	

Allocac' pro stipend' famulorum

In primis lotrici Collegij	v s
Item Johanni Tel' pro salario suo	xiij s iiij d
Summa xviij s iiij d	

Item computans petit allocari pro opere suo	x s

Summa omnium solucionum lxvij li iij d ob

Summa totalis omn' allocatorum ccxx li vij s j d ob q[a]

⟨Et sic computatis computandis et allocatis allocandis Computans debet Collegio q[a]

Willelmus Barow Cancellarius⟩

[*Quite a narrow roll of two membranes, in fair condition.*]

WHITSUN 4 HENRY V to WHITSUN 5 HENRY V (ROLL UC:BU1/F/27)

7 June 1416–30 May 1417

BURSAR: ADAM RADFORD

Radef'

Compotus M Ade Radefort Procuratoris Collegij Magistri Willelmi de Dunelm' magne aule universitatis vulgariter nuncupat' a Fest pentecost' inclusive Anno regni regis H[*enrici*] quinti quarto usque ad idem festum exclusive Anno revoluto

[*The Arrears are identical with the Allowances in* ***F/26*** *above, save for a few changes in spelling.*]

Summa omn' Arr' Precedenc' cliij li vj s x d q[a]

Redditus ten' eiusdem Collegij de Anno Reg' Regis Henrici quinti quarto

De Ten' nuper Alic' ffrench	l s
De Ten' Thome mayster Glover	iij li
De Ten' Galfridi Taylyour	xxvj s viij d
De Thoma Coke pro prat' quondam Th' maister	xxvj s viij d
De Ten' quond' holway	xv s
De Ten' Cambray	xv s viij d
De Ten' Johannis Royer	xij s
De Gardino Johannis Wychaym	iij s
De Gardino Ricardi Carior'	iiij s iiij d
De gardino Ade Riwer	iij s
De Novo Colleg' pro Maydyn' Hall'	x s[1]
De Gardino Th' Hampton' Sadlere	viij s
De Ten' quondam Roberti laycestr'	viij s
De gardino ex opposito ecclesie Sancti Egidij	x d
De gardino Ricardi Barbour	iij s
De Colleg' cantuar'	ij s vj d
De Abb' de Godstow pro quadam schoppa iuxta ecclesiam sancte fridiswyde	xx d

[1] [ADMC] A supplementary strip of parchment was once attached to the right margin here. There are 2 sets of holes with blue thread in it.

De Holdirnesse	iij li vj d
De Sprunt	xvj d
De Johanne Schawe pro prato yrelande	xxvj s viij d
De Mich' Taylyour	xv s
De Schoppa super angulum quadr'	xx s
De Ten' Philippi Corwyn'	xxvj s viij d
De Terris quond' Bayly mason	viij s
[2]De ten' phesand pro medietate anni	xvj s viij d

Summa xxj li v s ij d

Redditus de Essex eodem anno

De Essexe per Rectorem de margret Rodynges et Johannem Howtt' xx li

Summa patet

Redditus Aularum eodem anno

De Brasenose	iij li vj s viij d
De Aula Scuti	vj s viij d
De sancti Thome	x s
De parva Aula universitatis in vico scolarum	xxxiij s iiij d
De Hampton' Hall'	xl s
De Aula Edwardi	xxiiij s
De Drowdalhall'	xlv s
De Stauntonhall'	xiij s iiij d

Summa xj li xix s

Redditus camerarum eodem anno

De camera Scarll'	xvj s viij d
De camera Mich' Jamysse	xvj s viij d
De camera Appulton'	xiij s iiij d
De camera Kexby	xiij s iiij d
De camera Naffirton'	xvj s viij d
De camera Aass	x s
De camera Barton'	xx s
De camera hallom	xx s
De camera corff	xvj s viij d
	non tenuit illam per annum

Summa vij li iij s iiij d

[2] [ADMC] This entry is in a different ink.

Redditus scolarum de eodem anno		
	De scol' quondam Magistri Johannis Elys	viij s
	De scol' quondam Barnet	vj s viij d
	De scol' determinatorum	ij s iiij d
	Summa xvij s	
	Summa omn' reddituum lxj li iiij s vj d	

Sic computans rendet de xxx s et ix d, receptis pro granis in Essexe
Item rendet pro ij s receptis de Johanne laboror' pro camera sua

Summa xxxij s ix d

Summa omnium oneratorum ccxvj li iiij s j d q[a]

Allocaciones Ten' de Anno rr' Henrici quarti septimo		
	De Johe Barbur	xx d
+[3]	De Adam Ryver	iij s non debentur
	De Roberto laycestr'	ij s viij d
	De Holdernesse	vj d
+	De Cowley	xiij s iiij d
	Summa xxj s ij d	

Alloc' Aularum et Camerarum de eodem anno		
	De Aula Edwardi	vij s iiij d
	De camera canonici de Notley	iij s iiij d
	De Camera Morton'	iij s iiij d
	De Camera Nafferton'	iij s iiij d
	De Camera foston'	iij s iiij d
	De Camera Clesby	xiij s iiij d
	Summa xxxiiij s	

Alloc' ten' Anno predicti R' Henrici viij[vo]		
+	De Cowley	x s
	De Roberto lacestr'	viij s
	De Holdernesse	xij d
+	De Schoppa super anglo' quadr'	iiij d
	Summa xix s iiij d	

[3] Entries marked with a cross like this are all carried over to the arrears of **F/29** below. All the other allowances were copied on to the Arrears roll **F/28**, and never reappear in the main sequence of accounts.

Alloc' aularum eodem anno

	De droudelhall'	v s
	De Stauntonhall'	vj s viij d
	Summa xj s viij d	

Alloc' camerarum eodem anno

	De camera Naffirton'	iij s iiij d
	De camera ffoston'	xvj s viij d
	Summa xx s	

Alloc' ten' de anno eiusdem Regis henrici ix°

+	De ten' Cowley	xxx s
+	De Schoppa super Angulum quadr'	iiij d
+	De Adam Ryver	iij s non debentur
	De Roberto laycestr'	viij s
	De Holdernesse	xij d
	Summa xlij s iiij d	

Alloc' Aularum scolarum et camerarum eodem anno

	De staunton' Hall'	iij s iiij d
	De parva aula universitatis in alto vico	iij s iiij d
	De scol' frowik'	v s vj d[4]
	De camera nafferton'	x s
	Summa xxij s vij d	

Alloc' ten' de anno eiusdem Regis henrici decimo

	De Mercer	ij s vj d
+	De Glover	v li xij d
+	De schoppa super angulum quadr'	iiij d
+	De Adam Ryver	iij s non debentur
	De Roberto lacestr'	iij s
	De Holdernesse	xij d
	Summa v li x s x d	

Alloc' aularum et camerarum eodem Anno

	De parva aula universitatis in alto vico	iij s iiij d
	De camera Nafferton'	iij s iiij d
	De camera makeblyth	iij s iiij d
	Summa x s	

4 [ADMC] *Sic* – this figure ought to be v s xj d.

Alloc' ten' de anno eiusdem Regis xj°		
	De ten' Mercer	vij s vj d
	De Sprount	xvj d
+	De glover	xv s
+	De schoppa super angulum quadr'	iiij d
+	De Adam Ryver'	iij s non debentur
	De Holdernesse	xij d
	De cowley	x s
	De Roberto lacestr'	viij s
	Summa xlvj s ij d	
Alloc' de Esex		
	De anno decimo	xij li xiij s iiij d
	De anno undecimo	xx li xvij s j d per lyghtfote
	Summa xxxiij li x s v d	
[5]Alloc' Aularum		
	De Stantonhall'	vj s viij d
	De Parva Aula universitatis in alto vico	xxiij s iiij d per Brows
	Summa xxx s	
Alloc' scol' et camerarum eodem Anno		
	De scol' ponter	xvj d
	De camera Nafferton'	iij s iiij d
	De camera Beneham'	iij s iiij d
	De camera Makeblythe	x s
	Summa xviij s	
Alloc' ten' de anno eiusdem xij°		
	De glover	iij li xx d xliiij s iiij d[6]
+	De Adam Ryver	iij s non debentur
	De Roberto lacestr'	viij s
	De Holdernesse	xix s
	De Sprount	xvj d
	Summa iiij li xiij s	
Alloc' aularum de eodem anno		
+	De drowedelhall'	v s remittentur

[5] This section appears to have been inserted later; perhaps it had been first omitted in error.

[6] [ADMC] This second sum has been added in a different hand.

+	De hamptonhall'	iij s iiij d remittentur
	De Stauntonhall'	xiij s iiij d
+	De Scol' schotton'	vj s viij d
	Summa xxviij s iiij d	

Alloc' camerarum eodem anno

	De camera Nafferton'	iij s iiij d
	De camera Hurle	iiij s
	De camera Makeblythe	xiij s iiij d
	Summa xx s viij d	

Alloc' ten' de anno eiusdem Regis terciodecimo

	De glover	iij li v s viij d
+	De Schoppa super Angulum quadr'	iiij d
+	De Adam Ryver	iij s remittuntur
	De holdernesse	vij s viij d
	De sprount	xvj d
	De Rob' laycest'	v s viij d
	Summa iiij li iij s viij d	

Alloc' aularum et cameraum de eodem anno

	De Stauntonhall'	xiij s iiij d
	De camera hurle	iij s iiij d
	De camera nafferton'	iij s iiij d
	Summa xx s	

Alloc' ten' de anno eiusdem regis xiij°

	De glover	iij li viij d
+	De Adam Ryver	iij s non deb'
+	De Schoppa super anglo' quadr'	iiij d
	De Roberto laycestr'	vj s
	De holdernesse	vj d
	De sprount	xv d[7]
	Summa iij li xj s x d	

Alloc' aularum eodem Anno

	De aula Edwardi	iiij s
+	De drowdalhall'	vj s viij d remittuntur[8]
	De stanton hall'	xiij s iiij d

[7] [ADMC] *Sic* – presumably an error for xvj d.
[8] [ADMC] *Sic* – presumably for xj s viij d.

	De Hamtonhall'	xx s ix d per bon'
	Summa xlix s ix d	
Alloc' camerarum de eodem anno		
++	De Camera Scarle	viij s viij d Magister recepit
	De Camera nafferton'	iij s viij d
	De camera holwell	xiij s viij d
	De camera edwardi canonici	x s
+	De camera ensforth	viij s iiij d
		scilicet debet de isto anno iij s iiij d
	Summa xliij s viij d	
Alloc' de Essex' eodem anno		
	De Bode	xxij li xiij s iiij d
	Summa patet	
Alloc' scolarum eodem anno		
	De scol' scherp	ij s
	Summa patet	
Alloc' ten' de Anno p° Regis henrici quinti		
	De ten' Glover	iij li
	De terris Balle mason	iiij s
+	De gardino Ade Ryver	iij s non debentur
	De gardino Thome Hampton'	xx d
	De ten' Roberti laycestr'	viij s
	De holdernesse	vj d
	De Spront	xvj d
+	De Schoppa super angulum quadr'	iiij d
	Summa iij li xviij s x d	
Alloc' de Essex eodem anno		
	De Johanna Bod	xviij li vj s viij d
	Summa patet	
Alloc' aularum eodem anno		
+	De Drowdalhall'	v s remittuntur
	De staunton' hall'	xiij s iiij d
	Summa xviij s iiij d	
Alloc' camerarum eodem anno		
	De camera Bowbwyc	xvj s viij d
	De camera nafferton'	iij s iiij d

++	De Camera Ensforth	x s
	Summa xxx s	

Alloc' ten' de Anno Regis henrici quinti secundo

+++	De ten' Cawmberay	ij s vij d
	De ten' glov'	iij li
+	De gardino Ade Ryner	iij s non debentur[9]
	De ten' quond' Roberti laycestr'	viij s
	De holdernese	vj d
	De Spront	xvj d
+	De schoppa super angl' quadr'	iiij d
	De Baly mason	viij s
	Summa iiij li vj d ix d	

Alloc' de Essex' eodem Anno

	De bode	x li de termino sancti Mich'
	Summa patet	

Alloc' aularum eodem anno

+	De aula drowdall	v s remittuntur
	De Staunton hall'	xiij s iiij d
	Summa xviij s iiij d	

[*Dorse*]

Alloc' camerarum eodem Anno

	De camera Asse	vij s
	De came Nafferton'	iij s iiij d
	De camera ffytzhue	xx d
	De camera parryss	vj s viij d
+	De camera Ensford'	x s
	Summa xxviij s viij d	

Allocaciones ten' de anno Regis henrici quinti tercio

	De ten' glover	iij li
+++	De ten' Cawmberay	xij s ij d
+	De gardino Johannis Wycaym	ij s iij d
+	De gardino Ade Riwer	iij s non debentur
	De ten' quond' Roberti laycestr'	viij s
+++	De gardino ex opposito sancti egidij	iiij d

[9] [ADMC] A sum of 3s from the garden of Thomas Hampton must have been omitted in error.

	De holdernesse	vj d
	De Spront	xvj d
+	De ten' Mich' Taylyor	v s v d
+	De schoppa super angl' quadr'	iiij d
	De Baly mason	viij s
+	De gardino Ric' Barbour	xviij d
	Summa v li ij s ix d[10]	

Alloc' aularum de eodem Anno

	De aula staunton	xiij s iiij d
	Summa patet	

Allocaciones camerarum de eodem anno

	De Camera Nafferton'	xvj s viij d
	De camera domini Ricardi Petr'	x s remittuntur
+++	De camera laycester	x s
+	De camera Ensford'	x s
+++	De camera Barton'	v s
+++	De camera Mich' Jamys	vj s viij d
	Summa lviij s iiij d	

Allocaciones ten' eiusdem collegij anno regni Regis Henrici quinti quarto

	De ten' Thome mayster Glover	iij li
+++	De Cawmberay	xv s viij d
+	De gardino Johannis Wykam	iij s
+++	De gardino Ric' caryor	iiij s iiij d
+	De gardino Ade Riwer	iij s non debentur
	De ten' quondam Roberti laycestr'	viij s
+++	De gardino ex opposito ecclesie Sancti Egidij	x d
+	De gardino Ric' Barbour	iij s
+++	De holderness	iij li vj d
	De Spront	xvj d
	De Mich' Taylyour	xv s
	De Schoppa super angulum quadr'	iiij d
	De terris quond' Baly Mason	viij s
	De ten' phesand	x s

[10] [ADMC] The correct total is £5 2s 10d.

sed remanet [. . . .] in domo quam recepı ın parte solucionis istius summe xvj s viij d

Summa ix li xiij s

Allocaciones aularum de eodem anno

+++	De parva Aula universitatis in vico scolarum	x s
+++	De hampton' Hall'	xiij s iiij d
+++	De aula edwardi	xxiij s viij d
+	De drowdalhall'	xviij s x d sed remittuntur
	De Stanton hall'	xiij s iiij d

Summa iij li xix s ij d

Allocaciones camerarum de eodem anno

De camera Scarll'	xvj s viij d
De camera Mich' Jamysse	xvj s viij d
De camera apulton'	xiij s iiij d
De camera Kexby	xiij s iiij d
De camera naffirton'	xvj s viij d
De camera Barton'	x s
De camera hallom	xx s
De camera corff	xvj s viij d

hoc precio camera sed non debet totum

Summa vj li iij s iiij d

Allocaciones scolarum de eodem anno

De scol' quondam Magistri Johannis Elys iiij s viij d

Summa patet

Allocaciones comun' batell' et contribucionum Collegij a festo pent' inclusive Anno R' Regis Henrici quinti quarto usque ad idem festum exclusive xix li xix s

Summa patet

Allocaciones reparacionum infra collegium et extra xj li ij s vj d ob

Summa patet

Allocaciones expensarum infra collegium et extra iij li xij d

Summa patet

Allocaciones in solucionibus de eodem Anno

Abbathie de Osenay	ix s
Willelmo Wresteller et alteri in loco suo	ix d
Ecclesie beate virginis pro staunton hall	x d

Abbathie de Ensham	viij s
Abbathie de Abbyngton	iij s
Abbathie de godstow	xiiij s
Abbathie beate fridiswyde	vij s viij d
Sic collectoribus domini regis	iiij s
Summa xlvij s iij d	

Allocaciones pro pensionibus sociorum

In primis magistro collegij	iij li
Item magistro Roberto Burton	xl s
Item m Ade Redyforth'	xl s xiij d
Item magistro johanni Hamerton'	iiij s
Summa viij li xiij d	

Allocaciones pro stipend' famulorum eodem anno

In primis Johannis telm'	xxvj s viij d
Item thome coco pro tempore hamerton et meo	xx s
Item barbitonsori	v s
Item lotrici	v s
Summa lvj s viij d	

Item pro quodam libro quam incistavit magister Thoma Dufferd xxj s viij d

Item Computans petit allocari pro incepcione suo xx s
Item pro officio suo xx s

Summa omn' soluc' xlix li xix s ij d ob

Summa omn' allocac' ccxvj li iiij s j d ob

⟨Et sic computatis computandis et allocatis allocandis collegium debet computanti q[a]⟩

⟨Thomas Clare Cancellarius⟩

[*A roll of two membranes in fair condition, written in a neat, if small, hand.*]

ROLL LISTING ARREARS ON COLLEGE PROPERTY FOR 1405–1416 (ROLL UC:BU1/F/28)

[*This is the first extant arrears roll in the accounts, listing sums which are never recorded in later accounts. See Section 4 of the Introduction on this, and the other arrears rolls.*]

Arr' ab antiquo debita Magistro Aul' universitatis Oxon' de a° rr' henr' quarti vij°

De Johanne Barbur	xx d
De Rob' layc'	ij s viij d
De Holdernesse	vj d

Arr' aularum et camerarum de eodem anno

De Aula edwardi	vij s iiij d
De Camera canonici de Notley	iij s iiij d
De camera morton'	iij s iiij d
De camera Naffirton'	iij s iiij d
De Camera foston'	iij s iiij d
De Camera Clesby	xiij s iiij d

Arr' ten' anno predicti R' henrici viij^vo^

De Roberto lacestr'	viij s
De Holdernesse	xij d

Arr' aularum eodem anno

De stauntonhall'	vj s viij d

Arr' camerarum eodem anno

De camera Naffirton'	iij s iiij d
De camera ffoston'	xvj s viij d

Arr' ten' de anno eiusdem Regis henrici ix°

De Roberto leycest'	viij s
De Holdernesse	xij d

Arr' aularum scolarum et camerarum eodem anno

De staunton' Hall'	iij s iiij d
De parva aula universitatis in alto vico	iij s iiij d
De scol' frowik'	v s vj d
De camera Nafferton'	x s

Arr' ten' de anno eiusdem Regis henrici x°	
De Mercer	ij s vj d
De Roberto lacestr'	iij s
De Holdernesse	xij d
Arr' aularum et camerarum eodem Anno	
De parva aula universitatis in alto vico	iij s iiij d
De camera Naffirton'	iij s iiij d
De camera Makeblyth	iij s iiij d
Arr' ten' de anno eiusdem Regis henrici xj°	
De ten' Mercer	vij s vj d
De Sprount	xvj d
De Holdernesse	xij d
De Roberto lacestr'	viij s
Arr' de Esex	
De anno decimo	xij li xiij s iiij d
De anno undecimo	xx li xvij s j d per lyghtfote
Arr' Aularum	
De Stantonhall'	vj s viij d
De aula parva universitatis in alto vico	xxiij s iiij d per Brows
Arr' scol' et camerarum eodem anno	
De scol' ponter	xvj d
De camera Nafferton'	iij s iiij d
De camera Beneham'	iij s iiij d
De camera Makeblythe	x s
Arr' ten' de anno eiusdem xij°	
De glover	xxj s viij d ob[1]
De Roberto leycestr'	viij s
De Holdernesse	xix s
De Sprount	xvj d
Arr' aularum de eodem anno	
De Stauntonhall'	xiij s iiij d
Arr' camerarum eodem anno	
De camera Nafferton'	iij s iiij d
De camera Hurle	iiij s

[1] [ADMC] Written over an erasure.

De camera Makeblythe	xiij s iiij d
Arr' ten' de anno eiusdem Regis tercio decimo	
De glover	iij li v s viij d
De holdernesse	vij s viij d
De sprount	xvj d
De Rob' leycest'	v s viij d
Arr' aularum et camerarum de eodem anno	
De Staunton hall'	xiij s iiij d
De camera Hurle	iij s iiij d
De camera Nafferton'	iij s iiij d
Arr' ten' de anno eiusdem regis xiij°	
De glover	iij li viij d
De Roberto laycestr'	vj s
De holdernesse	vj d
De sprount	xvj d
Arr' aularum eodem Anno	
De aula Edwardi	iiij s
De stanton hall'	xiij s iiij d
De Hamptonhall'	xx s ix d per bon' ut patet in ult' ro' hamerton
Arr' camerarum de eodem anno	
De Camera Nafferton'	iij s viij d
De camera holwell	xiij s viij d
De camera Edwardi canonici	x s
Arr' de Essex' eodem anno	
De Bode	xxij li xiij s iiij d
Arr' scolarum eodem anno	
De scol' scherp	ij s
Arr' ten' de anno primo R' henrici quinti	
De ten' glover	iij li
De terris Balle mason	iiij s
+ De gardino Thome Hampton'	xx d ⟨sol' in ro hamerton ult'⟩
De ten' Roberti laycestr'	viij s
De holdernesse	vj d
De Spront	xvj d

Arr' de Essex eodem anno	
De Johanne Bode	xviij li vj s viij d
Arr' aularum eodem anno	
De staunton' hall'	xiij s iiij d
Arr' camerarum eodem anno	
De camera Bowbwyc	xvj s viij d
De camera Nafferton'	iij s iiij d
Arr' ten' de Anno Regis henrici quinti secundo	
De ten' glover	iij li
De ten' quond' Roberti laycestr'	viij s
De holdernese	vj d
De Sprunt	xvj d
De Baly mason	viij s
Arr' Essex' eodem Anno	
De bode	x li de termino sancti Mich'
Arr' aularum eodem anno	
De staunton hall'	xiij s iiij d
Arr' camerarum eodem anno	
De camera Asse	vij s sol'
De came Nafferton'	iij s iiij d
De camera ffytzhue	xx d
De camera parryss	vj s viij d
Arr' ten' de anno Regis henrici quinti tercio	
De ten' glover	iij li
De ten' quond' Roberti laycestr'	viij s
De holdernesse	vj d
De Spront	xvj d
De Baly mason	viij s
Arr' aularum de eodem Anno	
De aula staunton	xiij s iiij d
[*no heading*]	
De camera domini Ricardi Petr'	x s

[*Dorse*]

Arr' ten' eiusdem collegij de anno regni Regis Henrici quinti quarto

De ten' Thome maister Glover	iij li
De ten' quondam Roberti laycestr'	viij s
De Spront	xvj d
De terris quond' Baly Mason	viij s
De ten' phesand	x s

Arr' aularum de eodem anno

De Staunton hall'	xiij s iiij d

Summa vj^{xx} li x li xij s x d ob'

[2]Et memorand' quod isti 2 solverent plenarie scilicet Eynsford' et Mic' talyour et skarrel solvit omnia usque ad annum quintum rr' henr' quinti exclusive

Memorandum quod M Joh' Hamerton Procurator recepit de contentis in isto rotulo a^{o} rr' Henr' quinti sexto

In primis de Th hampton cliente	xx d
Item de Henr' Bon'	xx s
Item de Th' Master Glover	iij li

et memorandum quod dictus procurator de ista summa rendit in rotulo maiore

Memorandum quod M Rob' Burton' in rotulo suo anni octavi rr' h quinti [. . .] pro Thom' maister de debitis suis in isto rotulo xx s

Memorandum quod In tempore Magistri Joh' Castell' senioris collegij universitatis oxon' erat unum plac' de ferro arestatum in ten' Ric' Mercer pro decem solidis debitis Collegio pro Ricardo predicto et ista arestacio erat facta per Rogerum Chyddyslay generosum ~~sacre theologio~~ facultatis sacre theologie Anno regni Regis henrici quarti undecimo auctoritate magistri Willelmi Clynt tunc' Cancell'

[2] The rest of this roll was added later. Each entry is in a different hand, which suggests that the roll was retained for several years by successive Bursars, who each added these memoranda at different times.

Memorandum quod Robertus laycest' debet Collegio universitatis oxon pro annuali pencione exeunte de domo in qua moratur nunc Robertus lambherd' pro diversis annis ut in alio latere patet per parcel' iiij li xj s ij d

Item per alium rotulum ut patet parcell' xxiiij s

Memorandum quod Thomas mayster debet collegio universitatis oxon pro [. . .] sua ut patet parcell' in scriptis in alio latere rotuli xv li viij s ob

Item per alium rotulum ut patet parcell' xxxvj s iiij d

Memorandum quod Magister Thomas Naffirton' debet Collegio universitatis oxon ut patet parcell' ex alio latere rotuli - xl s

Memorandum quod Johannes Bale mason debet Collegio universitatis oxon ut patet parcell' ex alio latere rotuli - xxiiij s

Memorandum quod Hugo Benet debet Collegio universitatis oxon ut patet parcell' in Rotul' diversorum regum x li xiij s ij d

[*A narrow roll of one membrane, in good condition.*]

WHITSUN 5 HENRY V to WHITSUN 6 HENRY V (ROLL UC:BU1/F/29)

30 May 1417–15 May 1418

BURSAR: ROBERT BURTON

dat

Burton'

Computus M Rob' Burton' procuratoris Collegij M Willelmi de donolm' magn' Aul' universitatis Oxon' vulgariter nuncupat' A festo pent' inclusive anno r' r' henr' quinti post conquestum Angl' v^{to} usque ad id' festum exclusive Anno revolut'

Arr' ten' de A^{o} dicit domini nostri regis secundo	
De ten' Cawmbray	ij s vij d
Summa patet	
Arr' ten' de a^{o} eiusdem domini nostri regis tercio	
De ten' Cawmbray	xij s ij d
De Gard' ex o^{to} sancti Egidij	iiij d
Summa xij s vj d	
Arr' Cam' de eodem a^{o}	
De Cam' Nafferton'	xvj s viij d
De Cam' leyc'	x s
De Cam' barton'	v s
De Cam' Mich' james	vj s viij d
Summa xxxviij s iiij d	
Arr' ten' de A^{o} dicti domini regis quarto	
De Cawmbray	xv s viij d
De Gard' ric' caryor	iiij s iiij d
De gardino ex o^{to} sancti Egidij	x d
De Holderness	iij li vj d
Summa iiij li xvj d	
Arr' aul' eodem a^{o}	
De parv' Aul' universitatis in vico scol'	x s
De hampton' hal	xiij s iiij d

De Aul edwardi	xxiij s viij d
Summa xvlij s	
Arr' cam' de eodem a°	
De Cam' skarl'	xvj s viij d
De Cam' mic' james	xvj s viij d
De Cam' Apulton'	xiij s iiij d
De Cam' Cexby	xiij s iiij d
De Cam' Nafferton'	xvj s viij d
De Cam' barton'	x s
De Cam' Hallumb	xx s
De Cam' Corf'	xvj s viij d
Summa vj li iij s iiij d	
Arr' scol' eodem a°	
De scol' quond' magistri johannis eleys	iiij s viij d
Summa xv li ix s ix d	
Redditus ten' eiusdem Coll' de a° rr' dicti domini nostri quinto	
De ten' pyppard	l s
De ten' Thome mayst' Glov'	iij li
De ten' Galfrdi talyour	xxvj s viij d
De Alio ten' eiusdem quod fesaunt quond' tenuit	xxvj s viij d
De pratis retro Oseney	xxvj s viij d
De ten' quond' Holway	xv s
De ten' Cawmbray	xv s viij d
De ten' Roer	xij s
De Gardino Ric' Karyour	iiij s iiij d
De Gardino Ade ryver	iij s
De Novo Colleg' pro maydynhal'	x s
De Gard' Thom hampton' sadiller	viij s
De ten' quondam roberti layc'	viij d[1]
De Gard'ex ot° sancti egidij	x d
De Coll' Cant'	ij s vj d
De abb' de Godstow pro quadam schop' iuxta ecclesiam sancte frid'	xx d
De Holdernesse	iij li vj d
De spront	xvj d

[1] [ADMC] *Sic* – this should be viij s.

De shaw pro prato jrelande etc.	xxvj s viij d
De johanne Westbury[2]	xvj s
De shop' super ang' quadriv'	xx s
De uxor' philippi sut'	xxvj s viij d
De Rob' dudley	xxx s
De Goldfynch' pro terris in bello monte	viij s
De Esex'	xx li
Summa xliij li ij d	

Redditus Aul' eodem anno

De brasenose	iij li vj s viij d
De Aul' scuti	vj s viij d
De Aul' sancti Thom'	x s
De parva Aul' universitatis in vico scol'	xxxiij s iiij d
De Hampton' hal	xl s
De Aul' edwardi	xxiiij s
De drwdalhal	xlv s
De stauntonhal	xiij s iiij d
De parv' Aul' universitatis in alto vico	liij s iiij d
Summa xiiij li xij s iiij d	

Redditus Cam' eodem anno

De Cam' Skaryl	xvj s viij d
De Cam' lyle pro 3 terminis	x s
De Cam' Naffirton'	xvj s viij d
De Cam' Kexby	xiij s iiij d
De Cam' Corf'	xvj s viij d
De Cam' symond'	x s
Summa iiij li iij s iiij d	

Redditus scol' de eodem anno

De scol' bass quod' det' s marchal	ij s viij d
De scol' Altis ex o^{to} belfrontis de al' det'	ij s iij d
De Al' Altis scol' tradit' M Willelmo partrich	vj s viij d
Summa xj s vij d	

Summa omn' onerat' iij^{xx}li xvij li xvij s ij d

[2] On 4 September 1417, Wakeman's Tenement (now the site of 9 High Street) was leased to John Westbury, Manciple (**UC:E/E1/D/6**).

Item oneratus computans de diversis extra rotulum cum iij li ij s v d[3]

Allocaciones ten' de anno rr' henrici quinti ij^{o}	
De ten' Cawmbray	ij s vij d
All' ten' de Anno dict' domini nostri regis iij^{o}	
De ten' Cawmbray	xij s ij d
De Gard' ex o^{to} sancti egid'	iiij d
All' Cam' de eodem a^{o}	
De Cam' Nafferton'	iij s viij d
De Cam' leyc'	x s
De Cam' barton'	v s
De Cam' mic' james	xvj s viij d
Summa l s j d	
All' ten' de a^{o} dict' domini nostri regis iiij^{o}	
De ten' Cawmbray	xv s viij d
De Gard' ric' karyour	iiij s iiij d
De Gard' ex o^{to} sancti Egid'	ij d
All' aul' eodem a^{o}	
De Aul' edwardi	xxiij s viij d
Summa xxxix s vj d	
All' Cam' eodem anno	
De Cam' mic' james	xvj s viij d
De Cam' Apulton'	xiij s iiij d
De Cam' Kexby	vj s viij d
De Cam' Nafferton'	xvj s viij d
De Cam' Corf'	xvj s viij d
All' scol' eodem a^{o}	
De scol' quond' magistri joh' eleys	iiij s viij d
Summa iij li xiiij s viij d	
All' ten' de a^{o} eiusdem regis quinto	
De ten' Thom' Glover	xx s
De ten' Galfridi talyour	vj s viij d
De Alio ten' eiusdem	xxvj s viij d
De ten' roer	ix s

[3] [ADMC] i.e. the grand total for this section is £80 19s 17d.

De Gard' ric' karyour	iiij s iiij d
De Gard' Ade ryver	iij s
De ten' quondam rob' layc'	viij s
De Gard' ex ot° sancti Eg'	x d
De Holdernes	iij li vj d
De spront	xvj d
De shaw pro pratis	xiij s iiij d
De joh' Westby	viij s iiij d
De shop' super Ang' quad'	iiij d
De Goldfynch' pro terris in bello monte	viij s
Summa viij li x s iiij d	

All' Aul' eodem a°

De parva Aul' universitatis in vic' scol'	vj s viij d
De Hampton' hal	xx s
De Aul' edwardi	xxiiij s
De drwdalhal	xviij s iiij d
De stauntonhal	xiij s iiij d
De parv' Aul' universitatis in alto vico	xiij s iiij d
Summa iij li xvij s iiij d	

All' Cam' eodem a°

De Cam' Skaryl	xvj s viij d
De Cam' lyle	x s
De Cam' Naffirton'	xvj s viij d
De Cam' Kexby	xiij s iiij d
De Cam' Corf'	xvj s viij d
De Cam' symond'	x s
Summa iiij li iij s iiij d	

All' scol' eodem anno

De scol' partrich	vj s viij d
Summa patet	

All' comunarum et bat' etc. xx li viij d

All' reparaciones et aliarum expensarum infra et extra coll' xvij li xvj s iiij d ob

Arr' resolucionum

In primis Abb' de Abyngton	iij s
Abb' de Godstow	xiiij s
Ecclesie sancti petri	ix d

Eidem ecclesie	ij s x d
Collect' xvme domine regis prime ante Nat'	xvj d
Eisdem in quadragesima	ij s viij d
Ballivo extra portam borialem	xviij d
Abb' de Eynsham	viij d
Abb' de Oseney	iij s
In diversis expensis factis per Magistrum	v s vij d
Summa xlij s viij d	

All' pensionum magistro et soc'

In primis M johanni kastel	xlix s iiij d ob
M Rob' Burton'	iij li
M Ade redyford'	iij li xiij s iiij d
M jo hamerton'	xiij s iiij d
Summa ix li xvj s ob'	

All' pro stip' famulorum

In primis pincerne	xx s
Coco	xiij s iiij d
Lotrici	v s
Summa xxxviij s iiij d	

All' pro offic' proc'	x s

Summa omn' All' iij^{xx} li xvij li vj s

Item petit computans sibi Allocari pro reparac' factis per magistrum jo legh' xiij s iiij d
Item pet' allocari de xiij s iiij d solutis per Nafferton tempore M Ade redyford'
Item pet' sibi Allocari xiij d iiij d solut' M Johanni Castel
Et pet' [. . .] Allocari xiij s iiij d solut' M Ade redyford'
Et Allocari sibimet[4] solutis xx s iij d

⟨Et sic computatis computandis et allocatis allocandis ~~Colle~~ Computans nichil debet Collegio

W Trengof Cancellarius⟩

[*A roll of two membranes, in good condition, written in an untidy hand.*]

[4] This is Smith's reading; the original text is uncertain.

WHITSUN 6 HENRY V to WHITSUN 7 HENRY V (ROLL UC:BU1/F/30)

15 May 1418–4 June 1419

BURSAR: JOHN HAMERTON

dat

hamerton

Compotus M Johannis Hamerton' proc' Coll' M Willelmi de dunelm' Magne Aule universitatis Oxon' vulgariter nuncupat' a festo [*pent'*] inclusive anno r'r' Henr' quinti post conquestum Angl' Sexto usque ad idem festum exclusive anno resoluto

[*The Arrears are identical with the Allowances in* **F/29** *above, save for a few changes in spelling.*]

Summa omn' Arrerag' xxv li xxiij d

Redditus ten' de A° dicti domini nostri Regis Henr' sexto

De ten' Pyppard	liij s iiij d
De ten' Th' Master glover	iij li
De ten' Galfridi talior	xxvj s viij d
De alio ten' eiusdem quod fesaunt quondam tenuit pro dimidio anni	xiij s iiij d
De pratis retro Osney	xxvj s viij d
De ten' quondam Holway	xv s
De ten' Cawmbray	xv s viij d
De ten' Joh' Roer	xij s
De gard' Ricardi Kariour	iiij s iiij d
De gard' Ade ryver	iij s
De Novo Colleg' pro Madynhal'	x s
De gard' Thom' hampton' sadiller	viij s
De gard' Willelmi Bromton Marcer[1]	ij s
De ten' quondam Roberti layc'	viij s
De gard' ex opposito ecclesie sancti Egidij	x d
De Colleg' Cantuar'	ij s vj d

[1] On 25 March 1419, the garden in St. Thomas was leased to William Brompton, Burgess and Alderman of Oxford (**UC:E2/11/1D/2**).

De Abbat' de godstow pro quadam schoppa iuxta Ecclesiam sancte frides'	xx d
De Holdernesse	iij li vj d
De spronte	xvj d
De Schaw pro pratis Irelande	xxvj s viij d
De ten' Joh' Westbury	xxxj s viij d
De Schopa super angulum quadrivij	xx s
De uxore Philippi sutoris	xxvj s viij d
De Roberto Dudley	xxx s
De Goldfynch' pro terris in bello monte	viij s
De Essex'	xx li
Summa xliij li vij s x d	

Redditus Aul' eodem Anno

De Brasenose	iij li vj s [*viij d*]
De Aula scuti	vj s viij d
De Aula sancti thome	x s
De parva Aula universitatis in vico scol'	xxxiij s iiij d
De Hamptonhall'	xl s
De Aula Edwardi	xxiiij s
De drowdalehall'	xlv s
De Stauntonhall'	xx s
De parva Aula universitatis in Alto vico	liij s iiij d
Summa xiiij li xix s	

Redditus scol' eodem Anno

De scol' M. Th.' Juster'	viij s
De scol' M. Joh' Arnald'	vj s viij d
De scol' M. Joh' Modulton' de Aula Merton'	vj s viij d
Summa xxj s iiij d	

Redditus Camerarum eodem anno

De Camera M Joh' Corf'	xvj s viij d
De Camera Kexby et fytzwilliam	xiij s iiij d
De Camera M Willelmi Symond'	x s
De Camera M Th' Naffreton'	xvj s viij d
De Camera Suthwell'	xvj s viij d
De Camera Appulton'	xiij s iiij d
Summa iiij li vj s iiij d	

Item computans respondet de iiij s receptis de Bromton' Mercer. Item de Th' Hampton' cliente xx d
Item de Henr' Bon' quondam principale Hamptonhall – xx s Item de Th' Master Glover iij li

Summa omn' onerat' iiij^{xx}xiij li ij s v d

All' ten' de Anno dict' rr' Henr' quint' tercio

De ten' Cawmbray	x s v d
Summa patet	

Alloc' camerarum de eodem Anno

De Camera Naffreton'	iij s viij d
De Camera leycest'	x s
De Camera Mich' James	xvj s viij d
De Camera Barton'	v s
Summa xxxv s	

Alloc' ten' de a° dict' domini regis quarto

De ten' Cawmbray	xj s iiij d
Summa patet	

Alloc' Camerarum eodem anno

De Camera Mich' James	vj s viij d
De Camera Nafferton'	iij s iiij d
De Camera Corfe	xvj s viij d
Summa xxvj s viij d	

Alloc' scolarum eodem Anno

De Scol' quondam Magistri Joh' Elyse pro M Sawndr'	iiij s viij d
Summa patet	

Alloc' ten' de a° eiusdem Regis quinto

De ten' galfridi talyor	xiij s iiij d
De gard' Ade Ryver	iij s
De ten' quondam Roberti leyc'	viij s
De Spront'	xvj d
De Schopa super Angulum quadrivij	iiij d
Summa xxvj s	

Alloc' Aul' eodem Anno

De Drowdalehall'	v s
De Stauntonhal	xiij s iiij d
Summa xviij s iiij d	

Alloc' Camerarum eodem Anno	
De Camera Skaryle	xvj s viij d
De Camera Naffreton'	iij s iiij d
De Camera Kexby	xiij s iiij d scilicet remittuntur
De Camera Corfe	xvj s viij d
Summa l s	

Alloc' ten' de A° eiusdem domini regis vj[to]	
De ten' quondam Holway	xx d
De Gard' Ade Ryver	iij s
De ten' quondam Roberti layc'	viij s
De gard' ex opposito ecclesie sancti Egidij	x d
De Holdernesse	iij li vj d
De Spronte	xvj d
De ten' Joh' Westbury	xv s v d
De Schopa super angulum quadrivij	xij s
De Goldfynch' pro terris in bello monte	viij s
Summa v li x s ix d	

Alloc' Aularum eodem Anno	
De Hamptonhall'	xiij s ij d q[a]
De Aula Edwardi	iiij s
De Drowdalehall'	xviij s iiij d
De parva Aula universitatis in Alto vico	xiij s iiij d
Summa xlviij s x d q[a]	

Alloc' scolarum eodem Anno	
De Scol' M. Th.' Juster'	v s iiij d
De Scol' M. Joh' Modulton'	vj s viij d
Summa xij s	

Alloc' camerarum eodem anno	
De Camera M Joh' Corfe	xvj s viij d
De Camera Symond'	vj s viij d
De Camera Naffreton'	xvj s viij d
De Camera Suthwell'	viij s iiij d
De Camera Appulton'	xiij s iiij d
Summa iij li xx d	

Summa omn' Alloc' precedenc' xx li xv s viij d q[a]

Alloc' communarum et bat' xxiij li xviij s vj d

Alloc' reparacionum et aliarum expens' infra Collegium et extra xxxv li xvj d q[a]

Alloc' resoluc'

In prim' Abbatti de Abyngton' iij s
Abbatisse de Godstow xiiij s
Priori ecclesie sancti frideswide vj s viij d
Abbati de Osney de a[o] present vj s et in partem soluc' trium s' a retro de a[o] M R. Burton viij d
Procuratoribus ecclesie sancte virg' pro stantonhall' xij s
Abbati de Ensam' viij s
Pro firma quondam utterworde pro pratis retro Osney iij s viij d
Collect' xv[me] domini Regis in festo sancte Agnetis ij s viij d
Summa xlv s viij d

Alloc' pensionum Magistri et soc'

In primis M Johanni Castell' xlvj s viij d
Magistro Roberto Burton' iij li
Magistro Ade Redyforde xl s
Magistro Johanni Hamerton' xx s de anno presente et cj s viij d de A[o] M Burton
Summa viij li xiij s iiij d

Alloc' pro stip' famulorum

In primis Th' Carno pro stipendio suo xiij s iiij d
Item eidem Th' in recompensa laboris sui xiij s iiij d
Item Th' Barbitonsori v s
Item lotrici Collegij v s
Summa xxxvj s viij d

Alloc' pro officio procuratoris x s

Summa omn' Alloc' iiij[xx]xiij li xiiij d ob

⟨Et sic computatis computandis et allocatis allocandis computans debet collegio xiiij d ob. quos solvit magistro Roberto burton' procuratori huius collegij pro proximo anno sequenti

ffr' Robertus Colman Cancellarius⟩

[*A roll of two membranes, written on the front only; slightly stained, and written in an untidy hand.*]

WHITSUN 7 HENRY V to WHITSUN 8 HENRY V (ROLL UC:BU1/F/31)

4 June 1419–26 May 1420

BURSAR: ROBERT BURTON

dat

Compotus M Rob' Burton' procuratoris Coll' Willelmi de dunolm' in Oxon. Magn' Aul' universitatis vu[*lgariter nuncupat'*] a festo pent' inclusive anno r'r' Henr' quinti septimo usque ad idem festum exclusive anno revolu[*to*]

Arr' ten' de a° r'r' henr' quint' tercio	
De ten' Cawmbray	x s [*v d*]
Arr' Cam' eod' anno	
De Cam' Nafferton'	iij s [*iiij d*]
De Cam' laycest'	x [*s*]
De Cam' Mich' james	x[*vj s viij d*]
De Cam' Barton'	v s
Summa xlv s v d	
Arr' ten' de anno eiusdem iiij^to^	
De ten' Cawmbray	xj s iiij d
Arr' Cam' eod' anno	
De Cam' Mic' james	vj s viij d
De Cam' Nafferton'	iij s iiij d
De Cam' Corf'	xvj s viij d
Arr' scol' eod' a°	
De Scol' sawnd'	iiij s viij d
Summa xlij s viij d	
Arr' ten' de a° eiusd' regis quinto	
De Gard' Ade Ryver	iij s
De ten' quondam Rob' leycest' modo Rob' lamberd'	viij s
De Spront'	xvj d
Arr' cam' eod' Anno	
De Cam' skaryll'	xvj s viij d

De Cam' Nafferton'	iij s iiij d
De Cam' Corf'	xvj s viij d
Summa xlix s	

Arr' ten' de a° dicti domini regis vj^{to}

De ten' Holway	xx d
De Gard' Ade Ryver	iij s
De ten' quondam layc' modo lamberd'	viij s
De Gardino ex o^{to} sancti Egidij	x d
De Holderness	iij li vj d
De Sprount	xvj d
De ten' johannis Westbyry	xv s v d
De shopa super Angulum quadrivij	xij s
De Goldfinch' pro terris in bello monte	viij s
Summa v li x s ix d	

Arr' Aul' eod' Anno

De Hampton' hall'	xiij s ij d q^{a}
De Aul' Edwardi	iiij s
De drowdal hall'	xiij s iiij d
De parva Aul' universitatis in Alto vico	xiij s iiij d
Summa xliij s x d q^{a}	

Arr' scol' eodem anno

De Scol' Just'	v s iiij d
De Scol' Multon'	vj s viij d

Arr' Cam' eod' anno

De Cam' Corf'	xvj s viij d
De Cam' symond'	vj s viij d
De Cam' Nafferton'	xvj s viij d
De Cam' Suthwell'	viij s iiij d
De Cam' Appillton'	vij s viij d
Summa iij li vij d[1]	

Redditus ten' de a° dicti domini regis henrici quinti septimo

De pratis retro Osney	xxvj s viij d
De ten' pyppard	liij s iiij d
De ten' Thome mayst'	iij li
De ten' Galfridi talyour	xx s

[1] No grand total of arrears is given; it would be £17 12s 3½d.

De ten' quond' Holway	xv s
De ten' Cawmbray	xv s viij d
De ten' johannis Roer'	xij s
De gardino Ric' caryour	iiij s iiij d
De Gardino Ade Ryver	iij s
De Novo coll' pro Madyn' hall'	x s
De Gardino Hampton' sadal'	viij s
De Gardino Brompton merc'	ij s
De ten' quond' layc' modo lamberd'	viij s
De Gardino ex o^to ecclesie sancti Egidij	x d
De Coll' Cant'	ij s vj d
De abb' de godstow pro quadem schopa iuxta ecclesiam sancte frideswide	xx d
De Holderness	iij li vj d
De sprount	xvj d
De shaw pro pratis	xxvj s viij d
De ten' Westbury	xxxj s viij d
De schop' super angulum quadrivij	xx s
De uxore philippi sut'	xxvj s viij d
De ten' dudley	xxx s
De Goldfynch' pro terris in bello monte	viij s
De Esex'	xx li

Summa xlij li vij s x d

Redd' Aul' eod' Anno

De brasenose	iij li vj s viij d
De Aul' scuti	vj s viij d
De Aul' sancti thome	x s
De parva Aul' universitatis in vico scolarum	xxxiij s iiij d
De Hampton' hall'	xl s
De Aul' Edwardi	xxiiij s
De drowdale hall'	xlv s
De parva Aul' universitatis in alto vico	liij s iiij d

Summa xiij li xix s

Redd' scol' eodem anno

De scol' just'	viij s
De scol' Arnald'	vj s viij d
De scol' Wyresdall'	vj s viij d

Summa xxj s iiij d

Redditus Cam' eod' anno
De Cam' M Corf' xvj s viij d
De Cam' Symond' x s
De Cam' Nafferton' xvj s viij d
Summa xliij s iiij d

Summa omn' redd' lix li xj s vj d

Summa omn' onerat' iij^{xx}xvij li x s ij d q^{a}

Respondet idem computans receptis a fythwillyam – iij iiij d. et debet fythwilliam adhuc xx s
Respondet idem de all' pro arr' Ase in ro extracto – vij s Item respondet de xiiij ob. recept' in comp' hamerton.

Unde summa total' Onerat' iij^{xx}xviij li xx d ob q^{a}

Alloc' ten' de a^{o} rr' Henr' quint' iij^{o}
De ten' Cawmbray iij s v d

Alloc' Cam' eod' anno
De Cam' Naffereton' iij s viij d
De Cam' Mic' James xvj s viij d

Alloc' ten' de a^{o} dict' domini regis iiij^{to}
De ten' Cawmbray xj s iiij d

Alloc' Cam' eod' anno
De Cam' Mic' James vj s viij d
De Cam' Nafferton' iij s iiij d
De Cam' Corf' xvj s viij d

All' scol' eod' Anno
De Scol' sawnders iiij s viij d
Summa iij li vj s v d

Alloc' ten' de a^{o} dicti domini Regis v^{to}
De ten' quondam Rob' leyc' viij s
De Spront' xvj d

Alloc' Cam' eod' Anno
De Cam' skarell' xvj s viij d
De Cam' Nafferton' iij s iiij d
De Cam' Corf' xvj s viij d
Summa xlvj s

All' ten' de a^{o} dicti domini regis vj^{to}	
De Gardino Ade Ryver	iij s
De ten' quond' layc'	viij s
De Gard' ex o^{to} sancti Egidij	x d
De sprount	xvj d
All' Aul' eod' Anno	
De Aul' Edwardi	iiij s
De drowdalehall'	v s
All' scol' eod' Anno	
De scol' just'	v s iiij d
De scol' Multon'	vj s viij d
All' Cam' eod' anno	
De Cam' Corf'	xvj s viij d
De Cam' Symond'	vj s viij d
De Cam' Suthwell'	viij s iiij d
Summa iij li v s x d	
All' ten' de a^{o} dicti domini regis vij^{to}	
De ten' Cawmbray	xv s viij d
De ten' johannis Roer'	ix s
De Gardino Ric' karyour	xvj d
De novo coll' pro Maydenhall'	v s
De Gard' Brompton merc'	ij s
De ten' quond' layc'	viij s
De Gard' ex o^{to} sancti Egidij	x d
De Coll' Cant'	ij s vj d
De Holderness	iij li vj d
De sprount	xvj d
De shaw pro pratis jreland' etc.	xiij s iiij d
De ten' Westbury	ij d
De Goldfynch' pro terris in bello monte ~~solvend' in fest mic' sequente~~	viij s
Summa vj li vij s viij d	
All' Aul' eod' Anno	
De Hampton' Hall'	xiij s iiij d
De Aul' Edwardi	xxiiij s
De drowdalehall'	xxxj s viij d
De parva Aul' universitatis in alto vico	xxvj s viij d

All' scol' eod' anno
De scol' just' viij s
De scol' Arnald' iij s iiij d

All' Cam' eod' anno
De Cam' Corf' xvj s viij d
De Cam' Symond' x s
De Cam' Nafferton' xvj s viij d
Summa vij li x s iiij d

Summa omn' All' preced' xxij li xvj s iij d

Alloc' commun' eod' anno
In Gaud' sancti Cuthberti xj s x d
In communis et bat' Coll' xv li xj s
In communis servienc' soc' de exp' Coll' iiij li ix d

All' reparacionum et aliarum expensarum coll' eod' a°
In reparacionibus et alijs expensis infra Coll' et extra factis anno supradicto prout in paupiro dicti procuratoris xiij li ix s ix d ob
[2]Abb' de Abyngton' ij s
Abb' de Osney pro gard' pro hoc anno vj s et in part' sol' ij s' et iiij d a retro de tempore Burton xij s vij d

All' resoluc' eod' anno
In primis Abb' de Godstow xiiij s
Priori sancti frideswide pro omnibus debitis et arr' etc. ut in acquiet' inde fact' patet lvij s iiij d
Abb' de Eynsham' pro antiquo debito xvj s
Abb' de Eynsham' pro anno presenti viij s
Pro firma quond' otterworth iij s viij d
Collect' xvme domini regis ij s viij d
Summa v li x s viij d

All' pensionum sociorum eod' anno
In primis Castell' xx s
Burton' xij li vj s j d
Radyforth' xx s
Hamerton' xiij s iiij d
Summa xiiij li xix s v d

[2] [ADMC] These two entries were added later.

All' stipendiorum serviencium eod' a°

Ade Ryver iij s

Pincerne xx s

Coco pro servic' solito vj s viij d in reward' pro suo longo labor' xx s xxvj s viij d

lotrici v s

Summa liiij s viij d

All' pro officio proc' x s

Allocantur eidem computanti dat' Clerico nuper biblie in recessu suo iij s iiij d

Allocantur eidem computanti remiss' vidue ad angulum quadrivij viij d

All' eidem computanti pro debitis a retro eidem de anno r'r' Henr' quarti xiiij^mo quando dictus computans erat idem proc' xl s

Summa liiij s

Summa omn' Alloc' iiij^xx li xlviij s iiij d ob

⟨Et sic computatis computandis et allocandis [*sic*] Collegium debet computanto lxxxvj s vij d ob q^a

Walterus Trengof Cancellarius⟩

[*A roll of two membranes, in fair condition, but written in an untidy hand.*]

WHITSUN 8 HENRY V to WHITSUN 9 HENRY V (ROLL UC:BU1/F/32)

26 May 1420–11 May 1421

BURSAR: ROBERT BURTON[1]

dat'

Compotus procuratoris Collegij Willelmi de Dunelm' in Oxon' Magne Aula universitatis vulgariter nuncupat' a festo pent' inclusive anno rr' Henrici quinti octavo usque ad idem festum exclusive anno revoluto.

[*The Arrears are almost completely identical with the Allowances in* **F/31** *above, save for a few changes in spelling. The only difference is that the sums owed by Sprunt in the Arrears of tenements for 5–7 Hen are not 16d, but 13s 10½d for each year.*]

Summa omn' Arr' precend' xxiiij li viij s x d ob

Redditus ten' de Anno dicti domini Regis octavo

De Pratis retro oseney	xxvj s viij d
De ten' pypard'	liij s iiij d
De tenement' Thome Mayster	iij li
De ten' Bedford junioris	xxvj s viij d
De ten' Cawmbray	xx s
De ten' Johannis Roer'	xij s
De Gardino Ricardi Caryour	iiij s iiij d
De Gardino Ade River	iij s
De ten' Hugonis Benett	xx s
De Novo Collegio pro Maydyn' hall'	x s
De Gardino Hampton' Sedeler'	viij s
De Gardino Bromton Merc'	ij s
De ten' quond' lecest' modo lambherd'	viij s
De Gardino ex opposito ecclesie sancti Egidij	x d
De Collegio cantuar'	ij s vj d
De Abatissa de Godstowe pro quadam Schoppa iuxta ecclesiam sancte frideswide	xx d

[1] [ADMC] The evidence that Burton was Bursar in this year occurs in an additional entry to **F/28** above, the Roll of Arrears of 1416/7.

De holdernesse	iij li vj d[2]
De ten' Johannis Barber' quond' Stanton'hall'	xiij s iiij d
De Kentt' pell'	iiij s
De ten' Ricard' Sclatter' ar nat' dominic[3]	v s
De heredibus Johannis Sprount pro quond' mesuagio quod Johannes Bibury quond' tenuit	viij s x d ob
De Schawe pro pratis	xxvj s viij d
De ten' Westbury	xxxj s viij d
De uxore philippi Sutoris	xxvj s viij d
De ten' Dudelay	xxx s
De Goldfynche pro terris in bellomonte	viij s
De Bolde pro gardino quod ffulke Barbor' quond' tenuit	xx d
De Essex	xx li

Summa ten' precedencium xlv li viij s viij d ob

Redditus Aularum eod' Anno

De Brasynosse	iij li vj s viij d
De Aula Scuti	vj s viij d
De Aula sancti tho'	x s
De parva Aula universitatis in vico scolarum	xxxiij s iiij d
De hampton' hall'	xl s
De Aula Edwardi	xxiiij s
De Drowdalehall'	xlv s
De parva Aula universitatis in Alto vico	liij s iiij d

Summa xiij li xix s

Redditus Scolarum eodem anno

De Scolis qond' juster' de quodam determinatore s[*cilicet*] Benwell'	xxxij d
De Scolis quond' Arnalde modo Alwyn'	vj s viij d
De Scolis quond' Wyresdall' quodam determinatore s[*cilicet*] lymit'	ij s iij d

Summa xj s vij d

[2] [ADMC] Sewn onto the left edge of the roll is a slip which is clearly the Allowances for Room Rents for 12 Henry IV from roll **F**/23 of 1412/13 (see p. 224 above). It has been sewn onto the right edge of a roll and reads:

De cam' Nafferton'	iij s iiij d
De cam' Hurle	iiij s
De cam' makblith'	xiij s iiij d

Summa xx s viij d

[3] [ADMC] several erased words follow.

Redditus Cam' eod' anno

De Cam' Symonde x s

De Cam' Naffr' xvj s viij d

~~De Cam' Dinkley capt' ad festum peasche x s~~

~~De Cam' Sowthewell' capt' eciam ad festum pasche xvj s viij d~~

~~De Cam' Elswyk' capt' eciam ad festum pasche xiij s iiij d~~

Summa xxx s

[4]Item computans respondet de firma pro pratis retro Osney pro ij annis sibi all' vij s iiij d

Summa Omnium Reddituum iij^{xx} li xxix s iij d ob

Summa omn' oneratorum iiij^{xx} li xviij s ij d

Respondet computans eciam de receptis a antiquo rotulo per thom' mayster solut' xx s

All' ten' De Anno rr' Henrici quinti tercio

De ten' Cawmbray iij s ix d

All' Cam' eod' anno

De Cam' Naffr' iij s viij d

De Cam' Michaell' Jamys xvj s viij d

All' ten' de anno quarto

De ten' Cawmbray vj s iiij d

All' Cam' eod' Anno

De Cam' Michaell' Jamys vj s viij d

De Cam' Naffr' iij s iiij d

All' Scolarum eodem Anno

De Scol' Sawndyr' iiij s viij d

All' Ten' de Anno quinto

De ten' quond' laycest' viij s

De Spronтt' xiij s x d ob

All' Cam' eod' Anno

De Cam' Scharyll' xvj s viij d

De Cam' Naffr' iij s iiij d

[4] This, and the entry for 20s below, were added later.

All' Ten' de Anno sexto	
De Gardino Ade Ryver	iij s
De Ten' quond' laycestr'	viij s
De Gardino ex opposito sancti Egidij	x d
De Sprontt	xiij s x d ob
All' Aularum eod' A°	
De Aula Edwardi	iiij s
All' Scolarum eod' A°	
De Scol' Just'	v s iiij d
De Scoll' Multon'	vj s viij d
All' Cam' eod' Anno	
De Cam' Corffe	x s
De Cam' Symonde	vj s viij d
All' ten' de Anno Septimo	
De Ten' Cawmbray	xv s viij d
De Ten' Roer'	iiij s
De Gardino Ricardi Cariour	xvj d
De Gardino Brompton Merc'	ij s
De Ten' quond' laycest'	viij s
De Gardino ex opposito sancti Egidij	x d
De Sprontt	xiij s x d ob
De Ten' Westbury	ij d
De Goldfynch'	viij s
All' Aularum eod' Anno	
De aula Edwardy [*sic*]	iiij s
De Drowdallhall'	xxxj s viij d ~~xviij s iiij d~~
All' scolarum eod' anno	
De Scoll' Harnald'	iij s iiij d
All' Cam' eod' anno	
De Cam' Corffe	xvj s viij d
Summa Omn' All' Precedenc' xij li xiiij s vj d ob	
All' Ten' de anno octavo	
De pratis retro Oseney a thom' koke levand'	xiij s iiij d
De ten' Bedford' junioris	xiij s viij d
De ten' Cawmbray	xx s
De ten' Roer'	xij s

De Gardino Ricard' Caryor'	iiij s iiij d
De ten' Hugonis Benett'	xx s
De Gardino Hampton' Sadeler'	iiij s
De Gardino Browmpton Mercer	ij s
De Ten' quond' Laycest'	viij s
De Gardino ex opposito sancti Egidij	x d
De Collegio Cantuar'	x d
De Holdernesse	iij li vj d

[*Dorse*]

De Ricard' Sclatt' ad festum Nat' domini	x s
De Johannes Barbor'	viij s iiij d
De Kentt pell'	iiij s
De Swanne ~~pro mason~~ quond' Sprontt	v s
De hered' Sprontt pro novis ten'	viij s x d ob
De Schawe pro pratis	xiij s iiij d
De Westbury	v s
De Goldfynche	viij s
De Bolde pro Gardino	x d
De Essex	vj li xvj s viij d
Summa xvij li xij s vj d ob	

All' Scolarum eod' anno

De Scoll' Bassis Benwell'	xxxij d
De Scol' Halwyn'	vj s viij d
De Scoll' super bassas Scoll' hutt'	ij s iij d
Summa xj s vij d	

All' Aularum eod' Anno

De parva Aula universitatis in vico Scolarum	xx s
De Hampton' Hall'	xvj s viij d
De Aul' Edwardi	xxiiij s
De Drowdall' hall'	xxxj s viij d
De parva Aul' universitatis in Alto vico	xxvj s viij d
Summa v li xix s	

Aul' Cam' eod' Anno

De Cam' Symonde scilicet remittuntur v s	x s
De Naffr' pro Cam' in orto	iij s iiij d
Summa xiij s iiij d	

Summ' Omnium All' preceden' xxxvij li xj s

In Communis Sociorum et Batellis Collegij xiiij li vj s v d q[a]

In Reparacionibus et Expensis Collegij et intra et extra xxj li xiij s v d

In Resoluc' Reddituum

Abb' De Abyngton'	ij s
Abb' de Osseney	vj s
Abb' de Godstowe	xiiij s
Pro ffirma quond' Utterworth'	iij s viij d
Collect' quintodecimj domini Regis	ij s viij d

Summa xxviij s iiij d

In pensionibus Sociorum

Burton'	vij li vj s vij d ob q[a]
Redyford'	xl s
Elwyk'	xl s

Summa xj li vj s vij d ob q[a]

In Stipendijs ffamulorum

Pincerne	xiij s iiij d
Coco	xiij s iiij d
Barbitonsori	v s
lotrici	v s
Ade Ryver'	iij s

Summa xxxix s viij d

Pro Offic' procuratoris x s

Summa Total' omn' All' iiij[xx]viij li xv s vj d

⟨Et sic computatis computandis et allocandis allocandis collegium debet computanto – xxx s⟩

⟨Castell' Cancellarius⟩

[*A roll of two membranes, in good condition.*]

WHITSUN 9 HENRY V to WHITSUN 10 HENRY V (ROLL UC:BU1/F/33)

11 May 1421–31 May 1422

BURSAR: RICHARD WITTON

Compotus Ric' Wytton' procuratoris magne aule universitatis vulgariter nuncupat' a fest pent' inclusive a° rr' Henrici quinti nono usque ad idem festum exclusive anno revoluto

[*The Arrears are identical with the Allowances in* **F/32** *above, save for a few changes in spelling.*]

Summa omnium arr' precedencium xxxvij li xj s

Redditus ten' de Anno domini Regis Nono

De Pratis retro Oseney	xxvj s viij d
De Ten' Thome mayst'	iij li
De Ten' Pyppard'	liij s iiij d
De Ten' Bedforth'	xxvj s viij d
De Ten' Cawmbray	xx s
De Ten' Roer'	xij s
De Gardino Ric' Caryour	iiij s iiij d
De Ten' Hug' Benette	xx s
De Novo Collegio pro Madynhall'	x s
De Gardino Hampton' Sadler'	viij s
De Gardino Brompton Merc'	ij s
De Ten' quond' laycest'	viij s
De Gardino ex o^{to} ecclesie beati Egidij	x d
De Collegio Cantuar'	ij s vj d
De Abb' de Godstowe	xx d
De Holdyrnesse	iij li iij d
De Stanton Hall'	xiij s iiij d
De Kent' Pell'	iiij s
De Ric' Sclatter'	xiij s iiij d
De Swan pro manso quondam Sprount'	v s
De heredibus Johannis Sprount' pro quodam messuag' quod Joh' Bybery quondam tenuit	viij s x d ob
De Schawe pro pratis	xxvj s viij d
De Schopa super Angulum quatrivij [*sic*]	ij s

Redditus ten' eodem A°

De Gardino ade Ryv'	iij s
De Westbury[1]	xxxj s viij d
De Ten' quondam Philippi Suter	xxvj s viij d
De Ten' Dudley	xxx s
De Goldfynch' pro ten' in bello monte	viij s
De Gardino Bold'	xx d
De Esex	xxij li
De Ten' Johannis Rigton	vj s
Item computans respondet in receptis pro feno	xxxix s ij d

Summa om' Ten' precedencium xlvj li xvij s ij d ob[2]

Redditus aul' eod' A°

De Aul' Brasenoys	iij li vj s viij d
De Aul' Scuti	vj s viij d
De Aul' Sancti Thome	x s
De Parva Aula universitatis In vic' scolarum	xxxiij s iiij d
De Hampton' Hall'	xl s
De Aula Edwardi	xxiiij s
De Drowdell' hall'	xlv s
De parva Aul' universitatis in Alto vico	liij s iiij d

Summa Aul' xiij li xix s

Redditus scolarum Eodem Anno

De Scol' Magistri Roberti Woller'	viij s
De Scol' Magistri Roberti Halywell'	vj s viij d
De Scol' Magistri Hamundi Haydoke	vj s viij d

Summa xxj s iiij d

Redditus Cam' eod' A°

De Cam' Symonde	x s
De Cam' Redley	xvj s viij d
De Cam' Dyngley	x s
De Cam' Sowthwell'	xvj s viij d
De Cam' Elswyke	xiij s iiij d

[1] A lease of 29 September 1421 gives Westbury's property, Wakeman's tenement (now the site of 9 High Street), to John William, Glover (**UC:E/E1/D/8**). However, William does not appear in the accounts until 1424/5.

[2] [ADMC] This total has been altered, but is correct except that it does not include the last item. With this, the total would be £48 6s 4½d.

De Cam' Brerley	viij s
Summa iij li xiiij s viij d	
Summa omn' oneratorum cv li ij s ij d ob[3]	
All' ten' De A° Henrici quinti tercio	
De Cawmbray	iij s ix d
De Michaell' Jamis	xvj s viij d
All' de A° quarto	
De Cawmbray	vj s iiij d
De Cam' Michaell' Jamys	vj s viij d
All' cam' eodem A°	
De Cam' Naffr'	iij s iiij d
All' ten' de A° quinto	
De Ten' quondam laycest'	viij s
De Sprount'	xiij s x d ob
All' cam' eod' A°	
De Cam' Scharll'	xvj s viij d
De Cam' Naffr'	iij s iiij d
All' ten' de A° sexto	
De Gardino Ade Ryver	iij s
De Ten' quond' laycest'	viij s
De Gardino ex o^{to} ecclesie sancti Egidij	x d
De Sprount	xiij s x d ob
All' aul' eod' A°	
De Aul' edwardi	iiij s
All' scolarum eod' anno	
De Scol' Just'	v s iiij s
All' Cam' eod' A°	
De Cam' Corffe	x s
De Cam' Symond	vj s viij d
All' ten' de A° septimo	
De Ten' Cawmbray	xv s viij d
De Ten' quond' laycest'	viij s

[3] [ADMC] The correct total should be £105 2s 4½d.

De Gardino ex o^{to} sancti Egidij	x d
De Sprount	xiij s x d ob
De Ten' Westbury	ij d
All' aul' eod' A^{o}	
De Aula Edwardi	iiij s
De Drowdell Hall'	v s
All' cam' eod' A^{o}	
De Cam' Corffe	xvj s viij d
All' A^{o} octavo	
De Pratis retro Oseney	xiij s iiij d
De ten' Cawmbray	xx s
De ten' Roer'	xx s
De Ten' quond' laycest'	viij s
De Gardino ex o^{to} ecclesie sancti Egidij	x d
De Ricard' Sclatter	ij s viij d
~~De Her' Sprontt pro novis ten'~~	~~viij s x d ob~~
De Ten' Hugonis Benneth	xx s
De Johanne Barbour	vj s viij d
De Kent Pell'	xij d
De Swanne pro ten' quondam sprount	v d
De Her' Sprontt pro novis ten'	viij s x d ob
De Essex	xiij s iiij d
All' Aul' eod' A^{o}	
De Drowdell' hall'	xxxj s viij d
De Aula Edwardi	v d
Aul' cam' eod' A^{o}	
De Cam' Simond	x s
De Cam' Elswyke in orto	vj s viij d
[*No heading*]	
De Scol' de Thoma Hunter	ij s iij d

Summ' preceden' xvij li vj s xj d

[*Dorse*]

All' ten' de a^{o} nono	
De Thoma Mayster	xiij s
De Bedforth junioris	xix s iiij d

De Cawmbray	xx s
De Roer'	xij s
De Gardino Ric' Cariour	ij s iiij d
De Roberto Stretforth' pro gardino quondam Hampton sadler	ij s
De Mylton Talyour pro eodem gardino	viij d
De Bromton Merc'	ij s
De Ten' quond' laycest'	viij s
De Abb' de Godstowe	xx d
De Holdyrnesse	iij li iij d
De Stanton Hall'	xiij s iiij d
De Kent' pell'	iiij s
De Ric' Sclatter'	xiij s iiij d
De Swane pro manso quondam Sprount'	v s
De Heredibus spront pro quodam messuagio	viij s x d ob
De Schawe pro pratis	xxvj s viij d
De Westbery	xij s iij d
De Goldfynch' pro terris in bello monte	viij s
De Gardino Bold'	xx d
De Esex	iiij li x s
De Ten' Johannis Rigden	iij s
⟨All' pro feno non vendito	xxxj s iij d⟩

Summa precedenc' xix li x s ix d ob[4]

All' aularum eod' A°

De Aula Scuti	vj s viij d
De Parva Aul' universitatis in vic' scolarum	xiij s iiij d
De Aula Hampton'	xl s
De Aula Edwardi	xxiiij s
De Drowdell' hall'	xlv s
De Parva Aul' universitatis in alto vico	xxvj s viij d

Summa vij li xv s viij d

All' scol' eod' A°

De Scol' Magistri Roberti Woller'	viij s
De Scol' Magistri Roberti Halywell'	vj s viij d

[4] [ADMC] This total is 19s 1d too much. The entry against Westbury, of xij s iij d, has been altered, and in the Arrears for this year listed in **F/34** below, the figure is given as xxiij s iiij d. This gives the correct total.

De Scol' Magistri Hamundi Haydoke	vj s viij d
Summa xxj s iiij d	
All' cam' eod' A^{o}	
De Cam' Simond	x s
De Cam' Rydlay	xvj s viij d
De Cam' Southewell	xvj s viij d
~~De Cam' Elswyke in orto~~	~~vj s viij d~~
De Elswyke pro cam' quondam Bedyforth[5]	xiij s iiij d
De Magistro Roberto Dynkley	x s
Summa iij li vj s viij d	
Summa Omnium all' predendenc' xlix li xvj d ob	
In communis Sociorum et Batell'	xvj li iiij s xvj d ob
In Reparacionibus et expensis Collegij	xxij li iiij s viij d ob
In Resoluc' Reddituum	
Abb' De Abyngton'	ij s
Procuratoribus ecclesie beate marie pro stanton' hall' pro 2^{bus} annis et di' a retro	ij s vj d
Abb' de Osseney in plenum solucionem istius anno et omn' arr' a retro a principio mundi	xj s
Item collectoribus quintodecimo domini regis	xvj d
Item priori ffrideswide	xj s
Magistro Roberto Burton pro pecunijs mutuatis pro materia ufforth	iiij li
Summa v li vij s x d	
In Penc' Sociorum	
Magistro Roberto Burton'	iiij li ix s
Ric' Wytton'	xiij s iiij d
Thome Benwell'	xiij s iiij d
Johanni Ellwyke	xxx s
Magistro Willemo prentys	xiij s iiij d
Thome Boteler'	xiij s iiij d
Summa viij li xij s iiij d	
In Stipendijs ffamulorum	
Ade Ryver	iij s

[5] [ADMC] In the arrears in **F/34** below, this surname is spelt 'Redyford'.

Pincerne Johanni telme	xiij s iiij d
Coco	xx s
lotrici	v s
Thome barbour de Antiquo debito	vj s viij d
Summa xlviij s	

Item pro offic' procurat' x s

All' Ric Wytton pro incepcione sua xiij s iiij d

Summa totalis omnium all' cv li ij s v d ob

⟨Et sic computatis computandis et allocandis allocandis collegium debet computanto – iij d

Daventre commissarius venerabilis magistri M Johannis Castell' cancellarij⟩

[*A roll of two membranes, in good condition, and written in a neat hand.*]

WHITSUN 10 HENRY V to WHITSUN 1 HENRY VI (ROLL UC:BU1/F/34)

31 May 1422–23 May 1423

BURSAR THOMAS BENWELL

Compotus Thome Benewell' procuratoris Magne Aule Universitatis vulgariter nuncupat' a fest pentecost' inclusive a° rr' Henr' quinti decimo usque ad idem festum exclusive anno revoluto

[*The Arrears are identical with the Allowances in* **F/33** *above, save for a few changes in spelling.*]

Summa omn' arr' precedencium xlix li xvj d ob

Redditus ten' de a° r'r' H sexti primo

De Patris [*sic*] retro Osseney ⟨A° rr'H quinti decimo⟩	xxj s
De Ten' Thome mayst'	iij li
De Ten' Pyppard'	liij s iiij d
De Ten' Bedford	xx s
De Ten' Cawmbray	xx s
De Ten' Roer'	xij s
De gardino Ric' cariour	iiij s iiij d
De Ten' Hug' Benett	xx s
De Novo Collegio pro Maydenhall'	x s
De gardino hampton' sadeler	viij s
De Brampton marc'	ij s
De Ten' quond' laycest'	viij s
De gardino ex o^{to} ecclesie beati Egidij	x d
De Collegio Cantuar'	ij s vj d
De Abbat' de Godstowe	xx d
De Holdyrnesse	iij li iij d
De Stanton Hall'	xiij s iiij d
De Kent' pell'	iiij s
De Ric' Sclatter'	xiij s iiij d
De Swanne pro manso quondam Sprount'	v s
De heredibus Johannis Sprount' pro quodam messuag' quod Johannes bybery quondam tenuit	viij s x d ob
De Schawe pro pratis yreland etc.	xxvj s viij d
De Schopa super Angulum quatrivij [*sic*]	ij s iij d ob

De gardino Ad' Ryver	iij s
De Westbury	xxxj s viij d
De Ten' quond' Philippi Sut'	xxvj s viij d
De Ten' Dudley	xxx s
De goldfynch' pro terris in bello monte	viij s
De gardino Bolde	xx d
De Essex	xxij li
De Ten' Johannis Rygdon	vj s
Summa omn' precedencium xlvj li v s ij d	

Redditus Aul' eod' anno

De Aul' Brasenose	iij li vj s vij d
De Aul' Scuti	vj s viij d
De Aul' Sancti Thome	x s
De parva Aul' universitatis in vico scolarum	xxxiij s iiij d
De hampton' hall'	xl s
De Aula Edwardi	xxiiij s
De Drowdell' hall'	xlv s
De parva Aul' universitatis in alto vico	liij s iiij d
Summa Aul' xiij li xix s	

Redditus scolarum eod' anno

De Scol' magistri Ric' Wytton'	viij s
De Scol' magistri Roberti halywell'	vj s viij d
De Scol' magistri holgat'	vj s vi[*ij d*]
Summa xxj s iiij d	

Redditus cam' eod' a^{o}

De Camera Bap' Can'	vj s viij d
De Camera Mybbys	x s
De Camera Thome Rodley	xiij s iiij d
De Camera Symond'	xiij s iiij d
De Camera Hunfridi Rodley	xvj s viij d
De Camera Dynklay	x s
De Camera Sothwell'	xvj s [*viij d*]
De Camera thornton	iij s [*iiij d*]
De Camera Bowete	xvj s [*viij d*]
De Camera preston'	xiij s iiij d
De Camera Abbatis	xvj s viij d
De Camera tonge	xvj s viij [*d*]
De Camera Cracanthorp	xx s

De Camera Radclyfe	v s
Summa viij li xviij s iiij d	
Summa omn' oneratorum cxix li v s ij d ob	
All' ten' de a° H' quinti tercio	
De Cambray	[*iij s ix d*][1]
De Mich' Jamis	[*xvj s viij d*]
All' de a° quarto	
De Cambray	vj s [*iiij d*]
De Mich' Jamys	vj s [*viij d*]
All' cam' eodem a°	
De Camera Naffreton'	[*iij s iiij d*]
All' ten' de anno quinti [*sic*]	
De Ten' quondam Laycest'	[*viij s*]
De Sprount'	[*xiij s x d ob*]
All' cam' eod' a°	
De Cam' scharle	[*xvj s viij d*]
De Cam' Naffr'	[*iij s iiij d*]

[*Dorse*]

All' ten' de a° sexto	
De Gardino Ad' Ryver	[*iij s*]
De Ten' quond' laycest'	[*viij s*]
De gardino ex o^to^ ecclesie sancti Egidij	[*x d*]
De Sprount	[*xiij s x d ob*]
All' aul' eod' Anno	
De Aula Edwardi	[*iiij s*]
All' Scolarum eod' a°	
De scolis Just'	[*v s iiij s*]
All' Cam' eod' A°	
De Camera Croffe	x s
De Simond	vj s viij [*d*]

[1] [ADMC] The roll is torn at this point. However, the missing figures can largely be supplied from the arrears in **F**/35 below.

All' ten' de A^{o} septimo	
De Ten' Cambray	xv s vi[*ij d*]
De Ten' quond' laycest'	viij s
De gardino ex o^{to} ecclesie sancti Egidij	x d
De Sprount	xiij s x d [*ob*]
De Ten' Westbury	ij d
All' Aul' eod' A^{o}	
De Aula Edwardi	iiij s
De Drowdell Hall'	v s
All' cam' eod' A^{o}	
De Cam' Croffe	xvj s viij d
Summa precedencium ix li xiiij s vij d ob[2]	
All' A^{o} octavo	
De Pratis retro Osseney	xiij s iiij d
De Cambray	xx s
De Ten' quond' laycest'	viij s
De Gardino ex o^{to} ecclesie sancti Egidij	x d
De Ricard' sclatar'	ij s viij d
De Ten' Hug' Benett	xx s
De Johanne Barbour	vj s viij [*d*]
De Kent pell'	xij d
De Swanne pro ten' quondam sprount	v s
De heredibus Sprontt pro novis ten'	viij s x d ob
De Essex	xiij s iiij d
De Ten' Roer'	iij s
All' Aul' eod' A^{o}	
De Drowdall' Hall'	xviij s vij d
De Aul' Edwardi	v d
Aul' Cam' eod' A^{o}	
De Camera Symond	x s
De Camera Elswyke in orto	vj s viij [*d*]
All' scol' eod' a^{o}	
De Scol' thoma hunt'	ij s ii[*j d*]
Summa vij li v s ob	

[2] [ADMC] The correct total is £9 14s 6½d.

All' ten' de A° nono	
De Thoma Mayster	xiij s [*iiij d*]
De Cambray	xx s
De Hug' Benett	xx s
De Abbat' de Godstowe	x d
De Holdyrnesse	iiij s
De Kent' pell'	iiij s
De Ric' Sclatter'	xiij s iiij d
De Swanne pro manso quondam Sprount'	v s
De Heredibus spront pro quodam messuag'	viij s x d ob
De Westbery	xij s iij d
De gardino Bold'	xx d
De Goldynch pro ten' in bello monte	vj s
Summa v li vij s ob[3]	
All' Aul' eod' Anno	
De Drowdell' hall'	v s
All' scolarum eod' A°	
De Scol' M Roberti Woller'	xviij d
De Scol' M Roberti Halywell'	vj s viij d
De Scol' M hamundi haydok	iiij d
All' cam' eod' A°	
De Camera Symond°	x s
De Camera humfridi Rydlay	xl d
De Camera Sothwell	xvj s viij d
De Magra [*sic*] Roberto dynkley	x s
Summa liij s vj d	
All' ten' de A° p° regis H sexti	
De Pratis retro Osseney	iiij s iiij d
De Ten' Thome mayst'	xj s v[*j*] d
De Ten' filij eiusdem ⟨quondam bedford⟩	xviij s [*iiij d*]
De Ten' Cambray	vj s viij d
De ten' Roer'	xij s
De gardino Brampton Marc'	ij s
De Ten' Roberti lambart	viij s
De gardino ex o^{to} ecclesie sancti Egidij	x d

[3] [ADMC] The right sum ought to be £4 15s 11½d.

De Abb' de godstowe	xx d
De Holdyrnesse	iij li iij d
De Thome Barbour pro Stanton Hall'	xiij s iiij d
De Kent' pell'	iij s
De Ric' Sclatter'	xiij s iiij d
De Swanne pro manso quondam Sprount'	v s
De heredibus Johannis Sprount' pro quodam messuag' quod Joh' Bybery quondam tenuit	viij s x d ob
De Schawe pro pratis	xxvj s viij d
De gardino Ad' Ryv'	iij s
De Ten' Westbery	xxiij s viij d
De goldfynch' pro ten' in bello monte	viij s
De gardino Bold	xx d
De Ten' Johannis Rygdon'	iij s vj d
De Essex'	v li
Summa xvj li xvj s iiij d ob	

All' Aul' eod' a°

De parva Aula universitatis in vico scolarum	xx s
De Aula Hampton'	xxvj s viij d
De Aula Edwardi	xiiij s
De Drowdall' hall'	xxxviij s iiij d
De Parva Aula universitatis in alto vico	xxvij s viij d
Summa vj li v s viij d	

All' scolarum eod' a°

De Scol' M Ric' Wytton'	viij s
De Scol' M Roberti halywell'	vj s viij d
De Scol' M Thome holgate	vj s viij d
Summa xxj s iiij d	

All' cam' eod' A°

De Camera Humfridi Rodley	xvj s viij d
De Camera M Roberti Bowete	iij s iiij d
De Cam' M Nichi preston'	iiij s iiij d
De Cam' M Roberti Dynklay	x s
De Cam' abbatis de quibus abbas iiij s so[. . .] debet	xvj s viij d
De Cam' M Roberti tonge	xvj s viij d
De Camera thome Rodley	xiij s iiij d
De Camera M Thome Sothwell	xvj s viij d
De Cam' M Mebbys	x s

De Cam' Cracanthroppe	xx s
Summa vj li vij s viij d	
Summa all' precedenc' lv li iiij s viij d[4]	
In communis sociorum et batell' etc.	xvij li viij s j d q[a]
In reparacionibus et expensis Collegij	xvj li ix s viij d ob
In reparacionibus Essex'	xxvj s iiij d
In resoluc' reddituum	
In primis Abb' de Osseney	xx s xx d
Item Collectoribus quintodecimi domini regis	xvj d
Item Abbath' sancti ffrideswide	xij s x d
Item Abbath' de godstow	xxviij s
Item Magistro Collegij pro pecunijs mutuatis in materia Orford	iiij li
Item eidem Magistro pro salario alterius anni a retro et pro alijs debitis antiquis	iij li ij s xj d
Item pro pratis retro Osseney	iij s viij d
Item legisperitis londonijs	xiij s iiij d
Summa xij li x s j d[5]	
Item pencionum sociorum	
Item Magistro pro stipendio Magistratus et officio sacerdotali et alijs debitis	iij li xiiij s viij d
Magistro Ric' Wytton'	xiij s iiij d
Thome Benwell'	xiij s iiij d
Domino Johanni Ellwyk'	iij li vj s viij d
Magistro Willemo prentyse	xliij s iiij d
Thome Boteler'	xiij s iiij d
Thome Hunter'	xiij s iiij d
Summa xj li xviij s	
In stipendijs ffamulorum	
Johanni telme de antiquo debito	xxvj s viij d
Thome Barbour de antiquo debito	vj s
Johanni Barbour pro antiquo debito	iij s ix d
lotrici pro antiquo debito	xx d
Barbitonsori pro anno instanti	v s

[4] [ADMC] The correct total is apparently £55 6s 8d.
[5] [ADMC] The correct total is apparently £12 9s 1d.

Item Thome Coke pro Anno instanti xx s
Pro Officio procuratoris x s
Summa iij li xiiij d ix d

Summa omn' all' cxvij li v s iij d ob q[a]

⟨Memorandum quod computatis computandis et allocatis allocandis computans debet collegio – x s

Castell' Cancellarius⟩

[*A roll of two membranes, containing an unusually high number of incorect totals.*]

WHITSUN 1 HENRY VI to WHITSUN 2 HENRY VI (ROLL UC:BU1/F/35)

23 May 1423–11 June 1424

BURSAR: THOMAS BENWELL

⟨ non dat.⟩

Computus Thome Benewell' Procuratoris Collegij Magne Aule Universitatis Oxon' vulgariter nuncupat' A festo Pentecost' inclusive usque ad idem festum exclusive A° rr' Henrici sexti 2°.

[*Arrears are as in the Allowances of* **F/34**, *with the following alterations:*

Under Arrears of 4 Hen V, Cambray owes 3s 10d.

Under Arrears of Rooms for 6 Hen V and also 7 Hen V, the entries for Croffe are omitted.

The total for 4–7 Hen V is given as £8 7s 11½d.

Under Arrears of Halls for 8 Hen V, Drawda Hall now owes 18s 7d, and the total of arrears for this year is £7 5½d.

Under Arrears of Tenements for 9 Hen V, Westbury now owes 23s 4d, and the total for tenements is now £5 7½d.

Under Arrears of Rooms for the same year, Humfrey Rodley now owes 3s 4d, and the total for rooms is now 53s 6d.

Under Arrears of Tenements for 1 Hen VI, for Thomas Barbour, read John Barbour, and Westbury now owes 21s 8d; the total now is £16 14s 4½d.

Under Arrears of Rooms for the same year, the unnamed Abbot now owes 4s, and Robert Tonge 11s 8d, and the total is now £5 10s.]

Summa omnium Arr' precedencium liij li iiij d

Redditus Ten' de [*sic*] rr' H sexti secundo

De Pratis retro Osseney	xx s iiij d[1]
De Ten' Thome Mayst' ⟨ter' Nat' sancti johannis Bapt'⟩	iij li

[1] [ADMC] Written over erasure.

De Ten' Pippard ⟨ter' Nat' sancti jo Bapt' debet ij nobil'⟩ liij s iiij d
De Ten' ⟨filij Thome Mayst'⟩[2] ⟨ter' Nat' sancti jo Bapt'⟩ xx s
De Ten' Cawmbray xx s
De Ten' Roer ⟨ter' festum Michael'⟩ xij s
De Gardino Ric' Cariour ⟨ter' Johannis Bapt' debet xij d⟩ iiij s iiij d
De Ten' Hug' Benett ⟨ter' festum Nativitatis domini [. . .] debet [. . .] xxx s⟩ xx s
De Novo Collegio pro maydenhall' x s
De Gardino ⟨Roberti Stretford'⟩[3] ⟨ter' festum Michael'⟩ iiij s
De Gardino ⟨Vese⟩ ⟨ter' festum Michael'⟩ iiij s
De Gardino Brampton marc' ⟨ter' festum Annunciacionis debet ij s⟩ ij s
De Ten' quond' laycest' ⟨ter' festum Michael'⟩ iiij s
De Gardino ex o^{to} ecclesie sancti Egidij x d
De Collegio Cant' ij s vj d
De Abbat' de Godstowe xx d
De Holdyrnesse iij li iij d
De Stanton Halle ⟨ter' festum sancti johannis debet ij nobil'⟩ xiij s iiij d
De Kent' pell' ⟨ter' festum sancti johannis debet [*sic*]⟩ iiij s
De Ric' Sclatter' ⟨ter' festum Nativitatis domini . . . debet viij s x d⟩ xiij s iiij d
De Swanne pro manso quondam sprount v s
De heredibus Johannis Sprount pro quodam messuag' quod Johannes bybery quondam tenuit viij s x d ob
De Schawe pro pratis yreland etc. xxvj s viij d
De Schopa super anglum quadrivij ij s viij d
De Gardino ade Ryver iij s
De Westbury ⟨ter' festum sancti Johannis⟩ xxxj s viij d
De Ten' quond' philippi sut' ⟨ter' festum sancti Johannis debet⟩ xxvj s viij d
De Ten' Dudley ⟨ter' festum sancti Johannis debet⟩ xxx s
De ⟨~~Ten~~ de johanne Spyser'⟩[4] ⟨ter' festum sancti Michael'⟩ viij s

[2] [ADMC] Written over an erasure.
[3] [ADMC] Written over an erasure.
[4] [ADMC] Written over an erasure.

De Gardino Bolde ⟨ter' Annunciacionis⟩	xx d
De Essex	xx li
De Ten' Johannis Rygdon' ⟨ter' festum Michael'⟩	vj s

Item recepit computans de ~~eo~~ excrescencijs a° rr H sexti Secundo `et arr' de pede computi alterius'[5] xxxv s | xxxv s

Item recepit de communi cista pro certis negocijs Collegij | xxvj s viij d

Summa xlvij li xij s vj d ob[6]

Redditus Aul' eod' a°

De Aul' Brasenose	iij li vj s vij d
De Aul' Scuti	vj s viij d
De Aul' Sancti Thome	x s
De Parva aul' universitatis in vico scolarum	xxxiij s iiij d
De Hampton' Halle	xl s
De Aula Edwardi	xxiiij s
De Drowdell' hall'	xlv s
De Parva aul' universitatis in alto vico	liij s iiij d

Summa xiij li xix s

Redditus scol' eod' a°

De Scol' M Thome Elond	viij s
De Scol' M Johannis lyttyldon	vj s viij d
De Scol' M Willelmi sutton	vj s viij d
⟨Item computans respondet pro receptis de focalibus	viij s vj d⟩

Summa xxix s x d[7]

Summa omnium oneratorum [*blank*]

Redditus cam' eod' a°

De Camera Mebbys	x s
De Cam' Symon	xiij s iiij d
De Cam' Humfridi Rodeley	xvj s viij d
De Cam' Thome Bryd pro iij ter'	xij s viij d
De Cam' M Roberti Dynkeley	x s
De Cam' Kellow pro j ter'	iij s iiij d
De Cam' M Roberti Bowett	xvj s viij d

5 [ADMC] Interlineated as shown.
6 [ADMC] The correct total is £47 16s 6½d.
7 [ADMC] Figures written over an erasure.

De Cam' Preston	xiij s iiij d
De Cam' Crakynthroppe pro j termino	v s
⟨De Cam' domini Egidij pro uno termino	iiij s ij d⟩
Summa v li iiij s x d[8]	

Summa omnium oneratorum cxxj li vj s vj d ob

All' de a° rr' H' quinti tercio	
De Ten' Cambray	iij s x d
All' cam' eodem a°	
De Cam' Mich' Jamis	xvj s viij d
All' de a° quarto	
De Ten' Cambray	vj s iiij d
All' cam' eodem a°	
De Cam' Mich' Jamis	vj s viij d
De Cam' Naffreton'	iij s iiij d
All' ten' a° quinto	
De Ten' quondam laycestre	viij s +
De Sprount	xiij s x d ob
All' cam' de eodem a°	
De Cam' Scharle	xvj s viij d +
De Cam' Naffreton'	iij s iiij d
All' ten' de a° sexto	
De Gardino ade Ryver	iij s
De Ten' quond' laycest'	viij s +
De Gardino ex o^to ecclesie sancti Egidij	x d
De Sprount	xiij s x d ob
All' aul' eod' Anno	
De Aula ewardi [*sic*]	iiij s
All' scol' eodem a°	
De Scol' iuster	v s iiij s
All' cam' eodem a°	
De Camera Symon	vj s viij d +

[8] [ADMC] Last two figures written over an erasure.

All' ten' de a° sept'	
De Ten' Cambray	xv s viij d
De Ten' quond' laycest'	viij s
De Gardino ex o^to ecclesie sancti Egidij	x d
De De [*sic*] Sprount	xiij s x d ob
De Ten' Westbury	ij d +
All' Aul' de eodem a°	
De Aula Edwardi	iiij s
De Drowdall Hall'	v s
Summa viij li vij s xj d ob	
All' ten' de a° oct'	
De Pratis retro Osseney	xiij s iiij d
De Cambray	xx s
De Ten' quond' laycest'	viij s +
De Gardino ex o^to ecclesie sancti Egidij	x d
De Ric' sclattar'	ij s vj d
De Ten' Hug' Benett	xx s
De Johanne Barbour	vj s viij d
De Swanne pro ten' quondam sprount	v s
De heredibus sprount pro novis ten'	viij s x d ob
De Essex	xiij s iiij d
De Ten' Roer'	iij s
All' aul' eodem a°	
De Drowdall' Hall' ⟨Sorsby debet⟩	xviij s vij d
De Aul' Edwardi	v d
Aul' camerarum eodem a°	
De Cam' Symon	x s +
De Cam' elwyke in orto	vj s viij d
All' scol' eodem a°	
De Scol' Thoma Hunter	ij s iij d
Summa vj li xix s v d ob	
All' ten' de A° nono	
De Thoma Mayst'	xiij s iiij d
De Cambray	xx s
De Abbat' de godstow	x d
De Holdyrnesse	iiij s

De Swane pro manso quondam spront	v s
De heredibus sprount pro quodam messuag'	viij s x d ob
De Gardino Bold'	xx d
De Goldfynch' pro terris in bello monte	vj s
De Ten' Westbury	xij s iij d

[*Dorse*]

All' aularum eodem a^o^

De Drowdell' hall'	v s

All' scol' eodem a^o^

De Scol' M Roberti Woller'	xviij d
De Scol' M Haymundi Haydok	iiij d

All' cam' eodem a^o^

De Cam' Symon	x s +

Summa iiij li viij s ix d ob

All' ten' de a^o^ rr' H sexti p^o^

De Johanni Bosworth pro pratis retro Osseney	iiij s iiij d
De Ten' Thome Mayster	xj s vj d
De Ten' filij eiusdem quod tenuit Bedford iunior	xviij s iiij d
De Ten' Roer'	xij s
De Ten' Roberti lambart	viij s
De Gardino ex o^to^ ecclesie sancti Egidij	x d
De Abbat' de godstowe	xx d
De Holdyrnesse	ij s
De Ric' Sclatter'	xiij s
De Swanne pro manso sprount	v s
De heredibus sprountt pro quodam messuag' quod Johannes [*sic*] quondam tenuit	viij s x d ob
De Gardino ade Ryver	iij s
De Ten' Westbury	xv s
De Goldfynche pro terris in bello monte	xvj d +
De Gardino Bolde	xx d
De Ten' Johannis Rygdon'	iij s vj d
De Johanne Hunt in Essex' pro ⟨Roberto Schelmeford⟩	iij s
De Johanne Hunnte	ij li vj s viij d

Summa xvj li xix s viij d ob ⟨~~v li xiiij s ob~~⟩[9]

[9] [ADMC] Written in a very small, informal hand.

All' aularum eodem a°
De [*entry erased*]
De Aula Hampton' ⟨p'[. . .] lavandr' ffcd' [*sic*] cirotecarius in `cornerio ecclesie omnium sanctorum/⟩[10] iij s ij d
De [*entry erased*]
De Aul' Drowdale ⟨paderne deb'⟩ xxxv s
Summa [*blank*]

All' scol' eodem a°
De Scol' M^i Roberti Haliwelle vj s viij d
De [*blank*]

All' camera' eodem a°
[*blank*] Cam' M Nich' Preston' iiij s iiij d
De Cam' abbatis iiij s
De Cam' domini Thome Rodley iij s iiij d
De Cam' Mebbys x s
De Cam' crakintrope xx s
Summa iij li xvij s vj d

All' ten' de a° rr' H sexti secundo
De Ten' Thome Mayst' xj s vj d
De Ten' Roer cuius ter' `festum´ sancti Mich' futur' ij s viij d
De Ten' Hug' Benett cuius ter' natal' domini fuit xx s
De Gardino Brampton mercer cuius terminus festum annunciacionis beate preterit' ij s
De Ten' ex o^to ecclesie sancti Egidij x d
De Abbat' de Godstow xx d
De Holdirnesse cuius ter' assumpc' sancte Marie fut' iij li xij d
De Johanne Barbour pro staunton hall' xiij s iiij d +
[*an entry erased*]
De Swanne pro Ten' quondam [*sic*] v s
De Heredibus sprount pro quodam messuag' quod Johannes Bybery tenuit viij s x d ob
De Schaw pro pratis ireland xxvj s viij d +
De Gardino ade ryver iij s
De Johanne Spicer' ⟨pro terris in bello monte cuius ter' festum sancti Mich' fut'⟩ vj s ij d +
De Gardino Bolde xx d

10 [ADMC] Above line in text. [RHDS] The first three words of the addition are obscure.

⟨Item petit Johannes Rede de Exsex' all' pro Johanne Tyrelle⟩[11] x s
De Ten' Johannis Rygdon' iiij s ij d
Summa viij li xviij s vj d ob

All' Aul' eodem a°
De Aul' Scuti iij s iiij d
De Parva aul' universitatis in vico scolarum xxxiij s iiij d +
De Aul' Hampton' x s +
De Aul' Edwardi xviij s iiij d
De Drowdale Hall' v s
De Parva aul' universitatis in alto vico xxvj s viij d
Summa iiij li v s viij d

All' scolarum eodem a°
De Scol' M [*erasure*]

All' camer' eodem a°
De Camera Mebbys x s
De Camera M Roberti Bowett xvj d
De Camera Symond vj s viij d
De Camera Humfridi Roddeley cuius ter' festum sancte [*sic*] Cedde fut' xvj s viij d
De Camera Dynkley x s
De Camera preston xiij s iiij d
De Camera Crakynthroppe v s
Summa camerarum iij li iij s

Summa omnium All' precendencium xlviij li vij d ob

In communis et contribucionibus sociorum xv li v s ij d ob
Item in reparacionibus collegij et alijs expensis Collegij ix li xvij s vij d
Item in reparacionibus Essex et allocatis Johanni Rede et pro toga sua xx s xj d
Item in allocatis Johannis Hunt de Essex' pro toga et Sturdy xv s iiij d
Item in Edificacione domus apud Hampton Halle xxvj li xviij s vj d ob
Item in batellis laborancium Collegij iij li iij s ob q[a]
Summa lvij li vij d ob q[a]

[11] [ADMC] Written over an erasure.

Item in resolucionibus reddituum

Item abbat' de Osseneye	x s x d
Item Priori sancte ffrideswide	xiij s ij d[12]
Item in placitacionibus et iuris peritis	iiij li viij s iiij d ob
Item [*blank*] Harbarfylde pro pratis retro Osseney	iij s viij d
Summa v li xvj s ob	

Item in pencionibus sociorum

In primis M^{o} Ric^{o} Wytton	xiij s iiij d
Item Thome Benwell'	xiij s iiij d
Item domino Johanni Elwyke	ij li xiij s iiij d
Item M^{o} Willelmo Prentyse	ij li xiij s iiij d
Item Thome Boteler	xiij s iiij d
Item Thome Hunter	xiij s iiij d
Summa viij li	

Item in stipendijs ffamulorum

Item Thome Coke	xx s
Item Barbitonsori	ij s vj d
Item lotrici	v s
Item pro officio procuratoris Collegij	x s
Summa xxxvij s vj d	

Summa omn' all' ~~cxxvj~~ cxx li xiiij s ix d ob q^{a}

⟨Et sic computatis computandis et allocatis allocandis computans debet collegio – xj s viij s ob q^{a}⟩

⟨Memorandum predictus procurator pro utroque anno procuratorij sui satisfecit Collegio de Summa predicta exceptis v s quibus indebitatur collegio⟩

[*Very clear, though not very tidy. 2 membranes*]

12 [ADMC] Figures written over an erasure.

3 HENRY VI (ROLL UC:BU1/F/36)
11 June 1424–27 May 1425?[1]

BURSAR: JOHN ELWYK

⟨non dat⟩

Compotus Magistri Johannis Elwyk procuratoris Magne Aule Universitatis Oxon anno rr' Henrici Sexto Tercio

[*The Arrears are identical with the Allowances in* **F/35** *above, save for a few changes in spelling.*]

Summa omnium Arr' precedencium xlviij li vij d ob

Redditus Ten' de Anno tercio Regis Henr' Sexti

De Pratis retro oseney	xxvij s xj d
De Ten' Thome Mayst'	iij li
De Ten' Hug' Benett	xx s
De Ten' Roberti Dudley	xxx s
De Ten' Thome pipard'	liij s iiij d
De Ten' ffilij Thome Mayster in quo iam inhabitat Nicol' Schirburn'	xx s in manu Coll' per annum
De Ten' Ricardi Sclatter'	xiij s iiij d
De Ten' in quo inhabitavit Johannis Rygdon'	vj s in manu Coll'
De Ten' Kent' pell'	iiij s
De Johannis Wilyam glover[2]	xxxj s viij d
De Schopa quadrivij	xl s In manu Coll'
De Gardino Ricardi Carior	iiij s iiij d
De Gardino Johannis Barton Corveser'	xx d
De Gardino in Sewistwechyn	viij s In manu Coll'
De Gardino ex o^to^ ecclesie sancti Egidij	x d In manu Coll'
De Gardino Brampton Mercer	ij s
De Terris in Bello monte	viij s
De pratis yreland et Alrychesyd'	xxvj s viij d
De Swanne pro Ten' quondam Sprount	v s

[1] The roll is only dated to '3 Henry VI', but because the rolls to either side of it ran from one Whitsun to another, it is likely that this one did as well.

[2] John William, Glover, had been leased Wakeman's tenement (the site of 9 High Street) in 1421 (**UC:E/E1/D/8**), but this is his first appearance in the accounts.

De Heredibus Johannis Sprount pro ten' quod Johannes Bybery quondam tenuit viij s x d ob
De Roberto lambert viij s
De Johanne Barbour pro Stanton Hall xiij s iiij d
De Abbat' de Godstowe pro quadam Schopa iuxta portam sancte ffrediswide xx d
De Collegio Cantuar' ij s vj d
De Novo Collegio pro MaydinHall' x s
De Ten' Johannis Roer xij s
De Ten' Cambray xx s
De Holdernesse iij li iij d
De Essex xx li
De Ten' Alicie Corveser' quondam Philippi Suter xxvj s viij d
Summa xlvj li vj s ix d ob

Redditus Aularum eod' anno
De Aula Brasynose iij li vj s vij d
De Aula Scuti vj s viij d
De Aul' sancti Thome x s
De parva Aula universitatis in vico scolarum xxxiij s iiij d
De Hampton Hall' l s
De Aula Edwardi xxiiij s
De Drowdell' hall' xlv s
De parva Aula universitatis in alto vico liij s iiij d
Summa xiiij li ix s

Redditus scolarum eodem anno
De Scol' Magistri Thome Benwell' viij s
De Scol' M Johannis Elwyk vj s viij d
De Scol' M Thome Huntter vj s viij d
Summa xxj s iiij d

Redditus Camer' eodem anno
De Camera Magistri Roberti Bowett xvj s viij d
De Cam' Humfridi Rodley xvj s viij d
De Cam' M Walt' Blaket xiij s iiij d
De Cam' Dynkerlay x s
De Cam' domini Egidij Astley xvj s viij d
De Cam' Skelton' xvj s viij d
De Cam' Tong' xiij s iiij d
Summa v li iij s iiij d

⟨Item Respondet computans de receptis a communi cista et Alijs excrescencijs preter sortem domus v li xvj s viij d⟩

Summa omnium oneratorum cxx li xvij s ix d

All' de A° rr' H' quinti tercio	
De Ten' Cambray	iij s x d
All' Cam' eodem A°	
De Cam' Michael' Jamis	xvj s viij d
All' de A° quarto eiusdem	
De Ten' Cambray	vj s iiij d
All' cam' eodem A°	
De Cam' Michael' Jamis	vj s viij d
De Cam' Naffreton'	iij s iiij d
All' ten' de A° quinto	
De Ten' quondam laycestere	viij s
De Sprount	xiij s x d ob
All' Camer' eodem A°	
De Cam' Naffreton'	iij s iiij d
All' ten' de A° sexto	
De Gardino Ade Ryver	iij s
De Ten' quond' laycestere	viij s
De Gardino ex o^to^ ecclesie sancti Egidij	x d
De Sprount	xiij s x d ob
All' Aul' eodem' A°	
De Aula Edwardi	iiij s
All' scol' eodem A°	
De Scol' Juster	v s iiij s
All' ten' de A° septimo	
De Ten' Cambray	xv s viij d
De Ten' quond' laycestere	viij s
De Gardino ex o^to^ ecclesie sancti Egidij	x d
De Sprount	xiij s x d ob
All' Aul' eodem anno	
De Aula Edwardi	iiij s

De Drowdall' Hall'	v s
Summa vij li iiij s v d ob	
All' ten' de A^{o} octavo	
De Pratis Retro osenye	xiij s iiij d
De Cambray	xx s
De Ten' quond' laycestere	viij s
De Gardino ex o^{to} ecclesie sancti Egidij	x d
De Ricardo Sclatter	ij s vj d
De Ten' Hug' Benett	xx s
De Johanne Barbour	vj s viij d
De Swanne pro ten' quondam Sprount	v s
De Heredibus sprount pro novis ten'	viij s x d ob
De Essex	xiij s iiij d
All' Aularum eodem Anno	
De Drowdall' Hall'	xviij s vij d
De Aula Edwardi	v d
Aul' camerarum eodem A^{o}	
De Camera Elswyk in orto	vj s viij d
All' Scol' eodem A^{o}	
De Scolis Thome Huntter	ij s iij d
Summa vj li vj s v d ob	
All' ten' de A^{o} nono	
De Ten' Thoma Mayster	xiij s iiij d
De Cambray	xx s
De Holdernesse	iiij s
De Swanne pro Manso quondam Sprontt	v s
De Heredibus Sprount pro novis ten'	viij s x d ob
De Gardino Bolde	xx d
All' Aularum eodem anno	
De Drowdall' hall'	v s
All' scolarum eodem A^{o}	
De Scol' Magistri Roberti Woller'	xviij d
De Scol' Hamundi Haydok	iiij d
All' Camer' eodem A^{o}	
De Cam' Symond'	vj s viij d

All' ten' de A^{o} primo regis Henrici sexti

De Johanne Bosworth pro pratis retro oseney	iiij s iiij d
De Ten' Thome Mayster	xj s vj d
De Ten' ffilij eiusdem quod tenuit Bedford junior	v s
De Johanne Roer'	vj s iiij d
De Ten' Roberti lambart	viij s
De Gardino ex o^{to} ecclesie sancti Egidij	x d
De Holdernesse	ij s
De Ricardo Sclatter	xiij s
De Swanne pro Manso Sprount	v s
De Heredibus Sprount pro novis ten'	viij s x d ob
De Gardino Ade Ryver	iij s
De Gardino Bolde	xx d
De Ten' Johannis Rigdon'	iij s vj d
De Johanne Huntte in Essex'	xlvj s viij d
De Johanne Hunt de Exsex pro Roberto Chelmysford	iij s

All' Aul' eodem A^{o}

De Hampton' Hall	iiij s ij d
De Drowdall' Hall'	xj s viij d

All' scol' eodem A^{o}

De Scol' Magistri Roberti Halywell'	vj s viij d

All' Cam' eodem anno

De Camera Abbatis de Sulby	iiij s
De Cam' domini Thome Rodley	iij s iiij d
De Cam' Mebbys	x s
De Cam' Crakyntrope	xx s

Summa xij li viij s xj d

All' de A^{o} secundo regis H sexti

De Ten' Thome Mayster	xj s vj d
De Ten' Roer	ij s viij d
De Ten' Hug' Benett	xx s
De Ten' ex o^{to} ecclesie sancti Egidij	x d

[*Dorse*]

De Swanne pro ten' quondam Sprount	v s
De Heredibus sprount pro novis ten'	viij s x d ob
De Gardino Ade Ryver	iij s
De Johanne Rede de Exsex' pro Johanne Tyrelle	x s

De Johanne Rigdon patynmaker	iiij d
All' Aularum eodem Anno	
De Aula Drowdall'	v s
De Aula Scuti	iij s iiij d
All' camer' eodem Anno	
De Cam' Magistri Johannis Mebbys	x s
De Cam' Magistri Roberti Bowett	xvj d
De Cam' Symond	vj s viij d
De Camera Crakyntrope	v s
Summa iiij li xv s ij d ob	
Summa All' precendencium xxx li xv s ob	
All' ten' de Anno tercio Regis H Sexti	
De Ten' Thome Mayst'	iij li
De Ten' Thome Thundyer filij eius pro uno termino v s et tres termini in manu Coll'	xv s
De Ten' Dudley	vij s vj d Arrestantur
De Ten' Hug' Benett	vij s iiij d
De Ten' Thome pipart'	xiij s iiij d Arrestantur
De Ten' Johannis Wilyam glover	x s Arrestantur
~~De Ten' Ricardi Sclatter'~~	~~xiij s iiij d~~
De Ten' super Angulum quadrivij	xl s
De Swanne pro ten' quondam Sprount	v s
De heredibus Johannis Sprount pro novis ten'	viij s x d ob
De Gardino In Sewestwechyn	viij s
De Gardino Johannis Barton Corveser'	v d
De Gardino ex o^{to} ecclesie sancti Egidij	x d
De Johanne Spicer pro terris in bello monte	viij s
De Gardino Ade Ryver[3]	iij s
De Ten' Ricardi Sclatter	xv d
De Ten' Kentt' pell'	iij s
De Ten' Johannis Rigdon	vj s
De Johanne Schawe pro pratis yreland	xxvj s viij d
De Ten' Johannis Roer	vj s
De Ten' Cambray	xx s
De Ten' Johanne Barbour	xiij s iiij d

[3] [ADMC] This entry is omitted from the list of rents; no doubt in error.

De Ten' Roberti lambert viij s
De Holdernesse iij li iij d
De Essex xlj s
Summa xviij li xviij s vj d ob

All' Aul' eodem A°
De parva Aula universitatis in vico scolarum xiij s iiij d
De Aula Hampton' xx s iiij d
De Aula Edwardi xvj s
De Drowdall' hall' xxviij s iiij d
De parva Aula universitatis in Alto vico xx s
Summa iiij li xviij s

[*No heading*]
De Scol' M Benwell' viij s
De Scol' M Elwyk vj s viij d
De Scol' M Huntter vj s viij d
Summa xxj s iiij d

All' Camer' eodem anno
De Cam' Bowett xvj s viij d
De Cam' Humfridi rodley xvj s viij d
De Cam' Blakett xiij s iiij d
De Cam' Dynkley x s
De Cam' Skelton' x s
De Cam' Tong' xiij s iiij d
De Cam' domini Egidij pro ter' sancti Johannis futur' xvj s viij d
Summa iiij li xvj s viij d

Summa omnium All' precendencium lx li ix s vij d

Soluta pro diversis expensis factis per procuratorem In villa et extra
Summa Stauri empt' ad usum Colleg' viij s v s j d ob
Item in Reparacionibus et mutuatis ad extra x li xix s viij d ob
Item in Reparacionibus et expensis versus Exsex v li ix s ix d ob
Item in placitacionibus v li vij s vj d ob
Item in Expensis visitatorum batellis jurnellis contribucionibus et pro extranijs diversis iij li ix s vij d ob
Item in Communis sociorum xiiij li vj s v d q[a]
Item pro sera candel' et j torg' capell' vij s vj d ob
Summa xlviij li v s ix d ob[4]

[4] [ADMC] The correct sum is £48 5s 9¼d.

In Resolucionibus reddituum

In primis Abbati de Oseneye pro gardino infra Collegium vj s viij d

Item Abbati de Oseneye pro ten' Johannis Wilyam xv s

Item priori sancte ffredeswide xviij s viij d

Item pro redditu Besett pro pratis retro oseney iij s viij d

Item Abbati de Ensame pro antiquis Arr' pro Schopa quadrivij xx s

Item Abbati de oseney pro termino Annunciacionis preterito x s x d

Item Abbati de godstowe pro A° 3° R' H sexti xiiij s

Summa iiij li viij s x d

In stipendijs ffamulorum

Johanne heend' lotrici pro j termino xv d

Item Johanne Barbour pro ij anno v s

Item Juliane lotrici pro tribus terminis iij s ix d

Summa x s

Item ponitur in communi cista liij s iiij d

Item remanet Magister Ricardus in debit' ix s vij d Solut' est

Item peto Allocari pro Magistro Willelmo prentis xx d

In pencionibus Sociorum

Magistro Ricardo Wytton vj s viij d

Magistro Thome Benwell' xx s xiij s iiij d

Magistro Johanni Elwyke ij li xiij s iiij d

Magistro Willelmo P'rentis vj s viij d

Magistro Thome Buttler' vj s viij d

Magistro Thome Huntter vj s viij d

Item pro officio procuratoris x s

Item predicto procuratori pro labore suo ij s iij d ob

Summa omnium Allocatorum cxx li xvij s ix d

⟨Et sic computatis computandis et Allocatis Acomputans computans plene absolvitur et omnia eque inter domum et computantem penes istum compotum⟩

[*A very legible roll, slightly worn at the foot, and at the top of the dorse. All figures add up correctly, except for ¼d in 'Soluta pro diversis expensis'*]

WHITSUN 3 HENRY VI to WHITSUN 4 HENRY VI (ROLL UC:BU1/F/37)

27 May 1425–19 May 1426

BURSAR: THOMAS BENWELL

Compotus Magistri Thome Banwell' procuratoris Magne Aule universitatis Oxon' Anno rr' Henrici sexti quarto a ffesto Pentecost' inclusive usque ad item ffestum exclusive

[*The Arrears are identical with the Allowances in **F/36** above, save for a few changes in spelling.*]

Summa omnium arr' precedencium lx li ix s vij d

Redditus ten'

De Pratis retro Osyney'	xxvij s xj d
De Ten' Thome Master'	iij li
De Ten' Hugonis Benett	xx s
De Ten' Roberti Dudeley	xxx s
De Ten' Thome pippard'	liij s iiij d
De ten' Nicolai Scerburne annuatim	xx s
De Ten' Ric' Sclatter'	xiij s iiij d
De Ten' in quo inhabitavit Rigdon annuatim	vj s
De Ten' Kent' pelliparij	iiij s
De Ten' Johannis William glover	xxxj s viij d
De Gardino Ric' Cariour	iiij s iiij d
De Gardino Johannis Barton Corveser'	xx d
De Gardino Brompton Mercer	ij s
De Terris in Bello monte annuatim	viij s
De Pratis yreland' et alricheside annuatim	xxvj s viij d
De Sawnne [*sic*] pro ten' quondam sprount	v s
De Heredibus Sprount pro ten' quod Johannes Bybery quondam tenuit	viij s x d ob
De Roberto lambert'	viij s
De Johanne Barbour' pro stampton' Hall'	xiij s iiij d
De Abbatissa de Godstowe pro quadam schopa iuxta portam sancte ffrediswide xx d	
De Novo Collegio pro Mayden' Hall'	x s
De Ten' in quo habitavit Johannis Roer iam John' Coke	xij s

De Ten' Cambray	xx s
De Holdernesse	iij li iij d
De Manerio Mark' in Essex	xx li
De Ten' Allicie philippe'	xxvj s viij d
De Collegio Cantuar'	ij s vj d

Summa reddituum precedencium xliij li xvj s viij d ob

Redditus Aularum

De Aula Brasenose	iij li vj s vij d
De Aula scuti	vj s viij d
De Aula sancti Thome	x s
De parva Aula universitatis in vico scolarum	xxxiij s iiij d
De Aula Hampton	l s
De Aula Edwardi	xxiiij s
De Aula Drowdell'	xlv s
De parva Aula universitatis in alto vico	liij s iiij d

Summa xiiij li ix s

Redditus scolarum

De Scol' M Joh' Chadwyke'	vj s viij d
De Scol' Magistrorum Suedham et swaloe	vj s viij d
De Scol' quond' M Thome Benwe pro determinatore	v s
De [*entry erased*]	

Summa xviij s iiij d

Redditus camerarum

De Camera M Roberti Bowett iuxta promtuarium pro duobus terminis	iij s iiij d
De Magna Cam' qua iam habitat pro duobus terminis	x s
De Cam' Humfridi Rodley	xvj s viij d
De Cam' M Walteri Blaket	xiij s iiij d
De Cam' M Roberti Dynkelay	x s
De Cam' domini Egidij Astley	xvj s viij d
De Cam' Skelton'	xvj s viij d
De Cam' Tong'	xiij s iiij d

Summa v li

Item Respondet Computans de receptis de Johanne peys et Johanne Spicer pro pratis retro Oseney iij s ij d

Item pro focalibus de Thoma Talbot xiij s

Item de dimissis cum Rector' de Margaret rudyng in tempore

M Johannis Elwik ultra summam xlj s positam in rotulo dicti M Johannis iij s iiij d
Item de receptis pro schopa quadrivij vj d
Summa xxj s

Summa omnium oneratorum cxxv li xiiij s vij d ob

Redditus sequent' anno preterito erant in manu Coll' extra Scol' determinatoris ut prefertur sed iam dimittuntur quorum prius terminus est Nat' sancti Johannis Baptiste proximo fut'

De Gardino in Sewistwechyn	vij s
De Scol' M Symonis Row	viij s

Redditus sequent' anno preterito erant in manu Coll' et adhuc sunt

De Ten' super Angulum quadrivij	xl s
De Gardino ex o^{to} sancti Egidij	x d
De Gardino quond' Ade ryver	iij s

Allocat' de a^{o} rr' H' quinti tercio

De Cambray	iij s x d

Alloc' camerarum eodem anno

De Camera Michael' Jamis	xvj s viij d

Alloc' de a^{o} quarto eiusdem regis

De Cambray	vj s iiij d

[*Dorse*]

Alloc' camerarum eodem anno

De Camera Michael' Jamis	vj s viij d
De Camera Naffreton'	iij s iiij d

Allocat' ten' de anno quinto eiusdem regis

De Ten' quond' laycest'	viij s
De Sprount	xiij s x d ob

Allocat' camerarum eodem A^{o}

De Camera Naffreton'	iij s iiij d

Allocat' ten' de a^{o} sexto

De Gardino Ade Ryver	iij s
De Ten' quond' laycestere	viij s
De Gardino ex o^{to} ecclesie sancti Egidij	x d
De Sprount	xiij s x d ob

All' aul' eodem' a^{o}	
De Aula Edwardi	iiij s
All' scol' eodem a^{o}	
De Scol' Juster	v s iiij s
All' ten' de a^{o} septimo	
De Ten' Cambray	xv s viij d
De Ten' quond' laycest'	viij s
De Gardino \`ex o^{to}´ ecclesie sancti Egidij	x d
De Sprount	xiij s x d ob
All' aul' eodem anno	
De Aula Edwardi	iiij s
De Drowdall' Hall'	v s
Summa vij li iiij s v d ob	
All' ten' de a^{o} octavo	
De pratis retro Osyney	xiij s iiij d
De Cambray	xx s
De Ten' quond' laycest'	viij s
De Gardino ex o^{to} ecclesie sancti Egidij	x d
De Ric' Sclatter	ij s vj d
De Ten' Hug' Benet	xx s
De Johanne Barbour	vj s viij d
De Swanne pro ten' quond' Sprount	v s
De Heredibus sprount pro novis ten'	viij s x d ob
De Exsex	xiij s iiij d
All' aul' eodem a^{o}	
De Drowdall' Hall' ⟨Sorisby debet⟩	xviij s vij d
De aula edwardi	v d
All' camerarum eodem a^{o}	
De Camera Elswik in orto	vj s viij d
All' scol' eodem a^{o}	
De Scolis Thome Hunter quos debet M Robertus Burton	ij s iij d
Summa vj li vj s v d ob	
All' ten' de a^{o} nono	
De Ten' Thoma Master'	xiij s iiij d

De Cambray	xx s
De Holdernesse	iiij s
De Swanne pro Manso quond' Sprount	v s
De Heredibus Sprount pro novis ten'	viij s x d ob
De Gardino Bolde	xx d

All' aularum eodem a°

De Drowdall' hall'	v s

All' scolarum eodem anno

De Scol' M Roberti Woller'	xviij d
De Scol' Hamundi Haydok	iiij d

All' cam' eodem a°

De Cam' Simond'	vj s viij d

All' ten' de a° primo regis Henr' sexti

De Johanne Bosworth pro pratis retro Oseney	iiij s iiij d
De Ten' Thome Master	xj s vj d
De Ten' ffilij eiusdem quod tenuit Bedford junior	v s
De Johanne Roer'	vj s iiij d
De Ten' Roberti lambart	viij s
De Gardino ex o^to ecclesie sancti Egidij	x d
De Holdernesse	ij s
De Ricardo Sclatter	⟨x d⟩ vij s vj d
De Swanne pro Manso Sprount	v s
De Heredibus Sprount pro novis ten'	viij s x d ob
De Gardino Ade Ryver	iij s
De Gardino Bolde	xx d
De Ten' Johannis Rygdon'	iij s vj d
De Johanne Hunt in Essex quos debet Magister Robertus Burton	xlvj s viij d
De Johanne Hunt de Exsex pro Roberto Chelmsforde	iij s

All' aul' eodem anno

De Hampton' Hall	iiij s ij d
De Drowdall' Hall' ⟨Walterus paderne debet⟩	xj s viij d

All' scol' eodem a°

De Scol' M Roberti Halywell'	vj s viij d

[*no heading*]

De Camera Abbatis de Sulby	iiij s

De Cam' domini Thome Rodley	iij s iiij d
De Cam' Mebbis	x s
⟨Cam' Crakyntrope	iij s iiij d⟩
Summa xj li vj s ix d	

All' de a° secundo regis H sexti

De Ten' Hug' Benett	x s
De Ten' Thome Master	xj s vj d
De Ten' Roer	ij s viij d
De Ten' ex o^{to} ecclesie sancti Egidij	x d
De Swanne pro ten' quondam Sprount	v s
De Heredibus sprount pro novis ten'	viij s x d ob
De Gardino Ade Ryver	iij s
De Gardino Bolde	xx d
De Johanne Rede de Essex' pro Johanne Tyrell'	x s
De Johanne Rygdon patynmaker	iiij d

All' aul' eodem a°

De Aula Drowdall'	v s
De Aula Scuti	iij s iiij d

[*No heading*]

De Cam' M Johannis Mebbis	x s
De Cam' Symond	vj s viij d
De Cam' M Roberti Bowett	xvj d
[*no entry*]	⟨v s⟩ [*sic*]
Summa iiij li v s ij d ob	

[*No heading*]

De Ten' Thome Mayster	iij li
De Ten' Thome Thundy' filij eius pro uno termino v s et tres termini in manu Coll'	xv s
De Ten' Dudeley	vij s vj d arrestantur
De Ten' Hug' Benett	v s viij d arrestantur
De Ten' Thome pipard'	xiij s iiij d arrestantur
De Ten' Johannis William glover	x s arrestantur
De Ten' super Angulum quadrivij	xl s
De Swanne pro ten' quondam Sprount	v s
De Heredibus Sprount pro novis ten'	viij s x d ob
De Gardino in Sewestwechin	viij s
De Gardino Johannis Barton Corveser'	v d

De Gardino ex o^{to} ecclesie sancti Egidij	x d
De Johanne Spicer pro terris in bello monte	viij s
De Gardino Ade Ryver	iij s
De Ten' Ricardi Sclatter	xv d
De Ten' Kentt' pell'	iij s
De Ten' Johannis Rigdon	vj s
De Ten' Johannis Roer	vj s
De Ten' Cambray	xx s
De Ten' Johanne Barbour	xiij s iiij d
De Ten' Roberti lambert	viij s
Summa xij li viij s ij d ob	

Alloc' aul' eodem anno

De Aula Hampton'	xx s iiij d
De Aula Edwardi	iij s
De Drowdall' hall'	x s
De parva aula universitatis in vico scolarum	xiij s iiij d
Summa xxvj s viij d	

Alloc' camerarum eodem anno

De Cam' M Walteri Blakett	xiij s iiij d
De Cam' M Roberti Dyncley	x s
De Cam' M Roberti Tong'	xiij s iiij d
De Cam' domini Egidij Astley	xvj s viij d
De Cam' Umfridi Rodley	⟨iiij s ij d⟩ xvj s viij d
De Cam' Skelton'	viij s iiij d
Summa iij li xviij s iiij d	

All' ten' a° rr' H sexti quarto

De Ten' Johannis William Glover	vij s xj d arrestantur
De Ten' Thome Master'	iij li
De Ten' Roberti Dudeley	vij s vj d arrestantur
De Ten' Thome pippard'	xiij s iiij d arrestantur
De Ten' Nicolai Scherburn'	x s in manu Coll'
De Ten' in quo inhabitavit Rigdon patynmaker'	iiij s vj d in manu Coll'
De Ten' Kent' pell'	ij s iiij d
De Gardino Johannis Barton Corveser'	x d
De Gardino Brompton Mercer	ij s
De Johanne Spicer pro terris in bello monte	xvj d

De Schaw pro pratis yreland' cuius ultimus terminus est Assumpc' beate Marie futura xxvj s viij d
De Swanne pro ten' quondam sprount v s
De heredibus Sprount pro ten' quod Johannes Byber[1] quond' tenuit viij s x d ob
De Ten' Cambray xx s
De Holdernesse iij li iij d
De Essex quos Johannes Rede dabit Rectori de Margaret' Redyg xx s
Item de Exsex qui dimittuntur Rectori predicto ad edificacionem aule x s
Item pro Johanne Tirell' de Exsex petit dictus Red' allocari x s
Item item Red' petit allocari pro Roberto Chelmisforth' xij d

Summa xiij li x s iij d ob

All' aul' eodem anno

De Drowdell' Hall v s
De parva Aula Universitatis in alto vico xiij s iiij d

All' scol' eodem a°

De Scol' M Johannis Chadwyk vj s viij d

All' cam' eodem a°

De Cam' M Roberti Tong' xiij s iiij d
De Cam' M Roberti Dynclay x s

Summa xlviij s iiij d

Summa omnium Allocac' precedencium lx li liiij s viij d ob

In communis sociorum xij li vj s
Item in Batellis operariorum et contribucionibus et jurnellis sociorum iiij li ij d
Item in reparacionibus et expensis esex[2] v li ix s ix d
Item in Expensis versus Holdyrnese ij li iij s iiij d
Item in reparacionibus Aularum v li ix s xj d ob
Item in reparacionibus ten' et alijs expensis Collegij xxij li xvij s iij d

Summa liij li vj s v d ob

[1] [ADMC] Final letter has been altered.
[2] It was on this visit to Essex when Thomas Benwell's horse fell ill (see **UC:MA10/L2/1**, discussed on p. xix of the Introduction).

In resolucionibus reddituum

In primis Abbati de Oseney	xxj s viij d
Item abbatisse de Godstow	xiiij s
Item priori sancte ffredeswide	vj s viij d
Item pro redditu Besett de prato retro Oseney	iij s viij d
Summa xlvj s	

Item solut' socijs pro pencionibus a retro de anno ultimo preterito ij li

Item solut' in pensionibus sociorum de anno presenti

In primis M Ric' Wytton	xiij s iiij d
Magistro Thome Benwell'	xiij s iiij d
Magistro Johanni Elwik'	xiij s iiij d
Magistro Willelmo prentis	xlvj s viij d
Magistro Thome Butler'	vj s viij d
Magistro Thome Huntter	xiij s iiij d
⟨Item pro officio Magistratus	vj s viij d⟩
Item pro officio procuratoris	x s
Summa viij li iij s iiij d	

In stipendijs famulorum

In primis Thome Talbote	x s
Item barbintonsori	v s
Item Juliane lotrici	v s
Summa xxx s	

Summa omnium Alloc' precedencium cxxviij li vj d

⟨Et sic computatis computandis et allocatis allocandis domus est indebitatus computanti in summa xlv s x d ob

Chace Cancellarius⟩

[*Very clear roll, except at foot of the dorse, where rather worn. 2 membranes. All figures balance*]

WHITSUN 4 HENRY VI to WHITSUN 5 HENRY VI (ROLL UC:BU1/F/38)

19 May 1426–8 June 1427

BURSAR: THOMAS BUTLER

Compotus Magistri Thomas Botteler' Procuratoris magne Aule universitatis Oxon' Anno rr' Henrici sexto quinto a fest Pentecost' usque ad idem ffestum exclusive.

Arr' aularum a° sexto H quinti	
De Aula Edwardi quos debuit Johannes ardaghe	iij s iiij d
Arr' ten' a° octavo rr' H quinti	
De Ten' Ricardi Sclatter	ij s vj d
De Ten' Hugonis Benett	x s
Arr' ten' a° primo rr' H sexti	
De Johanne Bosworthe pro pratis retro osney	iiij s iiij d
De Ten' Ricardo Sclatter	x d
De Ten' Roberti Lambyrde	iiij s
Arr' cam' eodem a°	
De Camera Abbatis de Sowleby	iiij s
Arr' ten' de a° secundo H sexti	
De Ten' Hugonis Benett	x s
Arr' cam' eodem a°	
De Camera Magistri Roberti Benette	xvj d
Summa xl s iiij d	
Arr' ten' a° tercio eiusdem Regis	
De Gardino Johannis Barton Corveser'	v d
De Ten' Ricardi Sclatter	xv d
De Ten' Kentt' pelliparij	iij s
De Ten' Johanne Barbour pro Stampton Hall'	xiij s iiij d
De Johanne Spicer pro terris in parochia Egidijs viz in Bellomonte et alijs campis	vj s viij d
Arr' aularum eodem a°	
De Aula Edwardi	iij s

De Aula parva aula universitatis in vico scolarum xiij s iiij d

Arr' cam' eodem a°
De Camera Magistri Roberti Dynkley x s
De Camera Magister Roberti Tonge xiij s iiij d
De Camera Umfridi Rodeley iiij s ij d
De Camera Magistri Walteri Blakett xiij s iiij d
Summa iiij li xxij d

Arr' ten' de anno quarto eiusdem Regis
De Ten' Kent' pelliparij ij s iiij d
De Gardino Johannis Barton Corveser' x d
De Schaw pro pratis yrelande xiij s iiij d
De Essexya quos Johannes Rede dabit Rectori de Margarett Rudyg' xx s
De Exsexya qui dimittuntur cum predicto Rectore ad edificationem aule x s
De Exsexya pro Johanne Tyrell' petit dictus Rede allocari x s
De Essexya idem Rede petit allocari pro Rob' Chelmesford' xij d

Arr' scolarum eodem a°
De Scol' Magistri Johannis Chadewyk vj s viij d

Arr' aularum eodem a°
De Parva aula universitatis in alto vico xiij s iiij d

Arr' scolarum eodem a°
De Scolis Simoni Row a medie xlme usque ad festum sancti Thome ij s

Arr' cam' eodem a°
De Camera Magistri Roberti Tong' xiij s iiij d
De Camera Magistri Roberti Dynkley x s
De Camera Skelton viij s iiij d
Summa v li xj s iiij d

Summa omn' arr' precedencium xj li xiij s iiij d

Hec ten' sequencia sunt in parochia omnium sanctorum
De Ten' Johannis Willyam Glover xxxj s viij d
De Ten' Thome Mayster Glover iij li
De Ten' Nicholai Schirborne Cutteler xx s
De Ten' Roberti Dudeley xxx s

De Ten' Hugonis Bennet sariantte xx s
De Ten' Thome Pypparde Draper liij s iiij d
De Ten' Ricardi Sclatter xiij s iiij d
De Ten' Kentt Pelliparij pro uno termino xij d
De Ten' in quo inhabitavit Rigdon' iij s
Summa xj li xij s iiij d

In Paroch' sancti Martini
De Schopa super angulum quadrivij quo inhabitavit Nicholaus Strykmede xxvij s viij d annuatim
Sed procurator honoratus hoc anno pro duobus terminis tantum xiij s iiij d

In parochia sancte mildrede
De Gardino Ricardi Cariour quond' Holyfantte Hall' iiij s iiij d

In parochia sancte marie
De Stampton' Hall' in qua inhabitat Johannis Barbour xiij s iiij d
De Ten' Roberti Lalbyrde pincerne collegij mertonis in libero redditu viij s

In parochia sancti Petri in oriente
De Ten' Alicie Phylipe iuxta parvam aulam universitatis xxvj s viij d
De Ten' Cambray Glazyer xx s
De Ten' Johannis Cuke iuxta Cambray xij s
Summa iiij li xvij s viij d

Hec ten' sunt in suburbijs
De Gardino in parochia sancti Thome quod tenet Brampton' Mercer ij s
De Gardino in parochia sancte marie magdilene quod tenet Johannes Baron' corvisour xx d
De Pratis retro Osnay que tenuit Johannes Haynes de Henksey xxvj s viij d
De Pratis yrland et alrychesyde que tenet Johannes Schaw fychemanger xxvj s viij d

In parochia sancti petri in ballivo
De Johanne Sawn' pro ten' quond' Spronte v s
De Heredibus Sprontt pro ten' quod Johannes Bybery quondam tenuit viij s x d ob
De Gardino in Sewtwychyn' quod tenet Willelmus Hans vij s

In parochia [*blank*]
De Abbatissa de Godestowe pro quadam schopa ex op[to] sancte fredeswyde xx d
Summa iij li xix s vj d ob

De collegijs in liberis redditibus
De Novo Collegio pro maydyn' Hall in parochia sancti petri in oriente x s
De Collegio Cantuarii pro quadam parte terre in qua scituatur una camera eiusdem collegij ij s vj d
Summa xij s vj d

Redditus in partibus remotis
De Redditibus in pagula in Holdernys cuius ultimus terminus est Assumpcio sancte preterit' iij li xij d
De Maneria [*sic*] Merkys in exsexya cum suis pertinen' xix li iij s iiij d
De Molendinis Esexye xj s
De Subosco xj s j d
Summa xxiij li vj s v d

In parochia sante mildrede
Redditus Aulorum
De Aula Hampton' l s
De Aula Scuti vj s viij d
De Aula Sancti Thome x s
In parochia sancte marie
De Aula Brasynnose iij li vj s viij d
De Aula parva universitatis in vico scolarum xxxiij s iiij d
De Aula Edwardi xxiiij s
In parochia sancti petri in oriente
De Aula Drowdall' xlv s
De Aula parva universitatis in alto vico liij s iiij d
Summa xiiij li ix d

In parochia sancte marie
Redditus scolarum
De Scolis Simonis rowe viij s
De Scolis Magistri Johannis Lachen' vj s viij d
De Scolis Kyllom' determinatoris iij s iiij d
Summa xviij s

Infra collegium
Redditus camerarum

De Camera Magistri Roberti Bowet supra promptuarium xx s
solut' hoc anno usque ad festum sancti Thome futur'
De Camera Umfridi Rodley xvj s viij d
De Camera Magistri Walteri Blakett xiij s iiij d
De Camera Magistri Roberti Dynkley x s
De Camera domini Egidii Asteley xvj s viij d
De Camera domini Willelmi Skelton' xvj s viij d
De Camera domini Thome Clyffe pro duobus terminis scilicet a fest michaelis usque ad festum pasche viij s iiij d
De Camera Johannis ardaghe scilicet a festo Pur' usque ad invencionem sancte crucis ij s vj d
De Camera Johannis Hurlle a festo santi Michaelis preterito usque ad festum sancti Thome futur' xiij s iiij d
solut' hoc anno usque ad festum sancti Thome futur'
Summa vj li v s x d

Summa omnium reddituum lxvj li xxv d ob

Item respondet computans de quinque solidis quos recepit a M Thoma Benwell' quos idem Benwell debuit in pede compoti sui anno rr' H sexti secundo ut patet in eodem rotulo v s
Item respondet computans de Johanne Pece et Johanne Spicer pro pratis Oxnay iiij s ij d
Item respondet idem computans de receptis a communi Cista et pro focalibus iij li xviij s j d
Summa iiij li xxij d ob

Summa omnium oneratorum lxxxij li xxij d ob

Redditus hoc anno in manu collegij
In parochia sancti Egidij

De Gardino ex op^{to} ecclesie egidij x d
De Terris in bellomonte quos tenuit Johannes Spycer viij s

In parochia omnium Sanctorum

De Ten' Kentt pelleparij pro tribus terminis iij s
De Ten' in qui [*sic*] inhabitavit Rigdon' pro duobus terminis iij s

In parochia sancte mildrede

De Gardino quod quondam tenuit adam Rivere iij s

Allocat' ten' a° rr' H quarti [*sic*] octavo	
De Ten' Hugonis Benett	x s
De Ten' Ricardi Sclatter	xx d
Allocat' ten' a° primo rr' H sexti	
De Johanne Boseworth pro pratis osnay	iiij s iiij d
Allocat' ten' de a° secundo H sexti	
De Ten' Hugonis Benett	x s
Allocat' cam' eodem a°	
De Camera Magistri Roberti Bowett	xvj d
Allocat' a° tercio eiusdem Regis	
De Ten' Johanne Barbour	v s
De Gardino Johannis Barton corveser	v d
Allocat' cam' eodem a°	
De Camera Magistri Roberti Tonge	vj s viij d
De Camera Magistri Roberti Dynkley	x s
De Camera Umfridi Rodeley	iiij s ij d
De Camera Magistri Walteri Blakett	xiij s iiij d
Summa iij li vj s xj d	
Allocat' ten' de a° quarto eiusdem Regis	
De Gardino Johannis Barton Corvesere	x d
De Essexya petit Rede allocari pro Roberto Chelmesforde	xij d
Item idem Red' petit allocari pro Johanne Tirell	x s
Allocat' scolarum eodem anno	
De Scolis Magistri Johannis Chadwyke	x d
Allocat' camerarum eodem anno	
De Camera Magistri Roberti Tong'	xiij s iiij d
De Camera Magistri Roberti Dynkley	x s
Summa xxxvj s	
Allocat' ten' a° quinto eiusdem Regis	
De Ten' Thome Mayster	xxxix s iiij d
De Ten' Hugonis Bennet	xx s
De Johanne Spicer pro pratis Osnay	ij s j d
De Gardino Brampton' Mercer	ij s
De Gardino Barton' Corveser	xx d
De Pratis retro Osnay de Johanne Haynes	x s

De Schaw pro pratis de termino Annunciacionis sancti marie preterit' xiij s iiij d
De Swan' pro ten' quondam Sprontt v s
De Heredibus Sprontt pro ten' quondam Bybery viij s x d ob
De manerio Merkys in Exsexya pro Philippo Tyrrel et Johanne Symonds xij s
De Roberto lambyrd iiij s
De Ten' Thome Pypperde xiij s iiij d
[*An entry erased*]
Summa vj li xj s xj d ob

[*Dorse*]

De Exsexya de Johanne Umfray pro termino pasche iij li

Allocat' aularum eodem anno
De Aula Hampton' xxij s vj d
De Aula parva universitatis in vico scolarum vj s viij d
De Aula Drowdall' xxxv s
De Aula parva universitatis in alto vico xl s

Allocat' scolarum eodem a°
De Scolis Simonis Rowe pro tribus terminis preteritis vj s

Allocat' cam' eodem a°
De Camera Umfridi Rodley iij s iiij d
De Camera Magistri Walteri Blakett vj s viij d
De Camera Magistri Roberti Dynkley x s
De Camera domini Egidii Asteley iiij s ij d
De Camera Vicarij de Cuddesdon pro duobus terminis viij s iiij d
De Camera Johannis Ardaghe ij s vj d
De Camera domini Willelmi Skelton' v s
De Camera domini Thome Clyfe viij s viij d
Summa x li xviij s vj d

Summa omn' allocatorum precedencium xxij li xiij s iiij d ob

In communis Sociorum xiij li xvj s iij d ob q[a]
In batellis operariorum xxiij s xj d ob q[a]
Item in contribucionibus et iurnellis et convivio sancti Cutberti xxj s xj d ob
Item in reparacionibus Exsexye et expensis viij li xviij s vj d ob

Item in reparacionibus in villa et alijs expensis ix li vij s iiij d
Item in placitionibus circa materiam Osnay et alijs minutis expensis xxj s vj d ob
Item in expensis circa munimenta Esexye et pro equo conducto versus Holdern' xviij s iiij d

Summa xxvj li vij s vj d

In resolucionibus reddituum

In primis Abbati de Oseney in plenam solucionem xx s xx d
Item Abbati de Ennesam in plenam soluc' usque ad festum Michaelis x s
Item Abbatisse de Godstow xiiij s
Item Priori Sancte Fredeswide vj s viij d
Item procuratoribus sancti petri in oriente in plenam solucionem usque ad festum sancti Michaelis viij s vj d
Item Pro redditu Bassett pro pratis retro Osnay in plenam solucionem iij s viij d
Item pro redditu extra borialem in plenam solucionem iij s iiij d

Summa iij li vij s x d

Item soluc' sociorum

In primis Magistro Ricardo Wytton' pro placitacionibus officij magistratus xx s
Item eidem Magistro Ricardo Wytton' pro pencione officij sui a retro xiij s iiij d
Item eidem pro penc' anni presentis et officij magistratus xx s
Item M Thome Benwell' de pecunijs a retro in pede compot' sui viz de a° rr' Henrici quarto xlv s x d ob
Item eidem M Thome pro pensione anni presentis xiij s iiij d
Item M Johanni Elwyke pro pencione anni presentis liij s iiij d
Item M Willelmo Prentes pro antiquo debito a° rr' H sexti quarto liij s iiij d
Item eidem pro collato ad incepcionem xiij s iiij d
Item eidem pro anno presenti liij s iiij d
Item M Thome Butteler ex antiquo debito de a° rr' H sexti quarto vj s viij d
Item eidem pro pensione anni presentis xiij s iiij d
Item M Thome Hunter pro pensione anni presentis xiij s iiij d
Item Domino Johanni Alnwyk pro pensione anni presentis xxxiij s iiij d

Summa xvij li xij s vj d ob

In stipendijs famulorum

In primis Thome Talbott	xx s
Item Barbintonsori	v s
Item Lotrici ex antiquo et pro anno presenti	vj s vij d
Item pro Officio procuratoris	x s
Summa xlj s vij d	

Summa omnium allocatorum lxxxij li ij s x d

⟨Computatis computandis et allocatis allocandis domus debet computanti – xj d ob⟩

⟨Ric' Roderham commissarius M.T. Chace cancellar'⟩

[*Extremely clear roll, except where a little worn at the foot. 2 membranes. All figures balance*]

WHITSUN 5 HENRY VI to WHITSUN 6 HENRY VI (ROLL UC:BU1/F/39)
8 June 1427–23 May 1428

BURSAR: JOHN ALNWYK

Compotus dat' per Magistrum Ricardum Witton Magr [*sic*] Collegii magne Aule Universitatis in Oxon' tempore procuratorii domini Johannis Alnwek' procuratoris eiusdem Collegii Anno regni Regis Henrici sexti sexto A fest Pent' inclusive usque ad idem festum exclusive.

[*The Arrears are identical with the Allowances in* ***F/38*** *above, save for a few changes in spelling.*]

Summa totalis omnium Arr' precedencium xxij li xiij s iiij d ob

Redditus ten' in paroch' omnium sanctorum in Oxon' rr' H sexti sexto

De ten' Johannis Wilyam glover	xxxj s viij d
De ten' Thome Maister glover	iij li
De ten' Nicholai Schirborne cuttler'	xx s
De ten' Roberti Dudley glover	xxx s
De ten' hugonis Bennet sariante	xx s
De ten' Pypparde draper	liij s iiij d
De ten' Johannis Camey pro uno termino et di'	v s
De ten' Ric' Sclatter pro termino sancti Johannis Baptist'	iij s iiij d
De ten' quond' Kente pelliparij pro tribus ter'	iij s
De ten' quond' Riddon'	xx s

Redditus ten' in Paroch' sancti Martini et sancti Petri in Ballio in Oxon'

De Schopa super angulum quadrivij	xxviij s
De ten' Johannis Hans in sewystsychyn'	vij s

Redditus in Paroch' sancte Mildrede in Oxon'

De ten' Ric' Kariour vocat' Holifaunte Halle	iij s iiij d
De gardino ex o^to^ aule Hampton'	iij s

Redditus ten' in Paroch' sancte Marie in Oxon'

De Stampton' Hall' qua [*sic*] inhabitat Johannis Barbour	xiij s iiij d

Redditus ten' in Paroch' sancti Petri oriente [*sic*] in Oxon'
De ten' Alicie Philipe iuxta parvam aulam universitatis xxvj s viij d
De ten' Cambray glazier xvj s
De ten' Johannis Cok iuxta Cambray xij s

Redditus in suburbijs Oxon'
De gardino quod tenet Brompton' Mercer in paroch' sancti Thome ij s
De gardino quod tenet Barton' corvisour in paroch' Marie Magdelene xx d
De pratis retro Osney xxvj s viij d
De pratis in yrland et Alrychsyde que tenet schaw xxvj s viij d
De terris in bello monte pro j acre [*sic*] prati xx d
De gardino exo^{to} e ecclesie sancti Egidii x d
Summa xix li xviij s x d

Redditus Aulorum in Oxon' eodem Anno
De M' Johannis Legh' principalis Aul' Brasynhous iij li vj s viij d
De Aul' scuti vj s viij d
De Aul' sancti Thome x s
De Philippo Norres principali Aul' Universitatis vic' [*sic*] scolarum xxxiij s iiij d
De Michaele Trigurry principali Aul' Hampton' l s
De Johanne Mayo principali Aul' Edwardi xxiiij s
De M' Rogero Skybow principali Aul' Drowter' xl s
De M' Estyngtoun principali aule parve universitatis in alto vico liij s iiij d
Summa xiiij li iiij d

Redditus scolarum
De sc [*sic*] scola bassa a determinatore iij s viij d
De scolis [*sic*] superiori versus muros ville iij s
De scolis superiore [*blank*] pro j anno vj s viij d

Redditus camerarum infra Collegium eodem anno
De camera M' Roberti Bowet xx s
De camera M' Roberti Burton' xvj s viij d
De camera Humfridi Redly xvj s viij d
De camera M' Roberti Dyngley x s
De camera M' Egidii Astley pro tribus terminis xij s vj d
De camera M' Johannis Daventre pro ij^{bus} terminis viij s iiij d

De camera M' Walteri Blakett xiij s iiij d
De camera M' Willelmi Skelton' xvj s viij d
De camera M' Johannis Ardagh' xvj s viij d
De camera domini Thome Clyffe pro uno termino iiij s ij d
Summa vij li viij s iiij d

De Libero Redditu de ten' in Oxon' eodem anno
De godstow pro schopa exo^{to} porte ffridiswyde xx d
De Osney pro schopa iuxta Johannem Spicer in paroch' sancti Martini vj s viij d
De ten' Roberti Lambert in paroch' sancte Marie viij s
De Novo Colleg' pro Madyn'hall' x s
De Colleg' Cantuarii ij s vj d
De Swan' pro manso quond' Sprunt v s
De Heredibus Sprunt pro novis ten' viij s x d ob
De Johanne Spicer pro pratis retro Osney ij s j d
De Johanne Pays pro pratis retro Osney ij s j d
Summa xlvj s x d ob

Redditus in Esex et Holdernys eodem anno
De Johanne Humfray pro Merk' Hall in Esex xviij li vj s viij d
De Molendinis in Esex xxvj s viij d
De Subosco vendit' in Esex viij s
De Holdernys pro terris in pagula iij li xij d

Item oneratus computans de datis per M' Johannem Legh' cum xiiij s iiij d
Item respondet de Arr' Cambray in antiquo rotulo iiij s
Summa xxiij li xix s viij d

⟨Summa omn' onerat' lxxxx li x s j d⟩

All' de anno p^{o} H Sexti
De Johanne Bosworth pro pratis Osney iij s iiij d

All' de Anno secundo
De ten' Hugonis Bennet x s

All' came [*sic*]
De camera M' Roberti Bowet xvj d

All' ten' a^{o} tercio eisdem [*sic*] Regis
De ten' Johannis Barbour xx d
De gardino Barton' carvisour v d

All' a° quarto eisdem [*sic*] Regis	
Item de gardino Barton corvisour	x d
De scol' M' Johanis Chadwyke	x d
All' cam' eodem anno	
De camera Roberti Tonge	vj s viij d
All' ten' anno quinto	
De ten' Thome Mayster	xxxix s viij d
De ten' hugonis Bennet	xx s
De gardino Brompton' Mercer'	ij s
De gardino Barton' Corvisour	xx d
De ten' quond' Sprunt	v s
De heredibus Sprunt pro ten' quond' bibery	viij s x d ob
De Johanne Simond' in Essex	ij s
Summa v li v s iij d ob	
All' Aul' eodem anno	
De Aula drewgter' principali Skybow	xvij s ix d
All' cam' eodem anno	
De cam' M' Walteri Blakett	vj s viij d
De cam' Vicarii de Cudston'	viij s iiij d
De cam' M' Johannis Ardagh'	ij s vij d
Summa xxxv s iij d	
All ten' de a° sexto H. sexti	
De ten' Johannis Wilyam Glover	vij s xj d
De ten' Thome Mayster	xxvij s iiij d
De ten' Hugonis Bennet	xx s
De ten' quond' Kent Pelliparii	iij s
De Stampton hall' quam inhabitat Johannes Barbour	xiij s iiij d
De Ric' Slatter	iij s iiij d
De ten' Johannis Coke iuxta cambray	iij s
De gardino quod tenet Brampton' Mercer	ij s
De gardino quod tenet Barton' Corvisour	xx d
De Schaw pro pratis in yrlande et alrychsyd' pro ter' ann'	xiij s iiij d
De ten' Pipard' Drapour	xiij s iiij d
De Ric' Carriour	iiij s iiij d
Summa v li xij s vij d	

All' Aull' [*sic*] eodem anno

De parva aul' Universitatis in alto vico	xxvj s viij d
De Drewgtorhall'	xl s
De Parva aul' Universitatis in vico scolarum	xxij s iiij d
De Aul' Edwardi	viij s
Summa iiij li xvij s	

All' scolarum eodem anno

De Scol' Bassa a determinatore	iij s viij d
De Scol' superiori versus muros ville	iij s
De Scol' supra scolam Bassam versus ecclesiam sancte marie	vj s viij d
Summa xiij s iiij d	

All' Cam' infra Collegium eodem anno

De M' Roberti [*sic*] Bowet	xx s
De M' Roberto Burton'	xvj s viij d
De M' Humfridi [*sic*] Rodley	iiij s ij d
De M' Roberti [*sic*] Dyngley	x s
De M. Johannis [*sic*] Daventre pro 2 ter'	viij s iiij d
De M' Waltero Blakete	xiij s iiij d
De M. Egidii [*sic*] Astley	viij s iiij d
De M. Willelmo Skelton'	xj s viij d
De M' Johannis [*sic*] Ardagh'	x s
De Thome [*sic*] Clyff pro j ter'	iiij s ij d

All' ten' in manu Colleg' et de remissis ut patet in paupiro computandis ~~Summa~~ xxv s iij d

Summa vj li xj s xj d

All' liberi redditus Oxon' eodem anno

De Roberto Lambert	iiij s
De Swan' pro manso quond' sprunt	v s
De Heredibus Sprunt pro novis ten'	viij s x d ob
De Johanne Spicer pro pratis retro Osney	ij s j d
Summa xix s xj d ob	

[*no heading*]

De Humfrido pro Markhall' in Esex	vj li xiij s iiij d
De Molendinis in Esex	iiij s viij d
De Pecunijs quas recepit dominus Johannes Alnwyke	xx s

De Holdernes pro terris in pagula xij d
Summa vij li xix s

Summa omn' All' precedencium xxxiij li xiiij s iiij d

Item in Batellis contribucionibus et convivio in die sancti Cuthberti xlviij s q[a]
Item in communis ~~et Batellis et contribucionibus~~ xj li ix s ij d
Item in Expens' in Esex et perviam xlij s ij d
Item in Reparacionibus Aul' Hampton' viij li xj s viij d ob
Item in alijs reparacionibus et expensis ix li xix s vj d
Item in Placitacionibus xij li ij s vj d
Item in stauro xij li ij s x d ob
Summa [*blank – actually £54 14s 11¼d*]

[*Dorse*]

In Resolucionibus Reddituum
In primis Abbati de Osney in plenam solucionem xxj s viij d
Item Abbati de Ensam in plenam solucionem viij s
Item Abb' de Godstow xiiij s
Item ecclesie sancti Petri Oriente [*sic*] usque ad festum Michaelis ij s x d
Item Priori sancte ffridiswide usque ad festum annunciacionis preteritum xx s
Item Harberfeld' pro pratis retro Osney iij s viij d
Summa iij li x s ij d

Soluc' socijs Collegij
In primis M' Ric' Wytton' Magistro Collegii pro officio suo vj s viij d
Item eidem pro penc' in festo sancti Cuthberti et Annunciac' beate Marie xiij s iiij d
Item M' Thome Benewelle pro penc' sancti Cuthberti xiij s iiij d
Item M' Johanni Elwyke pro pencione sancti Cuthberti xiij s iiij d
Item eidem Johanni in partem salarii istius anni xx s
Item M' Willelmo Prentys pro pencione sancti Cuthberti xiij s iiij d
Item eidem Willelmo in partem salarii istius anni xx s
Item M' Thome Butler pro penc' sancti Cuthberti xiij s iiij d
Item Johanni Merton' pro eodem penc' xiij s iiij d

Item pro Offic' procuratoris x s

Summa [*blank*]

Soluc' servientibus Collegii

In primis lotrici vj s viij d

Summa vij li iij s iiij d

Summa omnium All' lxxxxij li xj s vj d ob q[a1]

⟨Computatis Computandis et allocatis allocandis domus debet computandi xlj s v d ob q[a]

Act' per Ric' Roderham commissarium M. Thome Chace Cancellarii⟩

[*Well written and well preserved roll; 2 membranes*]

[1] [ADMC] This total is 7s 4d too little. The group (at the top of this page) for which no total is given adds up to £48 11s d. Presumably the error is here, since all other totals are right. Possibly the Batells and contributions amounted to 7s 4d and were counted twice.

WHITSUN 6 HENRY VI to WHITSUN 7 HENRY VI (ROLL UC:BU1/F/40)
23 May 1428–15 May 1429

BURSAR: THOMAS BENWELL

[Compotus M^ri]¹ Thome Benwell magistri et procur[atoris . . . Anno regni Regis Henrici] sexti septimo. A festo Pent' [inclusive usque at idem festum exclusive]

[*Arrears are as in the Allocaciones* **F/39**, *with the following alterations:*

Arrears of 2 Hen VI: Hugh Bennet now owes 5s.

Arrears of tenements 5 Hen VI: the debts from Thomas Mayster, the house once of Sprount, the heirs of Sprount, and John Simond have all been paid.

Arrears of Halls 5 Hen VI – this debt has been paid.

Arrears of rooms 5 Hen VI – Walter Blakett and John Ardagh have paid their debts.

Arrears of tenements 6 Hen VI – Thomas Mayster has paid his debt.

Arrears of Halls 6 Hen VI – Drowda Hall now owes 30s.

Arrears of rooms 6 Hen VI – Walter Blakete now owes 6s 8d]

Summa omn' Arr' precedencium xxiiij li xx d

Redditus ten' in paroch' omnium sanctorum

De Ten' Johannis Wyllyam Glover	xxxj s viij d
De Ten' Thome Mayster Glover	iij li
De Ten' Nicholai Schirbourne Cuttler'	xx s
De Ten' Roberti Dudley	xxx s
De Ten' Hugonis Bennet seriantte	xx s
De Ten' Thome Pypparde Drapour	liij s iiij d
De Ten' Johannis Caume	xiij s iiij d
De Ten' Willelmi Tong' a fest Mich' usque pasc'[2]	ij s vj d

[1] [ADMC] Head of roll damaged. Words in square brackets from Smith Vol. VIII p. 108.
[2] [ADMC] Written over an erasure.

De Ten' Johannis lowell pro uno a° cuius primus terminus est festum Natal's jo bapt' iiij s

Summa xj li xiiij s viij d[3]

In parochia sancti martini

De Schopa super angulum quadrivij in qua inhabitat Ric' Strykmede xxviij s

De Schopa in qua quond' Cudston' corvesur habitavit pro libero redditu de Osenay vj s viij d

In parochia sancte mildrede

De Gardino Ricardi Cariour quond' Holefanthall iiij s iiij d

In parochia sancte marie

De Stampton' Hall' in qua inhabitat Johannis Barbour xiij s iiij d

De Ten' Roberti lambert pro libero redditu viij s

In parochia sancti petri in Oriente

De Ten' Alicie phylyppe iuxta parvam Aulam universitatis xxvj s viij d

De Ten' Caymbray Glasyur xvj s

De Ten' Johannis Cok iuxta Cambray xij s

Summa v li xv s

Hec sunt ten' in suburbijs et in parochia sancti Egidij et in campis Oxon'

De Gardino in paroch' sancti Thome quod tenet brompton mercer ij s

De Gardino in paroch' marie Magd' quod tenet Johannes Baron' Corveser xx d

De pratis retro Osney isto Anno quasi destructis per inundaciones aquarum solum in pecunia recepi[4] v s

De Pratis yrland et alrychsyde que tenet Johannes Schaw fychemonger xxvj s viij d

De Terris in bellomonte quas tenet Johannes Goldfynche pro dimidio unius anni `cuius primus terminus est festum Mich'' iij s vj d

In parochia sancti petri in ballivo

De Johanne Swayn' pro ten' quond' Spurunte v s

[3] [ADMC] The correct sum is £11 14s 10d.

[4] [ADMC] This is Smith's reading.

De Heredibus Spruntt de ten' quod Johannes Bybury quond' tenuit viij s x d ob

De Gardino in Sewtwychyn quod tenet Willelmus Hans vij s

In parochia [*blank*]

De Abbatissa de Godstaw pro quadem schopa ex o^{to} port' sancte ffrideswyde xx d

De collegijs Oxon' in liberis redditibus

De Novo Collegio pro Maydenhalle in paroch' sancti petri in oriente x s

De Collegio Cantuarie pro quadem parte terre in qua iam situata una camera eiusdem Collegij ij s vj d

Summa iij li xiij s x d ob

Redditus Aularum In parochia sancte Mildrede

De Aula Hampton' l s

De Aula Scuti vj s viij d

De Aula sancti Thome x s

In parochia sancte marie

De Aula Brasynnos iij li vj s viij d

De Parva Aula Universitatis in vico scolarum xxxiij s iiij d

De Aula Edwardi xxiiij s

In parochia sancti petri in oriente

De Aula Drowdagth' xl s[5]

De Parva Aula Universitatis in alto vico liij s iiij d

Summa xiiij li iiij s

Redditus sclorarum [*sic*] In parochia sante marie

De Scolis de scola bassa in qua legit Maynfurde viij s

De Scol' de scola australi in qua legit M J Marton' vj s viij d

De Scol' superiore boreali in qua legit W Stele vj s viij d

Summa xxj s iiij d

Infra Collegium Redditus camerarum

De Camera M Johannis Dawynstr' a pasc' usque ad festum Mich' viij s iiij d

De Camera M Domini Thome Clyfe a pasc' usque ad festum sancti Thome iiij s ij d

[5] [ADMC] Figure apparently altered from 'xlv s'.

De Camera Magistri Walteri Lambert' supra promptuarium scilicet pro terminis a fest Mich' usque ad pasc' x s
De C Umfridi Rodley pro anno cuius ultimus terminus est festum sancti Sedde preteritu xvj s viij d
De C M' Walteri Blaket pro anno cuius ultimus terminus est festum pasc' preteritum xiij s iiij d
De C M' Roberti Dynkley pro anno cuius ultimus terminus est festum pasc' preteritum x s
De C Johannis Johannis [*sic*] et roberti fflemmyng' pro uno termino scilicet a festo Nat' usque ad festum pasc' v s
De C domini [*sic*] Walteri lambert modo laysetyr' a pasc' usque ad festum Misc' viij s iiij d
De C M Thomas Hunter A festo Mich' usque pasc' v s
De Camera Domini Johannis laysetyr pro 2^bus terminis scilicet a festo Mich' usque ad festum pasc' preteritum viij s iij d
De C Domini Willelmi Skelton' pro uno anno cuius terminus [*blank*] xvj s viij d
De C Domini Johannis Ardagth' x s
De C Domini Thome Raymunde pro 2^bus terminis scilicet festo [*sic*] Mich' usque ad festum pasch' preteritum viij s iiij d
De C Thome de Gysburne pro uno termino scilicet a festo natalis usque ad pasch' preteritum ij s vj d
De C Domini Willelmi June pro 2^bus terminis scilicet a fest Nat' usque ad pasc' preteritum ij s vj d
De C M Roberti Dobbys pro duobus terminis scilicet a festo Mich' usque ad festum pasc' viij s iiij d

Summa vij li iij s iiij d

Redditus in partibus remotis

De Redditibus in pagula in Holdernesse cuius ultimus terminus est assumpcio beate marie preterita iij li xij d
De Maneria [*sic*] Markys in Esex' cum suis pertinencijs de Galfrido Athelham pro termino pasc' ultimo preterite x li
Item De Johanne Howmfray pro eodem Manerio [*sic*] De Merkse pro termino sancti Mich' ult' preteriti ix li iij s iiij d
Item De Molendinis eiusdem Manerij pro termino sancti Mich' ult' preteriti xiij s iiij d
Item Respondet computans de subbosco vendito per rectorem de Rodyng' Margaret iiij s viij d

Item respondet computans de focalibus receptis de quisquilijs venditis mancipio xiiij d

Summa xxiij li iij s vj d

Summa omn' redditum lxvj li ix s ob[6]

Summa omn' oneratorum lxxxx li x s viij d ob

In manu Collegij

De Gardino ex o^{to} sancti Egidij x d

In parochia sancti [*sic*] Mildrede

De Gardino ex o^{to} ~~se~~ Hampton Halle quod quond' tenuit Adam Ryver iij s

All' de A^{o} p^{o} Henr' Sexti

De Johanne Bosworth pro pratis Osney iiij s iiij d

All' Camerarum secundo A^{o} eiusdem regis

De Camera M Roberti Bowet xvj d

All' de A^{o} tercio eiusdem Regis

De Ten' Johannis Barbour xx d

De Gardino barton' Corvesur' v d

All' de A^{o} iiij^{o} eiusdem regis

De Gardino barton Corvesur x d

All' Scolarum eodem A^{o}

De Scolis M' Johannis Schadwyk x d

All' Camerarum eodem A^{o}

De Camera Roberti Tonge vj s viij d

All' de A^{o} v^{o} eiusdem regis

De Gardino barton' Corvesour xx d

All de A^{o} sexto eiusdem regis

De Ten' quod' inhabitavit Kent quos debet Joh' lowell' iij s

De Ten' Hug' Bennet xj s viij d

De ten' Johannis Coke iuxta Cambray iij s

De Schaw pro pratis yreland et Alrychsyds cuius terminus est Annunc' beate marie preterite xiij s iiij d

De Robert lambert iiij s

6 [ADMC] The correct total is £66 15 8½d.

All' Aularum eodem Anno

De Rogero Skebowe pro Aula Drowdagth'	v s

All' Camerarum eodem Anno

De Camera M' Roberti Bowet	xx s
De Camera M' Roberti Burton'	xvj s viij d
De Camera Humfridi Rodley	iiij s ij d
De Camera Domini Egidii Asteley	viij s iiij d
De Camera M' Walteri blakete	vj s viij d

[*No heading*]

De Johanne Tutbery de Hull' pro terris pagule in Holdernes	xij d

All' Ten' A° vij° eiusdem regis

De Ten' Thome Mayster	xj s viij d
De Ten' Hug' Bennet	xx s
De Ten' Thome Pypparde	xiij s iiij d
De Ten' Willelmi Tonge	xv d
De Johannis Barbour pro Stampton' Hall'	xiij s iiij d
De Ten' Alicie phylyppe	vj s viij d
De Ten' Cambray	xij s viij d
De Ten' Joh' Coke	xij s
De Brampton Mercer pro Gardino	ij s
De Johannes Schaw pro pratis ireland et Alryschsyde	vj s viij d
De Goldfynche pro terris in bellomonte	iij s vj d
De Heredibus spount pro ten' quond' sprount	v s
De Heredibus sprount pro ten' quod joh' bybyry quond' tenuit	viij s x d ob
De Abbatissa de Godstowe pro schopa ex o^{to} porte sancte ffrideswyde	xx d

Summa xj li xiij s ij d ob

[*Dorse*]

All' Aularum eodem A°

De Magistro Michaele tregurri pro Aula Hampton'	xiij s iiij d
De Magistris Philippo Norres principali Aule universitatis in vico scolarum et Roberto Glawsetyr occupante in eadem	xxv s x d
De Johanne Mayo pro Aula Edwardi	xv s
De Johanne Kylyngmersth' pro Aula Drowdagth'	xxxiij s iiij d

De Johanne Eslyngton pro parva Aula Universitatis in alto vico xxvj s viij d

Summa v li xiiij s ij d

All' Scolarum eodem A°

De M Johanne Maynysfurthe pro scola bassa viij s

De M Johanne Marton' pro scola superiori Australi vj s viij d

De M Willelmo Stele pro scola superiore boreali vj s viij d

Summa xxj s iiij d

All' Camerarum eodem A°

De Domino Waltero Lambert' pro mgna [*sic*] camera supra promptuarium ij s ij d

De Camera Humfridi Rodley iij s iiij d

De C M Roberti Dynkley ij s

De C Domini Johannis Ardagth' iij s iiij d

De C Domini Willelmi June xx s

De C Domini Thome Gysburne ij s vj d

Summa xv s

[*No heading*]

De Redditibus De pagula in Holdyrnes ij li [*sic*] xij d

De Galfrido Athelham de termino pasc' ult' preterit' pro manerio de Merks in Esex iiij Marc'

De Johanne Humfray de manerio de merkye vj s viij d

Item De Johanne Humfray pro Tyrell' xx s

Item De Johanne Humfray de Esex' de quo fit mencio in pede computi xxviij s

Summa vij li ix s

In communis sociorum xiij li v s ob

In batellis operariorum contribucionibus et convivio sancti Cuthberti iij li vj s viij d ob q[a]

Item in Edificacione Aule Hampton' et alijs reparacionibus in eadem aula iij li v s x d ob

Item in reparacionibus Aularum brasynnos et sancti Thome iiij li ix s

Item in reparacionibus Aule Drowdagth' et domus Cambray iij li iij s vj d

Item in factura pavimenti iiij li vij s vj d

Item in reparacionibus infra Collegium ij li v s j d ob

Item in expensis Capelle et pro receptis in grosso et stauro ij li xj s ob

Item in expensis circa pratum et pro cariagio romell' gardini quond' Ade river xvij s v d ob

Item in soluc' de debitis antiquis et juris peritis et M Ric' Wytton' bis eundo lond' x li v d

Item in solut' Johanni Milton' pro receptis ab eo et alijs parvis expensis xiij s xj d

Item in Expensis in Esex' in eundo et redeundo per viam ij li iij s ij d

Item in Expensis Esex' [*No entry*]

Item pro toga rectoris de Mergeret rodyng' x s

Item pro 2^{bus} togis joh' Humfray xiij s iiij d

Summa lj li xj s xj d q[a7]

In Resolucionibus Reddituum

In primis priori sancte fridiswide pro termino s Mich' ult' preteriti ix s iiij d

Item Abbathiie de Osney x s xj d

Item [*a word erased*] Byrseter pro pratis retro Osney iij s viij d

Item Camden' pro redditibus extra portem borialem xviij d

Item Collectoribus ecclesie sancti petri in oriente ij s x d

Summa xxviij s iij d

Soluta socijs Collegij

In primis pro officio Magistri vj s viij d

Item M' Thome benuell' M Collegij pro penc' in festo sancti cuthberti et Annunc' beate marie xiij s iiij d

Item eidem pro officij procuratoris x s

Item M' Johanni Elwyke pro pens' recept' in festis supradictis xiij s iiij d

Item eidem pro pens' a retro anni ult' preterit' xx s

Item eidem in partem soluc' anni instantis xx s

Item M Willelmo Prentis pro pens' recept' in predictis festis xiij s iiij d

Item eidem pro pens' a retro anni ult' preterit' xx s

Item eidem in partem soluc' anni instantis xx s

Item M' Thome Butteler pro penc' recept' in predictis festis xiij s iiij d

Item M' Thome Butteler in partem soluc' pens' qui incepit celeb' in crastino sancti Martini in hyeme xiij s iiij d

[7] [ADMC] The correct total is £51 11s 10¼d.

Item N Johanni Marton' pro penc' recept' in predictis festis xiij s iiij d

Summa viij li xvj s viij d

Solut' servientibus Collegii

In primis Waltero Spenser pro iij^{bus} terminus x s

Item seni Johanni Coke a pent' usque ad festum sancti Thome xij d

Item eidem Johanni a festo sancti Thome usque ad festum Mich' ij s

Item Ric' Coke a festo Mich' usque ad festum Nat' domini xx d

Item Waltero Coke a Nat' usque ad pasc' xx d

Item Johanne Hende lotrici a pasc' usque ad festum sancti Thome xx d

Item Agneti baly pro 2^{bus} terminis scilicet festi sancti Thome usque ad nat' domini iij s iiij d

Item Johanni Barbour pro uno anno v s

Summa xxviij s

Summa omnium Allocatorum precedenc' lxxxix li xvij s vj d ob q^{a}

⟨Computatis computandis et allocatis allocandis computans debet domum xiij s j d ob q^{a}⟩

⟨Memorandum quod de ista summa allocata dubitatur de xxviij s quos Joh' Humfray de Esex dicit se solvisse et quia nescitur an computans vel M Ric' Wytton illas pecunias recepit ideo discernunt auditores ulteriorem fieri de ista summa⟩

⟨Acta sunt hec per M Thomam Chace Cancellarium universitatis oxon'⟩

[*A wide roll (11.3 inches), very clearly, but not very beautifully written. The head of the roll damaged; otherwise in very good condition. 2 membranes*]

WHITSUN 7 HENRY VI to WHITSUN 8 HENRY VI (ROLL UC:BU1/F/41)

15 May 1429–4 June 1430

BURSAR: JOHN MARTYN

Compotus Magistri Johannis Marton' Procuratoris Magne Aule Universitatis Oxon' Anno Regni Regis Henrici sexti A festo Pent' inclusive usque ad idem festum exclusive

[*Arrears are as in Allowances for* **F/40**, *with the following differences:*

Arrears of Rooms 3 Hen VI – Robert Bowet has paid his debt.

Arrears of tenements 6 Hen VI – John Coke and John Shaw have both paid their debts.

Arrears of rooms 6 Hen VI – Robert Bowet and Robert Burton have both paid their debts, and Humphrey Rodley now only owes 20d.

Arrears of tenements 7 Hen VI – Cambray now owes 11s 8d, and John Shaw, and the heirs of Sprount have all paid their debts.

Arrears of Halls 7 Hen VI – Little University Hall in Schools Street now owes 32s 6d, and Drowda Hall 30s.

Arrears of rooms 7 Hen VI – John Ardagh has paid his debt.]

Summa omn' Arr' precedenc' xxij li xiiij s iiij d

Redditus ten' in paroch' Omnium Sanctorum

De Ten' Johannis Wyllyam Glover	xxxj s viij d
~~De Ten' quond' tenuit Thome Mayster Glover~~ ⟨nunc in manu Collegij[1]	[*Figure erased*]
De Ten' Nicholai Schirborne Cutteler	xx s
De Ten' Roberti Dudley	xxx s
De Ten' Hugonis Bennet seriantte	xx s
De Ten' Thome Pypparde Drapour	liij s iiij d
De Ten' Joh' Cayme ⟨et a Cayme pro duobus terminis[2]⟩	xiij s iiij d

[1] [ADMC] This entry added in a very small hand.
[2] [ADMC] This entry also added in a very small hand.

De Ten' Willelmi Tong' a festo Michaelis usque pasc' et a Joh' Cayme pro duobus terminis v s
De Ten' Joh' lowell pro uno anno cuius primus terminus est festum Nat' sancti Joh' bapt' iiij s
Summa viij li xvij s iiij d

In Parochia Sancti Martini
De Scopa super Angulum quadrivij in quo inhabitat Ric' Strykmede xxviij s
De Scopa in qua quondam Cudston' Corversur habitavit pro libero redditu de Oseney vj s viij d

In Parochia Sancte Mildrede
De Gardino Ric' Careur quond' Holefanthalle iiij s iiij d

In Parochia Sancte Marie
De Stampton' Hall' in qua inhabitat Joh' Barbour xiij s iiij d
De Ten' Roberti lambert pro libero redditu viij s

In Parochia Sancti Petri in oriente
De Ten' Alicie phylyppe iuxta parvam Aulam universitatis xxvj s viij d
De Ten' Alan Brome pro duobus terminis tantum et de Cam'a[3] pro Alijs duobus terminis xvj s viij d
De Ten' Johannis Coke iuxta Brome xij s
Summa v li xv s viij d

Hec sunt ten' in suburbijs et in Parochia sancti Egidij et in campis
De Gardino in parochia sancti Thome quod tenet brompton mercer ij s
De Gardino in parochia Marie Magd' quod tenet Joh' barton' Corvesur xx d
De pratis retro Osney xx s
De pratis yreland et alrychesyd' xxvj s viij d
De terris in bellomonte quas tenet Joh' Goldfynche ⟨vij s[4]⟩ vij s[5]

[3] [ADMC] *Sic* – clearly 'Cambray' is meant.
[4] [ADMC] This entry has also been added in a very small hand.
[5] [ADMC] This figure has been altered.

In Parochia Sancti Petri in ballivo
De Joh' Swayn pro ten' quond' Sprunte v s
De Heredibus Sprunte de ten' quod Joh' bybury quod [*sic*] tenuit viij s x s ob
De Gardino in Sewtwychyn' quod tenet Wyllelmus Hans vij s
De Abbatissa de Godstaw pro quadem schopa ex o^{to} port' sancte ffrideswyde xx d

De Collegijs Oxon' in liberis redditibus
De Novo Collegio pro mayden halle in paroch' sancti petri in oriente x s
De Collegio Cantuarie pro quadem parte terre in qua iam situata una camera eiusdem Collegij ij s vj d
Summa iiij li xij s iiij d ob

Redditus Aularum In parochia sancte Mildrede
De Aula Hampton' l s
De Aula Scuti vj s viij d
De Aula sancti Thome x s

In parochia sancte marie
De Aula Brasynnos iij li vj s viij d
De parva Aula Universitatis in vico scolarum xxxiij s iiij d
De Aula Edwardi xxiiij s

In parochia sancti petri in oriente
De Aula Drowdagth xl s
De Aula Universitatis in alto vico liij s iiij d
Summa xiiij li iiij s

Redditus scolarum In paroch' sante marie
De Scola bassa in qua legit Magister Rawlyns viij s
De scola superiore australi in qua legit M Joh' Barbour vj s viij d
De scola superiore boreali in qua legit M Ric' Grene vj s viij d
Summa xxj s iiij d

Infra Collegium Redditus camerarum
De Camera Magistri Johannis Marschall' pro uno termino iiij s
De Camera Joh' et Roberti fflemmyng' xx s
De Camera domini Thome Raymond xvj s viij d
De Camera domini Thome Cotome' x s
De Camera domini Willelmi Skelton' pro duobus terminis viij s iiij d

De Camera domini Joh' ardawgth' pro duobus terminis v s
De Camera domini Joh' laycetter pro duobus terminis viij s iiij d
De Camera Blaket xiij s iiij d
De Camera June pro duobus terminis viij s iiij d
De Camera Humfridi Rodeley a festo sancte Petronille usque ad festum sancti Michaelis ⟨vj s iiij d⟩ [*no entry*]
De Camera M' Roberti Dynkley x s
De Camera domini Walteri lamberte x s
De Camera M' Roberti Dobbys pro duobus terminis vj s viij d
Summa vj li iij s[6]

[*No heading*]

De Redditibus in pagula in Holdernesse cuius ultimus terminus est assumpcio beate marie preterita iij li xij d
De Manerio Merkys in Esex' cum suis pertinencijs de Galfrido Athelham xx li
Item Respondet computans pro pede compoti xiij s j d ob q[a]
Item de Rectore de Margrett' Rudyng' pro subbosco respondet computans v s vj d
Item de M[o] Roberto Gloucestr' pro clavibus respondet computans xx s
Item de Joh' pyese iij s
Item de principe parve Aule universitatis pro coquina vj s viij d
Item de priori sancte frideswyde xx d
Item de Johanne Couke pro lignis xij s
⟨Item respondet Comput' de missis a socijs per Ric' Elwyk Magistro Lond' pro placitis xx s⟩
Summa xxv li xiij s vij d ob q[a]

Summa omn' redditum precendencium lxvj li vij s iiij d ob q[a]

Summa Omn' Oneratorum Precendencium lxxxix[7] li xx d q[a]

In manu Collegij

De Ten' quod quond' tenuit Thomas Mayster nunc in manu Collegij iij li
De Gardino ex o[to] sancti Egidij x d

[6] [ADMC] Figure altered from 'vj li vij s'. £6 8d is the correct sum if the extra entry for Humphrey Rodley is disregarded; otherwise it is £6 7s.

[7] [ADMC] The 'ix' in 'lxxxix' written over an erasure.

In parochia sancte Mildrede
De Gardino ex o^{to} Hampton' Hall' quod quond' tenuit Adam Ryver — iij s

Alloc' de a^{o} p^{o} Henrici Sexti
De Johanne Bosworth pro pratis Osney — iiij s iiij d

All' de a^{o} tercio eiusdem Regis
De Ten' Joh' Barbour — xiiij d

All' scolarum a^{o} $iiij^{o}$ eiusdem Regis
De Scolis M' Johannis Schadwyk' — x d

Alloc' Camerarum eodem a^{o}
De Camera Magistri Roberti Tonge — vj s viij d

All' aularum de a^{o} Sexto eiusdem regis
De Rogero Skebow pro Aula drowdagh' — v s

Alloc' Camerarum eodem Anno
De Camera Egidii Asteley — viij s iiij d

[*No heading*]
De Tutbery de Hull' pro terris inpagul' [*sic*] in Holdernesse — xij d

All' ten' a^{o} septimo eiusdem regis
De Ten' Thome Mayster quod tenuit bellok' — xj s viij d
De Ten' Cambray — [*no entry*]
De Goldfynch' pro terris in bellomonte — iij s vj d
De Abbatissa de Godstowe pro Schopa ex o^{to} porte ffrideswyde — xx d
Summa xliiij s ij d

All Aularum eodem a^{o}
De Magistris philippo Norres principali aule universitatis in vico scolarum et Magistro [*sic*] Roberto Glowcester occupante de quibus Collegium debet Joh' lawles – vj s viij d pro reparacionibus factis per ipsum in brasnos — ix s ij d
De Joh' Mayo principali Aule Edwardi — v s
De Magistro Joh' Eslyngton — xx d

All' Scolarum eodem Anno
De M Johanne Maynsford' — xvj d

All' pro Redd' [*sic*]

De Pagula in Holdernes xj s

De Joh' Humfray de Manerio de Merk' quos ipse concedit se debere vj s viij d

Item de eodem Joh' Humfray quos dicit se solvisse hospitio georgij `iuxta´ fletbryge london' in tempore procuracionis Benwell' et quos idem Benwell' dicit se numquam recepisse xviij s

Summa lij s x d

All' ten' a° octavo eiusdem regis

De Joh' Wylliam Glover	v s v d
De Dudley	xxx d
De Hug' Bennett'	xviij s iiij d
De Ten' Joh' Lowell	xij d
De Joh' Barbour	xiij s iiij d
De Roberto Lambert	iiij s
De Cambray	xij d
De Brown'	iiij s iiij d
De Brampton' Mercer	ij s
De Bellok'	xx s

[*Dorse*]

De Schaw pro pratis yreland' et alryschyd'	[*no entry*]
De Goldfynch' pro terris in bellomonte	vij s
De Abbatissa de Godstow	xx d

Summa iiij li vij d

All' aularum eodem Anno

De principali Aule Hampton' xxvj s viij d

De principali parve Aule Universitatis in vico scolarum xiij s iiij d

De principali Aule Edwardi xvj s

De principali Aule drowdagth' xx s

De principali parve Aule in alto vico xxxiij s iiij d

Summa v li ix s iiij d

All' Scolarum eodem a°

De Magistro Rawlyns pro Scola bassa iiij s viij d

De Magistro Ric' Gren pro Scola superiore Australi iij s iiij d

Summa viij s

All' Camerarum eodem Anno

De Thome Cotum vij s vj d
De Magistro Roberto Dynkley vj s ij d
De Willelmo Skelton' x d
De Camera June iij s iiij d
Summa xvij s x d

All' Reddituum in partibus remotis

De pagula in Holdernes cuius ultimus terminus est Assumpcio beate Marie preterita iiij s iiij d
De Galfrido Athelham pro termino pasch' vj li xvj s viij d
Summa vj li xij d

Summa omnium alloc' precedencium xxij li xiij s ix d

All' in manu Collegij et de remissis ten' it' xx s vj d ob

In communis sociorum per totum Annum xvij li vij s vij d
In batellis operariorum contribucionibus detrimentis convivio sancti cuthberti et Ric' Elwyke ⟨et stipendijs servientium⟩[8] lix s[9]
Item in reparacione domus quam inhabitat dudley in edificacione parve domus in ten' quod inhabitat Joh' Cok' ix li xvij s ij d
Item in reparacionibus domorum Alani Brown' Joh' Cayne Alic' Phylippe et Thome Mayster xxxv s
Item in reparacionibus omnium Aularum et Scolarum iij li iiij s ij d ob
Item in reparacionibus infra Collegium pro receptis in grosso et stauro et pro expensis circa capellam et circa fenum iiij li iiij s ij d ob
Item in expensis versus Holdernes circa tractatus cameres [*sic*] et abyndon' et convivio maioris et Aliorum et in expensis cum Magistro xxxviij s ix d ob
Item in reparacionibus apud Exsex in expensis in eundo et redeundo et pro togis Rectoris et firmarij vij li iiij s x d ob
Item in placitis per totum annum ix li vij d
Item in diminutis expensis viij s xj d
Summa lviij li iiij d[10]

[8] [ADMC] These words erased but clearly legible.
[9] [ADMC] Figure has been altered.
[10] [ADMC] These figures written over an erasure.

In resolucione liberorum reddit'

In primis priori sancte fridiswide completa solucione anni septimi Henrici regis sexti ix s viij d
Item Canonico de oseney x s
Item Euynsham iiij s
Item Senescallo blakett' xviij d
Summa xxv s ij d

Solut' socijs Collegij

In primis Magistro pro officio Magistratus vj s viij d
Item Magistro Joh' Elwyke pro salario a retro Anni Septimi xx s
Item eidem Magistro pro salario in partem solucionis istius anni xxij s xj d
Item Magistro Willelmo Prent's pro salario a retro anni septimi xx s
Item pro pensione in die sancti cuthberti vj s viij d
Item pro salario in partem solucionis isto anno xvj d
Item M' Thome Butteler pro pencione a retro pro diebus sancti cuthberti et annunciacionis beate Marie et in partem solucionis isto Anno xlj s viij d
Summa v li xix s iij d

⟨In stipendijs famulorum
Summa xxx s vj d⟩

Summa omn' Expens' lxvij li xv s ix d ob

Summa omn' Allocatorum Precedenc' lxxxx li ix s vj d ob

⟨Computatis computandis et allocatis allocandis domus debet computanto xxvij s x d q[a]⟩

⟨Acta sunt hec per Ric' Roderham commissarium Magistri T Chace Cancellarij⟩

[*Another wide roll (eleven inches); 2 membranes. Very clear, though slightly damaged at the head of the roll*]

WHITSUN 8 HENRY VI to WHITSUN 9 HENRY VI (ROLL UC:BU1/F/42)

4 June 1430–20 May 1431

BURSAR: THOMAS BUTLER

Compotus Magistri Thome B[*oteler procuratoris Collegij sive Mag' Aule*] Universitatis Oxonie datus per M[*agistrum Thomam Benewell*] Magistrum predicti Collegij post promocionem predicti Magistri Thome Boteler Anno Regni Regis Henrici Sexti Nono a festo pentecost' inclusive usque ad idem ffestum exclusive

Arr' de anno primo Henrici Sexti
De Joh' Bosworth pro [*pratis*] Osney — iiij s iiij d

Arr' de anno tercio eiusdem Regis
De Ten' Joh' Barbour — xiiij d

Arr' scolarum Anno iiij^{o} eiusdem Regis
De Scola magistri Joh' Chadwyk' — x d

Arr' Camerarum Eodem Anno
De Camera Magistri Roberti Tong' — vj s viij d

Arr' Aularum Anno Sexto eiusdem Regis
De Rogero Skebow pro Aula drowdagh' — v s

Arr' Camerarum eod' Anno
De Camera domini Egidii Asteley — viij s iiij d

Arr' Ten' Anno Septimo eiusdem Regis
De Ten' Thome Mayster quod tenuit Bellok' — xj s viij d
De Goldfynch' pro terris in Bellomonte — iij s vj d
De Abbatissa de godstow pro Schopa ex o^{to} porte ffrideswyde — xx d

Summa xliiij s ij d

Arr' Aularum eod' Anno
De magistris philippo Norres principali Aule universitatis in vico Scolarum et magistro Roberto Glowcest' occupante — ix s ij d
occupante [*sic*] de quibus Collegium debet [*Joh' Lawles*] vj s viij d pro Reparacionibus factis per ipsum in Brasnos

De Joh' Mayo principali Aule Edwardi v s
De Magistro [*blank*] Estyngton xx d

Arr' Scolarum eod' Anno
De Magistro Joh' maynsfforde xvj d
De Joh' Humfray in Essex pro antiquo debito ex ultimo compotu inter ipsum et Magistrum Joh' Elwyk x s
Summa xxvij s ij d

Arr' ten' Anno octavo eiusdem Regis
De Joh' Wylliam Glover v s v d
De dudlay xxx d
De hug' Bennette xviij s iiij d
De ten' joh' lowell' xij d
De Joh' Barbour xiij s iiij d
De Roberto lambart iiij s
De Brown' iiij s iiij d
De Brampton' Merc' ij s
De Bellok[*e*] xx s
De Goldfynch' pro terris in Bellomonte vij s
De Abbatissa de Godstow xx d
Summa iij li xix s vij d

Arr' Aularum eod' Anno
De principali Aule Hampton' xxvj s viij d
De principali parve Aule universitatis in vico scolarum xiij s iiij d
De principali Aule Edwardi xvj s
De principali Aule drowdagh' xx s
De principali parve Aule in Alto Vico xxxiij s iiij d
Summa v li ix s iiij d

Arr' Scolarum eod' Anno
De Magistro Rawlyns pro Scola bass' iiij s viij d
De Magistro Ric' Gren pro Scola superiore Australi iij s iiij d
Summa viij s

Arr' Camerarum eod' Anno
De Thome Cotum vij s vj d
De Magistro Roberto dynkley vj s ij d
De Willelmo Skelton' x d
De Camera June iij s iiij d

Arr' Reddituum in partibus remotis

De Galfrido Athelham pro termino pasch' vj li xvj s viij d

Summa vij li xiiij s vj d

Summa omnium Arr' precedenc' xxj li xxj d

Redditus ten' in parochia omn' sanctorum

De Ten' David glover xxiij s iiij d

De Ten' Joh' Wylliam Glover xxxj s viij d

De Ten' Isabelle Colett' [*cuius*] redditus annuus est iij li [*xviij s sed*] pro ij [*term'*] preterit' quibus ibi habitavit xxxix s

De Ten' Nicho [*sic*] Schirborn Cutler' xx s

De Ten' Roberti dudeley xxx s

De Ten' Hug' Bennett Seriante xx s

De Ten' Thome pypparde drapour liij s iiij d

De Ten' Joh' Cayme xiij s iiij d

Item de eodem Joh' Cayme pro uno [*ten'*] in quo habitavit Willelmus Tong' v s

Item de Ten' in quo habitavit joh' lowell pro uno termino xij d

Item de Johanne lowell' pro eod' Ten' de eod' Ten' [*sic*] pro tribus term' iij s

⟨Summa x li s s viij d[1]⟩

In parochia Sancti Martini

De Scopa super Angulum quadrivii xxviij s

De Scopa in qua quondam Cudston' Corversur habitavit pro [. . .] vj s viij d

In parochia Sancte Mildrede

De Gardino Ricardi Careoure quond' holefanthalle iiij s iiij d

In Parochia Sancte Marie

De Stampton' Hall' in qua inhabitavit Joh' Barbour xiij s iiij d

De Ten' Roberti lambert pro libero redditu viij s

In Parochia Sancti Petri in oriente

De Ten' Alicie phylyppe iuxta parvam Aulam universitatis xxvj s viij d

De Ten' Alane Brome uno termino in manu Collegij iiij s ij d et tribus terminis inhabitat' xij s vj d

[1] [ADMC] The correct total is £11 19s 8d.

De Ten' Joh' Coke iuxta Brome xij s
Summa vj li xiiij s x d[2]

Hec sunt Ten' in suburbijs et in parochia sancti Egidij et [*camp*]is
De Gardino in parochia sancti Thome quod tenet Brampton Mercer ij s
De Gardino in parochia sancte marie magdalene quod tenet Joh' Barton' Corvesur xx d
De pratis retro Oseney xx s
De pratis yreland et Alrychesyd xxiij s iiij d
De terris in bellomonte quas tenet Joh' Goldfynche vij s

In parochia sancti petri in ballivo
De [*blank*] pro ten' quond' Sprunte v s
De heredibus Sprunte de ten' quod Joh' bybury quond' tenuit viij s x s ob
De Gardino in Sewtwychum' quod tenet Deylby Hans vij s
De Abbatissa de godstaw pro quadem schopa ex o^{to} port' sancte ffrideswyde xx d

De Colleg' Oxon' in liberis redditibus
De Novo Collegio pro Mayden hall' in paroch' sancti petri in oriente x s
De Collegio Cantuarie pro quadem parte terre [. . .] ij s vj d
Summa iiij li ix s ob

Redditus Aularum In parochia Sancte Mildrede
De Aula Hampton l s
De Aula Scuti vj s viij d
De Aula sancti Thome x s

In parochia sancte marie
De Aula Brasynnos iij li vj s viij d
De parva Aula Universitatis in vico scolarum xxxiij s iiij d
De Aula Edwardi xxiiij s

In parochia sancti petri in oriente
De Aula Drowdagh' xl s
De Aula universitatis in Alto Vico liij s iiij d
Summa xiiij li iiij s

[2] [ADMC] The correct total is £5 11s 6d.

Redditus scolarum In paroch' Sante Marie
De Scola bassa de Magistro Waltero pe [*blank*] pro uno termino cum di' iij s iiij d
De Scola magistri Joh' Goldsmyth pro duobus terminis iij s iiij d
De Scola superiore Australi in qua determinavit Robertus Croclynge' iij s iiij d
De Scola superiore boreali in qua determinavit Thomas huntte iij s iiij d
De Scola bassa in qua determinavit Joh' Madenhyll' iij s iiij d
Summa xvij s

Infra Collegium Redditus Camerarum
De Camera domini johannis laycestr' pro tribus terminis quorum finis est festum sancti Thome martiris futurum xij s vj d
De Camera domini thome Cotum' pro tribus terminis quorum finis est festum sancti Thome Martiris futurum xij s vj d
De Camera domini joh' Smethton' pro duobus terminis quorum finis est festum Annunciacionis beate Marie preteritum viij s iiij d
De Camera Roberti et Joh' fflemmyng' pro anno integro xx s
De Camera Magistri Johannis Marschall' xvj s viij d
⟨De Camera Magistri Roberti dynkley pro uno termino in fine anni ij s vj d⟩
Summa iij li xij s vj d

[*No heading*]
De Redditibus in pagula in holdernesse cuius ultimus terminus est Assumpcio beate Marie preterit' iij li xij d
De Manerio Merkys in Esex' cum fine pertin' de galfrido Athelham xx li
Item Respondet computans pro antiquo debito Scolarum de magistro Roberto Holywell iij s iiij d
Item Respondet computans de oct' denarijs receptis a soc' et commorantibus ad emendacionem vestiment' Altaris viij d
Item Respondet de receptis a joh' peys pro pratis retro osenay ij s ij d
Item Respondet computans de receptis a Willelmo Enerede pro debito antiquo Joh' Cambray xx s

Item respondet computans de receptis magistri joh' Ardage pro debito antiquo camere sue v s

Summa xxiiij li xiij s ij d

Summa omnium Redditum lxv li v s v d ob[3]

Summa Omnium Oneratorum precendenc' lxxxvj li vij s vij d ob

Ten' In manu Collegij

De Gardino ex o^{to} sancti Egidij x d

In parochia sancte Mildrede

De Gardino ex o^{to} Hampton' Hall' quod quond' tenuit Adam Ryver iij s

Alloc' Anno p^{o} Henrici Sexti

De Joh' Bosworthe pro pratis oseney iiij s iiij d

All' A^{o} 3° eiusdem Regis

De Joh' Barbour xiiij d

All' scolarum eod' Anno

De Scola Magistri Johannis Chadwyke x d

All' Camerarum eod' A^{o}

De Camera Magistri Roberti Tong' vj s viij d

All' Aularum A^{o} Sexto eiusd' R'

De Rogero Skebow pro aula drowdawgh' v s

All' Camerarum eod' Anno

De Camera domini Egidii Asteley viij s iiij d

All' Ten' A^{o} septimo eiusd' R'

De Goldfynch' pro terris in bellomonte iij s vj d

De Abbatissa de Godstowe xx d

All' Aularum eod' anno

De Magistris philippo Norres principali Aule universitatis in Vico Scolarum et [*Roberto Glowcester*] occupante de quibus Colleg' debet Joh' Lawles – vj s viij d pro [*reparacionibus factis per ipsum in*] Brasnoss ix s ij d

De Joh' Mayo principali Aule Edwardi v s

3 [ADMC] The correct total is £65 5s 10½d.

All' Scolarum eod' A°
De magistro maynfforde xvj d
De joh' humfray in Esex' pro antiquo debito in ultimo computo [*inter ipsum et Magistrum Joh' Elwyk*] x s
Summa ij li xviij s vij d

[*Dorse*]

All' ten' anno oct' eiusd' Regis
De Ten' dudeley xxx d
De Ten' Thome Bellok' v s
De Goldfynch' pro terris in bellomonte vij s
De Abbatissa de Godstow xx d

All' aularum eod' A°
De Michael tregur pro Aule Hampton' vj s viij d
De Joh' Mayo tunc principali Aule Edwardi ix s iiij d

All' Scolarum eod' A°
De M' Rawlyns pro Scola xvj d

All' camerarum eod' A°
De domino Thoma Cotum pro Camera bassa sub camera sua modo vij s vj d
De Camera domini Willelmi Skelton' x d
De Camera domini Willelmi June iij s iiij d

All' ten' in partibus remotis eod' A° eiusdem Reg'
Item Galfridus atteleham petit Allocari de Joh' terell' pro termino pasch' x s
Summa lv s ij d

All' ten' Anno Nono eiusdum Reg'
De Ten' Alicie Philyppe vj s viij d
De Ten' Joh' Willyams glov' xxiij s ix d
De Ten' Nicholai Scherbourne v s
De Ten' Hugon' Bennette vj s viij d
De Ten' Alane Brone xx d
De Joh' Barbour xiij s iiij d
De Roberto lambert iiij s
De Joh' Coke iuxta Alanum Brome xx d
De Gardino Brampton Mercer ij s
De Gardino Barton' Corveser xx d

De Goldfynche pro terris in bellomonte vij s
De pratis joh' hanys pro pratis oseney iij s iiij d
De Abbatissa de godstaw pro Schopa xx d
De Ten' Isabelle Colett' iiij s x d
⟨De Ten' Johannis lowell' xx d⟩
Summa iiij li iiij s xj d

All' Aularum eod' A°
De Magistro Willelmo chambyrlane pro Aula Hampton x s
De Magistro Joh' Corker' pro parva Aula universitatis in vico scolarum xvij s iiij d
De Magistro Joh' magg' pro Aula Edwardi xv s viij d
De Magistro Thoma Estyngton principali et magistro Roberto glowcestr' occupante parvam Aulam universitatis in alto vico xxix s viij d

All' Scolarum eod' A°
De Scola magistri Joh' Goldsmyth iij s iiij d

All' Camerarum eod' A°
De Camera domini Joh' Smethton' xx d
De Camera magistri Joh' Marschall' x d

All' ten' in remotis partibus eod' eiusdem Regis
De Galfrido atteleham quos petit allocari de Joh' terell pro termino sancto Michaelis ultime preterit' x s
De Galfrido atteleham pro manerio de Merkys de termino pasch' x li
Summa xiiij li viij s vj d

Summa omn' all' precedenc' xxiiij li vij s ij d

All' ten' in manu Colleg' eodem Anno eiusdem Regis
De Aula drowdawgh xl s

Item de dimissis tenentibus xx s vj d ob
Item de Holdernesse xij s
Summa iij li xviij d ob

In placitis l s iij d
In communis per totum Annum xij li xv s vij d
In batellis operariorum et jurnell' soc' et convivio sancti cuthberti iij li xviii d ob
Item in reparacione domus in qua habitat Isabella Colette x li xiv s vj d

Item in reparacione aliorum ten' et aularum in Oxon' et [. . .]
expensis v li xvj d
Item in reparacionibus Manerij de Merkys in essex' et in Alijs expensis
eiusdem manerij v li xij s viij d q[a]
Summa xxxix li xv s xj d ob q[a]

Soluta in antiquis debitis
In primis Johanni Mylton yrenmung' vj s viij d
Item matheo Carpentario x s ij d
Item Magistro Thome Chace Cancellario pro debito antiquo pavimenti quos recepit a Joh' Gayne x s ij d
Item ballivis ville Oxon' pro quinta decima domini Regis ij s viij d
Item Ricardo Gongfermor' debit' de tempore Magistro Ric' Wytton' iij s viij d
Item pro redempcione crateris inpignorate a° ultimo preterito xvj s viij d
Item Magistro Johanni Marton' in part' solucionis xxvij s x d q[a]
debit' sibi in pede Rotuli de A° ultimo preterit' xvj s viij d
Item margarete debbys pro cera ad capellam xj s viij d
Item pro debit' antiquis H.B. per dat' etc. iij s iiij d
Summa iij li xviij s ij d[4]

In resolucione liberorum Reddituum
Solut' in resolucionibus reddituum In primis priori sancte fridiswide xiij s iiij d
Item Abbati de Oseney pro gardino vj s
Item [*blank*] kyngysmylum pro redditu byrsette iij s viij d
Item ecclesie sancti petri in oriente ij s x d
Item Hampden' senescallo Blakete pro redditu extra portem borialem xviij d
Item Abbatie de Eneshame in partem solucionis etc.' xvj s
Summa xliij s iiij d

Solut' soc' Collegij
Inprimis Magistro Thome Benewell' magistro Collegij pro debit' anni ultimo preteriti xiij s iiij d
Item Magistro Johanni Elwyk pro completa solucione anni ultimi preteriti xxx s v d

[4] [ADMC] The correct total is £3 16s 2d.

Item eidem Magistro Johanni Elwyk in partem solucionis pensionis sacerdotalis et die sancti Cuthberti et Annunciacionis beate marie anni instantis xliij s x d
Item Magistro Johanni Marton' pro debito a retro anni ultimo preteriti xiij s iiij d
Item Magistro Johanni goldsmyth pro debito retro anni ultimo preteriti xiij s iiij d
Item Magistro Willelmo prentysse in plenam solucionem omnium et singulorum debit' sibi a Collegio lj s viij d
Item Magistro Thome Boteler' in plenam solucionem omnium et singulorum debit' sibi a Collegio l s
Summa x li xv s xj d

Solut' servientibus
Inprimis pro officio procuratoris x s
Item Johanni ffelton' pro officio pincerne et coci xxvj s viij d
Item Johannie Barbour pro officio Barbitonsoris v s
Item Alicie lotrici vj s viij d
Summa xlviij s iiij d

Item computans petit Allocari de dat' tenentibus in comput' cum eis xxj d

Summa omnium Expensarum una cum ten' in manu Collegij et dimissis lxij li ij s iij d q[a]

Summa omnium Allocatorum precedencium lxxxvj li xj s ij d q[a]

⟨Computatis computandis et allocatis allocandis domus debet computanto iij s vj d ob q[a]

Acta sunt hec per Thomam Chace [*Cancell*]arium universitatis oxon'⟩

[*An unusually wide roll – about 12 inches across; 2 membranes; written in a large hand and relatively untidy. Parts of the face of the roll are difficult to read owing either to smudging or to the flaking away of the ink*]

WHITSUN 9 HENRY VI to WHITSUN 10 HENRY VI (ROLL UC:BU1/F/43)
20 May 1431–8 June 1432

BURSAR: THOMAS BENWELL

[1]Compotus Thome [Benewell magistri et procuratoris Collegij quod vocatur] Magna Aula un[iversitatis in Oxon' anno rr' H 6] post conquestum decimo a ffesto [pent' inclusive ad idem festum exclusive]

[*The face of the first membrane is considerably damaged, smudged and faded, but enough can be read to show that the Arrears of Rents are the same as the Allowances of **F/42**, excluding those for tenements in the hands of the College.*]

Summa omnium arr' precend' xxiiij li vij s ij d

Redditus ten' in parochia omnium Sanctorum[2]

De ten' david glover	xxiij s iiij d
De ten' Isabelle Colett' cuius redditus unius anni	iij li xviij s
De ten' Joh' Wylliam glover	vij s xj d
De ten' Nichi Shirborne Co[*teler*]	xx s
De ten' Roberti dudeley	xxx s
De ten' Hug' bennett Seriante	xx s
De ten' Thome pipparde draper	iij li
De ten' Joh' Cayme	xiij s iiij d
Summa xiij li xix d	

In parochia Sancti [*martini*]

De Shopa super Angulum quadrivij in qua [*habitat Ric' Strykmed*] xxviij s

In parochia [*Sancte Mildrede*]

De Gardino Ric' Careour' quond' [*holefanthalle*] iiij s iiij d

[1] [ADMC] The head of the roll is badly damaged. Words in square brackets are from Smith Vol. VIII p. 115, except that he reads *a° rr' H 6 x° a fest pent'* whereas the roll shows ' . . .tum decimo'. Smith presumably omitted 'post conquestum'.

[2] [ADMC] Parts of the text are difficult to read and occasionally illegible. Missing words have been supplied from other entries in this and the immediately preceding or following rolls.

In parochia Sancte Marie
De Stampton' Halle in qua inhabitavit Johannes Barbour xiij s iiij d
De ten' Roberti lambert pro libero redditu viij s

In parochia Sancti petri in oriente
De ten' Roberti plu[*mer*] ubi Cameray habitavit pro uno termino iiij s
De ten' Johannis Coke iuxta [*brome*] xij s
De shopa Alicie Philippe ij s iiij d
De ten' Johannis Rede xxvj s viij d
Summa [*iiij li*] xix s viij d

Hec sunt Ten' in Suburbijs [*et*] in parochia Sancti Egidij et in Campijs
De Gardino in parochia Sancti Thome quod tenet [*Brampton*] Mercer ij s
De Gardino in parochia Sancte Marie Magdalen' quod tenet barton' xx d
De pratis retro Oseneye xiiij s viij d
De pratis yreland' et Alrychesyde xx s
De terris in bellomonte quas tenet Joh' goldefynche [*vij s*]
De Joh' Spiser pro pratis retro oseneye in libero redditu ij s ij d
Summa [*xlvij*] s vj d

In parochia Sancti petri in ballio
De Ten' quond' Spronte v s
De heredibus Spronte de ten' quod Joh' bybury tenuit viij s x s ob
De gardino in Sowttwythn' [*sic*] quod tenet Willelmus hanse vij s
De Abbatissa de Godstow pro quadem schopa [*parte*] Sancte ffrideswyde xx d

De Novo Colleg' in liberis redditibus
De novo Colleg' pro mayden hall' in paroch' Sancti petri in oriente x s
De Coll' Cantuar' pro quadem parte terre in qua situatur una Camera eiusdem Collegij ij s vj d
Summa xxxv s ob

Redditus Aularum In parochia Sancte myldrede

De Magistro Willelmus [*sic*] Chawmyrlane pro Aula Hampton l s

De Magistro Johanne Elwyke pro Aula Scuti vj s viij d

De Magistro Johanne legh' pro Aula sancti Thome x s

In parochia Sancte marie

De Magistro Joh' lee Aula brasenose iij li vj s viij d

De Magistro Joh' Coker' pro parva Aula universitatis in vico scolarum xxxiij s iiij d

De Joh' fitzRobert pro Aula Edwardi xxiiij s

In parochia Sancti petri in oriente

De pentaker pro Aula drowda' [*blank*] uno termino x s

De decano birgundinensi pro Aula drowdagh a [*blank*] beate Marie usque ad [*blank*] xx s

De magistro Roberto glowcest' et [*blank*] Ewene' pro parva Aula universitatis in alto vico vico [*sic*] liij s iiij d

Summa xiij li xiiij s

Redditus scolarum

De magistro Joh' goldesmyth pro Scola Australi superiori vj s viij d

De Magistro Willelmo karlele pro boriali superiori vj s viij d

De Thoma lemynton de [. . .] pro Scola bassa iij s iiij d

Summa xvj s viij d

[*No heading*]

De Camera domini d [*sic*] Thome Cotum Canonichi xvj s viij d

De Camera domini joh' Smethton' viij s iiij d

De Camera Magistri Joh' Marshall' pro tribus terminis xij s vj d

De Camera Roberti fflemmyng' xx s

De Camera graystoke pro tribus terminis viij s iiij d

De Camera Willelmi domini Kyllyngworth iij s iiij d

Summa iij li ix s ij d

De pagula in holdernesse cuius ultimus terminus est festum Assumpcionis Sancte marie preterit' iij li xij d
De manerio de Merkys in Esex' cum suis pertin' de galfrido Athelham xx li

Summa xxiij li xij d

Summa omnium reddit' lxiij li iiij s vij d ob

Item computans respondet de receptis ab Alicia philippe pro reparacionibus ultra reddit' annualem vj s viij d
Item computans respondet de receptis a Thoma pyppard pro reparacionibus iij s iiij d
Item computans de receptis a receptis [*sic*] a Joh' peys' pro pratis oseneye ij s ij d

Summa xij s ij d

Summa Redditus et receptorum preter summam reddituum lxiij li x[*vj*] s ix d ob

Summa Omnium Oneratorum lxxxviij li iij s xj d ob

[*No heading*]

De Abbate de Oseneye pro Shopa in quo Cuddiston quond' habitavit in parochia Sancti Martini vj s viij d
De ten' Joh' Wylliam tribus annis terminis in manu Collegij xxiij s ix d
De Gardino ex opposito Aule Hampton' quod Adam Ryver quondam tenuit in manu Collegij iij s

Alloc' Anno p° H Sexti

De Joh' ~~Barbour~~ Bosworth' pro pratis retro Oseneye iiij s iiij d

Alloc' a° 3° eiusd' Regis

De Joh' Barbour pro Stampton Halle xiiij d

Allocat' Scolarum eiusd' R' [*sic*]

De Scola magistri Joh' Chadwyke x d

Allocat' Camerarum eod' a°

De Camera magistri Roberti Tong' vj s viij d

Allocat' aularum de a° sexto

De Rogero Skybow pro Aula drowdagh v s

Allocat' Camerarum eod' a^o

De Camera domini Egidii Astley viij s iiij d

Allocat' ten' de a^o 7°

De Goldefynche pro terr' in bellomonte iij s vj d

De Abbatissa de Godstowe xx d

[*There is a change of handwriting at this point*]

Allocat' eodem anno

De magistris philippo Norres principali Aule universitatis in Vico Scolarum et Roberto Glowcett' occupante ix s ij d

De quibus Colleg' debet Joh' Lawles – vj s viij d pro reparacionibus per ipsum factis in brasnose

De Magistro Thoma Estlyngton pro parva aula universitatis oxon' in alto vico xx d

De Joh' Mayo pro Aule Edwardi v s

Allocat' Scol' eod' a^o

De Joh' Maynsforth pro scola xvj d

Allocat' Esex eod' a^o

De Joh' humfray in Esex' pro antiquis debitis ex ultimo comput' inter ipsum et ipsum magistrum [*sic*] Joh' Elwyke x s

Summa ij li xviij s vij d

Allocat' ten' de a^o oct' eiusdem Regis

De ten' dudeley xxx d

De ten' Thome Belloke v s

De goldefynch' pro terris in bellomonte vij s

De Abbatissa de godstow xx d

Allocat' Aularum eod' a^o

De Michael Tregurry pro Aula Hampton vj s viij d

De Joh' Mayo pro Aula Edwardi ix s iiij d

All' Scolarum eod' a^o

De Scola Magistri Rawlyns xvj d

All' camerarum eod' a^o

De domino Thoma Cotum pro Camera bassa in angulo vij s vj d

De Camera domini Willelmi Skelton' x d

De Camera domini Willelmi juyne iij s iiij d

Item Galfridus Atteleham in Esex' petit Allocari pro [*blank*] terell' x s

Summa lv s ij d

All' ten' a° nono eiusd' Regis

De Ten' Joh' William glover xxiij s ix d

De Ten' Nichi Shirborne de quibus petit allocari – xxx d pro dampnis suis in tempore sublevacionis domus dudeley v s

De Joh' Barbour pro Stampton Hall' xx d

De ten' Alan browne xx d

De gardino barton' Corveser viij d

De goldefynch' pro terr' in bellomonte vij s

De Abbatissa de godstaw pro Schopa xx d

De ten' ysabelle Colett iiij s x d

De ten' Joh' lowell' xx d

All' Aularum eod' a°

De Magistro Joh' magg' pro Aula Edwardi v s

De Magistro Thoma Estyngton principali et Roberto Chamyr pro parva aula universitatis in alto vico xvj s iiij d

[*Dorse*]

All' Scolarum eod' a°

De Scola Magistri Joh' Goldesmyth iij s iiij d

All' Camerarum eod' a°

De Camera magistri Joh' Marschall' x d

All' ten' in remotis partibus

De Galfrido Attleham quos petit allocari de Joh' Terell pro uno integro videlicet anno Nonno [*sic*] H Sexti xx s

Summa iiij li xiij s v d

All' ten' de a° decimo eiusdem regis

De ten' Joh' Wylliam glover vij s xj d

De ten' ysebelle Collett xxxiiij s iiij d

De ten' đavid glover vj s viij d

De ten' Rob' dudeley xvj s iiij d

De ten' Hugonis bennett xiij s iiij d

De ten' Joh' Cayme de quibus dicit quod solvit Magistro Thome Chace pro pavimento – iij s qui non ponuntur in summa total' Chace iiij s

De Joh' Barbour pro Stampton' Halle xiij s iiij d

De ten' Rob' lambarde v s iiij d
De ten' Joh' Coke iiij s viij d
De Gardino Brampton ij s
De Gardino barton' Corveser' xx d
De Joh' ffyscher' pro yreland' et Alrichesyde x s
De goldefynche pro terr' in bellomonte vij s
De Willelmo hanse pro gardino in sowthwychum iij s vj d
De Abbatissa de Godstow pro Schopa xx d
De Joh' Spic' pro pratis Oseneye ij s ij d
Summa vj li xiij s xj d[3]

All' Aularum eod' anno
De Magistro Willelmo Chawmerlayne pro Aula Hampton x s
De Magistro Joh' Corker' pro parva Aula universitatis oxon' in vico Scolarum vj s viij d
De Joh' fitzroberte pro Aula Edwardi xij s
De [*blank*]
De [*blank*] Ewen pro parva Aula universitatis in alto vico xiij s iiij d
De Magistro Roberto Glowcett' pro parva Aula universitatis pro quibus petit allocari circa xl d pro reparacionibus per ipsum ibi factis xx s

All' Scolarum eod' anno
De Scola Magistri Joh' goldesmyth vj s viij d
De Scola Magistri Willelmo karlele iij s viij d
Summa iij li xij s iiij d

All' Camerarum eod' [*sic*]
De Camera domini Willelmi kyllyngworth Canonici iij s iiij d
De Camera Magistri Joh' Marshall' iiij s ij d
Summa vij s vj d

All' ten' in remotis partibus
[4]De Galfrido Atteleham quos petit Allocari de Joh' Terell' pro termino sancti Mich' ultimo preterito x s
De Galfrido Atteleham pro manerio de Marks in Essex de termino pasch' x li

[3] [ADMC] This is underlined in red ink.
[4] In the original, one large 'De' is written, to cover both entries for Geoffrey Attleham.

De Joh' Tutteberye pro terris in pagula in Holdernesse iij li xij d
Summa xiij li xj d

Summa omnium Allocatorum precedencium xxxiiij li xj s xj d

Summa dimissa tenentibus xvj d

All' in dimissis Tenentibus
Item de heredibus etc.' xiij s x d ob

Soluta in reparacionibus in grosso minutis expensis et alijs factis infra oxon' vj li xij s j d
Solut' in ~~placitis~~ reparacionibus et expensis manerij de Merkes in Esex' vj li xij s v d
Solut' in placitis contra Abbatem Oseneye x li v s
Item pro iantaculis nostris peritorum et iuratorum et aliorum in eisdem placitis iij li vj d
Item in communis sociorum xj li xvj s x d q[a]
Item in batell' operariorum ij li xix s ix d
Item pro antiquo debito pavimenti primo debit' Magistro Thome Chace postea Magistro Georgio Ratheclyffe ultra Magistro Thome Boteler' et solvitur boteler' xvij s iiij d
Item in reparacionibus et Expensis factis per Magistrum Joh' Elwyke l s iij d
Summa xliiij li xiiij s ij d q[a]

In Resolucionibus Reddituum
In primis priori Sancte ffrydiswyde virginis viij s iiij d
Item Abbati de Oseney pro gardino vj s viij d
Item ecclesie sancti petri in Oriente ij s vj d
Item pro quintodecimo domini Regis iij s vij d
Summa xxj s j d

Solut' soc' Colleg'
In primis Magistro Colleg' pro festis Sancte Marie et Sancti Cuthberti de anno preterito xiij s iiij d
Item Magistro Joh' Elwyk in plenam solucionem debit' de anno ultimo preterito ix s vj d
Item eidem Magistro Joh' Elwyk in partem solucionis dierum sanctorum Cuthberti et Marie et stipendij sacerdotal' anni presentis xxxij s iiij d

Item Magistro Joh' Marton' pro diebus Sancti Cuthberti et Sancte Marie de anno preterito xiij s iiij d
Item Magistro Joh' Marton' in partem solucionis antiq' debit' sui xiij s iiij d
Item Magistro Joh' Goldesmyth' pro diebus Sancti Cuthberti et Sancte Marie de anno preterito xiij s iiij d
Item Magistro Thome Boteler' pro diebus Sancte Marie et Sancti Cuthberti de anno preterito xiij s iiij d
Summa v li xv s ij d[5]

Solut' servient' Collegij
In primis Joh' Coke famulo Smygtton xx d
Item Joh' Coke Seniori ij s
Item Joh' ffelton' xv s viij d
Item Thome yole v s
Item Alicie lotrici v s ij d
Item Joh' Tarlour' [*sic*] pro tercia parte anni xx d
Summa xxx s vj d

Summa omnium expensarum una cum ten' in manu Collegij liij li xvj s j d ob q^a

Summa Omnium Allocatorum lxx[xvij li viij s][6] ij d

[The remainder of the dorse is lost. The damage may have already been done by Smith's day, as his reading, and note of the conclusion of the roll (Vol. VIII p.118) is as follows:

Summa Omnium expens' una cum ten' in manu Collegij liij li xvj s j d
(Nihil de officio procuratoris hic anno)

Summa omnium allocatorum lxxxviij li viij s j d ob q^a
There is no Subscription to this Roll.

In the original, it is clear that the 'ob q^a*', which Smith places with the 'Summa omnium allocatorum', in fact belongs to the preceding total, Smith having perhaps been confused by the fact that those words occur in a lower line than the rest of the total, and are hence about on a level with the second total. £53 17s 1d is the correct total of Expenses. The grand total of 'Allocaciones' is actually £88 8 d, i.e. ¼d less than the figures given.*

5 [ADMC] The correct total is £5 8s 4d.
6 [ADMC] Roll torn; figures from Smith Vol. VIII p. 118.

A narrow roll; 2 membranes; the latter part of the face and the whole of the dorse, written in a neat legible hand; the first two-thirds of the face in an inferior hand, and the first membrane difficult to read through smudging and fading.]

WHITSUN 10 HENRY VI to WHITSUN 11 HENRY VI (ROLL UC:BU1/F/44)
8 June 1432–31 May 1433

BURSAR: JOHN MERTYN

Compotus magistr' johannis Merton' procurator [*sic*] collegij quod vocatur magna aula universitatis in oxon' Anno regni Regis Henrici sexti post conquestum undecimo a ffesto penticost' inclusive usque ad id' festum exclusive.

[*The Arrears are identical with the Allowances in* **F/43** *above, save for a few changes in spelling.*]

Summa Arrerag' precendencium xxxiiij li xj s xj d

Redditus ten' in paroch' omnium Sanctorum

De ten' david glover	xiij s iiij d
De ten' ysabelle Colet' cuius redditus unius anni	iij li xviij s[1]
De ten' joh' Wylyam glover	xxxj s viij d In manu collegij
De ten' Nichi Schirborne Coteler	xx s
De ten' Rob' dudley	xxx s
De ten' Hug' benet Serrante'	xx s
De ten' Th' piperd' draper	iij li
De ten' joh' Cayme	xxij s iiij d

Summa xij li xiij s viij d[2]

In parochia sancti Martini

De schopa super angulum quadrivii in qua inhabitat Ric' Stukemede xxviij s

In parochia sancte Mildrede

De Gardino Ric' Careoure quond' holefanthall iiij s iiij d

In parochia Sancte marie

De Stampton' Hall' in qua inhabitat Johannis Barbur	xiij s iiij d
De ten' Roberti lambert pro libero redditu	viij s

1 [ADMC] This latter figure written over an erasure.
2 [ADMC] This excludes the 31s 8d *in manu Collegij*.

In parochia sancti petri in oriente
De ten' Roberti plumer ubi Cameray habitavit[3] xvj s
De ten' joh' Coke[4] xij s
De schopa Alicije philip iij s iiij d
De ten' Johannis rede xxvj s viij d
Summa v li xj s viij d[5]

Hec sunt ten' in Suburbijs et in parochia Sancti Egidij et in campis
De Gardino in parochia sancti thome quod tene [*sic*] brampton mercer ij s
De Gardino in parochia sancte Marie Magdalene quod tenet Barton xx d
De pratis retro Oseneye xxx s in manu Collegij [*blank*]
De terris in bellmont quas tenet Wodeward' vij s
De johanne spicer pro pratis retro Oseney in libero redditu ij s ij d
⟨De pratis yreland' et alrichsyd'⟩ ⟨xxvj s viij d In Man' collegij⟩
Summa xij s x d[6]

In parochia sancti petri in ballio
De ten' quond' Spronte v s
De Heredibus Spronte de ten' quod johannes bibery tenuit viij s x s ob
De Gardino in Sewtwythum quod tenet Willelmus hanse' vij s
De Abatissa de godstow pro schopa ex parte sancte fridiswyde xx d

De collegijs in liberis redditibus
De Novo Colleg' pr [*sic*] Mayden Hall' in paroch' sancti petri in oriente x s
De Colleg' Cantuar' pro quadem parte terre in qua situatur una camera Eiusdem Colleg' ij s vj d
Summa xxxv s ob

Redditus Aularum In parochia Sancte Midrede [*sic*]
De Magistro Trewynnard' pro aula hampton' l s
De Magistro Joh' Elwycke pro aula scuti vj s viij d
De Magistro joh' lee pro Aula Sancti Thome x s

[3] [ADMC] A word deleted here.
[4] [ADMC] 2 words erased here.
[5] [ADMC] The correct total is £5 4s 4d.
[6] [ADMC] Excluding the £2 16s 8s *in manu Collegij*.

In parochia sancte marie

De Magistro johannis [*sic*] lee pro brasnose iij li vj s viij d

De Magistro Joh' Corker' pro parva aula universitatis in vico scolarum xxxiij s iiij d

De Joh' fitzRoberte pro Aula Edwardi xxiiij s

In parochia Sancti petri in Oriente

De decano Burgundinensi pro Aula drawda pro ij terminus xxv s

De Sucdon' pro parva Aula universitatis in Alto vico liij s

Summa xiij li ix s

De Scolis

De Gilberto[7] Kymere Cancellario universitatis oxon' pro scola inferiori vij s viij s [*sic*]

De Magistro pyge pro Scola boriali vj s viij d

De Magistro benedicto bowrth' pro scola Australi vj s viij d

Summa xxj s iiij d

De Cameris

De Camera flemyng xx s

De Camera dowson pro duobus terminis viij s

De Camera hunter pro duobus terminis iij s iiij d

De domino Abbate pro una camera inferiori pro termino natal' iij s iiij d

De dicto domino Abate pro una camera superiori pro termino pasch' iij s ij d

De domino Thoma ems monach' pro una camera inferiori iij s iiij d

De Rectore Stokpordie iij s iiij d

De Graystoke xj s

Summa lvij s ij d[8]

De pagula in Holdernesse cuius ultimus est festum assumpcionis sancte Marie preterit' iij li xij d

[7] [ADMC] Written over an erasure.

[8] [ADMC] Correct total £2 16s 6 d.

De Manerio de Merke in Esex' cum suis pertin' de Galfrido Atteleham xx li

Summa xxiij li xij d

Summa omnium Redituum jstius Anni iij^{xx} li xj s vj d ob[9]

Summa Omnium oneratorum iiij^{xx} li xv li iij s v d ob

Allocat' a^{o} j^{o} Henric' vj^{ti}

De Bosworth' pro pratis retro Oseney iiij s iiij d

Allocat' a^{o} iij^{o} eiusd' regis

De Johanne Barbour xiiij d

Allocat' scolarum eodem a^{o}

De Scola Magistri Johannis Chadwycke x d

Allocat' cam' eod' a^{o}

De Camera Magistri Roberti tong vj s viij d

Allocat' aularum de a^{o} vj^{to}

De Sybbow pro Aula drawda v s

Allocat' cam' eod' a^{o}

De Camera Egidii Asteley viij s iiij d

Allocat' ten' de a^{o} vij^{to} eiusd' regis

De Abatissa de godstow xx d

Allocat' aularum eod' a^{o}

De Magistro philippo Norres principal' Aule universitatis oxon' in vico scolarum et Roberto Glowcet' Ocupanti – ix s ij d. de quibus colleg' debet johanni lawles – vj s viij d pro reparacionibus per ipsum factis in brasnose

De Magistro Thoma Estyngton pro parva aula universitatis oxon' in alto vico xx d

De Johanne Mayo pro Aula Edwardi v s

Allocat' scolarum eod' a^{o}

De Joh' Maynyfforth' pro Scola xvj d

9 [ADMC] This total should apparently be £61 1s 8½d.

Allocat' Esex eod' a°
De Johanne Humfray in Esex' pro antiquis debitis ex ultimo copot' [*sic*] inter ipsum et magistrum Johannem Elwycke x s
Summa l s j d

Allocat' ten' de anno viij° eiusd' regis
De Thoma Belloke v s
De Abatissa de Godstow xx d

Allocat' Aularum eod' a°
De Mych' trigurr' pro Aula de hampton' iij s iiij d
De Johanne Mayo pro aula Edwardi ix s iiij d

Allocat' camerarum eod' a°
De Thoma Cotum pra [*sic*] camera bassa in angulo vij s vj d
De camera domini Willelmi Skelton' x d
De camera domini Willelmi juyne iij s iiij d
Summa xxxj s[10]

Allocat' ten' de a° ix°
~~De Johanne Willyam glover xviij s~~
De Barbur pro Stampton Hall' xx d
De Alano Brown' xx d
De Colet xiiij s vj d
De Abatissa de godstow xx d
⟨[*blank*] Johanne lowell' xx d⟩

Allocat' Aularum eod' a°
De Magistro Johanne Mag' [*sic*] pro Aula Edwardi v s
De Magistro Thoma Estyngton' et Roberto Chawmer pro parva Aula universitatis oxon' in alto vico xvj s iiij d

Allocat' camerarum
De Magistro johanne Marshall' x d

Allocat' de Esex
De terell' x s

⟨Summa totalis liij s iiij d⟩

Allocat' ten' a° x° eiusd' regis
De Johanne Barbur iij s x d ob

[10] [ADMC] This figure has been altered.

De Roberto lambert v s[11] iiij d
De Johanne Coke quos petit allocari pro salario debit' a flemmyng dowson et Marshall' iij s iiij d
De Abatissa de Godstow xx d
De Johanne spicer ij s ij d

Allocat' scolarum eod' a°
De Magistro Joh' Goldsmyth' vj s viij d
De Magistro Willelmo carleele iij s viij d

Allocat' Aularum eod' a°
De Johanne fitzRobert viij d

Allocat' camerarum eod' a°
De camera domini Ricardi Kyllyngworth' xvj d
De camera Magistri Johannis Marchal' iiij s ij d

Allocat' ten' in partibus remotis eod' a°
De Galfrid' ateleham quos petit allocari pro Johane tyrell' pro duobus terminis xx s
De johanne tutbere pro terris in holdernese xij d
Summa liij s vj d ob

Allocat' ten' a° xj° eiusd' regis
De david glover ix s iiij d
De ysabella colet iij li xviij s
De hugone benet vj s viij d
De Johanne Barbur pro stampton' hall' xiij s iiij d
De Rob' lambert pro libero reditu viij s
De thoma plummer iiij s
De Alicia phelip xx d
De johanne rede iij s iiij d
De Brampton ij s
De johanne Wodward' vij s
De Abatissa de Gostow [*sic*] xx d
De Johanne Spycer ij s ij d
Summa vj li xvij s ij d

Allocat' aularum eod' anno
De Magistro trewynard' xxiij s iiij d

[11] [ADMC] This figure has been altered.

De Magistro Johanne Corker xiij s iiij d
De Magistro Johanne legh vj s viij d
De Fitzrobert pro aula Edward' xxiiij s
De decano pro aula drawda v s
De Johanne Sugdon' pro parva Aula universitatis in alto vico xiij s iiij d

Summa iiij li v s viij d

Allocat' scolarum eod' anno

De Cancellario pro scola bassa viij s
De Magistro benedicto Burth' pro scola boreali v s
De Magistro Johanni [*sic*] pygge pro scola boriali iij s iiij d

Summa xvj s iiij d

Allocat' cam' eod' a°

De Abate pro duobus terminis vij s vj d
De domino thom' ems monacho v s
De Rectore de Stokport iij s iiij d
[*an entry erased*]

Summa xv s x d

Allocat' ten' in partibus remotis

De pagula in holdernese iij li xij d
De tyrell' xx s
De Galfrido atteleham vj li xv s

Summa totalis x li xv j s

Allocat' de dimissis tenementis Eod a°

De Strykemede xvj d
De Johanne William glover xxvj s ix d
De redibus [*sic*] sprunt xiij s x d ob
De dudeley xxx s

Summa xliiij s v d ob ⟨xxxv li viij s v d⟩

Summa Allocat' precedencium xxxv li viij s v d

[*Dorse*]

Solut'

In primis pro communis sociorum per totum Annum xij li iiij s j d ob
Item pro batell' operariorum detrimentorum et contribucionum xxxvij s viij d ob

Pro reparacionibus et expensis versus Exsex' et holdernese[12]
v li vij d ob
Item pro reparacionibus factis circa ten' laycor' ix li iij s ix d
Item pro reparacionibus scolarum et aularum lix s ix d ob
Item expensis fact' circa prata pro tegumina domorum
xxvj s vj d
Item In minutis expensis xxxj s xj d ob
In reparacionibus factis infra collegium lix s viij d ob
Summa xxxvij li iiij s ij d

Item Solut' pro Emptis in stauro v li ⟨6s ij d ob⟩
Item pro positis in Cista commune viij s ij d
Summa v li xiiij s iiij d ob

In resolucionibus Redit'
Item In primis priori Sancte fridiswide in plenam solucionem omnium debitorum et arr' xxxv s
Item Abati de Oseney pro gardino infra collegium vj s
Item Johanni herbertfeld' in plenam solucionem omnium arr' preterit' vij s iiij d
Item procuratoribus ecclesie Sancti petre [*sic*] in Oriente ij s x d
Item Senescallo hundred' extra portam borialem pro duobus annis iij s
Item Collectoribus quintodecime domini regis viij d
Summa liiij s x d

Solut' pro debitis antiquis
In primis Margarete dobbis xxvj s j d
Item hug' dawlibere ij s
Item Nich' Schirborne pro dampnis sue domus ij s vj d
Item Magistro Thom' Chase pro pavimento iij s
Summa xxxiij s vij d

Solut' pro debitis antiquijs socijs Colleg'
In primis Magistro Colleg' pro pecunijs de antiquo sibi debitis
xlix s viij d ob
Item johanni Elwycke pro pecunijs de antiquo debitis xx s

[12] The College archives include a letter of attorney, dated 16 August 1432 (ref. **UC:E1/3D/13**), which authorises John Elwyk to go up to Paull to collect the College's rent from its tenant John Tutbury, Burgess of Hull.

Item Magistro Joh' Merton' in part' soluc' ~~de~~ pro antiquis debitis iij s iiij d

Item Magistro Joh' Goldsmyth' in plenam solucionem pencionis anni preterit' xiij s iiij d

Summa iiij li vj s iiij d ob

Solut' pro pencionibus sociorum huius anni

In primis Magistro pro diebus Sancte marie et Cuthberti xiij s iiij d

⟨Item Magistro Johanni Elwycke xiij s iiij d⟩

Item Magistro Johanni Elwycke pro plena solucione pensionis sue sacerdotal' anni ult' preter' xl s

Item Magistro Johanni Merton pro diebus Sancti Cuthberti et sancte marie xiij s iiij d

Item Eidem Magistro Joh' Merton' pro plena solucione pensionis sacerdotal' xx s

Item Magistro Johanni Goldesmyth' pro die Sancti Cuthberti ann presentis vj s viij d

Summa totalis v li vj s viij d

Solut' servientibus Collegij et pro convivio sancti cuthb'

In primis ux' snawe xx d

Item Thome yole pro tribus terminis xv s

Item Henrico Coke pro uno termino ij s

Item Alicie lotrici scilicet Grikehowell' iij s iiij d

Item Willelmo barbut pro termino [*sic*] nat' et pasch' iij s iiij d

Item Johanni hunt' in partem soluc' termini quadrages' iij s iiij d

Item Willelmo lasbere pro termino quadrag' ij s

Item Johanni Cowke seni [*sic*] ix s

Item pro festo sancti Cuthberti xv s x d

Summa lv s vj d

Solut' pro stauro reparacionibus contribucionibus et stipendio pincerne

Item pro Calc' iij s vj d

Item pro factura fontis in parva Aule universitatis in alto vico xiiij d

Item pro contribucionibus termini pasche ij s xj d

Item johanni hunter pro stipendio termini pasch' ij s
Summa ix s vij d

Summa omnium Expensarum iij^{x} li v s j d

Summa omnium All' istius anni iiij^{x} li xv s xiij s vj d

⟨Computatis computandis et allocatis Allocandis domus debet computanti ix s ob[13]

Acta sunt hec per M Johannem Burbach' Comisssar' generalem venerabil' viri M Gilberti Kymer Cancell' universitatis Oxon'⟩

[*A very clearly written roll. 2 membranes*]

[13] [ADMC] The correct sum is 10s ½d.

WHITSUN 11 HENRY VI to WHITSUN 12 HENRY VI (ROLL UC:BU1/F/45)

31 May 1433–16 May 1434

BURSAR: JOHN GOLDSMYTH

Compotus Magistri Johannis Goldsmyth procuratoris Collegij quod vocatur Magna Aula universitatis in oxon' Anno regni Regis Henrici Sexti post conquestum duodecimo a ffesto pentecost' inclusive usque ad idem ffestum exclusive.

[*The Arrears are identical with the Allowances in* **F/44** *above, save for a few changes in spelling.*]

Summa Arr' precendencium xxxv li viij s v d

Redditus ten' in parochia omnium sanctorum	
De ten' ysabelle Colett cuius redditus unius anni	iij li xviij s
De ten' david glovere	xxiij s iiij d
De ten' Joh' Wylyam glover	xxxj s viij d
De ten' Nichi Shirborn' Coteler	xx s
De ten' Roberti dudeley	xxx s
De ten' Hug' benett Seriantte	xx s
De ten' ~~joh' perys glover~~ Th' pypparde draper	iij li
De ten' Joh' Cayme	xxij s iiij d
Summa xij li xiij s viij d[1]	
In parochia sancti Martini	
De schopa super Angulum quadrivii in qua habitat Ric' Strykemede	xxviij s
In parochia sancte Mildrede	
De Gardino Ric' Careour' quond' holefantthall'	iiij s iiij d
In parochia Sancte Marie	
De Stampton' halle in qua inhabitat joh' barbour'	xiij s iiij d
De ten' Roberti lambert pro libero redditu	viij s
In parochia sancti petri in oriente	
De ten' yrmanger in quo inhabitavit plummer	xvj s

[1] [ADMC] Excluding the 31s 8d from John William.

De ten' Joh' Coke xij s
⟨de ten' joh' redded pro tribus terminis xx s⟩
De ten' Roberti plumer in quo inhabitavit joh' Rede pro uno termino x s⟩ [*A sum erased*]
⟨v li xj s viij d⟩ Summa v li xj s viij d

Hec sunt ten' in suburbijs et in parochijs Sancti Egidij et in Campis
⟨de joh' peys in libero redditu ij s ij d⟩
De gardino in parochia Sancti Thome quod tenet brampton' mercer ij s
De gardino in parochia Sancte Marie Magdalene quod tenet barton' Corveser' ij s
De pratis retro Oseneye ~~in manu Collegij~~ xxiiij s vj d
De terris in bellmonte quas tenet Wodewarde vij s
De Joh' Spicer pro pratis retro oseneye in libero redditu ij s ij d
⟨de gardino ex opposito ecclesie sancti egidij viij d⟩
De pratis yrelande et alrychesyde xxvj s viij d
Summa iij li v s ij d[2]

In parochia sancti petri in ballio
De ten' quond' Sprownte v s
De heredibus sprounte de ten' quod joh' bibery tenuit viij s x s ob
De gardino in Sewtwythum quod tenet Willelmus hanse vij s
De Abbatissa de godstow pro Shopa ex parte sancte frideswyde virginis xx d

De Collegijs in liberis redditibus
De Novo Colleg' pro Mayden Halle in parochia sancti petri in oriente x s
De Colleg' Cantur' pro quadem parte terre in qua situatur una Camera eiusdem Colleg' ij s vj d
Summa xxxv s ob

Redditus Aularum In parochia Sancte Mildrede
De Magistro Truvennede pro Aula Hampton' l s
De Magistro joh' Elwyke pro Aula Scuti vj s viij d
De Magistro Joh' lee pro Aula sancti Thome xiij s iiij d

[2] [ADMC] The correct total is £3 7s 2d.

In parochia Sancte Marie

De Magistro Joh' lee pro brasnose iij li vj s viij d

De Magistro Joh' Corker' pro parva Aula universitatis in vico scolarum xxxiij s iiij d

De Joh' fitzroberte pro Aula Edwardi xxiiij s

In parochia sancti petri in oriente

De decano Burgundinensi pro Aula drowda pro duobus terminis xlv s

De Sugdon' pro parva Aula universitatis in Alto Vico liij s [*an erasure*]

Summa xiiij li xij s iiij d[3]

De Scolis

De Gilberto Kymer' Cancellario universitatis oxon' pro Scola inferiori ~~viij s~~

De Magistro ~~pyge~~ Wellys pro Scola boriali vj s viij d

De Magistro benedicto bowrthg' pro Scola Australi iij s iiij d

Summa x s

De Cameris

De Camera Roberti fflemyng' xx s

De Camera dowson pro duobus terminis xvj s viij d

De Camera Hunter pro duobus terminis ij s vj d – iij s iiij d [*sic*]

De domino Abbate pro una camera superiori ~~inferiori~~ pro termino natal' viij s iiij d

De dicto domino Abate pro una Camera superiori pro termino pasche [*blank*]

De domino Thoma ems monacho pro una Camera inferiori v s

De rectore stoppordie xiij s iiij d

Summa iij li v s x d[4]

[*No heading*]

De pagula in Holdernesse cuius ultimus est festum Assumpcionis beate Marie preterit' iij li xij d

[3] [ADMC] The correct total is £14 12s.

[4] [ADMC] Correct, if one takes 2s 6d, and not 3s 4d as Hunter's rent.

De Manerio de Merkes in Esex' cum suis pertinencijs de galfrido Atteleham xx li

Summa xxiij li xij d

Summa omnium Redituum iij^{x}iiij li xiiij s viij d ob

Summa Omnium Oneratorum c li ix s j d ob[5]

⟨iij^{x}iiij li xiiij s viij d ob⟩

[*Dorse*]

Allocat' a^{o} j^{o} Henric' vj^{ti}

De Bosworth' pro pratis retro Oseney iiij s

Allocat' a^{o} iij^{o} eiusdem regis

De joh' Barbour xiij d

All' Scolarum eodem a^{o}

De Scola Magistri ~~Elwyke~~ Chadwycke x d

All' Camerarum eo a^{o}

De Camera Magistri Roberti Tong' vj s viij d

All' aularum de a^{o} vj^{to}

De Skybow pro aula drowda iij s iiij d

All' Camerarum eodem a^{o}

De Camera Egidii asteley viij s iiij d

All' ten' de a^{o} vij^{o}

De Abbatissa de godstow xx d

All' aularum eod' a^{o}

De Magistro philippo Norres principali aule universitatis oxon' in vico Scolarum et Roberto glowcest' occupanti – ix s ij d. de quibus Collegium debet Johanni lawles vj s viij d pro reparacionibus per ipsum factis in brasnose

De Magistro Thoma Estyngton pro parva aula universitatis oxon' in alto vico xx d

De Joh' Mayo pro aula Edwardi v s

All' Scolarum eod' a^{o}

De Magistro Joh' Maynsforde pro Scola xvj d

[5] [ADMC] Apparently the correct total is £100 3s 1½d.

All' de Esex eodem a°
De joh' humfray in Esex' pro antiquis debitis ex ultimo compotu inter ipsum et Magistrum Johannem Elwyke x s
Summa liij s v d ⟨liij s j d⟩

Allocat' ten' de a° viij° eiusdem regis
De Thoma Belloke v s
De Abbatissa de godstow xx d

All' aularum eodem a°
De Mich' Trigur' pro Aula de Hampton' iij s iiij d
De Joh' Mayo pro aula Edwardi ix s iiij d

Allocat' Cam' eodem a°
De Thoma Cotom pro Camera bassa in Angulo vij s vj d
De Camera Willelmi Skelton x d
De Camera domini Willelmi juyne iij s iiij d
Summa xxxj s

All' ten' de a° ix°
De Barbour pro Stampton Halle xx d
De alano browne xx d
De Colett xiiij s vj d
De Abbatissa de godstow xx d
De Joh' lowell' xx d

All' aularum eodem a°
De Magistro Johanne Mag pro Aula Edwardi v s
De Magistro Thoma Estyngton' et Roberto Chawm' pro parva Aula universitatis in oxon' in alto vico xvj s iiij d

All' Camerarum
De Magistro joh' Marshall' x d

All' de Esex
De Tyrell' x s
Summa totalis liij s iiij d

All' ten' a° xij° [*sic*] eiusdem regis
De Joh' Barbour iij s x d ob
De Roberto lambert v s iiij d
De Joh' Cowke quos petit allocari pro salario debit' a fflemmyng' dowson et Marshall' iij s iiij d
De Abbatissa de godstow xx d

De joh' Spicer	ij s ij d
All' Scolarum eodem a°	
De Magistro Joh' goldsmyth'	vj s viij d
De Magistro Willelmo Carleele	iij s viij d
All' aularum eodem a°	
De Joh' fitzrobert	viij d
All' Camerarum eodem a°	
De Camera domini Ricardi Kyllyngworth'	xvj d
De Camera Magistri Johannis Marshalle	iiij s ij d
All' ten' in partibus remotis eodem a°	
De galfrido atteleham quos petit allocari pro Joh' tyrell' [*two or three words erased*]	x s
De Joh' Tutebery pro terris in holdernese	xij d
Summa xliij s vj d ob	
All' a° xj°	
De David glover	xxvj d[6]
De Hugone benett	vj s viij d
De Roberto lambert pro libero reditu	viij s
De Thoma plummer	ij s viij d
De Joh' Reede	xx s
De Joh' wodwart	vij s
De Abbatissa de godstow	xx d
De Joh' Spycer'	x d
Summa xxix s ij d[7]	
All' Aularum eodem anno	
De Mich' Triwynade pro Aula Hampton	xvj d
De fitzRobert pro aula Edwardi	xviij d
Summa ij s x d	
All' Scolarum eodem a°	
De Cancellario pro Scola bassa	viij s
De benedicto burgh' pro scola superiori Australi	xx d
Summa ix s viij d	

[6] [ADMC] *Sic* – presumably 16d is meant.
[7] [ADMC] This total is correct if David Glover owes 16d.

All' Camerarum eodem a°
De abbate pro duobus terminis v s
De Rectore Stopporde iij s iiij d
Summa viij s iiij d

All' ten' in partibus remotis
De pagula in Holdernese xij d
Summa xij d

All' de dimissis tenentibus eodem anno
De Strykemede xvj d
De Joh' Willyame glover xxvj s ix d
De Heredibus Sprownte xiij s x d ob
De dudeley xxx d
Summa xliiij s v d ob

All' ten' a° xij°
De ten' david glover viij s
de ten' ysabelle Colett ⟨quia vacabat per di'annum ex tempore⟩ xlvj s viij d
de ten' joh' Wylyam glover in manu Collegij xxxj s viij d
de roberto dudeley iij s iiij d
de ten' Thoma Pyppard xiij s iiij d
Summa v li iiij d[8]

[*No heading*]
de Ricardo Cariour' pro holefaunthall' iiij s iiij d
de Roberto lambert pro libero redditu viij s
Summa xij s iiij d

In parochia sancti petri in oriente
de ten' Roberti yrmanger `per unum terminum et per duos terminos de roberto plummer´ in quo quondam Cambray `per unum terminum de johanne sclatter´ inhabitavit in manu Collegij xij s
de Roberto plummer x s
Summa xxij s

Hec sunt ten' in suburbijs et in parochia Sancti Egidij et in Campis
de brampton' mercer ij s

[8] [ADMC] The correct sum is £5 3s.

de barton' Corveser' pro quodam gardino in parochia Sancte M^{e} magdalene ij s
~~de pratis retro oseneye in manu Collegij xxx s~~
de terris in bellomonte quas tenet Wodwart vij s
De Joh' Spycer pro pratis retro oseneye ij s ij d
⟨de quodam gardino viij d⟩
de quodam Gardino situato in parochia sancti Egidij viij d
Summa xiij s x d

[*No heading*]
de quondam Sprownte v s
de heredibus sprownte viij s x d ob
de gardino Swythyn' vij s
de abbatissa de godstow xx d
Summa xxij s vj d ob

[*No heading*]
De Aula Hampton de quibus provost debet iij s iiij d xxiij s iiij d
de Elwyke vj s viij d
Summa xxx s

[*No heading*]
de Magistro Cowpere pro Aula brasnose vj s viij d
de Magistro joh' Korker' iij s iiij d
de Aula Edwardi xvij s
Summa xxvij s

[*No heading*]
de aula sancti Thome iij s iiij d
de Sugdon' pro Aula universitatis in alto vico xiij s iiij d
Summa xvj s viij d

~~de Camera fflemyng' xx s~~
~~de Camera dowson xij s~~
~~de Camera hunter iij s iiij d~~

All' scolarum eodem a^{o}
de Scola bassa viij s
de Magistro novi Collegij iij s iiij d
de mytforth' iij s iiij d
Summa vj s viij d ⟨vj s viij d⟩

All' camerarum eodem anno

de Camera fflemmyng'	xx s
de Camera dowson	xij s
de Camera Hunter	x d
De Rectore Stopporde	xiij s iiij d
Summa xlv s ij d[9]	

All' de partibus remotis

de pagula in holdernesse	iij li xij d
De manerio de Merkes	vj li xvj s
de johanne tyrell'	x s
Summa x li vij s	

All' de dimissis tenentibus

de ten' forykines	xvj d

Solut'

In primis pro communis sociorum per totum annum	xiij li iij s vj d
Item pro batellis operariorum detrimentorum contribucionum	xlv s ij d
Item pro reparacionibus in esex	iiij li xvij s iiij d
Item pro expensis versus esex et holdernes	iiij li iiij s vij d ob
Item pro reparacionibus factis circa ten' laicorum	xxxiiij s vj d ob
Item pro reparacionibus scolarum et aularum	iij li xv d
Item expense facte circa prata	xxj s vj d
Item in minutis expensis	xxviij s vj d ob
Item in reparacionibus factis infra collegium	xxxviij s viij d ob
Item in reparacionem factam circa cameram ruinosam	xvij s vj d ob
Item in reparacionibus esex pro all' Galfrido et solutis plummer et alijs factis per magistrum et pro solucione johanni pes	vij li iij d v d ob
Item solut' pro emptis in stauro et pro factis in capella et circa ticaciones	xxxij s iiij d
Item in communis servientium in vacacione	viij s
Summa xlvj li iiij s ij d ob	

[9] [ADMC] The correct total is £2 6s 2d.

In resolucionibus reddituum

In primis priori sancte frideswyde in plenam solucionem xviij s viij d

Item abbati de osney pro gardino infra collegium ⟨et domo Willelmi glover⟩ ix s iiij d

Item procuratoribus ecclesie Sancti petri in oriente ij s x d

Item senescallo hundrede extra portam borialem xviij d

Item collectoribus quintadecime domini regis xvj d

Item roberto Wakfede procuratori de enyssam vj s viij d

Solut' pro debitis

In abbatisse de Godstow pro arr' in plenam solucionem xxvj s viij d

Item abbati de abbindon pro Aula Edwardi et in plenam solucionem omnium arr' ij s vj d

In primis [*sic*] margarete dobbys in plenam solucionem xvj s iiij d

Summa iiij li v s x d

Solut' pro debitis antiquijs soc' coll'

In primis magistro colleg' pro stipendio a retro vj s viij d

Item Magistro Johanni Merton in partem solucionis pro antiquis debitis xvj s ob

Item Magistro Johanni Goldsmyth pro plena solucione pencionis anni preteriti vj s viij d

Item Willelmo scharpe in plenam solucionem anni preteriti vj s viij d

Summa xxxvj s ob

Solut' pro pencione sociorum huius anni et pro recreacione eorundem

In primis Magistro collegij pro die sancte Marie et in partem solucionis pro officio Magistratus xj s viij d

Item Magistro Johanni elwyk pro eodem festo vj s viij d

Item Magistro Johanni elwyk in plenam solucionem pencionis sacerdotalis xl s

Item Magistro Johanni Merton pro eodem festo vj s viij d

Item Magistro Johanni Merton in stipendio sacerdotali trium terminorum xx s

Item Magistro Johanni Goldsmyth' pro officio procuratorio et die sancte Marie vj s viij d

Item Willelmo scharpe pro eodem festo vj s viij d
Summa v li xviij s iiij d

In recreacione sociorum
In primis pro recreacione Magistri iiij s
Item pro recreacione elwykk iiij s
Item pro recreacione Merton iiij s
Item pro recreacione Goldsmyth iiij s
Item pro Willelmo scharpe iiij s
Summa xx s

Solut' servientibus coll' et pro convivio sancti [*cuthberti*]
In primis lotrici scilicet uxori shawe et alter' pro uno anno vj s viij d
Item Johanni Cok pro duobus terminis vj s viij d
Item Johanni Cok seni pro uno termino xx d
Item Johanni hunter pro stipendio duorum terminorum x s viij d
Item Wyllelmo [*barbur*] viij d
Item pro festo sancti Cuthberti xj s iij d ob
Item pro [. . .] et [. . .] aliarum fact' per magistrum viij s iij d ob
Item pro soluc' procuratori [. . .]iarum suarum iiij s
[*Summa*] lvi s x d[10]

Summa omnium Expensarum iij^{x}ij li xxj d[11]

Summa precend' All' istius anni xxxix li iij s ix d ob[12]

Summa omn' all' istius anni cj li v s ij d ob

⟨Computatis computandis et a[*llocatis*] allocandis domus debet computanti xvj s vj d⟩

⟨Acta sunt hec per M Thomam Bourgchier Cancellarium universitatis Oxon'⟩[13]

[*A wide roll (11 inches), mostly clear, but worn and difficult to read at the foot of the dorse. 2 membranes*]

[10] [ADMC] The correct total is 56s 7d.
[11] [ADMC] The correct total is £62 1s 3d.
[12] [ADMC] The correct total is £39 3s 3½d.
[13] In 1439, however, Thomas Bourchier, now Bishop of Worcester, gave the College the right to ignore his ratification if they so wished (see **UC:S4/F1/1**).

WHITSUN 12 HENRY VI to WHITSUN 13 HENRY VI (ROLL UC:BU1/F/46)

16 May 1434–5 June 1435

BURSAR: THOMAS BENWELL

Compotus Magistri Thome Benwell' Magistri Magne Aule sive Collegij universitatis Oxon' et Magistri [. . .] socij aula sive Collegij Anno rr' henrici sexti terciodecimo a festo pent' incl[*usive usque ad idem*] festum exclusive anno revoluto.

Arr' de anno undecimo[1] regis henrici Sexti dat' predicto Magistro Thome Benwell' in scriptis a Magistro Joh' Goldsmyth' [*qui*] erat procurator dicte aule anno undecimo regis predicte.

Arr' ten' eodem anno

De david glover	viij s
De Hugone benett	vj s viij d
De Ricardo careour	iiij s iiij d
De Thome pippard pro ten' stoke'	x s
De Roberto lambert	xvj s
Summa xlv s	

Arr' Aularum eodem anno

De aula hampton de magistris joh' bernard' et petro provost ibid' illo anno principal' de quibus provost debet iij s iiij d pro penc'	xxiij s viij d
De aula brasnos de Magistro Thome Cowper	vj s viij d
De aula sancti Thome a magistro Thome cowper	iij s iiij d
De aula Edwardi videlicet dionisio principali	xvij s
Summa l s viij d	

Arr' scolarum eodem anno

De Nicholao mitford determinatore	iij s iiij d
De quodam Magistro novi collegij	iij s iiij d

[1] [ADMC] This should be the 12th year. [RHDS] There are far fewer Arrears in this roll than there were Allowances in **F/45** above; almost certainly an Arrears roll, now lost, was drawn up at this time, in the same manner as **F/28**, which would have recorded the missing sums.

Arr' camerarum eodem anno

De camera Magistri Willelmi dowson	xij s
De camera rectoris de stopeforde	xvj s viij d

Summa xxxv s iiij d

Arr' de pagula et esex eodem Anno

De pagula in Holdernes	iij li xij d
De Galfrido atletham pro manerio	vj li xvj s
De Joh' Terell'	x s

Summa x li vij s

Summa omnium arr' xvj li xviij s

Redditus ten' in parochia sancti Martini

De ten' Ric' strykmed	xxviij s

Redditus ten' in parochia omnium sanctorum

De ten' ysabelle colet	iij li xviij s
De ten' david glover	xxiij s iiij d
De ten' nich' scherburne	xx s
De ten' Thome dudlay	xxx s
De ten' hugonis benet	xx s
De ten' Stok'	xiij s iiij d
De ten' Joh' pars glover et stok'	ij li vj s viij d
De ten' Joh' caam'	xxij s iiij d
De gardino Ricardi cariour	iiij s iiij d

Summa xiiij li vj s

Redditus ten' in parochia sancte Marie

De ten' Roberti lambert in libero redditu	viij s
De ten' joh' barbur'	xiij s iiij d

Summa xxj s iiij d

Redditus ten' in parochia sancti petre [*sic*] in oriente

De ten' Roberti plummer'	xl s
De ten' Willelmi varyn'	xvj s
De ten' Joh' coke	xij s

Summa iij li viij s

[*Red*]ditus ten' in [*paroc*]hia sancti petri in ballio

De gardino Willelmi hans in sueria	vij s

[*D*]e ten' in suburbijs et campis oxon'

De gardino Willelmi brampton in parochia sancti Thome	ij s

De Joh' spicer pro pratis osney ij s j d
De Magistro joh' petynton pro pratis osney ij s j d
De Mert' fuller pro pratis osney xx s
De gardino barton' Corvesiur' xx d
De Wodward pro terris in bello monte vij s
Summa xlj s x d

[*R*]edditus leber'[*sic*]
De novo Colleg' pro madynhall' in parochia sancti petre in oriente x s
De Collegio cant' pro quadem camera in eodem Collegio ij s vj d
⟨De abbatissa godstw [*sic*] pro quadam shopa ex opposito[2] sancte frydeswyde xx d⟩
⟨Item de eadem pro redditu libero ten' quondam Thoma Master xiiij d⟩
Summa xv s iiij d

Redditus Aularum
De Magistro Thome cowper pro brasnos iij li vj s viij d
De eodem Magistro pro aula sancti thome xiij s iiij d
De eodem Magistro pro aula scuti vj s viij d
De aula Hampton videlicet Magistro joh' bernarde l s
De aula Edwardi a dionisio et jacobo leth' xxiiij s
De Magistro Joh' northfok et Joh' Sugden pro una quarta in parva aula universitatis in alto vico xiij s iiij d
De parva aula universitatis in vico scolarum a lancest' determinatore iij s iiij d
Summa viij li xvij s iiij d

Redditus Camerarum
De camera Roberti fflemyng xx s
De camera Magistri dowson xvj s viij d
Summa xxxvj s viij d

[*No heading*]
De Joh' Tutbery pro terris in holdernes iij li xij d

[2] [ADMC] Written in above a deletion.

De Galfrido attleham pro manerio de merkes xx li
Summa xxiij li xij d

Summa omnium reddituum huius anni lv li vij s vj d

Item computans oneratur de antiquo debito scolarum byllyngworth xvj d
Item Magister Joh' Elwyk recepit a cista communi ad reparacionem ten' Collegij iiij li xiiij d
Item Magister Collegij recepit a cista ad solvendum abbati de osney xxvj s viij d
Summa v li ix s ij d

Summa omnium oneratorum lxxvij li xiiij s viij d

Ten' in manu collegij eodem anno
De parva aula universitatis in vico scolarum xxxiij s iiij d
De parva aula universitatis in alto vico iiij marc'
De aula drawda xlv s
De ten' Joh' Willyam glover xxxj s viij d
De pratis yreland et alrechsett xxvj s viij d
De scolis xxj s iiij d
[*no total given*]

Alloc' ten de undecimo rr' H Sexti
De david glover viij s
De hugone benett vj s viij d
De Ricardo cariour iiij s iiij d
De Roberto lambert' viij s
Summa xxj s viij d

Alloc' aularum eodem anno
De aula hampton videlicet Joh' Bernarde et petro provest de quibus idem petrus debet iij s iiij d
Summa xxiij s viij d [*sic*]
De Magistro Thoma cowper pro aula Brasnos vj s viij d
De eodem Magistro Thoma cowper pro aula sancti Thome iij s iiij d
De dionisio selane principali aule Edwardi xij d
Summa xxxiiij s viij d

Alloc' Scolarum eodem anno
De Nych' Mytford determinatore iij s iiij d

De quodam Magistri novi Collegij	iij s iiij d
Summa vj s viij d	

Alloc' camerarum eodem anno

De camera Magistri Willelmi dowson dicit quod Magister Joh' Merton' recepit	xij s
De camera rectoris de Stopworth dicit quod Merton recepit	xvj s viij d
Summa viij s iiij d	

Alloc' esex eodem anno

De domino Joh' Terell	x s
Summa xxxviij s viij d	

Alloc' ten' de anno duodecimo eiusdem regis

De ten' ysabelle colet	xlviij s viij d
De nich' sherburne	iij s iiij d
De Thome dudlay	x s ij d
De ten' hugonis Benet	vj s viij d
De pippard de ten' stok'	vj s viij d
De Joh' caam'	iiij s viij d
De Ricardo cariour	iiij s iiij d
De ten' Roberti lambert	viij s
De ten' Joh' barbur'	xiij s iiij d
De ten' Roberti plummer'	v s
De ten' Willelmi Waryn'	vj s iiij d
Summa v li xiij s j d	

[*No heading*]

De gardino barton' corvesur'	xx d
De Martino fuller' pro pratis	vj s iiij d
De Wodwerd pro terris in bello monte	iij s viij d
De Abbatissa de godstow pro shopa et ten' colet	ij s x d
De Magistro Joh' petynton	ij s j d
De Joh' spicer	ij s j d
De gardino Willelmi hanse	vij s
Summa xxv s viij d	

[*Dorse*]

Alloc' Aularum eodem anno

De Magistro Thome cowper pro aula sancti Thome	xiij s iiij d
De eodem Magistro Thoma cowper pro aula scuti	iij s iiij d

De eodem Magistro Thoma cowper pro brasnos xlvj s viij d
De aula Hampton a Magistro joh' bernarde xxvj s viij d
De aula Edwardi a dionisio et Jacobo leth' xx s
Summa v li x s

Alloc' camerarum eodem anno
De camera fflemyng quos solvit Wakfeld vj s viij d
De camera Magistri Willelmi dowson viij s iiij d
Summa xv s

[*No heading*]
De Tutbery pro terris in holdernes iij li xij d
De Joh' Terell' xx s
De Galfrido atleham xvj li ij s viij d
Summa xx li iij d viij d

Summa omnium allocatorum precedencium xxxviij li ix s j d

Computans petit allocari de Ricardo strykmed quos expendit in reparacionibus in tempore procuratoris Magistri Goldsmyth' de termino sancti joh' baptist' post annum procuratoris dicti ~~Joh'~~ Magistri Joh' iiij s viij d
Item computans petit allocari de Roberto plumer quod expendit in reparacionibus in tempore procuratoris dicti Magistri Joh' Goldsmyth' de termino sancti Joh' bapt' post annum procuratoris docti Magistri Joh' iiij s

Solut' in partem solucionis ad novam cameram infra Collegium iij li xvij d ob
Item in reparacionibus ten' et in partem solucionis ad latrinam infra collegium xxix s iiij d ob
Item solut' in expensis esex et holdernes iij li xxij d ob
Item in emptos ad coquinam et promptuarium et in alijs solutis infra collegium x s v d
Summa viij li iij s j d ob

Solut' in resolucionibus reddituum in primis abbati de osney xxxvj s viij d
Item abbatisse de godstow v s vij d
Item priori sancte frideswyde x s
Item baly mason' pro redditu extra portam borialem xv d

Item pro quintadecima domini regis xvj d
Summa liiij s vj d[3]

Solut' pro communis sociorum a pent' usque ad terciamdecimam septimanam post natalem domini xj li iij s v d ob q[a]
Item pro batellis operariorum detrimentis contribucionibus a pent' usque ad terciamdecimam septimanam post natalem domini xxxvj s ix d ob
Item solut' in partem solucionis communarum sociorum et batell' operariorum a predicta terciadecima septimana post natalem domini usque in festum pent' tunc futurum ij li xvj s
Summa xv li xvj s ij d ob[4]

Solut' servientibus In primis Joh' Huntter pro antiquis debitis suis et servicio 2°bus terminis fer' huius anni xxxij s xj d ob
Item seni Joh' Cok vij s iij d
Item Roberto Cok xx d
Item Margarete cowbrig' lotrici ij s iiij d
Item Matilde lotrici pro terminis natalis domini et pasche iij s
Item Wyllelmo barbur' iij s iiij d
Summa xlv x vj d ob[5]

Item Magistro Joh' Elwyk quibus transiret esex iij s iiij d
Item posui in communi cista ij li xvj s viij d
Summa iij li

Summa totalis omnium harum Expensarum xxxj li xix s iiij d ob[6]

[*No more on the roll.*

A narrow roll of 2 membranes, legibly but not particularly neatly written. Note that there are no payments to Fellows this year]

[3] [ADMC] The correct total is 54s 10d.
[4] [ADMC] The correct total is £15 16s 3d.
[5] [ADMC] The correct total is 50s 6½d.
[6] [ADMC] The correct total is £70 8s 5½d. The Bursar presumably owes the College £7 6s 2½d.

WHITSUN 13 HENRY VI to WHITSUN 14 HENRY VI (ROLL UC:BU1/F/47)
5 June 1435–27 May 1436

BURSARS: THOMAS BENWELL AND JOHN ELWYK

Compotus Thome Benwell' Magistri Magne Aule sive Collegij universitatis Oxon' et Magistri Joh' Elwyk socij eiusdem collegij Anno rr' Henrici Sexti quarciodecimo[1] a festo pent' in[*clusive*] usque ad idem festum exclusive anno revoluto.

[*The Arrears are identical with the Allowances in* ***F/46*** *above, save for a few changes in spelling.*]

Summa omnium allocatorum [*sic*] precedencium xxxix li ix s j d

Redditus ten' in parochia sancti Martini	
De ten' Ric' strykmede	xxviij s
Redditus ten' in parochia omnium sanctorum	
De ten' ysabell' colet	iij li xviij s
De ten' david glover	xxiij s iiij d
De ten' nich' sherburne	xx s
De ten' Thome dudlay	xxx s
De ten' Hugonis benet	xx s
De ten' [*blank*] stokys	xiij s iiij d
De ten' payrs glover	ij li vj s viij d
De ten' Joh' caan'	xxij s iiij d
De gardino Ric' careour	iiij s iiij d
Summa xiiij li vj s	
Redditus ten' in parochia sancte Marie	
De ten' Roberti lambert in libero redditu	viij s
De ten' Joh' barbur'	xiij s iiij d
Summa xxj s iiij d	
Redditus ten' in parochia sancti petri in oriente	
De ten' Roberti plummar'	xl s
De ten' Willelmi Waryn'	xvj s

[1] [ADMC] *Sic*; looks as if altered from 'Terciodecimo'.

De ten' Joh' coke xij s

Summa iij li viij s

Redditus ten' in parochia sancti petri in ballio

De gardino Willelmi Hans in sueria vij s

De ten' in suburbijs et campis oxon'

De gardino Willelmi Brampton in parochia sancti Thome ij s

De Joh' spicer pro pratis osnay ij s j d

De Magistro joh' petynton pro pratis osnay ij s j d

De Martino fuller pro pratis osnay xx s

De gardino quodam [*sic*] barton' corvesor' ⟨modo alborum monachorum⟩ iiij s

De Wodward pro terris in bello monte vij s

Summa xliiij s ij d

Redditus liberi

De novo collegio pro madynhall' in parochia sancti petre in oriente x s

De collegio cant' pro quadem camera in eodem collegio ij s vj d

De Abbatissa de godstow pro quadam shopa ecclesie sancte frideswide xx d

Item de abbatissa de godstow pro quadam parte ten' in quo Thomas ~~quond'~~ Master quondam habitavit ad solvendum dominis feodi xiiij d

Summa xv s iiij d

Redditus Aularum

De [. . .] pro brasnose[2] iij li vj s viij d

De aula sancti Thome xiij s iiij d

De eodem Magistro pro aula scuti vj s viij d

De aula hampton videlicet Magistro joh' barnarde l s

De Aula Edwardi videlicet de jacobo leth' xxiiij s

De parva aula universitatis in alto vico videlicet de petro shothyrbroke pro duobus terminis xx s

De parva Aula universitatis in vico scolarum de filio everard qui idem determinavit iij s iiij d

Item hic respondit compotans pro receptis a Magistro Joh' corcar

[2] [ADMC] The first two entries under 'Redditus aularum' appear to have been altered to read 'De Magistro Thoma cowper pre brasenose' (as in the preceding year); but if so the ink has faded.

de eadem aula pro occupacione certarum camerarum in anno duodecimo rr' H Sexti iij s iiij d

Summa ix li vij s iiij d

Redditus Camerarum eodem anno

De camera Roberti fflemyng xx s

De camera Magistri Willelmi dowson xvj s viij d

De camera Magistri Joh' Gerves xiij s iij d

Summa l s

Redditus in partibus longinquis

De Joh' Tutbery de Hull' pro terris de pagula in Holdernes iij li xij d

De manerio de merkes in Esex videlicet de galfrido Atleham' pro demedio [*sic*] anni et joh' Stanes pro altero demedio anni xx li

Summa xxiij li xij d

Summa omnium reddituum huius anni lvj li xiij s ij d

Item computans oneratus de receptis a communi cista ad edificacionem nove camera infra collegium lvj s viij d

Item mutuatis a viccario sancti petri in oriente Oxon' ad edificacionem dicte camere adhuc debitis eidem viccario xx s

Item computans oneratus de receptis a Symone sompton' in elimosina iij s iij d

Item computans respondit de receptis a Joh' Telm' in elimosina x s

Item computans respondit de receptis a lucia Telme in elimosina xx d

[3]Item computans oneratus pro receptis a Waltero mason pro gardino ex opposito ecclesie sancti egidij xij d

Summa iiij li xij s viij d

Summa omnium oneratorum lxxxxix li xiiij s xj d

Ten' in manu Collegij eodem anno

De parva aula universitatis in vico scolarum xxxiij s iiij d

De parva aula universitatis in alto vico iiij marc'

De Aula drowda xlv s

De ten' Joh' glover Wyyllyam glover xxxj s viij d

De pratis yrland et alrechede xxvj s viij d

[3] This item appears to have been inserted later.

De scolis nostris xxj s iiij d
Summa x li x s iiij d[4]

Alloc' ten de anno rr' H Sexti undecimo
De david glover viij s
De Recard' [*sic*] cariour ⟨solut' commissario⟩ iiij s iiij d
De Roberto lambert' xvj d
Summa xiij s viij d

Alloc' Aullarum [*sic*] eodem anno
De aulla hampton videlicet de Magistro joh' bernarde et petro provest de quibus debet dictus petrus iij iiij d a colegio xxiij s viij d
De Magistro Thoma cowper pro aula brasnos vj s viij d
De eodem Magistro Thoma pro aula Sancti Thome iij s iiij d
Summa xxxiij s viij d

[*Dorse*]

Alloc' Scolarum eodem anno
De Nicola Mitforth' determinatore iij s iiij d
De camera Magistri Willelmi dowson quos ut dicit Magister joh' Merton' recepit xij s
De camera rectoris de stopworth quos idem Magister joh' Merton recepit xvj s viij d

Alloc' Esex eodem anno
De domino Joh' Terell x s
Summa xlij s

Alloc' ten' anno rr' H Sexti duodecimo
De ten' ysabelle colet xlviij s vij d
De Mertino fuller pro pratis retri osney iij s
De Wodwerd pro terris in bello montte [*sic*] iij s viij d
De abbatissa de godstow pro shopa et ten' colet xvij d
De joh' spicer pro pratis retro osney ij s j d
De gardino Ric' cariour xxij d
Summa iij li vij d

Alloc' Aularum eodem anno
De Magistro Thome cowper pro aula sancti Thome xiij s iiij d

[4] [ADMC] Correct total £10 11s 4d.

De eodem Magistro Thoma pro gardino de sheldhall'	iij s iiij d
De eodem Magistro Thoma pro aula brasnos	xxvj s viij d
De aula Hampton	xxvj s viij d
Summa iij li x s	

[*No heading*]

De joh' bedforth' pro terris in holdernes	iij li xij d
De domino Joh' Terell'	xx s
Summa iiij li xij d	

Summa omnium alloc' precedencium xv li xj d[5]

Alloc' ten' de anno terciodecimo eiusdem Regis

De ten' ysebell' colett	xxxvj s
De david glover	xij s ij d
De Thoma dudelay	xvij s iij d
De ten' Joh' caam	v s iiij d
De gardino Ric' cariour	iiij s iiij d
De Magistro Rogero skebow per ten' quondam lambert	iiij s
De ten' Joh' barbor'	xiij s iiij d
De ten' Willelmi Weryn'	xij s
De alicia [*blank*] pro ten' iuxta Waryn'	iij s iiij d
Summa v li vij s v d[6]	

[*No heading*]

De gardino Willelmi brampton	ij s
De Joh' spicer pro pratis osnay	ij s j d
De albis monachis pro gardino	ij s
De Wodwerd pro terris in bello monte	vij s
De godstow pro quadam shopa et ten' colett	ij s vj d
Summa xv s vij d	

Alloc' Aularum eodem anno

De Rogero gray pro brasnose	xxij s iij d
De eodem rogero pro gardino aule sheld	vj s viij d
De aula sancti Thome videlicet de Magistro Rogero Beethson' principali Magistro Thoma cowper et Rogero gray	xiij s iiij d
De aula edwardi	viij s
De aula hampton	xiij s

5 [ADMC] This sum excludes the 'Ten' in manu Collegij'.

6 [ADMC] This figure (v d) has been altered. The 'v' seems definite, though rather poorly shaped.

camerarum

De camera dowson viij s iiij d

Summa iij li xj s xj d

[*No heading*]

De Joh' bedforth' pro terris in Holdernes iij li xij d

De domino Joh' Terell' pro fedo militari in ramysden in esex xx s

De Joh' Stanes pro manerio de merkys ix li

Summa xiij li xij d

Summa omnium alloc' huius anno immediate precedentis xxij li xvj s iij d

Summa omnium et singulorum Redituum a retro hic alloc' xxxvij li xiiij s[7]

Item idem computans petit allocari pro reparacionibus factis in molendino ventretico Esexe pro Galfridum atteleham' vj li

Item computans allocari petit pro stacione molendini aquatici xxvij s

Item idem computans petit allocari pro toga Galfridi vj s viij d

Summa vij li xiij s viij d

Computans petit allocari pro dimissis Ric' strykmed xvj d

Item ~~id'~~ computans petit allocari pro mutuat' [*blank*] a vicario sancti petri in oriente cum quibus idem computans oneratus et patet superius quos Collegium adhuc debet predicto viccario xx s

Summa xxj s iiij d

Item in reparacione nove camera infra Collegium xiij li ob

Item pro reparacionibus latrine parietibus et alijs reparacionibus infra collegium xl s ix d ob

Item in reparacionibus aularum xliij s viij d

Item in reparacionibus ten' xlvij s vij d

Item in factura prati minutis expensis equitacionibus Esex' et in alijs debitis etc. xlij s ix d ob

Summa omnium reparacionum harum xxj li xiiij s x d ob

Solut' in resolucione reddit' in primis osney pro gardino vj s

Item abbatisse de godstow vij s

Item Willelmo Herberfeld pro pratis osney tribus annis xj s

[7] [ADMC] The correct total is £37 17s 2d.

Item priori sancte fridiswide xviij s
Summa xlij s viij d[8]

Solut' domino regi In primis pro d[. . .] quintadecima xvj d
Item pro nova collectione domini regis et expensis aput Wodstoke ix s ij s
Summa x s vj d

Solut' pro communis soc' a pent' usque pasch' exclusive viij li vij s ij d
Item solut' pro batellis operariorum a pent' usque pasch' exclusive iij li vj s xj d
Item solut' pro communis sancti Cudberti vj s j d
Item pincerne in partem soluc' communarum sociorum post pasch' xiiij s vj d ob
Summa xij li xiiij s viij d ob

Solut' soc' colleg' in primis Magistro Collegij [*blank*]
Item Magistro Joh' Elwyk vj s viij d
Item Magistro Joh' Merton' vj s viij d
Item Magistro Joh' Goldsmyth' vj s viij d
Item Magistro Willelmo Sharpe vj s viij d
Summa xxvj s viij d

Solut' servientibus Collegij in primis Roberto pincerne et coco xxvj s viij d
Item Wyllelmo barbur' v s
Item Matilde lotrici iiij s viij d
Summa xxvj s viij d[9]

Summa totalis solut' domino regi pro communis soc' et batellis pro stipendijs soc' et servientibus collegij xviij li x s x d ob[10]

[*The foot of the roll is defective*]

[8] [ADMC] The correct sum is 42s.
[9] [ADMC] The correct total is 30s 4d.
[10] [ADMC] The correct total is £18 11s 2½d.

WHITSUN 14 HENRY VI to WHITSUN 15 HENRY VI (ROLL UC:BU1/F/48)[1]
27 May 1436–19 May 1437

BURSAR: THOMAS BENWELL

In nomine patris et filij et spiritus sancti amen.

Compotus Magistri Thome Benwell' Magistri magne aule seu Collegij universitatis Oxon' de omnibus redditibus et proventibus dicti collegij receptis et expensis a festo pentecost' inclusive anno regni regis henrici sexti quartodecimo usque ad idem festum pentecoste exclusive anno eiusdem quintodecimo datus in die martis prox' post festum trinitatis predicto anno quintodecimo regis predicti[2]

Arr' ten

De david glover pro anno rr' henrici sexti undecimo viij s
Item de eodem david pro anno terciodecimo eiusdem regis xij s ij d

Summa xx s ij d

De Ric' cariour' pro anno undecimo regis predicti de gardino iiij s iiij d
Item de eodem Ric' pro anno duodecimo regis predicti de eodem gardino xxij d
Item de eodem Ric' pro anno terciodecimo eiusdem regis de eodem gardino xij d

Summa vij s iiij d

De lamberte pro anno undecimo De ten' nunc Magistro Rogeri skebow xvj d
Item de magistro Rogero skebow pro eodem ten' de anno terciodecimo regis predicti iiij s

Summa v s iiij d

[1] 1436/7 is unusual in having two account rolls. This roll, **F/48**, sets out its rents in the usual way, with arrears, rents and allowances, whereas the other roll, **F/49**, only lists 'receipts' (*recepta*) for its properties, which record the actual moneys received by the College. These sums can be calculated by deducting the Allowances in **F/48** from the combined Arrears and Rents there. The rest of the rolls' contents are almost identical. See p. xl of the Introduction.

[2] i.e. 4 June 1437.

De Isabelle colete pro anno duodecimo regis predicti xlviij s
Item de eadem Isabella pro anno terciodecimo eiusdem regis xxxvj s

Summa iiij li iij s vij d[3]

De Thoma dudeley pro anno terciodecimo eiusdem regis xvij s iij d
De Joh' cawne pro anno terciodecimo v s iiij d
De Joh' barbour' pro anno terciodecimo eiusdem regis xiij s iiij d
De alicia pro ten' iuxta Waryne pro anno terciodecimo v d
De Willelmo Waryne xij s
De Willelmo brampton' pro gardino pro anno terciodecimo eiusdem regis ij s
De albis monachis pro gardino ij s
De Martino Fuller' pro pratis retro [*sic*] de anno duodecimo iij s
De Abbata [*sic*] de godstow de anno duodecimo xvij d
De eadem abbata de godstow pro anno terceiodecimo ij s vj d

Summa iij s xj d

De Joh' spyser' pro novem annis preteritis xix s xj d
De Wodewarde pro terris de anno duodecimo iij s viij d
De Wodewarde pro eisdem de anno terciodecimo vij s

Summa x s viij d

Summa x li v s ix d[4]

Arr' aularum

De aula hampton videlicet de Magistro Johanne bernarde et petro provest de quibus dictus petrus debet collegio iij iiij d pro anno undecimo regis predicti xxiij s viij d
Item Magister Joh' bernard' debet pro anno duodecimo xxvj s viij d
Item Magister Joh' bernard' debet pro anno terciodecimo xiij s iiij d

Summa iij li iij s viij d

De Magistro Thoma Cowpere de aula sancti thome ⟨pro anno undecimo regis predicti⟩ vj s viij d

[3] [ADMC] The correct sum is £4 4s.
[4] [ADMC] The correct sum is £10 6s 5d.

Item de eodem Magistro Thoma Cowper predicto anno undecimo regis de gardino scheldehall iij s iiij d

De Magistro Thoma Cowper pro aula sancti Thome de anno duodecimo regis predicti xiij s iiij d

Item de eodem Magistro Thoma pro gardino de scheldhall' eodem anno vj s viij d

Item de eodem Magistro Thome pro aula brasnose de anno terciodecimo xxvj s viij d

De Magistro Rogero strey pro aula brasnose de anno terciodecimo regis predicti xxij s iij d

Item de Magistro Rogero strey et scolaribus suis pro gardino de scheldehall' de dicto anno terciodecimo regis vj s viij d

De Magistro Rogero beethson' principali aule sancti thome et dicto Magistro Rogero strey occupante dictam aulam sancti thome vj s viij d

De Nicholao Mythforde determinatore pro scola anno undecimo regis iij s iiij d

De Jacobo lethe principali aula Edwardi pro anno terciodecimo eiusdem regis viij s

Summa viij li vij s iij d

Arr' camerarum

De camera Magistri Willelmi dowson' pro anno undecimo dicti regis xij s

Item de eodem Magistro Willelmo dowson pro anno terciodecimo eiusdem regis viij s

Summa xx s

De camera rectoris de stopworthe xvj s viij d

Summa xxvj s viij d[5]

Arr' in partibus longinquis

De Johanne batforthe pro terris in Holdernesse pro anno duodecimo et terciodecimo eiusdem regis v li ij s

Item de domino Joh' terele milite de Esex pro quibus Magister Joh' Goldsmyte recepit acquietancias xxx s a collegio in tempore procuracionis sue Item de dicto Johanne terele pro annis duodecimo et terciodecimo xl s

Summa iij li x s[6]

[5] [ADMC] The correct total is £1 16s 8d.

[6] This total refers only to the arrears from Essex.

Summa ix li xij s

Summa omnium arr' xx li vij s v d[7]

Redditus ten' in parochia sancti Martini

De ten' Ricardi strykmede	xxviij s
De ten' david glover pro dimidio anno	xij s viij d
De ten' nicholai scherburne	xx s
De ten' Thome dudeley	xxx s
De ten' hugonis benete	xx s
De ten' stokys	xiij s iiij d
De ten' Joh' payrs glover	xlvj s viij d
De ten' Joh' caame	xxij s iiij d
De Magistro Joh' boke Rectore Lincolnienc' pro gardino	v s
Summa ix li xvij s[8]	

Ten' in parochia sancte marie virginis

De ten' Magistri Rogeri skebow in libero redditu	viij s
De ten' Joh' barbour'	xiij s iiij d
Summa xxj s iiij d	

Ten' in parochia sancti petri in oriente

De ten' Jacobi cariour'	xl s
⟨De ten' Augustini⟩	⟨xij s⟩
De ten' villelmi Waryene	xvj s
Summa iij li viij s	

Redditus ten' in parochia sancti petri in ballio

De gardino Willelmi hans in sueria	vij s

Redditus in suburbis [*sic*] et campis oxon'

De gardino Willelmi Brampton in parochia sancti Thome	ij s
De Joh' spicer pro pratis retro osnay	ij s j d
De Magistro Ric' petinton pro eisdem pratis	ij s j d
De Joh' hamys pro firma pratorum retro osney	v s
De gardino alborum monachorum	iiij s
De Joh' Wodwarde pro terris in campis de Walton'	vij s

[7] [ADMC] The correct total is £29 11s. If 10s is added for the obvious error in the third total, they would come to £30 1s 8d. The figure 'vij d' have apparently been altered.

[8] [ADMC] The correct total is £9 18s.

De Waltero mason' pro gardino ex opposito ecclesie sancti egidij vj d

Summa xxix s viij d

Redditus liberi

De novo collegio in parochia sancti petre in orient [*sic*] x s

De collegio cant' pro qua [*sic*] camera in eodem collegio ij s vj d

De abbata de godstow pro schopa ex opposito porte sancte frideswide xx d

Item de abbata de godstow in libero redditu pro ten' [*blank*] Thomas Master xiiij d

Summa xv s iiij d

Redditus Aularum et scolarum

De aula brasnose videlicet de Magistro Rogero Grey iij li vj s viij d

[9]De aula sancti Thome videlicet de Magistro rogero Grey ~~occup~~ principali et Magistro rogero occupante xiij s iiij d

De gardino aule schelde [*blank*] Magistro Rogero Grey et suis scolarius ipsum gardinum occupantibus vj s viij d

De aula hampton unde [*sic*] Magistro Thoma mor' principali ij li x s

De aula Edwardi videlicet de Jacobo lethe principali xxiiij s

De parva aula universitatis in alto vico videlicet de petro sothysbroke

prima medietate anni xx s

et pro secunda medietate eiusdem anni xiij s iiij d

De parva aula universitatis in vico scolarum a determinatore ij s ij d

Summa x li vj d

Redditus Camerarum

De camera domini Roberti fflemyng' xx s

De camera domini oliveri elton' x s

De camera Magistri Willelmi dowson' xvj s viij d

De camera Magistri Joh' chadworthe xvj s viij d

De camera Magistri Joh' Jerweyse xiij s iij d

Summa iij li xvj s viij d

[9] [ADMC] Subsequent entries show that this must be an error; Beetson was Principal and Gray occupant.

Redditus in longinquis partibus

De Joh' bedfurthe de Hulle pro terris in pagula in Holdernese iij li xij d

De Joh' stanis pro manerio de merkes in Esex xviij li iij s iiij d

De reddibus [*sic*] domini Joh' terell' militis pro libero redditu feodi militaris exeunte de villa rammysdynd' in comitatu dicte Esex' ad dictum manerium de merkys xx s

Summa xxij li iiij s iij d

Summa omnium reddituum huius anni lij li xij s x d

⟨Summa omnium onerat' lxxxiij li iij d⟩

Ten' in manu collegij

De ten' Isabelle colete iij li xviij s

De ten' ubi Joh' villiam habitavit xxj s viij s

De parva aula universitatis in vico scolarum xxxiij s iiij d

De aula druda xlv s

De pratis Irland' et alryche sete xxvj s viij d

De pratis retro osney xx s

Summa [*blank*]

Allocata ten'

De Isabella colete in quibus est condempnata coram Magistro Joh' burbache tunc commissario pro anni duodecimo et terciodecimo regni regis henrici sexti xxxviij s iiij d

De Thoma dudeley pro anno quartodecimo xxiiij s vj d

De nicholao scherburne pro anno quartodecimo iij s

De Hugone benete xiij s iiij d

De Joh' caame pro anno terciodecimo et quartodecimo xvij s iiij d

De Joh' perys glover pro anno quartodecimo xj s viij d

Summa v li viij s ij d

[*No heading*]

De Johanne barbure pro anno quartodecimo eiusdem regis xiij s iiij d

De Willelme Waryne pro anno quartodecimo vij s

De gardino Willelmi hans pro anno quartodecimo vij s

De Magistro Ricardi petinton' pro pratis retro osney de anno quartodecimo regis predicti ij s j d

De gardino Walteri Mason' pro anno quartodecimo vj d

De abbata de godstow pro anno duodecimo xvij d
Item de godstow pro anno terciodecimo ij s vj d
Item de eodem godstow pro schopa anno quartodecimo xx d
Item de eodem godstow pro ten' Thome maaster xiij d
Summa vj s ix d

De Joh' Hans pro pratis retro osney pro anno quartodecimo v s

Arr' [*sic*] aularum
De `magistro´ Joh' bernarde pro aula hampton[10] de anno terciodecimo r' Henrici sexti ix s viij d
De magistro thoma mor' pro aula de Hampton' pro anno quartodecimo r' regis predicti xxiij s
De magistro Rogero [*a deletion*] beetson' principali aule sancti thome et magistro Grey ocupante eandem aulam pro anno terciodecimo r' regis predicti vj s viij d
Item de predictis beetson' et Grey pro gardino de scheld' hall' vj s viij [*sic*]
De Magistro rogero Grey pro aula brasnose de anno quartodecimo predicti regis xij s iij d
De Magistro Rogert beetson' principali aule sancti thome et Magistro rogero occupante eandem aulam anno quartodecimo regis predicti vj s viij d

[*Dorse*]
De Magistro rogero Gray pro firma ecclesie sancte marie de annis terciodecimo et quartodecimo regis predicti [*blank*]
De Jacobo lethe principali aule edwardi pro anno quartodecimo regis predicti x s xj d
De petro schotysbroke pro parva aula universitatis in alto vico de anno quartodecimo regis predicti vj s viij d
De nicholao mitforde determinatore pro scola iij s iiij d
Summa iiij li xv s x d

Arr' [*sic*] camerarum
De camera Magistri Willelmi dowson' pro anno terciodecimo regis predicti viij s
De Magistro villelmo dowson' pro camera de anno quartodecimo viij d

10 [ADMC] Originally written 'sampton'.

De domino olyvere Elton' pro camera de anno quartodecimo iij s iiij d
De camera Magistri Joh' chadworth' pro anno quartodecimo ij s vj d
Summa xiij s vj d

Arr' [*sic*] redditus in partibus longinquis
De Joh' stanese pro manerio de markys in Esex' de termino epiphanie anno r' H sexti quartodecimo ix li xx d
De Joh' Bedforth' burgensi de Hull' pro terris in pagula in Holdernese de termino annunciacionis sancte Marie anno r H sexti quartodecimo iij li xij d
Summa xij li ij s vij d

Summa omnium alloc' precedencium xxv li ij s x d

Arr' [*sic*] in briga
De ysabella colet pro annis duodecimo et terciodecimo r' h sexti de quibus illa petit allocari pro se dicta colleg' et non ponitur in tallijs pincerne collegij et alijs [*blank*][11] que ipsa ysabella posuit in billa ij li v s iij d
De ten' Magistri Rogeri skebow pro anno terciodecimo iiij s
De eodem rogero pro anno duodecimo r' predicti viij s
De Roberto lamberte pro anno terciodecimo xvj d
De Joh' Wodwarde pro terris in campis de Walton de anno duodecimo regis predicti iij s viij d
Item de eodem Joh' Wodwarde pro eisdem terris de annos terciodecimo et quartodecimo r' predicti xiij s
Summa xvij s viij d
De david glover pro antiquo debito anni undecimi r' h sexti viij s
Item de eodem david pro redditu anni quartodecimi xij s ij d
Summa xx s ij d
De Joh' spicer pro decem annis preteritis xxj s ij d
Summa v li xvij s vj d[12]

Arr' [*sic*] aularum
De Magistro thoma colper pro anno undecimo r' h sexti de aula sancti Thome vj s viij d

[11] [ADMC] Smith (vol. VIII p. 127) reads 'evidencijs' here.
[12] [ADMC] The correct total is £5 18s 1d.

De eodem Magistro thoma eodem anno pro gardino de scheldhall' iij s iiij d

De eodem Magistro thoma pro aula sancti thome anno duodecimo r' predicti xiij s iij d

De eodem Magistro thoma eodem anno pro gardino de scheldehall' vj s viij d

De eodem Magistro thoma anno duodecimo r' h sexti pro Aula brasnose pro [*sic*] xxvj s viij d

Summa ij li xvj s viij d

Arr' [*sic*] reditus in partibus longinquis

De heredibus et executoribus domini Joh' terell' militis pro quibus Magister Joh' Goldsmyth tempore procuracionis sue recepit acquietancionis a collegio Summa xxx s

Item de heredibus et executoribus dicti Joh' terell' duodecimo terciodecimo et quartodecimo regis predicti iij li

Summa vij li vj s viij d

Summa alloc' omnium allocat' in briga xiij li iij s viij d[13]

Peticiones tenencium pro reparacionibus

In primis Willelmus Waryne pro factura unius terre parietis et alijs reparacionibus per ipsum factis xiij s

Item iacobus cariour petit allocari pro reparacionibus per ipsum factis xxiiij s

Item Magister Joh' barnarde petit pro reparacionibus per ipsum in Hampton' Hall' annis undecimo et duodecimo r' h sexti Summa iij li vij s iiij d

Item Magister rogerus Grey petit allocari pro reparacionibus per ipsum factis in brasnose anno quartodecimo regis predicti ix s j d

Item Jacobus lethe petit pro reparacionibus per ipsum factum in aula Edwardi anno quartodecimo r' predicti ix s j d

Summa v li ij s v d[14]

Summa omnium alloc' hic precedentium xliij li viij s xj d

Solut' eodem anno pro expensis dicti colleigj [*sic*] seu aule per predictum Magistrum Thomam Benwell'

In primis in reparacionibus infra collegium xv s vj d ob

[13] [ADMC] The correct total is £13 4s 2d.
[14] [ADMC] The correct total is £5 2s 6d.

Item in emptis in grosso silice calce et lattis et tegulis xj s ix d
Item in emptis ad coquinam et promptuarium xij s j d
Item in solutis infra capellam scilicet pro canvesse factura vestiment' et in partem solucionis pro cera v s vij d
Item in antiquis debitis et in renovcione [*sic*] caucionum incistarum xxiiij s j d
Summa [*blank*]

Item in reparacionibus ad domum iacobi cariour factis per magistrum collegij xj s ob
Item in reparacionibus aule brasnose xvj s vj d ob
Item in reparacionibus aule hampton' ix s v d
Summa [*blank*]

Item in solutis serviencibus collegij
In primis villelmo barbour' vj s viij d
Item roberto Joy pincerne pro duobus terminis xiij s iiij d
Item Willelmo coke pro uno termino scilicet natalis domini vj s viij d
Summa xxvj s viij d

Item in reparacionibus ad domum in qua habitavit ⟨Joh' William⟩ glover iij li xix s j d
Item in reparacionibus aule Edwardi ix d
Item in reparacionibus ad domum spennyg' xv d ob
Item in reparacionibus versus esex' et holdernesse xiiij s
Summa [*blank*]

In solutis socijs collegij
In primis Thome Benwell' Magistro collegij xvj s viij d
Item Magistro Joh' Elwyke xl s
Item Magistro Joh' Marton' oct' sancti laurentij iij s iiij d
Item eidem Magistro Joh' Marton' in festo sanctorum prothi et iacinti xiij s iiij d
Item Marton' recepit a Joh' pers glover xj s viij d
Item Marton' recepit a nich' scherburne iij s
Item Magister collegij solvit Marton' in festo sancti lini xx s
Item Magistro Joh' goldsmeth xvj s viij d
Item Magistro Willelmo scharpe xvj s viij d
Summa totalis hic soluta socijs vij li vj s viij d[15]

[15] [ADMC] The correct total is £7 1s 4d.

Item solut' in placitis

In primis placito latrine Joh' William contra dugwyll' xvij d

Item in placito contra Joh' spicer pro prato retro oseney viij d

Summa ij s j d

Solut' in resolucionibus reddituum

In primis Edmundo Wicum coquinario de oseney pro gardino infra collegij vj s

Item abbati de oseney in festo sanctorum fabiani et sebastiani xvj s x d

Item Thome sprong' pro redditu extra portam borialem xviij d

Item abbati de Enesham quos solvit schotysbroke xij s

Item abbate de godstowe xiij s

Item collectoribus quindecime domini regis viij d

Item in minutis expensis iij s j d

Solut' pro communis et batellis operariorum

In primis solut' roberto Joy de debitis sibi post pascha [*sic*] usque ad pentecost et a festo pentecoste usque ad festum sancti mich' v li xiij s v d

Item in soluc' Willelmo coke pro communis et batellis operariorum a fest mich' usque ad festum natalis domini iij li v s

Item Willelmo coke a festo natalis domini in partem soluc' communarum soc' et batellarum operariorum usque festum pentecost' v li vij s viij d

Summa [*blank*]

Summa totalis omnium soluc' precedencium xxxv li' xvj s vij d ob[16]

Item computans petit in isto compoto allocari sibi de sex libris ij s quas Magister Joh' goldsmyth recepit de redditibus pagule in holdernesse summam sequentem quam non solvit Magistro et soc' dicti collegij xxj s viij d

Item pro officio procuratoris huius anni x s

Summa xxxj s viij d

Item computans allocavit Magistro Joh' Marton' ad maiorem solucionem eorum que sibi debentur ut sequitur

In primis computans allocavit dicto Magistro Joh' Marton' quos recepit a Magistro Willelmo dowson xij s

[16] [ADMC] I think £35 15s 9d.

Item computans allocavit dicto Magistro Joh' Marton' quos idem Marton' recepit rectore stopfurde xvj s viij d
Item idem computans allocavit Matilde lotrici de redditu domus in qua habitat pro stipendio suo anni preteriti a retro et in plenam solucionem stipendij sui huius anni ix s
Item computans allocavit alicie stone de arr' suis pro emendacione vest' capelle ij s vij d
Summa xl s iiij d

Summa omnium expensarum xxxix li viij s vij d ob

Summa omnium allocatorum huius anni lxxij li xvj s xj d ob[17]

Computatis computandis et allocatis allocandis computans debet iij s iij d ob⟩

[*A wide roll (10½ inches), well preserved and very clearly written. Several totals appear to be inaccurate. 2 membranes.*]

[17] [ADMC] The correct total is £82 17s 6½d.

WHITSUN 14 HENRY VI to WHITSUN 15 HENRY VI (ROLL UC:BU1/F/49)

27 May 1436–19 May 1437

BURSAR: THOMAS BENWELL

In nomine patris et filij et spiritu sancti Amen

Compotus Magistri Thome Benwell' Magistri magne aule sue Collegij universitatis oxon' de omnibus redditibus et proventibus dicte Collegij seu Aule receptis et expensis per eundem Thomam a festo pent' exclusive Anno r'r' Henrici quartodecimo usque ad idem festum pentecost' exclusive Anno eiusdem regis quintodecimo datus in die martis proximo post festum trinitatis predicto Anno quintodecimo regis predicti[1].

[2]Recepta ten' in parochia sanctorum Martini et omnium sanctorum oxon' predicte

De ten' Ric' strykemede	xxvj s viij d
De ten' Thome dudeley	xxij s viij d
De ten' david glover	xij s ix d
De ten' nich' sherburne	xvij s
De ten' hugonis benet	vj s viij d
De thoma pyppert' pro ten' stokis	xiij s xj d
De ten' Joh' pers glover	xxxv s
De ten' Jon [*sic*] Caam	x s

Recepta ten' in parochijs sancte Mildrede sancte marie virginis et sancti petri in oriente

De ric' cariour' pro gardino	vij s iiij d
De magistro joh' Beke pro eodem gardino	v s
De joh' barbur' pro stamston hall'	xiij s iiij d
De ten' Jacobi cariour	xvj s viij d
De ten' Willelmi Warrn	viij s
De ten' augustine	iij s

[1] i.e. 4 June 1437.

[2] As explained at the start of **F/48**, this roll is unique (apart from that of 1383/4) among the account rolls in trying to record the exact amount received from each property. These amounts, called *recepta* as opposed to *redditus*, can be calculated by deducting the Allowances from the combined Arrears and Rents for each place in **F/48**. See further p. xl of the Introduction.

Recepta ten' in suburbijs oxon'	
De gardino Bramton'	iiij s
De martino fuller	iij s
Recepta de collegijs	
De novo collegio	x s
De collegij alborum monochorum [*sic*]	iiij s
De collegio cantuar'	ij s vj d
De godstowe abbata de godstow	xx d
Recepta aularum et scolarum	
De magistro rogero Grey pro aula brasnose	iij li xj s
De parva aula universitatis in vico scolarum	iiij s iiij d
De magistro Thoma more pro aula hampton	xxvij s
fit [*sic*] maweher' sutor in partem solucionis	vj s viij d
Antiqui debiti Magistri Joh' Barnard'	xij s[3]
De Jacobo leth' pro aula edwardi	[*blank*]
De petro shotysbroke pro parva aula universitatis [*sic*]	xxvj s viij d
De scola bassa a determinatore	ij s vj d
Recepta camerarum	
de domini roberti flemyng	xx s
De camera magistri Willelmi dowson'	xvj s
De camera cagistri Joh' chadword'	xiiij s
De camera magistri Joh' Gerveys	xiij s iiij d
De camera domini olyver' elton'	vj s viij d
Recepta in partibus remotis	xix li xx d[4]
In primis de Joh' Stanes in Esex	[*blank*]
Item Magister Joh' Goldesmyth' recepit a Magistro et socijs collegij duas acquietancias factas executoribus Joh' Tutteberi et Joh' Bedford' de Hull' pro hac summa ab eis recipienda De quibus solum deliberavit	iiij li xiij s iiij d
Item Magister Joh' Marton' recepit de antiquis debitis ut in subsequentibus patet	
In primis magister Marton a magistro Willelmo dowson	xij s
Item idem Joh' Marton recepit a rectore stopford'	xvj s viij d

[3] [ADMC] The sums 'vj s viij d' and 'xij s' are both clearly misplaced; the former should be opposite 'Barnard', the latter opposite 'aula edwardi'.

[4] [ADMC] Evidently this sum should be opposite the entry for John Stanes.

Item alloc' Matilde lotrice [*sic*] de redditu suo pro stipendio suo ix s
Item alloc' alice de redditu pro factura vestimentorum capelle et promptuarie ij s viij d

Summa omnium receptorum [*blank*]

Summa omnium alloc' hic precedentium xliij li viij s xj d

[*In a different hand*]

Solut' eodem anno pro expensis dicti collegij seu aule per predictum Magistrum Thomam Benwell'

In primis in reparacionibus infra collegium xv s vj d ob
Item in emptis in grasso silice calce et latis et tegulis xj s ix d
Item in emptis ad coquinam et promptuarium xij s j d
Item in solutis infra capellam scilicet pro canvesse factura vestiment' et in partem solucionis pro cera v s vij d
Item in antiquis debitis et in renovacione caucionum incistarum xxiiij s j d
Summa [*blank*]

Item in reparacionibus ad domum iacobi cariour factis per Magistrum collegij xj s ob
Item in reparacionibus aule brasnse [*sic*] xxj s vj d ob
Item in reparacionibus aule hampton' ix s v d
Summa [*blank*]

Item in solutis serviencibus collegij
In primis Willelmo Barrbur vj s viij d
Item Roberto Joi pincerne pro duobus terminis xiij s iiij d
Item Willelmo coke pro uno termino scilicet natalis domini vj s viij d
Summa xxvj s viij d

[*The original hand*]

Item in reparacionibus ad domum in qua habitavit Joh' Willyam glover ⟨in reparacionibus⟩ iij li xix s
Item ad aula [*sic*] Edwardi ix d
Item in reparacionibus ad domum spennyng' xv d ob
Item in equitacionibus versus Esex et Holdernesse xiiij s
Summa [*blank*]

In solutis socijs collegij

Thoma [*sic*] Benwell' In primis Magistro collegij xvj s viij d
Item Magistro Joh' Elewhyke xl s
Item Magistro Joh' Marton' oct' sancti laurentij iij s iiij d
Item eidem Magistro Joh' Marton' in festo sanctorum prothi et iacinti xiij s iiij d
Item ~~magistro W~~ Marton' recepit a Joh' pers glover xj s viij d
Item Marton' recepit a nich' Sharburne iij s
Item Magister Collegij solvit Marton' in festo sancti lini xx s
Item Magistro Joh' Goldesmyth' xv s viij d
Item Magistro Willelmo scharpe xvj s iij d
Summa totalis hic soluta socijs ~~vij li~~ vij li vj s viij d

Item solut' in placitis

In primis placito latrine Joh' William contra dagfyld' xvij d
Item in placito contra Johannem spicer pro prato retro oseney viij d
Summa ij s j d

[*Dorse*]

[*In a hand different from either of the preceding*]

Solut' in resolucionibus redituum

In primis Edmundo Wycum coquinario de oseney pro gardino infra colegium vj s
Item Abbati de Osney in festo fabiani et sebastiani xv s x d
Item Thome sprong' pro redditu extra portam borialem xviij d
Item abbati de Enesham quos solvit Shotysbroke xij s
Item Abbate de goddystowe xiij s
Item Colectoribus d [*sic*] quintidecym' domini regis viij d
Summa lj s[5]

Item in minutis expensis iij s j d

Soluc' pro communis soc' et batellis operariorum

In primis solut' Roberto Joy debitis [*sic*] sibi post pascha [*sic*] usque ad pentecost' et a festo pentecost' usque ad festum Sancti Michaelis v li xiij s v d

Pro communis et batellis operariorum

[5] [ADMC] This is only correct if the Abbot of Osney is paid 16s 10d, as he was in **F/48** above.

Item in [*sic*] solut' Willelmo Coke a festo Michael' usque ad festum Nat' domini iij li v s

Item Willelmo Coke a festo nat' domini in partem solucionis communarum sociorum et batellorum operariorum usque festum pentecosten' v li vij s viij d

Summa totalis omnium solucionum precedencium xxxv li' x s vij d ob[6]

Item computans petit in isto compoto allocari Sibi de sex libris ij s quas Magister Johannes Goldsmyth recepit de redditibus pagule in holdernes summam sequentem quam dictus Magister Joh' non solvit Magistro et soc' dicti collegij xxj s viij d

Item pro officio procuratoris huius anni x s

Summa xxxj s viij d Ric' bawdounuth

Item computans allocavit Magistro Joh' Marton' ad maiorem solucionem eorum que sibi debentur ut sequitur ⟨Summa h[. . .] est comedere et bibere quando est famelicus quis ex nobis⟩

In primis computans allocavit dicto Magistro Joh' Marton' quos recepit a magistro Willelmo dowson xij s

Item computans allocavit dicto Magistro Joh' Marton' quos idem Marton' recepit rectore Stopford viij d

Item idem computans allocavit Matilde lotrici de redditu domus in qua habitat pro stipendio suo anni preteriti a retro et in plenam solucionem stipendij sui huius anni jx s [*sic*]

Item computans allocavit alicie Stone de [*blank*] pro emendacione vest' capelle ij s vij d

Summa xl s iiij d

[*No more on the roll*]

[*Narrow roll (7 inches), 1 membrane; in good condition & very clear.*]

[6] [ADMC] I think £35 14s 11d as it stands.

WHITSUN 15 HENRY VI to WHITSUN 16 HENRY VI (ROLL UC:BU1/F/50)

19 May 1437–1 June 1438

BURSAR: WILLIAM SHARPE

In nomine patris et ffilij et spiritus sancti amen

Compotus Magistri Willelmi Sharpe procuratoris Magne Aule seu Collegij universitatis oxon' de omnibus redditibus et proventibus dicti collegij receptis et expensis a festo pentecost' inclusive anno regni regis Henrici Sexti quintodecimo usque ad idem festum pentecoste exclusive Anno eiusdem regis sextodecimo

[*The Arrears are identical with the Allowances in* ***F/48*** *above, except for the following small differences in content:*

(a) under Arrears of tenements, Thomas Dudeley's sum is noted as 15 Hen VI, not 14.
(b) William Waryne is called John Wayryn.
(c) The sum of ***Arr' in briga*** *is here £5 17s.*
(d) Under arrears of distant places in the first entry, ***heredibus*** *is replaced with* ***hereditatibus****.*]

Summa omnium arrerag' presedenc' [*sic*] xxxviij li vj s vj d

Redditus ten' in parochia omnium sanctorum

de thoma dudley de ten' quo Joh' Wyllyam nuper habitavit pro duobus terminis anni	xvj s viij d
de ten' Ric' strykemede	xxvj s viij d
de ten' ricard' spennyng	xx s
de ten' nicholai scherburne	xx s[1]
de ten' Thome dudley	xxx s
de ten' hugonis benet et pro gardino nuper conducto	xx s iij s iiij d
de ten' stokys	xiij s iiij d
de ten' Joh' Glover	xlvj s viij d
de ten' Joh' caame pro tribus terminis	xvj s ix d

[1] [ADMC] This figure has been altered.

de Magistro Joh' boke rectore collegij lincolnienc' pro gardino v s

Summa x li xviij s v d

Ten' in parochia sancte marie virginis

de ten' Magistri Rogeri skebow in libero redditu viij s

de ten' Joh' barbour' xiij s iiij d

Summa xxj s iiij d

Ten' in parochia sancti petri in oriente

de ten' Joh' auston xij s

de ten' Jacobi cariour' xl s

de ten' villelmi Waryene xvj s

Summa iij li viij s

[*No heading*]

de thoma harbyrfeld'[2] pratis [*sic*] yrelond' allerych'hett' xiij s iiij d

de gardino Willelmi hans in sueria vij s

de gardino Willelmi Brampton in parochia sancti Thome ij s

de Joh' spicer pro pratis retro osney ij s j d

de Magistro Ricardo petinton' pro eisdem pratis ij s j d

de Joh' hanys pro firma pratorum retro osney v s

de gardino alborum monacorum iiij s

de Thoma spreg'[3] pro terris in campis de Walton' vij s

de Waltero mason' pro gardino ex opposito ecclesie sancti egidij vj d

Summa ij li iij s

[*No heading*]

de novo collegio in parochia sancti petre in orienti x s

de collegio cant' pro quadam camera in eodem collegio ij s vj d

de abbata de godstowe pro schopa ex opposito porte sancte frydeswyd' xx d

Item de abbata de godstowe in libero redditu pro ten' [*blank*] Thoma maister xiiij d

Summa xv s iiij d[4]

[2] [ADMC] The name has been written over an erasure.

[3] [ADMC] Written over an erasure.

[4] [ADMC] Both these figures have been altered; the correct total is 14s 5d.

[*No heading*]

de aula brasnose videlicet de magistro Rogero grey iij li vj s viij d
de aula sancti Thome videlicet de Magistro rogero Grey principali et magistro rogero occupante xiij s iiij d
de gardino aule schelde magistro rogero grey et suis scolaribus ipsum gardinum occupantibus vj s viij d
de aula hampton videlicet Magistro Thoma More principali ij li x s
de parva aula universitatis in alto vico videlicet de petro shotisbroke pro meditate [*sic*] anni xxvj s viij d
⟨de aula edwardi videlicet de jacobo leche principali xxiiij s⟩
de parva aula universitatis in vico scolarum a determinatore iiij s iiij d
de pen[..]ar'[5] pro aula droda pro duobus terminis anni xx s

Summa x li xj s viij d

[*No heading*]

de camera Magistri petri prevost pro uno termino iij s iiij d
de camera Magistri Roberti fflemyng' xx s
de camera domini olyvery [*sic*] Elton' x s
de camera Magistri Willelmi dowson' xvj s viij d
de camera Magistri Joh' chadword' et domini Roberti hungerford' pro 3^{bus} terminis xxvij s ij d
de camera magistri Joh' gerveys xiij s iij d
de camera magistri Joh' Goldesmyth'[6] xvj s viij d
de camera magistri ioh' Wotton xiij s iiij d

Summa vj li vj d

[*No heading*]

de Joh' bedfurthe de hulle pro terris in pagula in Holdernese iij li xij d
de Joh' stanis pro manerio de merkes in Esex xviij li iij s iiij d
de redditibus domini Joh' terell' militis pro libero redditu feodi militaris exeuntis de villa de rammysdyne in Com' dicte Esex' ad dictum manerium de merkys xx s

Summa xxij li iiij s ij d

Summa omnium reddituum huius anni lvij li ij s vij d[7]

[5] [ADMC] The 4th letter has been overwritten and is illegible. Possibly it is meant to be deleted.

[6] [ADMC] Written over an erasure.

Item computans oneratur pro lignis que vendidit uxori hugonis
ij s xj d

Summa omnium oneratorum lxxxxv li xij s[8]

Ten' in manu collegij

De ten' ubi Isabella Colet habitavit	iij li xviij s
De ten' ubi Willelmus Wyllyam habitavit	xxxj s viij d
De ten' spendyng' diminuuntur	iij s iiij d
De ten' in quo Joh' Came habitavit	xxij s iiij d
De ten' in quo Joh' barbor habitavit	xiij s iiij d
De ten' gardini in sueria diminuuntur	iiij s
De pratis retro osney	xxxiij s iiij d
De pratis hyrelond' et alleryghayte unda [*sic*] sub'	xxvj s viij d

Summa x li xij s viij d

[*No heading, but also* ***in manu coll'***]

De aula drowdedas	l s
De parva aula universitatis in vico scolarum	xxxiij s iiij d
De parva universitatis [*sic*] in alto vico diminuuntur	xxvj s viij d
De aula hampton in manu collegij	ij li x s
De scolis	xxj s ij d
De cameris vacantibus infra collegium	iiij li vj s viij d

Summa xiij li vij s x d

Item diminuuntur de antiquo redditu manerio de merkys in Esexya
vij li xiij s iiij d

Summa omnium ten' in manu Collegij et diminucionum reddituum xxxj li xiij s x d

Allocata ten'

De Isabella colete in quibus est condempnata coram Joh' Burbag' tunc commissarium pro annis duodecimo et terciodecimo anno [*sic*] rr' Henr' sexti xxxviij s iiij d

De Nycholao schyrburne pro anno quintodecimo vj s

Item de dudeley pro anno quintodecimo xx s iij d

Item de eodem dudley quos dixit se solvisse mathe° carpentarios et quod idem matheus negavit ij s vj d

7 [ADMC] These figures altered.
8 [ADMC] These figures have also been altered.

Item de eodem Thoma dudley de anno dicti regis quintodecimo pro ten' ubi joh' Wysham habitavit xvj s viij d

Summa iiij li iij s ix d[9]

[*No heading*]

Item de peppard pro anno quintodecimo pro ten' stokys vj s viij d

Item de hugone Benett' pro anni quintodecimo et pro gardino eodem anno x s

Item de Joh' pers pro anno quintodecimo xxiij s iiij d

Item de Joh' Came pro anno quartodecimo et quinto^mo [*sic*] xxj s iij d

Item de Joh' barbour aula stampton pro anno quintodecimo xiij s iiij d

Item de skebowe pro annis terciodecimo quartodecimo et quintodecimo xvj s viij d

Item de Roberto lokyer et jacobo caryour pro anno quintodecimo xvij s iiij d

Item de Willelme Warenne pro anno quintodecimo vj s

Item de spendyng' v s

Item de gardino Willelmi Bramton ij s

[*Face of the roll*]

Item de magistro Ricardi petyngton' et [*sic*] anno quartodecimo et quintodecimo iiij s iiij d

Item de Joh' hanys pro pratis osney pro annis quartodecimo quintodecimo x s

Item de albis monachis pro gardino pro anno quintodecimo ij s

Item de Waltero Mason' pro anno quintodecimo vj d

Item de Thoma spryng pro terris in campis Walton pro anno quintodecimo vij s

Item abbata de godstow pro anno quartodecimo et quintodecimo de schopa [*blank*]

Item de eadem abbata pro ten' Thome mayster pro annis quartodecimo et quintodecimo [*blank*]

Item de novo Collegio pro anno quintodecimo v s

Item collegio cantuarij pro termino [*sic*] quintodecimo ij s vj d

9 [ADMC] These figures have been altered.

Item de abbata de godstow de shopa et ten' T Mayster de annis terciodecimo quarto quinto sexto ix s vij s

Summa viij li ij s vj d

Alloc' aularum

Item de magistro Joh' barnard' pro aula hampton de anno terciodecimo ix s viij d

Item de petro Shotisbroke pro anno quintodecimo iij s iiij d

Item de Jacobo leche pro aula edwardi pro anno quartodecimo x s xj d

Item de eodem Jacobo pro anno quintodecimo xxiiij s

Item de mytfurth' qui determinavit in parva aula universitatis in vico scolarum anno quinto° [*sic*] iiij s iiij d

Item de magistro rogero betson' principali aule sancti thome et magistro Rogero Grey ocupante eandem aulam pro anno terciodecimo regis predicti vj s viij d

Item de magistro Rogero Grey pro usu gardini de sheldehall' eodem anno vj s viij d

Item de magistro Rogero Grey pro aula brasnose pro anno quartodecimo regis predicti xxij s v d

Item de magistro Rogero betson' pro aula sancti Thome et Magistro Rogero Grey ocupante eandem aulam anno quartodecimo regis predicti vj s viij d

Item pro sheld'hall' de magistro Rogero grey anno quintodecimo regis predicti vj s viij d

Item de eodem magistro Rogero Grey pro aula sancti Thome anno quintodecimo regis predicti iij s iiij d

Item de magistro Thome cowper pro anno duodecimo regis predicti pro gardino sheld'hall' vj s viij d

Summa v li x s iiij d[10]

Allocata camerarum

Item de cameris infra collegium

De camera magistri Rob' flemyng' viij s iiij d

De camera domini olyvery Elton' pro anno quintodecimo vj s viij d

De camera Magistri Willelmi dowson' pro anno quartodecimo et quintodecimo xvij s iiij d

[10] [ADMC] The correct total is £5 11s 4d.

De camera Magistri Johannis Chadword' pro anno quintodecimo xx d
De camera magistri Johannis Gerverys pro anno quintodecimo vj s viij d
De camera magistri Joh' Wotton' pro anno quintodecimo xiij s iiij d
De camera Magistri Johannis goldesmyth' pro anno quintodecimo xvj s viij d
Summa iij li x s viij s [*sic*]

Allocat' in partibus longinquis
Item de Johanne Bedfurth' pro terris in holdernese pro anno quintodecimo ij li v s iiij d
Item de Joh' terell' pro anni decimo et undecimo regis predicti pro quibus magister Joh' Goldesmyth' tempore procuracionis sue recepit acquientancias a collegio xxx s
Item de eodem Johanne heredibus et exicutoribus [*sic*] suis pro annis duodecimo terciodecimo quartodecimo et quintodecimo regis predicti iiij li
Summa vij li xv s iiij d

⟨xxix li ij s vij d⟩ Summa omnium allocacionum presedentium [*sic*] xxx li xj d

[*No heading – in fact these are tenements* ***in briga*** *(i.e. in dispute)*]
Item Isabella Colette pro anis [*sic*] duodecimo et terciodecimo regis predicti de quibus illa petit allocari et non ponitur in tallijs pincerne Collegij nec in alijs evidencijs Collegij ij li v s iij d
Item de Roberto lambert pro anno terciodecimo regis predicti xvj d
Item de Johanne Wodward' pro terris in campis de Walton' pro anno duodecimo regis predicti iij s viij d
Item de eodem Johanne Wodward' pro eisdem terris de annos terciodecimo quartodecimo et quintodecimo xxj s
Item de david Glover pro antiquo debitu anni undecimi eiusdem regis viij s[11]
Item de eodem david pro redditu anni quartodecimi eiusdem regis xij s ij d

[11] [ADMC] Figure altered from vij s.

Item de Joh' Spyser pro pratis osney de undecim annis ultimo preteritis xxiij s ix d

Item de Joh' stanes pro manerio de merkys pro anno quarto decimo regis predicti quos dicit se solvisse magistro Johanni goldesmyth' v li viij s viij d

⟨Summa xj li ij s x d⟩[12]

Summa omnium allocat' et in briga xlj li iij s ix d

Peticiones tenencium pro reparacionibus

In primis Spendyng' petit xx d

Item Came petit allocari vij s

Item Willelmo hanse petit allocari xiij s

Item de magistro Thoma Cowper in relaxatis ei per arbitros xiiij s viij d

Item Thomas dudley petit allocari sibi v s iij d

Item de magistro Thoma more pro aula hampton xlvj s iiij d

Item de pyppard xiij d

Summa iij li xvij s j d

Summa omnium allocac' et in Briga una cum relaxatis premissis xlv li x d

Reparaciones ten' laycorum illo anno

In primis in domo Waryn et lockes xj d

Item in domo colettes xxiij s xj d

Item in domo Johannis Wyllyam glover xvj s iij d

Summa xlj s

Reparaciones aularum eodem anno

In primis in aula droda vj li v s ij d

Item in aula Edwardi iiij s vij d

Item in aula Hampton xiij d

Item in aula Brasnose xviij s j d

Summa vij li viij s xj d

[*No further headings are given in this roll*]

Item in reparacionibus factis infra Collegium vij s

Item pro emptis in grosso ad collegium xlvij s ij d ob

[12] [ADMC] The correct total is £11 3s 10d.

Item pro lignis emptis de Elewyke vj s viij d
Summa iij li x d ob

Item pro equitacionibus versus Esex l s ob
Item pro diminutis expenc' iij s xj d ob
Item pro solucione margarete dobbys et cera empta ad Capellam vij s x d
Item pro panno linnio empto ad promptuarium et eius factura vij s iij d
Item pro necessarijs emptis ad coquinam xj s viij d
Item pro candelis ad capellam tempore nat' j d ob
Summa iiij li x d ob

Item in reparacionibus factis per Magistri Collegij xlj s iiij d ob
In communis sociorum non solutis de anno preterito xxvij s j d q[a]
Item in convivio sancti Cutberti de anno preterito ultimo v s
Item in communis sociorum huius anni xiiij li ij s ix d ob
Item in batellis operariorum et contribucionibus huius anni iij li xix d ob q[a]
Summa xx li xvij s xj d

In resolucionibus redditum
In primis prior sancte frydeswyd' per manus magistri Collegij xvij s viij d
Item eidem priori per manus procuratoris collegij in plenam solucionem omnium debitorum xxx s iiij d
Item abbati de henesham viij s
Item abbati de osney vj s viij d
Summa totalis iij li ij s viij d

Item in solutis servientibus collegij
In primis Willelmo Coke pro stipendio xxxiij s iiij d
Item matylde lotrici vj s
Item Willelmi [*sic*] Barbitonsori vj s viij d
Summa xlvj s

Item in solutis sociorum Collegij
[13]In primis Magistro collegij in partem solucionis debiti sibi iij li xiij s iiij d

[13] [ADMC] The first entry has clearly been inserted later.

In primis Magister [*sic*] Joh' Elewyke pro debitis antiquis pro pencione in partem solucionis iiij li vj s viij d
Item Magistro Joh' Merton in partem solucionis debitorum sibi iij li vj s viij d
Item Magister [*sic*] Sharpe in plenam solucionem debitorum sibi pro anno quintodecimo xxiij s iiij d
Summa xij li x s

Item pro renovacione et redempcione caucionum iij li x s ij d

Summa omnium receptorum lviij li xij d

Summa omnium expensarum lviij li xix s v d

⟨Computatis computandis et allocatis allocandis Collegium debet computanti xviij s v d penes istum computem[14]
Acta sunt hec per M Thomam Carrier Cancellarium oxon' anno supradicto⟩

[*A very clear roll; 2 membranes; written with a thick pen. It begins on the dorse*]

[14] [ADMC] This final entry is heavily galled [RHDS: William Smith's work?], and can only just be made out. The figure 'xviij s' is confirmed by Smith, Vol. VIII p. 131, who however reads 'Carper' for 'Carriour' – very likely correctly.

WHITSUN 16 HENRY VI to WHITSUN 17 HENRY VI (ROLL UC:BU1/F/51)

1 June 1438–2 May 1439

BURSAR: JOHN MARTYN

[1][Compotus M^ri^ Johis Marton procuratoris M Aule] seu Collegij Oxon' de omnibus redditibus et proventibus dicti [Collegij a festo pentecost'] anno regni regi Henrici sexti Sextodecimo usque ad idem festum pentecost' [. . .

[*The first section of the Arrears is not wholly legible, but what survives is substantially identical with the first section of the Allowances of* ***F/50***]

Summa iiij li iij s ix d

[*No heading*]

De Thome pyppard drapur de anno quinto decimo pro ten' stokys vj s viij d

De Hugone Benett' de anno quintodecimo pro ten' suo et gardino v s

De Johanne Peris pro anno quintodecimo xvj s viij d

De Johanne Cayme pro annis terciodecimo quartodecimo et quintodecimo xxj s iij d

De Rogero Skybowe pro annis terciodecimo quartodecimo et quintodecimo xvj s viij d

De Johanne Barbor' pro Stampton' Hall' de anno quintodecimo xiij s iiij d

De Roberto lokyer et jacobo caryour pro anno quintodecimo xvij s iiij d

De Willelmo Waryne pro anno quintodecimo vj s

De Johanne Spendyng' pro anno quintodecimo v s

De Willelmo Bramton' mercer pro gardino ij s

De Magistro Ricardo Petyngton pro annis quartodecimo et quintodecimo pro pratis iiij s iiij d

De Johanne Hanys pro pratis osney pro annis quartodecimo et quintodecimo x s

[1] The first few lines are damaged and difficult to read. Readings in square brackets from Smith Vol. VIII p. 132.

De Albis monachis pro gardino pro anni quintodecimo ij s
De Waltero mason pro gardino pro anno quintodecimo vj d
De Thoma Spryg' pro terris in campis Walton' pro anno quintodecimo vij s
De Novo Collegio pro anno quintodecimo pro Maydenhall' v s
De Collegij cantuarij pro termino [*sic*] quintodecimo pro gardino [. . .] ij s vj d
De Abb' de Godstow de shopa et ten' T' mayster de [*annis terciodecimo quartodecimo quinto*]decimo sextodecimo ix s vij d
Summa vij li [. . .]

[*The Arrears for Halls, College Rooms, and places outside Oxford, are all identical with the similar Allowances in* ***F/50***]

Summa Arrer[*agi*]arum omnium xxix li xv s xj d

[*Reddi*]tus ten' laycorum in parochia omnium sanctorum in [. . .] Anno rr' Henrici sexti supradicto

[*De ten'*] Thome dudley in quo Johannes William h[*abi*]tavit xxxiij s iiij d
De eodem Thoma pro ten' in quo inhabitavit Robertus dudley pater eius xxx s
De Ten' Hugonis Benet' sargeant' et pro gardino xxiij s iiij d
De Ten' Johannis spendyng glover xx s
De Ten' Nicholayo [*sic*] Shurbyrne Cutteler xx s
De ~~Te~~ ten' Stokys hosier xiij s iiij d
De Ten' Johannis Perys Glover et Thome Pyppard draper xlvj s viij d
De Ten' Nicholayo S[. . .]th in quo Cayme inhabitavit pro duobus terminis viij s
Summa ix li xiij s viij d

Redditus ten' in parochia Sancti Martini et Sancti Petri in ballio in Oxon'

De ten' Ricardi Stocked [*sic*] super angulum quadrivij xxvj s viij d
De ten' Johannis hans Brower in sowstwychyn vij s viij d

Redditus ten' in parochia Sancte Marie in Oxon'

De ten' Roberti lambard vocato stanton' hall' pro duobus terminis viij s

Redditus ten' in parochia sancti Petri in oriente in Oxon'

[*De ten' Johannis*] laker et Willelmi Barbor quam quondam

inhabitavit Alicia phillipo iuxta parva aulam universitatis in alto vico xl s
[*De ten'*] Waryn yrymunger xvj s
[*De ten'*] Austenys cordwyner xij s
De ten' peter Schotysbruk xxvj s viij d

Redditus ten' in suburbijs in oxon'

De gardino quod tenet Brampton mercer in parochia Sancti Thome ultra castrum ij s
De Pratis retro Osney de Thoma Sprig' xx s
De terris in bellomonte de eodem Thoma vij s
De Pratis yirland' et Alrychsyde que tenet Johannis[2] [*sic*] dyer' xviij s
De Gardino exoposito ecclesie Sancti Egidij quod tenet Johannis [*sic*] mason vj d
Summa ~~xviij li xviij s xj d~~ ix li iij s x d[3]

Redditus Aularum in Oxon' eodem anno

De Aula Brasnose de magistro Rogero Grey principali iij li vj s viij d
De gardino Aule Scuti de eodem magistro vj s viij d
De Aula Sancti Thome de eodem magistro x s
De Aula Hampton' de magistro Johanne layley principali xl s
De Aula Edwardi de Jacobo legh principali xxiiij s
[*De parva*] Aula universitatis in vico Scolarum de magistro Calbuch' x s
Summa vij li xvij s iiij d

[*Redditus Camerarum in*]fra Collegium eodem anno

[*De Camera*] Magistri Roberti fflemyng' xx s
[*De*] Camera Magistri Willelmi Dowson' xvj s
[*De*] Camera Magistro Johannis Gerveys xiij s iiij d
[*De*] Camera Ascheby pro duobus terminis v s
De C[*amera*] Magistri Wotton xiij s iiij d
De [*Camera*] Magistri qwytfeld xiij s iiij d
De [*Camer*]a Magistri petri profest pro duobus terminis vj s viij d
De [*Camera*] Magistri Johannis Goldsmythe pro tribus terminis xij s

2 [ADMC] Written over an erasure.
3 [ADMC] The correct total should be £9 4s 6d.

De [*Camera M*]agistri Johannis Chadworth' xiij s iiij d
De [*Camera R*]oberti Ryseley infra gardinum pro duobus terminis iij s iiij d
Summa v li xvj s iiij d

Redditus pro libero redditu ten' in Oxon in suburbijs eodem anno
De Abbatissa de Godstow pro schopa exoposito porte ffrideswyde xx d
De Eadem Abbatissa de pecunijs quos recepit de ten' Thome Mayster ad solvendum abbati de Osney xij d
De Osney pro schopa iuxta Johannem spicer in parochia Sancti Martini in qua quondam habitabat Cudston' corviser' vj s viij d
De ten' quondam Skybow modo Collegij omnium animarum viij s
De novo Collegio pro maydynhall' x s
De Collegio Cantuarie ij s vj d
[*De albis mon*]achis pro uno gardino in quo camere in latere australi sporti [*edificant*]ur iiij s
[*De . . . N*]icol' pro gardino quod Ricardus kariour quondam tenuit v s
[*De . . .*] pro defalcacione prati retro Osney ij s ij d
[*De . . .*] Petyngton' pro defalcacione eiusdem prati ij s ij d
[*De ten'*] quondam sprunt in parochia Sancti Petri in balliolo v s
De heredibus Sprunt' pro novis ten' viij s x d ob
Summa lvij s ob

Redditus in Esex' et Holdernes eodem anno
De Johanne Stanys pro manerio de Marks et molendinis xviij li iij s iiij d
De Thoma Terell' armigero pro libero redditu de Ramysden' xx s
De Johanne Bedfurth burgensi de Hulle pro terris in pagula de Holdernes iij li xij d
Summa xxij li iiij s iiij d

Summa omnium reddituum istius anni lvij li xiij s vj d ob

. . .] cum quibus computans [. . .
De Scrisby v s
De uno bachillario pro camera sua in Aula Hampton' pro tribus terminis ij s

De [*Ma*]gistro karmardyn' pro camera in eadem Aula pro duobus terminis xvj d
[*De Magist*]ro Skryvener' pro camera sua in eadem aula xvj d
[*De* . . .]dyng' pro chyppys iiij d
[*De* . . .] Johannis Helyote pro chyppis iiij d
[*De* . . .] Johanne Marton' pro chyppis xiiij d
[*De* . . .]yer pro bosco vendito v s
Summa xvj s vj d

Summa omnium oneratorum istius anno lxxxviij li iiij s iij d ob[4]

[*Tenementa in manu*] Collegij
[*De ten' ubi*] Isabella Colet inhabitavit iij li xviij s
De Scolis xxj s iiij d
De Aula drowda xvl s
Summa vij li iiij s iiij d

Summa sequentes Magistro Johanni Marton procuratori predicto sunt allocate de onere predicto

Alloc' ten' laycorum
De ysabella colett' in quibus est condempnata coram magistro Johannis burbage tunc commissario pro anni duodecimo et terciodecimo regni regis Henrici sexti xxxviij s iij d
De Thoma dudelay pro anno quintodecimo iij d
De eodem Thoma dudley quod dixit se solvisse matheo carpentario et quod idem matheus negavit ij s vj d
De eodem Thoma dudley de anno dicti regis quintodecimo [*pro*] ten' ubi Johannes William' Glover habitavit xvj s viij d
De eodem Thoma pro eodem ten' de anno sextodecimo xxxiij s iiij d
De eodem Thoma pro ten' in quo pater suus inhabitavit vij s vj d
De Thoma pippard' de anno quintodecimo pro ten' stokes iij s iiij d
De eodem Thome pippard' de anno sextodecimo pro ten' Johannis Peers xxiij [*sic*] iiij d
De Nich' Smith alias castell' viij s
De Johanne Caym pro anno quartodecimo xv d

[4] [ADMC] The correct total is £88 5s 11½d.

De Johanne Barbor pro stanton' hall' pro anni quintodecimo xiij s iiij d
De Johanne lokyet et Willelmo Barbour de anno sextodecimo xxvij s
De Johanne Waryn' yrnmager' de anno quintodecimo vj s
De Willelmo Bramton mercer de anno sextodecimo ij s
De Johanne Haynes de anno quintodecimo v s
De Thoma sprig' de anno sextodecimo pro terris in bello monte vij s
De Abbatissa de godstow ix s vij d
De eadem abbatissa de anno sextodecimo xx d
De eadem abbatissa pro ten' Thoma Mayster eodem anno xij s
Summa x li vij s j d[5]

Alloc' aularum

De Magistro Johannis Barnard principali aula hampton' de anno terciodecimo ix s viij d
De Jacobo leche principali aule edwardi pro anno quartodecimo iij s xj d
De eodem Jacobo pro eadem aula de anno quintodecimo xxiiij s
De eodem Jacobo pro eadem aula de anno sextodecimo xxiiij s
De Magistro Rogero Betson' principali aula Sancti Thome et magistro Rogero Gery ocupante eandem aulam anno terciodecimo vj s viij d
De eodem Magistro pro eadem aula anno quartodecimo vj s viij d
De Magistro Rogero Grey pro usu gardini de schild hall' de anno terciodecimo vj s viij d
De eodem Magistro pro usu eiusdem gardini anno quartodecimo vj s viij d
De eodem Magistro pro aula sancti Thomi iij s iiij d
De eodem Magistro pro aula de Brasnose de anno sextodecimo xxij s v d
De eodem Magistro pro aula sancti Thome de eodem anno iij s iiij d
De eodem Magistro pro usu gardini de schyldhall' eodem anno vj s viij d

[5] [ADMC] Figures have been altered.

De Magistro Thoma Cowper pro anno duodecimo pro usu gardini de Schyldhall' vj s viij d

De Magistro Johanne leylay principali aula de hampton' de anno sextodecimo xxiij s iiij d

De Calbuch' pro parva aula universitatis in vico scolarum vj s viij d

Summa viij li viij d

Alloc' camerarum

De Camera flemmyg' pro anno quintodecimo viij s iiij d

De Camera Olivery rectoris de chylymysfoth pro eodem anno vj s viij d

De Camera Dowson' pro annis quartodecimo et quintodecimo xvij s iiij d

De Camera Chadworth' pro anno quintodecimo xx s

De Camera Goldsmith pro anno quintodecimo xj s viij d

De eiusdem Goldsmith pro tribus terminis in anno sextodecimo xij s vj d

De Camera Qwythfeld pro anno sextodecimo xiij s iiij d

De Camera Roberti scriptoris pro duobus terminis iij s iiij d

Summa iij li xix x d

Alloc' de partibus longinquis

De Johanne Bedfurth de Hull' pro anno quintodecimo xv s iiij d

De Johanne Terell' pro anno undecimo pro quibus Goldsmith recepit accquietancias tempore sui procuratoris [*sic*] xxx s

De eodem Johanne et eius executoribus pro anno quintodecimo iij s iiij d

De Thoma Thoma [*sic*] Terell' pro anno sextodecimo x s

Summa lviij s viij d[6]

Alloc' de liberis Redditibus

De ten' in quo Skybbowe habitavit modo Collegij omnium animarum pro termini Michaelis de anno ~~septimo~~ decimo sexto iiij s

De Johanne Spicer pro defalcacione retro Osney pro eodem anno ij s ij d

6 [ADMC] Figures have been altered.

De certis ten' in manu Collegij et de remissis tenentibus ut patet in parvo rotulo per computantem inde facto xlix s x d ob

Summa lvj s ob

Summa omnium allocatorum precedencium xxviij li ij s vj d q[a7]

Alloc' omnium expensarum et solucionum per annum predictum

~~Soluta pro reparacionibus infra Collegium factis~~

~~Soluta pro reparacionibus factis extra Collegium laycorum~~

~~Soluta pro reparacionibus factis in aulis~~

In primis infra Collegium pro capella xlvij s x d

Item pro camera fflemmyg' vij s ij d

Item pro reparacionibus aliarum camerarum infra Collegium et alijs necessarijs expensis xviij s ix d

Summa omnium reparacionum infra Collegium iij li xiij s ix d

Reparaciones ten' laycorum eodem anno

In primis pro nova domo facta in parochia omnium sanctorum et coquina vij li xvij s x d

Item pro reparacionibus factis in ten' Nycholay Castell' ubi inhabitavit xix s ij d

Item pro reparacionibus factis in domo Johannis Pers ubi Pyppard' quondam inhabitavit xxx s ij d ob

Item pro reparacionibus factis in ten' Rob' lambard' xiij s x d ob

Item pro reparacionibus factis in ten' Schotysbroke bidelli iiij s x d ob

Item pro reparacionibus factis in ten' ubi Isabella Colet inhabitavit xxiij s iiij d

Item pro reparacionibus factis in ten' Spendyng' et Nicholay Schirborn' iiij s vj d ob

Item pro reparacionibus factis in ten' Waryn' Strykmed et Willelmi barbour iij s ij d ob

Summa totalis reparacionum ten' laycorum xij li xvij s ob

Reparaciones aularum eodem anno

In primis pro reparacionibus factis in brasnos xvj s v d ob

Item pro reparacionibus factis in aula hampton' xviij s x d

[7] [ADMC] The correct total is £28 2a 3½d, excluding the £7 4s 4d at the top.

Item pro reparacionibus factis in aula drowda ix s viij d ob
Summa reparacionum aularum eodem anno ~~xliij s vj d~~ xlv s

Soluta pro emptis Collegio et pro placitis
In primis pro emptis in grosso ad Collegium v li iij s v d
Item pro emptis ad promtuarium et coquinam xvij s vj d ob
Item pro placitis factis per magistrium collegij et procuratorem xviij s xj d ob
Summa solutorum pro emptis in grosso et placitis vj li xix s xj d

Expence facte pro equitacionibus et reparacionibus in Esex eodem anno
In primis pro equitacionibus versus Esex' diversis vicibus et pro bina equitacione Johannis Cav[. . .]bus versus Hull' xlj s ix d ob
Item Johanni Stanys pro reparacionibus factis per ipsum in Esex l s x d
Summa iiij li xij s vij d ob

Soluta pro innovacione caucionum et pro capella et diminutis expensis
In primis pro innovacione caucionum iacencium in diversis cistis in universat' [*sic*] iiij s iiij d
In [*sic*] pro sera et candelis ad capellam ij s vj d
Item pro diminutis expencis v s j d
Item pro expensis factis per magistrum collegij iij s iiij d
Summa ~~xj s xj d~~ xv s iij d

Soluta pro communis sociorum et batellis operariorum iurnellis et contribucionibus per totum annum
In primis pro communis sociorum per totum annum xj li x s ix d ob
Item pro batellis contribucionibus iurnellis et detrimentis per totum annum xlix s q[a]
Item pro convivio sancti Cuthberti et pro Asplion' xij s
Summa totalis xiiij li xj s ix d ob q[a]

Resoluciones reddituum eodem anno
In primis priori sancte ffrydeswyde pro termino michaelis de anno sextodecimo regis predicti ix s iiij d
Iten canonico de Osney pro gardino de anno eiusdem regis decimo septimo vj s
Item id' [*sic*] canonico vel abbate [*sic*] de Osney pro ten' Johannis

William Glover pro annis eiusdem regis quarto quinti et sexto [*sic*] in plenam solucionem omnium arr' antiquorum iij li ij s[8]
Item id' [*sic*] abbati pro ten' Thome Mayster pro anno terciodecimo quartodecimo quintodecimo et sextodecimo iiij s viij d
Item abbatissa [*sic*] de Godstow pro eodem ten' in plenam solucionem de annis quintodecimo et sextodecimo eiusdem regis xv s viij d
Item uxori de harbyrfeld' pro anni quintodecimo et sextodecimo pro pratis retro osney vij s iiij d
Item Thome Spryg' subsasceri [*sic*] ballivo domini Regis pro annis quintodecimo et sextodecimo in plenam solucionem iij s
Item collectoribus quintodecime domini Regis xvj d
Item procuratoribus ecclesie beate marie virginis pro ten' Roberti lambart' de anno sextodecimo xij d
Summa totalis vij li iiij d[9]

Soluta servientibus Collegij eodem anno
Item [*sic*] primis Willelmo Cott seniori pro officio pincerni [*sic*] et coci pro termino sancti Thome vj s viij d
Item Johanni Galon' pro officio pincerne pro termino michaels v s
Item Willemo Coco iuniori pro officio coci pro eodem termino xx d
Item Waltero pincerne pro suo offficio [*sic*] pro termino natal' v s
Item Willelmo cote iuniori pro eodem termino xx d
Item eidem Willelmo pro termino pasche in partem solucionis stipendij sui xij d
Item Matilde Hawsten lotrici pro quatuor terminis vj s
Summa xxxiij s iiij d[10]

[*Dorse*]

Soluta socijs eodem anno
In primis magistro Collegij pro diebus Cuthberti et beate marie virginis anni quintodecimi xiij s iiij d

[8] [ADMC] This figure altered from *iiij li xij s*, which would give the correct total of £7 4d.
[9] [ADMC] As it stands the correct total is £5 10s 11d, but see the preceding note.
[10] [ADMC] The correct total is 33s 8d.

Item eidem Magistro pro die sancti Cuthberti de anno sextodecimo vj s viij d
Item eidem Magistro pro eodem anno in partem solucionis stipendij sacerdotalis xx s
Item Magistro Johanne Elwyk pro anno quintodecimo pro diebus sanctorum Cuthberti et beate marie virginis xiij s iiij d
Item Magistro Johanni Marton' pro diebus sanctorum Cuthberti et beate marie virginis pro anno quintodecimo xiij s iiij d
Item id' [*sic*] magistro pro die sancti Cuthberti de anno sextodecimo vj s viij d
Item id' Magistro in partem solucionis debite [*sic*] antiqui xxx s
Item Magistro Willemi Sharp' pro diebus sanctorum Cuthberti et beate marie virginis de anno quintodecimo xiij s iiij d
Item eidem Magistro ~~d~~ pro die sancti Cuthberti de anno sextodecimo vj s viij d
~~Item petit computans sibi allocari de tribus solidis et quatuor den' quos recepit Magister a tenentibus a eodem anno~~

Summa vj li iij s iiij d

Summa totalis Reparacionum et solutorum lx li xij s iiij d ob q^{a}

Summa omnium allocatorum et expensarum istius ann lxxxviij li xv s ij d ob q^{a}[11]

Computatis computandis et allocatis allocandis collegium debet computanti x s iiij d[12]

Acta sunt hec per Magistrum Johannem Burbach' Comissarium generalem venerabilis viri Magistri Johannis Norton Cancellarij universitatis Oxon'.

[*Very neatly written roll, two membranes; such an even hand that it looks like a contemporary fair copy of an original – especially as the totals and even the first two sentences of the dorse are in the same hand as the rest. First part of the roll is considerably damaged and some of the lettering blurred and difficult to read, I think because of inferior ink.*]

11 [ADMC] Figures altered. The correct total is £88 12s 11d.
12 [ADMC] The correct sum is 10s 11¼d.

WHITSUN 17 HENRY VI to WHITSUN 18 HENRY VI (ROLL UC:BU1/F/52)

23 May 1439–15 May 1440

BURSAR: WILLIAM ASPLYON

Decimo octavo

Compotus Magistri Willelmi Asplyon' procuratoris magne Aule seu Collegij Universitatis Oxon' de omnibus redditibus et proventibus dicti Collegij receptis et expensis a fest Penticost' inclusive Anno regni regis Henrici sexto septimodecimo usque ad idem festum penticost' exclusive Anno eiusdem regis Henrici Sexto decimooctavo

[*The Arrears are identical with the Allowances in* **F/51**, *with the following differences:*

Arrears of Tenements: the last two items read:]

De eadem abbatissa pro ten' Thome mayst' eodem anno pro anno sextodecimo xij d

De eadem abbatissa de eodem anno xx s

[*Arrears of Halls: the penultimate entry refers to a William Leylay.*

Arrears of Rooms: the second entry is written in a second time at the end.

Arrears of Free Rents: the entry for 49s 10½d is omitted.]

Summa omnium arraragiorum [*sic*] precedencium xxv li xij s v d

Redditus ten' laycorum in parochia omnium sanctorum in Oxon' Anno supradicto

De ten' Thome dudeley in quo Johannes Wylliam habitavit anno dicto xxxiij s[1] iiij d

De ten' Hugonis benett sariannte et pro gardino xxiij s iiij d

De ten' Rogeri spendynge glover cum celario xxiij s iiij d

De ten' Nicholai Schyrborne' cutteler' xx s

De ten' Johanni [*sic*] Wylliam glover et Johanni [*sic*] Stokys' Losyer quod quondam inhabitavit Johannes pers et Thomas Pyppard draper iij li

De ten' Nicholai Smyth in quo quondam habitavit cayme pro duobus terminis viij s

Summa viij li viij s

[1] [ADMC] The figure has been altered.

Redditus ten' in parochia sancti martini et sancti petri in balliolo in Oxon'

De ten' Ric' Strykemede super angulum quadrivij xxvj s viij d
De ten' Johannis hanse brower in sewstwychyn' vij s

Redditus ten' in parochia Sancte Marie in oxon'

De Ten' Roberti lambert vocato Stanton'hall' xvj s

Redditus ten' in parochia Sancti Petri in oriente in Oxon'

De Roberto lokyer pro termino sancti Johannis bapt' anno setimo [*sic*] decimo v s
De ten' Robert fuller pro tribus terminis eiusdem anni xv s
De ten' Johannis Waryn' yrenmoger xvj s
De ten' Rogeri Plommer' pro tribus terminis ix s
De Matilda hawsten' pro uno termino iij s
De ten' Schotysebroke xxvj s viij d
De ten' Willelmi barbor' xx s[2]

Redditus ten' in suburbijs in Oxon'

De brampton' mercer in parochia sancti Thome pro uno gardino ij s[3]
De Thoma Sprygge qui tenet prata retro Oseney xx s
De eodem Thoma pro terris in bellomonte' vij s
De mauricio cursitor' pro pratis yrelande et allrychsyde xx s
De Johanne Mason' pro gardino in parochia sancti egidij vj d
Summa ix li xiij s x d

Redditus aularum in oxon' anno predicto

De Aula brasnose de magistro Rogeri gray principali eiusdem iij li vj s viij d
De eodem magistro pro gardino aule scuti vj s viij d
De eodem magistro pro aula sancti Thome x s
De magistro Willelmo leyle principale [*sic*] aula hampton' l s
De Johanne ffeedobert pro aula edwardi xx s
De aula universitatis in vico scolarum xv d
De scolis nostris ibidem x s
De quatuor determinatoribus xiij s
Summa viij li xvij s vij d[4]

2 [ADMC] Originally xxx s. In this and the following case the erasure of the first figure is not very definite, but it must be intended, otherwise the total is 11s too much.

3 [ADMC] Originally iij s.

4 [ADMC] Several of the figures and the total have been altered.

Redditus Camerarum infra Collegium eodem anno

De camera magistri fflemyg' xx s
De camera magistri Dowson xvj s viij d
De camera magistri Gervese xiij s iiij d
De camera ascheby pro uno termino xx d
De camera magistri Whyttefelde xiij s iiij d
De camera magistri Chadeworth pro tribus terminis x s
De camera Ryseley pro ij^bus terminis iij s iiij d
Summa iij li xviij s iiij d

Redditus de liberis ten' in oxon' et in suburbijs eiusdem eodem anno

De Abbatissa de godstowe pro schopa exoposita porte frideswyde pro anno decimoseptimo xx d
De eadem abbatissa pro anuali redditu collegio solvendo pro `gardino´ ten' quondam Thome mayster pro eodem anno xiiij d
De oseney pro schopa iuxta Joh' Spicer quam quondam inhabitavit Cudston' corvis' pro dicto anno vj s viij d
De ten' quondam Skybbowe modo Collegij omnium animarum viij s
De novo Collegio pro Maydynhall' x s
De collegio Cant' ij s vj d
De albis monachis pro uno gardino in quo camere in latere australi edificantur ij s
De collegio lincoln' pro gardino quod quondam Ric' Karyour tenuit v s
De Johanne spicer pro defalcacione prati retro Oseney ij s ij d
De Magistro Johanne Petyngton' pro defalcacione eiusdem ij s
Summa xlj s ij d

Redditus in Essex et Holdernesse eodem anno

De Johanne Stanys pro manerio de Merkys et moldendinis xviij li iij s iiij d
De Thoma Terell' pro libero redditu exeunt' de Ramysdeyn' xx s
De Johanne Bedeforth de Hull pro terris in pagula de holdernesse iij li xij d
Summa xxij li iiij s iiij d

Summa omnium reddituum istius anni lv li iij s iij d

Recepta preter sortem domus cum quibus computans oneratur

De Magistro Dowson pro lignis	ij s x d
De Magistro Appylton'	xvj d
De Magistro Gerveys	v s
De David Glover	viij s
De Magistro Dyonys' ex legacione unius defuncti	vj s ij d
De thesauro collegij in festo undecim mill' virginum	viij li
De eodem thesauro alias	iij li
De lignis in collegio	xviij s ij d
De Magistro Northfolke pro uno rastro	iiij d
De eodem Magistro pro quatuor modijs calcis	x d
De Rogero carpentario pro chyppis	vj d

Summa xiij li iij s ij d

Tenementa in manu Collegij Anno antedicto

De ten' quod quondam inhabitavit ysabella Colett'	iij li xviij s
De ten' quod quondam inhabitavit Rob' Dudeley vacat'	xxx s
De parva aula universitatis in vico scolarum vacat'	xl s
De aula Droda vacavit [*sic*]	xlv s
De Camera Magistri Wotton' vacat'	xiij d iiij d
De camera Chadworth vacat' pro tribus terminis	x s
De camera Ryseley vacavit pro tribus terminis	v s
De heredibus Sprounte a quibus haberemus pro novo ten'	viij s x d ob

Summa ten' vacancium anno supradicto xj li xv s ij d ob[5]

Summa omnium oneratorum istius Anno lxxxxiij li ix s

Summe sequentes Magistro Willelmo Asplyon' predicto sunt allocat' de onere predicto

De Isabella colett in quibus est condemptat' [*sic*] coram [. . .] Magistro Johanne burbage tunc commissario pro annis duodecimo et terciodecimo — xxxviij s iiij d

De Thoma Dudeley pro ten' quod modo inhabitavit pro anno quintodecimo — xvj s viij d

De eodem Thome pro eodem ten' pro anno sextodecimo — xxxiij s iiij d

[5] [ADMC] The correct total is £11 10s 2½d.

De eodem Thome pro eodem ten' de anno septimodecimo viij s iiij d
De Rogero Spendyng' pro salario de anno decimoseptimo iij s iiij d
De Hugone Benett' pro gardino de eodem anno decimoseptimo iij s iiij d
De Johanne Willyam Glover de anno decimoseptimo x s
De Nich' Smyth alias castell' pro ten' quondam Johannis cayme pro eodem anno ij s viij d
De Johanne barbour pro stanton'hall' de anno quintodecimo xiij s iiij d
De Willelmo barbour pro ten' suo v s
De Willelmo Waryn viij s iij d
De Willelmo brampton' pro anno decimoseptimo ij s
De Thoma Spryg' pro terris in bella [*sic*] monte pro anno decimoseptimo ad terminum mich' proxim' futurum vij s
De Rogero Plummer pro anno decimoseptimo vj s
De Roberto ffuller pro ten' suo de eodem anno x s[6]
De Roberto lambert' pro ten' suo de anno decimoseptimo xj s
De Roberto lokyer iiij s
De Johanne Mason' pro gardino de anno decimoseptimo vj d
De Johanne hanse[7] brower de anno decimoseptimo iij s vj d

Summa allocat' de ten' in Oxon' ix li vj s vij d

Allocat'

De Magistro Johanne Barnard principali aule Hampton' pro anno terciodecimo ix s viij d
De Jacobo lech' principali aule Edwardi pro anno quartodecimo iij s xj d
De eodem Jacobo pro eadem aula de anno quintodecimo xxiiij s
De Magistro Rogero Grey pro aula brasynnose pro anno septimodecimo xxij s ij d ob
De eodem Magistro pro aula sancti Thome pro termino pasche iij s iiij d
De Scheldehall' gardyn' pro eodem termino eiusdem anni ij s ij d ob

6 [ADMC] Altered from xj s.
7 [ADMC] A correction made in this name.

De Magistro Thoma Cowper pro Schydlehall' gardyn pro anno duodecimo vj s viij d
De Magistro leyle principali aula hampton' solvend' in vig' nativitatis beate marie proximo futuro xx s
De Magistro Calbuch pro aula universitatis de anno sextodecimo vj s viij d
De fferoberd pro aula edwardi de anno decimoseptimo iij s iiij d
De novis scolis x s

Summa allocat' de aulis in oxon' v li xij s

Allocat' Camerarum

De Olivero rectore de chelmysforth pro camera de anno quintodecimo vj s viij d
De Magistro Dowson' pro annis quintodecimo sextodecimo et septimodecimo xiij s
De Magistro Qwytefeld' pro anno decimoseptimo xiij s iiij d
De Magistro Chadworth pro anno quintodecimo xx d
De eodem Magistro pro termino \`nat' domini´ in anno septimodecimo iij s iiij d
De Magistro Johanne Goldesmyth pro camera sua de anno quintodecimo xvj s viij d
De eodem Magistro pro eadem camera pro tribus terminis anni decimi sexti xij s vj d
De Magistro gervase pro anno decimoseptimo vj s viij d

Summa allocat' de cameris adintra iij li xiij s x d

Allocat' de partibus longinquis

De Johanne bedford' pro anno quintodecimo xv s iiij d
De Johanne Terell' de anno undecimo pro quibus Goldsmyth recepit acquietancias xxx s
De eodem Johanne et eius executoribus pro anno quintodecimo iij s iiij d
De Johanne Bedeford' de anno septimodecimo iiij s iiij d

Summa allocat' de partibus remotis liij s

Allocat' de liberis redditibus

De magistro Rogero Skybow pro termino mich' anni decimi sexti iiij s
De Johanne Spicer pro defalcacione prati retro Oseney pro duobus annis scilicet sextodecimo et decimoseptimo iiij s iiij d
De Abbatissa de godstowe de anno quintodecimo ix s vij d

De eadem de anno sextodecimo xx d
De eadem pro gardino ten' Thome Mayster de anno decimosexto xij d
De eadem pro ~~scop~~ schopa expo^{ta} porte ffrideswyde de anno decimoseptimo xx d
De eadem pro gardino ten' quondam Thome mayster xiiij d
De Osney pro schopa quam quondam Cudeston' Corviser inhabitavit vj s viij d
De Colleg^{io} Cantuar' pro anno decimoseptimo ij s vj d
Summa xxxij s vij d

Summa totalis omnium Allocatorum precedencium xxij li xviij s

Soluta et expens' facta circa reparaciones infra et extra collegium
In primis infra collegium pro capella v s ij d ob
Item circa liberarium xij s v d
Item circa coquinam et promptuarium ix s ix d ob
Summa xxvij s v d

In reparacionibus alijs Infra collegium
In primis in reparacionibus camerarum iij s xj d ob
Item in reparacionibus orti circa facturam muri voraginis xxv s iiij d
Summa xxix s iij d ob

De reparacionibus extra collegium
In primis de reparacionibus aularum xxiij s j d
Item in reparacionibus manerij de Merk in Esex xxvij s j d
Item in expenc' in varijs equitacionibus versus Esex et London xxxvij s vij d
Item Willelmo Hansce brewer quia dedit concessit inperpetuum et sua carta confirmavit dicto collegio unum introitum prout iacet sub et iuxta si[8] novas scolas dicti collegij in vico scolarum in parochia sancte marie virginis in Oxon x s

De reparacionibus ten' laycorum
In reparacionibus ten' laycorum Oxon' vj s vj d
Summa omnium reparacionum infra et extra collegium viij d xj d ob

[8] *Sic*; 'iv' is the number needed here (see below), but the roll's reading cannot produce this.

Circa edificium novarum scolarum
In edificio quatuor novarum scolarum xxix li iiij s ob

Expenc' circa pratum ~~in do~~ Dc minutis expencis
Item pro defalcacione pratorum et factura feni v s ix d
In minutis expensis xviij s ix d
Summa omnium reparacionum et edificiorum xxxviij li ix s vj d

Solut' de debitis antiquis
In primis Magistro Scharp pro lignis emptis in tempore Magistri Johannis Merton' xij d
Item famulo Magistro Willelmi Symond' pro tempore eodem ij s
Item Rogero Spendyng' pro duobus paribus serotecarum a Magistro receptis xx d
Item Margarete Dobys pro cereis ij s
Item Willelmo barbor' pro uno termino de antiquo xx d
Item Magistro fflemyg' in partem solucionis cuiusdam summi [*sic*] scilicet iij li iij s iiij d a collegio sibi debit' quam summam solvit pro redempcione caucionum collegij xxxj s viij d
Item eidem Magistro pro alia caucione quam recepit a magistro Johanne Appylton xiij s iiij d
Summa liij s iiij d

De annuis redditibus resolutis
In primis canonico de Oseney pro anno decimooctavo In festo Sancti dionisj xxij s x d
Item canonico ffrideswyde pro eodem anno xviij s viij d
Item pro secta curie pro Thoma Sprig' xviij d
Summa xliij s

Communis [*sic*] sociorum
In primis pro communibus sociorum per totum anni xiiij li xiiij s ix [*sic*] ob
Item pro convivio sancti Cuthberti xij s
Item ~~pro b~~ in detrimentis fficien' et R . . . in dicto ~~collegio~~ convivio iij s viij d
Item in batellis operarariorum xlj s ij d ob
Item in contribucionibus et detrimentis x s ix d ob
Summa omnium commun' batellarum contribucionum et detrimentorum xviij li ij s v d ob

Solut' servientibus collegij

In primis Thome mancipio pro duobus terminis x s

Item Ricardo Blythe pro uno termino et iiij^or ebdomadis alterius termini vj s ij d

Item Ricardo Barton vj s viij d

Item Johannie elese coco pro tribus terminis v s

Item Johanni coco pro uno termino xx s

Item Willelmo barbitonsori pro uno anno vj s viij d

Item lotrici pro eodem anno vj s viij d

Summa xlij s x d

Solut' Magistro et socijs collegij

In primis Magistro Thome Benwell' Magistro Collegij xxvj s viij d

Item Magistro Johanne Marton' xxvj s viij d

Item Magistro Willelmo Sharp' vj s viij d

Item Magistro Willelmo asplyon' vj s viij d

Item Magistro alexandro Surtayse vj s viij d

Summa iij li xiij s iiij d

Summa omnium expensarum istius anni lxvij li iiij s viij d ob

[*Dorse*]

Item Allocat' in dimissis tenencium

In primis Thome Pyppard iij s iiij d

Item Johanni Cayme xv s

Item Magistris Rogero Betsone et Rogero Grey xlj s iiij d ob

Item Thome Dudelay iij d

Item Willelmo Barbour xx d

Item Johanne Hansce pro pratis v s

Item Jacobo leche xxiiij s

Item Magistro Roberto fflemmyg' iij s viij d

Summa omnium dimiss' iiij li vj d ob

Summa omnium Allocatorum et dimiss' et expensarum lxxxxiiij li ij s viij d

⟨Allocatis allocandis post factum plenum compotum secundum modum et formam ordinacionis et statutorum collegij predicti Collegium debet computanti – xiij s viij d. Acta sunt hec coram nobis et per nos Ricardum Roderham theologie professorem cancellarium universitatis oxon'⟩

[*A broad roll (11½ inches), well written and well preserved. 2 membranes*]

WHITSUN 18 HENRY VI to WHITSUN 19 HENRY VI (ROLL UC:BU1/F/53)

15 May 1440–4 June 1441

BURSAR: ALEXANDER SURTAYS

Decimo nono

Compotus Magistri Alexandri Surtays nuper socij et procuratoris magne Aule seu Collegij Universitatis Oxon' datus per Magistrum Willelmum Sharp eiusdem Collegij socium de omnibus redditibus et proventibus dicti Collegij receptis et expensis a festo Penticost' inclusive Anno regni regis Henrici Sexti decimo octavo usque ad idem festum Penticost' exclusive Anno eiusdem regis Henrici Sexti decimo nono

[*The Arrears are identical with the Allowances in* **F/52**, *save for a few changes in spelling.*]

Summa totalis omnium arr' precedencium xxij li xviij s

Redditus ten' in parochia sanctorum Petri et Martini

De gardino quod tenet Willelmus hance in Seystwychne vij s

De ten' quod tenet Ricard Strikemede super angulum quadrivij xxvj s viij d

Summa xxxiij s viij d

Redditus in parochia omnium sanctorum

De ten' quod tenet Thomas Dudeley ubi Johannes William habitavit xxxiij s iiij d

De ten' quod tenet Ricardus Spendyng glover cum celario xxiij s iiij d

De ten' quod tenet Nicholaus Sherborne cuteler xx s

De ten' quod tenet Hugo Benet Shargent' cum gardino xxiij s iiij d

De ten' quod tenet Johannes William glover et Johannes Stokys hosier iij li iiij d

De ten' quod tenet Joh' Gower Taliour pro duobus terminis preteritis xj s viij d

De ten' quod tenet Joh' Chaum bedellus ix s

Summa ix li viij d

Redditus ten' in parochia Sancte Marie et parochia petri [*sic*] in oriente

De ten' quod tenet Robertus lambart in parochia Sancte Marie xvj s

De ten' quod tenet Robertus porter quod nunc tenet Henricus carior xx s

De ten' quod tenet Willelmus Coke ubi Robertus fuller nuper habitavit xx s

De ten' quod tenet Willelmus Waryn chandeler xvj s

De ten' quod tenet Rogerus plummer xij s

Summa iiij li iiij d

Redditus in suburbijs in campis oxon'

De executoribus Willelmi Brampton' pro gardino ij s

De terris in bello monte et campis de Walton quos tenet Thomas sprig' vij s

De eodem Thoma sprige pro pratis retro Osney xx s

De pratis in alrichehat que tenet [*blank*] dyer xvj s iij d

De Johanne Mason pro gardino ex parte orientali ecclesie sancti Egidij vj d

Summa xlv s ix d

Redditus aularum

De Aula Brasnose quam tenet Magister Rogerus Grey iij li vj s viij d

De Aula Sancti Thome quam tenet dictus Rogerus Grey x s

De Gardino Aule scuti quod tenet idem Rogerus vj s viij d

De Aula Hampton' quam tenet Magister Willelmus Leley l s

De Aula Edwardi quam tenet Joh' ffytzRobert xx s

De parva Aula universitatis in vico scolarum pro ~~determinatoribus et alio~~ scolar' inhabitante ij s viij d[1]

De Aula Droda quem tenet Cowper pro tribus terminis xxvj s viij d

De parva Aula universitatis in alto vico quem tenuit Petrus Shotysbroke cuius principal' est Magister Joh' Marton' xxvj s viij d

Summa x li ix s iiij d

Redditus camerarum infra collegium

De Camera Magistri Roberti fflemmyg' xx s

[1] [ADMC] Written over an erasure.

De Camera Magistri Willelmi Dowson' xvj s viij d
De Camera Domini Thome ffernys pro uno termino iiij s ij d
De Camera Magistri Johannis Gerveys xiij s iiij d
De Camera Nich' Serle pro uno termino ij s vj d
De Camera Magistri Thome Wyttefeld' xiij s iiij d
De Camera domini Johannis Typtot xxxiij s iiij d
De Camera Magistri Johannis Chadworth' xvj s viij d
De Camera Magistri Thome Boteler x s
Summa vj li x s

Redditus scolarum
De magistro kyppyng pro una novarum scolarum in anno predicto v s
De quatuor determinatoribus in eisdem iiij^{or} scolis eodem anno xiiij s iiij d
De alio determinatore in aula universitatis in vico scolarum iij s x d
Summa xxiij s ij d

Redditus de liberis tenementis in oxon' et suburbijs
De abbatissa de Godestowe pro uno schopa exposita [*sic*] magne porte frideswyde xx d
De eadem pro annuali redditu pro gardino ten' quondam Thome Mayster xiiij d
De abbate de Osney pro schopa iuxta Johannem Spicer vj s viij d
De ten' quondam skybbow modo collegio omnium animarum viij s
De novo collegio pro maydynhall' x s
De Collegio canturie [*sic*] ij s vj d
De Albis Monachis pro gardino in quo camere stant in parte Australi iiij s
De Collegio lincoln' pro gardino quod Ric' Kariour tenuit v s
De Johanne Tregmane pro defalcacione prati retro Osnay ij s ij d
De Magistro Ricardo petyngton' pro defalcacione eiusdem prati ij s ij d
De Colleigo [*sic*] animarum pro ten' quoddam [*sic*] Johannis Spront' in parochia sancti petri in ballivo v s
De Collegio ~~animarum~~ animarum pro gardino retro dict' ten' quond' dicti Joh' Spront' viij s x s ob
Summa ij li xvij s ij d ob

Redditus in Essex et Holdernes eodem anno

De Johanne Stanys pro manerio de Merkys et molendinis xviij li iij s iiij d

De Thoma Terell' pro libero Redditu exeunte de Rammysden' xx s

De Johanne Bedforth' de Hule pro terris de pagula in Holdernes iij li xij d

Summa xxij li iiij s iiij d

Recept' preter sortem domus

In primis de Magistro Goldsmyth xx s

De uxore hauberfeld' vj s viij d

De Magistro Thoma Wytefeld' pro quisquilijs xij d

De Magistro Goldesmyth pro tabulis v d

Summa xxviij s j d

Summa omnium reddituum et aliorum proventuum lxj li xvj s ij d ob

Summa omnium oneratorum lxxxiiij li xiiij s ij d ob

Ten' in manu collegij anno antedicto

De Ten' quod inhabitavit ysabella Colette iij li xviij s

De parva Aula universitatis in vico scolarum vacat' xl s

De Camera Magistri Wotton' vacavit per annum preteritum modo inhabitabatur [*blank*]

Summa [*blank*]

Alloc' aularum

De Magistro Johanne Barnard' pro aula Hamptoine de anno terciodecimo ix s viij d

De Jacobo leche principali aule Edwardi pro anno quartodecimo iij s xj d

De eodem pro eadem aula pro anno quintodecimo xxiiij s

De Magistro Rogero Grey vj s viij d

De Magistro Thoma Cowper pro gardino de Sheldhall' pro anno duodecimo vj s viij d

De Magistro Willelmo lelay pro aula Hampton' anno novo cuius ultimus terminus soluc' est nat' sancte Marie prox' futur' xxxvj s viij d

De Magistro Culbruche pro parva aula universitatis in vico scolarum de anno decimo et octavo vj s viij d

De Johanne ffetzRobert' pro aula edwardi de annis decimo octavo et decimo nono x s
De Petro Shotysbroke pro parva aula universitatis in alto vico pro anno decimo octavo xxvj s viij d
De Aula Droda vj s viij d
Summa vj li xvij s vij d

Alloc' camerarum

De domino olivero Elton' rectore chelmysford' pro camera de anno quintodecimo vj s viij d
De Magistro Willelmo Dowson' de arr' annorum quintodecimi et septimodecimi decimi octavi et decimi noni xvij s iiij d
De Magistro Thome Wytefeld' pro camera de anno de anno [*sic*] decimo octavo xiij s iiij d
De eodem Magistro Thoma pro camera de anno decimo nono xiij s iiij d
De Magistro Johanne Chadworthe pro camera de anno quintodecimo xx s
De eodem Magistro Joh' Chadworth pro camera ubi Johannis [*sic*] Golsmyth iacuit xvj s viij d
De eodem Magistro Johanne Chadworthe pro termino natal' domini in anno decimo octavo iij s iiij d
De camera Magistri Roberti fflemyg' xx s
Summa iiij li xij s viij d[2]

Allocat' scolarum

De Magistro kyppyng' pro scola in qua legebat in anno decimo nono iiij s iiij d
De Magistro Mitford pro alia scola pro anno decimo octavo iij s iiij d
Summa vij s viij d

Allocac' in liberis redditibus

De Magistro Rogero Skybbow pro termino Mich' anni decimi sexti iiij s
De Johanne Spicer pro defalcacione prati retro Osney pro anno decimo sexto residuum debiti dicto Johannis est in alio rotulo iij s iiij d

[2] [ADMC] The correct total is £4 12s 4d, as given in the Arrears of **F**/54.

[*An item erased*]
De abbate de osney pro Schopa ubi Cudston' habitavit de anno decimo nono vj s viij d
De ten' quod' [*sic*] Magistri Rogeri Skebbow modo colleg' animarum iiij s
[*An item erased*]
De Magistro Roberto petynton' pro defalcacione prati sui retro Osney iij s ij d
De Collegio animarum pro domo quond' Johannis Spront in quo nunc Joh' cor vynor [*sic*] inhabitat in parochia sancti petri in ballio v s
De eodem collegio animarum pro retro dicti ten' in quo cor' habitat viij s x d
Summa xxxiiij s x d

Alloc' de ten' in parochia omnium sanctorum
De ysabella colette in quibus condempnat' coram Magistro Joh' Burbage tunc commissario pro annis duodecimo et terciodecimo rr' regis Henrici sexti xxxviij s iiij d
De Thoma Dudelay pro ten' quod modo inhabitat pro anno quintodecimo xvj s viij d
De eodem Thoma pro eodem ten' de anno sextodecimo xxxiij s iiij d
De eodem Thoma pro eodem ten' de anno sextodecimo [*sic*] viij s iiij d
De Rogero Spendyng' pro celario de anno decimo nono eiusdem regis x d
De Nicholayo Sherborne Cuteler' pro anno decimo nono xx d
De Hugone Benet' pro gardino de anno decimo octavo ij s iiij d
De eodem Hugone pro ten' et gardino de anno decimonono vij s iiij d
De Johanne Willyam Glover de anno decimo [*sic*] x s
De eodem Johanne Willyam de anno decimo nono xv s
De Johanne Caam pro anno decimo nono v s
De Nicholayo catell' alias Smith mancipio pro ten' Caam de anno decimoseptimo ij s viij d
Summa vij li ij s vj d

Allocac' ten' in parochia sancti petri in oriente
De Johanne Barbour pro Stampton Hall' de anno quintodecimo xiij s iiij d

De Roberto lambart pro anno decimo octavo xj s
De eodem Roberto pro anno decimo nono iiij s viij d
De Willelmo Waryn pro anno decimo octavo viij s iij d
De eodem Willelmo Waryn' pro anno decimo nono xvj s
De Rogero Plumber pro anno decimo octavo vj s
De eodem Rogero plumber de anno decimo nono vj s
De Roberto ffuller pro ten' in quo habitat Willelmus Coke pro anno decimo octavo x s
De eodem Roberti ffuller pro anno decimo nono xiij s
De Roberto lokyer iiij s

Summa iiij li xij s iij d

Allocac' ten' in suburbijs et pratis et campis oxon'

De executoribus Willelmi Brampton' pro gardino in parochia Sancti Thome de anno decimo octavo ij s
De eisdem executoribus pro eodem gardino de anno decimo nono ij s
De eodem Thome Spryg pro terris in bello monte de anno decimo octavo vij s
De eodem Thome Spryg pro terris et pratis de anno decimo nono vj s viij d

Summa xvij s viij d

Summa totalis omnium allocatorum precedencium xxvj li v s[3] ij d

Item procurator petit allocari sequentes summas dimissis tenentibus et c'

De Willelmo Hans iij s iiij d
De camera Magistro Johannis Goldemyth [*sic*] pro diversis annis xxix s ij d
De Abbatissa de Godstow ut patet summa de diversis annis xv s viij d
De Abbate de Osney pro shopa quam quondam Ceddiston' habitavit vj s viij d
De Johanne terell' de Magistro Johanne Goldesmyt [*sic*] cepit a collegio acquietancias xxx s
De eodem eius executoribus pro anno quintodecimo iij s iiij d
De Johanne Bedford pro annis quintodecimo et decimoseptimo xix s viij d

[3] [ADMC] Written over an erasure.

De camera fernys	x d
Summa totalis v li viij s j d[4]	

[*Dorse*]

Reparaciones parva Aule in vico scolarum	vij li vij s v d
Reparaciones Aula Edwardi	x s iiij d
Reparaciones Aule Drowda	ij s x d ob
Reparaciones infra collegium	xviij s iiij d
Reparaciones capelle	ij s v d
Reparaciones Aula Brassenose	ij li iiij s v d
Reparaciones Aula Hampton'	vij s iiij d
Summa xj li xiij s j d ob	

Reparaciones domus Gower	xx d
Reparaciones domus Johanns Wyllyam	iij s j d
Reparaciones domus Waryn	ij s ij d
Reparaciones domus Willelmi Coke et Roberti Parker solut' per magistrum Willelmum Sharp'	viij s vj d
Item solut' pre Magistrum ad domum Willelmi cok	xxxvij s
Item solut' per Willelmum coke ad eandem domum et pro covintre	vij s vij d
Reparaciones domus Spendyng	xix d ob
Summa iij li xix d ob	

Solut' pro covintre et minutis expensis Magistri	iiij s vj d
Solut' in minutis expensis procuratoris	vj s iiij d
Summa x s x d	

Reparaciones Esex et stacione molendinorum	lvij s iij d
Expense versus esex in eundo et redeundo	xxxix s x d ob
Expense Holdernes et pro Johanne Terell'	v s
Summa iiij li xij s j d ob	

Soluta pro communis sociorum per totum annum	x li iij s ij d q[a]
Solut' pro batellis operariorum	xxviij s xj d q[a]
Solut' pro contribucionibus et detrimentis	vj s vj d
Solut' pro convivio sancti Cuthberti	xxj s ij d
Solut' pro communis et batellis Johannis tapster'	ix s j d
Summa xiij li viij s xj d[5]	

4 [ADMC] The correct total is £5 8s 8d.
5 [ADMC] The correct total is £13 8s 10½d.

Solut' pro stipendio Johannis tapstre vij s ix d
Item pro filo et instrumentis et alijs necessarijs ad artem suam viij s ix d
Summa xvj s vj d

In emptis in grosso iij li v s vij d ob
Expense facte per magistrum Alexandrum Surtays xxxj s ob
Summa iiij li xvj d viij d

Solut' pro redempcione biblio a cista rot'reburi'[6] xl s
Item pro debito Ricardi Sclat' quos capit Willelmus coke vij s x d ob
Item Willelmo Snowdon' xx d
In solutis domino regi ij s
Summa ij li xj s vj d ob

Solut' in liberis redditibus
In primis priori Sancti [*sic*] ffrideswyde ix s iiij d
Item abbati de Osney xvj s x d
Item abbatisse de godstowe xiiij s
Item ecclesie beate marie pro stampton hall' xij d
Item Margarete Herberfeld' pro pratis retro osney vij s iiij d
Item Thome Spryge pro hundredo extra portem borialem xviij d
Summa ij li x s

Solut' socijs collegij
In primis Magistro collegij xl s
Item Magistro Johanni Marton' xxxiij s iiij d
Item Magistro Willelmo Asplyon' xxxiij s iiij d
Item Magistro Willelmo Sharp xiij s iiij d
Item Magistro Johanne [*sic*] aspylton' xxxj s viij d
Summa totalis vij li xj s viij d

Solut' servientibus
In primis Willelmo cok pro offo [*sic*] pincerne et coci xxvj s viij d
Item Willelmo Barbour vj s viij d

[6] [ADMC] This is clearly the Robury loan chest. Just possibly the reading might be intended to be 'rotheburi'. [RHDS] On this, and other university loan chests, see *HUO I*, pp.274–287.

Item lotrici vj s viij d

Summa xl s

Summa omnium expensarum liij li xiij s

Summa omnium expensarum et allocatorum lxxxv li vj s iij d

⟨Computatis computandis et allocatis allocandis collegium debet computanti xij s ob

Acta sunt hec per Magistrum Robertum Thwaytes Commissarium venerabilis viri Magistri Willelmi Grey Cancell' universitatis Oxonie⟩

[*A well-preserved and neatly written roll of 2 membranes*]

WHITSUN 19 HENRY VI to WHITSUN 20 HENRY VI (ROLL UC:BU1/F/54)

4 June 1441–20 May 1442

BURSAR: THOMAS BENWELL

Compotus Magistri Thome Benwell Nuper Magistri et procuratoris magne aule seu collegij universitatis oxon' datus per magistrum Johannem Mertone eiusdem aule sive collegij socium de omnibus redditibus et proventibus dicte aule sive collegij receptis et expensis a festo penticost' inclusive Anno [rr' Henrici sexti decimo nono][1] ad idem festum penticost' exclusive Anno eiusdem Regis ~~vesimo~~ vicesimo

[*The Arrears are mostly the same as the Allowances of* **F/53**, *with the following differences:*

Arrears of Halls: parts of the text, and all figures are lost, but most figures appear to be the same. Item 4 is omitted.

Arrears of College Rooms:

In Item 2, for 'de arr' annorum quintodecimi et septimodecimi' etc., read 'de annis septimo decimi **[sic]** *decimi octavi et decimi noni'.*

In Item 3, after 'Wytefelde', read (only) 'pro decimo octavo anno'.

In Item 6, after Chadworth, read (only) 'pro anno sextodecimo'.

Arrears of Schools: in Item 1 after 'kyppyng', read (only) 'de anno decimo nono'.

Arrears of Free Rents:

In Item 2, after 'Osney', read (only) 'pro duobus annis', and for 'iiij s ij d' read 'iiij s iiij d' (an error for ij d).

In Item 7, for 'pro retro..' etc., read 'pro gardino retro dictum tenementum in quo cor' inhabitat', and for 'viij s x d', read 'viij s x d ob'.]

Arrears from the parish of All Saints:

In Items 3 & 4, read 'sextodecimo'.

Items 6 & 7 are listed in reverse order.

In Item 8, after 'Hugone', insert 'Benet'.

[1] [ADMC] The text is reconstructed from Smith Vol. VIII p. 143.

In Item 9, read 'decimo'.]

Summa omnium Arr' precendencium xxv li xviij s vij d ob[2]

Redditus ten' in parochia sanctorum petri et martini
De gardino quod tenet Willelmus hance in Swystwechene vij s
De tnt' [*sic*] quod tenet Richardus strykmede super angulum quadrivij xxvij s viij d
Summa xxxiij s viij d

Redditus ten' laicorum in parochis omnium sanctorum Anno' rr' Henrici sexti supradicto
De ten' quod tenet Thomas dudley xxxiij s iiij d
De ten' quod tenet Spendyng et pro solario xxiij s iiij d
De ten' quod tenet Nicholaus Schyrburn xx s
De ten' quod tenet Johannes Gowar' ⟨J. Bradmyre pro duobus ter' xj s viij d⟩[3] xxiij s iiij d
De ten' quod tenet Hugo Benet et pro gardino xxiij s iiij d
De ten' quod tenet Johannes William Glover et Johannes stokys hosier iij li
De ten' quod Johannes Caym Bedell tenet ⟨pro uno termino ij s iij d⟩ ix s
Summa ix li xij s iiij d

Redditus in parochia sancte marie et sancti petri in oriente
De ten' quod Robertus lambert tenet xvj s
De ten' quod tenet henricus Caryour' ⟨xxiij s iiij d⟩ xx s
De ten' quod tenet Willelmus Coke ⟨pro duobus ter' x s⟩ xx s
De ten' quod tenet Willelmus Warne ⟨Joh' Elys⟩ xvj s ⟨viij d⟩
De ten' quod tenuit rogerus plummer pro duobus terminis vj s
De eodem ten' quod modo tenet Thomas ⟨sprage⟩ coco pro duobus terminis ⟨xij s⟩ vij s
Summa iiij li iiij d

Redditus de insuburbijs [*sic*] et in Campis oxon' eodem Anno
De gardino iuxta castrum quem tenet uxor Willelmi Bramton mercer ij s
De terris in bello monte et campis de Walton quos tenet Thomas Spryg vij s

2 [ADMC] The correct total is £25 18s 2½d.
3 [ADMC] These, and the other entries represented in brackets, are in a different, and minute, hand. They are in fact notes of next year's tenants.

De pratis retro osnay que tenet Johannes Iuys malteman de osnay ⟨Keel Brewer⟩ xx s

De pratis alrycheset que tenet Thomas maunsipillus ⟨de yuhhall' xviij s⟩ xviij s

De gardino ex parte orientali [*sic*] ecclesie sancti egidij quem tenet Johannes mason vj d

Summa xlvj s vj d

Redditus aularum

De Aula Brasnes quam tenet Magister Rogerus Grey iij li vj s viij d

De Aula Thome quem tenet dictus Rogerus x s

De gardino Aule scuti quod tenet idem Rogerus vj s viij d

De aula Hampton quem tenet Magister Willelmus laylay l s

De aula edwardi quem tenet Johannes fytzRobart xx s

⟨de uno determinatore iij s ~~viij d~~ iiij d⟩[4]

De parva aula universitatis oxon' in vico scolarum quem tenuit dominus robertus cowper xx s

De aula drowda quem tenet Johannes cowper xxvij s viij d

De parva aula universitatis in alto vico quem tenet Magister robertus burton xxvj s viij d

Summa xj li vj s viij d

Redditus camerarum infra collegium eodem Anno

De camera Magistri Roberti flemmyg xx s

De camera Magistri Thome Benwell quem inhabitavit nicholaus serl pro duobus terminis x s

De eodem Nicholao pro camera quam modo tenet magister Johannes Crosby pro duobus terminis v s

De eadem camera de Magistro Johanne Crosby pro duobus terminis v s

De camera magistri Thome Botteler ⟨magistri Roberti toft⟩ x s

De camera Magistri Thome lamaton pro duobus terminis viij s

De camera lethum xiij s iiij d

De camera typtofft et hurle xxxiij s iiij d

De camera Wyttfeld' xiij s iiij d

De camera gervayse xiij s iiij d

De camera dowson xvj s viij d

[4] [ADMC] Inserted later between the lines.

De camera in gardino pro pueris Magistri Thome butteler ij s vj d
De camera fernes xvj s
Summa viij li iij s x d[5]

Redditus scolarum
De scola magistri aschby vj s viij d
De scolis Magistri alexandri de aula vitria vj s viij d
De scola Magistro Roberti Keele de neull' In[6] vj s viij d
De scolis Willelmi strete determinatoris iij s vj d
De scolis Johannis Thakyll' iij s
De scolis Ricardi Clerkson' iij s iiij d
De scolis determinatoris de aula sancte marie iij s iiij d
De Magistro regente de aula nigra vj s viij d
De determinatore in aula universitatis in vico scolarum iiij s
Summa xliij s x d

Redditus de liberis tenementis in oxon' suburbijs
De abbatissa de godsto pro una schopa exposita magne porte frideswyde xx d
De eadem pro annuali redditu pro gardino ten' quondam Thome magistri xiiij d
De abbate de osnay pro schopa iuxta Johannem spiser vj s viij d
De ten' quondam rogeri Skybbow modo collegij omnium animarum viij s
De novo collegio pro maydyn hall' x s
De collegio cantuarij[7] ij s vj d
De collegio lincolnie pro gardino oxon quem Ricardus carioure tenuit v s
De Johanne Treguram' pro defalcacione prati retro osney ij s ij d
De magistro Ricardo pedyngton' pro defalcacione eiusdem prati ij s ij d
De collegio Animarum pro ten' quondam Johannis Spront in parochia sancti petri in balliolo v s
De collegio animarum pro gardino retro dictum ten' quondam dicti Johannis Spront viij s x d ob

5 [ADMC] The correct total is £8 6s 6d.
6 [ADMC] Smith (Vol. VIII p. 143) reads 'Nevill Inne'.
7 [ADMC] The second 'j' has been overwritten; it may be meant to read 'o' or possibly 'e'.

De albus monachis pro gardino quem tenuit Barton corveser iiij s

Summa ij li xvij s ij d ob

Redditus in exsexcia et in [. . .][8] holdernes de eodem anno

De Johanne stanis pro Mannerio de Merx et Molendinis xviij li iij s iiij d

De Thoma Tyrell' pro libero redditu exeunte de rammysden xx s

De Johanne bedford' de hull pro terris de pugula [*sic*] in holdernesse iij li xij d

Summa xxij li iiij s iiij d

Summa omnium reddituum lxiiij li xij s iiij d ob

Recepta preter sortem domus

De Magistro Johanne Goldsmygte	xxvj s viij d
De Magistro Thoma Wytfeld' pro quisquilijs	xvj d
De Johanne Carpynter pro quisquilijs	iij s
De Johanne tanner pro libark	vj s
De Magistro Willelmo sharpe pro arboribus fracinis	viij d
De Johanne Ellyes pro fagotis	iiij d
De Magistro Willelmo scharpe	v s v d
De uxore Mores pro woddes	xviij d

Summa xliij s ix d

Summa omnium onoratorum istius Anni lxxxxiij li ij s[9]

Tenementum in manu collegij ysabelle colette iij li xviij s

Allocat' Aularum Anno vicesimo et Annis supradictis

De magistro Johanne Bernard' pro aula hampton pro anno tercio decimo ix s viij d

De jacobo leche principali Aule edwardi pro anno quartodecimo iij s xj d

De eodem pro eadem aule pro anno quintodecimo xxiiij s

De Magistro Thome cowper pro gardino de scheldhall' pro anno duodecimo vj s viij d

De Johanne fitz robert pro aula edwardi de anno vicesimo xij s iiij d

[8] [ADMC] There has been a deletion here.

[9] [ADMC] The correct total is £92 15s 8d.

De colbusch' pro parva aula universitatis in vico scolarum vj s viij d

De laylay pro aula hampton de anno vicesimo xl s ob

De Johanne Cowper pro aula drawda de anno decimo nono vj s viij d

De eodem Johanne pro eadem aula de anno vicesimo xxvj s viij d

De Rogero gray pro aula de brasnose de anno vicesimo xxij s ij d ob q[a]

De eodem pro aula sancti Thome eodem anno iij s iiij d

De eodem pro gardino aule scuti eodem anno vj s viij d

De executoribus domini Roberti cowper pro parva aula universitatis oxon' vj s viij d

Summa viij li xv s vj d q[a]

Allocat' camerarum eodem anno

De domino olivero Elton rectore de chelmisforth pro camera de anno quintodecimo vj s viij d

De magistro Willelmo dowson de arr' quintodecimo anno septimodecimi decimi octavi et decimi noni xvij s iiij d

De eodem magistro Willelmo pro camera sua de anno vicesimo xij s viij d

De magistro Thoma Whytfeld' pro camera de anno decimo nono iij s vj d

De eodem magistro Thoma pro camera sua de anno vicesimo xiij s iiij d

De camera magistri Johannis Chadworth' pro arr' anni decimi octavi et decimi noni viij s x d

De camera nicholai serl pro camera per introitum gardini de anno vicesimo pro duobus terminis v s

De eodem nicholao pro camera quam inhabitavit magister Thomas Benwell pro duobus terminis x s

De magistro Johanne Gerwys pro camera sua eodem anno xiij s iiij d

De domino Thoma lamaton pro camera sua eodem anno pro duobus terminis viij s

De Roberto flemmyng pro camera sua anno decimonono et anno vicesimo iiij s iiij d

De magistro Thoma Butler pro camera sua in gardino pro pueris suis pro duobus terminis eodem anno ij s vj d

De magistro Thoma ffernes pro camera eodem anno ij s viij d
Summa v li vij s x d[10]

Allocat' scolarum eodem anno
De magistro kyppyng pro scolis suis de anno decimo nono iiij s iiij d
De magistro myttforth pro alia scola in qua legebat eodem [*sic*] iij s iiij d
De magistro Ashby pro scola in qua legebat [*sic*] eodem vj s viij d
De magistro alexandro de Aula vitria pro scola in qua legebat vj s viij d
De magistro roberto keele de newill' In pro scola in qua legebat vj s viij d
De magistro [*blank*] de aula nigra pro parva aula universitatis in vico scolarum eodem anno vj s viij d
Summa totalis xxxiiij s iiij d

Allocat' de liberis redditibus
De Rogero Skybow pro termino michaelis anni decimi sexti iiij s
De Johanne spiser pro defalcacione prato retro osnay pro anno decimo sexto et residuum est in alio rotulo iiij s iiij d
De abbate de osney pro schopa ubi gutson habitavit de anno decimo nono vj s viij d
De magistro roberto petyngton pro defalcacione prati sui retro osnay ij s ij d
De collegio animarum pro domo quondam Johannis spront in quod nunc Johannes Coer bruer inhabitat in parochia sancti petri in ballio v s
De eodem collegio animarum pro gardino retro dictum ten' in quo cor' inhabitat viij s x d ob
De abbatissa de Goldstow pro schopa exposita magne porte frideswide de anno vicesimo xx d
De eadem pro annuali redditu pro gardino ten' quondam Thome mayster eodem anno xiiij d
De abbate de osney pro schopa iuxta Johannem Spicer eodem anno vj s viij d

[10] [ADMC] The correct total is £5 8s 2d.

De Johanne tregran pro defalcacione prati retro osney eodem anno ij s ij d
De magistro Ric' pedyngton pro defalcacione prati retro osney eodem anno ij s ij d
De collegio animarum pro ten' quondam Johannis spront in parochia sancti petri in ballio v s
De eodem collegio pro gardino retro dictum ten' quondam dicti Johannis spront viij s x d ob
Summa lviij s vij d[11]

Allocat' ten' laicorum eodem anno in parochia omnium sanctorum
De executoribus ysabelle colet in quibus condempnata fuerat coram magistro Johanne Burgagh tunc comissario pro annis duodecimo et terciodecimo rr' Henrici sexti xxxviij s iiij d
De Thoma dudley pro tenemento quod modo inhabitat pro anno quintodecimo xvj s viij d
De eodem pro eodem tenemento pro anno sextodecimo xxxiij s viij d
De eodem pro eodem tenemento pro anno decimo nono eiusdem regis viij s iiij d
De nicholao Shyrburn pro ten' quod inhabitat vij s viij d
De Johanne William Glower pro tenemento quod inhabitat pro anno decimoseptimo x s
[12]De eodem pro eodem ten' de anno vicesimo eiudem regis vj s viij d
De eodem Johanne pro eodem ten' pro anno vicesimo [*sic*] xv s
De nicholao smyth alias castell' mancipio pro ten' caam de anno decimoseptimo ij s iiij d
Summa vj li xix s

Alloc' ten' eodem anno in parochijs sancta marie et sancti petri in oriente
De Johanne barbour pro stanton hall' de anno quintodecimo regis xiij s iiij d
De roberto lambard pro eadem aula de anno vicesimo xvj s
De roberto fuller pro ten' in ~~h~~ quo habitat Willelmus Cooke de anno decimo octavo x s
De eodem roberto fuller' pro anno decimonono xiij s

[11] [ADMC] The correct total is 58s 9d.
[12] [ADMC] This entry refers to Thomas Dudley – see **F**/55 below.

De Willelmo Cooke pro suo ten' de anno vicesimo v s

[*Dorse*]

De henrico Cariour de ten' suo eodem anno iij s iiij d
De Thoma Cowper pro ten' suo eodem anno ij s viij d
Summa iij li iij s iiij d

Allat' [*sic*] ten' in suburbijs
De executoribus Willelmi Brampton mercer de anno decimo octavo ij s
De eisdem executoribus de anno decimo nono ij s
De eisdem executoribus de anno vicesimo ij s
De Johanne yvis maltman pratis [*sic*] retro osney eodem anno vj s ij d
Summa xij s ij d

Alloc' de exsex et de holdernes
De Johanne stanys de anno vicesimo iij li iij s iiij d
De bedforth de holdernese iiij s iiij d
Summa iij li vij s viij d

Summa totalis omnium Allocat' precedencium xxxij li xviij s xj d q[a][13]

Reparaciones facte per magistrum Thomam Benwell a festo penticostes usque ad festum Michael' et expens' sicut patet per suum papirum ix li v s vij d ob
Reparaciones et expense facte per magistrum Willelmum Scharpe a festo Michael' usque ad festum omnium sanctorum xxij s vj d
Reparaciones facte per magistrum Johannem merton eodem Anno a festo omnium sanctorum usque ad festum ascensionis domini
In primis in parva Aula universitatis in vico scolarum pro reparacionibus ibidem factis v li viij d ob
Item pro reparacionibus factis infra collegium lj s ix d
Item pro edificacione nove domus infra collegium ~~vj li~~ vj li xiij s x d ob
Item pro reparacionibus factis in Aula edwardi ~~v~~ vij s vij d ob
Item pro reparacionibus factis in Aula hampton xx s iiij d
Item pro reparacionibus in Aula Brasnose xij s xj d ob

[13] [ADMC] The correct total is £32 18s 5¼d.

Item pro reparacionibus factis in parva Aula universitatis in alto vico v s vj d

Summa xxvij li x d ob

Reparaciones facte in tenementis laicorum pre eundem Magistrum Johannem Merton eodem anno

In primis pro reparacionibus factis in domo Johannis William glover vj s viij d

Item pro reparacionibus factis in domo roberti lambert vj s iij d

Item pro reparacionibus factis in domo henrici cariour ij s xj d ob

Item pro reparacionibus factis in domo Johannis elis viij s vij d

Summa xxiiij s v d ob

Solut' pro capella et alijs diminutis expensis ix s viij d

Solut' pro antiquis debitis et redempcione trium caucionum renovacione [*sic*] v li v d

Solut' pro stauro ad collegium v li xvj s vij d

Solut' pro equitacionibus versus exsex et holdernes xlij s j d ob q[a]

Summa xiij li viij s ix d ob q[a]

Solut' in resolucionibus reddituum eodem anno in primis prior sancte frideswyde xij s viij d

Item abbati de osney xvj s x d

Item idem [*sic*] abbati vj d

Item collectoribus domini regis xv d

Item senescallo domini regis extra portam borialem xviij d

Item uxori harbirfeld' ~~iij s~~ iij s vj d

Summa xlj s ix d

Solut' pro communis omnium sociorum per totum annum vj li xiij s x d ob

Solut' pro batellis operariorum ~~iune~~ iurnellis et contribucionibus xxxviij s

Item pro convivijs sancti Cutberti xviij s iiij d ob

Summa ix li x s iij d

Solut' servientibus collegij per eundem magistrum xxxvj s viij d

Solut' socijs eodem anno per eundem magistrum In primis magistro Thome Benwell xj s ix d

Item magistro Johanni merton pro diebus sancti Cutberti et beate marie virginis xiij s iiij d

Item idem [*sic*] magistro Johanni pro antiquis debitis per manus schottisbruke et Magistri Thome Witfeld xliij s ij d
Item Magistro Willelmo scharpe pro diebus sancti Cutberti et beate marie virginis xiij s iiij d
Item idem [*sic*] magistro pro antiquis debitis xij s viij d
Item magistro Willelmo asplyon pro diebus sancti Cutberti et beate marie xiij s iiij d
Item idem [*sic*] magistro pro antiquis debitis xij s
Item magistro Johanni apilton xj s viij d
Summa viij li vij s xj d

Summa omnium expensarum lxj li xiiij s ob q[a]

Summa omnium expensarum et Allocat' lxxxxiiij li xiiij s iiij d[14]

⟨Computatis computandis et Allocatis allocandis Collegium debet computanti xxxij s iiij d

Acta sunt hec per magistrum Willelmum Babyngton Doctorem in decretis Comissarium generalem venerabilis viri magistri Willelmi Gray Cancellarij universtitatis Oxon'⟩

[*A clearly written roll, but damaged at the head and a few figures faded. 2 membranes*]

[14] The correct total is £94 13s.

WHITSUN 20 HENRY VI to WHITSUN 21 HENRY VI (ROLL UC:BU1/F/55)

20 May 1442–9 June 1443

BURSAR: JOHN MARTYN

Anno Regis Vicesimo Primo

Compotus Magistri Johannis Marton' Magistri et procuratoris [. . .] Oxon' datus per eundem Magistrum Johannem Marton' de omnibus redditibus [et proventibus . . .] receptis et expensis a festo Penticost' inclusive Anno [rr' Henrici sexti vicesimo usque ad] fest Penticost' exclusive Anno eiusdem Regis vicesimo [primo][1]

[*The Arrears are identical with the Allowances of* ***F/54****, save that some figures are illegible, and in the Arrears of properties in All Saints parish, after Item 4 occurs the entry:*

De eodem pro eodem ten' de anno vicesimo eiusdem regis vj s viij d

and Item 7 is omitted. These two alterations together mean that in 1441/2 6s 8d was wrongly charged against John William Glover instead of Thomas Dudley]

Summa vj li xix s

Summa totalis omnium arr' precedencium xxxij li xviij s v d q[a2]

Redditus ten' in parochia santorum Petri et Martini

De gardino quod tenet Willelmus Hance in Swy[. . .] [*vij s*][3]

De ten' quod tenet Ric' Strykmede super angulum quadrivij [*xxvj s*] viij d

Summa xxxiij s viij d

Redditus ten' laycorum in parochia omnium sanctorum anno regni regis Henrici Sexti [. . .]

De ten' quod tenet Thomas Dudley [*xxxiij s*] iiij d

De ten' quod tenet Spendyng' et pro solario xxiij s iiij d

De ten' quod tenet Nich' Schyrborn' xx s

[1] [ADMC] Parts of the heading of the roll are damaged and illegible. Some missing words have been supplied from Smith Vol. VIII p. 145.

[2] [ADMC] These figures are not clearly legible, but can be made out, except that the shillings might be 'xvj s'.

[3] [ADMC] Most figures in this section are not legible, or barely so. Some readings are from Smith Vol. VIII p. 145.

De ten' quod tenet Joh' Bradbyr' pro duobus terminis xj s vij d
De ten' quod tenet Hugo Benet et pro gardino xxiij s iiij d
De ten' quod tenet Johannes William Glover et Johannes Stokys Hosier iij li
De ten' quod Johannes ~~te~~ Caym' ~~tenet~~ Bedel tenet pro uno termino ij s iij d
Summa viij li xiij s xj d

Redditus in parochijs sancte Marie et Sancti Petri in oriente
De ten' quod tenet Robertus Lambert xvj s ⟨xviij s⟩[4]
De ten' quod tenet Henricus Cariour [*xxiij s iiij d*]
De ten' quod tenet Willelmus Cooke pro duobus terminis [*x s*]
De ten' quod tenet Joh' Elys [*xvj s viij d*]
De ten' quod tenet Thomas Sprag' alias Cowper [*xij s*]
Summa iij li xviij s

Redditus in suburbijs et in campis Oxon' eodem Anno
De gardino iuxta castrum quem tenet uxor Willelmi Brampton Mercer ij s
De terris in bello monte et campis de Walton quos tenet Thomas Spryg' vij s
De pratis retro Osney que tenet Joh' j Kell' Brower xx s
De pratis alrychset' que tenet Mansipill' de yng' hall' xviij s
De gardino ex parte orientali ecclesie sancte Egidij quem tenet Joh' Mason' vj d
Summa ij li vij s vj d

Redditus Aularum
De Aula Brasnose quem tenet Magister Rogerus Gray iij li vj s viij d
De Aula Sancti Thome quem tenet dictus Rogerus x s
De Gardino Aule scuti quod tenet idem Rogerus vj s viij d
De Aula Hampton quam tenet Magister Willelmus Laylay l s
De Aula Edwardi quem tenet Johannes ffytz Robert' xx s
De parva Aula universitatis Oxon' in vico scolarum d[*e uno determinatore*] iij s iiij d
De Aula Drowda quam tenet Johannis cowper et Johannes [*petriche flecher . . .*] xxvj s viij d

[4] [ADMC] 'xviij s' was apparently added against the original entry.

De parva Aula universitatis in alto vico quem tenet Magister [*Robertus Burton et Thomas Aweray*] xxx s

Summa x li xiij s iiij d

Redditus camerarum infra Collegium eodem anno

De camera ~~ea~~ Magistri Roberti fflemyg' xx s

De camera Magistri Thomas Benwell' quem inhabitavit Serl pro duobus terminis x s

~~De eodem Nich' pro Serl pro camera quem modo tenet Magister Joh' Crosby pro duobus terminis xv s~~[5]

De eadem camera de Magistro Johanne Crosby pro duobus terminis ~~v s~~ x s

De Camera Magistri Roberti Toft' ~~x s~~ v s

De camera Magistri Thome lematon xvj s viij d

De camera Bethwin' xiij s iiij d

De camera Typtot et hurle pro tribus terminis xxv s

De camera Gervays et Barbour xiij s iiij d

De camera Wyttfeld' xiij s iiij d

De camera Dowson' xvj s viij d

De camera ffernys xvj s

Summa viij li iij s viij d ⟨vij li xix s iiij d⟩[6]

Redditus scolarum

De scol' Magistri Willelmi Castell' vj s viij d

De scol' Magistri Willelmi Laghton' de aula vitria vj s viij d

De scol' Magistri de Oriell' v s

De scol' Magistri de Bem' Hall' v s

De scol' Betnam' determinatoris iiij s

De scol' Sabyr' determinatoris de collegio animarum iiij s

De scol' Bassall' determinatoris iij s vj ḍ

De scol' Rogerson determinatoris iij s vj d

Summa xxxviij s iiij d

Redditus de liberis tenementis in oxon' et suburbijs

De Abbatissa de Godstow pro una schopa exposito magne Aule [*sic*] ffrideswide xx d

De eadem pro annuali redditu pro gardino ten' quondam Thome Mayster xiiij s

[5] [ADMC] This entry almost certainly deleted, although Smith (Vol. VIII p. 146) does not read this entry as such.

[6] [ADMC] The first sum may have been intended to have been erased.

De Abbate de Osney pro schopa iuxta Johannem Spiser vj s viij d
De ten' quondam' Rogeri Skybbow modo Collegij omnium animarum viij s
De novo Collegio pro Maydyn Hall' x s
De Collegio Cantuarij ij s vj d
De Collegio Lincolnie pro gardino que Ric' cariour tenuit v s
De Johanne Treguran' pro defalcacione prati retro Osnay ij s ij d
De Magistro Ric' Pedyngton' pro defalcacione eiusdem prati ij s ij d
De collegio animarum pro ten' quondam' Joh' Spront in parochia sancti Petri in baliolo v s
De collegio animarum pro gardino retro dictum ten' quondam dicti Johannis Spront' viij s x d ob
De Albis monachis pro gardino quem tenuit Barton' corveser' in parochia sancte Marie Magd' iiij s
Summa ij li xvij s ij d ob

Redditus in Exsexcia et in Holdernes
De Johanne Stanys pro Manerio de Merx et Molendinis xviij li iij s iiij d
De Thoma Terell' et pro libero Redditu exeunte de Rammysden xx s
De Johanne Bedford' de Hull' pro terris de Pagula in Holdernes iij li xij d
Summa xxij li iiij s iiij d

Summa omnium reddituum lxij li ix s xj d ob

Recepta preter Sortem domus
In primis de Thoma Hall' pro quisquilijs v s
De Johanne Harres pro loppis [*vj s*] viij d
De Crosby [*xiiij d?*]
De Magistro Willelmo Dowson [*xiij d*]
De Thoma Hall et Thoma Sclater [*iiij d*]
De Johanne Harres pro loppis in Nowode iij s
De Thoma pincerna pro lignis et carbonibus hurle xx d
Item pro uno vendit' Thome Hall' xij d
De rectore de Bowe pro lignis iij s
Item pro lignis meis iiij s vj d

Item pro feno de irland' ij s vj d

Summa xxix s xj d

Summa omnium onoratorum lxxxxvj li xvj s viij d ob q[a][7]

Allocat' Aularum

De Magistro Johanne Barnard' pro anno terciodecimo [*ix s*] viij d

De Magistro Thoma Cowper pro gardino de Scheldhall pro [*anno duodecimo vj s viij d*]

De ~~Culbi~~ Calbusch pro parva aula universitatis in vico scolarum [*vj s viij d*]

De Laylay pro aula Hampton' [*l s*]

De Cowper pro Aula Drowda de anno decimonono vj s viij d

De eodem Cowper pro eodam Aula de anno vicesimo xxvj s viij d

De eodem Cowper pro eodam Aula de anno vicesimo primo xx s

De Johanne Pertryche fflechar' pro uno termino de anno vicesimo primo vj s viij d

De Rogero Grey pro aula ꝑ brasnose de anno vicesimo primo xxij s ij d ob q[a]

De eodem pro Aula sancti Thome eodem anno iij s iiij d

De eodem pro Gardino Aula scuti eodem anno vj s viij d

Summa viij li v s ij d ob q[a]

Allocat' Camerarum

De Magistro Willelmo Dowson' pro arr' quintidecimi septimodecimi decimi octavi et deciminoni xxij s iiij d

De eodem Magistro Willelmo pro anno vicesimo xij s

De eodem Magistro pro anno vicesimo primo xvj s viij d

De Magistro Thoma Whytfeld iij s iiij d

De Magistro Johanne Chadworth xx d

De Magistri Thome lamaton' pro duobus terminis de anno vicesimo viij s

De eodem Magistro de anno vicesimo primo xvj s viij d

De camera Magistri Thome Boteler' pro camera [*sic*] sua in

[7] [ADMC] Shillings and pence figures are not quite certain, particularly pence, which looks like 'viij d'; but the 'v' may be crossed out. £96 16s 3d is Smith's reading (Vol. VIII p. 147), and fits with the figures at the end of the roll. If correct, the total of arrears must be £32 16s 5¼d.

gardino pro pueris suis pro 2^{bus} terminus de anno vicesimo ij s vj d
De camera Tofft de anno vicesimo primo v s
De camera ffernys [. . .][8]
Summa iiij li ix s xj d

Allocat' de scolis
De scolis Magistri Castell' de anno vicesimo primo vj s viij d
De scolis Magistri Lawthton' pro eodem anno vj s viij d
De scolis Magistri de Oriell' v s
De scolis Magistri de Bemhall' v s
De Magistro Kell' xx d
De Magistro de nigra Aula pro parva Aula universitatis in vico scolarum vj s viij d
De Sebyr' determinatore de collegio animarum iiij s
Summa xxxv s viij d

Allocat' de liberis redditibus
De Rogeri Skybow pro terminis mich' anni decimi sexti pro ten' modo Collegij animarum iiij s
De Abbatissa de Godstowe pro annis vicesimo et vicesimo primo v s viij d
De Collegio Cantuarie ij s vj d
Summa xij s ij d

Allocat' ten' laycorum in paroch' omnium sanctorum et sancti martini
De executoribus Strykmed' pro anno vicesimo primo vj d viij d
De executoribus ysabelle Colet de annis duodecimo et terciodecimo xxxviij s iiij d
De Johanne William Glover pro anno decimoseptimo x s
De eodem Johanne pro anno ~~vise~~ vicesimo primo xv s
De Bradmyr[9] pro anno vicesimo xx d
De Nich' Smyth alias Castell' pro ten' in quo Caym' habitavit pro anno decimo septimo ij s viij d
Summa iij li xiiij s iiij d

[8] [ADMC] The figure is illegible, but it does not look like the 6s 9d which would be necessary to make the total correct.
[9] [ADMC] The 'm' of Bradmyr consists of 4 minims, presumably a mistake.

Allocat' in paroch' sancte marie et sancti petri in oriente

De Johanne Barbour pro Stanton Hall' pro anno quintodecimo xiij s iiij d

De Roberto lambard' pro eadem aula pro anno vicesimo primo xviij s

De Thoma Spyge cowper pro anno vicesimo primo vj s

De ~~Jh~~ Johanne Helys coco pro eodem anno xj s viij d

Summa xlix s

Allocat' ten' in suburbijs

De executoribus Willemi Brampton' pro quatuor annis viij s

De Johanne Mason' pro anno vicesimo vj d

[*Dorse*]

Allocat' de partibus remotis

De Bedforth' de anno vicesimo iiij s iiij d

De eodem pro anno vicesimo primo xxj s

Summa xxxiij s x d

Summa omnium allocatorum precedencium xxij li xviij s ij d ob q[a10]

Solut' et expense fact' per eundem Magistrum Johannem Marton' tam infra Collegium quam extra

In primis pro ~~Carr~~ carigio meremij a Stowod' et stanton' Wod et delacione quinque truncorum lvij s ix d

Item expense fact' pro nova domo scilicet storhows infra gardinum iiij li xviij s xj d

Item expense fact' pro reparacione Hampton Hall' vj li xvj s xj d

Item expense fact' pro domo ubi ysabelle Colette inhabitavit xj li v s ij d ob

Item expense fact' pro reparacione aularum scilicet Edwardi parve Aule universitatis in alto vico Brasnose et parve aula universitatis in vico scolarum lij s xj d ob

Item in reparacionibus ten' laycorum xxxij s v s ob

Item expense fact' pro reparacionibus factis infra Collegium et pro scolis vj s ij d

Item expense fact' pro pictura panni aularum et capella xlj s ij d

Item soluta pro emptis de novo ad coquinam et promptuarium et pro stauro ad collegium iij li xviij s vj d

[10] [ADMC] This could also be read as £22 18s 3d, but in any case the correct total is £23 1d.

Item soluta pro placitis et ~~dm~~ diminutis expensis xxij s vij d ob
Item soluta pro antiquis debitis et pro redempcione unius caucionis de Cista de Rotheberi lix s viij d
Item expense fact' pro reparacione per Johannem Stanys firmarium nostrum in Exsex iiij li xiij d
Item expense fact' in equitacionibus versus Exsex et Holdernes et pro licencia domini Regis circa laborem appropriacionis ecclesie de Harnclyffe vij li ix s x d ob
Item expense fact' per Magistrum Willelmum Sharp ix s ij d ob
Summa totalis lij li xij s vj d

Resoluciones facte eodem anno
In primis priori sancte ffrideswide in plenam solucionem anni vicesimi Regis supradicti x s
Item eidem priori in partem solucionis anni vicesimi primi ix s ij d
Item Abbati de Osney in completam solucionem anni vicesimi primi xxij s x d
Item Thome Spryg' xviij d
Item uxori de Harbyrfeld' iij s vj d
Item collectoribus domini regis pro quintodecimo xvj d
Summa xlvij s ij d[11]

Soluta ~~sol~~ socijs
In primis Magistro pro officio Magistratus vj s viij d
Item eidem Magistro pro diebus suis xiij s iiij d
Item Magistro Willelmo Sharpp eodem anno xiij s iiij d
Item Magistro Willelmo Aspylon eodem anno xiij s iiij d
Item Magistro Johanni Appylton' eodem anno xiij s
Summa lix s viij d

Soluta servientibus
In primis Johanni Cornyll' v s
Item Michaeli Gawyn' pro officio pincerne pro ~~tri~~ duobus terminis xv s
Item eidem Michaeli pro officio coci pro uno termino xx d
Item petro Barbour pro uno anno vj s viij d
Item uxori de Capper pro tribus terminis v s

[11] [ADMC] The correct total is 48s 4d.

Item ~~lotrici~~ lotrici yvine et uxori Johannis Cowper ij s
Summa xxxv s iiij d

Soluta pro communis sociorum per totum annum viij li iij s j d ob q^{a}
Soluta pro batellis operariorum per totum annum ~~vij~~ xvlij s ix d ob q^{a}
Soluta pro convivio sancti Cuthberti vij s vj d
Summa x li xviij s v d ob

Summa omnium expensarum lxx li xiiij s ob q^{a}

Extracta de arr' et ~~et~~ de onere precendentibus
De ~~Aulis~~ Jacobo leche de annis quartodecimo et quintodecimo ⟨pro Aula edvardi⟩ xxvij s xj d
De cameris
Soluciones Elton' Rectore de Chelforth de anno quintodecimo Regis Henrici Sexti vj s viij d
De Magistro Thoma Wythfeld pro dimissis sibi vj s viij d

De liberis redditibus
De Johanne Spicer pro defalcacione prati retro Osnay iiij s iiij d
De abbate de osney pro tribus annis xx s
~~De Magistro Ric' pytyngton' pro defalcacione prati retro osney iiij s iiij s~~ ~~[*sic*]~~
~~De Trygeram pro uno anno ij s ij d~~
De collegio animarum pro terris et ten' quondam spront' xlj s viij d ob

De ten' laycorum in paroch' omnium sanctorum et sancti petri in oriente
De Thoma Dudlay ~~p~~ in dimissis sibi in uno anno et dimidio xl s iiij d
De Nich' Schyrborn' xx d
De Roberto ffuller pro anno decimo oct' et decimo nono xvj s

De pratis retro osney
De Johanne ywys Maltman' pro anno vicesimo vj s ij d
Summa ix li xvj s ob q^{a}

Item in allocatis principali Aule de Hampton' pro reparacionibus factis per ipsum in eadem Aula anno regni Regis vicesimo xxx s

Summa omnium allocatorum et expensarum precedencium ciiij li iij s viij d q^{a}

⟨Computatis computandis et allocatis allocandis collegium debet computantibus vij li vij s iiij d ob

Acta sunt sunt hec coram nobis et per nos H Sever ~~et~~ sacre theologie professoris Cancellarium universitis Oxon'⟩

[*A roll of 2 membranes, now stuck together (not stitched). The dorse is very clear, but parts of the front are damaged or faded, particularly at the right hand edge.*]

WHITSUN 21 HENRY VI to WHITSUN 22 HENRY VI (ROLL UC:BU1/F/56)

9 June 1443–31 May 1444

BURSAR: WILLIAM CASTELL

⟨Will' Castell⟩

Compotus Magistri [Willelmi Castell procuratoris Magne Aule seu Collegij universitatis][1] Oxon' datus per eundem Magistrum Willelmum Cas[tell de omnibus redditibus et proventibus dicte Aule seu Collegij] receptis et expensis a festo Penticost' inclusive [anno rr' Henrici sexti vicesimo primo] usque ad item festum Penticost' anno eius [*sic*] regis vicesimo [secundo]

[*The Arrears are identical with the Allowances of* **F/55**, *although the whole of the first membrane is much damaged on the right hand edge, and very few figures are legible. However, the Arrears for Schools give slightly different names for the tenants from the Allowances, and are given here in full:*

Arr' de Scolis

De Scol' Magistri Castell' de anno vicesimo primo	[*vj s viij d*]
De Scol' Magistri Lawthton' de eodem anno	[*vj s viij d*]
De Scol' Magistri Camerlan' de eodem anno	[*v s*]
De Scol' Magistri ffree de eodem anno	[*v s*]
De Scol' Magistri Kell' de anno vicesimo	[*xx d*]
De Magistro lord pro parva aula universitatis in vico scolarum	[*vj s viij d*]
De Sabyt' determinatore de Collegio Animarum	[*iiij s*]

Summa xxxv s viij d

Summa omnium allocatorum [*sic*] precedencium xxij li xviij s ij d ob q[a]

Redditus ten' in paroch' sanctorum petri et Martini

De Gardino quod tenet Willelmus Hanse in Swynstwychne [*vij s?*]

[1] [ADMC] Both membranes are now badly damaged and the text is lost in numerous places. The damage had occured since Smith's day, and several lost entries are recoverable from Smith Vol. VIII pp. 148–152.

De ten' quod tenet teutonicus super angulum quadrivij pro duobus terminis[. . .] [xiij s iiij d]

Summa [*xx s iiij d?*]

Redditus ten' laicorum in paroch' omnium sanctorum anno regni Regis Henrici Sexti supra[*dicto*]

De ten' quod tenet Thomas Dudley [*xxxiij s iiij d*]

De ten' quod tenet Spendyng et pro solario [*xxiij s iiij d*]

De ten' quod tenet Nich' Schyrborn' xx s

De ten' quod tenet Joh' Bradmyr' pro tribus terminis xvij s vj d

De ten' quod tenet Hugo Benett et pro gardino xxiij s iiij d

De ten' quod tenet Johannes William Glover et Johannes Stokes Hosyer iij li

Summa viij li xvij s vj d

Redditus in paroch' sancte marie et Sancti Petri in oriente

De ten' quod tenet Robertus Lambert [*xviij s?*]

De ten' quod tenet Henricus Bath' pro uno [*anno* *xviij s iiij d*]

De ten' quod tenuit Joh' Swanys pro tribus [*terminis et una muliere pro uno termino*] [*xvj s*]

De ten' quod tenuit Thomas Sprag' alias Cow[*per* *xij s*]

Summa iij li xix s iiij d[2]

Redditus in suburbijs et in campis Oxon' eodem anno

De gardino iuxta castrum quod tenet Wyttfeld' preco laycorum [*ij s*]

De terris in bello monte et campis de Walton' quas tenet Thomas Spryg' [*vij s*]

De eodem pro pratis retro Osney xx s

De pratis Alrychset' que tenet Joh' Wykys et Thomas mansypyll' xviij s

De gardino ex parte orientali ecclesie sancte [*sic*] Egidij quem tenet Joh' Mason [. . .] [*vj d*]

[*2nd membrane*]

Summa xlvij s vj d

Redditus aularum

[De Aula] Brasnose quam tenet Magister Robertus Merkham iij li vj s viij d

[2] [ADMC] The 'iiij d' is not quite certain.

[De Aula Sancti Thome quam] tenet idem Magister x s
[De Gardino Aule scuti quem] tenet idem Magister vj s viij d
[De Aula Hampton' quem tenet] Magister Willemus Laylay l s
[De eodem Magistro pro ten' annexo] eidem aule xx s
De parva universitatis [*sic*] Oxon' in vico scolarum de Willelmo Chyrch determinatore iiij s
De aula Edwardi quam tenet Johannus ffytz Robert xx s
De aula Drowda quem tenet Johannes Partrych fflecher' xxvj s viij d
De [aula] universitatis in alto vico quam tenuit Thomas Averay pro duobus terminis xvj s viij d
Summa xj li viij d

Redditus [Camerarum infra Coll]egium eodem anno
[De camera Magistri Roberti] Flemyng xx s
[De camera Magistri Willelmi Dow]son' xvj s viij d
[De Magistro Roberto Tofte pro tribus] terminis in bassa camera vij s vj d
[De eodem Magistro pro camera Typtofte . . .[3]] pro uno termino iij s iiij d
[De Robert Bothwyn] pro duobus terminis in bassa camera vj s viij d
De eodem pro duobus terminis in alta camera viij s
De Magistro joh' Barbour pro duobus terminis vj s viij d
De eadem camera de Magistro Roberto Chesman' pro uno termino iij s iiij d
De Cam' Magistri Whytfeld' pro duobus terminis vj s viij d
De eadem Camera de Magistro Roberto Metford pro duobus terminis vj s viij d
[De Camera] Magistri Nicholai Medgorth pro duobus terminis viij s iiij d
[De Camera Magistri Johannis] Crosby x s
[De Camera Roet de Bowe] pro duobus terminis viij s
[De Camera fernys] ij s viij d
[Summa] v li xiiij s vj d

Redditus scolarum
[De scol'] Magistri Willelmi ~~Castell vj s viij d~~
~~De scol' Magistri Willelmi Laghton' vj s viij d~~

[3] [ADMC] Smith was uncertain of the next word.

De scol' Magistro Camerlan v s
De scol' Magistri Willelmi ffree v s
De scol' Magistri Swan de Oriell' vj s viij d
De scol' Norton' determinatore iij s iiij d
[De scol'] Hesyldon' determinatore iiij s
[De scol' Thome] famulo Ensgwyn' determinatore iij s iiij d
[Summa] xxvij s iiij d

Redditus [*de liberis tenementis*][4]
[*De Abbatissa de Godstow pro*] una schopa exposita mage [*sic*] porte ffrideswide xx d
[*De eadem pro annuali*] redditu pro gardino ten' quondam Thome Mayster xiiij d
De Abbate de Osney pro schopa iuxta Johannem Spiser vj s viij d
De ten' quondam Rogeri Skybow modo Collegij animarum viij s
De Novo Collegio pro Maydyn' Hall' x s
De Collegio Cantuarij ij s vj d
De Collegio lincolnie pro gardino v s
De Joh' Tregurum' pro defalcacione prati retro Osney ij s ij d
[*De collegio animarum*] pro ten' quondam Joh' Spront in paroch' sancti Petri in balliolo v s
[*De eodem collegio pro gar*]dino retro dictum ten' quondam dicti Johannis Spront viij s x d ob
[*De albis monachis pro gardino*] quem tenuit Barton' corveser in paroch' sancte Marie Magd' iiij s
De Magistro Ric' Pedyngton pro' defalcacione prati retro Osney ij s ij d
[*Summa*] lvij s ij d ob

Redditus [*in Essex et Holdernes*]
De Johanne Stanys pro manerio de Merx et Molendinis xviij li iij s iiij d
De Thome Terell' et pro libero redditu exeunte de Rammysden xx s

[4] [ADMC] Square bracket readings in this section are supplied from the similar section in **F**/55 above, as Smith (Vol. VIII p. 149) indicates that they were the same.

De Johanne yowerd' de pagula in Holdernes iij li xij d
Summa xxij li iiij s iiij d

Summa omnium Reddituum lix li viij s viij d ob

Recepta [preter sortem domus]
[In primis pro quisquilijs de lignis] antiquis venditis diversis vicibus x s
[De una caucione ex mutuo] iiij li
[De Magistro Johanne Castell] iiij li
De executoribus Magistri Ricardi Heth' iij li vj s viij d
De Magistro Johanne Marchall' vj s viij d
De Domino nostro speciali episcopo Exon' x li
Summa xxij li iij s iiij d

Summa omnium oneratorum ciiij li x s iij d q[a]

Allocaciones Aularum[5]
[*De Magistro*] Johanne Bernard pro anno terciodecimo ix s viij d
[*De Magistro Thoma Co*]wper pro anno duodecimo vj s viij d
[*De Magistro Calbuch' pro par*]va aula universitatis in vico scolarum vj s viij d
[*De Magistro Willelmo laylay*] pro anno vicesimo secundo xvj s viij d
[*De Cowper pro Aula Drowda*] pro annis decimo nono vicesimo et vicesimo primo xlix [*s*] j d
[*De Johanne Pertrysch' pro annis vicesimo primo et secundo*] viij s iiij d
[*De Magistro Robert*] Merk'ham pro Brasnose de anno vicesimo secundo xxij s ij d ob q[a]
[*De eo*]dem pro aula sancti Thome eodem anno iij s iiij d
[*De*] eodem pro Gardino aule scuti ij s ij d od q[a]
Summa vj li iiij s x d ob

Allocacionis Camerarum
De Magistro Willelmo Dowson pro annis vicesimo vicesimo primo et vicesimo secundo xl s iiij d
De camera Magistri Roberti fflemyng xx d
De camera Magistri Joh' Chadworth' xx d
De camera lematon' pro anno vicesimo et vicesimo primo xxj s

[5] [ADMC] Bracketed readings from this section are based on the Arrears in **F**/57 below.

[*De camera Magistri Roberti*] Tofte v s x d
[*De camera Magistri Roberti M*]edforth' vj s viij d
[*De camera Magistri Nicholai Me*]dforth' viij s iiij d
[*Summa*] iiij li v s vj d

[*Allocaciones scolarum*]
[*De scola Magistri Willelmi Keell' pro anno vicesimo*] xx d
[*De scola lorde pro eodem*] anno vj s viij d
[*De scola Magistri*] Camerton pro anno vicesimo secundo v s
[*De*] scol' Magistri ffree pro eodem anno v s
[*De*] scol' Magistri Rosemay pro eodem anno vj s viij d
[*De*] scol' Magistri Swan eodem anno vj s viij d
[*De*] scol' Norton' determinatore iij s iiij d
De scol' Thome famuli Gasgwyn' determinatore iij s iiij d
Summa xxxviij s iiij d

Allocaciones [*in parochia*] Omnium sanctorum
[*De*] executoribus ysebelle Colet de annis duodecimo et terciodecimo xxxviij s iiij d
[*De Johanne Barbour pro*] Stanton' Hall' xiij s iiij d
[*De Johanne Wilyam Glover pro*] anno decimo septimo x s
[*De eodem Johanne Wilyam pro*] anno vicesimo secundo xv s
[*De Bradmyre pro anno vicesimo secundo*] v s
[*De Nicholao Schyrborn pro anno vicesimo secundo*] xj s
[*Summa*] iiij li xiij s ij d

Allocaciones [*in paroch' beate*] Marie [*et sancti petri in*] oriente
[*De*] Roberto lambert pro anno vicesimo secundo xviij s
[*De He*]nrico Bath' pro eodem anno xx s
[*De*] Thoma Sprag' pro eodem anno iij s ~~vij s vj d~~
[*De*] Joh' Swaynse pro eodem anno ij s j d ob
[*De*] Joh' Elys xx d
[*De*] Nich' Smyth ij s viij d
Summa xlvij s v s ob

Allocaciones in sub[*urbijs*] et campis [*oxon' et*] partibus [*remotis*]
[*De*] Thome mancipio pro alrycheset' ij s
[*De Wytfeld' prec*]one maioris pro gardino iuxta castrum vj s
[*De Johanne Stanys de*] Esexia xvj s viij d
[*Summa*] xxiiij s viij d

[*Allocacionis de liberis redditibus*]

[*De Schybbow*] iiij s

[*De Abbatissa de Godstow pro tribus annis*] viij s vj d

[*De Collegio Cantuarie pro anno vicesimo secundo*] ij s vj d

[*De Collegio animarum pro ten'*] quondam Spront v s

[*De eodem Collegio pro gard*]ino retro dictum ten' viij s x d ob

[*Summa*] xxviij s x d ob

[*Sum*]ma omnium allocatorum xxij li ij s x d ob

[*Dorse of second membrane*]

[*Reparaciones facte*] pre eundum Magistrum Willelmum Castell' tam infra Collegium quam extra

[*Reparaciones facte?*] apud Brasnose et solutis Magistro Rogero Grey pro [*parva aula universitatis?*] in vico scolarum [. . . .]

. . .] anno et anno preterito xliij s[6] vij d

. . .] iij s j d

. . .]da[7] lviij s iiij d

[*Summa*] vij li xvij s x d

Resol[*uciones*] fact' eodem anno

[*In primis Abbati*] de Osney pro anno vicesimo secundo xxij s x d

[*Item priori sancte*] ffrideswide in plenam solucionem anni vicesimi primi ix s iiij d

Item eidem priori in partem solucionis anni vicesimi secundi vj s viij d

Item Collectoribus domini Regis pro quintodecima [*sic*] xvj d

Summa xl s ij d

Soluc' [*et ex*]pense facte pro reparacionibus ten' laicorum

In primis pro reparacionibus factis in domo Johannis Waskew xij li xiij s v d

[*Item*] pro una latrina facta in domo Johannis William ij s

[*Item*] pro reparacionibus factis in domo Roberti lambard' vj s

[*Item*] pro reparacionibus factis apud esexiam et pro stacione molendini iij li iij s viij d ob

[*Item pro reparacionibus factis*] apud holdernese xxviij s

[Summa xvij] li xiij s j d ob

6 [ADMC] Possibly not 'xliij' but 'liij'.

7 [ADMC] Smith Vol. VIII p. 150 notes 'de reparac' de Drowdahall 2–18–iiij d'.

[In expensis infra Collegium in Capella[8]] xliiij s iiij d ob
. . .]iarium iiij s x d
. . .]pro uno veru [. . . ij s
[In stauro] et Reparacionibus factis infra Collegium iiij li xj s ix d ob
Summa vij li iij s

Soluciones socijs eodem anno
In primis Magistro Collegij pro pencione sacerdotali xxvj s viij d
Item eidem Magistro pro die sancti Cuthberti vj s viij d
Item Magistro Willelmo Sharp pro eodem die vj s viij d
Item Magistro Willelmo Castell' pro pencione sacerdotali in partem solucionis xx s
Summa iij li

[Soluc' servientibus]
[In primis Thome Walker pincerne pro tribus termi]nis xv s
[Item Joh' Telme pro uno termino] v s
[Item Roberto Coke pro duobus terminis] iij s iiij d
[Item Thome Coco pro uno termino] xx d
[Item Joh' Coco pro uno termino] xx d
[Item Barbiton]sori pro toto anno vj s viij d
[Item] lotrici pro toto anno vj s viij d
Item eidem lotrici pro locione Capelle viij d
Item Johanni helys pro stipendio suo de anno vicesimo primo vj s
Summa xlvj s viij d

Expense facte in equitacionibus versus exsexiam per Magistrum Collegij et Magistrum W Sharp iij li v s viij d
[*Item*] expense facte per Magistrum Sharp et M Willelmum Asplyon circa appropriacionem ecclesie de Arnclyff xviij li xiiij s iij d
[*Item*] soluc' pro antiquis debitis predicto Magistro W. Asplyon' xliiij s iij d
Summa xxiiij li iiij s ij d

[In communis sociorum a festo Pent'] inclusive usque ad festum Pasche exclusive xij li ix s vij d ob q[a]
[In Batellis operariorum jornellis et contri]bucionibus per idem tempus lix s iij d ob q[a]

[8] [ADMC] This is Smith's version, but is not necessarily the actual text. Some of the figures in this section are not quite certain.

[Item pro convivio sancti Cuthberti] xiij s viij d ob
[Summa] xvj li ij s viij d

Soluc' pro plac[*itis et in*][9] minutis expensis
In primis pro expensis extraniorum xxxiij s ix d ob q[a]
Item pro placitis vj s ij d
Item in resolutis tenentibus ij s vj d
Item solut' Thome Sprag' pro hupys ad vasa panduxatoria x s
Item in pecunijs dimissis tenentibus vj s viij d
Summa lix s j d ob q[a]

[*Summa omnium*] expensarum lxxxiij li vj s ix d q[a]

Summa omnium allocatorum et expensarum precedencium xv li ix s vij d ob q[a]

⟨Computatis computandis et allocatis allocandis collegium debet computanti xix s iiij d ob
[Acta sunt hec coram] nobie Magistro Willelmo Dowson sacre theologie professore commissario generalem Magistri [Thome Gascoyne cancellarij universitatis oxon']⟩

[*A roll of 2 separate membrances stitched together at the head; no writing on the dorse of the first membrane.*]

9 [ADMC] Reading not certain.

EASTER 22 HENRY VI to WHITSUN 23 HENRY VI (ROLL UC:BU1/F/57)
12 April 1444–16 May 1445

BURSAR: ROBERT HARTILPOLE

Compotus Roberti Hertilpoll' Procuratoris Collegij seu magne Aule universitatis oxon' datus per eundem Robertum Hertilpoll' de omnibus redditibus et proventibus dicte Aule seu Collegij receptis et expensis a festo Pasche Anno Regni Regis Henrici sexti xxij° usque ad festum Pentecost' exclusive Anno eiusdem Regis xxiij°

[*The Arrears are, as far as can be judged, identical with the Allowances in* ***F/56****, if one bears in mind the poor condition of the previous roll*]

Summa omnium arr' xxij li ij s x d ob

Redditus ten' in parochia sanctorum Petri et Martini Anno Regni Regis Henrici sexti xxiij°

De ten' quod tenet Willelmus Hance in Swynstwechn'	vij s
De ten' quod tenet Teutonicus super angulum quadrivij pro uno anno	xxvj s viij d
Summa xxxiij s viij d	

Redditus ten' laicorum in parochia omnium sanctorum Anno rr' Henrici sexti supradicto

De ten' quod tenet Thomas Dudley	xxxiij s iiij d
De ten' quod tenet Spendyng' pro ten' pro solario	xxiij s iiij d
De Hugone Benett pro uno anno	xxvj s viij d
De Johanne Wilyam Glover pro uno termino	xv s
De Willelmo Stokys pro tribus terminis	xxxv s
De Johanne Wilyam Glover pro ten' in quo commoratur pro tribus terminis	xvij s vj d
De ten' quod tenet Weskew pro uno anno	liij s iiij d
De Hosier iuxta stokys pro uno termino	iiij s ij d
Summa x li viij s iiij d	

Redditus in parochia sancte Marie et sancti petri in oriente

De ten' quod tenet Robertus lambert	xvij s
De ten' quod tenet Henricus Bayth'	xl s
De Johanne Cuke pro uno anno	xvj s viij d

De Thoma Sprage Cowper xij s
Summa iiij li vj s viij d

Redditus in suburbijs et campis oxon' anno supradicto
De gardino iuxta castrum quod tenet Wytfelde ij s
De terris in bello monte et campis de Walton quas tenet Thomas Spryge vij s
De eodem pro pratis retro osnay xx s
De priori fratrum predicatorum pro pratis scilicet alryschette xviij s iiij d
De gardino ex parte orientale ecclesie sancti Egidij quod tenet Johannes Mayson vj d
De Gyllotte pro prato vocato yrland xx d
Summa xlix s vj d

Redditus Aularum
De Aula Brasnos quem tenet Magister Robertus Merkhamm pro uno anno iij li vj s viij d
De Aula sancti Thome quam tenet idem magister x s
De gardino aule scuti quod tenet idem magister vj s viij d
De Aula Hampton' quam tenet Magister Willelmus leylay l s
De eodem magistro pro ten' quondam tenure chaym bedelli xx s
De parva aula universitatis in vico scolarum pro uno anno xx s
De Aula Edwardi xx s
De Aula Drowda quam tenet Joh' pertrysch' xxvj s viij d
De parva aula universitatis in alto vico xl s
Summa xiij li

Redditus camerarum infra Collegium
De Magistro Willelmo Dowson' xvj s viij d
De Magistro Roberto Tofte xiij s iiij d
De Rectore bethom pro uno termino iiij s
De Magistro Robert fflemyng' pro uno termino v s
De Magistro Johanne Crosby v s
De Magistro Roberto Medforde pro duobus terminis anni xxiij vj s viij d
Summa l s viij d

Redditus scolarum
De scola Magistri Swan de Oryall' vj s viij d
De Magistro Willelmo Dalton vj s viij d

De Willelm Shyryfe determinatore iiij s
De Clopton' determinatore iiij s
De kyng' determinatore iiij s
De Marschall' determinatore iiij s
Summa xxix s iiij d

Redditus de liberis ten' in oxonia et suburbijs
De abbatissa de godstow pro parva shoppa exposita magne porte ffrydeswyde xx d
De eadem pro annuali redditu pro gardino ten' quondam Thome Mayster xiiij d
De Abbate de Osnay pro schoppa iuxta Johannem Spisere vj s viij d
De ten' quondam Rogeri Skybbow mo°do [*sic*] Collegij animarum viij s
De novo Collegio pro Maydynhall' x s
De Collegio Cantuar' pro sylverhall' ij s vj d
De Collegio lincoln' pro gardino v s
De Pedyngton' pro defalcacione prati retro Osnay ij s ij d
De Collegio animarum pro ten' quondam Johannis Spronte in parochia sancti petri in balliolo v s
De eodem Collegio pro gardino retro dictum ten' quondam dicti Johannis Spronte viij s x d ob
De albis monachis pro gardino quod tenuit Barton Corvysere in parochia sancte Marie Magdalen' iiij s
De Henrico Salmon pro defalcacione prati retro Osnay ij s ij d
Summa lvij s ij d ob

Redditus in exsexia et Holderness'
De Johanne stanes pro Manerio de Merx et molendinis xviij li iij s iiij d
De Thoma Terell' pro libero [*sic*] exeunte de Rammysden' xx s
De terris in Holdernes iij li xij d
Summa xxij li iiij s iiij d

Summa omnium Reddituum lx li xix s viij d ob

Recepta preter sortem domus
In primis de Magistro Ric' Wytton' pro quisquilijs vj s viij d
De uxore Johannis Telm senioris vj s viij d
De Thoma Walkere pro focalibus ij s ij d

De stephano de Aula stapilina pro uno studio xx d
Summa xvij s ij d

Summa omnium oneratorum lxxxiij li xix s ix d

Allocaciones aularum
De Magistro Johanne Bernard pro anno terciodecimo ix s viij d
De Magistro Thoma Cowper pro anno duodecimo vj s viij d
De Magistro Calbuch' pro parva aula universitatis in vico scolarum vj s viij d
De Magistro Willelmo leylay pro anno xxiij° xxiij s iiij d
De Couper pro aula drouda pro annis decimo nono vicesimo et vicesimo primo xlix s j d
De Johanne pertrysch' pro annis vicesimo primo et secundo viij s iiij d
De eodem pro anno xxiij° iij s iiij d
De Magistro Roberto Merkham pro aula brasynnos xxij s ij d ob q[a]
De eodem pro aula sancti Thome iij s iiij d
De eodem pro gardino aule scuti ij s ij d ob q[a]
De parva aula universitatis in vico scolarum vj s viij d
De parva aula universitatis in alto vico xiij s iiij d
Summa vij li xiiij s x d ob

Alloc' camerarum
De Magistro Willelmo Douson' pro annis xx[mo] xxj° et xxij° xl s iiij d
De eodem pro anno xxiij° vj s viij d
De camera Magistri Johannis Chadworth' xx d
De camera lematon pro anno xx[mo] et xxj° xxj s
De camera Magistri Toft v s v d
De Magistri Medforth' xiij s iiij d
De camera Magistri Nicholai Medforth' viij s iiij d
Summa iiij li xvij s ij d

Alloc' scolarum
De scola magistri Willelmi Keell' pro anno vicesimo xx d
De scola lorde pro eodem anno vj s viij d
De scola Magistri swan' de Oriall' pro anni xxij° et xxiij° xiij s iiij d
De scola Magistri Willelmi Dalton vj s viij d
Summa xxvij s iiij d

Alloc' in parochia omnium sanctorum

De executoribus jsabelle Colette pro annis duodecimo et terciodecimo xxxviij s iiij d

De Johanne Barbour pro staynton' hall' xiij s iiij d

De Johanne Wilyam Glover pro anno decimo septimo x s

De eodem pro anno vicesimo secundo xv s

De Willelmo stokys vij s iiij d

De hosyer iuxta stokys iiij s iiij d

De Spendyng pro solario iij s iiij d

De Hugone Benett vij s vj d

De Weskew xlivj s viij d

De Bradmyre iij s vj d

Summa vij li ix s ij d

Alloc' in paroch' beate Marie et sancti Petri in oriente

De Roberto lambert xvij s

De Henrico Bayth' pro anno xxij° xx s

De eodem pro anno xxiij° vij s ij d

De Thoma Sprag' pro annis xxij° et xxiij° ix s

De Johanne swanys pro anno xxij° ij s j d ob

De Johanne Cuke pro anno xxiij° x s

De Nicholao Smyth' ij s viij d

Summa iij li ix s xj d ob

Alloc' in suburbijs et campis oxon'

De Thoma Mancipio de pro alrychesette ij s

De Wytfeld precone maioris pro quatuor annis viij s

De Pedyngtin pro defalcacione prati retro Osnay ij s ij d

De Thoma Spryge ij s

De Johanne Mayson pro gardino ex parte orientali ecclesie sancti egidij vj d

De Gyllotte pro yrlande xx d

Summa xvj s iiij d

Alloc' de liberis ten'

De Schybbow iiij s

De Collegio animarum pro ten' quondam schybbow pro anno xxiij° iiij s

De eodem Collegio pro ten' quondam johannis spronte in parochia sancti petri in balliolo v s

De eodem Collegio pro gardino retro dictum ten' viij s x d ob

De eodem Collegio animarium pro dictum ten' quondam spronte v s
De eodem Collegio pro gardino eiusdem viij s x d ob
De Willelmo Hance pro anno xxiij° vij s
Summa xlij s ix d

Alloc' de partibus remotis scilicet de holdernes et exsexia
De terris in holdernes iij li xij d
De Johanne Stannys xviij s iiij d
De Thoma Terell' xx s
Summa iiij li xix s iiij d

Summa omnium allocatorum xxxij li xviij s xj d

[1]De Magistro Camerlan pro scola iiij d
De Rosmay pro scola viij d

[*Dorse*]

Solut' et expense facte per eundem Robertum tam infra Collegium quem extra Anno rr' xxiij°

Reparac' aularum
In primis pro reparacionibus factis apud Braynnos vj s ix d ob
Item pro reparacionibus factis in aula parva universitatis in vico scolarum v s
Item pro reparacionibus factis apud Hampton' Hall' xxj s ij d
Item pro reparacionibus factis apud aulam sancti Edwardi vj s ij d ob
Item pro reparacionibus factis apud aulam Drowda ij s vij d[2]
Item pro reparacionibus factis in parva aula universitatis in alto vico iuxta collegium xxix s iiij d
Summa iij li xj s j d

Resolucionis facte eodem anno
In primis abbati de Osney pro anno xxiij° xxij s x d
Item Priori sancte ffrydeswide in plenam solucionem anni xxij xij s
Item eidem Priori in partem solucionis anni xxiij vj s viij d
Item Abbatisse de Godstow v s

[1] [ADMC] These entries have been added on as if previously omitted in error.
[2] [ADMC] The MS reads 'vijj d' – clearly intended to be altered to 'vij d'.

Item procuratoris ecclesie beate Marie pro ten' Roberti almbert xij d

Summa xlvij s vj d

Solut' et expense facte pro reparacionibus ten' laycorum

Item primis pro reparacionibus factis in domo Willelmi Stokys iij li iij s viij d

Item pro reparacionibus factis in domo Weskew et vasis pandoxatorijs xxij s viij d ob

Item pro factura pavimenti apud quadrivium et alijs reparacionibus factis circa ten' super anglum quadrivij xj s xj d

Item pro reparacionibus factis in ten' in quo moratur jacobus teutonicus quondem tenure N Schyrborn' xvj d

Item pro reparacionibus factis in domo Johannis Wilyam xvij d

Item pro reparacionibus factis in domo Henrici Bayth' iij s ix d

Item pro reparacionibus factis apud exsexiam xxxij s xj d

Summa vj l xvij s viij d ob

Solut' et expense facte infra collegium

In primis pro capella vj s v d ob

Item pro fabricacione gradus librarie xiij s ob

Item pro bretyssyng' circa aulam et fixione eiusdem iij s vij d

Item pro m[. . .]cione vasorum in promptuario v s j d

Item pro emptis ad coquinam ij s x d

Item pro stauro et reparacionibus factis infra collegium et mundifficacione de lysport infra collegium xvj s viij s ob

Item pro Esyng' burde iij s viij d

Summa xlxj [*sic*] s iiij d ob

Solut' socijs eodem anno

In primis Magistro Collegij pro pensione sacerdotali xxvj s viij d

Item pro die sancti Cuthberti vj s viij d

Item Magistro Willelmo scharpe pro eodem die vj s viij d

Item Magistro Willelmo Castell' pro pensione sacerdotali xx s

Item eidem Magistro pro die sancti Cuthberti vj s viij d

Item Magistro Gilberto Haydoke pro eodem die vj s viij d

Item Magistro Willelmo Dalton' pro eodem die iij s iiij d

Item Thome Pray pro eodem die vj s viij d

Item Roberto Hertilpole pro eodem die vj s viij d

Item eidem Roberto pro officio procuratoris x s

Summa v li

Solut' servientibus per totum annum

In primis Johannie Telm pro uno termino	v s
Item Thome Walker pincerne pro tribus terminis	xv s
Item Thome Clerke coco pro 3[bus] terminis	v s
Item Johanni Newbright coco pro uno termino	xx d
Item Petro Barbitonsori pro toto anno	vj s viij d
Item lotrici pro toto anno	vj s viij d
Summa xl s	

Expense facte versus exsexiam et london'

In primis per Magistrum Collegij versus exsexiam	xlj s iiij d
Item per Magistrum W Scharpe pro ratificacione ecclesie paroch' de Arnecliffe	xxvj s viij d
Item in equitacione Magistri Collegij et magistri Willelmi Scharpe versus london' et silvam	ij s vij d
Summa iij li x s vij d	

Solut' et expense facte pro communis sociorum et batellis operariorum a fest pasche inclusive anno rr' henrici sexti xxij° usque ad festum pentecost' anno eiusdem rr' xxiij°

In primis pro communis sociorum	xviij li x s xj d ob q[a]
Item pro batellis operariorum jornellis et contribucionibus per idem tempus	iij li vj d ~~ob q~~[a]
Item in die sancti Cuthberti	vj s ij d
Summa xxj li xvij s viij d[3]	

Solut' pro alijs expensis

In primis pro expensis Magistri Willelmi Kyrkby et aliorum extraneorum	xxij s
Item pro renovacione caucionum	v s
Item pro placitis	xx d
Item in resolutis tenentibus	xxj d ob
Item pro ficubus et alloc' et cariagio tempore quadragesimali	xiij s j d
Item in funere Hugonis Benette pro oblacionibus	ij d
Item in allocatis pro cervisia Hugoni Benette	xvj d
Item in pecunijs dimissis tenentibus	xviij s
Item in allocatis de pecunijs et pecunijs lucie Telm	iiij d
Item pro una clavi ad scolam Magistri Willelmi ffree	ij d

[3] [ADMC] The correct total is £21 17s 7d.

Item Thome Pray procuratori xvj d

Summa iij li iiij s xj d ob

Summa omnium expensarum lj li x d ob

Summa omnium allocatorum et expensarum precedencium lxxxiij li xix s ix d ob

[*A very clear and well-preserved roll of 2 membranes stuck together (not stitched). With the exception of a farthing in the last section but one, all totals etc. are correct. The roll is not signed by the Chancellor, and consequently no balance is given; in fact there is a deficit of ½d.*]

WHITSUN 23 HENRY VI to WHITSUN 24 HENRY VI (ROLL UC:BU1/F/58)
16 May 1445–5 June 1446

BURSAR: THOMAS PRAY

Compotus Thome Pray [Procuratoris Collegij seu Magne Aule universitatis oxon' datus per eundem Thomam Pray de omnibus redditibus et proventibus dicte Aule sue Collegij receptis] a festo Pentecost' [inclusive anno Regni Regis Henrici Sexti xxiij° ad idem festum exclusive Anno] eiusdem Regis xxiiij°[1].

[*The Arrears section of this roll is heavily damaged on the right hand side, so that no figures can be read against individual items, and parts of the text are illegible. Totals of four sections can be read in whole or in part. The figures clearly agree throughout with the Allowances of* **F/57**, *and there are a few very minor differences in the text*]

Summa omn' arr' xxxij li xviij s xj d[2]

Redditus tenencium in parochia ~~omnium~~ sanctorum petri in balliolo et m[*artini* . . .

De ten' quod Willelmus Hans tenet in [*Swynstwychun*][3]

De ten' quod tenet [*blank*]

Summa [. . .

Redditus ten' laicorum in parochia omnium sanctorum anno rr' Henrici sexti [*xxiiij°*]

De ten' quod tenet Thomas Dudley

De ten' quod tenet spendyng et pro solario

De ten' quod tenet hug' benet pro tribus terminis

De ten' quod tenet Willelmus furbyour pro uno termino

[1] [ADMC] This roll has been heavily damaged down the right hand side of the roll, both face and dorse. Not a single figure or total is completely legible, and the later part of the text of many entries is also lost. Some material can be recovered from Smith, Vol. VIII pp. 155–157, and this is given in square brackets. With the exception of the words not bracketed, the heading is reconstructed from Smith Vol. VIII p. 155: 'Compotus Tho Pray procur +c ut in preced' Rotulo a fest Pent a° rr H 7 23° ad etc. 24°'.

[2] [ADMC] The sums at the end of the Allowances in **F/57**, of 4d and 8d, do not appear to be included in the list of Arrears. This total in **F/57** included this extra shilling.

[3] No figures are legible in this section. Some sums given in Smith (Vol. VIII pp. 155–156) are given in square brackets. The rest has been deduced from **F/57** and **F/59**.

De ten' quod tenet Johannes William glover
De ten' quod tenet Willelmus stokys
De ten' quod tenet Westkew
De ten' quod tenet Johannes frane pro tribus terminis
De ten' quod tenet iacobus
[*Summa* . . .

[*Redditus*] in parochia beate marie et sancti petri in oriente [. . .
De ten' quod tenet Robertus lambert
De ten' quod tenet Henricus Bath'
De Johanne Kuke carpent' pro ij terminis
De ten' quod tenet Ricardus carpent' pro iij terminis
De eodem pro ten' in quo Johannes Kuke habitavit pro uno termino
Summa [. . .

Redditus in suburbijs et campis oxon' anno supradicto
De gardino iuxta castrum quod tenet qw[*ytfelde*]
De terris in bello monte et campis et [*Walton quas tenet Thomas Spryg'*]
De eodem pro pratis retro osnay [xx s]
De priore fratrum predicatorum pro pratis [*scilicet Alrychsett*] [xviij s iiij d]
De gardino ex parte orientali ecclesie [*sancti Egidij quod tenet Johannes Mason*]
De gyllote pro prato vocato ireland
Summa [. . .

Redditus aularum
De Brasynnose quam tenet magister Robertus Markham
De aula sancti Thome quam tenet idem magister
De gardino aule scuti quam tenet idem magister
De aula hampton' quam tenet magister Willelmus leylay
De eodem magistro pro ten' quond' tenure cham [*bedelli*]
De parva aula universitatis in vico scolarum [xxvj s viij d]
De aule edwardi
De aula drowda quam tenet Johannes [*pertrycche*]
Summa [. . .

Redditus [*camer*]arum infra collegium
De magistro Willelmo dowson [xvj s viij d]
De magistro Roberto Burton [xx s]

De magistro Roberto Tofte pro tribus terminis [x s]
De magistro Roberto langerst [xvj s viij d]
De magistro Johanne Crosby pro duobus terminis [v s]
De magistro Ricardo Newbrygge pro ij terminis [vj s viij d]
[Summa iij li xv s]

Redditus scolarum
De magistro Johanne sagefeld [vj s viij d]
De magistro Johanne Scherburn [vj s viij d]
De magistro Henrico Smyth [vj s viij d]
De magistro Roberto scharpe [vj s viij d]
De domino Johanne ston' determinatore [iiij s]
De domino Henrico ffych' [iij s viij d]
De domino Johanne Sparwell' [iij s viij d]
De domino Ricardo Calme [iij s viij d]
[Summa xlj s viij d]

Redditus de liberis tenementis in oxon' et suburbijs
De abbatissa de godstow pro parva schopa [exposita magne porte ffrydeswide] [xx d]
De eadem pro annuali redditu pro gardino ten' quond' [Thome Maystyre xiiij d]
De abbate de osnay pro schopa iuxta Johanne Spycer' [viij s vij d]
De ten' quond' Rogeri Skybbow modo collegij animarum [viij s]
De novo Collegio pro maydynhall' [x s]
De colleg' Cantuarens' pro sylverhall' [ij s vj d]
De colleg' linc' pro gardino [v s]
De magistro Johanne tryguram' pro defalcacione [prati retro osney] [ij s ij d]
De patyngton' pro defalcacione prati retro osney [ij s ij d]
De colleg' animarum pro ten' quond' Johannis Spront' [v s]
De eodem colleg' pro gardino retro dictum ten' [quondam dicti Johannis Spront'] [viij s x d ob]
De albis monachis pro gardino quod tenuit [Barton Corvysere] [iiij s]
Summa lvij s [ij d ob]

Redditus in exsexia et Holdyrnesse
De Johanne Stanys pro manerio de merx et molendinis

De domino Thoma Tyrell' pro libero ten' exeunte de Rammysden'
De terris in Holdyrnesse
Summa [*by deduction £22 4s 4d*]

Summa omn' Redd[*ituum by deduction £62 2s 6½d*]

Recept' preter sortem domus
De Roberto hertylpol
De Stephano pro focalibus
De principali de Brasynnose [iiij d]
De principali de Aula Hampton' [iiij d]
De luto [j d]
De cista communi [v li vj s viij d]
De pecunijs mutuatis Magistri Willelmi scharp' [de manibus magistri Burton'] [xiij s iiij d]
De mutuatis de cista Wyntonie [lviij s ix d]
De pecunijs datis a magistro Ricardo Wytton' [x s]
De [pecunijs] mutuatis de [Rectore de Newbery] [xiij s iiij d]
Summa [x li xj s ix d ob]

Summa omn' oneratorum cv li xiij s [iij d]

[*In the Allowances section, no figures for individual items and no totals can be read; parts of the text are also damaged, though nearly all of it can be read. With no significant differences, all entries appear to be exactly as the Arrears on* ***F/59*** *below. But the 'Summa Allocat' reddituum' as given by Smith Vol. VIII p.156 is 2s 6d more than the Arrears figure below. The list of Allowances continues on the dorse of this roll.*]

Summa Allocatorum reddituum [xxxvij li v s iij d ob]

Soluciones et expense facte per eundum Thomam tam infra collegium [*quam extra*]

Reparaciones aularum
In primis pro reparacionibus factis apud Brasynnose
Item pro reparacionibus factis in parva aula universitatis in vico scolarum
Item pro reparacionibus factis apud hampton' hall'
Item pro reparacionibus factis in aula sancti edwardi
Item pro reparacionibus [*factis in aula drowda*][4]

[4] [ADMC] Reading not quite certain.

Item pro reparacionibus factis in aula universitatis [*in alto vico*] [x li vj s xj d ob]

[Summa tot' xvj[5] li xvj s viij d]

Soluciones et expense facte pro reparacionibus ten' laicorum

In primis pro reparacionibus factis in domo Willelmi stokys

Item pro reparacionibus factis in domo Henrici Bath'

Item pro reparacionibus [*factis in domo Hans*][6]

Item pro reparacionibus factis in domo Richardi Car[*penter*]

Item pro reparacionibus factis in domo Johannis [. . .

Item pro reparacionibus factis in domo dudley

Item pro reparacionibus factis apud exsexia'

Item pro reparacionibus factis apud Holdyrnesse [. . .

Summa [l s j d]

Soluciones et expense facte infra collegium

In primis pro capella	[vj s vj d ob]
Item pro reparacionibus capelle	[xviij s vij d]
Item pro novis cameris	[xxix s]
Item circa librarium	[vj s]
Item pro reparacionibus factis camere magistri Burton'	
Item pro necessarijs coquine	
Item pro mundificacione camerarum orti et sporti	[xiiij d]
Item pro burdys ad novas cameras	[xv s ij d]
Item circa ortum et instrumenta eiusdem	
Item circa murum de luto	
Item circa mundificacionem latrine	[xvj s]
Item pro necessarijs emptis promptuarie	
Item pro emendacione pavimenti aularum	
Item pro ligacione librorum	[vj s]
Item in vigilia sancti nicholai	[vj d]
Item Thome Walker pinc' pro sacell[. . .	
Item solutum [*per magistrum*] pro [*nova camera*]	[xiij s iiij d]

[Summa vij li xix d ob]

Resoluciones facte eodem anno

In primis abbati de osnay pro anno xxiiij°

Item priore sancte frideswyde in plenam solucionem anni xxiij

~~Item eidem priori in partem solucionem anni xxiiij~~

[5] [ADMC] This figure of Smith's could be 'xij li'.

[6] [ADMC] Reading not quite certain.

Item abbati [*sic*] de godstow
Item procuratoribus ecclesie beate marie pro ten' Roberti lambert
Item Johanni Bode in parochia sancti Thome [iij s iiij d]
[*Summa* . . .

[. . .]acione lignorum in silva
In primis [*blank*]
Item Henrico bath' pro lignis emptis ab eo
[*Summa* . . .

Solut' socijs anno xxiiij°[7]
In primis magistro Collegij pro pensione sacerdotali [xx s]
Item magister Willelmus Castell' recepit in partem solucionis [xx s]
Item magistro dalton' solutum est' [iij s iiij d]
Item Thome Pray procuratori pro officio [eius] [x s]
~~Item solutum~~ Magistro Willelmo scharpe [de pecunijs receptis de Lematon] [xxj s]
Item solutum magistro Willelmo ~~Castell~~ [scharpe de pecunijs recepits de Mytford] [xiiij s]
Item solutum magistro Willelmo [Castell de pecunijs recepits de Mytford] [viij s]
Item eidem magistro [de pecunijs receptis de domini Johanne Stone determinatore] [iiij s]
~~Item solutum est magistro~~
[Summa iij li xx s]

[*Solut' servient*]ibus per totum annum
In primis Stephano Brown' pro ij terminis
Item Ricardi collyng pincerne pro ij terminis
Item Johanne Kuke pro iij terminis
Item Thome Kuke pro uno termino
Item petri barbitonsori pro toto anno
Item lotrici pro toto anno
[*Summa* . . .

Expense facte versus london' exsexiam et exciter
In primis magistro pro expensis versus exsexiam [. . .

[7] [ADMC] Smith (Vol. VIII p. 157) noted of this section 'Some of the summes seem added after ye totall summe was set downe'. In the original, only the first four entries are easily legible.

~~Item magistro~~ Willelmo scharpe pro expensis [circa appropriacionem Ecclesie de Arnclyffe] [xxx s]
Item magistro de pecunijs receptis de trig[*uram*]
Item Willelmo Kuke pro equis
Item Magistro Willelmo scharpe scilicet [. . .]
Item Magistro scharpe pro cirotecis [v s viij d]
Item pro equis [vj d]
Item pro casio london'
Item Magistro Willelmo versus exciter [xiij s iiij d]
Item Magistro pro expensis abindon' [iiij d]
[Summa iiij li ij s viij d]

Soluc' et expense pro communis et batellis operariorum a festo pentec' inclusive anno [. . .
In primis pro communis [xj li vij s vj d]
Item pro batellis [xxxiij s iiij d ob]
Item pro contribucionibus [pro tribus terminis ix s ix d]
Item in die sancti cuthberti [xvij s viij d ob]
[Summa xiij li viij s viij d ob[8]]

[*Solut' pro*] alijs expensis
In primis pro necessarijs emptis domui
Item pro placitis [xxxviij s ij d]
Item pro resolutus tenentibus
Item pro oblacionibus
Item pro pergameo scriptura et adducione librorum
Item pro decimis regalibus [xvj d]
+Item Magistro Willelmo scharpe de pecunijs receptis[9]
+Item eidem magistro de pecunijs receptis de magistro
+Item magistro Wyllelmo Castell'
+Item eidem magistro de pecunijs receptis [. . .
Item priori fratrum predicatorum pro Wyll[ons et dykyng] [ij s vj d]
[Summa liij s iiij d]

[*Solut' pro*] reparacionibus in exsexia pre magistrum Collegij
In primis pro factura unius ~~horrei~~ horrij [x li]

8 [ADMC] The correct total is £14 8s 4d.
9 [ADMC] On the roll Smith has noted, roughly, against the items marked with a cross 'Vide total de solut' sociorum supra'. May this possibly account for the error in that total?

Item pro reparacionibus pro molendin[o ventritico][10] [lviij s]
Item pro deliberatis firmario nostro scil[icet Willelmo pond ad emendos equos] [xiij s iiij d]
Item pro reparacionibus apud Holdyrnesse
[*Summa* . . .

Soluc' facte pro equitacione ~~facta versus~~ Magistri Willelmi Scharpe versus [*Novum Castrum*]
In primis pro prandio sui et servi eius et [populo [*sic*] equorum xix s iij d]
Item pro conductione equorum [xj s]
Item pro cirotecis et famulo [et circa vicarium de paul' v s v d]
Item pro equitacionibus versus exciter de p[ecunijs Lamaton xxj s]
[Summa lvj s viij d]

Summa omnium Solut' et expens' [lxix li ix s vj s ob]

Summa omn' allocatorum et expensarum pre[teritarum cvj li xiiij s x d]

⟨Computatis computandis et allocatis allocandis collegium [nihil debet computanti]⟩

⟨Acta sunt hec per M W Dow[son Doctorem sacre Theologie ac commissarium in hoc computo] venerabilis viri Magistri Roberti [Thwaytys Cancellarij universitatis oxon']⟩

[*A neatly written roll; 2 membranes. Heavily damaged down the right hand side of the roll, both face and dorse. Not a single figure or total is completely legible, and the later part of the text of many entries is also lost. Although the Credit side of the roll totals £105 13s 3d ,and the Debt side £106 14s 10d, they are said, in the penultimate entry, to balance exactly. Smith (Vol. VIII p.158) also notes this discrepancy.*]

[10] [ADMC] Smith actually reads 'pro reparat molendini ventritici'; this must be a condensed version.

WHITSUN 24 HENRY VI to WHITSUN 25 HENRY VI (ROLL UC:BU1/F/59)

5 June 1446–28 May 1447

BURSAR: GILBERT HAYDOCK

[1][Compotus Magistri Gi]lberti Haydok datus per [Ricard]um collyng [datus per collectorem pe]cuniarum collegij Magistri Willelm de dunelmia [quod vulgariter nuncupatur] Magna aula universitatis oxon' de omnibus redditibus et [proventibus] dicte aule [seu coll]egij receptis et expensis a festo [pentecostes anno] rr' Henrici Sexti xxiiij° ad idem fest' pent' [exclusive] anno eiusdem regis xxv°

[*Arr' Aularum*]

[*De Magistro*] Johanne Barnard pro anno ~~xii~~ terciodecimo — ix s viij d
De Magistro Thoma Cowper pro anno duodecimo — vj s viij d
De magistro Galbuch' pro parva aula universitatis in vico scolarum — vj s viij d
De magistro Willelmo leylay pro anno vicesimo quarto — xxxv s
[*De Couper pro Aula Drowda pro annis*] decimo nono vicesimo et vicesimo primo — xlix s
De Johanne pertrych' pro anno vicesimo quarto — xviij s iiij d
[*De Magistro Roberto Merkham pro aule de*] Brasnose — xxij s ij d ob q[a]
[*De eodem pro Aula sancti Thome*] — [*iij*] s iiij d
[*De eodem pro gardino aule scuti*] — ij s ij d ob q[a]
[*De parva aula universitatis*] in vico scolarum — ix s ij d
[*De Aula Edwardi pro anno vicesimo quarto*] de magistro gramaticali Russelle — v s

Summa viij li vij s iiij d ob

Arr' camerarum

De Magistro Willelmo ~~Dwson~~ Dowson pro annis xx° ~~primo~~ xxj° et xxij° — xl s iiij d
De eodem pro anno vicesimo tercio — vj s viij d
De eodem pro anno vicesimo quarto — vij s viij d
De camera magistri Chadworth — xx d

[1] [ADMC] The heading of the roll is much damaged. Bracketed words are from Smith Vol. VIII p.158, who underlines the words 'per Ricardum collyng datus per collectorem'.

De camera magistri Toffte pro anno vicesimo quarto	ij s vj d
De camera magistri Burton' pro eodem anno	v s
De camera magistri Ricardi Newbryge pro duobus terminis	vj s viij d
De camera magistri [*Roberti lang*]rych'[2]	iij s iiij d
Summa iij li xiij s x d	

Arr' scolarum

De magistro Willelmo Keele pro anno vic[*esimo*]	xx d
De scola magistri Lorde [*eodem anno*]	vj s viij d
De scola magistri swan' pro anno vicesimo tercio	vj s viij d
De scola magistri Willelmi Dawlton	iij s viij d
De scola magistri Johannis Scherburn'	vj s viij d
De scola magistri Henrici smyth'	vj s viij d
De scola magistri Roberti Sharpe	vj s viij d
Summa xlv s	

Arr' in parochia omnium sanctorum

De executoribus ysabelle Colet pro annis xij^{o} et x^{o}iij^{o}	xxxviij s iiij d
De Johanne Barber pro stanton' hall'	xiij s iiij d
De Johanne Wilyam pro anno x^{o}vij^{o}	x s
De [*eodem pro*] anno vicesimo secundo	xv s
De Johanne ffrayn' pro anno vicesimo quarto	ij s vj d
De Willelmo Stokys pro anno vicesimo secundo	vij s iiij d
De Spendyng' pro solario pro annis xx^{o}iij^{o} et xx^{o}iiij^{o}	vj s viij d
De Hugone Benette	xxvij s vj d
De Westkow pro anno vicesimo tercio	xlvj s viij d
De eodem pro anno vicesimo quarto	xxvij s ix d
De bradbyr'	iij s vj d
Summa ix li xviij s iij d[3]	

Arr' [*in paroch' beate marie et sancti petri in oriente*]

De uxore lambert'[4] pro annis xxiij^{o} et xxiiij^{o}	xxvij s
De Henrico bath' pro anno xxij^{o}	xx s
De eodem pro anno xxiij^{o}	viij s ij d
De eodem pro anno xxiiij^{o}	xxij s iiij d

[2] [ADMC] Supplied from the Allowances in **F/58**.

[3] [ADMC] The correct total is £9 18s 6d.

[4] Agnes Lambert, Widow of Robert, and John Morley of Oxford, Barber, were leased a house once known as Stanton Hall on 23 May 1446 (**UC:E/A5/D/3**).

De Thoma Sprag pro annis xxij° et xxiij°	ix s
De Johanne Swayns pro anno xxij°	ij s j d ob
De Johanne Kuke carpentario	xiij s x d
De Nicholao Smyth	ij s viij d
De Ricardo carpentario pro uno termino	iiij s ij d
Summa v li ix s iij d ob	

Arr' in suburbijs et campis oxonie

De [*Thoma*] mancipio pro alrych'sell [*sic*]	ij s
De queytfelde precone maioris	iiij s iiij d
De pedyngton' pro annis xxiij° et xxiiij	iiij s iiij d
De Thoma Spryg pro eisdem annis	vj s iiij d
De Hans	v d
De Johanne mason' pro gardino ex parte orientali ecclesie sancti egidij	xij d
De gyllotte pro yrlande pro annis xxiij° et xxiiij°	v s
Summa xxiij s v d	

Arr' de liberis tenentibus

De S[kybbow[5]]	iiij s
De Collegio animarum pro ten' quondam Johannis spronte in parochia sancti petri in balliolo	v s
De eodem Collegio pro gardino retro dictum ten'	viij s x d ob
De eodem Collegio animarum pro dicto ten' quondam Johannis spronte	v s
De eodem Collegio pro gardino eiusdem	viij s x d ob
De eodem Collegio animarum pro dicto ten' quondam Johannis spronte	v s
De eodem pro gardino retro dictum tenementum	viij s x s ob
De abbatissa de godstow pro parva shopa exposita magne porte ffrideswyde	xx d
De eadem pro annuali redditu pro gardino quondam ten' Thome maystyr'	xiiij d
De abbate de osnay pro schop iuxta Johannem spycer	vj s viij d
De [*Collegio linc'*] pro gardino anno xxiiij°	ij s vj d
Summa lv s j d ob[6]	

[5] [ADMC] This is Smith's reading (Vol. VIII p.158). But it looks more like 'Talyor', and cf. the entry in the Allowances below.

[6] [ADMC] The correct total is 57s 7½d.

Arr' in partibus remotis viz de Holdyrnesse et exsexia
De terris in Holdernesse iij li x s vj d
De Johanne Stanys [*blank*]
De domino Thoma tyrell' [*blank*]
Summa iij li x s vj d

Summa omnium Arr' xxxvij li ij s ix d ob

[*Redditus ten' in paroch' sanctorum Petri et Mart*]ini anno rr' Henrici sexti xxiiij° [*sic*]
[*De ten' quod*] Willelmus hans tenet in Swynstwychen vij s
[*De ten' quod tenet go*]sse super angulum quadrivij xxvj s viij d
Summa xxxiij s viij d

Redditus ten' laicorum in parochia omnium sanctorum anno rr' Henrici sexti supradicto
De ten' quod tenet Thomas Dudlay xxxiij s iiij d
De ten' quod tenet spendyng' et pro solario xxxiij s iiij d
De ten' quod tenet hugo benet pro tribus terminis [*blank*]
De ten' quod tenet Willelmus ffurbyour' xvj s viij d
De ten' quod tenet Johannes William glover pro uno termino v s x d
De eodem ten' quod tenet Thomas Hosyer pro uno termino v s x d
De ten' quod tenet Willelmus Stokys xlvj s viij d
De ten' quod tenet Westkew pro duobus terminis xxvj s viij d
De eodem ten' quod tenet Willelmus dagwyll' pro duobus terminis xxvj s viij d
De ten' quod tenet Willelmus [*Calizor*] xvj s viij d
Summa x li xx d

Redditus in parochia beate marie et sancti petri in oriente
De ten' quod tenet Johannes Morland pro tribus terminis xiij s vj d
De ten' quod tenet Henricus Bathe xl s
De ten' quod tenet Ricardus Carpent' pro duobus terminis viij s
De eodem ten' quod tenet Westkew pro 2°bus terminis viij s
De ten' quod tenet Johannes Sclatter pro uno termino iij s
De eodem ten' quod tenet Johannes Sadeler' pro uno termino iij s

De eodem ten' quod tenet Ricardus Mancipil pro 2°bus terminis vj s

Summa iiij li xviij d

Redditus in suburbijs et campis oxon' anno predicto

De gardino iuxta Castrum quod tenet qwitfeld ij s

De terris in bellomonte et Campis de Walton quas tenet Thomas Spryg' vij s

De eodem pro pratis retro Osnay xviij s

De priore fratrum predicatorum pro pratis scilicet Alrychset xviij s iiij d

De gardino ex parte orientali ecclesie sancti egidij quod tenet Johannes Mason vj d

De Gillotte pro prato vocato Ireland [*blank*]

Summa xlv s x d

Redditus aularum [. . .

[*De Brasynnos*] quem tenet Magister Robertus Markham iij li vj s viij d

De Aule sancte [*sic*] Thome quam tenet idem magister x s

De gardino aule scuti quod tenet idem magister vj s viij d

De Aula Hampton quam tenet magister Willelmus Leylay l s

De eodem Magistro pro ten' quondam tenure Caym bedelli xx s

De parva aula universitatis in vico scolarum xxvj s viij d

De aula edwardi xx s

De aula Drowda quam tenet Johannes Partriche xxvj s viij d

Summa xj li vj s viij d

Redditus camerarum infra Collegium

De Magistro Willelmo Dowson xvj s viij d

De Magistro Roberto Borton xx s

De lodowico pro uno termino iiij s

De Nicholao qwite pro uno termino iiij s

De Thoma Chaundre pro 2°bus terminis vj s viij d

De domino Willelmo Danyel pro uno termino iiij s

[*De Magistro Johanne Crosby*] ~~pro tribus terminis~~ x s

[*De Magistro Roberto Langrysch*] xiij s iiij d

[*De Magistro Ricardo Mewbr*]yghe pro 2°bus terminis vj s viij d

Summa iiij li v s iiij d

Redditus scolarum

De Magistro Petto vj s viij d

De Magistro Stephano tilar ~~iij s iiij d~~ vj s viij d

De Magistro Roberto Hartilpole pro 2°bus terminis ~~vj s viij d~~ iij s iiij d

De Magistro Thoma pray pro 2°bus terminis ~~vj s viij d~~ iij s iiij d

De domino Thoma Balm determinatore iij s iiij d

De Johanne Chamnur determinatore iij s iiij d

De Stephano Brown iij s viij d

De person iij s viij d

Summa xxxiiij s iiij d

Redditus de liberis ten' in oxon' et suburbijs

De abbatissa de godstoe pro parva shopa ex opposito porte fridiswide xx d

De eadem pro annuali redditu pro gardino ten' quondam Thome Mayster xiiij d

De abbate de osnay pro schopa iuxta Johannem spiser vj s viij d

De ten' quondam Rogeri Skybbow modo collegij animarum viij s

De novo collegio pro Maydinhall' x s

De collegio cantuariensi pro silverhal ij s vj d

De collegio linc' pro gardino v s

De Magistro Johanne Triguryan pro defalcacione prati retro osnay ij s ij d

De petinton pro defalcacione prati retro osnay ij s ij d

De collegio animarum pro ten' quondam Johannis Spronte in parochia sancti petri in balliolo v s

De eodem collegio pro gardino retro dictum ten' quondam Johannis spronte viij s x d ob

De Albus monachis pro gardino quod tenuit Barton Cornisar in parochia Sancte Marie Magdalene iiij s

Summa lvjj [*sic*] s ij d ob

Redditus in Exsexia et Holdernesse

De Willelmo Pede [. . .] pro manerio de markys et molendinis xviij li iij s iiij d

De domino Thome Tyrel pro libero ten' exeunte de Ramisdangray xx s

De terris in Holdernes	iij li xij d
Summa xxij li iiij s iiij d	

Summa omnium reddituum lx li x s vj d ob

Recepta preter sortem domus

De Magistro [*to*]bilfeld pro focalibus	iiij d
De Ricardo Collyng	xij s ix d
[*De Margareta*] bathe	xij d
De Thoma Hawll'	ij d
De Magistro Willelmo Scharpe	iiij li
De Magistro Johanne Marton	iij li ij s iiij d
De eodem ex domo magistri Johannis Castell'	xl s
De Magistro Johanne Goldsmyth	liij s iiij d
[*De Magistro Hadok*]	xxxv s ix d
[. . .] onerat	[*blank*]
Summa xiiij li v s viij d	

Summa omnium oneratorum cxj li xix s[7]

Allocaciones aularum

De Magistro Johanne Barnard pro anno xiij°	ix s viij d
De Magistro Thoma Cowper pro anno xij°	vj s viij d
[*De Magistro Calbuch*] pro aula universitatis in vico scolarum	vj s viij d
[*De Magistro Willelmo leylay*] pro annis xx°iiij° et xx°v°	iij li xvij s vj d
De Cowper pro aula druda pro annis xviiij° [*sic*] xx° et xxj°	xlix s j d
De Johanne partriche pro annis xxiiij° et xxv°	xxj s viij d
De Magistro Roberto Marham pro aula brasinnos	xxij s ij d ob q^a
De eodem pro aula sancte [*sic*] Thome	iij s iiij d
De eodem pro gardino aule scutei	ij s ij d ob q^a
[*De parva aula univ*]ersitatis in vico scolarum	ix s ij d
[*De Aula Edwardi*] pro anno xxiiij° de magistro grammaticali Russel	v s
Summa x li xiij s ij d ob	

7 [ADMC] The shilling figure has been altered, and a pence figure apparently deleted.

Allocaciones camerarum

De Magistro Willelmmo Dowson pro annis xxj° et xxj° et xxij°	xl s iiij d
[*De eodem*] pro anno xxiij°	vj s viij d
[*De eodem pro anno*] xxiiij°	vij s viij d
[*De eodem pro anno*] xxv°	ix s viij d
De Camera Magistri Chadworth	xx d
De Camera Magistri Tofte pro anno xxiiij°	ij s vj d
De Camera Magistri Burton pro annis xxiiij° et xxv°	xxv s
De Camera Magistri Ricardi Newbriche	xiij s iiij d
[*De Magistro*] Johanne Crosby	v s
Summa v li xj s x d	

Allocaciones scolarum

De Magistro Willelmo Kell pro anno xx°	xx d
De scola Magistri Lord pro eodem anno	vj s viij d
De scola Magistri Swan pro anno xxiij°	vj s viij d
[*De*] scola Magistri Willelmi Dawton	iij s iiij d
[. . .]	vj s viij d
[*De scola*] Magistri stephani tilar	vj s viij d
De scola Magistri Roberti Hertilpole	iij s iiij d
De scola Magistri Thome pray	iij s viij d
De stephano brown	iij s viij d
[. . .]	iij s viij d
Summa xlv s viij d	

[*Dorse*]

Allocaciones in parochia omnium sanctorum

De Willelmo Dagwill'	vj s viij d
De executoribus Isabelle Collete pro annis xij° et xiij°	xxxviij s iiij d
De Johanne Barbur pro staynton hall'	xiij s iiij d
De Johanne Willyam pro anni xvij°	x s
De eodem pro anno xxij°	xv s
De [*Willelmo*] S[*tok*]ys pro anno xxij°	vij s iiij d
De eodem pro annio xxv°	xx d
De spendung pro solario pro annis xxiij° xxiiij° et xxv°	x s
De Hugone Benet	xxvij s vj d
De Westkow pro anni xxiij°	xlvj s viij d
[*De eodem pro anno*] xx°iiij	xxvij s x d

[*De eodem pro anno*] xxv°	xj s iiij d
De Bradmyr	iij s vj d
De Willelmo talyor	iiij s ij d
De Willelmo forbur	iij s iiij d
Summa xj li vj s vij d[8]	

Allocaciones [*in paroch' beate Marie*] et sancti petri in oriente

[*De uxore lambert*] pro annis xxiij° et xxiiij°	iiij s viij d
[*An illegible entry, deleted*]	~~iiij s vj d~~
De Johanne Morland pro anno xxv°	ix s
De Henrico Bathe pro anno xxij°	xx s
De eodem pro anno xxiij°	viij s ij d
De eodem pro anno xxiiij°	xxij s iiij d
[*De eodem pro anno*] xxv°	xiv s vij d
[*De Thoma Sprag'*] pro annis xxij° et xxiij°	ix s
De Johanne Swayns pro anno xxij°	ij s j d ob
De Johanne Coke carpentario	xiij s x d
De Nicholao Smith	[*blank*]
De Ricardo Carpentir pro uno termino	iiij s ij d
[*De eodem pro*] anno xxv°	viij s ~~iiij d~~
Summa v li xv s x d ob	

Allocaciones in suburbijs et campis oxon'

De Thoma Mancipil pro alrychset	ij s
De Qwitfeld precone maioris	iiij s iiij d
De Petinton pro annis xxiij° et xxiijj° [*sic*]	iiij s iiij d
[*An illegible entry, deleted*]	~~ij s ij d~~
[*An illegible entry*]	[*blank*]
De Hans	v d
De Johanne Mason pro gardino ex parte orientali ecclesie sancti egidij	vj d
De Gillote pro irland pro annis xxiijj° et xxiiij°	v s
De [*eodem*] pro anno xxv°	[*an entry erased here*]
De Magistro Johanne Triguravn pro defalcacione prati retro osnay	ij s ij d
Summa xviij s ix d	

Allocaciones de liberis [*tenentibus*]

De S[*kybbow?*]	iiij s

[8] [ADMC] The correct total is £11 7s 8d.

De Collegio animarum ~~quo~~ pro ten' quondam Johannis spront in parochia sancti patri in baliolo v s
De eodem collegio pro gardino retro dictum ten' viij s x d ob
De eodem collegio pro dicto ten' quondam Johannis Spront v s
De eodem collegio pro gardino eiusdem viij s x d ob
De eodem collegio pro dicto ten' quondam Johannis Spront v s
[*De eodem pro gardino*] retro dictum ten' viij s x d ob
[*De eodem pro dicto*] ten' quondam Johannis Spront v s
[*De eodem*] pro gardino retro dictum ten' viij s x d ob
De abbatissa de godestow pro parva schopa exopposita magne parte fridiswide pro annis xxiiij^{o} et xxv^{o} xx d
De eadem pro annuali redditu pro gardino quondam ten' Thome Mayster xiij d
De abbate de osnay pro schopa iuxta Johannem Spiser vj s viij d
De collegio linc' pro gardino anno xxiiij^{o} [*an entry erased*]
De Albis monachis ij s
Summa iij li xj s

Allocaciones [*de partibus remotis viz de*] exsexia et Holdirnesse
De terris in Holdirness iiij li iiij s x d
De Willelmo Ponde xviij s iiij d
Summa iiij li xiiij s x d

Summa omnium Allocatorum xliiij li xvij s ix d

Soluciones et ex[*pense facte per Ricardum*] Collyng' tam infra collegium quam extra anno supradicto
[*Repar' in parva Aula*] universitatis in alto vico xiij li xiij s x d q^{a}
[*Item*] apud [*Brassennose*] xviij s iiij d
[*Item*] pro aul drud' et edwardi xxj d
Summa xiiij li xiij s xj d q^{a}

Reparaciones infra collegium
In primis pro capella xij d
Item pro ceris emptis et novas cameras et factura unius [. . .]tarij xj s iiij d
Summa xij s iiij d

Reparacionis facte in ten' [*laicorum per eundem*] Ricardum
In primis [. . .]el xlj s j d ob
Item pro [*tenemento*] stokis vij s ix d

Item pro ten' Hance gos dudlay Benet Hosear et aliorum tenencium xiij s j d ob
Summa iij li ij s

Soluta pro cariagio lignorum de a beklay et schottower et sarracione eorundem et alijs expensis circa eadem
In primis danieli et eius fratri pro bigacione x s
Item pro quatuor serratoribus vj s vjj d [*sic*]
[*Item pro* . . .]ibis xvj d ob
[*Item* . . .] in solvend' red [*sic*] viij s iij d ob
[*Item* . . .] x d
Summa xxvij s j d

Soluta pro equitacione versus exsexiam et episcopum exoniensem[9] xv s vij d ob
Item Soluta pro plastis[10] vj s xj d
Item pro abbate de sallay ij s vj d
Item pro diminutis expensis v s vij d
Summa xxx s ⟨vij d⟩ ob

Soluta servientibus
In primis Ricardo Collyng' pro officio suo xx s
Item [*Thome coco*] v s
Item [*lotrici*] v s
Summa xxx s

Soluta pro communis sociorum et batellis operariorum Jurnellis et contribucionibus
In primis pro communis sociorum x li xviij s ~~vij d~~ ⟨ij d⟩
Item in batellis xxxix s iij d q[a]
[*Item in*] contribucionibus vj s iij d
[*Item pro convivio sancti Cuth*]berti xij s vij d ob
Summa xiij li xvj s iij d ob q[a]

Resoluciones facte eodem anno per eundem Ricardum
In primis Abbati de osnay xiij s iiij d
Item priori sancte fridiswide xij s

9 [ADMC] The Episcopal Register of Edmund Lacy, Bishop of Exeter (and former Fellow of the College), shows that he was in Devonshire for the whole of 25 Hen VI, but on 12 Jul 1446 he was at 'Calyse prope Londo'; 14 July at Acton; 16 Jul at Oxford; 4 and 15–16 August at Gloucester.

10 [ADMC] Smith reads 'pastis', I think wrongly.

Item abbatisse de godstow v s
Item Johanni Wode iij s viij d
Summa xxxiiij s

Solute per eundum Ricardum Collyng'
Magistro Collegij et Magistro Willelmo Scharp xxxij s
Item pro tegulis emptis a fratre iij s x d
Item pro salario procuratoris x s
Summa xlv s x d

Soluta in dimissis tenentibus
Nicholao Smyth[11] xij d
[*Thome Sprig*] ij s
Item [*abbati*] de osnay vj s viij d
Item abbatisse de godstow ij s x d
Summa xij s vj d

Summa omnium expensarum Ricardi Collyng xlj li iiij s vij d ob

Expense deliberate per Magistrum Johannem Marton Magistrum collegij predicti
In primis Ricardo carpentario et Willelmo socio eius pro 2°bus septimanis xij s
Item priori sancte fridiswide ~~x~~ vj s viij d
Item pro pictura crucifixi et armorum johannis Wode et expensis cum iohanne low ij s ix d
Item [solut' pro placitis[12] apud London] post festum michael' contra executores Heugonis benet iiij li xj s
[Item pro materia Alicie Balisise et co]mitis northumbrie et ducis bukyngannie xxviij s x d ob
[*Item* . . .] de Margretrudyng' ij s ob
Item Magistro [*Johanne*] Crosby pro mutuatis ab ipso iij li vj s viij d
Item pro reparacionibus factis in exsexia iij s iiij d
Summa x li xiij s iiij d

Expense facte per eundum Magistrum a festo natal' usque ad festum pentecoste
In primis pro equitacione versus novum castrum et labore circa

[11] [ADMC] Apparently no 'In primis' was written here.
[12] Smith read 'pastis' here, but ADMC preferred 'placitis', I think rightly.

execucionem unius brevis vocati ad quod dampnum iiij li iiij s vij d
Item Magistro Willelmo Scharp ad redimendum cauciones impignoratas pro edificacione parve aule universitatis iij li
Item pro expensis eiusdem Magistri [*factis*] londonijs vj s x d
Item [*Ricardo*] Coll[*in*]g' [*pro communis*] sociorum xxxiij s iiij d
[*Item Rogero Cowper pro emendacione va*]sorum pandoxatorum x s viij d
[*Item Magistro Collegij pro caucionibus sibi impi*]gnoratis xlvj s viij d
Item [. . .] carpentarijs xvij s vj d
Item abbatisse de godstow x s
Item abbati de osnay vj s viij d
Item pro pabulo equi apud domum Mauricij barice ix d
Item Carnaby xij d
Item Thome sclatter viij d
Item pro clavis ij d
Item Sex laborarijs pro uno die ij s
Item apud beklay in domo Weston ij d
Item Magistro Willelmo Scharp in vigilia sancti cuthberti xx s
Item [*Thome Hawl in*] vigilia pentecostes iij s
Item [. . .] vj s viij d
Item [. . .] ad ly wyket xiiij d
Item [. . .] iiij d
Item Johanne Smyth pro factura de ly twyst xv d
Item pro clavis ad idem ostium iiij d

Summa xv li vj s ix d[13]

Summa omnium expensarum xxvj li j d

Solut' per Magistrum Gilbertum Hadok a festo Michaelis usque ad festum natalis v li viij s vj d ob

Summa omnium solutorum et expensarum lxxij li xiij s iij d

[*Summa omnium*] allocatorum solutorum et expensarum precendencium cxvij li xj s

⟨Computatis computandis et allocatis allocandis Collegium debet computanti v li xij s

[13] [ADMC] The correct sum is £15 12s 9d.

Acta sunt hec pro M W Dowson sacre theologie professorem ac commissarium in hoc computo venerabilis Magistri Magistri [*sic*] Gilberti Kymer' Cancellarij Universitiatis oxon⟩

[*A roll of 2 membranes, parts of which have become illegible since Smith.*]

[*The roll for 1447/1448 was missing even in Smith's day.*]

27 HENRY VI (ROLL UC:BU1/F/60)
c.12 May 1448–1 Jun 1449?[1]

BURSAR: ROBERT HERTILPOLL

Compotus M Roberti Hertilpoll' procuratoris Collegij sive Magne aule universitatis oxonie Anno rr' Henrici sexto vicesimo septimo

Arr' aularum

In primis de Johanne fflecchere pro aula drowda	xij s
Item de M Johanne Barnarde pro anno terciodecimo	ix s viij d
Item de M Thome Cowper pro anno duodecimo	vj s viij d
Item de M Calbuch' pro parva aula universitatis in vico scolarum	vj s viij d
Item de Cowper pro Aula drouda pro annis nonodecimo vicesimo et vicesimo primo	xlix s j d
Item de M Church pro Aula Brassynnos	xxij s ij d ob q[a]
Item de eodem pro aula sancti thome	iij s iiij d
Item de eodem pro gardino aule scuti	ij s ij d ob q[a]
Item de parva aula universitatis in vico scolarum	ix s ij d
Item de Aula Edwardi pro anno vicesimo quarto de Russell' magistro gramaticali	v s
Item de Church'	vj s viij d
Summa vj li xij s viij d ob	

Arr' camerarum

De Magistro Willelmo douson pro annis xx[mo] xxj et xxij[o]	xl s iiij d
De eodem pro anno vicesimo tercio	vj s viij d
De eodem pro anno vicesimo quarto	vij s viij d
De eodem pro anno vicesimo quinto	ix s viij d
De eodem pro anno vicesimo sexto	xj s viij d
De M Chadworth'	xx d
De Magistro Toft pro anno vicesimo quarto	ij s vj d
De M Burton pro annis vicesimo quarto et vicesimo quinto	xxv s

[1] The rolls from 1448–1472 are only dated by regnal year, whereas those before and after are usually dated to Pentecost. Since it is very probable that the 1448–1472 rolls also ended at the Pentecost of the regnal year given here, the dates of Pentecost are given throughout this period to provide a rough idea of the College's financial year.

De eodem pro anno vicesimo sexto	xx s
De Magistro Roberto fflemyng'	iiij s
De Magistro Willelmo Danyell'	xij s
De M Thome Elslake	iij s iiij d
De Nicholao qwytte	iiij s
Summa vij li xj s	

Arr' scolarum

De M Willelmo Keyll' pro anno vicesimo	xx d
De scola M lorde pro eodem anno	vj s viij d
De scola M Swan pro anno vicesimo tercio	vj s viij d
De scola M Willelmi dalton	iij s iiij d
De scola M petri	vj s viij d
De scola M hertilpoll'	iij s iiij d
De eodem pro anno vicesimo sexto	vj s viij d
De scola Magistri pray	iij s iiij d
De eodem pro anno vicesimo sexto	vj s viij d
De stephano Broun	iij s viij d
De duxfeld	iij s viij d
De Willelmo Wrangwych'	iij s viij d
Summa lvj s	

Arr' in paroch' omnium sanctorum

De Willelmo Dagvyll'	xxvj s viij d
De exsecutoribus ysabelle Colette pro annis duodecimo terciodecimo	xxxvij s iiij d
De Johanne Barbour pro staynton hall'	xiij s iiij d
De Johanne Wilyam pro anno xvij^{o}	x s
De eodem pro anno xxij^{o}	xv s
De Willelmo Stokys pro anno vicesimo secundo	vij s iiij d
De eodem pro anno xxv^{to}	xx d
De eodem pro anno vicesimo sexto	xxj s vj d
De spendyng pro solario pro annis vicesimo tercio quarto quinto et sexto	xiij s iiij d
De Hugone Benett	xxvij s vj d
De Westhew	vj s iiij d
De Bradmyre	iij s vj d
De Willelmo ffrubyour	x d
Summa ix li v s iiij d	

Arr' in paroch' sancte Marie et sancti petri in oriente

De Thoma preston	vij d
De henrico Bayth'	xxx s ix d
De Thoma Sprag' pro annis vicesimo secundo et tercio	ix s
De Johanne swanys pro anno vicesimo secundo	ij s j d ob
De Johanne Coke carpentario	xiij s x d
De Ric' carpentario	viij s ix d
Summa iij li v s ob	

Arr' in suburbijs et campis oxon'

De Thoma Maunsypyll' pro alryschette	ij s
De qwyttfeld precone maioris	iiij s iiij d
De pydyngton pro annis xxiij^{o} xxiiij^{o} et xxvj^{o}	vj s vij d
De Thoma spryg'	xj s viij d
De hans	v d
De eodem pro anno vicesimo sexto	iij s vj d
De Johanne Mason pro Gardino ex parte orientali ecclesie sancti egidij	xij d
De Gyllott pro yrlande pro annis xxiij^{o} et xxiiij^{o}	v s
De M Johanne Tryguram	iiij s iiij d
Summa xxxviij s ix d[2]	

Arr' de liberis tenementis

De schybbow	iiij s
De collegio animarum ~~pro tenemento quondam Johannis spront in parochia sancti petri in orienti balym~~[3] pro annis xxij^{o} xxiij^{o} xxiiij^{o} xxv^{o} et xxvj^{o}	xxv s
De eodem collegio pro gardino retro dictum tenementum pro annis xxij^{o} xxiij^{o} quarto quinto et sexto	xliij s iiij d ob
De abbatissa de godstow pro parva schoppa ~~ex opposito~~ pro annis xxiiij^{o} quinto et sexto	xx d
De eadem pro annuali redditu pro gardino quondam tenure Thome maister xiiij d	
De abbate de osnay pro schopa iuxta Johannem spyser	vj s viij d
De collegio lincoln' pro gardino pro anno xxvj^{to}	ij s vj d
De albis monachis	ij s
De collegio Cantuar'	ij s vj d

[2] [ADMC] The correct total is 38s 10d.
[3] [ADMC] Possibly not intended to be deleted.

De collegio animarum pro tenemento quondam skybbow pro anno xxvj^{to} viij s

Summa iiij li xvij s x d ob

Arr' de partibus remotis

De Willelmi pounde pro manerio nostro in exsex' xj s viij d

De terris in holdernes vj li iiij s x d

Summa vj li xvj s vj d

Summa omnium Arr' xliij li iij s ij d ob

Redditus ten' in parochia sanctorum petri in ball' et Martini anno rr' Henrici sexti [*blank*]

De tenemento quod Willelmus Hans tenet in swynshewtyn' vij s

De tenemento quod tenet gos teutonicus super anglum quadrivij xxvj s viij d

Summa xxxiij s viij d

Redditus tenementorum laycorum in parochia omnium sanctorum anno supradicto

De tenemento quod tenet Thomas Dudley xxxiij s iiij d

\+ De tenemento quod tenet spendyng'[4] et pro solario xxiij s iiij d

De tenemento quod tenuit Johannes Gower quod iam tenet Thomas xvj s viij d

De ten' quod tenet Thomas ffurd' xxiij s iiij d

De ten' quod tenet Willelmus stokys xlvj s viij d

De ten' quod tenet Willelmus Dagvyll' liij s iiij d

De ten' quod tenet Willelmus Talyour xvj s viij d

Summa x li xiij s iiij d

Redditus in parochia sancte Marie et sancti petri in oriente

De ten' quod tenet Johannes Morland xviij s

De ten' quod tenet Henricus bayth' xl s

De ten' quod tenet Johannes Cuke xvj s

De ten' quod tenet Ric' Carpenter xij s

Summa iiij li vj s

[4] On 15 June 1449, the westernmost of the three 'Gonwardby' houses on High Street (see pp. xxiv–xxvi of the Introduction) was leased to Richard Spendyng, Glover. However, Richard himself had been living there since 1440/1, and other members of his family before then.

Redditus in suburbijs et campis oxonie

De gardino iuxta castrum quod tenet qwytfeld ij s

De terris in bello monte et campis de Walton quas tenet Thomas spryg' vij s

De eodem pro pratis retro osnay xviij s

De priori fratrum predicatorum pro pratis scilicet allryschsette xviij s iiij d

De gardino ex parte orientali ecclesie sancti egidij quod t [*sic*] vj d

Summa xlv s x d

Redditus aularum

De Magistro Church' pro Brassynnqs iij li vj s viij d

De eodem pro aula sancti Thome x s

De gardino Aule scuti quod tenet item magister vj s viij d

De Aula Hampton quam tenet M Rounk l s

De eodem magistro pro ten' quondam tenure chaym xx s

De parva Aule universitatis in vico scolarum xxvj s viij d

De Aula Edwardi xx s

De Aule drowda xx s

Summa xj li

Redditus camerarum infra collegium

De Magistro Willelmo Douson xvj s viij d

De Magistro Roberto Burton xx s

De Magistro Johanne Crosby x s

De Magistro Thoma Elslake xiij s iiij d

Summa iij li

Redditus scolarum

De Magistro Thoma sutton vj s viij d

De Magistro Johanne Curtes vj s viij d

De Magistro Johanne Chepman vj s viij d

De Reginaldo toyne determinatore iij s viij d

De Johanne Clyfford determinatore iij s viij d

De Johanne Salway iij s viij d

De domino Johanne Stanys iij s viij d

Summa xxxiiij s ~~li~~ viij d

Redditus de liberis ten' in oxonia et suburbijs

De abbatissa de Godstow pro shopa ex opposito magne porte ffrideswyde xx d

De eadem pro annuali redditu pro gardino ten' quondam thome mastyre xiiij d

De abbate de osnay pro schoppa iuxta johannem Spysere vj s viij d

De ten' quondam' Rogeri Skybbow modo Collegij animarum viij s

De novo Collegio pro Maydynhall' x s

De Collegio Cant' pro silverhall' ij s vj d

De Collegio lincoln' pro gardino v s

De Magistro Johanne Triguran pro defalcacione prati retro osnay ij s ij d

De pedyngton' pro defalcacione prati retro osnay ij s ij d

De Collegio animarum pro ten' quondam Johannis Spront in paroch' sancti petri in ball' v s

De eodem Collegio animarum pro Gardino retro dictum ten' quondam Johannis Spront' viij s x d ob

De albis monachis pro gardino quod tenuit Barton' corvysere iiij s

Summa lvij s ij d ob

Redditus de exsexia et holdernes

De Willelmo ponde pro Manerio de Merkys et Molendinis xviij li iij s iiij d

De domino Thoma Tyrell' pro libero ten' existent' de Ramysdongrave xx s

De terris in Holdernes iij li xij d

Summa xxij li iiij s iiij d

Summa omnium Reddituum lix li xv s ob

Recepta preter sortem domus

Pro lignis xiiij d

De petro barbitonsore pro ald lattys ij s

Summa xvj d

Summa omnium oneratorum cij li xix s vij d

Allocaciones aularum

De Magistro Johanne Barnarde pro anno xiij° ix s viij d

De M Thoma Cowper pro anno xij° vj s viij d

De M Calbuch' pro parva aula universitatis in vico scolarum vj s viij d

De Cowper pro aula drowda pro annis xix xx^{o} et xxj^{o} xlix s j d
De M Church pro aula Brassynnos xxij s ij d ob q^{a}
De eodem pro aula sancti thome iij s iiij d
De eodem pro Gardino aule scuti ij s ij d ob q^{a}
De parva aula universitatis in ~~alto~~ vico scolarum ix s ij d
De Magistro Church pro anno vicesimo septimo pro Brassynos ~~x d~~ x s
De eodem pro parva aula universitatis in vico scolarum pro eodem anno vj s viij d
De Aula Edwardi pro anno xxiiij^{o} de M gramaticali Russell' v s
De Mauricio Caryour pro anni xxvij^{o} ij s ij d
De M Rounk' pro ten' quondam tenure chaym xx s
Summa vij li xij s x d ob

Allocaciones camerarum

De Magistro Willelmo douson pro annis xx^{o} xxj^{o} et xxij^{o} xl s iiij d
De eodem pro anno xxiij^{o} vj s viij d
De eodem pro anno xxiiij^{o} vij s viij d
De eodem pro anno xxv^{to} ix s viij d
De eodem pro anno xxvj^{to} xj s viij d
De eodem pro anni xxvij^{o} iiij s viij d
De M Chadworth' xx d
De M Roberto Toft pro ann~~is~~o xxiiij^{o} ~~et xxv^{to}~~ ij s vj d
De M Burton pro annis xxiiij et xxv^{to} xxv s
De eodem pro anno xxvj^{to} xx s
De eodem pro anno xxvij^{to} ix s vj d
De M Johanne Crosby ij s vj d
De M Roberto ffemmyng' iiij s
De Magistro Willelmo Danyell' xij s
De Nicholao Qwytte iiij s
De M Thoma Elslake iij s iiij d
Summa viij li v s vj d

Allocaciones scolarum

De M Willelmo Keyll' pro anno xx xx d
De scola Magistri lorde pro eodem anno vj s viij d
De scola M Swan pro anno xxiij^{o} vj s viij d
De scola M Willelmi Dalton iij s iiij d
De scola M petri vj s viij d
De scola M Hertilpoll' iij s iiij d

De eodem pro anno xxvj	vj s viij d
De scola M pray	iij s iiij d
De eodem pro anno xvij^{to}	vj s viij d
De stephano Broun	iij s viij d
De Duxfelde	iij s viij d
De M Johanne Curtes pro anni xxvij^{o}	vj s viij d
De M Johanne Chepman pro eodem anno	vj s viij d
De domino Johanne Stanys determinatore pro eodem anno	iij s viij d

Summa iij li ix s iiij d

[*Dorse*]

Allocaciones in parochia omnium sanctorum

De Willelmo Dagvyll'	xviij s x d
De exsecutoribus ysabelle Colett' pro annis xij^{o} xiij^{o}	xxxvij s iiij d
De johanne Barbour pro staynton hall'	xiij s iiij d
De johanne Wylyam pro anno xvij^{o}	x s
De eodem	xv s
De Willelmo Stokys pro anno xxij^{o}	vij s iiij d
De eodem pro anno xxv^{to}	xx d ij d [*sic*][5]
De Spendyng pro solario pro annis xxiij^{o} xxiiij^{o} xxv et xxvj^{to}	xiij s iiij d
De Hugone Benett	xxvij s vj d
De Weschew	vj s iiij d
De Bradmyre	iij s vj d
De Willelmo ffurbyour	x d
De dudley pro anno xxvij^{o}	viij s iiij d
De spendyng pro salario [*sic*] pro anno xxvij^{o}	iij s iiij d

Summa viij li vij s x d

Alloc' in parochia beate Marie et sancti petri in oriente

De Thoma preston	vij d
De henrico Bayth'	xxx s ix d
De Thoma Sprag' pro annis xxij^{o} et xxiij^{o}	ix s
De Johanne Swanys pro annis [*sic*] xxij^{o}	ij s j d ob
De Johanne Coke carpentare	xiij s x d
De Ricardo Carpent'	viij s ix d

[5] [ADMC] Although the corresponding entry in the Arrears is 'xx d', xxij d is needed here to make the total correct.

De eodem pro anni xxvij° xij s
De johanne Morland pro anno xxvij° viij s
Summa vj li iiij d ob[6]

Allocaciones in suburbijs et campis oxonie
De Thoma Mauncypyll' pro alryschette ij s
De qwytfeld precone maioris iiij s iiij d
De eodem pro anno xxvij° ij s
De pedyngton pro annis vicesimo tercio xxiiij° et xxvj° vj s vj d[7]
De eodem pro anni xxvij° viij s iiij d
De Thoma Spryg' xj s viij d
De hans v d
De eodem pro anno xxvij° iij s vj d[8]
De Johanne Mayson pro gardino ex parte orientali ecclesie sancti Egidij xij d
De eodem pro eodem Gardino vj d
De gillotte pro yrland pro annis xxiij° et xxiiij° v s
De Magistro Johanne Tryguram iiij s iiij d
De eodem pro anno xxvij° ij s ij d
Summa liij s xj d

Allocaciones de liberis tenementis
De Schybbow iiij s
De collegio animarum pro tenemento quondam johannis spronte in parochia sancti petri in balliolo pro annis xxij xxiij xxiiij° xxv^to^ et xxv^to^ [*sic*] xxv s
De eodem Collegio pro gardino retro dictum tenementum pro eisdem annis supradictis xliiij s iiij d ob
De ~~abbatiss~~ eodem Collego pro ten' quondam spronte pro anno xxvij° v s
pro gardino infra dictum ten' pro eodem anno viij s x d ob
De Abbatissa de godstow pro parva schoppa ex opposito magne porte ffrid' xx d
De eadem pro annuali redditu pro gardino quondam ten' Th' Maist' xiiij d
De eadem pro anno xxvij° xx d

6 [ADMC] The correct total is £5 10s 4½d.
7 [ADMC] The MS reads 'vji d', but evidently 'vj d' is intended.
8 [ADMC] As above, 'vij d' is written, but 'vj d' is intended.

De eadem pro annuali redditu pro gardino quondam ten' Th' mayst' xiiij d
De abbate de osnay pro schopa iuxta Johannem Spyser vj s viij d
De eodem pro eodem shopa vj s viij d
De collegio linc' pro anno xxvij° ij s vj d
De albis monachis pro anno xxvij° ij s
De Collegio Cantuar' pro eodem anno ij s vj d
De Collegio animarum pro ten' quondam schybbow pro anno xxvij^to viij s
Summa vj li xij d

Allocaciones in partibus remotis
De Willelmo pounde pro manerio nostro in exsex' [*no entry*]
De terris holdyrnes iij li xij d
Summa iij li xij d

Summa omnium allocatorum xlv li xij s j d

Soluciones et expense facte per Robertum Hertilpoll' tam infra collegium quam extra

Reparaciones aularum
In primis pro aula hampton et tenemento quondam tenure chaym xxix s x d ob
Item in aula de Brassynnos xxvj s viij d
Item in aula Edwardi ix s v d
Item in aula Drowda xv d
Summa iij li vij s ij d ob

Reparaciones facte circa tenementa laicorum in parochia omnium sanctorum
In primis in domo dudley ij s iiij d
Item in domo Dagvyll' v s viij d
Item in domo spendyng' x s vij d
In domo Willelmi talyour et Thome hosyere iuxta stokys ix d
Item circa ly pentes Thome ffurde xix s
In domo Stokys xl s ij s
Summa iij li xiij d

Expense facte infra collegium circa cameras capellam et librariam
In primis circa cameras iiij s x d
Item circa librariam ꝑ et pro libris redemptis a monacho collegij Gloucestr' xvj s ix d

Item circa capellam iiij s xj d ob
Summa xxxj s x d

Expense facte circa novam aulam promptuarium et coquinam et circa ortum

In primis pro coopertura murorum nove aule iiij s x d
Item circa meremium ad eandem aulam xxx s iij d
Item pro emptis ad coquinam et promptuarium xj s vj d ob
Item pro discoopertura murorum nove Aule et mundificacione orti xvij d
Summa xlviij s ob

Expense facte pro placitis diminutis expensis et pro stauro empto

In primis pro placitis xiij s vij d ob
Item in diminutis expensis xv s vj d ob
Item pro calce et lattys emptis collegio xxiiij s vj s ob
Item in resolutis tenentibus iij s ix d
Item pro quinta decima domini regis xvj d
Summa lviij s ix d ob

Expense facte circa muros ortorum et novas ~~aul~~ scolas et pro renovacione caucionum

In primis pro muris factis in gardino quod tenet hans et collegium lincoln et gardino iuxta ecclesiam sancti egidij ij s xj d
Item pro quatuor novis clavibus ad novas scolas xij d
Item pro renovacione caucionum vij s iiij d
Summa xj s iij d

Solut' socijs

In primis solutum est magistro lv s
In ~~primis~~ M Thome pray xiij s iiij d
Item M Roberto Hertilpoll' xiij s iiij d
Item solutum est magistro [*blank*]
Summa iiij li xx d

Solut' servientibus

In primis pincerne xx s
Item lotrici vj s viij d
Item Barbitonsori vj s viij d
Item Johanni Cuke v s
Item alteri Johanni vj d

Item procuratori	x s
Summa xlviij s x d	

Resoluciones facte

In primis priori sancte ffrideswyde pro anno xxvj°	xviij s viij d
Item eidem pro anno xxvij°	xviij s viij d
Item Abbati de osnay	xxij s x d
Item Abbati [*sic*] de Godstow	x s
Item Roberto Wodde pro terris Byssett	iij s viij d
Summa iij li xiij s x d	

Soluta pro communis sociorum batellis operariorum et contribucionibus

In communis sociorum	vij li xvj s iij d
Item in batellis	xxxij s j d ob
Item in contribucionibus	viij s x d ob
Item in convivio sancti Cuthberti	xij s vij d
Summa x li ix s x d	

Solut' alicie Belasys et magistro johanni Crosby

Item solut' Crosby pro redempcione cratere	x s
Item alice Belasys	v li xvj s viij d
Summa vj li vj s viij d	

Expense facte in equitacionibus

In primis in equitacione magistri ed exsexiam festo sancti johannis Baptiste	x s ix d ob
Item in equitacione magistri ad partes boriales pro ecclesia de arnclyffe	iij li vij d
Item in expensis Magistri in materia comitis oxon' apud london' post festum purificacionis	xx s xj d ob
Summa iiij li xij s iiij d	

Reparaciones et allocaciones facte in exsexia et holdernes

Pro clausura silve et tectura horreorum et stacione molendini in exsex'	xxvj s viij d
Item in allocatis firmario de exsex' pro reparacionibus factis ibidem	xxxij s vij d
Item in solutis firmario de exsex' pro labore suo in materia comitis oxonie	iiij s
Item in resolutis vicario de paull'	xvij s ix d

Item pro factura de ly see dykys iij li

Summa vij li xij d

Solut' pecunie[9] ad reparacionem nove aule

In primis ad illius aule facturam iij li xv s

Item ad eandem facturam eius [*sic*] aule ~~xl s~~ xvj s viij d

Summa v li ~~xv s~~ x d[10]

Summa omnium allocatorum et expensarum ciij li vj s j d ob

⟨Computatis computandis et allocatis allocandis domus debet procuratori computanti vj s viij d ob[11]

Acta sunt in capella domus predicte per doctorem Wylley commissarium generalem venerabilis viri Magistri Gilberti Kymer' cancellarij universitatis oxon' xj die Junij Anno supradicto regni regis Henrici vj[ti]⟩

[*A very clear and well-preserved roll; 2 membranes*]

[*The Roll for 1449/1450 was missing even in Smith's day*]

9 [ADMC] Apparently written 'pecturie' in the MS.
10 [ADMC] The correct total, as amended, is £4 11s 8d.
11 [ADMC] The correct total is 6s 6½d.

29 HENRY VI (ROLL UC:BU1/F/61)
c. 24 May 1450–13 Jun 1451?[1]

BURSAR: THOMAS PRAY

[This roll is much damaged, but some of the text can be recovered from Smith Vol. VII p. 165. The roll itself appears never to have had the usual type of heading; simply the year. It is misleadingly endorsed '1436' (not contemporary). It is certainly 29 Hen VI, as the lists of Arrears and Allowances show. The evidence that Thomas Pray was Bursar is the fact the the payments made (on the dorse of the roll) are made by him.]

Anno rr' [. . .

Arr' aularum[2]

De magistro Johanne Barnarde pro anno terciodecimo
De magistro Thoma Cowper pro anno duodecimo
De eodem pro aula drowda pro annis xix xx et xxj
De ma[. . .] pro anni xxvij^{o}
De [. . .] tenure caym
De [. . .
De [. . .
De [. . .
De [. . .
. . . *pro gardino*] aule scuti
[*Several lines lost*]
Summa viij li vj s ij d

Arr' camerarum

De magistro Willelmo [*Dowson*] pro annis xx xxj et xxij
De eodem pro anno xxiij et xxiiij
De eodem [*pro anno xxv^{to}*] xxvj^{to} et xxvij^{mo}
De eodem [. . .
De [. . .
De magistro Roberto Toft pro anno xxiiij^{to}
De magistro Roberto B[*urton* . . .

[1] The dates of Pentecost for 1450–1451. See the note at the head of **F/60** above for their inclusion here.

[2] Most of the totals on this roll are now lost; only a few are legible.

De magistro Johanne Crosby [. . .
De [. . .
De magistro [. . .
De Nycollao Wyde
De magistro Thoma [. . .][3] pro anno xxviij°
De magistro Roberto Burton pro anno xxviij°
Summa x li vij s ij d [*?*]

Arr' scolarum
De Magistro keyll' pro anno xx°
De scola magistri lord pro eodem anno
De scola M Swan pro anno xxiij°
De scola M Wyllelmi Dawam [*sic*]
De scola M petri
De [*scola M Hertilpoll'*]
De eodem pro anno xxvj°
De Stephano Brown'
De duxfeyld
De domino Johanne Stanys
De Magistro Sutton'
De Magistro Georgio
De Magistro Stokys
De Magistro Grafton'
De Jacabo [*sic*] Baynbyrge
Summa iiij li vj s iiij d

Arr' in paroch' omnium sanctorum
De Willelmo dagwyll'
De exsecutoribus Isabelle Colette pro annis xij° [*xiij°*
De Johanne Barbour pro Staynton Hall
De Johanne Wylliam pro anno xvij°
De eodem
De Willelmo Stokys pro anno xxij°
De eodem pro anno [*xxv°* . . .
De spendyng pro solario pro annis xxiij° xxiiij° xxv et xxvj^to^
De Hugone Benett xxvij s vij d
De Wesskew vj s iij d
De Bradener [. . .] ix d

3 [ADMC] This name, which might be made out, does not look like 'Elslake', which is the name expected here.

De Willelmo ffurbiore
De dodelay pro anno xxviij
De spendyng pro solario pro anno xxvij^{o}
De Wyllelmo Taylour pro anno xxviij^{o}
De Johanne Gowre
De Thoma Spyreche
De Thome ffores
Summa ix li [. . .

Arr' in parochia beate Marie et sancti petri in oriente
De Thoma preston
De henrico Bathe
De eodem pro anno xxvij^{o}
De Thoma Spragge pro annis xxij et xxiij^{o} ix s
De Johanne Swanys pro anno xxij^{o} ij s j d ob
De Johanne Cryke carpentare xiij s [. . .
De Rycardo carpentare
De eodem pro anno xxvj^{o} et xxviij^{o}
De Henrico Baythe pro anno xxviij^{o}
De Johanne Morland
Summa vij li xvj s ob

Arr' in suburbijs et campis [. . .
De Thoma Mancypyll' pro a[*lryschette* . . .
De qwyttfelld
De petyngton pro annis xxiij xxiiij^{o} et xxvj^{to}
De eodem pro anno xxvij^{o} ij s ij d
De eodem pro anno xxviij^{o} ij s ij d
De Thoma Sprygge pro anno xxviij^{o} [..] s vij d
De Hannse v d
De Johanne Mason pro gardino ex parte orientali ecclesie sancti egidij
De eodem pro eodem gardino pro anno xxviij^{o}
De Gyllotte pro Irland pro annis xxiij^{o} et xxiiij^{to}
De Magistro Johanne Tryguram
De eodem pro anno xxvij^{o}
De eodem pro anno xxviij^{o}
⟨Summa arrerag' notat' in dorso(?) rotuli⟩
[*An illegible total*]

Summa xliiij li ix d[*?*]

De Hanse [*sic*]

Redditus ten' in paroch' sanctorum petri in balliolo [*et Martini* . . .
De ten' quod Wod tenet in s[. . . prius Hanse][4] [vj s]
De ten' quod Goose tenet [*teutonicum*] super angulum quadrivij [xxv s xj d]
Summa xxxj s xj d

Redditus ten' laicorum in parochia omnium sanctorum anno supradicto
De ten' quod Thomas dudlay tenet . . .] iiij d
De ten' quod tenet Spendyng xxxj s vij d
De ten' quod tenet Thomas Spyrcole [. . .] viij d
De ten' quod tenet Johannes Gowyr xxiij s iiij d
De ten' quod tenet Wyllelmus Stokys xlvj s viij d
De ten' quod tenet Wyllelmus Dagwyll' pro ij^{bus} terminis
De ten' quod tenet Wyllelmus Taylour [xvj s viij d]
De ten' quod tenet predictus Wyllelmus nuper inhabitavit [Hugo Benet xvj s]
De Brysto[w] pro ten' quondam tenure [Dagvyle pro ij ter' xxvj s viij d]
Summa [xj li vij s viij d]

Redditus in parochia sancte marie et sancti petri in oriente
De ten' quod tenet Johannes [*Morland*]
De ten' quod tenet henricus [*Bayth*]
De ten' quod tenet Johannes [*Cuke*]
De ten' quod tenuit Ricardus [*carpenter*?] et modo domini [. . .
Summa [. . .

Redditus in subarbijs [*sic*] et in campis oxonie
De gardino iuxta Castrum quod qwythfyld tenet
De terris in bellomonte et in campis de Walton quas tenet [. . .
De eodem pro pratis retro oseney xviij s
De priore fratrum predicatorum pro pratis scilicet Allryschette[5] xviij s iiij d
De gardino ex parte orientale ecclesie sancti egidij ⟨quod tenet [. . .

[4] On 20 March 1449/1450, the garden in Sewy Street had been leased to Robert atte Wood (**UC:E2/12/1D/2**).

[5] On 1 April 1451, these meadows were leased to the Dominicans (**UC:E2/10/1D/2**), although they had been paying rent on them since 1444/5.

De hibernico [. . .] ⟨pro [. . .
Summa xlvj s iiij d

Redditus Aularum
De Magistro church pro Brasynnose
De eodem pro Aula sancti Thome
De gardino Aule scuti quod tenet idem magister
De Aula Hampton' quam tenet M [. . .
De eodem Magistro pro ten' quondam tenure Cayme
De parva Aule universitatis in vico scolarum
De Aula edwardi
De Aula drowda
Summa xj li ij s viij d

Redditus camerarum infra collegium
De Magistro Willelmi dowson' pro 3^{bus} terminis xij s vj d
~~De Magistro Roberto Burton' pro duobus terminis~~
~~De Magistro Johanne Crosby pro tribus terminis~~
De Magistro Thoma Elslake ⟨pro duobus terminis⟩ [vj s viij d]
[*Summa*] xix s ij d

~~Summa xlvij s vj d~~

Redditus scolarum
De Magistro Balme [vj s viij d]
De Magistro Chambyr [vj s viij d]
De Magistro Wilgryth [vj s viij d]
~~De Magistro Grif~~
De domino [Roberto Wr]yght [iij s viij d]
De Thoma Aschbye [iij s viij d]
De Domino Th[oma] [iij s viij d]
De domino Johanne payntour [iij s viij d]
Summa xxxiiij s [viij d]

Redditus de liberis ten' in oxonia et suburbijs
De Abatissa de Godstow pro schopa ex o^{to} magne porte fr[ideswide . . .
De eadem pro annuali redditu pro gardino ten [. . .
De Abbate de Oseney pro shopa iuxta [. . .
De ten' quondam Rogeri Schybbow modo collegij animarum
De novo collegio pro Maydyn halle
De collegio cantuar' pro Sylvyr Halle

De collegio lincolln' pro gardino
De Magistro Johanne Tryguran pro defalcacione prato retro Oseney
De Petyngton' pro defalcacione prato retro Oseney
De collegio Animarum pro ten' quondam Johannis Spronte in parochia sancti petri in ball'
De eodem collegio pro gardino retro dicti [*sic*] Johannis Sprunte quondam te[. . .
De Albis monachis pro gardino quod tenuit Barton' Corveser
Summa lvij s [?]

Redditus de exsexia et holdernysse
De Wyllelmo ponde pro manerio de Marykys et molendinis [xviij li iij s iiij d]
De domino Thome Tyrell' pro libero ten' exeun' de Ramys[-*den*] [xx s]
De terrys in holdyrnesse [iij li xij d]
⟨De Novo castro v li xv s vj d⟩[6]
Summa [xxviij li vj s x d ob]

Summa omnium reddituum lxiiij li [. . .

~~Recept' preter sortem domus In primis de novo castro~~
Recepta de cistis [v li xvj s]
Recepta de episcopo exonie [v li xvj s]
[*Another entry erased*]
Summa x li ~~xx s~~ xvj s

Summa omnium oneratorum [cxxix li x d]

Alloacaciones aularum
De magistro Johanne Barnarde pro anno terciodecimo
De magistro Thoma Cowper pro anno duodecimo
De cowper pro aula druda pro annis xix xx° et xxj°
De mauricio karyour pro anni xxvij°
De magistro Runk pro tenemento quondam tenure Ch[*aym*]
De magistro Runk pro tenemento quondam tenure [. . .
De magistro chyrche pro Brasnose
De eodem pro aula sancti Thome

[6] This is the first mention of a rent from the property at Newcastle upon Tyne which the College was given by Alice de Bellasis in 1447.

De eodem pro gardino aule scuti
De parva aula universitatis in vico scolarum
De eodem [*sic*] pro parva aula universitatis in vico scolarum pro anno xxvij^{o}
De eodem pro anno xxviij^{o}
De aula edwardi pro anno xxiiij^{o} de russell magistro grammaticali
\+ ~~De m~~aurico karyour pro anno xxviij^{o}
De Magistro Church pro anno vicesimo nono
Summa viij li [. . .

Allocaciones camerarum
De magistro Willelmo dowsyn pro annis xx xxj et xxij^{o}
De eodem pro annis xxviij et xxix
De eodem pro anno xxv xxvj et xxvij
De eodem pro anno xxviij^{o} et [. . .
De magistro chadworth'
De magistro tofte pro anno xxiiij^{o}
\+ ~~De magistro Roberto Burton pro annis xxiiij^{o} xxv xxvj et xxvij^{o}~~
De magistro Joh Crosby pro 3bus terminis
De magistro Roberto fflemmyng
De magistro W Camel
De nicholao qwyte
De magistro Thoma elslak
~~De magistro~~ Roberto Burton pro anno xxviij^{o} pro ij^{bus} terminis
Summa [. . .

Allocaciones scolarum
De magistro keyll' pro anno xx^{o}
De magistro lord pro eodem anno
De scola magistri swan pro anno xxiij^{o}
De scola magistri dalton
De scola magistri petri
\+ ~~De scola magistri Hertilpoll'~~
\+ ~~De scola magistri Pray~~
\+ ~~De magistro Hertilpoll' pro anno xxvj^{o}~~
\+ ~~De magistro pray pro eodem~~
De stephano Brown'
De duxfeyld
De domino joh' Stanys
De Magistro Balme

De Magistro Chambr'
De Magistro Wylgrysse
De domino Roberto Wryght'
De Thoma Aschby
Summa [. . .

Allocaciones in paroch' omnium sanctorum
\+ ~~De dagvyld' ex dimisso per landu' xxiij s iiij d~~
De executoribus ysabelle colett pro annis xij et xiij^{o} xxxviij s iiij d
De Johanne Barbour pro stanton' hall'
De Johanne William pro anno xvij^{o}
De eodem
De Willelmo Stokys pro anno xxij^{o}
De spendyng pro solario pro annis xxiij xxiiij xxv et xxvj
De hugone benet'
De weskew
De Bradmer
De Willelmo furbyour
De spendyng pro solario pro anno xxvij^{o} iij s iiij d
De Wyllelmo Taylour pro anno xxviij^{o} et xxix^{o} x s xj d
De Joh' Gower pro annis xxviij^{o} et xxix^{o} v s ij d
De spyrkok pro annis ~~xxviii~~ xxviii et xxix^{o} xij d
Summa vij li [. . .

Allocaciones in parochia beate marie et sancti petri in oriente
De Thoma preston
De henrico Bathe
De eodem pro anno xxvij^{o} xxv s
De eodem pro anno xxviij^{o} xxvj s
De eodem pro anno xxix^{o} vj s
De Thoma Spragge pro annis xxij et xxiij^{o} ix s
De Johanne Swayns pro anno xxij^{o} ij s j d ob
De Johanne Cuk carpent' xiij s [. . .
De Ricardo carpent' xxvj xxvij et xxviij^{o} et xxix^{o} xxx s
De morland' pro anno xxviij et xxix^{o}
De Joh' cuke pro anno xxix^{o} xiij s
De ~~symone~~ domino symone pro ten' quondam ten' ricardi carpent' xij s
Summa [. . .

Allocaciones in suburbijs et campis oxon'

De Thoma mancipyll' pro alrychsed

De Thoma Sprygge pro annis xxviij et xxix^{o}

De tryguram pro annis xxvj xxviij et xxix viij s

De qwytfeld' pro anno xxix^{o}

De petyngton pro annis xxiij xiiij [*sic*] xxvj xxvij xxviij et xxix

De hanse

De Johanne mason pro gardino ex parte orientali ecclesie sancti egidij

De eodem pro eodem gardino pro anno xxvij et xxviij^{o}

De eodem [. . .] pro eodem de [. . .

De gyllot pro iruland pro annis xxiij et xxiiij^{to}

~~De hibernico pro [. . .]~~ terris in bellimonte [*sic*]

De Roberto Wade

Summa [. . .

Allocaciones de liberis tenementis

De schybbow iiij s

De collegio animarum pro tenementis quondam Joh' spronte in parochia sancti petri [*in balliolo*] pro annis xxij xxiij xxiiij xxv et xxvj xxv[?] s

De eodem collegio pro gardino infra dictum ten' pro eisdem annis

De eodem collegio pro anno xxvij^{o}

De eodem collegio pro gardino infra dictum ten' pro eodem anno

De eodem collegio pro ten' quondam joh' spronte in eadem p[*arochia* . . .

De eodem collegio pro gardino infra dictum ten' pro eodem anno

De abbatissa de godstow pro parva schopa ex o^{to} magne porte [. . .

De eadem pro annuali redditu pro gardino quondam Thome mayst'

De eodem [*sic*] pro anno xxvij^{o}

De eodem pro annuali redditu pro anno xxviij^{o} pro gardino quondam Thome mayst'

De eodem pro anno xxviij^{o}

De eodem pro annuali redditu pro predicto anno pro gardino quondam Thome mayst'

De abbate de osnay pro schopa iuxta johannem spyser

De eodem pro eadem schopa iuxta johannem spyser
De eodem pro eadem schopa
De collegio animarum pro tenemento quondam schybbow pro anno xxix
De albis monachis pro annis xxviij et xxix°
De abbatissa de godstow pro anno xxix° pro schopa predicta xx d
De eadem pro annuali redditu pro gardino quondam Thome mayst' xiij d
De abbate de osnay pro schopa iuxta joh' spyser vj s viij d
De collegio animarum pro gardino retro dictum ten' v s
\+ ~~De collegio animarum pro ten' quondam joh' schybbow~~
Summa viij li [. . .

Alloc' in partibus remotis
De terris holdyrnesse pro annis xxviij et xxix° v[. . .
De terris Novi cast' lv s iiij d
Summa [*blank*]

Summa omnium allocatorum [. . .

[*Dorse*]

[Soluciones facte per magistrum Thomam Pray infra Collegium quam extra]

. . .] xx d
. . .] redditu pro predicto anno q[. . . xiiij d
. . .] pro schopa iuxta Johannem spyser vj s viij d
. . .] joh' spiser vj s viij d
[. . . vj s viij d
. . .] xxviij°(?) iiij s
Summa vj li [. . .] s vij d ob

. . .]iiij li xvj s

[*The next several inches of the dorse are lost*]

[Reparaciones Aularum]
[. . .] xxiij s ij d
[. . .] iiij s ix d ob
[. . .] iiij s iij s ob
Summa xxxij s v d [ob]

[Reparaciones ten'] laycorum	
[In domo Dudley]	vij li xv s ij d
[. . .]	xvj s vj d ob
[. . .]	vj d
[. . .]	ij s vij d
[. . .]	xiij s vij d ob
[. . .]	ij s ix d
Summa ix li xj s ij d	
. . .]ellam et cameras[7]	
[Inprimis pro reparationibus in nova Aula et Capella]	ix li xvij d ob
[In capella]	x s j d ob
[Summa] ix li xj s vij d	
[. . .]	v s
Summa x s viij d ob	
. . .] expensis et [. . .	
[. . .]	lij s xj d ob
[. . .]	xix s ix d
[. . .]	xxj s x d
[Pro subsidijs regis]	vj s viij d
Summa [. . .] xiiij d ob	
[Expens' circa renovatione caucionum]	
[In primis pro lincoe [*sic*] et renovacione] caucionum	vj li xv s j d
[Summa] vj li xv s j d	
[Solut' Sociorum]	
[M^{ro} Collegij]	xlj s iij d ob
[M^{ro} Hertilpoll]	[x s]
[M^{ro} pray]	[x s]
[Summa] iij li xv d ob	
[*Sol*]ut' servientibus	
[*In*] primis pincerne	xx s
Item coco	vij s x d
Item Barbitonsori	vj s viij d
Item lotrici	vj s viij d

[7] Smith gives this section the heading *expens' infra Coll'* – almost certainly a paraphrase of the original.

Item procuratori	x s
Summa lj s ij d	
[. . .]	
[. . .]	vj s viij d
[. . .]	xvj s viij d
[. . .]	x s
[. . .]	iij s viij d
[. . .]	iij s
Summa iij li iij s iiij d	

[In communis sociorum]	x li v s [v d] ob
[In Batellis]	xxiij s ij d
[In contribucionibus]	x s vij d ob
[In Jurnellis]	[v] s [ij] d ob
[In die Sancti Cuthberti]	x s vj d
[. . .]	iij s iiij d
Summa xij li xviij s iiij d	

[Expens' in equitacionibus]

[In equitacione M[ri] versus Esex duobus] vicibus et equis et f[. . .] et firmario	iij li x s v d ob
[Eidem pro equitacionibus versus Exeter]	xxiij s j d ob
[M[ro] versus Eboracum]	iij li xvj s j d ob
[Item M[ro] Burton pro Lira][8]	[iij li iiij s x d]
[Summa xij li xiiij s[9]]	

Summa omnium expensarum 72 li 7 s iiij [d]

Summa omnium allocatorum et expensarum cxxviij li xij s vj d

[Computatis computandis et] allocatis allocandis computans debet Collegio] xviij s [iiij d]

[⟨Acta sunt hec per Magistrum] Joh' [Merton] mag[istrum se]u senior[em Collegij predict' ex auctoritate et mandato] venerab[il' doctoris Magistri Gilberti Kyme Cancellarij] universitatis oxon'⟩

[8] Smith notes that this is almost certainly a copy of Nicholas de Lyra's commentary on the bible, a copy of which had been given to the College by Walter Skirlaw, Bishop of Durham.

[9] *Sic* Smith; however, an 'ob' is legible on the roll here, and the entries, as Smith gives them, suggest a total of £11 14s 6½d.

[A badly damaged roll of 2 membranes. Most of the right hand side of the face of the roll is lost, and only fragments of the dorse are legible. The damage has occurred since Smith's day.]

30 HENRY VI (ROLL UC:BU1/F/62)
c.13 June 1451–28 May 1452?[1]

BURSAR: ROBERT HARTILPOLE

[*The original roll is now missing. What follows is the condensed version of the text in Smith Vol. VIII pp.166–169.*]

Compotus M^{ri} Roberti Hertilpole procur' Mag' Aule seu $Coll^{ij}$ Un^{tis} Oxon datus per eundem magistrum a^{o} regni regis Henrici sexto post conquestum tricesimo

Arr 13 H 6

Summa arrerag' lvj li v s ij d

Redditus in parochia S petri et S Martini

de Ten. quod tenet Robertus Wod' in Swynschewton	vj s
prius [*habuit ille*][2] etiam in Rotulo precedente	

Ten' in par' omn' sanctorum

ten. Tho. Dudley	1.13.4
Brestow	liij s iiij d
Spending	xxvj s viij d
Will' Taylor	xvj s vij d
quondam Hug' Benet	xviij s
Joh' Gower	xxiij s iiij d
Tho' Spyrcock	xvj s viij d
Willus [*sic*] Stokes	xlvj s viij d
Summa xj li ix s viij d	

Red' camerarum de magistro Johanne	ij s vj d

Redditus Scolarum

De magistro Roberto Coky	vj s viij d
De magistro Jo. Davison	vj s viij d
De magistro Willelmo Wrangwesse	vj s viij d
De magistro Galfrido Close	vj d viij d Galf Close

[1] The dates of Pentecost for 1451–1452. See the note at the head of **F/60** above for their inclusion here.

[2] [ADMC] These words are uncertain; they come at the bottom of the page, which has been cut through them.

George Hergill vj s viij d ⟨2.00.8d⟩
Jo. Brampton iij s viij d
Willelmo Gregfort iij s viij d
Bartlett iij s viij d
Summa xlj s iiij d

De terris in Bello monte `et campis Walton´ quas tenet unus Hibernicus vij s
Robertus fuller pro gardino ex parte orientali ecclesie S Egidij xij d

Inter red. post de novo castro v li xv s vj d
de magistro Tho Pray (nihil scribitur)

Summa reddituum lxiiij li xix [*sic*] xj d ob

2[3]Summa omn' oneratorum cxxj li ix [*sic*] x d ob

1 preter sortem pro cumbustibilibus ix d
de vas' plumbei de inhabitanti Aula Edward iiij s
Summa iiij s ix d

Allocat' red Summa lxviij li xv s vj d ob

Expens' infra Coll' circa novam Aulam muros Collegij capellam et coquinam
Summa totalis xxj s ob

Collectoribus domini Regis et pro scriptura libri Augustini xxij s

Pro renovatione cautionum vj s

Solut' Socijs Collegij
in primis Magistro iij li
magistro Hertilpole xiij s iiij d
magistro Pray xiij s iiij d
item magistro Johanni Davison xlvj s viij d
Summa vj li xiij [*sic*] iiij d

Pro liberis ten' abbat de Osney xvij s vj d
(1[a] mentio) Item Abbatisse Studley ij s

In communis Sociorum xj li v s x d ob
In Batellis et Jurnell' xxvj s j d ob q[a]
In Contribucionibus xix s j d

[3] [ADMC] These two items were presumably intended to be in reverse order.

In die Sancti Cuthberti xj s viij d ob

Solut' Alisie Ballyssis v li xvj s viij d

Expens' circa Ecclesiam de Harncliffe

In primis pro Littera adquisita ab episcopo Ebor' pro dimissione beneficij ad firmam xxx s
In equitacione Magistri pray et Exsexiam ad circa adquisitionem ejusdam Littere xviij s
Item in equitatione Magistri pray in fest Michaelis circa Ecclesiam Harncliffe iiij li vij s ob
Item famulo secum equitanti iij s x d
In equitatione Magistri Hertilpole et M Davyson ix s ij d
In equis iij s x d
Item Georg' pro labore et ocrijs ejus xix d
Item magistro Davyson versus London et Hertilpole ad Magistrum Rouke ij s iiij d
Summa vij li xv s viij d ob[4]

Pro Redemptione cautionum

In primis Doctori Bukley pro quadem Cautione xxvj s viij d
Summa xxvj s viij d

Summa omn' Expens' lij li xiiij s ij d ob q[a]

Summa omn' Allocationum et expens' cxxj li ix s viij d ob

Et sic computatis computandis et allocatis allocandis rem' de claro ob q[a]

Acta sunt hec per Johannem [. . .[5]] doctorem in decretis et commissarium M Gilberto Keym' Cancellar' universitatis Oxon'.

[4] [ADMC] The correct total is £7 15s 9½d.
[5] [ADMC] This word was evidently not legible to Smith.

31 HENRY VI (ROLL UC:BU1/F/63)
c.28 May 1452–20 May 1453?[1]

BURSAR: HENRY STROTHER

[*The roll is very badly damaged. A few extra details can be supplied from Smith (Vol. VIII pp.169–171).*]

[Compotus Henr' Strother procuratoris mag' Aul' seu Collegij Universitatis Oxon' datus per eundem Henricum anno regni regis Henrici sexto post conquestum Ang' tricesimo primo.]

Arr' Aularum[2]

De M Johanne Bernard pro anno terciodecimo
De M Thoma Couper pro anno duodecimo
De Cowper pro aula druda pro annis xix xx [. . .
De Morico Cariour pro anno xxvij°
De M Runke pro ten' quondam tenure [*cayme*?] pro a[. . .
De eodem pro Aula Hampton et ten' q[*uondam*] Cay pro a[. . .
De M Chyrche pro aula [. . .
De eodem pro aula [. . .
De eodem de parva aula [. . .
De eodem de parva aula [. . .
De eodem pro anno [. . .
De eodem [. . .
De eodem pro [. . .
De Russell mr gram[. . .
De M Antonio pro aula Hampton [. . .
De eodem pro ten' quondam tenure Came [. . .
De Aula Drowda pro anno xxx [. . .
Summa [. . .

Arr' Camerarum

De M Willelmo Dowson pro anno [. . .
De eodem pro annis xxv xxvj [. . .
De eodem pro anno [. . .
De M Chadworth [. . .

[1] The dates of Pentecost for 1452–1453. See the note at the head of **F/60** above for their inclusion here.
[2] Next to no figures are legible on the original roll.

De M Toft [. . .
De M Johanne C[*rosby* . . .
De M Roberto fflem[*ing* . . .
De M [. . .
De Nicholao [. . .
De M Eleys [. . .
Summa [. . .

Arr' Scolarum
De M Kele
De M Lord
De M Swan
De M Dalton
De M Patr'
De Stephano [*Brown* . . .
De Duxfeld
De D[. . .
De domino [. . .
De M Johanne [. . .
De M Roberto(?) [. . .
De Galfrido Clo[. . .
De Willelmo Grayforth
De Johanne Brampton
Summa [. . .

Arr' in parochia Omnium sanctorum
De execut' Isabelle Colet pro annis xij xiij [. . .
De Johanne Barbor' pro Stayntonh[*all* . . .
De Johanne William
De Willelmo Sotkes pro annis [. . .
De Spendyng [*pro solario pro annis* . . .
De Hugone B[*enet* . . .
De Wesch[*ew* . . .
De Bradmer' [. . .
De Willelmo ff[*urbyour* . . .
De Willelmo Taliour' pro annis [. . .
De Johanne Gower' pro annis xx[. . .
De eodem pro anni tricesimo
De Spitcok' pro Annis xxviij et xxix
De eodem pro anno xxxo^mo^

De Dudley
Summa [. . .

Arr' in paroch' beate Marie et Sancti Petri in Oriente
De Thoma Preston
De Henrico Bath'
De eodem pro anni xxvij
De eodem pro anno xxviij xxix [. . .
De domo Henrici Bath' pro ann[. . .
De Thoma Sprag' pro annis [. . .
De Johanne Swanose pro [. . .
De Johanne Cuke carpent[. . .
De Ricardo carpent'
De Morland' pro annis xxviij xxix
De eodem pro annis xxx
De domo Johannis Cuke pro anno xxix
De eodem domo pro anno xxx
De ten' quondam in tenur' Ric' Carpent[. . .
De eodem ten' pro anno xxx
Summa [. . .

Arr' in Suburbijs et Campis Oxon'
De Thoma Maunciple pro Alrychs[. . .
De Thoma Spryge pro anno xxviij(?) [. . .
De Trigrano pro annis [. . .
De Qwytfeld' pro [. . .
De Petyngton pro annis [. . .
De eodem pro anno xxx [. . .
De Hanse
De Johanne Mason pro gardino ex parte orientali [. . .
De Roberto fuller' pro eodem
De eodem pro gardino pro anno xxx
De Gyllot pro Iruland' pro annis xx[. . .
De Ibernico pro pratis [*in bello monte* . . .
De Roberto wode
De eodem pro anno xxx
Summa [. . .

Arr' de liberis ten'
De Schybbow

De collegio animarum pro [*tenementis quondam Johannis Sprunt pro anno . . .*
De eodem collegio pro gardino [*infra dictum ten' pro eodem anno . . .*
De eodem collegio pro anno xxvij° (?)
De eodem collegio pro gardino infra dictum [*ten' pro eodem anno*
De eodem pro anno xxviij°
De eodem pro eodem gardino eodem anno
De Abbatissa de Godstow pro parva s[*hopa (opposite St. Frideswide)* . . .
De eadem pro annuali redd' pro gardino quondam [*Thome Maister . . .*
De eadem pro anno xxvij°
De eadem pro annuali red[. . .
De eadem pro anno xxviij°
De eadem pro annuali red[. . .
De Abbate de Osney [. . .

[*Dorse of 2nd membrane*]

De eodem pro annis [. . .
De eodem [. . .
De albis [*monachis . . .*] pro annis xxviij et xxx [. . .
De abbatissa [. . .] pro annis xxix [. . .
De eadem pro an[. . .
De Abbate de Osney pro shopa [*Johannis Spyser . . .*
De collegio animarum pro ten' quondam [. . .] pro anni xxix°
De eodem pro gardino dicti ten'
De Abbatissa de Godstow pro [. . .
De eadem pro predict' anuali red[. . .
De Abbate de Osney pro schopa iuxta [. . .
De Collegio animarum pro ten' [. . .
De eodem pro gardino [. . .
Summa ix (?) li [. . .

Arr' in partibus remotis
De terris in Holdernes pro annis xxviij° et xxix[. . .
De terris Novicastri [. . .
De terris in Holder[*nes*] pro anno xxx
De terris Novicastri pro anno xxx
Summa xiiij li ij s iiij d

Summa omnium Arr' lxviij li [xv s vj d ob]

Redditus in paroch' Sanctorum petri et martini [*anno*] regni Regis Henrici sexti [*tr*]icesimo primo

De ten' quod tenet Robertus wod [(*in Sewy Street*) . . .

De ten' quod tenet Tutonicus super angulum quadrivij

Summa xxx[. . .

Redditus ten' laicorum in paroch' omnium sanctorum

De ten' quod tenet Thomas Dudley

De ten' quod tenet Bristow

De ten' quod tenet Spendyng'

De ten' quod tenet Willelmus Taliour

De eodem pro ten' quondam tenure Hugone Benet(?)

De ten' quod tenet Joh' Gower pro duobus terminis

De Willelmo Taliour pro eodem ten' pro duobus [*terminis* . . .

De ten' quod tenuit Th Spircol pro ijbus terminis [. . .

De [*blank*] pro uno [*termino* . . .

De ten' quod ten' Will' Stokes

Summa xj(?) li xj s viij d

Redditus in paroch' beate Marie et sancti petri in Oriente

De ten' quod tene^t [*sic*] Johannes Morland

De ten' quod tenet Henricus Bath

De ten' quod tenet Johannes Cuke

De ten' quod tenuit [. . .

Summa iiij li vj s

Redd' Aularum

De M Chirch pro Aula Brasynnose	
De eodem pro Aula Sancti Thome	
De eodem pro gardino Aule S[*cuti*]	vj s viij d[3]
De M Antonio pro Aule Hampton' pro uno termino	xvj s viij d
De M Browne pro eodem Aula pro uno [. . .	xvj s viij d
De M Donislay pro uno termino	
De M Antonio pro ten' quondam tenur' Came	vj s viij d
De M Browne pro eodem ten' pro uno termino	vj s [. . .
De M Bemeslay pro eodem ten' pro i term	vj s [. . .
De M Chirch pro parva aula universitatis in vico scolarum	xx [. . .
De M Semer pro parva Aula universitatis in alto [. . .	viij s [. . .

[3] A few figures in this section are legible.

Item de eodem magistro pro duobus terminis eiusdem [*aule*? . . .
De Aula Edwardi
De Aula Drowda
[*Summa* . . .

Redditus camerarum
De M Johanne [Sl [*sic*] pro tribus terminis] [vij s vj d]
S[umma patet]

Redd' Scolarum

De M Wymark'	[vj s viij d]
De M Petro	[vj s viij d]
De M Roo	[vj s viij d]
De M Marschall'	[vj s viij d]
De domino Willelmo Lyndesey	[iij s iiij d]
De Burley[4]	[iij s iiij d]
De Willelmo Preston	[iij s iiij d]
De Johanne Bl[ox]h[am]	[iij s iiij d]

Summa xlj s iiij d

Redd' in suburbijs et in Camp' Oxon'
De gardino quod tenet Whytfeld iuxta castrum
De terris in bellomonte et in campis de Walton quas tenet [. . .
De pratis retro Osney
De priore fratrum predicatorum pro pratis [. . .] Alryshet et Irland'
Summa xix s viij d

Reddit' de liberis ten' in Oxon'
De abbatissa de Godstow pro [*schopa*] ex opposito magne parte sancte fridiswyde
De eadem pro annuali [. . .
De collegio animarum pro [(*Schybbow's former house*) . . .
De Novo collegio pro Maydyn H[*all* . . .
De Collegio Cantuar' pro Sylver Hall'
De Collegio Lincoln' pro gardino
De johanne Trygrane pro [*defalcacione prati retro Osney* . . .
De petyngton pro defalcacione prati retro Osney
De Collegio Animarum pro [(*John Sprunt's house in St. Peter-le-Bailey*) . . .

[4] Smith reads this name as 'Hurley'.

De eodem Collegio pro [*(the garden behind the above*) . . .
De albis monachis pro gardino [*(once of Barton)* . . .
Summa [. . .

Redd' in partibus remotis
De Willelmo Pond' pro manerio de [*Merkys*] et molendinis
De domino Thoma Tyrell'
De terris in Hold'
De Novocastro
De Ecclesia de Arncly[ffe] [xx li]
Summa [xlviij li vj d]

Summa omnium [reddituum] lxxx[vj li xvij s vij d ob]

Recept' preter sortem domus
De inhabitante A[. . .
Item pro fu[. . .
Summa [. . .

[*Face of 2nd membrane*]

Allocaciones Aularum
De Cowper pro aula druda pro annis [. . .
De Morico Cariour pro anno xxvij°
De M Church pro Aula Brasyn[. . .
De eodem pro aula Sancti Thome [. . .
De eodem pro gardino Aule Scuti [. . .
De eodem pro parva Aula universitatis in vico Scolarum [*pro anno* . . .
De eodem pro parva Aula universitatis in vico Scolarum pro anno xxvij°
De eodem pro anno xxviij°
De eodem pro anno xxx°
De eodem pro anno xxxj°
De M Browne pro Aula Hampton et ten' annex' x s [. . .
De M Bemesley pro Aula Hampton iiij s [. . .
De eodem pro ten' quondam tenure Came vj s [. . .
De M Antonio pro ten' quondam tenur' Came xj s [. . .
De M Semer pro parva Aula universitatis in alto vico pro anno xxxj° viij s [. . .
De Aula Drouda pro annis xxx et xxj

De Rusell M grammaticali pro aula Edwardi
Summa x li v s vij d

Allocaciones Camerarum
De M Willelmo Dowson pro annis xx xxj xxij
De eodem pro annis xxv xxvj et xxvij
De eodem pro annis xxviij et xxx
De M Roberto fflemynge
De M Willelmo Daynyul'
Summa [. . .

Allocaciones Scolarum
De M K[*ele* . . .
De M Lord
De M Swanne
De M Petro
De Stephano Br[*own* . . .
De [. . .] Willelmo
De Willelmo Grayforth
De M Roo
De M Wymun
De M Ricardo Marchall'
De M Petro
Summa lvij s iiij d

Allocacaciones in parochia Omnium sanctorum
De Johanne Barbor' [*(for Stanton Hall)* . . .
De [. . .
De Bradmer' [. . .
De Willelmo Taliour [. . .
De eodem pro annis xx[. . .
De Johanne [. . .] pro annis [. . .
Summa xlv s vij d

Allocaciones in paroch' beate Marie et Sancti Petri in Oriente
De Henrico Bathe
De eodem pro anni xxvij[?]
De eodem pro anno xxviij et xx[. . .
De domo Henrici [*Bath pro anno* . . .
De Ricardo carpent'
De Morland' pro annis xx[. . .
De eodem pro annis xxx° et xxxj

De domo Johannis Cuke pro annis xxix et xxx°[?]
De eodem domo pro anno xxxj
De ten' quondam in tenur' [*Ric' Carpenter* . . .
Summa xiij [. . .

Allocaciones in Suburbijs et Campis Oxon'
De Thoma [*Maunsipel*] pro [*Alry*]chsed'
De tryg[. . .] annis xxv[. . .] xxviij et xxix°
De Wytfeld' pro annis xx[. . .
De Petyngton [. . .
De Symons [. . .
De Roberto fuller' pro gardino pro annis xx[. . .] xxx et xxxj°
De Gyllot pro Iruland' pro annis x[. . .] et xx[. . .
De Roberto Wode
De eodem pro annis xxx et xxx[. . .
Summa xliiij s ij d

Allocaciones de liberis ten'
De albis monachis pro anno xxvj [?]
De Collegio lincoln' pro gardino pro anno xxxj[?]
Summa vj s iij d[?]

Allocaciones in partibus remotis
De terris in Holdernes pro ann[. . . vij li xij s ij d [?]
De terris Novicastri [. . . lij s viij d
De terris in Holdern[. . .
De terris Novicastri pro annis xxx et xxxj
Summa xvj li [. . .

Summa totalis all[ocac' lv li xv s x d ob]

Soluciones facte Reparaciones Aularum
In primis in Aula Brasynnose
Item in parva Aula universitatis in alto vico
Item pro reparacionibus factis in eadem Aula
Item in Aula Hampton'
Item in Aula Drouda
Summa xl s[?] iiij d ob

Reparaciones [. . .]orum
In primis in domo Bris[. . .
Item in reparacionibus factis [. . .
Item in domo Willelmi [. . .

Item in domo Willelmi [. . .
Item in domo [. . .]yngc
Item in Scolis M Johannis [. . .
Summa [. . .

Expens' facta infra Collegium
In primis in expensis infra Coll[egium per procuratorem et per cistam] [xx li xj s iij d]
Item in Capella [xj s j d]
Item in coquin[a] [iiij s iiij d ob]
Item Spry[ge et] pro [vect]ur' la[pidum] [viij s]
Summa [xx li xix s ob]

Expens' facte [. . .] pro [Stauro] et reso[. . .[5]
In Primis [. . .] S[. . .
Item in d[. . .] ex [. . .
Item pro renovacione c[*aucionum*]
Item in resoluc' pro stau[. . .
Summa [iiij li xij s vj d]

Soluc' facte socijs collegij
In primis Magistro Collegij [iij li]
Item pro antiquis debitis [xx s]
Item Magistro Hertilp[ole] [xiij s iiij d]
Item M Pray[6]
Item M Joh' [Davyson] [xliij s iiij d]
Item eidem [M^ro Joh' pro scola] [vj s viij d]
Item Henr' S[trother pro officio procuratoris] [x s]
[Summa vij li xiij s iiij d]

[*Dorse of 1st membrane*]

Solut' servientibus
In primis [. . .
Item Pincerne
Item Johanni Coco
Item lotrici

[5] Smith has a heading here 'Expens' in Staturo'. 'Staturo' is presumably an error for 'Stauro', and the heading only a paraphrase.

[6] Smith leaves the amount paid to Pray blank, but the total is correct as the figures stand.

Item Petro Barbitonsori
Summa [. . .

Resoluc' facte
In primis Abbati de Osney
Item priori sancte ffrideswyde
Item Abbatisse de Godstow
Item ecclesie beate marie
Summa [. . .

Solut' pro communis batellis et contribuc'
In primis [pro] communis soc[iorum] [xiiij li xiij s iij d]
Item in batellis et jur[nellis] [l s vij d ob q[a]]
Item in contribucionibus [xij s vj d ob]
Item in die Sancti Cuthberti [*v s iiij d ob*][7]
Item in recepcione ext[raneorum] [xvj s ij d ob q[a]]
Summa [xix li viij s ob]

[*Soluc'*] Alicie Belasise
In primis eedem [*sic*] Alicie Belasise [iiij li xvj s iiij d]
Summa [*patet*]

Expens' facte in equit'
In primis procuratori pro equitacione ver[sus essex] [x s x d ob]
Item in equitac' M Th pray pro [acquisitione littere pro . . . de Arncliffe] [x s]
Item eidem M pro equitac' Lond[on] [xx s]
Item pro cere[ticis][8] de[liberatis] sibi [iij s iiij d]
Item in equit' procuratoris versus Es[sex circa festum Mich'] [v s viij d]
Item alia vice in equit' eiusdem [xvj s ij d ob]
Item alia vice in equitacione pro[curatoris] [viij s]
Summa iij li vij s viij d

Expens' facte in Estsex'
In primis firmario pro reparacionibus molend' [iij li]
Item eidem firmar [*sic*] allocac' pro libers ten' pro u[. . .
Item Allocac' pro dimidio anni
[Summa iiij li viij s iiij d ob]

[7] Smith omits this entry. However, since the four entries which he does give total £18 12s 8d, this sum of 5s 4½d makes up the difference with the final total.
[8] Smith suggested that this was meant to read 'chirotecis'.

In dimissis ten'

In primis [dimissis tenementis] [xxvj li viij s ob]

Item remanet in c[ista] [xlj s iij d][9]

S[umma patet]

Summa omnium exp[ensorum[10]

Summa omnium Allocatorum et [expens'

[*Smith wrote at the end of his summary 'Nothing more added in ye Roll'.*

This roll consists of 2 quite separate membranes, now sewn together at the head. The order in which they should be read is: membrane 1, face; membrane 2, dorse; membrane 2, face; membrane 1, dorse. The face and dorse of both membranes is very badly damaged on the right hand side, and practically none of the right hand of the roll can be read at any point. The damage has occurred since Smith's time.]

[9] Smith wrote of this entry: 'This summe seems added'.

[10] Smith gives no totals for this or the following entry.

32 HENRY VI (ROLL UC:BU1/F/64)
c.20 May 1453–9 June 1454?[1]

BURSAR: RICHARD MARSHALL

[*The original roll is now missing. What follows is the condensed version of the text in Smith Vol. VIII pp.176–178.*]

A° 1453	(Compotus Magistri Ric' Marshall procuratoris Magne
1454	(Aule sive Collegij universitatis oxon' datus per eundem
	(magistrum Ricardum a° r' H 6 32°

Arr' aul +c.

arr' de liberis tenementis

de monachis pro a° 31	iiij d
de coll' Lincoln pro a° 31	ij s vj d
Summa vj s vj d	

vid' reditus remissos a° et Rotulo precendente scilicet 21 li 00 08 d ob

Redd' Camerarum

de magistro Weyght	xvj s viij d
de magistro Pray	xiij s iiij d
de magistro Stringer pro 2 ter'	v s
Summa xxxiiij s iiij d[2]	

Red Scol'

de magistro Tolbot	2s	
De Goodall	3 8d	
Cowpere	3 8d	
Clyfton	3 8d	15s 8d[3]
Carpenter de Aul' Hampton	3 8	

[1] The dates of Pentecost for 1453–1454. See the note at the head of **F/60** above for their inclusion here.

[2] [ADMC] The correct total is 35s.

[3] [ADMC] The correct total is 16s 8d.

The rents which should hear follow (the roll not being sowed but onely pasted together) + y[e] allocat' are wanting

Expens' in repar' Aul'	2 16 7
Expens' in repar' laicorum	5 5 8

Infra Coll'

In primis in expens factis infra coll' per cistam	xj li vj s iiij d
In libraria et capella	xiij s iiij d ob
In proptuario [*sic*] et coquina	iiij s vj d ob
Summa xij li iiij s iij d	

In reparationibus et novis edificijs pro procurator'		4 14 6 ob
In renovatione Cautionum	xxiiij s j d	added 3 li 4 s 4 d
In redemptione unius cautionis	xl s	

In communis Sociorum	xx li xvij s vj d ob q[a]
In Batellis et jurnellis	3 17 8
In contributionibus	1 0 9
In die sancti Cuthberti	1 4 6 ob
In receptione extraneorum	0 8 4 ob
Summa xxvij li viij s x d[4]	

Solut' fact' Socijs

In primis Magistro Coll'	l s
Item Magistro Hertylpole	xxiij s iiij d
Magistro Davyson	xlvj s viij d
Magistro Marschal (whose name being writt here + summe enterded [*sic*] is interlined below between Greyford & Hull, the Roll being of his own Bursarshipp)	
Henrico Strothere	x s
Magistro Ricardo Marshall	xvj s viij d
domino Johannis Hull	xvj s viij d
Johanni Mercere	xvj s viij d
Item M' Ric' Marshall pro officio procuratoris	x s
Summa x li vj s viij d	

pincerne	xx s (anno prox. xxvj s 1455)
coco	x s
lotrici et Barbitonsori cuilibet	vj s viij d

[4] [ADMC] The correct total is £27 8s 9d.

pro equitacione procuratoris bis versus Essex xxiij s xj d
versus M' Tho Dunham xiiij s
versus Northampton x s vj d
Summa xlix s v d[5]

firmario de Essex in alloc pro liberis reparat' cirothecis stipendio senescalli et toga firmarij xiiij s iiij d
firmario de Holderness vj s iiij d
de Arncliffe xxxiij s iiij d

In dimissis Tenement' xvj li x s ij d
In remanentibus in cista xx s Summa xvij li x [*sic*] ij d
Sum [*blank*]

Summa omn' expens' lxxxvij li xxiij d

Et sic computatis computandis et allocatis allocandis Collegium indebitetur [*sic*] procuratori in vij s ix d

Acta sunt hec per Georgium Nevill artium magistrum Cancellarium universitat' oxon.

Inter dimissa tenentibus hic a° 32 H 6ti hec computanda videntur viz. Johanni Cowper pro aul' Drouda a° 19 20 21 H6 2.9.1
magistro Brome pro aul' Hampton + [*sic*] x s et alijs nescio quibus

[5] [ADMC] The correct total is 48s 5d.

33 HENRY VI (ROLL UC:BU1/F/65)
c.9 June 1454–25 May 1455?[1]

BURSAR: JOHN HULLE

[*This roll is so much damaged that the surviving fragments are mostly not worth transcribing. It is much the narrowest roll to date (4.9 inches), and consists of 2 membranes, which are now wrongly sewn together. The order should be (1) face of 1st membrane (entirely arrears); (2) dorse of 2nd membrane (rents); face of 2nd membrane (allowances); (4) dorse of 1st membrane (payments and expenses).*

Since, therefore, the original is so damaged, almost all of the following is taken from the summary in Smith Vol. VIII pp.172–175.]

a° 1454 (Compotus Magistri Jo Hull procuratoris Mag. Aul. sive
1455 (Collegij universitatis oxon datus per eundem Magistrum
(Johannem a° H 6ti post conquestum Angl' 33°

Incipit cum arr' a° H 6 Aularum

[*Arrears: The first 2 or 3 words only are legible or semi-legible in a fair number of entries; the rest is completely lost. This section can give no information beyound the following:*

Arrears of Halls – nothing decipherable
Arrears of Rooms – M William dow[son] and others illegible
Arrears of Schools – M lord; M. Swanne; M Peter. Other illegible names, and two which might conceivably be read.
Arrears of property rents No names clearly legible. In All Saints parish an entry 'De West . . .'. Smith only supplies the following extracts:]

Arr' camerarum viz.

De magistro Willelmo Dowson pro annis 20 21 22 25 26 27 28 et 29 – 5 li 7s + 6d in alloc' ejusdem an tantum iiij li xiij s ij d nec aliquid occurit inter Recept'

de magistro Roberto fflemyng	iiij s
de magistro Will' Daniell'	xij s
de magistro Wryght	viij s

[1] The dates of Pentecost for 1454–1455. See the note at the head of **F/60** above for their inclusion here.

de magistro Strynger v s
Summa vj li xvj s x d

Arr' Scolarum de duodecim Magistris +c Summa l s

Seq' ar' parochiarum
Ar' de liberis ten' de Albis monachis pro a° 31 et a° 32 8 s
De Abbatissa de Godstow xx d et xiiij d
De Abb' de osney vj s viij d an' domini non adject'
De Collegio Animarum 5s et viij s x d ob
Summa xxxj s iiij d ob

de ar' in partibus remotis scil. de Holdernes et novo castro
Summa xix li vij s viij d nihil de Essex et Arncliffe

Summa omn' arrerag' xlvj li iij s v d

[*Nothing whatever of the Rents and Allowances are legible except parts of the marginal headings.*]

Red an 33 H 6 in paroch' S Petri et S Martini ut supra

de par' omn' Sanctorum	
de ten' quod tenet Tho Dudley	1.13.4
Bristow	2.13.4
Spending	1.1.8
Will' Taylour pro 3 ter	12.6
quond' Hug Benet pro 3 ter	15.0
de Jo Lewys pro eodem ten' pro uno ter	0.10.0
quondam Gower pro 3 ter	1.00.0
de ten' quod tenet [*blank*]	0.16.8
de ten' quod tenet W. Stokes	2.6.8
De Spender pro quadam camera pro 1 ter	0.0.10

Summa 11.16.8[2]

Red' Aul
De Jo Ware pro aule Edwardi pro 2 ter x s
De Magistro Jo Warde pro eadem Aul pro 2 ter xvij s viij d
De Johanne Dalton pro aula drowda xxvj s vij d
Omn' Aularum reddit Summa xiiij li vij s viij d

[2] [ADMC] The correct total is £11 10s.

Red' Camerarum de magistro Pray	xiij s iiij d
de magistro Wyght	xvj s viij d
de magistro Bylsdon pro 2 ter	vj s viij d
Summa xxxvj s v [*sic*][3]	

Red. Scolarum	
de magistro Hen Stroder	vj s viij d
de magistro Jo Hull	vj s viij d
de magistro [*blank*]	vj s viij d
de Ric. fulwod	iij s viij d
Ric' Dikson	iij s viij d
Cerne	iij s viij d
Smyth	iij s viij d
	- al. 33 Magistro Jo
Summa xxxiiij s viij d	

redd' liberi et in partibus remotis ut supra

Summa omn' reddituum lxxxviij li xvij s x d ob

red' preter sortem domus	
de cista	xx s
De Magistro Davyson	iij s iiij d
De Magistro [. . .][4]	xxiij d
De Byrkhed Rect' de Harow of ye hyll	xxxiij s iiij d
Summa lviij s vj d[5]	

Summa omn' oneratorum cxxxvij li xix s ix d ob

Alloc' summa xlv li vj s ob

[*The original has at this point the words:*]

Expense facte circa facturam [. . .
In primis [. . .

[3] [ADMC] The correct total is 36s 8d.
[4] [ADMC] An ink blot obscures this name.
[5] [ADMC] The correct total is 58s 7d.

[*These might be linked with the following entry in Smith, or refer to a section which he did not summarise.*]

Repar' laicorum In primis pro domo Bristow pro reparationis [*sic*] factis tempore procuratoris Marschall	vj s viij d
In renovatione Cautionum	viij s
Solutiones facte Socijs Collegij	
In primis Magistro Collegij	liij s iiij d
Item Magistro Hertylpole	xx s
Item Magistro Dawyson	liij s iiij d
Item Magistro Stroder	xvj s viij d
Item domino Jacobo Baynbrygg	xxxiij s iiij d
Item W. Gregforth	xvj s viij d
Item M Ric' Marschall	xvj s viij d
Item Magistro Johanne Hull	xvj s viij d
Item Magistro Johanni Mercer	iij s iiij d
Item Magistro Jo Hull pro officio procur'	x s
Summa xij li	
pincerne	xxx [*sic*]
Barbiton'	vj s viij d
Coco	ix s ij d
Lotrici	vj s viij d
Summa lij s vj d	
Abb' de osney	xxix s vj d
Priori S Frideswyde	xviij s viij d
Abbatisse de Godstow	x s
Summa lviij s ij d	
In primis in communis sociorum	xxj li iij s ij d ob
In Batell et Jurnell	xxix s x s q[a]
In Contribucionibus	xx s
In die sancte Trinitatis	iij s viij d ob
Summa xxiij li xvj s ix d q[a]	
Alicie Belacysse	v li xvj s viij d
In equitacione magistri et procur' versus Essex	xxxij s vj d
——— procuratoris versus petworth	xvij s xj d
——— magistri 2 vice [*sic*] versus Essex et Wilcotts	iij li xij s ix d
magistri versus Northumberland	iiij li vj s x d

In equitacione Tho Taylour	xxvj s vj d
magistri Hertylpole et Davyson versus dunkon	iij s
Summa xj s [*sic; recte li*] xix s vj d	

Expens' in Essex alloc' firmario pro liberis tenementis	xxxvij s iiij d
firmario de Arnclyyffe pro reparationibus	vij li
In repar' in novo castro et stipend' Collect redd	iij li ij s viij d
In reparacionibus factis in Holdernes et alijs expens'	v li xvj s
1ª mentio reparatibus	
Summa xvij li xvj d	

In dimissis tenentibus	xlij s
In remanentibus in cista	iij li xvij s
Summa v li xix s	

Summa omn' expens' lxxxxj li xiij s viij d ob

Summa omn' Allocatorum et expensarum cxxxvij li ix d qª[6]

Computatis Computandis et allocatis allocandis computans est obnoxius dicto Collegio seu Magne Aule Universitatis predicte in xix s cum qª.

Acta sunt hec per M Thomam Saundres Commissarium prenobilis viri magistri Georgij Nevill anno et mense supra specificatis.

[6] [ADMC] The correct total is £137 9d.

34 HENRY VI (ROLL UC:BU1/F/66)
c.25 May 1455–16 May 1456?[1]

BURSAR: JAMES BAYNBRYGE

[The roll is very badly damaged, but some parts can be reconstructed from Smith Vol. VIII pp.178a, 179a and 170b.]

Compotus domini Jacobi Baynbryge procuratoris Magne Aula sive Collegij [. . .] Anno Regni regis Henrici Sexti post conquestum [tricesimo quarto]

[Heading lost; presumably 'Aul' Aularum'
About 6 or 8 lines missing; no figures are legible]

. . .] eodem pro parva aula universitatis in vico scolarum pro anno xxxij°

De eodem pro anno xxxiij°
De Mro Beymslay pro Aula H[. . .]ton pro anno xxxiij°
De eodem pro ten' quond' tenure Came pro anno xxxj
De eodem pro eodem ten' pro anno xxxij°
De eodem pro eodem ten' pro anno xxxiij°
De Mro Antonio Clayton' pro ten' q[*uondam ten*]ur' Came
De Mro Semer pro parva Aula [*universitatis*] in alto [*vico* . . .
De eodem pro anno xxxij° [?]

[About 7 illegible lines follow, in which the Arrears of Halls end, and the Arrears for College Rooms begin]

De Mro [. . .
De Mro [. . .
De Mro Wyrthe [. . .
De Mro Strynger
Summa vj li xv s vij d

[Arr' Scolarum]
De Mro Keler (?) [. . .
De Mro lorde [. . .
De Mro Swanne [. . .

[1] The dates of Pentecost for 1455–1456. See the note at the head of **F/60** above for their inclusion here.

De Mro Petro [. . .
De St[. . .
De [. . .

[*About 3 or 4 illegible lines*]

De [. . .
De Mro [. . .
De Mro J Sug[. . .
De Mro Tallour [. . .
Summa iij li iij s iiij d

[*Arrears for All Saints*]
De Johanne barbor' [. . .
De Wasskhew [. . .
De Bradmer [. . .
De Joh' [. . .

[*About 4 illegible lines, in which probably the All Saints Arrears end, and the St. Mary the Virgin and St. Peter in the East ones begin*]

De [. . .
De Johanne [. . .
De eodem pro anno xxxiij[. . .
Summa xlvij s

[*Arrears for the suburbs and fields of Oxford*]
De Thome Mansypyll' pro Allrychsed' [. . .
De Trygrano pro annis xxvij° xxviij et xxix°
De Pedyngton'
De symone M[. . .
De Roberto ful[. . .

[*About 3 illegible lines follow*]

De Hu[. . .
De cam[. . .
[*Summa*] lvj s x [*d*]

[*Arrears for free tenements*]
De Abbatissa de godstow pro schopa exopposito magne porte fridiswide pro ann[. . .
De eadem pro annuali redditu pro gardino quond' tenure [*Thome*] mayster [. . .

De abbati de osney pro schopa iuxta J. spisere
De collegio animarum quond' tenure J. Spront'
De eodem pro gardino [. . .
[*Summa* . . .

[*About 2 illegible lines follow, in which the Arrears from distant places probably begin.*]

De eisdem pro [. . .
De Willelmo [. . .
Summa x li xx s viij d

Summa omn' A[*rr'*] xlv li vj s ob

Redditus in paroch' sanctorum petri in balliolo et martini anno rr' Henrici sexti tercio quarto

De ten' quod tenet Ric[. . .
De ten' quod tenet [. . .
[*This is probably last entry of this section. Any total is illegible*]

Redditus ten' laycorum in parochia omn' sanctorum

[*Possibly an entry here*]
De ten' [. . .
De ten' quod tenet [. . .
De ten' quod tenet Spen[*dyng* . . .
De eodem Spendyng pro quadam camera pro uno anno [. . .
De Johanne lewys pro ten' quond' tenuer' [*sic*] Hugon' Benet pro tribus terminis
De Johanne Harthe pro ten' quond' ten[. . .]r' J Gower pro tribus terminis[2]
De Cifford [. . .
De ten' quod tenuit [. . .
De ten' quod tenet [. . .
[*Summa* . . .

Redditus [*in paroch' beate*] marie et sancti petri [*in*] oriente

[*About 2 or 3 lines illegible*]
De ten' [. . .
[*Summa* . . .

[2] On 8 April 1454, the central of the three 'Gonwardby' houses on High Street (see pp. xxiv–xxvi of the Introduction), which had been rented to John Gowere, Barber, was leased to John Hartt, Mason (**UC:E2/7/2D/2**).

Redditus Aularum
De Mro Church [. . .
De [. . .
De eodem [. . .
De eodem [. . .
[*One line illegible*]
De eodem [. . .
De Mro [. . .
De Johanne Ware pro Aule Edwardi
De Mro Johanne Ward' pro eadem Aula pro [. . .
De Johanne fletcher' pro Aula drowda ⟨pro duobus term'⟩
Summa [. . .

Redditus camerarum

De Mro [pray]	[xiij s iiij d]
De Mro [Wyghte pro duobus terminis]	[viij s iiij d]
[De Mro Bylsdon pro duobus terminis]	[vj s viij d]
[Summa xxviij s iiij d]	

Redditus scolarum

De Mro Willelmo [Staynton]	[vj s viij d]
De Mro langhorn	[vj s viij d]
De Mro Henric' Boste'	[vj s viij d]
De Mro Thoma [Loo]	[vj s viij d]
De Johanne payn[ter]	[iij s viij d]
De Sawhal[d]	[iij s viij d][3]
De tylling	[iij s viij d]
De [Hudson]	[iij s viij d]
[Summa xlj s iiij d]	

Redditus suburbijs [*sic*] et campis oxon'
De [. . .
De terris [. . .
De pratis retro osnay [. . .
De priori fratrum predicatorum pro [. . .] Irland'
Summa [. . .

Redditus de liberis ten' in oxon'
De Abbatissa de godstow pro schopa ex op^{to} magne aule sancte fridiswide

[3] Smith adds here the words 'Sawghold all' pro a^{o}'.

De eadem [. . .
De Abba[. . .
De coll[*(Canterbury College for Silver Hall)* . . .
De [*n*]ov[*o collegio pro (Maiden Hall)*
De coll[. . .
De collegio linc'[. . .
De Johanne trygrane pro def[*alcacione*] [ij s ij d]
De Pedyngton pro defalcacione [ij s ij d]
De collegio animarum pro ten' quond' tenure J Spronte in parochia sancti petri in ball[. . .
De eodem collegio pro gardino retro dictum ten'
De albis [*monachis pro gardino*] quond' tenure Barton'
[*Summa* . . .

Redditus in partibus remotis
[*3 illegible lines follow*]
De novo castro
De ecclesia in Arnclyffe
Summa xlviij li [. . .

Summa Omn' Reddituum [lxxxvij li vij s ix d]

Recepta p[*reter*] sortem domus
Recept' [de cista] [iij li xvij s]
[Item de Abbate de Sollay] [liij s iiij d]
[De execut' episcopi exon'] [vj s viij d]
[De calce de stramine] [vj d]
~~Item de Humfrido~~
Summa vj li x[vij s vj d]

Summa omnium oneratorum cxxxix li xj s iij d][4]

Allocaciones Aularum[5]
De Moricio carior' [*x d*]
De Mro Chris' pro Aula Brasnosse [*xxij s ij d ob q*[a]]
De eodem pro parva Aula universitatis in vico scolarum [*ix s ij d*]
De eodem pro Aula [*sancti Thome iij s iiij d*]
De eodem pro Gardino [*aule scuti ij s ij d ob q*[a]]
De eodem pro parva [. . .

[4] [ADMC] The correct total is £139 11s 11d.
[5] Although almost all the sums in this section are missing, several can be deduced from the arrears of **F/67** below.

De eodem pro Anno xxviij
De eodem pro Anno xxx
De eodem pro Anno xxxj°
De eodem pro parva Aula universitatis in vico scolarum pro anno xxxij°
De eodem pro Anno xxxiij°
De eodem pro Anno xxxiiij° [*xviij s[?] viij d*]
De Mro Bemyslay pro Aula H[*ampton*] [*xiiij s iiij d*]
De eodem pro ten' quond' tenur' [*Cayme*] anno [. . . [*vj s viij d*]
De eodem pro eodem ten' [*pro anno xxxij* *xx s*]
De eodem pro eodem ten' [*pro anno xxxiij* *xx s*]
De eodem pro Aula Hampton et Sykyll Hall pro Anno xxxiiij [xxviij s ij d]
De Mro Anton' Claton' [*xj s viij d*]
De Mro Semar' pro Anno xxxiiij° [*xviij s j d ob*]
De Russell [*mro*] grammaticali pro Aula Edwardi [*v s*]
De Johanne Dalton pro Aula drowda [*xx s*]
De Johanne flecher pro Aula [. . .] xxxiiij° [*x s[?] iiij d*]
De M Ward pro [. . .
[*Summa* . . .

Allocaciones camerarum
De doctor' dowson' pro annis xx° xxj° xxij° xxv° xxvj° xxvij° xxviij° et xxix [iiij li xiiij s vj d]
De Mro Roberto flemyng [*iiij s*]
De Mro Willelmo d[*an*]yell' [*xij s*]
De Mro Wryght' [*xij d*]
De Mro Strynger [*iij s iiij d*]
Summa [*v li xiiij s xj d*]

[*Face of Roll*]

Allocaciones scolarum
De Mro Kele [*xx d*]
De Mro lord' [*vj s viij d*]
De Mro Swan' [*vj s viij d*]
De Mro Petro [*vj s viij d*]
De Stephane Brown'
De Mro Wrangwysch
De Carver
De Clyfton

De Mro H Stroker	[*vj d viij d*]
De Mro Hull'	[*vj s viij d*]
De Mro Sowtham	[*viij d*]
De Mro Talbot	[*ij s*]
De Mro W Staynton'	[*vj s viij d*]
De Mro Langhorn'	[*vj s viij d*]
De Mro H Boste	[*vj s viij d*]
De Mro Thoma Leo[. . .	[*iij s viij d*]
De saw[. . .	[*iij s viij d*]
De tylyng	
De [*hu*]dson	
Summa [. . .	

Allocaciones in parochia omnium sanctorum

De Johanne Barbour	
De Westk[*ew* . . .	[*vj s viij d*]
De Brad[*myr* . . .	[*xj s vj d*]
De Johanne G[. . .	[*vj s*[?] *ij d*]
De Johanne Hart[. . .	[*xij s viij d*]
De J. lewys pro ten' quond' tenure Hugonis Benyt	[*x s*]
[*Summa* . . .	

Allocaciones in paroch' sancte marie et sancti patri in oriente

[*About 3 illegible lines follow*]

[*Summa*] xlvij [*s* . . .

Allocacionies in [*suburbijs*] et campis [*oxon'*]

De T[. . .] Alrychsed'	[*ij s*]
. . .] xxvj [?] xxviij et xxix°	[*viij s x d*]
[*2 illegible lines follow*]	
De [. . .] xxix xxx et xxxj	
De Gylote [. . .	
De Roberto Wode	
De eodem pro Annis xxx° xxxj° xxxij° et xxxiij°	
De eodem pro Anno xxxiiij°	
De qwytfeld' [. . .	
De [. . .] xxxiij°	
. . .] pro Anno xxxiij	
. . .] Anno xxxiiij° [. . .	
De R[. . .] in bellom[*onte* . . .	

[*Probably one more line, now illegible*]
Summa [. . .

Allocaciones de liberis ten'
De [. . .
. . .] tenure [. . .
[*2 lines indecipherable*]
De abbati [. . .
De eodem pro eodem s[. . .
De collegio animarum pro ten' quond' tenure Skybowe
De collegio linc' pro gardino
De collegio animarum pro ten' [*quond'*] tenure J Spront' x s
De eodem pro gardino xv[. . .
. . .] viij s x [. . .
[*About 2 lines indecipherable*]
[*Summa* . . .]ij li iij s [. . .

Allocaciones in partibus remotis
De terris in Holdernesse pro Anno xxxiij° xlj s [*viij d*]
De eisdem pro Anno xxxiiij° [*xxj s viij d*]
De terris novi castri [*lvj s iiij d(?)*]
De eidem pro Annos xxx° xxxj° et xxxij° xiiij s [*vij d(?)*]
De exsexya [. . . iiij li [*xix s*]
[*About 6 lines, not clearly decipherable*]
[*Summa*] xiiij li vj s [. . .

Summa omn' Allocatorum [lv li xvij d]

Soluciones facte per procuratorem
[*5 or 6 lines illegible*]
Item in parva Aula universitatis [. . .
Item in Aula Edwardi
Item in Aula drowda
[*Summa* . . .

[*No heading discernable, then 5 or 6 illegible lines, and an illegible total. At this point Smith notes two payments he found of interest, namely one of £4 14s 6d to John Morlay's former tenement (once Stanton Hall), and the other of 13s for the renewal of caution moneys* (**cautiones**).]

Reparaciones facte in paroch' sancte marie
In domo quond' tenuere J. William [. . .

Item in scolis
[*Summa* . . .

. . .] colleg[. . .
[*About 4 or 5 lines illegible*]
Item in Aula
Item in coquina
[*Summa* . . .

Expense facte circa staurum pro [. . .
In primis [. . .
[*About 5 lines illegible*]
Summa [. . .

Soluciones facte socijs collegij

In Primis Magistro	[iij li vj s viij d]
Item Mro Hartyllpoll'	[xxvj s viij d]
Item M Henrico [Stroder]	[xxvj s viij d]
Item [domino Jacobo Baynbrygge]	[iij li vj s viij d]
[Willelmo Gregforth]	[xxvj s viij d]
[M[ro] Joh' Hull]	[xx s]
[Item Procuratori pro officio ejus]	[x s]
[Item M' in partem solucionis sue indenture]	[xx s]

[Summa xiiij li x s]

Solut' servientibus
In primis pincerne
Item Coco
Item barbitonsori
Item lotrici
[*Summa* . . .

[*No heading discernable, then about 6 illegible lines*]
Summa [. . .

Solut' pro communis batellis et contribucionibus

In primis in communis sociorum	[xvj li vij s xj s ob]
Item in batellis et jurnellis	[xxxviij s iij d q[a]]
Item in [contribucionibus]	[xix s ix d ob]
[In festo Sancti Cuthberti tempore M[ri] Hull]	[xij s ix d]
[In eodem festo hoc a[o]]	[xij s vij s ob]
[In festo sancte Trinitatis]	[ij s vj d ob]

[Summa xx li xiij s xj s q[a]]

[Alicie Bellasis in 3 solutionibus][6] [viij li x s]

Expense facte in equitacionibus

In primis in equitacione Magistri et procuratoris ad exsexiam [xix s vij d ob]

Item in equitacione M et M Johannis Hull' ad exoniam' [xxij s ix d ob]

Item in equitacione M Ric' M[arshall ad exoniam] [vj s ij d]

Item in equitacione M Ric Marschall' *[xvj s vij d ob]*[7]

Item in equitacione M [Johannis] Hull [ad Arncliffe] [xxj s]

[Item Henr' pro pecunijs a M^ro^ Ric' Marshall missis] [ij s viij d]

[Item Thoma Lau pro pecunijs a novo castro portatis] [xx d]

[Summa iiij li x s vj d ob]

Item thome d[ikson firmario] [vj s viij d]

[remanet in cista] [vj li xv s iij d]

Summa omn' expensarum [lxxxiij li vij s v d]

[Summa omnium Allocat' et expens' cxxxviij li viij s x d ob q^a^][8]

[A roll of 2 membranes, written in a small hand. The damage is very bad for the right two-thirds of the roll, face and dorse.

The roll now ends with the total of expenses. However Smith ends his summary with the following comment:

Note yt by a small peice of parchmt wch was loose and unpasted [now lost] I find this subscription w^h^ belongs to ye fore going as I find by ye agreem^t^ of ye same remaining

*Computatis computandis allocatis allocandis prefatus computans est obnoxius magne Aule un^tis^ oxon in xx li 2^bus^ s quatuor d cum q^a^*[9]

Acta sunt hec per Thomam Saundress Comissarium prenobilis domini domini Georgij Nevill Cancell' alme Universitatis oxon anno et mense suprascriptis.]

6 These are Smith's words, very probably a paraphrase of the original.

7 Smith forgot to write in this entry. However, it can be deduced by subtracting the totals which he did include from the final sum.

8 [ADMC] The correct total is £138 8s 10d.

9 [ADMC] Presumably an error for 22 s 4¼d, which would be the correct figure.

35 HENRY VI (ROLL UC:BU1/F/67)
c.16 May 1456–5 June 1457?[1]

BURSAR: WILLIAM GREGFORD

[*The roll is badly damaged. Some extra material is supplied from Smith's summary (Vol. VIII pp.170b-172b).*]

[*The roll begins on the dorse.*]

[Compotus Willelmi Gregforth procuratoris Collegij Willel]mi de dunelm' [magne Aule universitatis oxonie vulgariter nuncupat' d]atus per eundem Willelmum [anno regni regis Henrici s]exti post conquestum [A]nglie trecesimo quinto

[*No original headings, and no texts of entries are legible, unless otherwise indicated. The contents of some have been deduced from other rolls, in particular the Allowances of* **F/66**.]

[*These first totals are for Arrears from Halls*]

[*De Moricio carior'*]	x d
[*De Mro Chris' pro Aula Brasnosse*]	xxij s ij d ob q^{a}
[*De eodem pro parva Aula universitatis in vico scolarum*]	ix s ij d
[*De eodem pro Aula sancti Thome*]	iij s iiij d
[*De eodem pro Gardino aule scuti*]	ij s ij d ob q^{a}
[*De eodem pro parva . . .*	
[*De eodem pro Anno xxviij . . .*	
[*De eodem pro Anno xxx . . .*	
[*De eodem pro Anno xxxj*^{o} *. . .*	
[*De eodem pro parva Aula universitatis in vico scolarum pro anno xxxij*^{o} *. . .*	
[*De eodem pro Anno xxxiij*^{o} *. . .*	
[*De eodem pro Anno xxxiiij*^{o}]	xviij s[?] viij d
[*De Mro Bemyslay pro Aula Hampton*]	xiiij s iiij d
[*De eodem pro ten' quond' tenur' Cayme anno . . .*]	[*vj s*] viij d[2]
[(*from Hampton Hall for 32 Hen VI*)]	xx s
[(*from Hampton Hall for 33 Hen VI*)]	xx s

[1] The dates of Pentecost for 1456–1457. See the note at the head of **F/60** above for their inclusion here.

[2] ADMC proposed 'ij s' as a doubtful reading here; the Allowances below suggest that 'vj s' should be read.

[*De eodem pro Aula Hampton et Sykyll Hall*] pro anno xxxiiij°
xxviij s ij d
[*(from Master Anthony Clayton)*] xj s viij d
[*De Mro Semar' pro Anno xxxiiij°*] xviij s j d ob
[*De Russell mro grammaticali pro Aula Edwardi*] v s
[*De Johanne Dalton pro Aula drowda*] xx s
[*De Johanne flecher pro Aula . . . xxxiiij°*] x s[?] iiij d
[*De M Ward pro . . .*
[*Summa . . .*

[*Arr' Aularum*]
[*De doctor' dowson' pro annis xx° xxj° xxij° xxv° xxvj° xxvij° xxviij° et xxix*] [*iiij li xiii*] s vij d
[*De Mro Roberto flemyng*] iiij s
[*De Mro Willelmo danyell'*] xij s
[*De Mro Wryght'*] xij d
[*De Mro Strynger*] iij s iiij d
[*Summa*] v li xiiij s xj d

[*Arr' Scolarum*]
[*De Mro Kele*] xx d
[*De Mro lord'*] vj s viij d
[*De Mro Swan'*] vj s viij d
[*De Mro Petro*] vj s viij d
[*De Stephane Brown' . . .*
[*De Mro Wrangwysch . . .*
[*De Carver . . .*
[*De Clyfton . . .*
[*De Mro H Stroker*] vj d viij d
[*De Mro Hull'*] vj s viij d
[*De Mro Sowtham*] viij d
[*De Mro Talbot*] ij s
[*De Mro W Staynton'*] vj s viij d
[*De Mro Langhorn'*] vj s viij d
[*De Mro H Boste*] vj s viij d
[*De Mro Thoma Leo*] . . . iij s viij d
[*De saw*] . . . iij s viij d
[*De tylyng . . .*
[*De hudson. . . .*
[*Summa . . .*

[*(Arrears from All Saints)*]

[*De Johanne Barbour* . . .	
[*De Westkew*] . . .	vj s viij d
[*De Bradmyr*] . . .	xj s vj d
[*De Johanne G*] . . .	vj s[?] ij d
[*De Johanne Hart*] . . .	xij s viij d
[*De J. lewys pro ten' quond' tenure Hugonis Benyt*]	x s
[*Summa*] xlix s iiij d	

[*(Arrears of tenements in St. Mary and St. Peter)*]

	xxx s ij d
	iij s iiij d
	xiij s vj d
[*Summa*] xlvij s	

[*(Arrears from the suburbs and fields of Oxford)*]

[*De T . . Alrychsed'*]	ij s
. . . [*xxvj [?] xxviij et xxix°*]	viij s x d
	vj s [?] ij d

[*One, or possibly two, lines not clearly legible*]

	v s
	vj s
	xxiiij s
	vj s
	xij d
	xij d
	ij s ij d
	xx d
	v s
	iiij d
[*Summa* . . .	

[*About 1½ inches are illegible; the Arrears from Quit Rents start here, but it is not possible to link them exactly with the Allowances in* ***F/66***]

	xvj s[?] iiij d
	vj s viij d
	viij s
	v s
	x s
	xvij s ix d

v s
viij s x d ob

[*Summa* . . .]j d ob

[*Arr' in partibus remotis*]

[*De terris in Holdernesse pro Anno xxxiij°*	*xl s*] viij d[3]
[*De eisdem pro Anno xxxiiij°*]	xxj s viij d
[*De terris novi castri*]	lvj s iiij d[?]
[*De eidem pro Annos xxx° xxxj° et xxxij°*	*xiiij s]* vij d[?][4]
[*De exsexya*] . . .	iiij li xix s
	iij li ij s ij d
	v s ij d

[*Summa*] xiiij li[?] xvj s viij d

[Summa omnium arrerag' lv li xvij d]

[*Redditus in parochia Sancti Martini anno rr Henrici*] tricesimo quinto

[*(Robert Wode's house in Sewy Street)*]	vj s
[*(the house on the corner of Carfax)*]	xxxj s viij d

[*Apparently no further entries for 2 inches to the foot of the first membrane, nor for 1½ inches at the top of the 2nd membrane; then rents from All Saints' parish*]

iij s[?] iiij d

[*2½ inches not clearly decipherable; rents from St. Mary and St. Peter in the East start here*]

[*(Tenement of Henry Bath)*]	xl s
	xvj s
	xij s

[*Summa*] iij li viij s

[*Redditus Aularum*]

[*(for Brasenose)*]	iij li vj s viij d
[*(for St. Thomas Hall)*]	x s
[*(for the garden of Sheld Hall?)*]	xvj s viij d[5]
[*(for Little University Hall in Schools Street)*]	xxvj s viij d
[*(for Hampton Hall)*]	l s[?]

[3] ADMC proposed 'xl s' as a doubtful reading here; **F/66** seems to read 'xlj s' instead.
[4] ADMC proposed 'xxij s' as a doubtful reading here; **F/66** seems to read 'xiiij s' instead.
[5] By the 1450s, the rent from Sheld Hall is usually much smaller than this.

[*(for the tenement once occupied by Chaym)*]	xx s
[*(for Little University Hall in High Street?)*]	lvj s iiij d
[*(for Edward Hall)*]	xxxiij s iiij d
[*(for Drowda Hall)*]	xxvj s viij d
[*Summa*] xiiij li[?] xiij s[?] iiij d[?]	

[*Redditus Camerarum*]

De M^ro^ Pray	xiij s iiij d
[Summa xiij] s iiij d	

[Redditus scolarum]

[De M^ro^ Carpenter]	vj s viij d
[De M^ro^ Willelmo Hastyngys]	vj s viij d
[De M^ro^ Davy fayrceatyr pro uno ter']	ij s
[De Roberto Rors]	iij s viij d
[De Thome Proctor]	iij s viij d
[De J. Maydayne]	iij s viij d
[De Dobbys]	iij s viij d
[Summa xxx s]	

[*Redditus in suburbijs et campis oxon'*]

[*(for the garden next to the castle)*]	ij s
[*(for fields in Beaumont)*]	vij s
[*(for the fields behind Osney)*]	xix s viij d
[*(for the fields on the islands in the Thames)*]	xxj s viij d
[*Summa*] l s iiij d	

[*About 5 lines not decipherable, during which the list of Quit Rents begins*]

[*(from New College for Maiden Hall)*]	x s
[*(from Canterbury College for Silver Hall)*]	ij s vj d
[*(from Lincoln College for a garden)*]	v s
[*(from Trygrame or Pedyngton for mowing)*]	ij s ij d
[*(from Trygrame or Pedyngton for mowing)*]	ij s ij d
[*(from All Souls for a house once occupied by Sprount)*]	v s
[*(from All Souls for a garden behind the above property)*]	viij s x d ob
[*(from the Cistercians for a garden once occupied by Barton)*]	vj s
[*Summa . .*]ij d ob	

[*Redditus in partibus remotis*]

[*(for the Manor of Marks Hall)*]	xviij li iij s iiij d
[*(from Thomas Tirrell?)*]	xx s
[*(from Holderness)*]	iij li xx d

[*(from Newcastle)*] v li xv s vj d
[*(from Arnecliffe)*] xx li
[*Summa*] xlviij li vj d

[Summa Reddituum lxxxvj] li vij s x d ob

[*Recepta preter sortem domus*]
[Recepta de cista] [v li xv s vj d]
xv s iij d
[*One line illegible*]
xij d
xiiij d
iij s
[Summa vij li xix (*sic*)]

[Summa omnium oneratorum cxlviij li vij s x d ob]

[*About 2½ inches illegible; then the Allowances of Halls begin; many entries from the Allowances can be deduced from the Arrears of* **F/68** *below*]
[*De Mro Chris' pro Aula Brasnosse*] xxij s ij d ob q[a]
[*De eodem pro parva Aula universitatis in vico scolarum*] ix s ij d
[*De eodem pro Aula sancti Thome*] iij s iiij d
[*De eodem pro Gardino aule scuti*] ij s ij d ob q[a]
[*De eodem pro parva aula universitatis in vico scolarum pro anno vicesimo septimo*] vj s viij d
[*De eodem pro anno xxviij°*] xiij s iiij d
[*De eodem pro anno xxx°*] xvj s iiij d[6]
[*De eodem pro anno xxxj°*] xxv s [. . .
[*De eodem pro parva aula universitatis in vico scolarum*] xxvj s viij d
[*De eodem pro anno xxxiij°*] xxxvj s viij d
[*De eodem pro anno xxxiiij°*] xxxiij s viij d
[*De Mro Bemyslay pro Aula Hampton*] xiiij s iiij d
[*De eodem pro ten' quond' tenur' Cayme anno . . .*] vj s viij d
[*(from Hampton Hall for 32 Hen VI)*] xx s
[*(from Hampton Hall for 33 Hen VI)*] xx s
[*De eodem pro Aula Hampton et Sykyll Hall pro anno xxxiiij°*]
xxviij s ij d
[*De eodem pro aula hampton pro anno tricesimo 5°*] x s

[6] The Arrears of **F/68** suggest that this sum was *xiij s.*

[*De eodem pro ten' quond' tenure chaym pro anno tricesimo 5°*] xx s
[(*From Anthony Clayton for Hampton Hall; year not given*)][7]
xj s viij d
[*De M^ro^ Seymour pro anno tricesimo 4°* iiij d
[*De eodem pro anno tricesimo quinto*] xvij s ix d ob
[*De Russell mro grammaticali pro Aula Edwardi*] v s
xvj s[?] viij d
vij s[?] iiij d

[*One line illegible*]
[*Summa*] xix li xvij s[?] [. . .

[*Face of roll*]

[*Alloc' camerarum*]
[*De Doctore Dowson pro annis xx° xxj° xxv xxvj°*] xxvij xxviij° et xx[*ix*] [*iiij*] li xiiij s vij d
[*De M. Roberto ffemyng*] [*iiij*] s
[*De M Willelmo Danyell'*] xij s
[*De M Wyght'*] xij d
[*Summa v li*] xj s vij d

[*Alloc' scolarum*]
[*De M^ro^ Kele*] xx d
[?*De M^ro^ Lorde*] vj s viij d
[?*De M^ro^ Swan'*] vj s viij d
[*De M^ro^ Petro* *vj s*] viij d
[*De Stephano Brown* *iij s*] viij d
[*De M^ro^ Wrangwysch* *xx*] d
[*De Carver* *iij*] s viij d
[*De Clyfton'*] iij s viij d
[*De M^ro^ Henrico Stroder*] vj s viij d
[*De M^ro^ Johanne Hull'*] vj s viij d
[*De M^ro^*] . . . viij d
[*De M' T*] . . . ij s
[*De*] . . . iij s viij d
[*De M' Davy Fayr . . . pro uno termino* *ij*] s
vj s [*viij d*]
iij s viij d

[7] Smith's exact words for this entry are: 'Inter arr' [*sic*] Aularum de m^ro^ Antonio Clayton xj s viij d pro Aula Hampton ut videtur sine anno'. It is unclear why this is the only entry from the Allowances section which he chose to copy out.

[*One line illegible*]

[*Summa iij li*] ix s vij d

[*Alloc' in paroch' omnium sanctorum*]

[*De Johanne Barbour*]	xiij s iiij d
[*De Westkew*]	vj s viij d
[*De Bradmyre*]	iij s vj d
[*De Joh' Gower*]	iij s ij d
[*De Johanne Hart pro anno xxxiij°*]	xij s viij d
[*De Johanne leuwys pro ten' quond' H*]ugonis Benette	x s
[*De Spendyng' pro anno tricesimo quinto*]	v s v d
[*De Doby pro una camera pro uno termino*]	x d
[*Summa lv s vij d*]	

[*One line illegible; these are Allowances for St. Mary and St. Peter; however, the totals do not match up very well with those on the Arrears of* ***F/68***]

	xxv s ij d
	vj s iiij d
	xvij s[?] ij d
. . .] quinto	xj s iiij d
[*Summa*] lviij s iiij d	

[*Alloc' in suburbijs et campis*]

[*De Thoma Maunsipyll' pro Allryschscheytte*]	ij s
[*De . . . pro annis xxvij° xxviij° xxix*]	viij s x d
[*De . . .*]	iij s ij d
[*De eodem pro anno tricesimo quarto*]	ij s ij d
[*De eodem pro anno tricesimo quinto*]	ij s ij d
[*De simone Mancypylle*	*ij*] s ij d
[*De Roberto ffullere pro gardino pro*] annis xxix xxx et xxxj°	iij s
De Gylotte pro yreland pro annis vicesi]imo tercio et xxiiij°	[*v s*]
[*De qwytfeld' pro anno xxix°*]	xij d
[*De eodem pro anno xxxiiij*]	xij s
[*Summa*] xxx s vj d	

[*Alloc' de liberis tenementis*]

[*De Abbatissa de godstow pro schopa ex o^to^*] magne porte frid[*is-wide*]	iij s iiij d
[*De eadem pro annuali redditu pro ten'*] quond' tenur' Thome Master	ij s iiij d
[*De eadem Abbatisse*]	xx d

[*De eadem pro annuali redditu quond' tenur' Thome Master*] xiiij d
[*De eadem pro anno xxxv°*] xx s
[*De eadem pro eodem anno pro annuali redditu quond'*] tenur' Thome Master xiiij s
[*De abbate de osnay pro schopa iuxta Johannem Spy*]sere xiij s iiij d
[*De eodem pro eadem schopa*] vj s viij d
[*De eodem pro eadem schopa pro anno xxxv°*] vj s viij d
[*De colleg' animarum pro ten' quond' tenur' skybbow pro a° xxxv°*] viij s
[*De eodem pro ten' quond' tenur' Johannis spronte*] x s
[*De eodem pro gardino retro dictum ten'*] xvij s ix d
[*De eodem pro ten' quond' tenur' spronte*] v s
[*De eodem pro gardino retro dictum ten'*] viij s x d ob
[*De eodem pro ten' quond' tenur' spronte*] v s
[*De eodem pro gardino retro dictum ten'*] viij s x d ob
[*De albis monachis pro anno xxxv°*] iiij s
[*Summa*] v li v s vj d

[*Alloc' in partibus remotis*]
[*De Holdyrnysse pro anno xxxiij*] xlj s viij d
[*De eisdem pro anno tricesimo quarto*] xxj s viij d
[*De eisdem anno xxxv°*] xxviij s iiij d
[*De eisdem anno . . .*] liij s viij d
[*De eisdem pro annis xxx xxxj xxxij*] xiij s iiij d
[*De eisdem pro anno xxxiij*] iiij li xix s
[*De eisdem pro anno xxxiiij*] iij li ij s ij d
v li xv s vj d
xl s
[*(From the manor of Mark)*]shall' pro anno xxxiij° v s ij d
[*Summa xxiiij li vj d*]

[Summa allocat' red'] lxv li iiij s viij d ob

[*Two inches probably with no entries*]

xix s ix d

[*2 lines illegible. Probably at around this point Smith found a payment of 10s for the renewal of the* ***Cautiones*** *(pledges).*]

iiij s [. . .
[*Summa . . .*

[*Perhaps one entry illegible*]

iij s x d
xiiij s ix d ob
iiij s viij d
iiij s xj d
xj s x d
ij s
xj s xj d ob
xxv s[?] viij d[?]
xij s [. . .

[*3 inches, to the foot of the 1st membrane, illegible.*]

[*Summa*] xv li xv s xj d ob

vj s iiij d
iiij s x d
x s j d ob
x s xj d ob
[. . .] s v d ob

[*One or possiby two lines not clearly legible.*]

[*Summa*] xlvj s viij d ob

xxxj s ix d
viij s x d ob
vj s iiij d
x d

[*Summa* . . .] s xj d ob

[Solut' facte socijs]

[Magistro]	xx s
[Mro Hertilpoll]	[xxvj] s viij d
[Mro Stroder]	[xxvj s viij d]
[Domino Jacobo Baynbryge]	[l s]
[Willelmo Gregforthe]	xxvj s viij d
[Mo Marshall]	xxvj s viij d
[Mo Hull]	xxvj s viij d
[Mo Watson]	xx s
[Procuratori pro officio suo]	x s

[Summa] xj li xiij s iiij d

xxvj s viij d

x s[?]

vj s[?] viij d

[. . .] s viij d

[*One inch, illegible. Probably around here were the payments of quit rents, where Smith noted a payment of 3s 4d to Richard Wode for Basset Fee, and one to Alice Bellasis of 58s 4d.*]

xxxij s x d

xviij s viij d

x s

xij d

iij s viij d

[*Summa*] lvj s[?] ij d

[In communis sociorum] [x]vj li xviij s xj d

[In Batell' et Jornell'] [xliij s vij d]

[In Contribucionibus] [xxj s ix d ob]

[Pro festo Sancte Trinitatis] [vij s ij d q[a]]

[Pro festo Sancti Cuthberti] [x]xvij s iiij d

[*Summa*..]xij li ix s [.]d ob[8]

lviij s iiij d

[*Summa*] lviij s iiij d

xiij s iiij d

xij s ij d ob

xxxix s[?] vij d

[*Possibly one or two lines illegible, then possibly an illegible total. Around here would have been the entries for riding expenses, for which Smith gives a total of £3 5s 9½d.*]

. . .]vientibus[?]

vj s ij d

xxj s ij d

[Domino Ric' Bernnys pecunie demisse pro ten' in parochia sancti] petri in oriente xxij s viij d

[Roberto at Wode pecunie dimisse] xxxvj s

viij s

ij s

[8] Smith's figures suggest a total of £21 18s 9¾d.

[Pro licentia dimissionis Arnclyffe ad firmam] [xxiij s iiij d]

[*Summa*] iiij li xvj s

[*Nothing decipherable for 1½ or 2 inches.*]

[Summa omnium expens'] lxxxiij li xv s viij d q[a]

[Summa omn' Allocat' et] expensarum cxlix li iiij d ob q[a]

[Acta sunt Hec coram nobis Thome Saundrees sacrorum Canonum professore Commissario venerabili [*sic*] domini domini Georgij Nevyll Episcopi Exon' Cancellarij Alme un[tis] oxon' anno supradicto Computatis computandis Allocatis allocandis prefatum Collegium extitit obnoxium predicto computanti in ix s vj d ob[9].]

[*The roll is a rather narrow one of 2 membranes. For the most part only the left hand edges of both face and dorse is legible. Some of the figures here transcribed are possibly wrongly read.*]

[9] [ADMC] The correct total is 9s 6d.

36 HENRY VI (ROLL UC:BU1/F/68)
c.5 June 1457–21 May 1458?[1]

BURSAR: JOHN HULLE

[*This roll is badly damaged in many places. A good many entries can be reconstructed, and all the entries in Smith Vol. VIII pp.173b-174b which cannot now be read in the original have been incorporated in the text of the roll here. More material has been supplied from other rolls.*]

[*Face of first membrane*]

. . .] Collegij Magistri Willelmi [. . .] vulgariter nuncupat' Datus [. . .] sexti post conquestum Anglie

[*Arr' Aularum*]

[*De Moricio carior'*]	x d
De M° Church pro aula [*brasnose*]	xxij s ij d ob q^a
De eodem pro parva aula universitatis in vico scolarum	ix s ij d
De eodem pro aula sancti Thome	ij s iiij d
De eodem pro gardino aule scuti	ij s ij d ob q^a
De [*eodem*] pro parva aula universitatis [*in vico scolarum*] pro anno vicesimo septimo	vj s viij d
[*De eodem pro anno xxviij°*]	xiij s iiij d
[*De eodem pro anno xxx°*]	xiij s iiij d
[*De eodem pro anno xxxj°*]	xxv s ij d
[*De eodem pro parva aula*] universitatis in vico scolarum[2]	xxvj s viij d
[*De eodem pro anno xxxiij°*]	xxxvj s viij d
[*De eodem pro anno xxxiiij°*]	xxxiij s viij d
[*?De M^{ro} Benyslay pro Aula Hampton' pro a° xxxiij°*]	[*xiij s*] iiij d
[*?De eodem pro ten' quond' tenure Came pro anno*] tricesimo primo	vj s viij d
[*?De eodem pro eodem ten' pro anno*] tricesimo 2°	xx s
[*?De eodem pro eodem ten'*] pro [*anno*] tricesimo 3°	xx s

[1] The dates of Pentecost for 1457–1458. See the note at the head of **F/60** above for their inclusion here.

[2] [ADMC] 'In vico scolarum' are the last words of this entry, but from the length of the entry it looks as if 'pro anno xxxij°' (which in the Allowances of **F/66** comes at the end) probably came here after 'De eodem'.

De eodem pro aula hampton et sekyllhall' pro anno tricesimo 4° xxviij s ij d
De eodem pro aula hampton pro anno tricesimo 5° x s
De eodem pro ten' quond' tenure chaym pro anno tricesimo 5° xx s
De [*Mro*] Antonio Clayton xj s viij d
De [*Mro*] Seymour pro anno tricesimo 4° iiij d
De eodem pro anno tricesimo quinto xvij s ix d ob
[*De Russell magistro grammaticali*] pro aula edwardi v s
[*?De Johanne Dalton pro aula drow*]da xvj s viij d
[. . . *pro anno*] tricesimo 4° xiij s iiij d
[. . . *pro anno xxxv°*] xv s viij d
[. . . *pro aula Edwardi pro anno*] tricesimo 4° v d ob

[*Summa*] xix li xiij s iiij d ob

Arr' camerarum

De [. . . *dowson*] pro annis xx xxj xxij xxv xxvj° xxvij xxviij et xxix iiij li xiiij s vij d
De M' [*Roberto*] ffiemyng' iiij s
De M' Willelmo Danyell' xij s
De M' Wyght' xij d

Summa v li xj s vij d

[*Arr' scolarum*]

[*De Mro Kele*] xx d
[*?De Mro Lorde*] vj s viij d
[*?De Mro Swan'*] vj s viij d
[*De Mro Petro*] vj s viij d
[*De Stephano Brown*] iij s viij d
[*De Mro Wrangwysch*] xx d
[*De Carver*] iij s viij d
[*De Clyfton'*] iij s viij d
[*De Mro Henrico Stroder*] vj s viij d
[*De Mro Johanne*] Hull' vj s viij d
De Mro [. . .] viij d
De M' T[. . . ij s
De [. . . iij s viij d
De M' [*Davy*] Fayr[. . .] pro uno termino ij s
[*De* . . . vj s viij d
[*De* . . . vj s viij d

[*Summa iij*] li ix s iiij d

[*Arr' in paroch' omnium sanctorum*]

[*De Johanne Barbour*]	xiij s iiij d
[*De Westkew*]	vj s viij d
[*De Bradmyre*]	iij s vj d
[*De Joh' Gower*]	iij s ij d
De Johanne Hart pro anno xxxiij°	xij s viij d
De Johanne lewys pro ten' quond' Hugonis Benette	x s
De [*Spen*]dyng' pro anno tricesimo quinto	v s v d
De [*Doby*] pro una camera pro uno termino	x d

Summa lv s vij d

[*Arr' in paroch' sancte Marie et sancti Petri in oriente*]

[*De Ric' Carpenter*]	xxx s ij d
[*De Johanne Morlay*]	iij s iiij d
[*De eodem pro anno xxxiiij°*]	xiij s vj d
[*De . . . pro anno tri*]cesimo quinto	xj s iiij d

[*Summa lviij*] s iiij d

[*Arr' in suburbijs*] et campis

[*De*] Thoma [*Maunsipy*]ll' pro Allryschscheytte	ij s
[*De . . .*] pro annis xxvij° xxviij° xxix	viij s x d
[*De . . .*]	iij s ij d
De eodem pro anno tricesimo quarto	ij s ij d
De eodem pro anno tricesimo quinto	ij s ij d
De simone Mancypylle	ij s ij d
De Roberto ffullere pro gardino pro annis xxix° xxx et xxxj°	iij s
De [*Gylotte*] pro yreland pro annis xxiij et xxiiij°	v s
[*De qwytfeld' pro anno xxix°*]	xij d
[*De eodem pro anno xxxiiij*]	xij s

[*Summa xx*]x s vj d

[*Arr' de liberis ten'*]

[*De Abbatissa de godstow*] pro [*scho*]pa ex o^to^ magne porte ffrideswide	iij s iiij d
[*De eadem pro annuali redditu pro ten'*] quond' tenur' Thome Master	ij s iiij d
[*De eadem Abbatisse*]	xx d
[*De eadem*] pro annuali redditu quond' tenur' Thome Master	xiiij d
De eadem pro anno xxxv°	xx s

De eadem pro eodem anno pro annuali redditu quond' tenur' Thome Master xiiij s

De abbate de osnay pro schopa iuxta Johannem Spyser xiij s iiij d

De eodem pro eadem schopa vj s viij d

De eodem pro eadem schopa pro anno xxxv° vj s viij d

[*De colleg' animarum pro ten'*] quond' tenur' skybbow pro a° xxxv° viij s

[*De eodem pro ten' quond' tenur'*] Johannis spronte x s

[*De eodem pro gardino retro dictum*] ten' xvij s ix d

[*De eodem pro ten' quond' tenur' spronte*] v s

[*De eodem pro gardino retro dictum*] ten' viij s x d ob

[*De eodem pro ten' quond'*] tenur' spronte v s

[*De eodem pro gardino*] retro dictum ten' viij s x d ob

De albis monachis pro anno xxxv° iiij s

Summa v li v s vj d

Arr' in partibus remotis

De [*Holdyrn*]ysse pro anno xxxiij xlj s viij d

De eisdem pro anno tricesimo quarto xxj s viij d

[*De eisdem anno*] xxxv° xxviij s iiij d

[*De eisdem anno . . .*] liij s viij d

[*De eisdem pro annis xxx xxxj xxxij*] xiij s iiij d

[*De eisdem pro anno xxxiij*] iiij li xix s

[*De eisdem pro anno xxxiiij*] iij li ij s ij d

[*De . . .*] v li xv s vj d

[*De . . .*] a° xxxv xl s

[*De . . .*]ound pro manerio de Merkyshall' pro a° xxxiij v s ij d

Summa xxiiij li vj d

Summa omn' Arreragiorum lxv li iiij s viij d ob

Redditus in parochia sancti Martini Anno rr Henrici sexti xxxvj°

[*De ten' quod*] tenet Robertus Wode in Swynshewton vj s

[*De ten' quod*] tenet [*teuto*]nicus [*super*] angulum quadrivij xxvj s viij d

[*Summa*] xxxij s viij d

[*Redditus ten' laicorum*] in parochia omn' sanctorum

[*De ten' . . .*] Thomas Dudlay xxxiij s iiij d

[*De ten' . . . Tho*]mas Brystow liij s iiij d

De te[*n' quod*] tenet Spendyng' xxj s viij d

De ten' [*quod*] tenet Thomas Mores talyour xl s
De ten' quod tenet Ric' Wode xxvj s viij d
De ten' quod tenet Willelmus Barbour xvj s viij d
[*De ten'*] quod [. . .] xlvj s viij d
[*Summa*] xj li xviij s iiij d

[*Redditus in paroch' beate Marie et sancti*] petri in oriente
[De ten' quod tenet Henricus Bath[3]] xl s
[*De ten'* . . .] xvj s
[*De ten* . . .] M' Hugo ffoster M' grammatical' xij s
Summa iij li viij s

[*Face of second membrane*]

[*Redditus Aularum*]
[*(for Brasenose)*] iij li vj s viij d
[*(for St. Thomas' Hall)*] x s
[*(for the garden of Sheld Hall)*] vj s viij d
[*De parva aula*] universitatis in vico scolarum xxvj s viij d
De [*?M' Beneslay pro*] Aula Hampton l s
De eodem pro ten' quond' tenure chayme xx s
De M' Seymour pro parva aula universitatis in alto vico liij s iiij d
[*De M' ?Ward pro*] aula Edwardi xxxiij s iiij d
[*(for Drowda Hall)*] xxvj s viij d
[*(for Stanton Hall)*] xvj s viij d
[*Summa xv li*] x s

[*Redditus Camerarum*]
[De M^{ro}] Pray xiij s iiij d
De domino Alano Bayton [pro 2 ter'] vj s viij d
Summa xx s

[Redditus Scolarum]
[De m^{ro} David fayrwater] vj s viij d
[De m^{ro} Willelmo Gregforth] vj s viij d
[De m^{ro} [*blank*] Lynsay] vj s viij d
[De m^{ro} Ric' Granger] vj s viij d
[De Johanne Pylyng] iij s viij d
[De [*blank*]] iij s viij d

3 [ADMC] Reading from Smith Vol. VIII p. 173b; Smith notes that the reading under 'Reparacione ten' laicorum' is 'pro domo quond' Henrici Bayth'.

De [duobus] determinatoribus	vij s iiij d
[Summa] xlj s iiij d	

[*Redditus in suburbijs et in campis*] oxon'

[*De . . . pro gardino*] iuxta castrum	ij s
[*De . . .*] Walton	vij s
De Pratis retro [*Osnay*]	xix s viij d
De [. . .] ⟨pro pratis alrysshet et yrland⟩	xxj s viij d
[*Summa*] l s iiij d	

[*Redditus de liberis ten' in oxon'*]

[*De Abbatissa de Godstow pro shopa*] ex opp^{to} magne porte sancte frideswyde	xx d
[*De . . .*] quond' tenur' Thome Maister	xiij s
[*De . . .*] Johannem Spyser	vj s viij d
De [*Novo Collegio pro*] Madynhall'	x s
De [*Collegio Cant'*] pro [*silver*]hall'	ij s vj d
[*De . . .*]	v s
[*De . . .*] Osnay	ij s ij d
[*De . . .*]	ij s ij d
[*(from All Souls' College for a house once in the)*] tenur' Sprount in paroch' sancti petri in balliolo	v s
[*(from the same for a garden behind the)*] dictum ten'	viij s x d ob
[*De Albis monachis pro*] gardino quond' tenur' Barton	iiij s
Summa lvij s ij d ob	

[*Redditus in partibus remotis*]

[*?De Johanne Pound pro*] manerio de Merkyshall' et Molendinis	xviij li iij s iiij d
[*?De domino Thome Tirrell'*]	xx s
[*?De terris in Holdernesse*]	iij li xx d
[*?De Novo Castro*]	v li xv s vj d
[*?De Ecclesia de Arnec*]lyff	xx li
Summa xlviij li vj s	

[*Summa*] omn' reddituum lxxxviij li xviij s iiij d ob

[*Recepta preter sortem domus*]

[*De cista*]	v li ix d ob
[*De . . .*] de pypard pro equo	xvj s
[*De . . .*]	xj d

[*De . . .*]	j d ob
Summa v li xvij s x d	

[*Summa omnium*] oneratorum clx li xj d

[*Allocaciones Aularum*]

[*De Moricio carior'*]	x d
[*De Magistro Church pro aula*] Brasynnose	xxij s ij d ob q^{a}
[*De eodem pro parva aula*] universitatis in vico scolarum	ix s ij d
[*De eodem pro aula sancti Thome*]	iij s iiij d
[*De eodem pro gardino aule scuti*]	ij s ij d ob q^{a}
[*De eodem pro parva aula*] universitatis in vico scolarum pro anno xxvij^{o}	vj s viij d
[*De eodem pro anno*] xxviij^{o}	xiij s iiij d
[*De eodem pro anno xxx^{o}*]	xiij s iiij d
[*De eodem pro anno*] xxxj^{o}	xxv s ij d
[*De eodem pro parva aula*] universitatis in vico scolarum pro anno xxxij^{o}	xxvj s viij d
[*De eodem pro anno xxxiij^{o}*]	xxxvj s viij d
[*De eodem pro anno xxxiiij^{o}*]	xxxiij s viij d
[*De . . .*]	xlv s viij d
[*?De M^{ro} Benyslay pro Aula Hampton' pro a^{o} xxxiij^{o}?*]	vj s viij d
[*?De eodem pro ten' quond' tenure Came pro anno*] xxxj^{o}	vj s viij d
[*?De eodem pro eodem ten' pro anno*] xxxij^{o}	xx s
[*?De eodem pro eodem ten' pro anno*] xxxiij^{o}	xx s
[*De eodem pro aula hampton et*] sekyll' hall' pro anno xxx^{o} iiij	xxviij s ij d
De eodem pro [. . .]^{o}	iiij s viij d
[*De eodem pro ten' quond' tenure chaym pro*] anno xxxv^{o}	xx s
[*De eodem pro ten' quond' tenure chaym pro anno*] xxxvj^{o}	xx s
[*De Magistro Antonio Clayton'*]	xj s viij d
[*De Magistro Seymour pro anno xxxiiij^{o}*]	iiij d
[*?De eodem pro anno tricesimo sext?*]^{o}	liij s iiij d
[*De Russell magistro grammaticali*] pro aula Edwardi	v s
[*?De Johanne Dalton pro aula*] drowda	xvj s viij d
[*De . . . pro*] a^{o} xxxiiij^{o}	xiij s iiij d
[*De . . .*] pro anno xxxv^{o}	xv s viij d
[*De . . .*] xxxvj	vij s viij d
[*De . . .*] pro aula Edwardi pro anno a^{o} xxxiiij	v d ob
[*De . . . pro*] eadem aula pro a^{o} xxxvj^{o}	xxij s iij d

[*De . . .*] pro aula staunton pro a° xxxvj° xvj s viij d

Summa xxvj li xv s x d

[*Alloc' camerarum*]

De [. . . *dowson pro annis*] xx xxj xxij xxv xxvj° xxvij° xxviij° et xxix° iiij li xiiij s vij d

[*De magistro Roberto ffłem*]myng' iiij s

De M' Wyght' xij d

De [*domino Alano Baytson*] vj s viij d

Summa v li ~~xj s vij d~~ xviij s iij d

[*Dorse of second membrane*]

[*Alloc' scolarum*]

[*De Magistro Kele*] xx d

[*?De magistro Lorde*] vj s viij d

[*?De magistro Swan'*] vj s viij d

De m[*agistro*] Petro vj s viij d

[*De Steph*]ano Brown iij s viij d

[*De magistro Wr*]angwych xx d

[*De Carver*] iij s viij d

[*De Clyfton'*] iij s viij d

[*De magistro*] Henrico Stroder vj s viij d

[*De magistro*] Johanne Hull' vj s viij d

[*De magistro . . .*] viij d

[*De magistro T . . .*] ij s

[*De . . .*] iij s viij d

[*De magistro Davidio fair*]ether pro annis xxxv et xxxvj° viij s viij d

De [. . .] carpent' viij d

De magistro [*W*] gregforth' vj s viij d

De [. . .] vj s viij d

[*De . . .*] iij s viij d

Summa iiij li vij s

[*Alloc' in paroch'*] omnium sanctorum et sancti martini

[*De Johanne Barbour*] xiij s iiij d

[*De Westkew*] vj s viij d

De Bradmyre iij s vj d

De Johanne Gower iij s ij d

[*De Johanne Hart*] pro a° xxxiij° xij s viij d

[*De Joh' lewys*] pro ten' quond' tenure Hugonis Benette x s

[*De Spendyng'*] pro anno xxxv	v s v d
De [. . .] pro una camera pro uno termino ⟨pro eodem a^{o}⟩	x d
De eodem pro anno xxxvj^{o}	iiij s xj d
De Brystow pro anno xxxvj^{o}	xiiij s
De [. . .] Warne	vj s viij d
[*De Roberto Wo*]de pro a^{o} xxxvj	vj s
Summa iiij li x s xj d	

Allocaciones in parochia sancte Marie et sancti Petri in oriente

De Ricardo Carpenter	xxx s ij d
De Johanne Morlay	iij s iiij d
[*De eodem pro anno*] xxxiiij^{o}	xiij s vj d
[*De* . . .] pro anno xxxv^{o}	xj s iiij d
[*De* . . .]	xviij s viij d
Summa iij li xvij s	

Allocaciones in suburbijs et campis oxon'

De Thoma Mauncypyll' pro alrychhett'	ij s
[*De* . . .] annis xxvij^{o} xxviij^{o} et xxix^{o}	viij s x d
D[*e* . . .]	iij s ij d
De [*eodem pro anno xxxiiij^{o}*]	ij s ij d
De [*eodem*] pro annis xxxv^{o} et xxxvj^{o}	iiij s iiij d
De simone Mauncypyll'	ij s ij d
De Roberto ffuller pro Gardino pro annis xxix^{o} xxx et xxxj^{o}	iij s
De Gyllotte pro yreland' pro annis xxiij et xxiiij^{o}	v s
De qwytfeld' pro anno xxix^{o}	xij d
De [*eodem*] pro anno xxxiiij	xij d
[*De* . . .]	iij s vj d
[*De Pratis retro Osnay pro anno xxxvj^{o}*]	xix s viij d
[*Summa*] lv s x d	

Allocaciones de liberis ten'

De Abbatissa de godstow pro schopa ex opo^{to} magne porte frydeswyde	iij s iiij d
De eadem pro annuali redditu pro ten' quond' tenur' Thome Mayster	ij s iiij d
De eadem Abbatissa	xx d
De eadem pro annuali redditu quond' tenur' Thome Mayster	xiiij d
[*De eadem pro anno x*]xxv^{o}	xx d

[*De eadem pro eodem a^{o}*] pro annuali r' quond' tenur' T. Mayster xiiij d
[*De abbate*] de Ossney pro schopa iuxta Johannem Spyser xiij s iiij d
De eodem pro eadem schopa vj s viij d
De eodem pro eadem schopa pro annis xxxv^{o} et xxxvj^{o} xiij s iiij d
De Collegio animarum pro ten' quond' tenur' skybbow pro a^{o} xxxvj viij s
De eodem pro ten' quond' tenur' Joh' Spront x s
[*De eodem pro*] Gardino retro dict' ten' xvij s ix d
[*De eodem pro ten' quond' ten*]ur' Spront' v s
[*De eodem pro gardino*] retro dictum ten' viij s x d ob
[*De eodem pro ten' quond' tenur' S*]pront v s
[*De eodem pro gardino retro dict'*] ten' viij s x d ob
De Albis monachis pro anno xxxvj^{o} iiij s
De Collegio linc' pro Gardino pro eodem a^{o} ij s vj d
Summa vj li xj s iiij d ob

[*Allocaciones in partibus*] remotis
De holdernysse xlvj s viij d
De [. . .] Novi Castri liij s viij d
De eisdem pro annis xxx xxxj xxxij xiij s iiij d
De eisdem pro anno xxxiij iiij li xix s
De [. . .] pro anno xxxiiij iij li ij s ij d
[*De* . . .] iij li xvj s ix d
[*De* . . .]erio de Merkyshall' pro a^{o} xxxiij^{o} v s ij d
[*De* . . .] de Holdernysse iij s iiij d
Summa xviij li [*j*] d ~~ix d~~[4]

Summa Omn' Allocatorum lxxij li xvj s iij d ob

[*Soluciones facte per*] Procuratorem
[. . .] xj s ix d
[. . .] iij s x d
[. . .] xvj d
Summa xvj s xj d

[4] [ADMC] The figure has certainly once been 'xj d', but has been more or less erased. 'j d' would be the correct figure.

In reparacionibus ten' laicorum in parochia omn' sanctorum	
In domo Spendyng'	vj d
[. . .]	iiij d
[. . .]	iiij s vj d
[*Summa*] v s iiij d	

[*Dorse of first membrane*]

In reparacionibus facte in paroch' [*beate*] Marie et sancti petri in oriente	
In domo [. . .]y[. . .]l	viij s ix d
Item [pro domo quond' Henrici B]ayth	viij li xviij d
[. . .] solucionis pro a° ollyvery	iiij s
[*Summa*] viij li [*xiij s iij d*]	

[*Repara*]ciones fact[*e infra*] collegium	
[*In primis*] pro [. . .] Collegij	xxxiij s xj d
In capella	vij s
Item pro lignis emptis a Jonge de tempore baynbryg'	x s
Item phillippo nasch pro camera supra promptuarium	iiij s
Summa liij s xj d	

[. . .] expensis et resolutis tenentibus et in renovacione caucionum	
[. . .]	iij li v s xj d
[. . .	xj s viij d ob
[. . .	iiij s viij d ob
[In renovacione caucionum]	viij s
Summa iiij li xj s iiij d	

In solucionibus factis socijs	
In primis Magistro Collegij pro tempore Gregforth	vj s viij d
Item Magistri	xxvj s viij d
[Item Magistro Her]tilpole	xxvj s viij d
[Item M' Strothur]	xxvj s viij d
[Item domino Jacobo Bay]nbryg'	iij li vj s viij d
[Item Magistro Gregforth]	xxvj s viij d
[Item Magistro Marshall]	xx s
[Item Magistro Hulle]	xlvj s viij d
[Item Magistro Watson]	iij li vj s viij d
Item Magistro in par[tem] soluc' indenture sue	xxiiij s j d[5]

[5] [ADMC] See OHS Vol. XCIII (1932), pp. 354–5 for a text of this document.

Item procuratori pro officio suo	x s
Summa xvij li vij s v d	
[*In*] soluc' factis servientibus	
[. . . *pinc*]erne	xiiij s ix d
[. . .]	x s
[. . .]	vj s viij d
[. . .]	vj s viij d
Summa xxxviij s j d	
In resolucionibus factis	
Abbati de osnay	xxij s x d
Priori sancte ffridiswide	ix s iiij d
Abbatisse de Godstow	x s
Ecclesie beate Marie	xij d
Summa xliij s ij d	
[*In communis batellis et contrib*]ucionibus	
[*In communis sociorum*]	xv li xiiij s iij d q[a]
[*Item in batellis*]	xxx s ob
In jurnell[*is*]	vij s xj d q[a]
In contribucionibus	xix s v d
Pro festo sancte trinitatis	v s vij d
Pro festo sancti Cuthberti	xxvij s v d
Pro [. . .] extraneorum	viij s ix d q[a]
[*Summa*] xx li xiij s v d q[a]	
[*(paid to Alice Belacys)*]	viij li xv s
[*Summa*] viij li xv s	
In equitacionibus	
In equitacione procuratoris ad exsexiam	xj s iiij d
In equitacione Magistri Hertylpolle ad novum castrum et pro equo	iij li iiij s viij d
Item pro pabulo equi suo [. . .]	v d
In equitacione [. . .] ad Arnnclyff	x s
[. . .] ad cariag' [. . .] pecuniarum	iij s iiij d
Summa iiij li xvj s xj d	
[*In reparacionibus factis in ex*]sexia et dimissis tenentibus	
[. . .]	vj s viij d
Pecunia dimissa domino Ric' Bernnys pro ten' in parochia sancti petri	ix s iiij d

Item in dimissis determinatoribus xij s
Item pro domo quond' tenur' Henrici bayth in man' Collegij xl s
Item in reparacionibus factis in exsexia vij s vij d
Item in p[*arochia*] sancti Egidij iij d
Summa iij li iiij s x d

[Summa remanens in cista] x li xiiij s viij d ob
[Pro pecunijs defectuosis] viij d

[Summa expens'] lxxxvj li xv s xj d ob q[a]

Summa omn' Allocatorum et Expensarum clix li xij s iij d q[a]

Et sic computatis computandis et allocatis allocandis procurator indebitatur collegio in viij s vij d ob q[a]

Acta sunt hec coram nobis magistro Waltero Wy'hale[6] commissario magistro Thome chandelore Cancellar' [univ][7]ersitatis Oxon' anno supradicto

[*A roll of two separate membranes. All are heavily damaged on the left hand side, the damage having occurred since Smith's time. All figures in this roll balance.*]

[6] [ADMC] Smith's reading. It could either be 'Weryhale' or 'Werphale'.

[7] [ADMC] In the original it looks as though there is an illegible word (possbly an erasure?) between 'Cancellar' and 'universitatis', but Smith does not suggest this.

37 HENRY VI (ROLL UC:BU1/F/69)
c.21 May 1458–13 May 1459?[1]

BURSAR: HENRY STROTHER

[*The original roll is now missing. The following is the condensed text from Smith Vol. VIII pp.174b-176b.*]

a° 1458 (Compotus M^ri Strother procur' Collegij sive magne Aule
1459 (Universitatis oxon datus per eundum Henricum a° rr H
(6^ti – 37.

Arr' camerarum de doct' Dowson – 4.14.7 this debt is omitted in ye following Rolls as also Mr Wygt 12d

Arr' lxxij li xvj s iij d ob

red' Camerarum de M^ro Pray	xiij s iiij d
Summa patet	
Red' Scolarum	
M Cutter	vj s viij d
M' Burlay	vj s viij d
~~M~~	iij s viij [*sic*]
	iij s viij d
de alijs determinatoribus	vij s iiij d
Summa xxvij s iiij d	
De Willelmo Pownde pro manerio de Merkys et molendinis	xviij li iij s iiij d
De domino Tho Tyrell	xx s
De terris in Holdernes	iij li xx d
De novo castro	v li xv s vj d
De Ecclesie de Arneclyffe	xx li
Summa xlviij li vj d	

Summa omn' reddituum lxxxiij li viij s xj d

[1] The dates of Pentecost for 1458–1459. See the note at the head of **F/60** above for their inclusion here.

recepta de cista	x li xiiij s viij d ob[2]
pro quisquilijs	iij s vj d
De Holdernesse	xv s
Summa xj li xiij s ij d ob	

Summa omn' oneratorum clxvij li xviij s v d

Inter Ar' necnon red. de Mr Church de 3 Aulis pro 2 ter	
Item de M^{ro} Broggis pro 1 ter'	
Arr' Mr Church pro an ante 27 H 6	xxxvj s xj d ob
et sub nomine parva Aul' un^{tis} pro a^{o} 27 28 30 31 32 33 34 36 27 [*sic*]	ad Summam xij li xij s j d ob
arr' de novo castro pro a^{o} 30 31 32	xiij s iiij d
pro a^{o} 33 34 35 37 [*sic*]	xv li vj s ix d

Summa Alloct' [*sic*] lxxxj li iiij s iiij d ob

In reparationibus pro domo quond' Henr' Bayth	xxvj li ix s ix d

In solut' fact' socijs	
In primis M^{ro} pro officio magistratus pro annis [*sic*]	xx s
Item M^{ro}	xxvj s viij d
Item M^{ro} in partem solucionis Indenture	iiij li vj s viij d
Item M^{ro} Hen Strother	xxvj s viij d
Item M^{ro} Willelmo Gregforth	xxvj s viij d
Item M^{ro} Ric Marshall	xxvj s viij d
Item M^{ro} Jo Hull	iij li vj s viij d
Item procuratori pro officio suo	x s
Summa xiiij li x s	

In communis Sociorum	xiiij li xiij d
Batell'	[*blank*]
Jurnell'	v s vj d
In Contributionibus	xxviij s viij d
Pro convivio sancte trinitatis	v s iiij d ob
Pro festo Sancti Cuthberti	x s ix d

[2] [ADMC] This is evidently the sum 'remanens in cista' (£10 13s 8½d), which occurred at the end of the previous roll, carried forward. Smith has erroneously written 'xiiij s' but the error of 1s in the total for this section shows that 'xiij s' was the original entry.

Supple in Batell' 5 li 5 s od
Summa 21 16 4 ob

Summa Expens' lxxxvj li viij s j d ob

Summa Expenc' omn' Allocat' et expens' clxvj li xij [*sic*] vj d

Et sic computatis computatandis et allocatis allocandis procurator indebitatur Collegio in v s vj d

Acta sunt Hec coram nobis M° Tho[a] Chaundeler Cancellario Universitatis oxon Anno supradicto

[*After the above notes, at Vol. VIII p.176b, Smith wrote the following important notes on this roll, and those for the two following years (1459/60 and 1460/61), viz.:*]

a° 1459 1460	The roll for this year is wanting when M[r] Strother seems to have been again Bursar		
a° 1458 1459	Arr' [*This must mean* **Alloc'**] Aularum in rot' hujus anni 30 li 00 00 d		
1460	Arr' Aularum		17 12 01 d[3]
1461	Ar' Camerarum	– 5.18.3 [*i.e. Allowances for 1458/9*] 1.2.8 [*i.e. Arrears for 1460/1*]	
	Scolarum	– 3.16.4 [*i.e. Allowances for 1458/9*] 1.11.4 [*i.e. Arrears for 1460/1*]	
	Ar' liberorum ten'	7.8.4 *i.e. Allowances for 1458/9*] 1.19.4 ob [*i.e. Arrears for 1460/1*]	

out of w[ch] great summes these following are deducted viz.

from the arrears of y[e] Abby of Godstow	0.14.2
from arrears of oseney	1.13.4
from y[e] arrears of All Souls for Sprount ten[ts]	3.09.4 d

[3] [ADMC] The actual figure in **F/70** is £18 12 1½. The other figures of the 1460/1 Arrears are correct.

I have not time to examine ye rest wch I suppose were most of y^{m} disparate [*sic*]; those y^{t} were not looked upon as such being continued; as appears by ye arrears of New castle; wh were 18 li 13s 9d. by ye rent for ye 36 H 6 being omitted in this roll (if another roll be not wanting ~~as I think y^{re} is not~~) the summe quoted hence (from Mr Strother Roll) a^{o} 1459 or 1460, make ye arrears 21 li 15s 11d

I conceive ye Roll of Mr Stother Bursarship ye 2^{d} year (1459 & 1460) is wanting

I suppose yr was a distinct Roll of desparate arrears made at y^{s} time & yrefore not entered in ye Roll of 1459 & 1460 (ult^{o} H 6^{ti} et 1 Ed 4^{ti}) wch summe of desparate debts must have been 19 li 4 4d so much being struck out, as appear by ye difference bet' ye summes in calce hujus et in fronte sequentis Rotuli.

[*As explained above, the Roll for 1459/60 was missing even in Smith's day. The evidence that Strother was Bursar in 1459/60 is the entry about the Newcastle arrears for the past nine years 'per rotulam M H Strother'. The 1458/9 roll shows that the earliest Newcastle arrears outstanding were for 30 H 6. and the year 1459/60 (38 Hen VI) would therefore be the last of the nine years referred to. Strother's second Bursarship seems to be a strong probability rather than an a certainty – as Smith rightly implies.*]

1 EDWARD IV (ROLL UC:BU1/F/70)
c.1 June 1460–24 May 1461?[1]

BURSAR: JOHN HULLE

Compotus Magistri Johannis Hull' Procuratoris Collegij sive Magne Aule universitatis Oxonie; Datus per eundem Magistrum Johannem Anno Regni Regis Edwardi quarti Primo.

Arr' laycorum

In primis de Dudlay	iij s ix d
Item de Spendyng'	viij s iij d
Item de Stokes	xx d
Item de Thoma taylyour pro anno xxxviij°	v s
Item de Johanne Morlay	iij s iiij d
Item de eodem pro anno xxxiij	xiij s vj d
Item de Johanne Mancypyll' pro a° xxxviij	xvj d
Item de Johanne flecher	l s
Item de uxore Johannis Cooke	viij s
Item de Roberto ffuller	vij s viij d
Item de Ruschbery pro a° xxxvj°	xvj s viij d
Item de Nicholao Weyr carpent'	xxx s ij d
Item de Thoma Mancypyll' pro alrychhet	ij s
Item de pedyngton pro antiquis debiti	xj s x d
Item de Symone Mancypyll'	ij s ij d
Item de Gyllott pro yrlond	v s
Item de Palmer	iij s ij d
Item de Johanne Gower	iij s ij d
Item de Johanne Harth	xij s viij d
Item de lewys	x d
Item de Baylyamason	xvj d
Summa x li viij d	

Arr' Aularum

In primis de M Bragges pro aula Brasynnose	xlvij s ij d ob
Item de M Bemyslay pro aula Hampton pro annis preteritis	xix s ij d

[1] The dates of Pentecost for 1460–1461. See the note at the head of **F/60** above for their inclusion here. Edward IV's regnal year started on 4 March.

Item de eodem pro anno xxxviij°	l s
Item de eodem pro sekyll' hall'	vj li vj s viij d
Item de M Antonio et alijs occupantibus sekyll' hall' pro a° xxxviij°	xx s
Item de M Semer	lj s j d q[a]
Item de M Warde pro aula Edwardi pro a° xxxiiij	vj d ob
Item de eodem pro a° xxxvj°	xxij s iij d
Item de eodem pro a° xxxvij°	xj s j d q[a]
Item de Roberto Wrygt	xij s vj d
Item de M Antonio Clayton	xj s viij d
Summa xviij li xij s j d ob	

Arr' scolarum

In primis de M Keel	xx d
Item de Stephano Browne	iij s viij d
Item de Carver	iij s viij d
Item de Clyffton	iij s viij d
Item de Sawghed'	iij s viij d
Item de M Greanger	xx d
Item de M Cutler	vj s viij d
Item de M Carver	vj s viij d
Summa xxxj s iiij d	

Arr' cam'

In primis de M Roberto fflemyng	iiij s
Item de M W. Danyell'	xij s
Item de domino Alano Baytson	vj s viij d
Summa xxij s viij d	

Arr' de lib' ten'

In primis de Albis monachis	viij s
Item de Collegio Animarum	viij s
Item de Abbatissa de Godstowe	xx d
Item de eadem	xiiij d
Item de ten' Johannis Spront modo tenur' Collegij animarum	v s
Item de eodem Collegio pro Gardino retro dict' ten'	viij s x d ob
Item de abbato do osnay	vj s viij d
Summa xxxix s iiij d	

[*No heading*]

In primis de novo Castro in parte pro ix annis ut patet per rotulum M H Strother xxj li xv s xj d
Item de exsex pro anno xxxviij° xxvj s viij d
Item de Thoma Brown de pecunijs de Holdernysse iij s iiij d
Item petit allocari de Cista v li vij s xj d
Summa xxviij li xiij s x d

Summa Omn' Arreragiorum [*sic*] lxij li

Rentale

De ten' quod tenet Robertus Wood in Swythwychlayn vj s
De ten' super Angulum quadrivij quod tenet teutonicus xxvj s viij d
Summa xxxij s viij d

Redditus in parochia omnium sanctorum

De ten' quod tenet Thomas dudlay xxxiij s iiij d
De ten' quod tenet Byrstow liij s iiij d
De ten' quod tenet Spendyng' xxj s viij d
De ten' quod tenet Thomas Morrys taylyour xl s
De ten' quod tenet Ric' Woode xxvj s viij d
De ten' quod [*sic*] W Bayrbour xvj s viij d
De ten' quod [*sic*] W Stokys xlvj s viij d
Summa xj li xviij s iiij d

Redditus in parochia beate Marie et sancti Petri in oriente

De ten' quod tenet Ɉ Thomas Web xxvj s viij d
De ten' quod tenet Johannes flecher xxvj s viij d
De ten' quod tenet Ric' ffyshe pro 2^{bus} ter' xiij s iiij d
De ten' quod tenuit Johannes Coke pro 2^{bus} ter' viij s
De Wappys pro eodem ten' pro 2^{bus} ter' viij s
De W qwythe pro 2^{bus} ter' vj s viij d
~~De M lyonell vj s viij d~~
De Owyn pro ten' quond' tenur' Ric' fyche pro uno ter' vj s viij d
Summa iiij li xvj s

Redditus Aularum

De M Bragges pro aula Brasynnose iij li vj s viij d
De eodem pro aula sancti Thome x s
De eodem pro Gardino aula scuti vj s viij d

De eodem pro parva aula universitatis in vico scolarum xxvj s viij d
De M Bemyslay pro aula Hampton pro uno ter' xvj s viij d
De M Paunton pro eadem aula pro 2bus ter' xxxiij s iiij d
De M Antonio et alijs occupantibus sekylhall' xx s
De Mancipio de Brasynnose pro aula Edwardi xx s
De Roberto Wrygt pro parva aula universitatis in alto vico xlvj s viij d
Summa xij li vj s viij d

Red' camerarum et scol'

De M Pray	xiij s iiij d
De M Mawer	vj s viij d
De Qwyth	iij s iiij d
De Kyrkby	iij s iiij d
De M Lyonel	vj s iiij d
De freston'	iij s iiij d
De kenrosse	iij s iiij d

Summa xl s

[*No heading*]

De qwytfeld pro Gardino iuxta castrum ij s
De Baylyamason pro terris in bellomonte et gardino viij s
De Priore ffratrum predicatorum pro pratis yrland et alrychhett xxj s viij d
De Johanne Jennys ⟨pro pratis retro osnay⟩ xix s viij d
Summa lj s iiij d

[*No heading*]

De Abbatissa de Godstow pro schopa ex oto magne porte sancte ffrideswyde xx d
De annuali redditu pro gardino quond' tenur' Thome Mayster xiiij d
De abbate de Ossnay pro schopa iuxta Johannem Spyser vj s viij d
De Collegio animarum pro ten' quond' tenuer' [*sic*] Skybbow viij s
De novo Collegio pro Madynhall' x s
De Collegio Cantuarie pro silverhall' ij s vj d
De Collegio lincoln' pro Gardino v s
De Collegio animarum pro ten' quond' tenur' J spronte v s

De eodem Collegio pro Gardino retro dictum ten' viij s x d ob
De Albis monachis pro Gardino quond' tenur' Burton iiij s
Summa lij s x d ob

[*No heading*]
De Willelmo Pownde pro Manerio de merkes hall' et molendinis xviij li iij s iiij d
De domino Thoma Tyrell' xx s
De terris in Holdernysse iij li xx d
De novo castro v li xv s vj d
De ecclesia de Arnclyffe xx li
Summa xlviij li vj d

Summa omn' Reddituum – lxxxv li xviij s iiij d ob

Preter sortem domus
Item de Reyff de Elsfield vj s viij d

Summa Omn' Oneratorum – cxlviij li v s ob

Allocaciones M J Hull'
In primis de Dudlay iij s ix d
Item de eodem pro anno xxxix ⟨pro 2^{bus} ter⟩ xvj s viij d
Item de Spendyng' ⟨pro a^{o} xxxv^{o} et $xxxvj^{o}$⟩ viij s iij d
Item de eodem pro anno xxxix pro ~~2^{bus} ter~~ vj s v d
Item de Byrstow pro a^{o} xxxix^{o} xx d
Item de Stokes xx d
Item de eodem pro a^{o} xxxix xj s viij d
Item de T taylyour pro a^{o} $xxxviij^{o}$ v s
Item de eodem pro anno xxxix v s
Item de Ric' Woode xiij s iiij d
Item de W Barbour iiij s ij d
Item de Johanne Morlay iij s iiij d
Item de eodem pro anno xxxiij xiij s vj d
Item de Johanne Mancypyll' pro a^{o} $xxxviij^{o}$ xvj d
Item de T Webb ij s viij d
Item de Johanne fflecher l s
Item de eodem pro a^{o} xxxix^{o} xvj s viij d
Item de uxore J Cooke viij s
Item de Roberto ffuller xx d
Item de J Cook iiij s iij d
Item de Ruschbery xvj s viij d

Item de Nicholao Veyr carpent'	xxx s ij d
Item de Wappys pro 2[obus] terminis	viij s
Item de W Qwyth	iij s iiij d
Item de Thoma Mancypyll' pro alrychhet	ij s
Item de Pedyngton pro antiquis debitis	xj s x d
Item de Symone Mancypyll'	ij s ij d
Item de Gyllott pro yrlond	v s
Item de Palmer	ij s vj d
Item de Johanne Gower	iij s ij d
Item de Johanne Harth	xij s viij d
Item de lewys	x s
Item de Baylyamason	xvj d
Item de eodem pro terris in bellomonte et gardino pro a[o] xxxix	viij s
Item de Roberto Wood	vj s viij d
Item de owyn pro a[o] xxxix	vj s viij d
Item de J Jenynsse	xix s viij d
Summa xvj li viij s ix d	

[*Dorse*]

[*No heading*]

In primis de M Bragges pro aula Brasynnose	xlvij s ij d ob
Item de eodem pro anno xxxix[o]	liij s iiij d
Item de M[o] Bemyslay pro aula Hampton pro annis preteritis	xix s ij d
Item de eodem pro anno xxxviij[o]	l s
Item de eodem pro sekyll' hall'	vj li vj s viij d
Item de eodem pro anno xxxix[o]	x s
Item de M Antonio et alijs occupantibus sekyll' hall' pro anno xxxviij	xx s
Item de eisdem pro anno xxxix[o] ⟨pro eadem aula⟩	xx s
Item de M[o] Pawnton pro aula Hampton pro a[o] xxxix pro 2[bus] terminis	xx s
Item de M Semer	lj s j d q[a]
Item de M Warde pro aula Edwardi pro a[o] xxxiiij[o]	v d ob
Item de eodem pro a[o] xxxvj[o]	xxij s iij d
Item de eodem pro a[o] xxxvij[o]	xj s j d q[a]
Item de Roberto Wrygt	xij s vj d
Item de eodem pro a[o] xxxix	xx s
Item de Mancipio de Brasynnose pro a[o] xxxix	v s

Item de M^{o} antonio clayton	xj s viij d
[*An entry erased*]	~~xx s~~
Summa xxv li v d ob	

[*No heading*]

Item de M Keel	xx d
Item de Stephano Browne	iij s viij d
Item de Carver	iij s viij d
Item de Clyffton	iij s viij d
Item de Sawgheld'	iij s viij d
Item de M Granger	xx d
Item de M Cutler	vj s viij d
Item de M Carver	vj s viij d
Item de M Mawer	vj s viij d
Item de Qwyth	iij s iiij d
Item de Kyrkby	iij s iiij d
Item de M lyonel	vj s viij d
Item de freston	iij s iiij d
Item de kenrosse	iij s iiij d
Summa liiij s viij d	

[*No heading*]

In primis de M Roberto fflemyng	iiij s
Item de M W. Danyell'	xij s
Item de domino Alano Baytson	vj s viij d
Summa xxij s viij d	

[*No heading*]

[2]Item de Collegio Cant'	ij s vj d
Item de albis monachis	viij s
Item de Collegio Animarum	viij s
Item de ten' johannis Spront modo tenur' Collegij animarum	v s
Item de eodem Collegio pro Gardino retro dict' ten'	viij s x d ob
Item de abbatissa de godstow	xx d
Item de eadem	xiiij d
Item de abbato do osnay	vj s viij d
Item de Collegio novo	x s

[2] [ADMC] This entry looks as if it may have been added, and the group total altered accordingly.

Item de Collegio linc'	ij s vj d
Summa xlix s iiij d ob	

[*No heading*]

In primis de novo Castro in parte pro ix annis ut patet per rotulum M H Strother	xxj li xv s xj d
Item de exsex pro anno xxxviij°	xxvj s viij d
Item de eodem pro anno xxxix	ix li xj s viij d
Item de Thoma Brown de pecunijs de Holdernis	iij s iiij d
Item de terris in Holdernys	iij li xx d
Item de novo castro pro a° xxxix°	v li xv s vj d
Item de ecclesia de Arnclyff	xx li
Item de domino T Tyrell'	x s
Summa lxij li iiij s x d	

Summa Omn' Allocacionum cx li iiij d[3]

[*No heading*]

In primis in Aula Brasynnose	ij s x d
Item in Aula Edwardi	v s ob
Item in parva aula universitatis in alto vico	v s iij d ob
Item in Aula drowwht'	ij s
Summa xv s ij d	

[*No heading*]

Item in domo Dudlay	ij d
Item in domo T Taylyour	iiij s x d
Item in domo W Stokes	ij s viij d
Item in domo T Webb	v s
Item in domo J Coke	xiiij d
Item in domo W Qwyth	vj d
Item in domo Ric' ffyche	vj s viij d

3 [ADMC] The figures originally read 'cix li iiij d', and the correct total is £110 8d. Evidently, however, the item of 2s 6d against Canterbury College, which appears to have been added, or altered in some way, should not be included in the account, as it does not appear in the Arrears of 1461/2. If this 2s 6d item is omitted, and the error of 4d in the total corrected, the Summa Omn' Allocacionum comes to £109 18s 2d; and this added to the total Expenses figure of £37 19s 10½d gives the correct grand total of £147 18s 0½d. (In the Arrears of 1461/2 the Arrears total is given as £109 17s 6d, but this total has been altered from £109 18s 2d, which is the figure produced by adding the totals of the different sections. 8s has in fact been deducted from one entry, presumably after the sectional totals were written in, and the Summa Omn' Arr' has been altered accordingly, hence the discrepancy).

Item in domo iuxta aulam universitatis in alto vico	ij s xj d[4]
~~Item d~~	
Summa xxiij s xj d	

[*No heading*]

Item in Capella pro cera	v s j d ob
Item in emp' infra Collegium	iiij s viij d
Item in Aula promptuario coquina et orto	xv s viij d
Item pro stauro	xxij d
Item pro renovacione caucionum	vj s
Item in diminutis expensis	iij s ij d
Item in resolucione ten'	iiij s
Item Alicie Bellacysse	lviij s iiij d
Item solut' infra Collegium	vij li ij s
Summa xij li ix s ob	

[*No heading*]

In primis pincerne	xx s
Item Thome coco	vij s vj d
Item Barbetonsori	v s
Item lotrici	v s
Summa xxxvij s vj d	

[*No heading*]

In primis Magistro Collegij	vj s viij d
Item M Hartylpole	vj s viij d
Item M Stroder	vj s viij d
Item M Gregford	vj s viij d
Item M Marschall'	vj s viij d
Item M Hull'	vj s viij d
Item M Watson	vj s viij d
Item Baynbryg'	vj s viij d
Item M Watson	xx s
Item M Hull pro officio procuratoris	x s
Summa iiij li iij s iiij d	

[*No heading*]

In primis pro communis sociorum	xij li ix s vj d ob
Item in batellis	xl s iiij d ob q[a]

[4] [ADMC] These figures have been altered from 'iiij s' (certain) 'j d' (some doubt).

Item in jurnellis	iij s iiij d
Item in contribucionibus	xxiiij s iiij d
Item pro festo sancte trinitatis	v s vj d ob
Item pro festo sancti Cuthberti	viij s ix d
Summa xvj li xj s x d ob q^a	

[*No heading*]

Item pro equitacionibus	xxj s iij d
Item M Johanni Coke pro placitis	vj s
Summa xxvij s iij d	

Summa Omn' Expensarum xxxvij li xix s x d q^a

Summa Omn' Allocatorum et Expensarum cxlvij li xviij s q^a[5]

⟨Et sic computatis computandis et allocatis allocandis Magister Johannes Hull' indebitatur Collegio in Summa vij s -[6] q^a. Acta sunt hec coram nobis M Willelmo Ive Reverendi in Christo Patris et domini domino Georgij dei gratia Exon' Episcopi et Universitatis Oxon Cancellarij Commissario generali ibidem Anno suprascripto presentibus nobiscum Magistris Willelmo Tybarde et Willelmo ffenton sacre Theologie Bacularijs⟩

[*A very clear and well-preserved roll; 2 membranes.*

All figures in it would balance, except for the Total of Allowances.]

5 [ADMC] The correct total is £143 2¼d.

6 [ADMC] This dash is apparently written over an erasure.

2 EDWARD IV (ROLL UC:BU1/F/71)
c.24 May 1461–6 June 1462?[1]

BURSAR: RICHARD MARSHALL

Computus Magistri Ricardi Marshall' Procuratoris Collegii Magistri Willelmi de Dunelm' Magne Aule sive Collegii Universitatis Oxonie vulgariter dict'. Datus per eundem Magistrum Ricardum Anno Regni Regis Edwardi quarto secundo.

[*The Arrears are identical with the Allowances in* **F/70** *above, save for a few changes in spelling.*]

Summa omn' Arreregiorum cix li xvij s vj d[2]

Rentale in parochia sancti martini

De ten' quod tenuit Robertus Wood in Swythwychlayn'	vj s
De ten' super angulum quadrivii quod tenet tutonicus	xxvj s viij d
Summa xxxij ł s viij d	

Redditus in parochia omn' sanctorum

De ten' quod tenet Thomas Dudlay	xxxiij s iiij d
De ten' quod tenet Brystow	liij s iiij d
De ten' quod tenet Spendyng'	xxj s viij d
De ten' quod tenet Thomas Mores Talyour	xl s
De ten' quod tenet Ric' Wood	xxvj s viij d
De ten' quod tenet Willelmus Barbour	xvj s viij d
De ten' quod tenet Willelmus Stokes	xlvj s viij d
Summa xl li xviij s iiij d	

Redditus in parochia beate [*sic*] et sancti petri in oriente

De ten' quod tenuit Thomas Webe pro uno termino	vj s viiij d
De Jacobo vector' pro eodem ten' pro ij^bus terminis	xiiij s iiij d
De ten' quod tenet Johannes fflecher'	xxvj s viij d
De owino pro ten' quondam tenur' Ricardi ffyssh pro 2^obus terminis	xiij s iiij d

[1] The dates of Pentecost for 1461–1462. See the note at the head of **F/60** above for their inclusion here.

[2] [ADMC] Although this sum is correct, it is not the sum of the section totals of the Arrears.

De Wappys pro ten' quond' tenure Johannis Cooke	xvj s
De Coga pro ij^{bus} terminis	vj s viij d
Summa iiij li ij s viij d	

Redditus Aularum[3]

De M' Bragg' pro aula brasynnose	iij li vj s viij d
De eodem pro Aule sancti Thome	x s
De eodem pro gardino Aule scuti	vj s viij d
De eodem pro parva aula universitatis in vico scolarum	xxvj s viij d
De M' Pawnton' pro Aula Hampton'	l s
De M' Antonio Clayton' et alijs occupantibus Sekyllhall'	xx s
De Mancipio de brasynnose pro aula edwardi pro iij^{bus} terminis	xv s
De alio Mancipio pro eadem pro j termino	v s
De Roberto Wrygth pro parva aula universitatis in alto vico	xlvj s viij d
Summa xij li vj s viij d	

Redditus cam'

Redditus scolarum

De M' Pray	vj s viij d
De Magistro Johanne Paynter	vj s viij d
De M' Dobbys	vj s viij d
De M' Wych	vj s viij d
De M' Herberd'	vj s viij d
De baculario de domo sancti Johannis	iij s viij d
De domino Willelmo Smyth	iij s viij d
De Appylton'	iij s viij d
De Morsley	iij s viij d
De domino Thoma Podyam	iij s viij d
Summa l s	

Redditus in suburbijs et campis

De Whytfyld' pro gardino iuxta castrum	ij s
De Balyhamason' pro terris in bellomonte et gardino pro ii^{bus} terminis	iiij s
De Barton' pro eijsdem [*sic*] pro 2^{bus} terminis	iiij s

3 [ADMC] Underlined in text.

[4]De prior' fratrum predicatorum pro pratis yrlond' et Allrychhet xxj s viij d
De Johanne Jennynse pro pratis retro Osnay x s
Summa xlj s viij d

Redditus liberorum tenementorum
De abbatissa de Godstow pro shopa ex o^to^ magne porte sancte ffrydeswyde xx d
De annuali redditu pro gardino quondam Thome Mayster xiiij d
De abbate de Osnay pro shopa iuxta Johannem Spysere vj s viij d
De collegio animarum pro ten' quondam tenure Schybbow ~~x s~~ viij s
De novo collegio ⟨pro Madynhall'⟩ x s
De collegio cantuar' pro silverhall ij s vj d
De collegio lincoln' pro gardino v s
De collegio animarum pro ten' quond' tenur' Johannis Sprount v s
De eodem collegio pro gardino retro dictum ten' viij s x d ob
De Albis monachis pro gardino quondam tenure Barton' iiij s
Summa lij s x d ob

Redditus in partibus remotis
De Johanne pounnd' pro Manerio de Merkyshall' et molendinis xliij li iij s iiij d
De Domino Thoma Tirell' xx s
De terris in Holdernes iij li xx d
De novo castro v li xv s vj d
De Ecclesia de Arnnclyfe xx li
Summa xlviij li vj d

Summa omn' Reddituum lxxxv li v s iiij d ob

Recepta preter sortem domus
In primis pro calce x d
Item de bonis M' church' de M' Hertylpoll' vij s ij d
Item de M' Gregfurth' viij s iiij d
Item de M' Marshall' xiij s vj d

[4] [ADMC] The entry is underlined & a note of a few words are written against it in an 18th century (?) hand, not Smith's.

Item de M' Hull' ij s
Summa xxxj s x d

Summa omn' oneratorum clxxxxvj li xiij s viij d ob[5]

Allocaciones Magistri Ric' Marshall'
In primis de Roberto Wood' viij s
Item de Dudley iij s ix d
Item de Spendyng' pro annis xxxv et xxxvj^to viij s iij d
Item de Stok' xx d
Item de Thoma Taylyour pro a^o xxxviij^o v s
Item de Ricardo Wood pro annis primo et secundo Regis Edwardi quarti xx s
Item de Johanne Morlay iij s iiij d
Item de eodem pro a^o xxxiij^o xiij s vj d
Item de Johanne Mancypyll' pro a^o xxxviij^o xvj d
Item de Thoma Webe pro a^o xxxix ij s viij d
Item de eodem pro a^o secundo regis Edwardi quarti iij s v d
Item de Johanne fflecher l s
Item de eodem pro a^o xxxix xvj s
Item de eodem pro a^o secundo Regis Edwardi quarti x s
Item de uxor' Johannis Cooke viij s
[6]Item de Spendyng' pro anno primo Regis Edwardi quarti xij d

[*Dorse*]

Item de Roberto ffullere xx d
Item de Johanne Cooke iiij s ij d
Item de Ricardo Weyre carpent' xxx s ij d
Item de Wappys pro ij^bus terminis a^o xxxix^o viij s ij d
Item de eodem pro anno secundo Regis Edwardi quarti xvj s
Item de Willelmo qwhyet pro a^o xxxix^o iij s iiij d
Item de ~~d~~ Thoma Mancipyll' pro Alryshet ij s
Item de Pedyngton' pro antiquis debitis xj s x d
Item de Simone Mancipyll' ij s ij d
Item de Gyllot pro yrlonnd' v s
Item de Johanne Gower iij s ij d
Item de Johanne Hart xij s viij d
Item de lews x s

[5] Shillings & pence in this figure have apparently been written over an erasure.
[6] [ADMC] This item in a different ink.

Item de Balyhamason' pro a° xxxviiij° xvj d
Item de eodem pro a° xxxix° pro terris in bellomonte et gardino viij s
Item de eodem pro eijsdem A° primo Regis Edwarti[*sic*] quarti pro ii^bus^ terminis iiij s
Item de Barton' pro eijsdem pro 2^obus^ terminis primo anno et secundo dicti Edwardi iiij s
Item de qwhytfyld' pro a° ~~secundo p~~ secundo edwardi quarti ij s
~~Item de Roberto Wood'~~
Item de Jacobo vectore vj s viij d
Item de Johanne Jennyns pro pratis retro Osney pro a° xxxix° xix s viij d

Summa xv li xij s v d

Allocaciones Aularum

In primis de M' Bragg' pro aula Brasynnose pro a° ~~xxxix°~~ xxxviij° xlvij s ij d ob
Item de eodem pro a° xxxix° liij s iiij d
Item de eodem pro anno secundo regis Edwardi quarti iij li v s
Item de M' Bemeslay pro annis preteritis pro Aula Hampton' xix s ij d
Item de eodem pro ~~Sekylhall'~~ anno xxxviij° pro eadem l s
Item de eodem pro Sekylhall' vj li vj s viij d
Item de M' Antonio Clayton et alijs occupantibus sekylhall pro a° xxxviij° xx s
Item de eodem et alijs ut supra pro a° xxxix xx s
Item de Aula Sykkyll' in manibus collegij xvij s
Item de M' Pawnton' pro aula hampton pro 2^obus^ terminis pro a° xxxix xx s
Item de eodem pro anno secundo regis Edwardi quarti xxxvj s viij d
Item de Magistro Semer lj s j d q^a^
va Item de ~~eodem~~ M' Ward' pro aula Edwardi pro a° xxxiiij^to^ – cat [*no entry*]
Item de Roberto Wrygth' pro anno xxxviij° xij s vj d
Item de eodem pro a° xxxix° xx s
Item de eodem pro anno secundo regis Edwardi quarti xxxvj s iiij d[7]

[7] [ADMC] Figures have been altered.

Item de Mancipio de Brasynnose pro Aula Edwardi pro a° xxxix° — v s
Item de eodem pro anno primo regis edwardi quarti — xj s viij d
Item de M' Antonio Clayton' — xj s viij d
[8]Item de M' Benneslay — x s
Summa xxxj li x s iij d ob qª

Allocaciones scolarum
De M' Keell' — xx d
De Stephano Brownn' — iij s viij d
De Carver — viij s viij d
De Clyfton' — iij s viij d
De Sawgheld' — iij s viij d
De M' Granger — xx d
De M' Cutter — vj s viij d
De M' Carver — xx d
De qwhyth' — xx d
De M' lionell' — vj s viij d
De M' Paynter — iij s viij d
De M' Wych' — vj s viij d
De M' Dobbys — vj s viij d
De M' W. Herberd' — vj s viij d
De Ricardo Appylby et Morsley in collegio dunelm' — vj s viij d[9]
De ~~Alto~~ ⟨domino Thoma Podyam[10] — ~~iij s~~ xx d⟩
Summa iij li vj s iiij d

Allocaciones camerarum
In primis de M' Roberto fflemyng' — iiij s
Item de M' W. Daniel — xij s
Item de domino Alano Baytson' — vj s viij d
Item de M' Pray — vj s viij d[11]
Summa xxix s iiij d[12]

Allocaciones liberorum tenementorum
In primis de albis monachis — viij s
Item de eijsdem pro a° ⟨secundo regis Edwardi quarti⟩ — iiij s

[8] [ADMC] This item is written in a different ink.
[9] [ADMC] These figures have been altered.
[10] [ADMC] This is written in a different ink.
[11] [ADMC] All this item is witten in a different ink.
[12] [ADMC] Figures have been altered.

Item de collegio animarum pro a° xxxix° iiij s
Item de ten' Johannis Sprount modo tenure collegij animarum pro a° xxxix v s
Item de eijsdem pro eodem a° ~~x~~ ⟨secundo regis Edwardi quarti⟩ v s
Item de eodem collegio pro gardino retro dict' ten' pro a° xxxix° viij s x d ob
Item de eodem pro dict' gardino ~~a°~~ ⟨pro a° secundo regis Edwardi quarti⟩ viij s x d ob
Item de abbatissa de Godstow pro a° xxxix° xx d
Item de eadem pro eodem a° xiiij d
Item de eadem pro a° ⟨secundo regis Edwardi quarti⟩ xx d
Item de eadem pro eodem a° xiiij d
Item de abbate de Osnay pro a° xxxix vj s viij d
Item de eodem pro anno ⟨secundo regis Edwardi quarti⟩ vj s viij d

Summa iij li ij s ix d

Allocaciones in partibus remotis

In primis de novocastro in parte pro ix annos ut patet in rotula Magistri H. Stroder xxj li xv s xj d
Item de eodem pro a° xxxix v li xv s vj d
Item de eodem pro a° secundo regis Edwardi quarti xxxv s x d
Item de Arnnclyf pro a° secundo regis Edwardi quarti iiij li xiij s iiij d
Item de Thoma Brown' de pecunijs de Holdernes iij s iiij d
Item de terris in Holdernes pro a° xxxix° iij li xx d
Item de eijsdem pro a° secundo regis Edwardi quarti iij li xx d
~~Item de novo castro pro a° xxxix v li xv s vj d~~
[13]Item de exsex' pro a° xxxix xxxvij s viij d
Item de exsex' pro a° secundo regis Edwardi quarti iij li xvij s v d

Summa xlv li xvj d

Summa omnium Allocacionum lxxxxviij li xiij s j d ob q[a14]

[13] [ADMC] This and the next entry have apparently been added later.
[14] [ADMC] The actual sum is £100 2s 5d. The difference between these totals, namely £1 9s 4d, is the exact figure for the section totals for the Allowances of College Rooms. This error is repeated in the Arrears of the next roll.

Allocaciones edificiorum et reparacionum

In primis in Aula Universitatis in ~~alt~~ vico scolarum	xxxj li xij s j d
Item in Aula enea	ix d
Item in Aula Hampton'	v s ix d
Item in Aula Edwardi	v s iij d
Item in Aula ~~Do~~ Drowda	xvj d
Item in Aula Universitatis in alto vico	ix d
Summa xxij li v s xj d	

Allcaciones pro reparacionibus laicorum[15]

In primis pro pavimento apud quadrivium	v s ix d
Item in domo Dudley	xj d
Item in domo Brystow	xxx s j d ob
Item in domo Spendyng'	iij d ob
Item in domo Ricardi Wood'	v s
Item in domo Willelmi Barbour	ij s xj d
Item in domo Stokes	xij s vj d
Item in domo Wappys	vj s vj d
[16]Item in ten' quond' in tenur' owini	iiij s
Item in alio novo ten'	ij s x d
Item in domo Thome Thalyour	xviij s iij d ob
Item tegularijs	xx s iij d
Summa v li ix s iiij d ob	

Allocaciones expensarum infra collegium

In primis in capella pro cera	vj s ij d
Item pro stauro	liij s ij d
Item pro reparacionibus murorum et aliorum infra collegium	vj li xj s ob
Item in coquina	ij s ix d
Item pro dealbacione capelle et Aule	iij s viij d
Summa ix li ~~v~~ xvj s ix d ob	

Allocaciones solucionum sociorum

In primis Magistro Collegij	xxxvj s viij d
Item M' Hertylpoll'	xliij s ~~v~~ iiij d
Item domino Jacobo Baynbryg'	l s

[15] [ADMC] This and the next section are continuous in the MS, probably because the later entries of the earlier section have been squeezed in. The total of the earlier section, in the right hand margin, is additional to that at the foot of the later section.

[16] [ADMC] This last 4 entries have all to some extent been written over deletions.

Item M' Gregfurth	xliij s iiij d
Item M' Marshall'	xlvj s viij d
Item M' Hull'	xx s
Item M' Hertylpoll de bonis M' church	vij s ij d
Item M' Gregfurth de eijsdem	viij s iiij d
Item M' Marshall' de eijsdem	xiij s vj d
Item M' Hull' de eijsdem	ij s
Item M' Marshall pro officio procuratoris	x s
Summa xiij li xj s	

Allocaciones solucionum serviencium

In primis pincerne	xxvj s viij d
Item coco	x s
Item barbitonsori	viij s iiij d
Item lotrici	viij s iiij d
Item Willelmo Wotton	vij s iij d
Summa iij li vij d	

Allocaciones resolucionum

In primis abbati de Osnay	xliiij s iiij d
Item Abbatisse de Godstow	x s
Summa liiij s iiij d	

Allocaciones solucionum Alicie Bellacyse

Solut' ~~alice~~ Alicie Bellacyse	viij li xv s
Summa viij li xv s	

Allocaciones equitacionum

Solut' pro equitacionibus	iij li xv s iiij d ob
Summa iij li xv s iiij d ob	

Allocaciones communarum sociorum

In primis pro communis sociorum	xvij li xiiij s iij d ob
Item in batellis	xliiij s x d
Item in iornellis	iij s iiij d
Item in contribucionibus	xvj s ij d
Item pro festo sancti trinitatis	iij s viij d ob
Item pro festo sancti Cuthberti	xiiij s j d ob
Item pro communis carpentarii	xlj s iij d ob q[a]
Summa xxiij li xvij s ix d q[a][17]	

[17] Figures in this total have been changed.

Allocaciones diminutarum expensarum et dimissorum tenentibus

Solut' pro diminutis expensis et dimissis tenentibus xxxix s ij d q^{a}

Summa xxxix ij d q^{a}

Item petit allocari de pecunijs remanentibus in cista xxxiiij s iij d

Summa xxxiiij s iij d

Summa omnium expensarum cvj li xix s vij d

Summa omnium Allocatorum et expensarum ccv li xij s viij d ob q^{a}

⟨Et sic computatis computandis et allocatis allocandis Collegium indebitatur Procuratori computanti in viij li xviij s q^{a}. Acta sunt hec coram nobis Magistro Willelmo Ive Reverendi in Xpo Patris et domini domini Georgij dei gratia Exon' episcopi et Cancellarij Universatitis Oxon' Commissario generali ibidem secundo die Septembr' Anno infrascript'⟩

[*At foot of roll, and written the other way up, occurs the endorsement*]:

2^{dus} annus Ed iiij^{ti}

[*Clear & well-preserved roll of 2 membranes. Totals etc. are all correct, except for the totals of Arrears and Allowances.*]

3 EDWARD IV (ROLL UC:BU1/F/72)
c.6 June 1462–29 May 1463?[1]

BURSAR: WILLIAM GREGFORD

[This roll begins on the second membrane of the dorse (as at present rolled), the first membrane being a very short one.]

Compotus M' Willelmi Gregfurth Procuratoris collegij M' Willelmi de dunelm' magne aula universitatis in oxon' vulgariter nuncupat' datus per eundem M' Willelmum A° rr' edwardi iiij^ti^ post conqestum tercio[2].

*[The Arrears are identical with the Allowances in **F/71** above, save for a few changes in spelling, except in the Arrears from remote places, In Items 3 & 4, the figure (35s 10d) of Item 3, and the text of Item 4 are omitted, the figure 'iiij li xiij s iiij d', which in **F/71** s entered against item 4 being here entered against Item 3. Since Item 3 in effect occurs in a new entry (see below), the text here presumably should refer to Arncliffe.*

Item 8 is omitted.

After Item 10, a new item, written in a different hand, is added, viz.:]

Item de ~~eodem~~ novo castro pro a° 2° regis edwardi quarti xxxv s x d[3]

Summa xlv li xvj d

Summa Omnium arr' lxxxxviij li xiij s j d ob q^a[4]

Rentale

De Ten' quod tenuit Robertus Wood in Swynsheton'	vj s

Redditus in parochia omnium sanctorum

De ten' quod tenet Thomas Dudley	xxxiij s iiij d
De ten' quod tenet Brystow	liij s iiij d
De ten' quod tenet Spendyng'	xxj s viij d
De ten' quod tenet Thomas Mores Taylyour	xl s
De ten' quod tenet Ricardus Wod'	xxvj s viij d
De ten' quod tenet Willelmus Barbour	xvj s viij d

[1] The dates of Pentecost for 1462–1463. See the note at the head of **F/60** above for their inclusion here, and **F/73**, which runs from Pentecost 1463.

[2] [ADMC] A short erasure between 'conquestum' and 'tercio'.

[3] The word *vacat* has been written alongside this entry, probably to indicate that the property was empty.

[4] [ADMC] The correct total is £100 2s 5d (see note 14 in roll **F/72** above on this).

De ten' quod tenet Willelmus Stokes xlvj s viij d
Summa xj li xviij s iiij d

Redditus in parochia ~~S~~ beate Marie et sancti petri in or'
De ten' quod tenet Thomas Chandler xxvj s viij d
De ten' quod tenet Jacobus Vector xxvj s viij d
De ten' quod tenet Henricus bath xxvj s viij d
De ten' quod tenet Joh' fflecher xxvj s viij d
De ten' quod tenet Wappys xvj s viij d
Summa vj li iij s iiij d ⟨vj li iij s iiij d⟩

Redditus aularum ~~de M Mulendre~~
[5]De M' Brages pro aula Brasynnose pro uno termino xxij s ij s ob q^{a}
De eodem pro aula sancti Thome pro uno termino iij s iiij d
De eodem pro Gardino aule Scuti ij s ij d ob
De eodem pro aula universitatis pro uno termino ~~xlj s~~ xiij s iiij d
~~Pro aula~~ De M' Mulenars pro aula Brasynnose pro ij^{bus} terminis xliij s v d ob
De eodem pro aula sancti Thome pro ij^{bus} terminis vj s viij d
De eodem pro gardino aule Scuti pro ij^{bus} terminis iiij s v d ob q^{a}
De eodem pro parva aula universitatis in vico scolarum pro ij^{bus} terminis xxvj s viij d
De M' Summaster pro aula Hampton' pro ij^{bus} terminis xxxiij s iiij d
De eodem pro Sykyllhall' pro ij^{bus} terminis xiij s iiij d
De quodam Mancipio pro aula edwardi pro ij^{bus} terminis x s
De M' Mawer pro eadem aula pro ij^{bus} terminis xx s
De Roberto Wryght pro parva aula universitatis in alto vico xlvj s viij d
De M' Pawneton' pro aula Hampton' et Sykkilhall' pro uno termino xxiij s iiij d
Summa xiij li x s ob ⟨xiij li x s ob⟩

[*There are no room rents recorded for this year.*]

Redditus scolarum
De M' Joh' Carter vj s viij d
De M' Appylby vj s viij d
De M' [*blank*] vj s viij d

[5] [ADMC] These first four items were apparently added later.

De M' Willelmo Russell' vj s viij d
De Domino langton' iij s iiij d
De Domino bacar iij s iiij d
De Domino [*blank*] iij s iiij d
De Domino [*blank*] iij s iiij d
De M' Sharpp vj s viij d
Summa xlvj s viij d ⟨xlvj s viij d⟩

Redditus in suburbijs et campis
De qwytfeld' pro gardino iuxta castrum ij s
De Barton' pro terris in bellomonte viij s
De Priore fratrum predicatorum pro pratis yreland' et Alryshete xxj s viij d
De Joh' Kettyll' pro pratis retro Osnay xx s
Summa lj s viij d ⟨lj s viij d⟩

Redditus liberorum tenementorum
De Abbatissa de Godstow pro Schoppa ex o^{to} magne porte sancte ffridiss. xx d
De annuali redditu pro gardino quond' Thome Mayst' xiiij d
De Abbate de Osnay pro schopa iuxta Johannem Spycer vj s viij d
De Collegio animarum pro ten' quond' ten' Skybow viij s
De novo collegio pro Maydyn'hall' x s
De Collegio Cantuar' pro Sylv'hall' ij s vj d
De Collegio lincoln' pro Gardino v s
De Collegio animarum pro ten' quond' tenure Joh' Sprount' v s
De eodem Collegio pro Gardino retro dictum ten' viij s x d ob
De Albis monachis pro Gardino quond' ten' Barton' iiij s
De Pedyngton' pro defalcac' prati retro osnay ij s ij d
De Trygrave pro defalcacione prati retro osnay ij s ij d
Summa lvij s ij d[6]

Redditus in part' remotis
De Joh' Pownde pro manerio De Merkishall' et molendinis xviij li iij s iiij d
De Domino Thoma Terell' xx s
De Terris in Holdyrnes iij li xx d
De Novo caustro [*sic*] v li xv s vj d

[6] [ADMC] The correct total is 57s 2½d.

De ecclesia de Aronclyff	xx li
Summa xlviij li vj d	

Summa Omnium reddit' lxxxvij li xiij s ix d[7]

Recept' preter sortem domus

Item De M' Bragis	vj s viij d
Item De pincerna	iij s x d
Recept' de sista	xxiiij s iij d
Item In sista De Donkane	iij li vj s viij d
Item recept' de firmario exsex'	vj s viij d
Summa v li xvij s j d[8]	

Summa Omnium oneratorum cxcij li iij s xj d ob q[a]

[*Face of Roll*]

Allocac' M Willelmi Gregforth

In primis de Roberto Wode	viij s
De eodem pro anno ~~xxxiij~~ tercio regis edwardi iiij[ti]	vj s
Item De Dudelay	iij s ix d
Item De Spendyng' pro annis xxxv et xxxvj	viij s iij d
Item De Stokys	xx d
Item De Thoma Taylyour pro anno xxxviij[o]	v s
Item De Ricardo Wode pro annis i[o] et ij[o] Regis edwardi iiij[ti]	xx s
Item De Joh' Morelay	iij s iiij d
Item De eodem pro anno xxxiij[o]	xiij s vj d
Item De Joh' Mancipill' pro a[o] xxxviij[o]	xvj d
Item De Thoma Web pro a[o] xxxix[o]	ij s viij d
Item De eodem pro anno ij[o] Reg' edwardi iiij[ti]	iij s v d
Item De Joh' fflechar	l s
Item De eodem pro a[o] xxxix[o]	xvj s viij d
Item De eodem pro a[o] ij[o] Reg' edwardi iiij[ti]	x s
Item De eodem pro a[o] iij[o] Reg' edwardi iiij[ti]	vj s viij d
Item De Spendyng' pro a[o] primo Reg' edwardi iiij[ti]	xij d
Item De Roberto ffuller	xx d
Item De Johanne Coke	iiij s ij d

[7] [ADMC] The correct total is £87 13s 8½d.

[8] [ADMC] The shillings figure appears to have been altered, and the correct total is £5 18s 1d.

Item De Ricardo Were carpent'	xxx s ij d
Item De Wappys pro ij^{bus} terminis pro a^{o} xxxix^{o}	viij s
Item De eodem pro a^{o} ij^{o} Reg' edwardi iiij^{ti}	xvj s
Item De eodem pro a^{o} iij^{o} Reg' edwardi iiij^{ti}	xiij s iiij d
Item De Willelmo Whyte pro anno xxxix^{o}	iij s iiij d
Item De Thoma Mancipill' pro alrysheytt	ij s
Item De Pedyngton' pro antiquis debitis	xj s x d
Item De eodem pro A^{o} iij^{o} reg' edwardi iiij^{ti}	ij s ij d
Item De Trygrave pro a^{o} iij^{o} Reg' edwardi iiij^{ti}	ij s ij d
Item De Symone Mancipill'	ij s ij d
Item De Gyllott pro Ireland'	v s
Item De Joh' Gower	iij s ij d
Item De Joh' Hertt	xij s viij d
Item De bale Mason pro A^{o} xxxviij^{o}	xvj d
Item De eodem pro A^{o} xxxix pro terris in bellomonte et gardino	viij s
Item De eodem pro eisdem terris a^{o} i^{o} edwardi iiij^{ti} pro ij terminis	iiij s
Item De Barton pro eisdem pro ij terminis primi Anni et ij edwardi iiij^{ti}	iiij s
Item De Whytfeld' pro A^{o} ij^{o} edwardi iiij^{ti}	ij s
Item De eodem pro A^{o} iij^{o} Reg' edwardi iiij^{ti}	iiij d
Item De Jacobo Vectore	vj s viij d
Item De eodem pro A^{o} iij^{o} Reg' edwardi iiij^{ti}	xvj s viij d
Item De Joh' Jenens pro pratis retro Osnay pro A^{o} xxxix	xix s viij d
Item De ux' Joh' Coke	viij s
Item De Joh' Chaundlar	xxvj s viij d
Item De Henric' bath'	xx s
Item De Joh' Byrstow	xiij s iiij d
Item De Collegio lincoln' pro uno termino	ij s vj d
Summa [*blank*]	⟨xx li xvj s iij d⟩
Summa xx li xiij s iij d	

Allocaciones aularum

In primis de M' Mulenars	lv s vij d q^{a}
De M' Seymer	lj s j d q^{a}
De Roberto Wryght pro anno xxxviij^{o}	xij s vj d
De eodem pro a^{o} xxxix	xx s
De eodem pro Anno ij^{o} Regis edwardi iiij^{ti}	xxxiij s iiij d

De eodem pro Anno iij^{o} Regis edwardi iiij^{ti}	xl s
De Mancipio de brasynnose pro aula edwardi pro A^{o} xxxix	v s
De eodem pro primo Anno Regis edwardi quarti	xj s viij d
De M' Summayster pro aula Hampton' pro ij^{bus} terminis	xxxiij s iiij d
De eodem pro Sykkyl Hall' pro ij^{bus} terminis	xiij s iiij d
De M' Mawer pro aula edwardi pro A^{o} iij^{o} Regis edwardi quarti	xij s vj d
Summa xiiij li viij s iiij d ob	

Allocaciones Scolarum

De M' Keyll'	xx d
De Stephano Brown'	iij s viij d
De Kerver	iij s viij d
De Clyffton'	iij s viij d
De Sawkeld'	iij s viij d
De Graynger	xx d
De M' Cutter	vj s viij d
De M' Kerver	xx d
De Whyte	xx d
De M' lyonell'	vj s viij d
De M' paynter	~~vj s~~ iij s iiij d
De M Wyteyhe	vj s viij d
De Thoma Podyanne	xx d
De M' Karter	vj s viij d
De M' Appylby	vj s viij d
De M' Martok	vj s viij d
De M' Russell'	vj s viij d
De M' Scharpp	vj s viij d
Summa iij li xix s viij d	

Allocaciones camerarum

⟨Ista magna summa	De M' fflemmyng'	iiij s
camerarum ut patet	De M' Danyell'	xij s
per parcellas inde	De Domino Alano Bateson'	vj s viij d
proband' etc –	De M' Pray	vj s viij d
xxix s iiij d⟩[10]	Summa xix s iiij d[9]	

[9] [ADMC] This marginal entry is, I think, in the same hand as the auditor's certificate at the foot of the roll.

[10] [ADMC] The correct total is 29s 4d.

Allocaciones liberorum ten'

De Colleg' Animarum pro A° xxxix°	iiij s
De Ten' Joh' Sprounte – nunc in tenura collegij Animarum	v s
De eodem pro A° ij° Regis edwardi quarti	v s
De eodem pro A° iij° Regis edwardi quarti	v s
De eodem Colleg' pro Gardino retro dictum ten' pro A° xxxix	viij s x d ob
De eodem pro dicto gardino pro A° ij° Regis edwardi quarti	viij s x d ob
De eodem pro dicto gardino pro A° iij° Regis edwardi quarti	viij s x d ob
De Abbatissa de Godstow pro A° xxxix	xx d
De eadem pro eodem A°	xiiij d
De eadem pro A° ij° Regis edwardi quarti	xx d
De eadem pro A° ij° Regis edwardi quarti	xiiij d
De eadem pro A° iij° Regis edwardi quarti	xx d
De eadem pro A° iij° Regis edwardi quarti	xiiij d
De Abbate de Osnay pro A° xxxix	vj s viij d
De eodem pro A° ij° Regis edwardo quarti	vj s viij d
De eodem pro A° iij° Regis edwardo quarti	vj s viij d
Summa iij li xiiij s j d ob	

Allocaciones in partibus remotis

De novo castro ut patet in rotulo M' Henrici Stroder	xxj li xv s xj d
De Eodem pro A° xxxix	v li xv s vj d
De Eodem pro A° ij° Regis Edwardi quarti	xxv s x d
De Eodem pro A° iij° Regis Edwardi quarti	v li xv s vj d
De Willelmo Dixson' et Thoma Dixson'	xxviij s viij d
De Thoma Brown' de pecunijs de holderness	iij s
De Terris in Holdernes pro a° xxxix°	iij li xx d
De Joh' Pownde pro A° iij° Regis edwardi quarti	xxviij s ob
Summa xl li xiiij s v d ob	⟨xl li xiiij s v d ob⟩

Summa omnium Allocacionum lxxxiiij li ix s ij d ob[11]

Expens' fact' per procurat'

[11] [ADMC] An erasure here. The total includes the incorrect sum for the allowances on rooms.

In reparacionibus Aularum

In Aula Brasynnose	iij li ix s j d
In Aule Edwardi	xix s viij d

Summa iiij li viij s ix d

In reparacionibus ten' laicorum

In domo quadrivij	xj li xvij d
In domo Byrstow	xx s j d
In domo Spendyng'	ij d
In domo Thome Taylyour	xix s vj d
In domo Willelmi Barbour	ij d
In domo Stokys	iij d
In domo Wappys	ij s viij d
In domo lampray	iij s ob
In domo Margaret' bath	xiiij d
In domo Roberti Best	vij s v d

Summa xiij li xvj s ij d ob

Expens' infra Collegium et reparaciones

In capella	xxiiij s v d
In promptuario	xj s xj d
In coquina	xiij s xj d ob
In stauro[12]	xxj s vj d
In reparacionibus camerarum [*fenest'*?] et Aliorum infra colleg'	xxj s

Summa iiij li xij s ix d[13]

Solut' socijs

M' loci pro meremio	xxvj s viij d
M' pro suis devidenc'	xx s
M' Baynbryg'	liij s iiij d
M' Marschall'	xx s
M' Hull'	xliij s iiij d
M' Hartilpoll' pro suis debitis	x s
M' Gregforth pro suo officio	x s
M' gregforth'	xliij s iiij d

Summa xj li vj s viij d

[12] [ADMC] There is a stain on the MS here, and it is not certain whether the semi-legible letters after 'stauro' are in fact on the other side of the Roll. In the last line, the semi-obliterated word *may* be 'fenestr'.

[13] [ADMC] The correct total is £4 12s 9½d.

Solut' servientibus	
Pincerne	xxvj s viij d
Item Coco	xj s
Item barbitonsori	vij s
Item lotrici	vj s viij d
M' Wallyngford'	iij s iiij d
Pro taxacione Aule edwardi	xx d
Summa lvj s iiij d	
Resoluciones fact'	
Abbati de Osnay	xxij s x d
Priori sancte fridisswide	xviij s viij d
Abbatisse de Godstow	x s
Summa lj s vj d	
Solut' Allic' ~~dele~~ Belasyse	
Item Alic' belicis'	lviij s iiij d
Summa lviij s iiij d	
Item in equitacionibus	lviij s vij d
Summa lxvij s vij d	
In reparacionibus fact' in exsex' et holdernes Et dimissis tenentibus et alijs locis	
In primis reparacionibus fact' in exsex' pro A^{o} j^{o} et ij^{o} regis edwardi quarti	iij li xvij s v d
Item in Anno eodem	xxvj s viij d
Item in A^{o} iij^{o} regis edwardi iiij^{ti}	xxxviij s iij d
Item pro toga firmarij et expensis veniendi oxon'	x s
Item in reparacionibus de terris in holdernes pro A^{o} iij^{o} regis edwardi quarti	xxxiij s iiij d
Item pro multacione ecclesie de Aronclyff	xxvj s viij d
Item pro falcacione prati retro Osnay	xj s
Item in expensis datis dixson'	v s
Item dat' pincerne pro batellis M' Hull'	v s
Summa xj li xij s iiij d	
Item in renovacione caucionum	xiiij s
Summa xiiij s	
In communis sociorum	xviij li xv s vij d
In batellis	xxxvij s iiij d ob q^{a}
In jornellis	v s viij d ob

In contribucionibus	xxviij s viij d ob
In fest' sancte trinitatis	iiij s viij d
In fest' sancti Cuthberti	xvj s iij d ob
Summa xxiij li viij s iiij d qª	
In diminut' expensis	xxvij s v d
Summa xxvij s v d	
In dimissis ten' aularum	
In primis M' Brages	viij li xiij s iij d ob qª
Item M' Pampton'	xxvj s viij d
Item M' Bemyslay	ix li ix s iiij d
Item pro Sykkilhall' In manibus colleg'	xvij s
Item M' Antonio Clayton'	xxxiij s viij d
Summa xxij li[14]	
Item Pecun' dimissis in Cista	iiij li xj s ix d
Summa iiij li xj s ix d	

Summa omnium expens' cix li ij s xj d ob qª

Summa Omnium ~~ex~~ Allocatorum et expens' cxciij li xij s j d ob[15]

⟨Et sic computatis computandis et allocatis allocandis Collegium ind[*ebitatur Procuratori*] xxviij s ob qª. Acta sunt hec coram nobis Thom[*a . . . reverendi Christo Patris*] et domini domini Georgij dei gratia Exon' Episcopi [et Cancellarij Universitatis Oxon'] Commissario generali ibidem xxiij° die [. . .

[*Clear and mostly well-reserved roll of 3 membranes, written on rather flimsy parchment.*]

[14] [ADMC] The correct total is £21 19s 11d.
[15] [ADMC] The correct total is £193 12s 2½d.

WHITSUN to MARTINMAS 4 EDWARD IV [*SIC*; *RECTE* 3 EDWARD IV] (ROLL UC:BU1/F/73)[1]

29 May 1463–11 November 1463

BURSAR: JAMES BAYNBRYGE

Compotus M' Jacobi Baynbryg' pro 2^bus terminis

[*Space of about 4 inches*]

Compotus Magistri Jacobi Banbryge a festo pentecost' Anno regni Regis Edwardi quarti quarto usque ad festum sancti Martini in yeme[2]

[*The Arrears are substantially as in the Allowances of* **F/72**, *with only a few differences in spelling. The totals are all as in* **F/72**, *except for the total for College Rooms, which is 29s 4d (as opposed to the erroneous 19s 4d above), and the final total is now correct.*]

Summa omnium Arr' lxxxiiij li xix s ij d ob

Rentale
In paroch' omnium sanctorum

De Edwardo Wode pro Gardino quod tenet in Swynscheton' pro ij^bus terminis	iij s
De Ten' quod tenet Thomas dudlay pro ij^bus terminis	xvj s viij d
De Ten' quod tenet Brystoe bruer' pro ij^bus terminis	xxvj s viij d
De Ten' quod tenet Spendyng' pro ij^bus terminis	x s x d
De Ten' quod tenet Thomas Tayliour pro ij^bus terminis	xvj s viij d
De Ten' quod tenet Ric' Wode pro ij^bus terminis	xiij s iiij d
De Ten' quod tenet Willelmus Barbur pro ij^bus terminis	viij s iiij d
De Ten' quod tenet stokys pro ij^bus terminis	xx s
Summa v li xviij s x d[3]	

[1] This roll is dated to Whitsun-Martinmas 4 Edward IV (i.e. to the second half of 1464). However, this must certainly an error for *3* Edward IV: there is already a roll covering this period, namely **F/75**, and the roll's actual contents make it fit exactly between **F/72** and **F/74** i.e. May to November 1463.

[2] [ADMC] Entries in the Arrears in **F/74** below (and the Allowances here) show that Baynbrigge's 2 terms as Bursar are also referred to as falling in 3 Edw IV.

[3] [ADMC] The correct total is £5 15s 6d.

In paroch' beate Marie et sancti petri in oriente

De Ten' quod tenet lampray pro ij^{bus} terminis x s
De Ten' quod tenet jacobus vector' pro ij^{bus} terminis xiij s iiij d
De Ten' quod tenet Robertus best pro ij^{bus} terminis x s
De Ten' quod tenet Henr' Bath' pro uxore sua vj s viij d
De Ten' quod tenet joh' ffleschar' pro ij^{bus} terminis xiij s iiij d
De Ten' quod tenet Wappys pro ij^{bus} terminis viij s iiij d
Summa iij li xx d

Redditus Aularum

De M' Molennars pro Brasynnos pro uno termino xxij s ij s ob q^{a}
De eodem pro Aula sancti Thome pro uno termino iij s iiij d
De eodem pro Gardino Aula scuti pro uno termino ij s ij d ob q^{a}
De parva Aula universitatis in vico scolarum in manu colleg' xiij s iiij d
De Sumayster pro Aula Hampton' pro uno termino xvj s viij d
~~De Sykyll' Hall n^{hil} n^{hil}~~
De M' Mawer pro Aula Edwardi pro uno termino x s
De Roberto Wryght pro parva Aula universitatis in alto vico pro ij^{bus} terminis xxiij s iiij d
Summa iiij li xj s j d ob

[*No heading*]

De Scolis xxxiij s iiij d
De Cameris nichil
Summa patet

[*Redd*]itus in sub[*urb*]ijs et campis

De qwytfeld' pro Gardino iuxta castrum pro ij^{bus} terminis xij d
De palmer pro terris in bellimonte [*sic*] pro ij^{bus} terminis iiij s
De priore predicametorum pro ij^{bus} terminis xxj s viij d
De Corry pro prato retro osnay xvij s
Summa xliij s viij d

[*Red*]ditus liberorum [*ten'*]

De Abbatissa de Godstow pro schoppa ex o^{to} magne porte fridiss' x d
De eadem pro Gardino quond' Thome Mayster vij d
De Abbate de osnay pro schoppa iuxta johannem spicer iij s iiij d

De Colleg' animarum pro ten' quond' Rogeri skybbow pro ij[bus] terminis iiij s
De Novo Colleg' pro Maydyn' Hall' pro ij[bus] terminis v s
De Colleg' Cantuarie pro ij[bus] terminis pro sylver Hall' xv d
De Colleg' animarum pro quodam Ten' quond' tenure johannis Spront in paroch' sancti petri ij s vj d
De eodem Colleg' pro quodam Gardino retro dictum ten' quond' de tenura eiusdem Johannis Spront in eadem parochia pro ij[bus] terminis iiij s v d q[a]
De Albis Monachis pro Gardino quond' Tenure Johannis Barton' sutoris pro ij[bus] terminis ij s
De Pyttyngton pro defalcacione prati retro osnay ij s ij d
De Trygrane pro defalcacione eiusdem prati ij s ij d
Summa xxx s ix d q[a]

[*Redditus in partibus remotis*]
[*De*] Johanne pownde pro manerio de Markyshawe et Molendinis in exsexeia pro ij[bus] terminis ix li xx d
[*De T*]home Terell' pro libero redditu pro ij[bus] terminis x s
[*De T*]erris in Holdernes pro ij[bus] terminis xxx s x d
[*De N*]ovo Castro pro ij[bus] terminis lvij s ix d
[*De Ec*]clesia de Aronclyff x li
Summa xxiij li iij d

Summa omnium reddit' xlij li xij s ob q[a4]

[*Rec*]epta de Cista iiij li xj s ix d
[*Pre*]ter sortem [*dom*]us xvij s ix d ob q[a5]

[*Summa*] omnium Oneratorum cxxxij li ~~ix s~~ ix s viij d q[a]

[. . .] Oneratorum cxxxiij li vij s vj d

[*Dorse*]

[*Allocacion*]es M' Jac[*obi B*]anbryg'
[*De Roberto Wode*] [*viij s*]
[*De eodem pro ao iij[o] Reg' Edwardi*] iiij[ti] [*v s*]

[4] [ADMC] The correct total is £42 19s 4d.
[5] [ADMC] Uncertain readings here. The 'Preter sortem domus' entri is in a different ink, as is the 'ix s' written over the total, which is erased because not clearly written. The 'q[a]' in square brackets is not certain.

[*De Dudelay*]	[*iij s ix d*]
[*De Spendyng' pro annis*] xxxv^{to} et xxxvj^{to}	[*viij s iiij d*]
[*De eodem pro a^{o} primo R'*] E' iiij^{ti}	xij [*d*]
[*De Stokys*]	xx [*d*]
[*De Thoma Tayly*]our pro A^{o} xxxviij^{o}	v s
[*De eodem pro a^{o} i*]ij^{o} r' E' iiij^{ti}	iiij s viij d
[*De Ric' Wode*] pro annis primo et ij^{o} r' E' iiij^{ti}	xx s
[*De eodem pro A^{o}*] iij^{o} r' E' iiij^{ti}	ij s
[*De Morlay*]	iij s iiij d
[*De eodem pro*] A^{o} xxxiij^{o}	xiij s vj d
[*De Johanne*] Mancypull' pro A^{o} xxxviij^{o}	xvj d
[*De Thoma*] Webb pro A^{o} xxxix^{o}	ij s viij d
[*De eodem*] pro A^{o} ij^{o} r' E' iiij^{ti}	iij s v d
[*De Jo*]hanne flechar	l s
[*De eo*]dem pro A^{o} xxxix^{o}	xvj s viij d
[*De eo*]dem pro A^{o} ij^{o} r' E' iiij^{ti}	x s
[*De eo*]dem pro A^{o} iij^{o} r' E' iiij^{ti}	vj s viij d
[*De eo*]dem pro eodem a^{o}	iij s iiij d
[*De Ro*]berto ffuller pro quodam Gardino	xx d
[*De J*]ohanne Cooke	iiij s ij d
[*De R*]icardo Wer' carpentario	xxx s ij d
[*De W*]appys pro ij^{bus} terminis pro a^{o} xxxix^{o}	viij s
[*De*] eodem pro a^{o} ij^{o} r' E' iiij^{ti}	xvj s
[*De*] eodem pro A^{o} iij^{o} r' E' iiij^{ti} pro tempore M' Gregforde	xiiij s iiij d
De eodem pro tempore meo	vij s iiij d
De Willelmo Whych'	iij s iiij d
De Thoma Mancypull' pro Alryscheyt	ij s iiij d
De Pedyngton'	viij s iiij d
De Trygrande pro A^{o} iij^{o} r' E' iiij^{ti}	ij s ij d
De Symone Mancypull'	ij s ij d
De M' Gyllott pro jrelande	v s
De Gowar'	iij s ij d
De Johanne Harte	xij s viij d
De Balymason pro A^{o} xxxviij^{o}	xvj d
De eodem pro a^{o} xxxix^{o} pro terris in bellomonte et Gardino	viij s
De eodem pro eisdem terris A^{o} primo r' E' iiij^{ti}	iiij s
De Barton pro eisdem eisdem primo A^{o} et ij^{i} r' E' iiij^{ti}	iiij s
De eodem pro A^{o} iij^{o} r' E' iiij^{ti}	iiij d

De eodem in tempore meo	xij d
[6]⟨De Whytfeld' pro a^{o} 2° Edwardi $iiij^{ti}$	ij s⟩
De Jacobo vector'	vj s viij d
De Johanne Senens [*sic*] pro A^{o} xxxix^{o}	xix s viij d
De uxore johannis Cooke	viij s
De Johanne schandlar'	xxvj s viij d
De Henrico Bathe	xx s
De eodem pro Alio ten'	vj s viij d
De Joh' Byrstow pro A^{o} iij^{o} r' E' $iiij^{ti}$	xiij s iiij d
⟨Item de eodem pro tempore meo	xiij s iiij d⟩
De Palmer pro ~~A°~~ terris in bellimonte	iiij s
De lampray	iiij s
De Roberto Beste	x s
De Corre	x s
Summa xxiij li x s ix d[7]	

Allegate [*sic*] ~~Allocca~~ ⟨Aularum⟩

De M' Molennars pro tempore M' Gregforde	viij s xj d q^{a}
De eodem pro uno termino pro tempore M' Banbryg'	xxvij s ix d ob
De Symmayster pro tempore procuracionis M' gregford' in allecatis [*sic*] sibi	xxx s
De M' Seymer	lj s j d q^{a}
De Roberto Wryght pro A^{o} $xxxviij^{o}$	xij s vj d
De eodem pro A^{o} xxxix^{o}	xx s
De eodem pro A^{o} ij^{o} r' E' $iiij^{ti}$	xxxiij s iiij d
De eodem pro A^{o} iij^{o} r' E' $iiij^{ti}$ pro tempore procuracionis M' Gregforde	xl s
De eodem pro tempore procuracionis M Banbryg'	xxiij s iiij d
De Mancipio de Brasynnos pro Aula Edwardi pro a^{o} xxxix^{o}	v s
De eodem pro primo a^{o} r' E' $iiij^{ti}$	xj s viij d
De Summayster pro Sykkyl Hall'	xiij s iiij d
De Mawer pro Aula Edwardi pro a^{o} iij^{o} r' E' $iiij^{ti}$	vij s
De eodem pro uno termino in tempore M Banbryg'	x s
Item pro parva Aula universitatis in vico scolarum	xiij s iiij d
Summa xv li vij s iiij d	

[6] This, and the next entry in hooked brackets, were both added later in the margin of the roll.

[7] [ADMC] The correct total is £23 10s 10d.

Allocaciones Scolarum

De M' Keyll'	xx d
De Stephano Brown'	iij s viij d
De Kerwar'	iij s viij d
De Clyfton'	iij s viij d
De Sawkett'	iij s viij d
De Graynger	xx d
De M' Cutter	vj s viij d
De M' Kerver	xx d
De Whytt	xx d
De M' lyonell'	vj s viij d
De M' paynter	iij s iiij d
De M Wyche ⟨quondam aule beate Marie⟩	vj s viij d
De Thoma Podyam'	xx d
De M' Medlay	vj s viij d
De M fratre suo	vj s viij d
De M [*blank*] de Aula cervina	vj s viij d
De M' Baynbryg'	vj s viij d
De M [*blank*] Colleg' animarum	vj s viij d
De M' Appylby	vj s viij d
De M' Martoke	vj s viij d
De M' Russell'	vj s viij d
Summa iiij li xix s viij d	

Allocaciones camerarum

De M' fflemmyng'	iiij s
De M' Danyell'	xij s
De domino Alano Battson'	vj s viij d
De M' Pray	vj s viij d
Summa xxix s iiij d	

Allocaciones liberorum Ten'

De Colleg' Animarum pro A° xxxix°	iiij s
De Ten' Joh' Sprounte et nunc in tenur' colleg' animarum	v s
De eodem pro A° ij° r' E' iiij^ti	v s
De eodem pro A° iij° r' E' iiij^ti	v s
De eodem Colleg' pro Gardino retro dictum ten' pro A° xxxix°	viij s x d ob
De eodem pro dicto gardino pro A° ij° r' E' iiij^ti	viij s x d ob
De eodem pro dicto gardino pro A° iij° r' E' iiij^ti	viij s x d ob
De eodem Colleg' in tempore meo pro Ten' Sprownte	ij s vj d

De eodem pro Gardino retro dictum Ten'	iiij s v d q^{a}
De Abbatissa de Godstow pro A^{o} xxxix^{o}	xx d
De eadem pro tempore meo pro quodam Gardino	vj d
De eadem pro eodem A^{o}	xiiij d
De eadem pro A^{o} ij^{o} r' E' iiij^{ti}	xx d
De eadem pro A^{o} ij^{o} r' E' iiij^{ti}	xiiij d
De eadem pro A^{o} iij^{o} r' E' iiij^{ti}	xx d
De eadem pro A^{o} iij^{o} r' E' iiij^{ti}	xiiij d
De eadem pro tempore Banbryg'	x d
De Abbate de Osnay pro A^{o} xxxix^{o}	vj s viij d
De eodem pro A^{o} ij^{o} r' E' iiij^{ti}	vj s viij d
De eodem pro A^{o} iij^{o} r' E' iiij^{ti}	vj s viij d
De eodem pro tempore Banbryg'	iij s iiij d
Summa iiij li v s ix d ob q^{a}	

Allocaciones in partibus remotis

De novo castro	xxj li xv s xj d
De eodem pro A^{o} xxxix^{o}	v li xv s vj d
De eodem pro A^{o} ij^{o} r' E' iiij^{ti}	xxv s x d
De eodem pro A^{o} iij^{o} r' E' iiij^{ti}	v li xv s vj d
De eodem pro ij^{bus} terminis in tempore Banbryg'	lvij s ix d
De Willelmo Dixson' et Thoma Dixson'	xxviij s viij d
De eisdem pro ij^{bus} terminis	x li
De Thoma Brown' de pecunijs de Holdernes	iij s iiij d
De Terris in Holdernes pro A^{o} xxxix^{o}	iij li xx d
De eisdem pro Tempore Banbryg'	xxx s x d
De Johanne Pownde pro A^{o} iij^{o} r' E' iiij^{ti}	xxviij s ob
Summa lv li iij s ob	⟨xl li xiiij s v d ob⟩

Summa omnium Allocacionum ciiij li xv s xj d q^{a}

Expens' facte in reparacionibus Aularum

In de [*sic*] Brasynnose et parva Aula universitatis in vico scolarum	v li xvij d ob
Item in Expens' factis circa mutacionem Aule Hamptonie	iij s j d ob
Item in parva Aula universitatis in Alto vico	viij d
Summa vj li v s iij d	

In reparacionibus Ten' laycorum

In domo quadrivij	ix li ix s ix d ob

Item in Tenemento lampray et Thome Taylyour ij s vij d
Summa ix li xij s iiij d ob

Expens' infra Collegium
In reparacionibus Camerarum et Aliorum infra Collegium xvij s iiij d

Soluc' socij
In primis Magistro vj s viij d
Item Banbryg' vj s viij d
Item Magistro Gregforde vj s viij d
Item Magistro Marschall' vj s viij d
Item Magistro Hull' vj s viij d
Item Magistro Thurby vj s viij d
Item Magistro Banbryg' vj s viij d
Item Magistro Gregforde pro eadem soluc' vj s viij d
Item Magistro Hull' pro eadem soluc' vj s viij d
Item Magistro Banbryg' pro officio procuratoris v s
Summa iij li v s

Soluc' servientibus
In primis pincerne vj s viij d
Item Johanne Coco vj s
Item Barbitonsori iij s vij d
Item Magistro Wallyngforde iij s iiij d
Summa xix s vij d

Resoluc' facte
In primis priori sancte frideswyde vj s viij d
Item Alicie Belisis xxx s iiij d
Summa xxxvij s

In Equitacionibus
In primis Magistro Marschall' vj s xj d
Item Magistro Hull' xij s vj d
Item Johanne Portar' qu[. . .] equitavit Magistro Bragges ix d
Summa xx s ij d

In resolutis Tenentibus ij s
In diminutis Expens' ix s x d
Summe patent

[8]Pro communis sociorum in absencia Roberti Best pro tribus septimanis xxj s
Item in jurnellis ij d
Item in batellis domus ij s iij d ob q[a]
Item in communis sociorum Johanni Porter pro decem septimanis xlix s xj d ob
Item in batellis v s xj d ob
Item in jurnellis eodem tempore iij s vij d
Summa iiij li ij s xj d ob q[a]

Summa Omnium Expensarum xxviij li xj s vj d q[a]

Summa Omnium Allocatorum et Expensarum cxxxiij li vij s vj d ob[9]

[*The Roll is not signed*]

[*A rapidly and untidily written roll of 3 membranes (one of them very short). Mostly in good condition, but damaged at the foot, and at the top of the dorse.*

The figures on the Credit side of the roll are puzzling, and apparantly cannot be made to balance. The Arrears total (£84 19s 2½d) is correct. In Rents, the All Saints total is given as £5 18s 10d; the items in this section actually come to £5 15s 6d. The total of Rents is given as £42 12s d; the combined section totals in fact amount to £42 19s 7d.

From the MS it looks as of the 'Recepta preter sortem domus' may have been added. The first grand total (£132 9s 8¼d) would in that case represent Arrears and Rent and Chest, although it in that case (or, I think, in any other) an incorrect figure (£84 19s 2½d + £42 12s d + £4 11s 9d = £132 3s 0¼d). The second grand total (£133 7s 7d) is clearly the first plus the amount of 'Recepta preter sortem' (17s 9d).

N.B. The 'ix s' written, in a different ink, over the 'ix s' of the first grand total is possibly merely a rewriting of the figure for clarity. But the roll is damaged here, and it is just possible that it represents another item written under 'Recepta preter sortem', the other 'ix s' not being intended to be deleted. If so, it is hard to see how it fits in.]

[8] [ADMC] The remainder of roll, from this point, is in a different hand.
[9] [ADMC] The correct total is £132 7s 5½d.

4 EDWARD IV (ROLL UC:BU1/F/74)
c.11 November 1463–20 May 1464?[1]

BURSAR: THOMAS THURLBY

Compotus Magistri Thome Thorleby Procuratoris Collegij sive Magne Aula universitatis Oxon'. Datus per eundem magistro A^{o} Regni Regis Edwardi quarti quarto

[*The Arrears are identical with the Allowances in* **F/74** *above, save for a few changes in spelling.*]

Summa Omnium Arr' ciiij li xv s xj d q^{a}

Rentale

[*None of these sections has a heading*]

De Edwardo Wode pro gardino quod tenet in Swynscheton pro 2^{bus} ter' iij s
De paulo teutonico pro ij^{bus} ter' xx s
De ten' quod tenet Thomas Dudlay pro ij^{bus} ter' xvj s viij d
De ten' quod tenet Byrstow Breuer' pro ij^{bus} ter' xxvj s viij d
De ten' quod tenet Spendyng' pro ij^{bus} ter' x s x d
De ten' quod tenet Thomas Tayliour pro ij^{bus} ter' xvj s viij d
De ten' quod tenet Johannes Hall' pro ij^{bus} ter' xiij s iiij d
De Ten' quod tenet Willelmus Barbor pro ij^{bus} ter' viij s
De Ten' quod tenet Stokys pro ij^{bus} ter' xx s
Summa v li xv s ij d

De ten' quod tenet lampray pro ij^{bus} ter' x s
De ten' quod tenet Ric' Cocus pro ij^{bus} ter' x s
De ten' quod tenet Joh' fflecher' pro ij^{bus} ter' xiij s iiij d
De ten' quod tenet Wappys pro ij^{bus} ter' viij s iiij d
Summa xlj s viij d

De M Adam pro Brasynnosse pro uno ter' ante taxacionem xxij s ij s ob q^{a}
De eodem pro aula sancti Thome pro eodem ter' iij s iiij d

[1] The dates of Martinmas for 1463, and Pentecost for 1464. See the note at the head of **F/60** above for their inclusion here; in this case, since the previous roll ended at Martinmas 1463, and the present roll only covers rents for two terms, it is assumed that this roll ran from St. Martin's Day 1463 to Pentecost 1464.

De eodem pro gardino aula scuti pro eodem ter' ij s ij d ob q^{a}
De eodem pro Brasynnosse pro uno ter' ante taxacionem
xv s vj s ob q^{a}
De eodem pro aula sancti Thome pro eodem ter' vj s
De eodem pro Gardino Aula scuti pro eodem ter' ij s ij d ob q^{a}
De M Proketer pro aula universitatis in alto vico pro ij^{bus} ter'
xxxv s vj d ob

Summa iiij li vij s j d ob

De Scolis xvj s viij d

Summa patet

De Qwytfeld' pro Gardino iuxta Castrum pro ij^{bus} ter' xij d
De Palmer pro terris in bellamonte [*sic*] pro ij^{bus} ter' iiij s

Summa v s

De Abbatissa de godstow pro schopa exo^{to} magne porte fridiss'
x d
De eadem pro Gardino quond' Thome Mayster vij d
De abbate de Osnay pro schopa iuxta johannem Spiser iij s iiij d
De Collegio Animarum pro ten' quond' Rogeri Skybbow pro ij^{bus} ter' iiij s
De eodem pro ten' quond' tenur' Johannis Sprownt in paroch' sancti petri ij s vj d
De eodem Colleg' pro quodam Gardino retro dict' ten' eiusdem Johannis Spront pro ij^{bus} ter' iiij s v d q^{a}
De novo Collegio pro Maydyn Hall' pro ij^{bus} ter' v s
De Colleg' Cantuarie ij s vj d
De Albis Monachys pro Gardino quond' Tenure Johannis Barton' ij s
De Collegio linc' pro 2^{bus} ter' xxiij s iiij d

Summa xlviij s vj d q^{a}

De Johanne Pownde pro Manerio de Markyshall' et molendinis in exsexeia pro ij^{bus} ter' ix li xx d
De Thome Terell' pro ij^{bus} ter' x s
De terris in Holdernes pro ij^{bus} ter' xxx s x d
De Novo Castro pro ij^{bus} ter' lvij s ix d
De ecclesia de Aranclyff x li

Summa xxiij li iij d

De Camera A Adam pro 2[bus] ter'	viij s
De M Henrico Barfforth pro 2[bus] ter'	v s iiij d
De M Potter pro 2[bus] ter'	v s iiij d
De M fforde pro 2[bus] ter'	iiij s viij d
De Suttontysse pro 2[bus] ter'	v s
De Camara [*sic*] quam occupant bidelli	iij s
De Alia Camera Edwardi lupton	iiij s
Summa xxxv s iiij d	

Summa omnium reddit' xlij li ix s viij s ob q[a]

Preter sortem domus

De M Bragges	xxvj s viij d
De M Baybryg	iiij s viij d
De Bemyslay	xj s v d
De Collegio Animarum pro antiquis debitis	iiij s
Summa xlvj s ix d	

Summa omnium Oneratorum cxlix li xij s v d

[*Dorse*]

R M Th' Thorleby[2]

In primis de Roberto Wode	viij s
Item de paulo teutonico	xx d
De Roberto Wode pro a[o] 3[o] Regis Edwardi iiij[ti]	v s
De eodem pro ij[bus] ter'	iij s
De Dudlay	iij s ix d
De eodem pro tempore M Thorleby	x s
De Spendyng' pro annis xxxv et xxxvj[o]	viij s iiij d
De eodem pro a[o] primo R' Edwardi iiij[ti]	xij d
De Byrstow pro a[o] iij[o] R' Edwardi iiij[ti]	xiij s iiij d
De eodem pro tempore M Baynbryg'	xiij s iiij d
De Thoma Taylyour pro a[o] xxxviij[o]	v s
De eodem pro a[o] iij[o] r' E' iiij[ti]	x d
De Ric' Woode	xij s iiij d
De eodem pro a[o] iij[o] r' E' iiij[ti] ⟨pro tempore baynbryg'⟩	ij s
De Johanne hall' ⟨pro ij[bus] ter'⟩	xiij s iiij d

[2] [ADMC] This is written in large letters, and was probably the endorsement on the outside of the roll when rolled up.

De Stokes	xx d
De Morlay	iij s iiij d
De eodem pro a^{o} xxxiij^{o}	xiij s vj d
De Johanne Mancypyll' pro a^{o} xxxviij^{o}	xvj d
De Thoma Webbe pro a^{o} xxxix^{o}	ij s viij d
De eodem pro a^{o} ij^{o} r' E' iiij^{ti}	iij s v d
De Johanne fflecher	l s
De eodem pro a^{o} xxxix^{o}	xvj s viij d
De eodem pro a^{o} ij^{o} r' E' iiij^{ti}	x s
De eodem pro a^{o} iij^{o} r' E' iiij^{ti}	vj s viij d
De eodem pro tempore Baynbryg'	iij s iiij d
De eodem pro tempore meo	x s
De Roberto ffuller pro quodam gardino	xx d
De Johanne Coke	iiij s ij d
De Ricardo Wer' carpentario	xxx s ij d
De Wappys pro ij^{bus} terminis pro a^{o} xxxix^{o}	viij s
De eodem pro a^{o} 2° et 3° r' E' iiij^{ti} et pro tempore M Gregford	xxx s iiij d
De eodem pro tempore M Baynbryg'	vij s iiij d
De eodem pro tempore meo	iiij s iiij d
De Willelmo Wyche	iij s iiij d
De Thoma Mauncypyll' pro alrychet	ij s
De Pedyngton'	viij s iiij d
De Trygrane pro a^{o} 3° r' E' iiij^{ti}	ij s ij d
De Symone Mancypyll'	ij s ij d
De M' Gyllot pro yreland'	v s
De Gower	ij s ij d
De Johanne Harth	xij s viij d
De Baylyamason pro annis xxxviij^{o} et xxxix^{o} pro terris in bellomonte et gardino	ix s iiij d
De eodem pro a^{o} primo r' E' iiij^{ti} pro eisdem terris	iiij s
De Barton pro eisdem terris primo primo et 2° r' E' iiij^{ti}	iiij s
De Whytefel pro a^{o} 2° rr' E' iiij^{ti}	ij s
De eadem [*sic*] pro a^{o} 3°	iiij d
De eadem pro ij^{bus} ter' in tempore M Baynbryg' et pro 2^{bus} ter' in tempore meo	ij s
De jacobo vectore	xj s viij d
De johanne Jenyns pro a^{o} xxxix^{o}	xix s viij d
De uxore johannis Cooke	viij s
De Johanne Schaunler'	xxvj s viij d

De Henrico Bayth xx s
De eodem pro alio ten' vj s viij d
De Palmer pro terris in bellimonte iiij s
De eodem pro tempore meo iiij s
De lampray pro tempore M baynbryg' x s
De eodem pro tempore meo vj s
De Roberto Beste x s
De Ric' Coke ij s
De Corre iiij s
Summa xxv li xx d

Allocaciones Aularum

De M' Molennars pro tempore M' Gregforde viij s xj d q^{a}
De eodem pro uno termino pro tempore M' Baynbryg' xxvij s ix d ob
De M Adam pro brasynnose aula sancti Thome et pro gardino pro 2^{bus} ter' ante tax' et post tax' iiij s xj d
De M Prokter pro parva Aula universitatis in alto vico pro 2^{bus} ter' viij s x s ob
De M Summayster xv s
De eodem pro Sekyll' Hall' xiij s iiij d
De M' Semar lj s j d q^{a}
De Roberto Wryght pro annis xxxviij^{o} et xxxix xxxij s vj d
De eodem pro annis 2° et 3° r' E' iiij^{ti} iij li xiij s iiij d
De eodem pro tempore M Baynbryg' xxiij s iiij d
De Mancipio de Brasynnosse pro Aula Edwardi pro a^{o} xxxix v s
De eodem pro a^{o} primo r' E' iiij^{ti} xj s viij d
De M Mawer pro Aula Edwardi xvij s
De parva Aula universitatis in vico scolarum xiij s iiij d
De M Baynbryg' pro camera M fford' in aula universitatis in vico scolarum xx d
De M fford pro eadem camera xv d
De Cameris in aula universitatis in vico scolarum xxx s[3] viij d
Summa xvj li xix s viij d ob

Allocaciones Scolarum

De M' Keell' xx d
De ~~M~~ Stephano Brown' iij s viij d

[3] [ADMC] Altered from 'xxxij s'.

De Kervar'	iij s viij d
De Clyffton'	iij s viij d
De Sawkell'	iij s viij d
De Grawnger	xx d
De M' Cutter	vj s viij d
De M' Kerver	xx d
De Whyte	xx d
De lyonell'	vj s viij d
De M' Paynter	iij s iiij d
De M Wyche quond' Aule Beate Marie	vj s viij d
De Thoma Podyane	xx d
De M' Medlay	vj s viij d
De M fratre suo	vj s viij d
De M Wryter aule cervine	vj s viij d
De M' Baynbryg'	vj s viij d
De M Crosse Collegij Animarum	vj s viij d
De M' Appylbe	vj s viij d
De M' Martoke	vj s viij d
De M' Russell'	vj s viij d
De Willelmo Barker de Colleg' dunelm'	iij s iiij d
Summa v li iij s	

Allocaciones camerarum

De M' fflemmyng'	iiij s
De M' Daniell'	xij s
De Alano Batson'	vj s viij d
De M' Pray	vj s viij d
Summa xxix s iiij d	

Allocaciones liberorum Ten'

In primis de Colleg' Animarum pro a° xxxix°	iiij s
De eodem Colleg' pro ten' Johannis Sprount	v s
De eodem pro annis 2° et 3° r' E' iiij[ti]	x s
De eodem pro Gardino retro dictum ten' pro a° xxxix°	viij s x d ob
De eodem pro dict' gardino pro annis 2° et 3° r' E' iiij[ti]	xvij s ix d
De eodem pro ten' Johannis Sprount in tempore Baynbryg'	ij s vj d
De eodem pro Gardino retro dictum ten' in tempore Baynbryg'	iiij s v d q[a]
De eodem pro ten' Johannis Sprount pro tempore meo	ij s vj d

De eodem pro gardino retro dict' ten' eiusdem Johannis pro 2^{bus} ter'	iiij s v d q^{a}
De Abbatissa de Godstow pro a^{o} xxxix^{o}	xx d
De eadem pro gardino pro tempore M Baynbryg'	viij d
De eadem pro eodem a^{o}	xiiij d
De eadem pro A^{o} 2° r' E' iiij^{ti}	xx d
De eadem pro annis 2° et 3° r' E' iiij^{ti}	iiij s
De eadem pro tempore M Baynbryg'	x d
De eadem pro tempore meo	x d
De Abbate de Osnay pro a^{o} xxxix	vj s viij d
De eodem pro annis 2° et 3° r' E' iiij^{ti}	xiij s iiij d
De eodem pro tempore M Baynbryg'	iij s iiij d
De eodem pro tempore meo	iij s iiij d
De albis Monachis pro ij^{bus} ter'	ij s

Summa iiij li xix s vj d

Allocaciones in partibus remotis

In primis de novo castro	xxj li xv s xj d
De eodem pro a^{o} xxxix^{o}	v li xv s vj d
De eodem pro annis 2° et 3° r' E' iiij^{ti}	vij li xvj d
De eodem pro 2^{bus} ter' in tempore M Banbryg'	lvij s ix d
De eodem pro 2^{bus} ter' in tempore meo	xj s j d
De Thoma Browne de pecunijs de Holdernesse	iij s iiij d
De Johanne Pownde pro a^{o} 3° r' E' iiij^{ti}	xxviij s ob
De domino Thome Tyrell'	x s
De terris in Holdernysse	iij li xx d

Summa xliij li iiij s vij d ob

Summa omnium Allocatorum lxxxxvj li xvij s x d

Reparacionis Aularum et scolarum

In primis in Aula Brasynnose	iij li ij s iij d ob
Item in Aula universitatis in alto vico	xvj s xj d
Item in aula Edwardi	iiij d
Item in scolis	xiiij s

Summa iiij li viij d ob

Reparaciones ten' laycorum

In primis in domo super quadrivium	lviij s iiij d ob
Item in domibus spendyng' et Byrstow	ij s xj d
Item in domibus Thome Taylyour et stokes	vj s xj d ob
Item in domo Johanne fflecher	iij s

Item in domo Ric' Coke	xij s viij d
Summa iiij li iij s xj d	

Expens' infra Collegium

In primis in Camera doctoris	xvij s xj d
Summa patet	

Soluc' socijs

In primis M loci	xx s
Item M Gregford	xx s
Item M Marschall'	xx s
Item M Hull'	xx s
Item M thorleby	xx s
Item M Gregford in part' penc' sue	xxxiij s iiij d
Item M Hull' in part' penc' sue	xxxiij s iiij d
Item M Thorleby pro officio procuratoris	x s
Summa ix li xx d	

Soluciones servientibus

In primis Pincerne pro 2^{bus} ter'	xiij s iiij d
Item Rogero coco pro 2^{bus} ter'	vj s
Item barbetonsori	iij s iiij d
Item M Wallyngford	iij s iiij d
Item taxatoribus pro taxacione aula universitatis in vico scolarum	vj s viij d
Summa xxxij s[4] viij d	

Resoluc'

In primis abbati de osnay	xxij s x d
Item priori ffrideswyde	xxx s viij d
Item abbatisse de godstow	x s
Item Alicie Bellacysse	lviij s iiij d
Summa vj li xxij d	

In equitacionibus et alijs

In primis M loci	xxiiij s ix d ob
Item firmario de Exsex' pro toga et expensis	x s
Item Thome Law	xij d
Item pro reparacione unius Molendini	xiij s iij d
Item Dikson pro multacione et expensis suis	xxxiij s iiij d

[4] [ADMC] Altered from 'xxxiij s'.

Item pro debitis antiquis M Baynbryg' uxori Coddi et alijs laborarijs	x s xj d
Item in stauro	xlviij s xj d
Item uxori dagfeld pro tempore Best	viij s x d
Item in capella aula promptuario et in orto	xv s xj d
Item in diminutis expensis Resoluc' ten' et renovacione caucionum	xj s iiij d
Summa viij li xviij s iij d ob	

In Communis sociorum	viij li xiij s vij d
Item in batellis	xxj s xj d ob
Item in jurnellis	vj s vj d ob
Item in Contribucionibus	ix s vij d
Item pro festo sancti Cuthberti	xj s vj d ob
Summa xj li iij s ij d ob	

Summa Omnium Expens' xlvj li ij d ob

Item de pecunijs dimissis in cista	vj li vij s ix d
Item pro expensis fact' per M in tempore M Gregford	vj s viij d
Summa v li xiiij s v d	

Summa Omnium Allocatorum et Expensarum cxlix li xij s v d ob

⟨Et sic computatis computandis et Allocatis Allocandis collegium indebitatur computanti – ob. Acta sunt Hec coram nobis Johanne Mulcaster Reverendi in X° patris et domini domini Georgij dei gratia Exon' episcopi et Cancellarij universitatis Oxon' Commissario generali penultimo die mensis Maij Anno Infrascripto⟩

[*Very clear roll, and in very good condition. 2 membranes. Except for a discrepancy of 1d in the Arrears, all figures balance.*]

5 EDWARD IV (ROLL UC:BU1/F/75)
c.20 May 1464–2 June 1465?[1]

BURSAR: JOHN HULLE

Compotus Magistri Johannis Hull' Procuratoris Collegij sive Magne Aule universitatis Oxon' Datus per eundem Magistrum Regni Regis Edwardi quarti quinto.

Arr'

[*These are just as in the Allowances in* **F/74** *above, save that Robert Wood in the first items is here called Edward Wood, and that all references in the Allowances to 'tempore meo' are replaced by ones to 'tempore M Thorleby'.*]

Summa omnium Arr' lxxxxvj li xvij s x d

Rentale

[*No heading*]

De Edwardo Wood pro gardino in Swynscheton vj s ⟨a⟩[2]
De Antonio Hardwarnian super quadrivium pro tribus ter' et di' xxxv s
De ten' quod tenet Thomas Dudlay xxxiij s iiij d ⟨a⟩
De ten' quod tenet Birstow breuer liij s iiij d
De ten' quod tenet Spendyng' xxj s viij d
De ten' quod tenet Thomas Taylyour xxxviij s iiij d
De ten' quod tenet W Barbor xvj s viij d
De ten' quod tenet Stokys xl s
Summa xij li iiij s iiij d ⟨xij li iij s viij d⟩[3]

De ten' quod tenet lampray xx s ⟨a⟩
De ten' quod tenet Ric' Cocus pro 3^{bus} ter' xv s ⟨a⟩
De eodem ten' quod iam tenet pincerna Collegij Mertonis pro uno ter' v s ⟨a⟩
De ten' quod tenet Johannes flecher pro ij^{bus} ter'' xiij s iiij d ⟨a⟩
De eodem ten' quod iam tenet Johannes Baker pro ij^{bus} ter' x s

[1] The dates of Pentecost for 1464–1465. See the note at the head of **F/60** above for their inclusion here.

[2] [ADMC] Many items in the Rental are marked 'a', possibly in the hand in which the text of the roll is written; certainly not in the same hand as the marginal totals.

[3] [ADMC] These marginal totals are in a very small and informal hand.

De ten' quod tenet Wappys xvj s viij s ⟨a⟩
Summa iiij li ⟨iiij li⟩

De Magistro Adam pro brasynnosse xlvj s viij d
De eodem pro Aula sancti Thome xviij s
De eodem pro Gardino aula scuti vj s viij d
De Magistro prokter pro aula universitatis in alto vico liij s iiij d ⟨a⟩
Summa vj li iiij s viij d ⟨vj li iiij s viij d⟩

De cameris Aule universitatis in vico scolarum
In primis De Camera M[i] Adam x s ⟨a⟩
De Magistro Henrico Barforth et M[o] layn viij s ⟨a⟩
De Magistro Potter vj s
De Suttonse vij s ⟨a⟩
De Stephano Clyff vij s ⟨a⟩
De Edwardo lupton iiij s ⟨a⟩
De Camera quam occupant bidelli iij s ⟨a⟩
Summa xlv s ⟨xlv s⟩

De scolis
In primis de Magistro ffreston vj s viij d ⟨a⟩
Item de quatuor determinatoribus xij s
Item [*blank*]
Summa xviij s viij d ⟨xviij s viij d⟩

De suburbijs et campis
In primis de uxore de Qwytfeld' pro Gardino iuxta Castrum ij s ⟨a⟩
Item de Palmer pro terris in bellomonte viij d ⟨a⟩
Item de Priore fratrum predicatorum pro pratis yreland et alryschete xxj s viij d
Item de Joh' kettyll' pro pratis retro ossnay xx s
Item de perkyns pro Gardino in parochia sancti Egidij xvj d
Summa liij s ⟨lj s viij d⟩

De liberis ten'
In primis de Abbatissa de godstow pro schopa ex opposito magne porte sancte ffridiswide xx d
De eadem pro Gardino quondam Thome Mayster xiiij d
De Abbate de Osnay pro schopa iuxta johannem Spycer vj s viij d

De Collegio Animarum pro ten' quond' Rogeri Skybbow viij s
De eodem pro ten' quond' Johannis Sprounte v s
De eodem pro Gardino retro dict' ten' viij s x d ob
De novo Collegio pro Madyn Hall' x s
De Colleg' Cantuarie pro sylverhall' ij s vj d
De Collegio linc' xlvj s viij d
De Albis Monachys pro Gardino quond' tenure Barton' iiij s
De Pedyngton pro defalcacione prati retro osnay ij s ij d
De Trygrane pro defalcacione prati retro osnay ij s ij d
Summa iiij li xviij s x d ob

De partibus remotis
De Johanne Pownd pro manerio de Merkyshall' et molendinis xviij li iij s iiij d
De domino Thome Terell' xx s ⟨a⟩
De terris in Holdernysse iij li xx d ⟨a⟩
De novo castro v li xv s vj d ⟨a⟩
De ecclesia de Aranclyff xx li
Summa xlviij li vj d

Summa Omnium Reddit' lxxxj li v s ob

Recepta preter sortem domus
In Primis pro quisquilijs vij s ij d
~~Item de Johanne Hall' ij s~~
Item in excresenc' pec' xvj d
Summa viij s vj d

Item ~~de~~ In Cista pecunias recepi vj li xvj s viij d ⟨a⟩
Summa patet

Summa Omnium Oneratorum clxxxv li viij s ob

[*Dorse*]

M J Hull Anno V^{o} E^{di} $iiij^{ti}$[4]

Allocaciones M^{i} J Hull
In primis de Edwardo Wode viij s
De Roberto Wode pro a^{o} tercio regis E' $iiij^{ti}$ v s
De eodem pro ij^{bus} ter' M^{i} Thorleby iij s

[4] [ADMC] Title written on the outside of the roll when rolled up.

De eodem pro anno meo	iij s viij d
De paulo teutonico	xx d
De Dudlay	iij s ix d
De eodem pro a^{o} meo	viij s iiij d
De Byrstow pro a^{o} 3° R' E' iiij^{ti}	xiij s iiij d
De eodem pro tempore M Baynbryg'	xiij s iiij d
De Thoma Taylyour pro a^{o} xxxviij^{o}	v s
De eodem pro a^{o} 3° R' E' iiij^{ti}	x d
De Ric' Wood	xij s
De eodem pro tempore M Baynbryg'	ij s
De Johanne hall'	xj s iiij d
De Stokes	xx d
De Morlay	xvj s x d
De Johanne Mancypyll' pro a^{o} xxxviij^{o}	xvj d
De Thoma Webb pro annis xxxix 2° ~~et 3°~~ Rr' E' iiij^{ti}	vj s j d
De Johanne fflecher	l s ⟨viij li vij s⟩
De eodem pro a^{o} xxxix^{o} 2° et 3° R' E' iiij^{ti}	xxxiij s iiij d
De eodem pro tempore Baynbryg' et thorleby	xiij s iiij d
De eodem pro tempore meo	vj s viij d
De Roberto ffuller pro quodam gardino	xx d
De Johanne Cooke	iiij s ij d
De Ric' Wer carpentario	xxx s ij d
De Wappys pro 2^{bus} terminis et pro annis xxxix^{o} 2° et 3° R' E' iiij^{ti} et pro tempore M Gregford	xxxviij s iiij d
De eodem pro tempore Magistrorum Baynbryg' et Thorleby	xj s viij d
De eodem pro tempore meo	ix s x d
De Willelmo Wyche	iij s iiij d
De Thoma Mauncypyll' pro alrychet	ij s
De Pedyngton'	viij s iiij d
De Trygrane pro a^{o} 3° R' E' iiij^{ti}	ij s ij d
De Symone Mancypyll'	ij s ij d
De Pedyngton et Trygrane pro tempore meo	iiij s iiij d
De M Gyllot pro yrland	v s
De Gower	ij s ij d
De Johanne Harth	xij s viij d
De Baylyamason pro annis xxxviij^{o} et xxxix^{o} et primo R' E' iiij^{ti} pro bellomonte	xiij s iiij d
De Barton pro eisdem terris pro annis primo et 2° R' E' iiij^{ti}	iiij s

De qwytfeld pro annis 2° et 3° R’ E’ iiij^{ti} ij s iiij d
De eadem pro 2^{bus} ter’ Baynbryg’ et pro 2^{bus} ter’ Thorleby ij s
De eadem pro tempore meo ij s
De Jacobo vectore viij d
De Johanne Jenynse xiij s x d
De uxore Johannis Cooke viij s
De Johanne Schaunler xxvj s viij d
De Henrico Bayth xxvj s viij d
De Palmer x d
De lampray pro tempore Magistrorum baynbryg’ et Thorleby xvj s
De eodem pro tempore meo x s
De Roberto Beste x s
De Ric’ Coke ij s viij d
De Corre iiij s
De Perkynse in parochia sancti Egidij xvj d
Summa xxv li vij s x d ⟨xvij li viij d⟩

Allocaciones Aularum

De M^{o} Mollyners pro tempore M^{i} Gregford viij s xj d q^{a}
De eodem pro tempore M^{i} Baynbryg’ pro uno ter’ xxvij s ix d ob
De M^{o} prokter pro parva Aula universitatis in alto vico pro 2^{bus} ter’ viij s x s ob
De eodem pro tempore M^{i} J Hull’ xiij s iiij d
De M^{o} Summaster xv s
De eodem pro Sekyll’ Hall’ xiij s iiij d
De M’ Semar lj s j d q^{a}
De Roberto Wryght ut patet in arr’ vj li ix s ij d
De Mancipio de Brasynnosse pro Aula Edwardi pro annis xxxix^{o} et primo R’ E’ 4^{ti} xvj s viij d
De parva aula universitatis in vico scolarum xiij s iiij d
De M Baynbryg’ pro camera M^{i} fford’ in eadem aula xx d
De Cameris in Aula universitatis in vico scolarum xx s viij d
De M Adam pro tempore M^{i} Hull’ pro ca [*sic*] x s
De Magistris Henrico Barforth et layn viij s
De Suttonse pro tempore meo iiij d
De Stephano Clyff pro tempore meo vij s
De Edwardo lupton pro tempore meo iiij s
De Camera quam occupant bidelli ij s
Summa xvij li xj s x d ob ⟨xvij li xj s x d ob⟩

Allocaciones Scolarum

De M° Keell'	xx d
De M [*sic*] Stephano Brown'	iij s viij d
De Kerver'	iij s viij d
De Clyffton'	iij s viij d
De Sawkell'	iij s viij d
De grawnger	xx d
De M' Cutter	vj s viij d
De M' Kerver	xx d
De Whyte	xx d
De M lyonell'	vj s viij d
De M' paynter	iij s iiij d
De M Wyche quond' Aule Beate Marie	vj s viij d
De T Podyane	xx d
De M Wryter aule cervine	vj s viij d
De M' Baynbryg'	vj s viij d
De M' Russell'	vj s viij d
De Willelmo Barker	iij s iiij d
De M ffreston'	vj s viij d
Summa iij li xvj s iiij d	

Allocaciones camerarum

De M' fflemmyng'	iiij s
De M' Danyell'	xij s
De Alano Baytson'	vj s viij d
De M' Pray	vj s viij d
Summa xxix s iiij d	

Allocaciones liberorum ten'

In primis de Collegio Animarum pro a° xxxix°	iiij s
De eodem pro ten' quond' Johannis Sprount	v s
De eodem pro annis 2° et 3° R' E' iiij[ti]	x s
De eodem pro gardino retro dictum ten' pro a° xxxix	viij s x d ob
De eodem pro dict' gardino pro annis 2° et 3° r' E' iiij[ti]	xvij s ix d
De eodem pro ten' J' Sprount in tempore M[i] Baynbryg'	ij s vj d
De eodem pro gardino retro dictum ten' in tempore Baynbryg'	iiij s v d q[a]
De eodem pro ten' Johannis Sprount pro tempore M[i] Thorleby	ij s vj d

De eodem pro gardino retro dict' ten' pro 2[bus] ter' eiusdem M[i] iiij s v d q[a]
De eodem pro ten' quond' johannis Sprount pro tempore meo v s
De eodem pro gardino retro dict' ten' pro a[o] meo viij s x d ob
De Abbatissa de Godstow pro a[o] xxxix[o] xx d
De eadem pro gardino pro tempore M Baynbryg' vij d
De eadem pro eodem anno xiiij d
De eadem pro a[o] 2[o] R' E' iiij[ti] xx d
De eadem pro annis 2[o] et 3[o] R' E' iiij[ti] iiij s
De eadem pro tempore M Baynbryg' et Thorleby xx d
De eadem pro gardino quond' T Mayster vij d
De eadem pro schopa ex opposito Magne porta sancte ffridiswide pro a[o] meo xx d
De Abbate de Osnay pro a[o] xxxix vj s viij d
De eodem pro annis 2[o] et 3[o] R' E' iiij[ti] xiij s iiij d
De eodem pro A[o] M Baynbryg' et Thorleby vj s viij d
De eodem pro schopa iuxta J Spyser pro tempore meo vj s viij d
De albis Monachis pro 2[bus] ter' ij s
De eisdem pro tempore meo iiij s
Summa vj li vj s x d ob

Allocaciones in partibus remotis
In primis de novo Castro xxj li xv s xj d
Item de eodem pro a[o] xxxix[o] v li xv s vj d
De eodem pro annis 2[o] et 3[o] R' E' iiij[ti] vij li xvj d
De eodem pro a[o] M Banbryg' et Thorleby iij li viij s x d
De eodem pro a[o] meo v li xv s vj d
De Thoma Browne de pec' de Holdernesse iij s iiij d
De Johanne Pownde pro a[o] 3[o] R' E' iiij[ti] xxviij s ob
De terris in Holdernysse pro annis Magistrorum Baynbryg' Thorleby et Hull' vj li iij s iiij d
De domino Thome Tyrell' xx s
Summa lij li xj s ix d ob

Summa omnium Allocatorum cvij li iiij s ob

Reparaciones Aularum et scolarum
In primis in Aula Brasynnosse xxxiiij s ix d
Item in Aula universitatis in vico scolarum vj s vj d
Item in Aula Edwardi ix d

Item in Aula universitatis in Alto vico — iiij s iiij d
Item in scolis — ix d
Summa xlvij s j d

Reparac' ten' laycorum

In primis In domo Antonij Hardwarnian super quadrivium — vij s j d ob
Item in domo Byrstow — vij s iiij d
Item in domo Spendyng — xix d
Item in domo Thome Taylyour — xv li xv s ij d ob
Item in domo Stokes — v li xx d
Item in domo Torver — vij d
Item in domo Johannis fflecher — iiij s
Item in domo quond' Johannis Coke — xij s iij d
Summa xxij li ix s ix d

Reparac' infra Collegium

In primis In Capella — viij s ix d
Item propter rem[. . .]ciones fact' in sporto — xviij d
In in [*sic*] Aula — xxij d
Item in promptuario — ix d
Item in quoquina — xiij d
Item in orto — ij s j d
Item in stauro — xxviij s ix d ob
Item in Cameris — vij s j d
Summa lj s x d ob

Soluc' socijs

In primis M^{o} Johanni Marton — xxvj s viij d
Item M^{o} Gregford — xxvj s viij d
Item M^{o} Marschall' — xxvj s viij d
Item M^{o} Hull — xxvj s viij d
Item M^{o} Thorleby — xxvj s viij d
Item Doctori Molcaster — xxvj s viij d
Item M^{o} Gregford — xl s
Item M^{o} Hull — xl s
Item M^{o} Hull pro officio procuratoris — x s
Summa xij li x s

Soluc' servientibus

In primis Johanni Pincerne — xxvj s viij d
Item Cocis — xiiij s

Item barbetonsori	vij s iiij d
Item M° Wallyngford	iij s iiij d
Summa lj s iiij d	⟨lj s iiij d⟩

Resol' fact'

In primis Ecclesie beate Marie	vj s
Item Abbati de Osnay	xxij s x d
Item priori sancte ffridiswide ⟨pro 3^bus ter'⟩	xxviij s
Item generose[5] scilicet Alicie Bellicyss	v li xvj s viij d
Summa viij li xiij s vj d	

Reparaciones fact' in Exsex'	v s
Item in renovacione caucionum	xiij s
Item in diminutis expensis	xvj s iiij d ob
Item in resolutis tenentibus	vij s ix d
Item in equitacionibus	xxij s
Item Dicson pro multacione et expensis	xiij s iiij d
Summa iij l xvij s v d ob	

In Communis sociorum	xij li v d
Item in batellis	xxxvij s ix d
Item in jurnellis	x s iiij d
Item in Contribucionibus	xiij s ij d
Item pro festo Trinitatis	vj s v d
Item pro festo sancti Cuthberti	xj s vj d ob
Summa xv li xix s vij d ob	

In dimissis tenentibus

In primis Spendyng	v s iiij d
Summa patet	

Item Summa Remanens in cista	vj li xvj s viij d

Summa Omnium Expensarum lxxviij li ij s vij d ob

Summa Omnium Allocatorum et Expensarum clxxxv li vj s viij d

[5] [ADMC] 'gn'ose' in MS.

⟨Et sic computatis computandis et allocatis allocandis computans indebitatur collegio in sexdecim denar' cum ob'. Acta sunt hec coram nobis M Thoma Smyth Reverendi in christo patris et domini domini Georgij dei gratia episcopi et electi Ebor' Cancellar' universitatis Oxon' commissario generali xj die junij Anno infra scripto⟩

[*Very clear roll; 2 membranes. All totals balance.*]

6 EDWARD IV (ROLL UC:BU1/F/76)
c.2 June 1465–25 May 1466?[1]

BURSAR: ROBERT MIDDELHAM

Compotus M^i^ Roberti Medyllham procuratoris collegij sive Magne Aula [univer]sitatis in Oxon' Redditus per eundem Magistrum Anno Regni R[egis Edward]i Quarti Sexto

[*Arrears are as in the Allowances of* **F/75** *above, without any significant differences. Totals added in the small hand in the right hand margin are omitted, and 'pro anno/tempore meo' is replaced by 'pro tempore M^i^ Hull' or 'pro tempore M^i^ J Hull', or, when such an entry is consecutive, on another one 'pro anno eodem'.*]

Summa Omnium Arr' cvij li iiij s ob

Rentale

De edwardo Wood' pro gardino in Swynscheton	vj s
De Antonio super quadrivium	xl s
De ten' quod tenet Thomas Dudley	xxxiij s iiij d
De ten' quod tenet Brystow brewer	liij s iiij d
De ten' quod tenet spendyng'	xxj s viij d
De eodem pro camera pertinente ad ten' quond' Thoma Taylor pro 3^bus^ ter'	ij s vj d
De ten' quod tenet Thomas Taylur' pro uno ter'	x s
De ten' quod tenet W Barbur'	xvj s viij d
De ten' quod tenet Stokys	xl s
Summa xj li iij s vj d	

De ten' quod tenet lampray	xx s
De ten' quod tenet ~~Ric' C~~ Mancipius Collegij Mertonis	xx s
De ten' quod tenet Johannes baker pro 2^bus^ ter'	x s
De ten' quod tenet Wappys	xvj s viij d
De ten' quod tenet torver	xx s
Summa iiij li vj s viij d	

[1] The dates of Pentecost for 1465–1466. See the note at the head of **F/60** above for their inclusion here.

De ~~M° Adam~~ brasynosse xlvj s viij d
De eodem pro Aula sancti Thome xviij s
De eodem pro Gardino aula scuti vj s viij d
De M° proktor' pro Aula universitatis in alto vico xl s
De Warde Mancipio pro Aula Edwardi ⟨pro 2^{bus} ter'⟩ ~~xvj s~~ viij s[2]
Summa ~~vj li vij s iiij d~~ v li xix s iiij d

De cameris Aule universitatis
~~Item de M° Hyll'~~
In primis de M° potter et consocio eiusdem pro ij^{bus} ter' iiij s
De camera quam occupant bidelli iij s
Summa vij s

de scolis
Item de M° Hyll' vj s viij d
In primis de M° petro frank vj s viij d
Item de 4^{or} determinatoribus xij s viij d
Summa xxvj s ~~iiij d~~

de suburbijs et campis
In primis de uxore Qwytfeld' pro gardino iuxta castrum ij s
Item de J. rede pro terris in bellomonte viij s
Item de priore fratrum predicatorum pro pratis yrland' et Alryschete xxj s viij d
Item de Johanne Kettyll' pro pratis retro osnay xx s
Item de perkyns pro gardino in parochia sancti Egidij xvj d
Summa ~~xx~~ liij s

De liberis ten'
In primis de abbatissa de godstow pro schopa ex^{to} magne porte sancte fridiswide xx d
Item de eodem [*sic*] pro gardino quond' Thome Mayster xiiij d
De Abbate de osnay pro schopa iuxta Johannem spicer vj s viij d
Item De Collegio animarum pro ten' quond' Rogeri Skybbow viij s
Item De eodem pro ten' quond' Johannis Sprounte v s
Item De eodem pro Gardino retro dicti [*sic*] ten' viij s x d ob
Item De novo collegio pro MadynHall' x s
Item De colleg' cantuarie pro sylilhall' [*sic*] ij s vj d

2 [ADMC] See next note.

Item De Collegio lincoln' xlvj s viij d
Item De albis Monachis pro Gardino quond' ten' barton' iiij s
Item De pedyngton' pro defalcacione prati retro osnay ij s ij d
Item De trygrane pro defalcacione prati retro osnay ij s ij d
Summa iiij li xviij s x d ob

De partibus remotis

In primis de Johanne pownd' pro Manerio de Makyshall' et Molendino [*sic*] xviij li iij s iiij d
Item de domino Thome Terell' xx s
Item de terris in Holdernysse iij li xx d
Item de novo castro v li xv s vj d
Item de ecclesia de Arnnclyff xx li
Summa xlviij li vj d

Summa Omnium Reddit' lxxix li ij s x d ob[3]

Recepta preter sortem domus

In primis pro quisquilijs vj s viij d
Item in Cista pecunie recepte vj li xvj s viij d
Summa vij li iij s iiij d

Recepta preter sortem domus de M° barforth et Ric' Cooke viij s iiij d

Summa Omnium Oneratorum clxxxxiij li x s iij d

[*Dorse*]

A° 6 E[i] 4[ti4]

Allocaciones M[i] Roberti Medylham

[*In primis*] de edwardo Wode viij s
[*Item de eodem pro*] a° [*3°*] R' E' iiij[ti] v s
[*Item de eodem pro 2[bus] ter'*] M[i] Thorleby iij s
[*Item de eodem pro a° M[i] Hull'*] iij s viij d

[3] [ADMC] The total of Rents is given as £79 2s 10½d. It should be £78 14s 10½d – i.e. the total is 8s too much. This is accounted for by the alteration in Rents of Halls (see above) of the rent for Edward's Hall from 16s to 8s, the change having presumably been made after the total had been added up. The entry at the end of Receipts (8s 4d), though in the same hand as the rest, is in a different ink. It has evidently been added after the 'Summa Omnium Oneratorum' figure (£193 10s 3d) has been entered, since the latter total is 8s 4d too low, though it includes 8s too much for Edward's Hall.

[4] [ADMC] The endorsement on the outside of the roll when rolled up.

[*Item de eodem pro*] a^{o} M^{i} Medylham	vj s
[*Item de*] paulo teutonico	xx d
Item de dudley	iij s ix d
Item de eodem pro a^{o} M^{i} Hull	viij s iii d
Item de brystow pro a^{o} 3° R' E' iiij^{ti}	xiij s iiij d
Item de eodem pro tempore M^{i} Baynbryg'	xiij s iiij d
Item de Thoma Taylur' pro a^{o} xxxviij^{o}	v s
Item de eodem pro a^{o} 3° R' E' iiij^{ti}	x d
Item de Ric' Wood	xij s
Item de eodem pro tempore M^{i} Baynbryg'	ij s
Item de J Hall'	xj s iiij d
Item de Stokes	xx d
Item de eodem pro a^{o} M^{i} Mydylham	iiij s
Item de Morlay	xvj s x d
Item de J Mancipyll' pro a^{o} xxxviij^{o}	xvj d
Item de Thoma Webe pro annis xxxix 2° R' E' iiij^{ti}	vj s j d
Item de J flecher	l s
Item de eodem pro a^{o} xxxix^{o} 2° et 3° R' E' iiij^{ti}	xxxiij s iiij d
Item de eodem pro tempore M^{i} Hull'	vj s viij d
Item de Roberto ffuller pro quodam gardino	xx d
Item de J Cooke	iiij s ij d
Item de Ric' Wer carpentario	xxx s ij d
Item de Wappys pro 2^{bus} terminis et pro annis xxxix^{o} 2° et 3° R' E' iiij^{ti} et pro tempore M^{i} gregforth	xxxviij s ~~iiij d~~
Item de eodem pro a^{o} Magistrorum Baynbryg' et Thorleby	xj s viij d
Item de eodem pro tempore M^{i} Hull'	ix s x d
~~Item de Roberto ffuller pro quodam gardino~~	~~xx d~~
~~Item de J Cooke~~	~~iiij s ij d~~
Item de Wych	iij s iiij d
Item de T Mancipyll' pro Alryschet	ij s
Item de pedyngton'	viij s iiij d
Item de Trygrane pro a^{o} 3° R' E' iiij^{ti}	ij s ij d
Item de Simone Mancipyll'	ij s ij d
Item de pedyngton et Trygrane pro tempore M^{i} Hull'	iiij s iiij d
Item de pedyngton et Trygrane pro a^{o} M^{i} Medylham	iiij s ~~ij d~~ iiij d
Item de M^{o} Gyllot pro yrland'	v s
Item de Gower	ij s ij d
Item de J Harth	xij s viij d

Item de balyamason pro annis xxxviij° et xxxix° et primo R' E' 4[ti] xiij s iiij d
Item de Barton pro eisdem terris pro annis primo et 2° R' E' iiij[ti] iiij s
Item de qwytfeld pro annis 2° et 3° R' E' iiij[ti] ij s iiij d
Item de eadem pro 2[bus] ter' baynbryg' et pro 2[bus] ter' Thorleby ij s
Item de eadem pro tempore M[i] Hull' ij s
Item de eadem pro a° M[i] Medylham ij s
Item de Jacobo Ɉ vectore viij d
Item de J Jenyns xiij s x d
Item de uxore J Cook viij s
Item de J Schawnler' xxvj s viij d
Item de henrico bathe xxvj s viij d
Item de palmer x d
Item de lampray pro a° Magistrorum baynbryg' et Thorleby xvj s
Item de eodem pro tempore ~~meo~~ M[i] Hull' x s
Item de Roberto Best' x s
Item de Ric' Coke xij d
Item de Corre iiij s
Item de perkyns in parochia sancti Egidij xvj d
Summa xxv li viij s x d ⟨xvij li viij d⟩

Allocaciones Aularum

In primis de M° Mollynerys pro tempore M[i] Gregford viij s xj d q[a]
Item de eodem pro tempore M[i] Baynbryg' xxvij s ix d ob
Item de M° prokter pro parva Aula universitatis in alto vico pro 2[bus] ter' viij s x s ob
Item de eodem pro tempore M[i] J Hull' xiij s iiij d
Item de M° summayster xv s
Item de eodem pro sekyll' hall' xiij s iiij d
Item de M° semer lj s j d q[a]
Item de Roberto Wryght ut patet in Arr' vj li ix s ij d
Item de Mancipio de brasynose pro Aula Edwardi pro annis xxxix° et primo R' E' iiij[ti] xvj s viij d
Item de parva Aula universitatis in vico scolarum xiij s iiij d
Item de M° Baynbryg' pro ca. M[i] furd' in eadem Aula xx d
Item de cameris in aula universitatis in vico scolarum xx s viij d

Item de M^{o} Adam pro tempore M^{i} Hull' pro ca	x s
Item de M^{o} layn'	viij s
Item de Suttonse	iiij d
Item de stephano Clyf pro tempore M^{i} Hull'	vij s
Item de Edwardo lupton pro tempore M^{i} Hull'	xij d
Item de Camera quam occupant Bedelli pro annis Magistrorum Hull' et Medylham	vj s
Item de War' Mancipio pro Aula Edwardi pro 2^{bus} ter'	viij s
Item de brasynose de sutton	xxvij s vij d
Summa ~~xvij li xix s x d ob~~ xix li vij s v d ob	

Allocaciones ~~aularum~~ scolarum

Item de M^{o} Keell'	xx d
Item de M^{o} stephano Brown'	iij s viij d
Item de kerver'	iij s viij d
Item de Clyfton'	iij s viij d
Item de sakyll'	iij s viij d
Item de Grawnger	xx d
Item de M^{o} Cutter	vj s viij d
Item de M^{o} Kerver	xx d
Item de Wytte	xx d
Item de M^{o} leonell'	vj s viij d
Item de M^{o} paynter	iij s iiij d
Item de M^{o} Wyche quond' Aule beate Marie	~~iij s iiij s~~ vj s viij d
Item de T Podyane	xx d
Item de M^{o} Wryter Aule cervine	vj s viij d
Item de M^{o} baynbryg'	vj s viij d
Item de M^{o} Russell'	vj s viij d
Item de Willelmo Barker'	iiij d
Item de M^{o} freston'	vj s viij d
Summa iiij li	

Allocaciones camerarum

Item de M^{o} flemmyng'	iiij s
Item de M^{o} danyell'	xij s
Item de Alano Batson'	vj s viij d
Item de M^{o} pray	vj s viij d
Summa xxix s iiij d	

Allocaciones liberorum ten'

In primis de Collegio animarum pro anno xxxix^{o}	iiij s

Item de eodem pro ten' quond' J sprounte v s
Item de eodem pro annis 2° et 3° regis Edwardi 4^{ti} x s
Item de eodem pro gardino retro dictum ten' pro a^{o} xxxix^{o}
viij s x d ob
Item de eodem pro dicto gardino pro annis 2° et 3° R' E' $iiij^{ti}$
xvij s ix d
Item de eodem pro ten' J' sprounte in tempore M^{i} baynbryg'
ij s vj d
⟨4 li 7 s 3 d⟩[5]
Item de eodem pro gardino retro dict' ten' in tempore baynbryg' iiij s v d q^{a}
Item de eodem pro ten' J sprounte pro tempore M^{i} Thorleby
ij s vj d
Item de eodem pro gardino retro dict' ten' pro 2^{bus} ter' eiusdem M^{i} iiij s v d q^{a}
Item de eodem pro ten' quond' J Sprount pro tempore M^{i} Hull' v s
Item de eodem pro gardino retro dict' ten' pro a^{o} M^{i} Hull'
viij s x d ob
Item de eodem pro ten' quond' J Sprount pro a^{o} M^{i} Mydlam
v s
Item de eodem pro gardino retro dict' ten' pro a^{o} M^{i} Mydhylham viij s x d ob
Item de abbatissa de godstow pro a^{o} xxxix^{o} xx d
Item de eadem pro gardino pro tempore M^{i} baynbryg' vij d
Item de eadem pro eodem a^{o} xiiij d
Item de eadem pro a^{o} 2° regis E' $iiij^{ti}$ xx d
Item de eadem pro annis 2° et 3° R' E' $iiij^{ti}$ iiij s
⟨7 s⟩
Item de eadem pro tempore Magistrorum baynbryg' et Thorleby xx d
Item de eadem pro gardino quond' Thome Mayster vij d
Item de eadem pro schopa ex^{to} Magne porta sancte fridyswyde pro a^{o} M^{i} Hull' xx d
Item de eadem pro gardino quond' Thome Mayster xiiij d
Item de eadem pro schoppa pro tempore M^{i} Mydylham xx d

[5] This, and the other two sums in Arabic numerals inserted in this section, are subtotals for all the Allowances due from All Souls College, the Abbess of Godstow and the Abbot of Osney respectively.

Item de eadem pro gardino pro tempore M^{i} Mydylham xiiij d
Item de Abbate de Osnay pro a^{o} xxxix^{o} vj s viij d
Item de eodem pro annis 2° et 3° R' E' $iiij^{ti}$ xiij s iiij d
⟨44 s⟩
Item de eodem pro tempore M^{i} baynbryg' et thorleby vj s viij d
Item de eodem pro schopa iuxta J Spyser pro M^{i} Hull' vj s viij d
Item de eodem pro schopa pro a^{o} M^{i} Mydylham vj s viij d
Item de albis Monachis pro 2^{bus} ter' ij s
Item de eisdem pro tempore ~~meo~~ M^{i} Hull' iiij s
Item de eisdem pro a^{o} meo iiij s
Summa vij li xiiij s iij d

Allocaciones in partibus remotis
In primis de novo Castro xxj li xv s xj d
Item de eodem pro a^{o} xxxix^{o} v li xv s vj d
Item de eodem pro annis 2° et 3° R' E' $iiij^{ti}$ vij li ~~iij s xij d~~ xvj d
Item de eodem pro a^{o} Magistrorum Baynbryg' et Thorleby
iij li viij s x d
Item de eodem pro a^{o} M^{i} Hull' iiij li ij s ij d
Item de T Brown' de pecunijs de Holdernes' iij s iiij d
Item de J Pownd' pro a^{o} 3° R' E' $iiij^{ti}$ xxviij s ob
Item de terris de Holdernysse pro annis Magistrorum Baynbryg' Thorleby et Hull' vj li iij s iiij d
Item de domino Thome Tyrell' pro a^{o} meo x s
Item de pownd' pro a^{o} meo lv s
Summa liij li iij s v d

Summa omnium Allocatorum cxj li ~~xv s ix d~~ iij s iiij d

Reparaciones aularum
In primis in Aula brasynose viij s iiij d
Item in parva Aula universitatis in vico scolarum xiiij d
Item in scolis v d
Summa ix s xj d

[*No heading*]
In primis in domo tutonici vij s xj d
Item in domo Brystow ij s iij d
Item in domo Spendyng xxij d
Item in domo Barbetonsoris xiiij d
Item in domo T Cissor' iiij s ix d
Item in domo stokes xxv li xj s xj d ob

Item in domo Collegij Mertonis xxj d
Summa xxvj li xj s vij d ob

[*No heading*]
In primis in Capella ix s
Item pro turre et sporto x s iij d ob
Item in Aula vij d
Item in promptuario vj d
Item in Coquina xxvij d ob
Item in Orto iiij d
Item pro latrina ij s iiij d
Item in Camera M^i^ Medylham iij s v d
Summa xxix s iiij d[6]

Solut' servientibus
In primis pincerne xxvj s viij d
Item Cocis xvij s iiij d
Item barbetonsori vij s iiij d
Item lotrici vj s viij d
Summa lviij s

Solut' socijs
In primis M^o^ Johannis Marton xxvj s viij d
Item M^o^ gregforth xxvj s viij d
Item M^o^ Marchall' xxvj s viij d
Item M^o^ thorleby xxvj s viij d
Item M^o^ [*sic*] Mulcaster xxvj s viij d
Item M^o^ Medylham vj s viij d
Item M^o^ Hull' xl s
Item M^o^ Medylham xl s
Item M^o^ Medylham pro officio procuratoris x s
Summa xiij li xvj s viij d

Resoluciones
Item Abbati de Osnay xxij s x d
Item priori sancte frydiswide ix s iiij d
Item abbatisse de godstow pro annis M^i^ Hull' et M^i^ Medylham xx s
Item generose scilicet alicie Bellacysse lviij s iiij d
Summa v li x s vj d

[6] [ADMC] The correct total is £1 10s 2d.

Reparaciones facte in exsex'	xxij s ix d
Item in diminutis expensis	ij s j d
Item in resolutis tenentibus	vj s
Item in equitacionibus	v li viij s j d ob
Item pro Multacione et licencia ad ponendam ecclesiam nostram ad firmam	xxxix s iiij d
Summa viij li xviij s iij d ob	
In communis sociorum	xiij li ix s ij d ob
In batellis	xlvj s vij d ob
Item in jurnellis	xiij s vj s ob
Item pro contribucionibus	xv s viij d ob
Item pro festo trinitatis	vij s ij d
Item pro festo sancti Cubberti	xij s iiij d
Summa xviij li iiij s vij d	
Summa remanens in cista	iij li xij s iiij d

Summa Omnium Expensarum lxxvij li xviij s xj d

Summa Omnium Allocatorum et expensarum clxxxxij li xiiij s vij d

⟨Et sic computatis computandis et allocatis ~~allocatis~~ allocandis computans indebitatus collegio in quindecim s. et octo denarijs / Acta sunt hec coram nobis Thoma Chaundeler' Reverendi in Christo patris et domini domini Georgij dei gratia Eboracen' Archiepiscopi Cancellarij universitatis Oxon' Commissario generali viij^{o} die mensis Junij Anno ~~supra~~ Infrascripto⟩

[*A clear, but not very neat roll. 2 full membranes, plus a strip of about 4 inches attached because there was insufficient room at the foot of the dorse for the auditor's statement.*]

7 EDWARD IV (ROLL UC:BU1/F/77)
c.25 May 1466–17 May 1467?[1]

BURSAR: CHRISTOPHER ALMGYLL

Compotus Magistri Christofer almgyll' procuratoris collegij sive Magne Aula universitatis in Oxon' redditus per eundem Magistrum Anno Regni Regis Edwardi Quarti Septimo

[*Arrears are exactly as in **F/76** above, save that references to 'anno meo' are replaced by ones to 'anno Magistri Mydylham'.*]

Summa Omnum Arr' cxj li iij s iiij d

Rentale

In parochijs sancti Martini et omnium sanctorum

In primis de Edwardo Wodward' pro gardino quod tenet in Sweswychyn vj s
Item de Antonio tutonico pro tenemento apud quadrivium pro duobus terminis xx s
Item de Tenemento quod tenet Thomas Dudley xxxiij s iiij d
Item de ten' quod tenet Johannes Brystowe liij s iiij d
Item de ten' quod tenet Spendyng' xxj s viij d
Item de eodem pro camera pertinente ad ten' quondam tenure Thoma Taylyour iij s iiij d
Item de tenemento quod tenuit Ricardus Wood' xxvj s viij d
Item de tenemento quod tenet Willelmus Barbour xvj s viij d
Item de tenemento quod tenet Willelmus Stokes pro duobus terminis xx s
Item de eodem pro eodem ten' pro alijs duobus terminis xxiij s iiij d
Item de tenemento quondam Thome Talyour in manibus collegij xl s

Summa xiij li iiij s iiij d

In parochijs sancte marie et sancti petri in oriente

In primis de ten' quod ~~tey~~ tenet lampray xx s

[1] The dates of Pentecost for 1466–1467. See the note at the head of **F/60** above for their inclusion here.

Item de ten' quod tenet pincerna Collegij Martonis xx s
Item de ten' quod tenet Ricardus Brownn' pro duobus terminis x s[2]
Item de ten' quod tenet Mathew Mason pro duobus terminis vj s viij d
Item de ten' quod tenet Turner' xx s
Item de ten' quod tenuit Scogan iam in manibus collegij xij s
Summa iiij li viij s viij d

Aularum
In primis de Magistro Willelmo Sutton' pro aula enea xlvj s viij d
Item de eodem pro aula sancti Thome xviij s
Item de eodem pro gardino aula scuti vj s viij d
Item pro aula universitatis in vico scolarum in manibus collegij liij s iiij d
Item de Johanne War' mancipio pro aula ~~sancti~~ Edwardi xvj s
Item pro aula universitatis in alto vico in manibus collegij liij s iiij d
[3]Item pro camera quam occupant bedelli ij s
Summa ix li xvij s

Scolarum
In primis de Magistro Whytlay vj s viij d
Item de Magistro Thoma Sutton vj s viij d
Item de Magistro Bonyfannte vj s viij d
Item de Magistro Hyll vj s viij d
Item de tribus determinatoribus x s
Item de ~~Hatton'~~ Hayton' iij s iiij d
Item de Cartmell' collegij regine iij s iiij d
Summa xliij s iiij d

Camerarum
In primis de Abbate de Ensham pro duobus terminis ix s[4]
Item de magistro Johanne Pawy pro duobus terminis iiij s ij d
Summa xiij s ij d[5]

[2] [ADMC] Altered from 'xx s'.
[3] This entry was added later.
[4] This figure has been altered.
[5] Both these figures have been altered.

In suburbijs et campis

In primis de uxore qwhytfyld' pro gardino iuxta castrum ij s
Item de Johanne Reed pro terris in bellomonte viij s
Item de priore fratrum predicatorum pro pratis yrland' et Alryschet xxj s viij d
Item de Johanne Kettyll' pro pratis retro Osnay xx s
Item de Perkynns pro gardino in parochia sancti Egidij xvj d
Summa liij s

In liberis tenementis

In primis de abbatissa de Godstowe pro schopa ex opposito magne porte sancte ffridiswyde xx d
Item de eadem pro gardino quond' Thome Mayster xiiij d
Item de Abbate de Osnay pro schopa iuxta Johannem Spycer vj s viij d
Item de Collegio animarum pro tenemento quond' rogeri Skybbow viij s
Item de eodem pro ten' quondam Johannis Sprounte v s
Item de eodem pro Gardino retro dict' tenementum viij s x d ob
Item de novo Collegio pro Madynhall' x s
Item de Colleg' Cantuarie pro Sylver Hall' ij s vj d
Item de Collegio lincoln' pro aulis Hampton et Sykkell' et gardino xlvj s viij d
Item de albis Monachis pro gardino quond' tenur' Barton' iiij s
Item de Pedyngton' pro defalcacione prati retro Osnay ij s ij d
Item de Trygranne pro defalcacione prati retro Osnay ij s ij d
Summa iiij li xviij s x d ob

In partibus remotis

In primis de Johanne Pownnd' pro manerio et molendinis de Merkyshall' xviij li iij s iiij d
Item de domino Thome Tyrell' milite xx s
Item de terris in Holdernes iij li xx d
Item de novo Castro v li xv s vj d
Item de Ecclesia de Arnnclyfe xx li
Summa xlvij li vij s ij d[6]

Summa totalis reddituum lxxxv li v s vj d ob

6 [ADMC] The correct total is £47 2s 2d.

Recepta preter sortem domus

Pro una pelve	iij s viij d
Item in pecunijs reman[*entibus in ci*][7]sta	iij li xij s iiij d

Summa omnium oneratorum [*cc li*] ~~ob~~ iiij s x d ob

[*Dorse*]

A^{o} 7mo E^{d} 4^{ti}[8]

Allocaciones Magistri Christoferi Almgyll'

In primis de paulo tutonico	xx d
Item de Dudley	iij s ix d
Item de eodem pro anno Magistri Hull	viij s iii d
Item de Brystow pro a^{o} 3° regis Edwardi 4^{ti}	xiij s iiij d
Item de eodem pro tempore Magistri Baynbryge	xiij s iiij d
Item de Thoma Talyour pro anno tricesimo octavo	v s
Item de eodem pro anno 3° Regis Edwardo 4^{ti}	x d
Item de Ricardo Wood'	xij s
Item de eodem pro tempore Magistri Baynbryge	ij s
Item de Johanne Hall	xj s iiij d
Item de Willelmo Stokes	xx d
Item de eodem pro anno Magistri Myddylham	iiij s
Item de Morlay	xvj s x d
Item de Johanne Mancypyll' pro a^{o} xxxviij^{o}	xvj d
~~Item de Thoma Webe pro annis xxxix et 2° R' Ed' 4^{ti}~~	~~vj s j d~~
~~Item de Johanne fflecher~~	[*blank*]
Item de Roberto ffuller' pro quodam gardino	xx d
Item de Johanne Cooke	iiij s ij d
Item de Ricardo Were carpentario	xxx s ij d
Item de Wappys	xxxviij s ij d
Item de Wych	iij s iiij d
Item de Thoma Mancypyll' pro Alryschete	ij s
Item de Pedyngton'	viij s iiij d
Item de Trygrane pro anno 3° R' Ed' 4^{ti}	ij s ij d
~~Item de Simone Mancypyll'~~	~~ij s ij d~~
Item de Pedyngton et Trigrane pro tempore Magistri Hull'	iiij s iiij d

7 [ADMC] The roll is torn here.
8 [ADMC] The endorsement on the outside of the roll when rolled up.

Item de eijsdem pro a^{o} Magistri ~~Myddyha~~ Myddylham iiij s iiij d
Item de eisdem pro anno vij R' Ed 4^{ti} iiij s iiij d
Item de Magistro Gyllote pro yrlaund' v s
Item de Johanne Gower ij s ij d
Item de Johanne Harte xij s viij d
Item de Balyhamason pro annis 38 39 et primo Regis Ed' 4^{ti} xiij s iiij d
Item de Barton pro terris in bellomonte pro annis j et 2° R' Ed' 4^{ti} iiij s
Item de uxor' Whytfyld' pro ~~xxx~~ annis 5to et 6to R' Ed' 4^{ti} iiij s
Item de eadem pro anno 7mo R' Ed' 4^{ti} iij s
~~Item de Jacobo vector' viij d~~
Item de Johanne Jennyns xiij s x d
~~Item de uxor' Johanne Coke viij s~~
Item de J Chawnndelar' xxvj s viij d
Item de Henrico Bayth xxvj s viij d
Item de Palmer x d
Item de lampray pro anno Magistrorum Baynbryg' et Thorleby xvj s
Item de eodem pro tempore M^{i} Hull' x s
Item de eodem pro anno 7mo R' Ed. 4^{ti} iij s iiij d
Item de Roberto Best x s
Item de Ricardo Coke xij d
Item de Corry iiij s
Item de perkyns brewer pro gardino in parochia sancti Egidij xvj d
Item de eodem pro anno 7mo R' Ed. 4^{ti} xvj d
Item de Ricardo Brownn pro aula ~~drouda~~ drowda pro a^{o} 7° R' Ed 4^{ti} iiij s
~~Item de tenemento apud quadrivium in manibus collegij xvj d~~
Item de tenemento quondam Ricardi Wood' et iam in manibus collegij xxvj s viij d
Item de ten' quondam Thome Talyour et iam in manibus collegij xl s
Item de ten' quondam Scogan et iam in manibus collegij xij s
Item de Willelmo Atkyns quarrario pro bonis Wappys xiij s iiij d
Item de Turnere pro bonis Johannis fflecher xxj s viij d

Item de pincerna collegij Martonis pro a° 7mo R' Ed 4^ti v s
Summa xxiij li xiiij s iij d

Allocaciones Aularum

In primis de M' Johanne Molynerys pro annis Magistrorum Gregfurth et baynbryg' xxxvj s viij d ob q^a

Item de M' Thoma proctur' pro parva aula universitatis in alto vico xxij s ij d ob

Item de eodem pro a° 7mo R' E 4^ti xiij s iiij d

Item pro eadem in manibus collegij xl s

Item de M' Summayster pro aula Hampton et Sykyll' xxviij s iiij d

Item de M' Johanne Seymer pro aula universitatis in alto vico lj s j d q^a

Item de Roberto Wryghth' bedello iij li

Item de mancipio de aula enea pro aula edwardi pro annis xxxix° R' H 6^ti et primo R' E' 4^ti xvj s viij d

Item de M' Baynbryge pro camera Magistri fford' in aula universitatis in vico scolarum xx d

Item de M' layn' pro camera in eadem viij s

Item de Stephano Clyfe et Edwardo lupton pro tempore M^i Hull' vj s

Item de camera quam occupant bidelli pro annis Magistrorum Hull' et Myddylham vj s

Item de eijsdem pro eadem camera pro a° 7mo iij s

Item de Ward' mancipio pro aula Edwardi pro 2^obus terminis viij s

Item de collegij pro parva aula universitatis in vico scolarum in manibus eiusdem liij s iiij d

Item de Ward' mancipio pro aula Edwardi pro anno 7mo xvj s
Summa xviij li xij s iiij d ob

Allocaciones Scolarum

Item de Carver \`de aula Hampton'' iij s viij d

Item de Clyfton \`Collegij regine' iij s viij d

Item de Sakyl \`de eodem' iij s viij d

Item de M' Grawnger xx d

Item de M' Cutter vj s viij d

Item de M' Carver xx d

Item de M' lyonell' vj s viij d

Item de M' Johanne Paynter iij s iiij d

Item de M' Wych quondam aule beate marie vj s viij d
Item de M' Wrytter aule cervine vj s viij d
Item de M' Baynbrige vj s viij d
Item de M' Russell' vj s viij d
Item de M' W ffreston' vj s viij d
Item de M' Thoma Sutton pro anno 7mo vj s viij d
Item de M' Bonygaunte pro eodem anno vj s viij d
Item de Cartmell' collegij Regine pro eodem anno iij s iiij d
Item de Wyte ~~iij s~~ xx s
Summa iiij li vj s

Allocaciones Camerarum
In primis de M' fflemmyng' iiij s
Item de M' Willemo Danyel xij s
Item de domino Alano Batson' vj s viij d
Item de M' Thoma Pray vj s viij d
Item de abbate de Ensham `pro duobus terminis´ ix s
~~Item de M' Johanne Pawy iiij s ij d~~
Summa xxxviij s iiij d

Allocaciones liberorum ten'
In primis de Collegio animarum pro diversis arr' ut patet in rotula facta vj^{to} anno Regis Edwardi 4^{ti} iiij li vij s[9] iij d
Item de eodem pro a^{o} 7mo pro tenemento Johannis Spronte v s
Item de eodem pro gardino retro dict' ten' viij s x d ob
Item de Abbatissa de Godstow pro diversis arr' in rotula supradicta xvij s
Item de eadem pro a^{o} 7mo pro shopa ex opposito magne porte sancte ffrideswyde xx d
Item de eadem pro gardino quondam Thome Mayster xiiij d
Item de abbate de Osnay pro diversis arr' in rotula predicta xl s
Item de eodem pro anno 7mo vj s viij d
Item de albis Monachis pro anno 7mo iiij s
Summa viij li ~~vij s~~ xj s vij d ob

Allocaciones in partibus remotis
In primis de novo castro xxj li xv s xj d
Item de eodem pro anno xxxix^{o} v li xv s vj d
Item de eodem pro annis 2° et 3° regis Edwardi quarti vij li xvj d

[9] [ADMC] Altered from 'xvij s'.

Item de eodem pro anno Magistrorum Baynbryge et Thorleby
iij li viij s x d
Item de eodem pro anno M^{i} Hull' iiij li ij s ij d
Item de eodem pro anno 7mo R' Edwardi iiij^{ti} xxj s vj d
Item de Thoma Brown' de pecunijs de Holdernes iij s iiij d
Item de Holdernes xxx s x d
Item de Johanne Pownnd' pro anno 3° R' Edwardi 4^{ti} xxviij s ob
Item de eodem pro ~~anno~~ annis [*sic*] 6to[10] lv s
Item de terris de Holdernysse pro anno 7mo iij li xx d
Item de Johanne pownd' pro anno 7mo vij li iij s iiij d
Summa lix li vij s v d ob

Summa omnium Allocatorum cxvj li x s ob

Reparaciones Aularum
Expense facte per Magistrum Christoferum Almgyll'
In primis in aula enea xix s
Item in parva aula universitatis in vico scolarum ij s viij d
Item in aula drowda xvij s vij d ob
Item in parva aula universitatis in alto vico ix s x d
Summa xlix s j d ob

Reparaciones tenementorum laicorum
In primis in domo Willelmi Barbour xix s
Item in domo Spendyng' iij s iij d
Item in domo Brystow' viij s ij d ob
Item in domo quondam Thoma Talyour xxxviij s v d
Item in domo Johannis Stokes viij s v d ob
Item in domo lampray iij s x d
Item in domo Mathei latham xxiij s iij d
Item in domo pincerne Collegij Martonis xvj d
Summa iiij li viij s iiij d

Expense facte infra Collegium
In primis in capella aula promptuario et coquina xxxix s ~~iiij d~~ xj d
Item in reparacionibus et alijs expensis infra collegium
v li xiiij s ij d ob
Item in stauro xv s xj d
Item in diminutis expensis xij s vj d ob

[10] [ADMC] '6to' is followed by an erasure.

Item in renovacionibus et redempcionibus caucionum v li xvij s ~~x d ob~~
Item in libraria pro cathenis librorum ij s vj d
Summa xv li ij s j d

Solut' servientibus
In primo pincerne xxvj s viij d
Item coco xx s
Item barbitonsori vij s iiij d
Item lotrici vj s viij d
Summa iij li viij d

Solut' socijs
In primis Magistro Johanni Marton' xxxiij s iiij d
Item Magistro Gregfurth xxxv s
Item M' Marchall' xxvj s viij d
Item M' Hull' xiij s iiij d
Item eidem pro stipendio xl s
Item M' Thorleby xxvj s viij d
Item M' Mulcaster xxvj s viij d
Item M' Mydylham xxvj s viij d
Item eidem pro stipendio xl s
Item M' Almgyll' vj s viij d
Item eidem pro stipendio xl s
Item eidem pro officio procuratoris x s
Summa xvj li v s

Resoluciones
In primis priori sancte ffrideswyde pro uno termino ix s iiij d
Item abbatisse de Godstow x s
Item Alicie Belacyse lviij s iiij d
Summa iij li xvij s viij d

Item in diminutis expensis xij s vj d ob
Item in resolutis tenentibus iij s ix d
Item in dimissis tenentibus vij li xix s j d
Item in equitacionibus xlij s x d
Item in allocatis firmarijs de Arnnclyfe viij s iiij d
Item in allocatis firmario de Pawll' vj d
Summa xj li vij s ob

In communis sociorum xij li v s viij d q[a]

In batellis	xlvj s iiij d
Item in jurnellis	xvj s iiij d ob q[a]
Item in contribucionibus	xxj s iij d ob
Item pro festo trinitatis	iiij s j d
Item pro festo sancti Cuthberti	xv s iij d ob

Summa xvij li ix s j d

Summa omnium expensarum lxxiij li xix s

Summa remanens in cista vij li xv s vij d

Summa omnium Allocatorum et expensarum clxxxxviij li iiij s vij d ob

⟨Et sic computatis Computandis et Allocatis allocandis computans indebitatur Collegio in xl s et iij d. Acta sunt hec coram nobis Thoma Chaundeler' Reverendissimi in Christo patris et domini domini Georgij permissione divina Eboracens' Archiepiscopi Cancellarij universitatis Oxon commissario generali xxvj[to] die mensis maij Anno infrascripto.⟩

[*A very clear and well-preserved roll. 3 membranes, the third a small one (about 6 inches). All figures would balance, except that the rents 'in partibus remotis' are wrongly added, to make £47 7s 2d instead of £47 2s 2d; and this error of 5s is included in the total of rents and the grand total of the Credit side.*]

8 EDWARD IV (ROLL UC:BU1/F/78)
c.17 May 1467–5 June 1468?[1]

BURSAR: RICHARD WITTON

Compotus Ricar[di Wytton . . .][2] universitatis in Oxon' [*redditus per eundum Magistrum Anno Regni Regis*] Edwardi quarti [Octavo . . .

[*Arrears are as in the Allowances for* **F**/*77, except for a few spelling changes.*]

Summa omnium Arre' cxvj li x s ob

Rentale

In parochijs sancti martini et omnium sanctorum

In primis de Edwardo Wodward' pro gardino quod tenet in sweswychyn vj s

Item de tenemento quod tenuit Antonius tutonicus apud quadrivium iam in manibus collegij xlvj s viij d

Item de tenemento quod [*sic*] Thomas Dudley xxxiij s iiij d

Item de ten' quod tenet Johannes Brystow liij s iiij d

Item de ten' quod tenet Spendyng' xxj s viij d

Item de eodem pro camera pertinente ad tenementum quond' tenure Thoma Taylyour iij s iiij d

Item de ten' quod tenet filius Stokes pro ij^obus terminis x s

Item de ten' quod tenet Willelmus Barbur xvj s viij d

Item de ten' quod tenet Willelmus Stokes xlvj s viij d

Item de ten' quondam Thome Talyour et iam in manibus Collegij xl s

Summa xiij li xvij s viij d

In parochijs sancte Marie et sancti petri in oriente

In primis de Tenemento quod tenet Johannes Mortimer' pro tribus terminis xv s

Item de Ten' quod tenet pincerna quondam Collegij Mertonis xx s

[1] The dates of Pentecost for 1467–1468. See the note at the head of **F**/60 above for their inclusion here.

[2] [ADMC] The head of the roll is damaged. Some words are taken from Smith Vol. VIII p. 196.

Item de ten' quod tenet Janyn' Coke pro ij^{obus} terminis ix s
Item de ten' quod tenet Mathew Mason xiij s iiij d
Item de ten' quod tenet Turner' xx s
Item de ten' quod tenuit scogan' iam in manibus collegij ix s
Summa iiij li vj s iiij d

Aularum

In primis de Magistro Willelmo Sutton pro aula enea xlvj s viij d
Item de eodem pro aula sancti Thome xviij s
Item de eodem pro gardino Aula scuti vj s viij d
Item pro parva aula universitatis in vico scolarum pro ij^{obus} terminis xx s
Item de Johanne Ware Mancipio pro aula Edwardi xvj s
Item de domino Symkokkes pro Aula universitatis in alto vico pro ij^{obus} terminis xxvj s viij d
Item pro Camera quam occupant bedelli pro duobus terminis ij s
Summa vj li xvj s

Scolarum

In primis de Magistro pyrnywr' de Collegio beate Marie Magdalene vj s viij d
Item de Magistro Mure de Aula Hamptonia vj s viij d
Item de domino lassy de Aula enea iij s iiij d
Item de domino Smyth' de Aula beate Marie iij s iiij d
Item de domino Ricardo ludwych iij s
Item de alio Bachulario eiusdem Collegij iij s
Summa xxvj s

Camerarum

In primis de Magistro Johanne Pawy viij s iiij d
Item de Magistro Cowper ij s
Item de abbate de Ennsham iiij s vj d
Summa xiiij s x d

In suburbijs et campis

In primis de uxore qwhytfyld' pro gardino iuxta castrum ij s
Item de Johanne Rede pro terris in bellomonte viij s
Item de priore fratrum predicatorum pro pratis yerland' et alryschet xxj s viij d
Item de Johanne Ketyll' pro pratis retro Osnay xx s

Item de Gardino in parochia sancti egidij quod tenuit perkyns brewer' in manibus Collegij xvj d

Summa xlxiij s[3]

In liberis tenementis

In primis de abbatissa de Godstowe pro schopa ex opposito magne porte sancte ffredeswyde xx d

Item de eadem pro gardino quondam Thome Mayster xiiij d

Item de abbate de Osnay pro schopa iuxta Johannem Spycer vj s viij d

Item de Collegio Animarum pro tenemento quond' Rogeri Skybbow viij s

Item de eodem pro tenemento quondam Johannis Sprowte v s

Item de eodem pro gardino retro dictum Tenement' viij s x d ob

Item de novo Collegio pro madyn hall' x s

Item de Collegio Cantuarie pro Sylver Hall' ij s vj d

Item de Collegio lincoln' pro aulis Hampto [*sic*] et Sykkell' et gardino xlvj s viij d

Item de Albis Monachis pro gardino quondam tenur' Barton' iiij s

Item de Pettyngton pro defalcacione prati retro Osnay ij s ij d

Item de Trygranne pro defalcacione prati retro Osnay ij s ij d

Summa iiij li xviij s x d ob

In partibus Remotis

In primis de Johanne Pownnd' pro manerio et molendinis de Merkyshall' xviij li iij s iiij d

Item de Domino Thome Tyrell' milite xx s

Item de Terris in Holdernes iij li xx d

Item de Novo Castro v li xv s vj d

Item de Ecclesia de Arnnclyfe xx li

Summa xlvij li ij s ij d

Summa totalis reddituum lxxxj li xiiij s x d ob

[3] [ADMC] *Sic*; it is in fact another way of writing 'liij s'.

Recepta preter sortem domus iij s iiij d

Item in pecunijs remanentibus in cista vij li xv s vij d

Summa omnium oneratorum ccvj li iij s x d

[*Dorse*]

[*Allocaciones Magistri Ricardi Witton*][4]

[*In primis de paulo tutonico*]	xx d
[*Item de tenemento quod tenuit Antonius tutonicus apud quadrivium iam in man*]ibus Collegij	xlvj s viij d
[*Item de Dudley*]	iij s ix d
[*Item de eodem pro anno Magistri Hull*]	viij s iii d
[*Item de Brystow pro a° 3° regis Edwardi 4ti*]	*xiij s*] iiij d
[*Item de eodem pro tempore Magistri Baynbryge*]	x[*iij s iiij*] d
[*Item de Thoma Talyour pro anno tricesimo octavo*]	v s
[*Item de eodem pro anno 3° Regis Edwardo 4ti*]	x d
[*Item de Ricardo Wood'*]	xij s
[*Item de eodem pro tempore Magistri Baynbryge*]	ij s
[*Item de Johanne Hall*]	xj s iiij d
[*Item de Willelmo Stokes*]	xx d
[*Item de eodem pro anno Magistri Myddylham*]	iiij s
[*Item de Morlay*]	xvj s x d
[*Item de Johanne Mancypyll' pro a° xxxviij°*]	xvj d
[*Item de Roberto ffuller' pro quodam gardino*]	xx d
[*Item de Johanne Cooke*]	iiij s ij d
[*Item de Ricardo Were car*]pentario	xxx s ij d
[*Item de Wappys*]	xxxviij s ij d
[*Item de Wych*]	iij s iiij d
[*Item*] de Thoma Mancypil pro Alryschete	ij s
[*Item*] de Pedyngton'	viij s iiij d
Item de Trygrane pro anno 3° Regis Edwardi [*4ti*]	ij s ij d
Item de Pedyngton et Trigrane pro tempore Magistri Hull'	iiij s iiij d
Item de eijsdem pro [*a° Magistri*] Myddylham	iiij s iiij d
Item de eisdem pro a° vij° Regis Edwardi [*4ti*]	iiij s iiij d
Item de eidem pro a° octavo Regis Edwardi 4ti	iiij s iiij d

[4] [ADMC] The early part of the dorse is lost; text in square brackets is derived from the Arrears of **F**/79 below.

Item de Magistro G[*yllote pro*] yrlaund' v s
Item de Johanne Gower ij s ij d
Item de Johanne Harte xij s viij d
Item de Balyhamason pro annis 38 39 et primo R. Ed' 4^ti^ xiij s iiij d
Item de Barton pro terris in bellomonte pro annis primo et 2° R' Ed' 4^ti^ iiij s
Item de uxore Whytfyld' pro annis 5to et 6to R' Ed' 4^ti^ iij s
Item de eadem pro anno 7mo R' Ed' 4^ti^ ij s
Item de eadem pro anno octavo Regis Edwardi 4^ti^ ij s
Item de Johanne Jannyns xiij s x d
Item de Johanne Chawnndelar xxvj s viij d
Item de Henrico Bayth xxvj s viij d
Item de Palmer x d
Item de lampray pro anno Magistrorum Baynbryge et Thorleby ix s iiij d
Item de eodem pro tempore Magistri Hull' x s
Item de eodem pro anno 7mo R' Ed. 4^ti^ iij s iiij d
Item de roberto Best x s
Item de Ricardo Coke xij d
Item de Corry iiij s
Item de Perkyns brewer' pro gardino in parochia sancti Egidij xvj d
Item de eodem pro anno 7mo R' Ed. 4^ti^ xvj d
Item de Collegio pro eodem gardino pro anno Octavo R' Edwardi 4^ti^ xvj d
Item de Ricardo Brown' pro aula drowda pro a^o^ 7mo R' Ed 4^ti^ iiij s
Item de tenemento quondam Ricardi Wood et alijs ten' iam in manibus collegij pro a^o^ 7mo iij li xviij s viij d
Item de tenemento quondam Thome Talyour in manibus collegij pro a^o^ Octavo R' Ed' 4^ti^ xl s
Item de tenemento quod tenuit Scogan in manibus collegij pro a^o^ 8° R' Ed' 4^ti^ ix s
Item de Johanne Mortimer pro duobus terminis pro a^o^ Octavo R' Ed. 4^ti^ x s
Item de Mathew Mason pro anno Octavo R' Edwardi 4^ti^ iij s iiij d
Item de Willelmo Atkyns quarrario pro bonis Wappys xiiij s iiij d

Item de Turner' pro bonis Johannis fflecher xviij s x d

Summa xxviij li xvj s v d

Allocaciones Aularum

In primis de M' Johanne Molyners pro annis Magistrorum Gregfurth et baynbryge xxxvj s viij d ob q^{a}

Item de M' Thoma procture pro parva Aula universitatis in alto vico xxij s ij d ob

Item de eodem pro a^{o} 7mo R' E 4^{ti} xiij s iiij d

Item de Collegio pro eadem in manibus Collegij pro a^{o} 7° R' Ed. 4^{ti} xl s

Item de M' Summayster pro aula hamton et Sykyll' xxviij s iiij d

Item de M' Johanne Semer' pro aula universitatis in alto vico lj s j d q^{a}

Item de Roberto Wrygth' bedello iij li

Item de Mancipio de Aula enea pro aula Edwardi pro annis xxxix^{o} R' H 6^{ti} et primo R' E' 4^{ti} xvj s viij d

Item de baynbryge pro camera Magistri fford' in Aula universitatis in vico scolarum xx d

Item de M' layn' pro camera In eadem viij s

Item de stephano Clyfe et Edwardo lupton pro tempore Magistri Hull' viij s

Item de camera quam occupant bidelli pro annis Magistrorum Hull' et Myddylham vj s

Item de eisdem pro eadem camera pro a^{o} 7mo iij s

Item de eisdem pro eadem camera pro duobus terminis pro a^{o} octavo R' Ed' 4^{ti} ij s

Item de Collegio pro parva Aula universitatis in vico scolarum in manibus Collegij pro a^{o} 7mo R' Ed' 4^{ti} liij s iiij d

Item de M' ~~S~~ Willelmo Sutton pro Aula enea Aula sancti Thome Aula parva universitatis in vico scolarum et pro gardino Aula scuti pro anno Octavo R' Ed' 4^{ti} iij li v s iiij d

Item de Ward Mancipio pro Aula Edwardi pro anno 7mo xvj s

Item de eodem pro eadem aula pro a^{o} Octavo R' Ed. 4^{ti} xvj s

Summa xxij li vij s viij d ob

Allocaciones Scolarum

In primis de Carver de Aula Hampton' iij s viij d

Item de clyfton Collegij regine iij s viij d

Item de Sakyll' de eodem iij s viij d

Item de M' Granger xx d

Item de M' Cutter vj s viij d
Item de M' Carver xx d
Item de M' lyonell' vj s viij d
Item de M' Johanne Paynter iij s iiij d
Item de M' Wycces quondam aule beate marie vj s viij d
Item de M' Wrytter Aule cervine vj s viij d
Item de M' baynbryge vj s viij d
Item de M' Russell' vj s viij d
Item de M' Willemo ffreston' vj s viij d
Item de M' Bonyfannte pro anno 7mo R' Ed' 4^ti vj s viij d
Item de Hyton pro eodem anno iij s iiij d
Item de Wytte xx d
Item de M' Purwynr' de Collegio beate Marie Magdalene pro a^o Octavo R' Ed' 4^ti vj s viij d
Item de M' Mure de Aula Hamptonia pro eodem anno vj s viij d
Summa iiij li ix s iiij d

Allocaciones Camerarum
In primis de M' fflemmyng' iiij s
Item de M' Willemo Danyell' xij s
Item de domino Alano Batson' vj s viij d
Item de M' Thoma Pray vj s viij d
Item de Abbate de Ensham pro duobus terminis pro a^o 7mo R' Ed' 4^ti ix s
Item de eodem pro uno termino pro anno Octavo Regis Ed' 4^ti iiij s vj d
Summa xlij s x d

Allocaciones liberorum ten'
In primis de Collegio animarum pro diversis arr' ut patet in rotula facta vj^to anno R.' Ed' 4^ti iiij li vij s iij d
Item de eodem pro anno 7mo pro tenemento Johannis Spronte v s
Item de eodem pro anno Octavo pro tenemento [*Joh'*][5] Spronte v s
Item de eodem pro gardino retro dict' ten' [*pro*] a^o 7mo viij s.x d ob
Item de eodem pro gardino retro dict' ten' pro a^o Octavo R' Ed 4^ti viij s x d ob

[5] [ADMC] The Roll is damaged here.

Item de abbatissa de Godstow pro diversis arr' in rotula supradicta xvij s
Item de eadem pro a^{o} 7mo pro shopa ex opposito Magne porte sancte ffrideswyde xx d
Item de eadem pro gardino quondam Thome Mayster xiiij d
Item de eadem pro a^{o} Octavo pro shopa exopposito Magne porte sancte ffrideswyde xx d
Item de eadem pro gardino quondam Thome Mayster pro a^{o} octavo R' Ed' 4^{ti} xiiij d
Item de abbate de Osnay pro diversis Arr' in rotula predicta xl s
Item de eodem pro anno 7mo vj s viij d
Item de eodem pro una shopa iuxta Johannem Spycer pro a^{o} octavo R' Ed. 4^{ti} vj s viij d
Item de albis Monachis pro anno 7mo iiij s
Item de eijsdem pro a^{o} Octavo R' Ed. 4^{ti} iiij s
Summa ix li xix s

Allocaciones in partibus remotis

In primis de novo castro xxj li xv s xj d
Item de eodem pro anno xxxix^{o} v li xv s vj d
Item de eodem pro annis 2° et 3° R' Ed' 4^{ti} vij li xvj d
Item de eodem pro annis Magistrorum Baynbryge et Thorleby iij li viij s x d
Item de eodem pro anno Magistri Hull' iiij li ij s ij d
Item de eodem pro anno 7mo R' Ed' 4^{ti} xxj s vj d
Item de eodem pro anno Octavo R' Ed' 4^{ti} xix s iiij d
Item de Thoma Browne de pecunijs de Holdernes iij s iiij d
Item de Holdernes xxx s x d
Item de Holdernes pro a^{o} 7mo iij li xx d
Item de Holdernes pro a^{o} octavo R' Ed' 4^{ti} viij s iiij d
[6]+Item de Johanne Pownnd' pro a^{o} 3° R' Edwardi 4^{ti} xxviij s ob
+Item de eodem pro anno 6to lv s
Item de eodem pro anno Octavo R' Ed 4^{ti} xlvj s iiij d
Item de domino Thoma Tyrell' pro a^{o} octavo R' Ed' 4^{ti} x s

[6] [ADMC] These two items, both marked '+', are clearly intended to be deleted; otherwise the total is wrong.

⟨Item de Holdernes viij s iiij d⟩
Summa lij li xiij s v d[7]

Summa omnium Allocatorum cxx li viij s viij d ob

[*Re*]paraciones [*Au*]larum
Expense facte per Ricardum Witon

In primis in Aula Enea	xij s xj s ob
Item in Aula parva universitatis in vico scolarum	v s vj s ob
Item in Aula drowda	xvij s vj d
Item in parva Aula universitatis in alto vico	xix s ix d
Summa lv s ix d	

Reparaciones tenementorum laicorum

In primis In domo quondam tenur' Thome Talyour	ij s vij d
Item In domo filij stokes	iij s ix d ob
Item In domo Dudley	vj d
Item In domo Spendynges	xvj s xj d ob
Item In domo Brystow	vj s viij d
Item In domo Willelmi Barbour	vj d
Item In domo Willelmi Stokys	x s viij d
Item In domo Mortymer'	iiij s iij d
Item In domo Thome Spencer	xviij d
Item In domo Wattys	v s vij d
Item In domo Mathe Mason	xxiij s vij d
Summa iij li xvj s vij d	

Expense facte infra Collegium

In primis in Capella Aula promptuario et coquina	xxxvj s v d ob
Item in Reparacionibus et alijs expensis infra Collegium	xxxv s ij d
Item in stauro	xxj s iij d ob
Item in diminutis expensis	iiij s x d
Item in renovacionibus et redempcionibus caucionum	iij li viij s
Summa viij li v s ix d	

Solut' servientibus

In primis pincerne	xxvj s viij d
Item Coco	xx s
Item barbitonsori	vij s iiij d

7 [ADMC] This total is correct if the items intended to be deleted are excluded.

Item lotrici pro termino xx d
Summa lv s viij d

Solut' socijs
In primis Magistro Johanni Marton xxxiij s iiij d
Item Magistro Gregfurth' xxvj s viij d
Item Magistro Marchall' xxvj s viij d
Item Magistro Hull' xxxiij s iiij d
Item eidem pro stipendio xl s
Item M' Thorleby xxvj s viij d
Item M' Mulcaster xxvj s viij d
Item M' Mydylham xxvj s viij d
Item eidem pro stipendio xl s
Item M' almgyll' xxvj s viij d
Item eidem pro stipendio xl s
Item Ricardo Witton pro officio procuratoris x s
Summa xvij li xvj s viij d

Resoluciones
In primis priori sancte frideswyde pro uno termino anni 7^{i} R' ed' 4^{ti} ix s iiij d
Item eidem pro anno Octavo R' Ed' 4^{ti} xviij s viij d
Item alycie Belacyse liij s iiij d
Item Edwardo Wodward iiij s iiij d
Item Abbatisse de Godstow x s
Summa iiij li xv s viij d

Item In diminutis expensis nichil
Item In Resolutis tenentibus iij s iiij d
Item In dimissis tenentibus ~~Johanni Pownd~~ Johanni Pownd ix li ij s iiij d ob
Item in equitacionibus xxvj s x d ob
Item in allocatis firmarijs de arnnclyfe x s x d
Item in allocatis firmario de Exsex' viij s viij d
Item in solutis procuratoribus novi castri xvj s viij d
Summa xij li viij s ix d

In communis sociorum xx li ij s x d q^{a}
In batellis xxvij s iiij d q^{a}
Item in Jurnellis xxix s ij d ob
Item in contribucionibus xxxj s ij d q^{a}
Item pro festo trinitatis ix s viij d ob

Item pro festo sancti Cuthberti xx s viij d

Summa xxvj li xj d ob q^{a}

Summa omnium Expensarum lxxix li iiij s j d ob q^{a}[8]

Summa remanens in cista vj li vij s vij d ob

Summa omnium Allocatorum et Expensarum ccv li xij s j d ob q^{a}

⟨Et sic computatis computandis et allocatis allocandis computans indebitatur collegio xj s viij d ob q^{a}. Acta sunt hec coram nobis M Thoma Stephyn sacre theologie professor' reverendissimi in Christo patris et domini domini Georgij eborac' archiepiscopi cancellarij universitatis oxon' commissario generali xvj^{o} die Junij Anno infrascripto.⟩

[*This roll is badly damaged for a few inches at the top (face and dorse), and the top of the dorse is also worn. These parts can be recovered from the Allowances of* **F/77** *and the Arrears of* **F/79**. *Otherwise clear and in good condition. 3 membranes, the last a short one.*

All figures in the roll would balance, but the 'Summa omnium Expensarum' has been altered to £79 4s 1d. The correct figure would be £78 15s 9d – 8s 4d less, and this is the total which is used in arriving at the 'Summa omnium Allocatorum et Expensarum'; this grand total is therefore right.

Presumably the error of 8s 4d in the 'Summa omnium Expensarum' is due to the addition of the final item (Holdernes – 8s 4d) to the Allowances from distant places. This added item had already been taken into account in arriving at the total of Allowances; it looks as though a double error was made when it was added (a) in altering a total at all (b) in altering the total of Expenses, instead of the total of Allowances.]

[8] [ADMC] The correct total is £78 15s 9 d. This total has been altered, although it is written in the same hand as the rest of the roll.

9 EDWARD IV (ROLL UC:BU1/F/79)
c.5 June 1468–21 May 1469?[1]

BURSAR: SIMON BAXTER

Compotus Magistri Simonis Baxter procuratoris Collegij sive Magne aule universitatis in Oxon' Redditus per eundem Magistrum Simonem Anno Regni regis Edwardi quarti Nono

[*Arrears appear to identical with the Allowances of* **F/78** *above, save for a few alterations in spelling, except that in the Arrears from distant places, the first eight items are just as in the Allowances, but the rest of the section reads:*]

Item de Holdyrnesse	xxx s x d
Item de Holdyrnesse pro Anno 7°	iij li xx d
+Item de Holdernesse pro Anno 8° R' ed 4^ti^	viij s iiij d
+Item de eodem pro anno 6°	lv s
Item de eodem pro Anno 8° R' ed 4^ti^	xlvj s iiij d
Item de domino Thoma Tyrelle pro Anno 8° R' ed. 4^ti^	x s
Item de Holdyrnesse	viij s iiij d
+Item de Johanne Pownde pro A° 3° Regis ed 4^ti^	xxviij s ob
Summa lij li xiij s v d[2]	

Summa Omnium Arr' cxx li viij s viij d ob

Rentale

In paroch' sancti Martini et omnium sanctorum

In primis de Edwardo Wodward' pro Gardino quod tenet in Sweswychyn	vj s
Item de tenemento quod tenuit Antonius tutonicus Apud quadrivium jam in manibus collegij	xlvj s viij d
Item de tenemento Thome Dudley	xxxiij s iiij d

[1] The dates of Pentecost for 1468–1469. See the note at the head of **F/60** above for their inclusion here.

[2] [ADMC] The final item is clearly accidentally misplaced, and should follow the Arrears from Holderness for 8 Edw IV. The 'eodem' of the item below this refers to John Pownde, not to Holderness; this is confirmed by the Allowances below. Presumably the '+' against the last Holderness entry was intended to be marked against the misplaced John Pownde item, as in the Allowances in **F/78**. As in the Allowances in **F/78**, the total is only correct if the two entries intended to be marked are omitted. Both those figures, however, appear in the Allowances of **F/78**, and are included in the total there.

Item de ten' quod tenet ~~Thomas~~ Johannes Brestow liij s iiij d
Item de ten' quod tenet Spendyng' xxj s viij d
Item de eodem pro Camera pertinente ad ten' quondam Thome Taylyour iij s iiij d
Item de ten' quod tenet filius Stokes ~~pro terminis duobus~~ xx s
Item de ten' Willelmi Barbour xvj s viij d
Item de ten' quod tenet Willelmus Stokys xlvj s viij d
Item de muliere tenente ten' quondam Thome Talyour pro ij^{bus} terminis xxx s

Summa xiij li xvij s viij d

In paroch' sancte marie et sancti petri in oriente

In primis de ten' quod tenet Johannes Mortimer xx s
Item de ten' quod tenet pincerna quondam Collegij Martonis xx s
Item de ten' quod tenet Jannyn Cooke ix s
Item de Thoma Sondyrlaund' pardoner pro ten' quod tenuit Mathew Mason pro ij^{bus} terminis vj s viij d
Item pro eadem domo sive ten' de Edmundo Steyner pro uno termino iij s iiij d
Item de ten' quod tenet Turner xx s
Item de ten' quod tenet Wappys ix s

Summa iiij li xvij s

Aularum

In primis de Magistro Willelmo Sutton pro Aula enea xlvj s viij d
Item de Eodem pro Aula sancti Thome xviij s
Item de eodem pro Gardino aule scuti vj s viij d
Item pro parva aula universitatis in vico scolarum xxx s
Item de Johanne Ware Mancipio pro Aula edwardi xvj s
Item de domino Symkokkys pro aula universitatis xl s

Summa vij li xij s iiij d[3]

Scolarum

In primis de Magistro Christofero leyk' de loco sancti Johannis vj s viij d
Item de Magistro Maybourne de Collegio lync' vj s viij d
Item de M Bakyr de Aula tabina vj s viij d

[3] [ADMC] The correct total is £4 17s 4d.

Item de M Henrico Thomas de Aula beate marie vj s viij d
Item de Domino Hardyng de Aula enea iij s iiij d
Item de domino preeke de aula albani iij s iiij d
Item de domino raakure de aula beate marie iij s iiij d
Item de domino lawse de eadem aula iij s iiij d
Summa xl s

Camerarum

In primis de Magistro Pavy viij s iiij d
Item de M Knyght Rectore de Chyllevey xvj s
Item de M ffyppys pro dimidio unius termini et termino Annunciacionis beate marie vj s
Item de Magistro Johanne Jonys pro termino Annunciacionis beate marie iij s iiij d
Item de Rettore Aschynden' pro terminis natal' domini et Annunciacionis beate marie v s
Summa xxxviij s viij d

In Suburbijs et campis

In primis de uxor' Whittfeld' pro Gardino iuxta castrum pro dimidio Anni 8^{i} xij d
Item de M Pavy pro eodem Gardino pro dimidio dicti Anni altero xviij d
Item de Johanne Reede pro terris in bellomonte viij s
Item de priore ffratrum predicatorum pro pratis yerlaund' et Alryschet' xxj s viij d
Item de Johanne Ketyll' pro pratis retro Osnay xx s
Item de Johanne Reede pro gardino in parochia sancti Egidij quod tenuit perkyns pro dimidio anni 8^{i} viij d
Summa lij s ~~x~~ x d

In liberis tenementis

In primis de Abbatissa de Godstow pro schopa ex o^{to} magne porte sancte frideswide xx d
Item de Eadem pro gardino quondam Thome Mayster xiiij d
Item de Abbate de Osnay pro shopa iuxta Johannem Spycer vj s viij d
Item de Collegio Animarum pro ten' quond' Rogeri Skybbow viij s
Item de Eodem pro ten' quondam Johannis Sprowte v s
Item de eodem pro gardino retro dictum ten' viij s x d ob

Item de novo Collegio pro Madyn Halle x s
Item de Collegio Cantuariensi pro Silver Halle ij s vj d
Item de Collegio Linc' pro aulis Hampton et Sykkell' et gardino xlvj s viij d
Item de albis Monachis pro gardino quondam tenur' Barton' iiij s
Item de pettyngton pro defalcacione prati retro Osnay ij s ij d
Item de Trygranne pro defalcacione prati retro Osnay ij s ij d
Summa iiij li xviij s x d ob

In partibus Remotis
In primis de Johanne Pownnd' pro Manerio et molendinis de Merkyshall' xviij li iij s iiij d
Item de domino Thome Tyrell' milite xx s
Item de terris in Holdernes iij li xx d
Item de novo Castro iiij li xvij s ij d
Item de ecclesia de Arnnclyfe xx li
Summa xlvij li ij s ij d

Summa totalis Reddituum lxxxiiij li xix s vj d ob

Recepta preter sortem domus xlv s x d

Item In pecunijs remanentibus in cista vj li vij s vij d ob

Summa omnium Oneratorum ccxiiij li xx d ob

[*Dorse*]

Allocaciones Magistri Baxter A^{o} nono
Item de tenemento super quadrivium xlvj s viij d
Item de Thoma Brown' pro ten' quod tenuit Sondyrland' xx d
Item de Thoma Spencer pro Anno nono R' ed' iiij^{ti} xx s
Item de Edmundo Stayner pro termino Annunciacionis beate marie Anno 9^{i} iij s iiij d
Item de [. . .][4] pro ij^{bus} terminis Anno 9^{i} R' ed iiij^{ti} [. . .
Item de Johanne Mortimere pro termino Annunciacionis beate marie Anni 9^{i} [. . .
In p[. . .]aulo Tutonico xx d

[4] [ADMC] Stain on MS; some words here not legible.

Item de ten' quod tenuit Antonius tutonicus Apud quadrivium iam in manibus Collegij a° octavo	xlvj [*s*] viij d
Item de Dudley	iij s ix d
Item de eodem pro Anno Magistri Hulle	viij s iii d
Item Brystow [*sic*] pro Anno 3° Regis Edwardi 4ti	xiij s iiij d
Item de Eodem pro tempore M Baynbryge	xiij s iiij d
Item de Thoma Talyour pro Anno tricesimo octavo	v s
Item de Eodem pro Anno 3° R' Edwardo 4ti	x d
Item de Ricardo Wodde	xij s
Item de Eodem pro tempore Magistri Baynbryge	ij s
Item de Johanne Halle	xj s iiij d
Item de Willelmo Stokys	xx d
Item de eodem pro anno M Middylham	iiij s
Item de Morlay	xvj s x d
Item de Johanne Manciple pro Ann° xxxviij°	xvj d
Item de Roberto ffuller pro quodam Gardino	xx d
Item de Johanne Cooke	iiij s ij d
Item de Ricardo Were Carpentario	xxx s ij d
Item de Wappys	xxxviij s ij d
Item de Wrych	iij s iiij d
Item de Thoma Mancyple pro Alryschete	ij s
Item de pedyngton'	viij s iiij d
Item de Trigranne pro Anno 3° R' Edwardi 4ti	ij s ij d
Item de pedyngtone et trigranne pro tempore M Hulle	iiij s iiij d
Item de eijsdem pro Anno Magistri Myddylham	iiij s iiij d
Item de eijdem [*sic*] pro Anno vij° R' Edwardi 4ti	iiij s iiij d
Item de eijsdem pro Anno viij° R' Ed. 4ti	iiij s iiij d
Item de Magistro Gyllote pro yrlaund'	v s
Item de Johanne Gowere	ij s ij d
Item de Johanne Harte	xij s viij d
Item de Balehamason pro Annis 38 39 et primo Regis Edwardi iiijti	xiij s iiij d
Item de Barton pro terris in bellomonte pro Annis primo et 2° R' Ed' 4ti	iiij s
Item de uxor' Whytfeld' pro annis 5° et 6° R' ed' 4ti	ij s
Item de Eadem pro Anno vij° R' edwardi iiijti	ij s
Item de Eadem pro Anno viij° R' ed iiijti	ij s
Item de Johanne Jannyns	xiij s x d
Item de Johanne Chaundeler	xxvj s viij d

Item de Henrico Bayth xxvj s viij d

Item de Palmer x d

Item de Lampray pro Annis Magistrorum Baynbryge et Thorleby ix s iiij d

Item de Eodem pro tempore M Hulle x s

Item de Eodem pro Anno vij^{o} R' edwardi iiij^{ti} iij s iiij d

Item de Roberto Beste x s

Item de Ricardo Cooke xij d

Item de Corry iiij s

Item de perkyns Brewer pro gardino in parochia sancti Egidij xvj d

Item de pro [*sic*] eodem pro vij^{o} Regis edwardi 4^{ti} xvj d

Item de Ricardo Brown pro Aula drowda pro A^{o} vij^{o} R' edwardi 4^{ti} iiij s

Item de ten' quondam Ricardi Wodde et alijs ten' iam in manibus Collegij pro Anno vij^{o} iij li xviij s viij d

Item de ten' quondam Thome Talyour in manibus collegij pro Anno viij^{o} R' ed' 4^{ti} xl s

Item de ten' quod tenuit Scogan in manibus collegij pro A^{o} viij^{o} R' Ed' 4^{ti} ix s

Item de Matheo Mason pro Anno 8° Regis edwardi iiij^{ti} iij s iiij d

Item de Willelmo Attkyns quarrario pro bonis Wappys xiiij s iiij d

⟨Item de Edwardo Wodward' pro Anno nono vj s⟩

Summa xxxij li xvij s ix d

Allocaciones Aularum

⟨Item de M' Sutton pro A^{o} nono⟩ ⟨xviij s⟩

~~In primis de Carver pro aula Hampton' iij s viij d~~

In primis de M' Johanne Molyners pro Annis Magistrorum Gregfurth et Baynbryge xxxvj s viij d ob q^{a}

Item de Magistro Thoma procture pro parva Aula universitatis in alto vico xxij s ij d ob

Item de eodem pro Anno vij^{o} R' ed iiij^{ti} xiij s iiij d

Item de Collegio pro eadem in manibus Collegij pro A^{o} vij^{o} R' ed. 4^{ti} xl s

Item de Magistro Summayster pro aula Hampton et Sykill' xxviij s iiij d

Item de Magistro Johanne Semer' pro aula universitatis in alto vico lj s j d q[a]
Item de Roberto Wryght Bedello xxx s
Item de Mancipio de aula enea pro aula edwardi pro annis xxxix[o] R' Henr' 6[ti] et primo R' ed iiij[ti] xvj s viij d
Item de Baynbryge pro camera M forde in Aula universitatis in vico scolarum xx d
Item de Magistro lane pro camera in eadem viij s
Item de Stephano Clyfe et edwardo Lupton pro tempore M Hull' viij s
Item de Camera quam occupant Bedelli pro tempore M Hull' et Myddylham vj s
Item de eijsdem pro eadem camera pro Anno vij[o] iij s
Item de eijsdem pro eadem camera pro ij[bus] terminis pro a[o] 8[o] R' ed' iiij[ti] ij s
Item de Collegio pro parva aula universitatis in vico scolarum in manibus Collegij pro a[o] vij[o] R' Ed' iiij[ti] liij s iiij d
Item de Magistro Willelmo Sutton' pro aula enea aula sancti Thome Aula parva universitatis in vico scolarum et pro Gardino Aula scuti pro anno 8[o] Regis edwardo iiij[ti] iij li v s iiij d
Item de Warde Mancipio pro Aula edwardi pro Anno vij[o] xvj s
Item de eodem pro eadem aula pro Anno Octavo R' ed. iiij[ti] xvj s
⟨Item de eodem pro duobus terminis pro a[o] nono⟩ ⟨viij s⟩
⟨Item de Symkokes pro a[o] nono⟩ ⟨vj s viij d⟩

Summa xxij li x s iiij d ob

Allocaciones Scolarum

In primis de Carver de Aula Hampton' iij s viij d
Item de Clifton Collegij Regine iij s viij d
Item de Saughyld' de eodem iij s viij d
Item de M' Granger xx d
Item de M' Carver xx d
Item de M' Cutter vj s viij d
Item de Magistro lyonell' vj s viij d
Item de M' J payntour iij s iiij d
Item de M' quondam aule beate marie vj s viij d
Item de M' Wrytter Aule Cervine vj s viij d
Item de M' Baynbryge vj s viij d
Item de Magistro Russell' vj s viij d

Item de M' Willemo ffreeston' vj s viij d
Item de M' Bonifawnt pro Anno vij° R' ed' iiij^ti vj s viij d
Item de Hyton pro eodem Anno iij s iiij d
Item de Wytte xx d
Item de Magistro Mayborn de Collegio linc' vj s viij d
Item de M Christofero [*blank*] de loco sancti Johannis vj s viij d
Item de M Barker de Aula trabina vj s viij d
Item de H Henrico Thomas de aula sancte marie vj s viij d
Item de domino Preeke de aula albani iij s iiij d
Item de domino Hardyng de aula enea iij s iiij d
Summa v li ix s viij d

Allocaciones Camerarum

In primis de Magistro fflemmyng iiij s
Item de M' Willemo Danyell' xij s
Item de domino Alano Batson' vj s viij d
Item de M' Thoma pray vj s viij d
Item de Abbate de Ensham pro ij^bus terminis pro Anno vij° R' ed' iiij^ti ix s
Item de eodem pro uno termino pro a° 8° R ed' iiij^ti iiij s vj d
Item de M W ffyppys pro dimidio unius termino [*sic*] et termino Annunciacionis beate marie vj s
Item de Rectore Aschynden pro terminis natal' domini et annunciacionis beate marie v s
Summa liij s x d

Allocaciones liberorum ten'

In primis de Collegio Animarum pro diversis arr' ut patet in Rotula facta vj^to anno R ꝫ ed' 4^ti iiij li vij s iij d
Item de eodem pro Anno vij° pro ten' Johannis Spronte v s
Item de eodem pro Anno 8° pro eodem ten' eiusdem Spronte v s
Item de eodem pro gardino retro dict' ten' pro Anno 7° viij s x d ob
Item de eodem pro gardino retro dictum ten' pro a° 8° R' ed iiij^ti viij s x d ob
Item de Abbatissa de Godstow pro diversis Arr' in Rotula supradicta xvij s
Item de eadem pro Anno vij° pro shopa ex opposito magne porte sancte ffrideswide xx d
Item de eadem pro gardino quondam Thome Maister xiiij d

Item de eadem pro Anno octavo pro shopa ex o^{to} magne porte sancte frideswide xx d
Item de eadem pro gardino quondam Thome Mayster pro Anno 8° R' ed' $iiij^{ti}$ xiiij d
Item de Abbate de Osnay pro diversis Arr' in Rotula predicta xl s
Item de eodem pro Anno vij^{o} vj s viij d
Item de eodem pro una shopa iuxta Johannem Spycer pro A^{o} 8° R' ed. $iiij^{ti}$ vj s viij d
Item de Abbatissa de Gostow pro shopa ex o^{to} magne porte sancte frideswyde xx d
Item de eadem pro gardino quond' Thome Mayster xiiij d
Item de Abbate de Osney pro shopa iuxta Johanne Spycer vj s viij d
Item de Collegio Animarum pro ten' quond' Johanis Spronte v s
Item de eodem pro gardino retro dictum ten' viij s x s ob
Item de albis Monachis pro a^{o} 9° r' ed $iiij^{ti}$ ij s
Item de petyngton pro defalcacione prati retro Osney ij s ij d
Item de Trigranne pro defalcacione prati retro Osney ij s ij d
⟨Item de Johanne Reed'⟩ ⟨viij d⟩
⟨Item de uxore qwytfeld'⟩ ⟨xij d⟩
Summa xj li ij s iiij d ob

Allocaciones in partibus remotis

In primis de Novo Castro xxj li xv s xj d
Item de Eodem pro Anno xxxix^{o} v li xv s vj d
Item de Eodem pro Annis 2° et 3° R' Ed' 4^{ti} vij li xvj d
Item de Eodem pro Annis Magistrorum Baynbryge et Thorleby iij li viij s x d
Item de eodem pro Anno M Hull' iiij li ij s ij d
Item de eodem pro Anno vij^{o} R' ed' $iiij^{ti}$ xxj s vj d
Item de eodem pro Anno $viij^{o}$ R' ed' $iiij^{ti}$ xix s iiij d
Item de Thoma Browne de pecunijs de Holdernesse iij s iiij d
Item de Holdyrnesse xxx s x d
Item de Holdernes pro Anno vij^{o} iij li xx d
Item de Holdernes pro Anno $viij^{o}$ R' ed' $iiij^{ti}$ viij s iiij d
Item de Johanne Pownnd' pro a^{o} 3° R' ed $iiij^{ti}$ xxviij s ob
Item de Eodem pro Anno 6° lv s
Item de Eodem pro Anno $viij^{o}$ R' ed $iiij^{ti}$ xlvj s iiij d

item de domino Thoma Tyrell' pro Anno viij° R' ed' iiij^ti	x s
Item de Holdernesse	viij s iiij d
Item de Johanne Pownnd' pro Anno nono R' ed iiij^ti	vij li xv s
Item de Terris in Holdernesse pro Anno nono	iij li xx d
Item de Novo Castro pro A° nono	iiij li xvij s ij d
Summa lxxij li x s iij d ob	

Summa omnium Allocatorum cxlvij li iiij s iij d ob[5]

Reparaciones facte per M Baxter

Reparaciones Aularum

In primis in Aula Enea	x s
Item in Aula universitatis in Alto vico	xvij s vij d ob
Item In Aula Drowda	ij s
Summa xxix s vij d ob	

Reparaciones tenementorum laicorum

In primis In domo Dudley	iiij s iij d ob
⟨Item⟩ In domo super Quadrivium	iij d
Item In domo Spendynges	viij d
Item In domo filij Stokys	xvj d
Item In domo Stokys	vj d
Item In domo Mulieris tenentis tenementum quond' Thome taylour	xij d
Item In domo Thome Sondirlaund' pardoner	vj s
Item In domo Wattys	iij d
Item In domo Turnour	ij s viij d
I [*sic*]	
Summa xvj s xj d ob	

Expense facte Infra Collegium

In primis In Reparacionibus infra Collegium	xlvj s ix d ob
Item In Aula et Capella	xix d
Item In Stauro	xxxvj s
Item In diminutis Expensis	iiij s
Item In Renovacionibus Caucionum	xviij s
Summa v li vj s iiij d ob	

Solucionis servientibus

In primis Barbitonsori	vij s iiij d

5 [ADMC] The figures of this total have been altered.

Item Pincerne	xx s
Item Coco	xx s
Item lotrici	x s
Summa lvij s iiij d	

Soluc' socijs

In primis Magistro loci	xxxiij s iiij d
Item M Gregfurth	xxvj s viij d
Item M Marshall'	xxvj s viij d
Item `M´ Thorleby	xxvj s viij d
Item M Molkastre	xxvj s viij d
Item M Mydylham	xxvj s viij d
Item Eidem pro Stipendio	xl s
Item M Ricardo Wytton	xx s
Item M Baxster	xx s
Item Eidem pro Officio Procuratoris	x s
Item Domino Hyton'	xx s
Item Eidem pro stipendio	xxx s
Item M Hynmarse	xx s
Summa xvj li vj s viij d	

Resoluciones

In primis Priori sancte frideswyde pro uno termino	ix s iiij d
Item Abbati de Osney	xxij s ij d
Item Abbatisse de Godstow	x s
Item Alic' Belacyis	lviij s iiij d
Item pro Quintadecima domini Regis	xvj d
Summa v li xiiij d	

[*No heading*]

In primis In diminutis Expensis	iiij s
Item Resolucionibus [*sic*]	v s iij d
Item In dimissis tenentibus	x s
Item In remuneratis firmar' de Arnncliffe	v s
Item pro Sinodo Eidem	iij s iiij d
Item In Equitacionibus	x s ij d
Summa xxxvij s ix d	

In Communis Sociorum	xviij li xix s vj d ob
In Batellis domus	xiiij s xj d ob
In Jurnellis	xix s x d ob
In Contribucionibus	xviij s vj d ob

In ffesto sancte Trinitatis v s viij d ob
In ffesto sancti Cuthberti xviij s j d ob
Summa xxij li xvj s ix d

Summa omnium Expensarum lvj li xij s vij d ob

Summa remanens in Cista x li iiij s ix d ob

Summa omnium Allocatorum et Expensarum ccxiiij li xx d ob

⟨Et sic computatis computandis et allocatis et [*sic*] allocandis computans nichil indebitatur Collegio. Acta sunt hec coram nobis Roberto dei gratia Menevensis Episcopo Ac universitatis Commissario generali Oxon' xx°ix° die Mensis Maij Anno infrascripto.⟩

[*A clear and well-preserved roll, except for a few small brown stains and considerable wear at the top of the dorse. 3 membranes.*

There appears to be an error of 5s in the Rents of Halls total. Otherwise all figures balance, with the important exception that the arrears of rent owed by John Pownde for Marks Hall for 3 and 6 Edw IV, totalling £4 3s 0½d, are not included in the total of Arrears, but are included in the total of Allowances.

These two items, which appear but are not counted in the Arrears of 1468/9 and the Allowances of 1467/8, appeared and were counted in the Arrears of 1467/8. Possibly a mistake was made in the Allowances of 1467/8, and was rectified by not counting the entry in the Arrears of 1468/9, but including it in the Allowances of 1468/9 – this last entry this balancing the Arrears entry of the preceding roll.

Many of the sections in the Debit side of the 1468/9 roll have an unofficial total figure, which in all cases has been more or less erased, in the right hand margin.]

[*The roll for 1469/70 was lost even in Smith's day.*]

11 EDWARD IV (ROLL UC:BU1/F/80)
c.10 June 1470–2 June 1471?[1]

BURSAR: SIMON BAXTER

Compotus M Baxter procuratoris Collegij sive magne Aula universitatis in Oxon' Redditus per eundem M Anno regni Regis Edwardi iiij^{ti} undecimo

Arr' ten'

In primis De Tenemento super Quadrivium pro Anno Nono xlvj s viij d
Item De Edmundo Steyne pro Anno decimo Regis edwardi iiij^{ti} xiij s iiij d
Item De Thomas Walis quondam pincerna Collegij [*sic*] Mertonis pro A^{o} decimo xvj s
Item De Thome Talyouer pro Anno decimo x s
Item De Surrurgio Manente in ten' quond' Stokys xj s viij d
Item De Dudley pro termino Annunciacionis beate Marie Anni decimi viij s iiij d
Item De Turnour pro Anno decimo R' Ed iiij^{ti} xx s
Item De Hore pro opella quondam Thome Talour v s
Item De Paulo Tutonico xx d
Item De ten' quod Tenuit Antonius Tutonicus apud quadrivium iam in manibus Collegij xlvj s viij d
Item De Dudley iij s ix d
Item De Eodem pro Anno Magistri Hulle viij s iii d
Item De Brystow pro A^{o} Tercio R' ed iiij^{ti} xiij s iiij d
Item De Eodem pro Anno Magistri ~~Dan~~ Banebryge xiij s iiij d
Item De Thoma Thalyour pro Anno tricesimo octavo v s
Item De Eodem pro anno `tercio´ R' ed iiij^{ti} x d
Item De Ricardo Wodde xij s
Item De Eodem pro tempore Magistri Banbryge ij s
Item De Johanne Halle xj s iiij d
Item De Willelmo Stokys xx d
Item De Moreley xvj s x d
Item De Johanne Manciple pro Anno xxxviij^{o} xvj d

[1] The dates of Pentecost for 1470–1471. See the note at the head of **F/60** above for their inclusion here.

Item De Roberto ffuller' pro quodam Gardino	xx d
Item De Johanne Cooke	iiij s ij d
Item De Ricardo Ware Carpentario	xxx s ij d
Item De Wappys	xxxviij s ij d
Item De Wryche	iij s iiij d
Item De Thoma Mancyple pro Allrychyte	ij s
Item De Pedyngtone	viij s iiij d
Item De Trygrane pro Anno quarto R' ed iiij^{ti}	ij s ij d
Item De pedyngtone Trygrane pro Anno Magistri Hulle	iiij s iiij d
Item De Eijsdem pro Anno Magistri Mydyleham	iiij s iiij d
Item De Eijsdem pro Anno Octavo R' ed iiij^{ti}	iiij s iiij d
Item De Eijsdem pro Anno Septimo R' ed. iiij^{ti}	iiij s iiij d
Item De Magistro Gyllote pro yrland'	v s
Item De Johanne Gower'	ij s ij d
Item De Johanne Herte	xij s viij d
Item De Baly Masone pro Annis 38 39 et primo R ed iiij^{ti}	xiij s iiij d
Item De Barton' pro terris in bellomonte pro Annis primo et secundo ed' iiij^{ti}	iiij s
Item De Uxor' Whytfeld' pro Annis 5° et 6° R' ed' iiij^{ti}	iij s
Item De Eadem pro Anno vij^{o} R' ed iiij^{ti}	ij s
Item De Eadem pro A^{o} viij^{o} R' ed iiij^{ti}	ij s
Item De Johanne Janyns	xiij s x d
Item De Johanne Chandeler'	xxvj s viij d
Item De Henrico Bathe	xxvj s viij d
Item De Palmer	x d
Item De Lampray pro Annis Magistrorum Banbrige et Thorlby	ix s iiij d
Item De Eodem pro tempore Magistri Hulle	x s
Item De Eodem pro anno vij^{o} R' ed iiij^{ti}	iij s iiij d
Item De Roberto Beste	x s
Item De Ricardo Cooke	xij d
Item De Corry	iiij s
Item De perkyns Brewer pro Gardino in parochia sancti Egidij	xvj d
Item De Eodem pro Anno vij^{o} R ed iiij^{ti}	xvj d
Item De Ricardo Brown pro Aula drowda pro A^{o} vij^{o} R' ed iiij^{ti}	iiij s

Item De Ten' quondam Ricard [*sic*] Wodde et alijs ten' iam in Manibus Collegij pro A° vij° iij li xviij s viij d
Item De Ten' quondam Thome Talyour in Manibus Collegij Anno Octavo R' ed' iiij[ti] xl s
Item De Ten' quod tenuit Scogan in Manibus collegij pro A° octavo R' ed' iiij[ti] ix s
Item De Willelmo Atkyns quarrario pro bonis Wappys xiij s iiij d
Item De Turnour pro bonis Johannis ffletcher' xviij s x d
Item De Edwardo Wodwarde pro A° decimo vj s
Item De Matheo Masone xiij d
Summa xxxiij li xv s x d

Arr' Aularum

In primis pro anno nono de Magistro Sutton' xviij s
Item De Magistro Molinerys pro Annis Magistrorum Gregford' et banbryge xxxvj s viij d ob q[a]
Item De Magistro Thoma proctour pro parva aula universitatis in alto vico xxij s ij d ob
Item De Eodem pro Anno vij° R' ed iiij[ti] xiij s iiij d
Item De Collegio ~~in manibus~~ pro eadem in manibus Collegij pro A° vij° R' ed iiij[ti] xl [*sic*]
Item De Magistro Summaster pro aula hampton et Sykyll' xxviij s iiij d
Item De Magistro Semer' pro aula universitatis in alto vico lj s j d q[a]
Item De Mancipio aule enee pro aula edwardi pro annis xxxix° R' henrici et primo R' ed iiij[ti] xvj s viij d
Item De Banbrig pro camera Magistri fford' in aula universitatis in vico scolarum xx d
Item De Magistro Lane pro camera in eadem viij s
Item De [*an erasure*] Stephano Clyfe et edwardo Lupton pro tempore Magistri Hull' viij s
Item De Camera quam occupant bedelli pro tempore M Hull' et Medleham vj s
Item De Eijsdem pro eadem camera pro anno vij° ij s
Item De eijsdem pro eadem camera pro ij[bus] terminis pro a° viij° ij s
Item De Colligio pro parva aula universitatis in vico scolarum in manibus collegij a° vij° liij s iiij d

Item De Magistro Willelmo Sutton' pro Aula Enea Aula sancti Thome Aula parva universitatis in vico scolarum Et pro gardino Aula scuti pro Anno octavo R ed iiij^{ti} iij li v s iiij d
Item De Wayer Mancipio pro eula edwardi pro Anno vij^{o} iiij s
Item De eodem pro eadem aula pro anno octavo R' ed. iiij^{ti} xvj s
Item De eodem pro ij^{bus} terminis pro anno nono viij s
Item De Symcokys pro Anno decimo vj s viij d
Summa xx li viij s iiij d ob

Arr' Scolarum

In primis de Carver de aula Hampton'	iij s viij d
Item De Clyftene Colligij Regine	iij s viij d
Item De Savghyld' de eodem	iij s viij d
Item De Magistro Granger	xx d
Item De M' Carver	xx d
Item De Magisto Cutter	vj s viij d
Item De M Lionell'	vj s viij d
Item De M Johanne Pantour	iij s iiij d
Item De M' quondam aule beate Marie	vj s viij d
Item De M' Wrytter Aule Cervine	vj s viij d
Item De Magistro Banbryg	vj s viij d
Item De M' Russell'	vj s viij d
Item De Magistro Willemo ffrestone	vj s viij d
Item De Hytone pro anno vij^{o}	iij s iiij d
Item De Wytte	xx d
Item De M Bakyr	vj s viij d
Item De M Witton	vj s viij d
Item De M Bakstre	vj s viij d
Item De M Keyll' de aula beate marie	vj s viij d

Summa iiij li xviij s[2]

Arr' Camerarum

In primis De Magistro fflemmyng	iiij s
Item De M' Willemo daniell'	xij s
Item De domino Alano Batsone	vj s viij d
Item De M' Thoma Pray	vj s viij d
Item De abbate de Ensham pro duobus terminis Anno vij^{o}	ix s

[2] [ADMC] The correct total is £4 17s 8d.

Item De eodem pro uno termino ann^{o} octavo iiij s vj d
Item De Magistro fippys pro di' unius termini et alio termino vj s
Item De eodem pro anno decimo xvj s
Item De M Thorlby vij s vj d
Item de Rector' asschyndenne v s
Summa iij li xvij s iiij d

Arr' liberorum ten'

In primis de Colligio animarum pro diversis Arr' ut patet in rotula facta vj^{to} Anno Regis ed' iiij^{ti} iiij li vij s iij d
Item De eodem pro anno vij^{o} pro ten' Johannis spronte v s
Item De eodem pro anno octavo pro eodem ten' eiusdem spronte v s
Item De eodem pro gardino retro dict' ten' pro anno vij^{o} viij s x d ob
Item De eodem pro gardino retro dictum ten' pro A^{o} 8° Regis ed iiij^{ti} viij s x d ob
Item De Abbatissa de Godstow pro diversis arr' in Rotula supradicta xvij s
Item De eadem pro anno vij^{o} pro shopa ex opposito magne porte sancte frideswide xx d
Item De eadem pro gardino quondam Maister xiiij d
Item De eadem pro anno octavo pro shopa ex opposito magne porte sancte frideswide xx d
Item De eadem pro gardino quondam Thome mayster pro A^{o} 8° R' ed' iiij^{ti} xiiij d
Item De Abbate de Osnay pro diversis Arr' in rotula predicta xl s
Item De eodem pro Anno vij^{o} vj s viij d
Item De eodem pro una shopa iuxta Johannem Spicer pro A^{o} viij^{o} R' ed. iiij^{ti} vj s viij d
Item De abbatissa de godstow pro shopa ex opposito magne porte sancte frideswide xx d
Item De eadem pro gardino quond' Thome Maister xiiij d
Item De Abbate de Osney pro shopa iuxta Johannem Spicer vj s viij d
[3]Item De Colligio animarum pro ten' quondam Spronte v s

[3] [ADMC] Entries from this point to the end of section were written very close together.

Item De eodem pro gardino retro dictum ten' viij s x s ob
Item De abbatissa de godstow pro Shopa ex opposito magne porte sancte frideswide pro a° decimo xx d
Item De eadem pro gardino quondam Thome Maister xiiij d
Item De abbate de Osney pro shopa iuxta Johannem Spicer vj s viij d
Item De Colligio animarum pro ten' quondam Johannis Spronte v s
Item De eodem pro gardino quondam retro dictum ten' viij s x s ob
Item De uxore Whytfeld' xij d
Item De Johanne Reede pro Anni decimo viij d
Item De albis Monachis pro anno decimo iiij s
Summa xij li iij s v d

Arr' in partibus remotis
In primis De Novo Castro xxj li xv s xj d
Item De Eodem pro Anno xxxix° v li xv s vj d
Item De eodem pro Annis 2° et 3° R' ed' 4ti vij li xvj d
Item De eodem pro Annis M Banbrig et Thorlby iij li viij s x d
Item De eodem pro Anno M Hull' iiij li ij s ij d
Item De eodem pro Anno vij° R' ed' iiijti xxj s vj d
Item De eodem pro Anno viij° R' Ed' iiijti xix s iiij d
Item De Thoma Brown' de pecunijs de Holdyrnesse iij s iiij d
Item De Holdyrnesse xij s vj d
Item De Holdyrnesse pro Anno vij° iij li xx d
Item De Holdernesse pro Anno viij° R' ed' iiijti viij s iiij d
Item De Johanne pownne pro Anno iij° R' ed iiijti xxviij s ob
Item De eodem pro Anno [*blank*] lv s
Item De eodem pro Anno viij° R' ed iiijti xlvj s iiij d
item de domino Thoma Tyrell' pro a° decimo x s
Item De Holdernesse viij s iiij d
Item De Johanne pownde pro Anno nono R' ed iiijti vij li xv s
Item De eodem pro Anno decimo R' ed iiijti viij li
Item De terris in Holdernesse pro Anno decimo iij li xx d
Item De Novo Castro pro Anno nono xx d
Item de eodem pro Anno decimo iiij li xvij s ij d
Summa lxxix li xiiij s ob

Summa omnium Arr' cxlxv li xvij s

Rentale

In parochia sancti Martini et omnium sanctorum

In primis de Edwardo Wodward' pro gardino quem [*sic*] tenet in Sweswynchyn vj s

Item De Ten' super quadrivium de Elizabeth Irynmonger' xxxiij s iiij d

Item De Ten' Thome Dudley xxxiij s iiij d

Item De ten' Johannis Brystow liij s iiij d

Item De ten' Spendyng' xxj s viij d

Item De eodem pro Camera pertinente ad ten' quondam Thome Taylyour iij s iiij d

Item De Throppe talyour xx s

Item De ten' Willelmi Barburr' xvj s viij d

Item De Surrurgico et Willelmo Cateryke xlvj s viij d

Item De ten' Thome talyour xl s

Summa xiij li xiiij s iiij d

In parochia sancte marie et sancti petri in oriente

In primis De ten' quod tenet Johannes Mortimar' xx s

Item De ten' Thomas Walys xx s

Item De ten' quod tenet Janyn Cooke xviij s

Item De Roberti ffletcher' xij s

Item De ten' quod tenet Turnour xx s

Item De ten' quod tenet Wattys ix s

Summa iiij li xix s

Aularum

In primis de M Willelmo Sutton pro Aula Enea xlvj s viij d

Item De Eodem pro Aula sancti Thome xviij s

Item De Eodem pro Gardino Aule scuti vj s viij d

Item De eodem pro parva aula universitatis in vico scolarum xxx s

Item De clerico ecclesie beate marie xvj s

Item De Domino Symcok' pro Aula universitatis in Alto vico xl s

Summa vij li xvij s iiij d

Scolarum

In primis de M Johanne Cartmale de Colligio Regine vj s viij d

Item De M Hanneley de Colligio Regali vj s viij d

Item De M Holcote eiusdem Colligij vj s viij d
Item De Domino Byrde de Colligio Dunell' iij s iiij d
Item De D ffox de Aula beate marie iij s iiij d
Item De d gilbert eiusdem Aula iij s iiij d
Item De d david eiusdem aula iij s iiij d
Summa xxxiij s iiij d

Camerarum
In primis De M Pavy viij s iiij d
Item De M Knyght et grysakyrys xvj s
Item De M ffyppys viij s
Item De Magistro Johanne Jonys `pro iij^bus terminis´ x s
Item De Rectore Aschyndene x s
Item De M Thorlby x s
Item De M Kyng viij s vj d
Item De doctore Bukmothe `pro ij^bus terminis´ viij s
Summa iij li xviij s x d

In Suburbijs et Campis
Item De M Pavy pro Gardino iuxta Castrum iij s
Item De Johanne Reede pro terris in bellomonte viij s
Item De eodem pro gardino in parochia sancti egidij xvj d
Item De priore ffratrum predicatorum pro pratis in yrland' et Arischytte xxj s viij d
Item De Johanne Ketyll' pro pratis retro Osnay xx s
Summa liiij s

In liberis tenementis
In primis de Abbatissa de Godstow pro Shopa ex opposito magne porte sancte frideswide xx d
Item De Eadem pro gardino quondam Thome Maister xiiij d
Item De Abbate de Osnay pro Shopa iuxta Johannem Spicer vj s viij d
Item De Collig' Animarum pro ten' quondam Rogeri Skybbow viij s
– Item De eodem pro ~~ten'~~ pro gardino retro dictum ten' viij s x d ob
Item De Novo Collig' pro Maydyn Hall' x s
Item De Collig' Cantuariens' pro Silverhall' ij s vj d
Item De Collig' Linc' pro Aul' Hampton sekkyll' hall' et gardino xlvj s viij d

Item De Albis Monachis pro gardino quondam tempore [*sic*] Bertone iiij s

[4]+ Item de eodem pro ten' quondam Johannis Spronte v s

Item De Johanne Jenyns pro defalcacione prati retro Osney iiij s iiij d

Summa iiij li xviij s x d ob

In partibus remotis

In primis de Johanne Pownde pro Manerio et molendinis de Merkyshall' xviij li iij s iiij d

Item De domino Thome Tyrell' milite xx s

Item De terris in Holdyrnesse iij li xx d

Item De Novocastro iiij li xvij s ij d

Item De Ecclesia de Arnclyff xx li

Summa xlvij li ij s ij d

Summa totalis Reddituum lxxxvj li xvij s x d ob

Recepta preter sortem domus xij li xv s

Item In pecunijs remanentibus in Cista viij li xij s vj d ob[5]

Summa Omnium Oneratorum cclxiij li ij s v d

[*Face of Roll*]

Allocaciones M Bakster[6]

In primis De Thome Talyour `pro a° undecimo' v s

Item De Surrurgico pro ten' quondam Willelmi Stokes `pro a° 11°/ xj s viij d

Item De Turnour pro Anno undecimo x s

Item De Mortimare pro eodem Anno x s

Item De Thome Walys pro eodem Anno xvj s

. Item De Ten' super quadrivium pro Anno 9° xlvj s viij d

Item De Valys pro Anno decimo xvj s

Item De Turnour pro Anno decimo xx s

. Item De Paulo Tutonico xx d

[4] [ADMC] This entry refers to All Souls, as marks in the margin indicate.

[5] [ADMC] An erased figure between 'xij s' and 'vj d'.

[6] [ADMC] All the items with dots against them in the Allowances section are transferred to the Arrears Roll F/81 below.

. Item De ten' quod tenuit antonius tutonicus apud quadrivium iam in manibus Collegij xlvj s viij d
. Item De dudley iij s ix d
. Item De Eodem pro Anno M Hulle viij s iii d
. Item De Brystow pro anno 3° R' ed iiij[ti] xiij s iiij d
. Item De Eodem pro tempore M Banbryge xiij s iiij d
. Item De Thoma Talour pro Anno tricesimo octavo v s
Item De Eodem pro Anno 3° R' Ed iiij[ti] x d
Item De Ricardo Wodde xij s
Item De Eodem pro tempore M Banbryge ij s
[7]. Item De Johanne Hall' xj s iiij d
. Item De Willelmo Stokys xx d
. Item De Morelay xvj s x d
. Item De Johanne Mancipyll' pro Anno xxxviij xvj d
. Item De Roberto ffullerr' pro quodam gardino xx d
. Item De Johanne Cooke iiij s ij d
. Item De Ricardo Ware Carpentario xxx s ij d
. Item De Wappys xxxviij s ij d
. Item De Wryche iij s iiij d
. Item De Thoma Mancipyll' pro Allrychytte ij s
. Item De pedyn`g´tone viij s iiij d
. Item De trygrane pro Anno 3° R' ed iiij[ti] ij s ij d
. Item De pedyngtone et trygrane pro A° M Hull' iiij s iiij d
. Item De Eijsdem pro Anno Magistri Medleham iiij s iiij d
. Item De eijsdem pro Anno vijj° R' Ed iiij[ti] iiij s iiij d
. Item De Eijsdem pro Anno vij° R' Ed. iiij[ti] iiij s iiij d
. Item De Magistro ~~pro yrland~~ Gyllotte pro yrland' v s
. Item De Johanne Gower' ij s ij d
. Item De Johanne Herte xij s viij d
. Item De Balymason' pro Annis 38 39 et primo R ed iiij[ti] xiij s iiij d
. Item De Bartone pro terris in bellomonte pro Annis primo et 2° R' ed' iiij[ti] iiij s
. Item De uxor' Whtfeld' pro Annis 5° et 6° R' ed' iiij[ti] iij s
. Item De ~~Edem~~ eadem pro Anno vij° R' Ed iiij[ti] ij s
. Item De Eadem pro Anno viij° R' Ed iiij[ti] ij s
. Item De Johanne Jannyns xiij s x d

[7] There is a large hole in the parchment around the next ten entries or so; it must have been there when the parchment was first written, as all the entries are written around it.

. Item De Johanne Chawndeler' xxvj s viij d

Item De Henrico Bathe xxvj s viij d

. Item De Palmer x d

. Item De Lampray pro Annis M banbrige et Thorlby ix s iiij d

. Item De Eodem pro tempore M Hulle x s

. Item De Eodem pro Anno vij^{o} R' ed iiij^{ti} iij s iiij d

. Item De Roberto Beste x s

. Item De Ricardo Cooke xij d

Item De Corry iiij s

Item De Perkyns Brewer' pro Gardino in parochia sancti Egidij xvj d

Item De Eodem pro Anno vij^{o} R Ed iiij^{ti} xvj d

. Item De Ricardo Brown pro Aula drowda pro Anno vij^{o} R' Ed iiij^{ti} iiij s

. Item De Ten' quondam Ricardi Wodde et alijs ten' iam in Manibus Collegij Anno vij^{o} iij li xviij s viij d

. Item De ten' quondam Thome Talyour in manibus Collig' Anno viij^{o} R' Ed' iiij^{ti} xl s

. Item De ten' quod tenuit Scogane in manibus Collig' pro A^{o} viij^{o} R' Ed' iiij^{ti} ix s

. Item De Willelmo Atkyns quarrario pro bonis Wappys xiij s iiij d

Item De Turnour pro bonis Johannis ffletchere xviij s x d

Item De Matheo Masone xiij d

Summa xxxiij li xiiij s ij d

Allocaciones Aularum

. In primis De M Sutton' pro Anno nono xviij s

Item De M Molyners pro Annis Magistrorum Gregford' et banbryge xxxvj s viij d ob q^{a}

Item De M Thoma Proctour pro parva aula universitatis in alto vico xxij s ij d ob

Item De Eodem pro Anno vij^{o} R' Ed iiij^{ti} xiij s iiij d

Item De Collig' pro eadem in manibus Collig' pro A^{o} vij^{o} R' ed iiij^{ti} xl s

Item De M Summayster pro Aula Hampton et Sykyll' xxviij s iiij d

Item De M Semer' pro aula universitatis in alto vico lj s j d q^{a}

. Item De Mancipio de aula enea pro Aula edwardi pro Annis xxxix^{o} R' Henr' et primo R' ed iiij^{ti} xvj s viij d

. Item De banbryg pro camera M fford in aula universitatis in vico scolarum xx d
Item De M Lane pro Camera in eadem viij s
Item De Stephano Clyffe et Edwardo Lupton pro tempore M Hull' viij s
Item De Camera quam Occupant bedelli pro tempore M Hull' et Medleham vj s
+ Item De Eijsdem pro Eadem Camera pro ij^{bus} terminis pro Anno Octavo iij s
. Item De Collig' pro parva Aula universitatis in vico scolarum in manibus collegij a^{o} vij^{o} liij s iiij d
. Item De M Willelmo Sutton' pro aula enea aula sancti thome parva aula universitatis in vico scolarum et pro gardino Aula scuti pro Anno octavo R ed iiij^{ti} iij li v s iiij d
. Item De Ware mancipio pro Aula edwardi pro Anno vij^{o} iiij s
. Item De Eodem pro eadem aula pro Anno octavo R' ed. iiij^{ti} xvj s
. Item De Eodem pro ij^{bus} terminis pro Anno nono viij s
Item De Symcokes pro Anno decimo vj s viij d
+ Item De Eijsdem pro Eadem Camera pro A^{o} vij^{o} ij s
Summa xx li viij s iiij d ob

Allocaciones Scolarum
In Primis De M Cartmale de Collig' Regine vj s viij d
Item De M Hanley de Colleg' Regali vj s viij d
Item De M Holcote eiusdem Collig' vj s viij d
Item De domino ffox de aula beate marie iij s iiij d
Item De domino Gylbert eiusdem Aule iij s iiij d
Item De domino david eiusdem Aule iij s iiij d
. Item De M Carver de Aula Hampton' iij s viij d
. Item De Clyftone de Collig' Regine iij s viij d
Item De Saughyll' de eodem iij s viij d
Item De M' Carver xx d
. Item De M Cutter vj s viij d
. Item De M lyonell' vj s viij d
. Item De M `J´ Payntour iij s iiij d
. Item De M' `Ware´ quondam aule beate Marie vj s viij d
. Item De M' Wryter Aule Cervine vj s viij d
. Item De M Banbryg vj s viij d
. Item De M' Russell' vj s viij d

Item De M Willemo ffrestone vj s viij d
. Item De White xx d
Item De M Bakar' vj s viij d
Item De M Wyttone vj s viij d
Item De M Bakster vj s viij d
Item De M Hyndemarssh' vj s viij d
Item De M Granger' xx d
Summa vj li ij s viij d

Allocaciones Camerarum

. In primis De M fflemmynge iiij s
. Item De M' daniell' xij s
. Item De M Batson vj s viij d
. Item De M' Pray vj s viij d
. Item De Abbate Ensham pro ij^{bus} terminis 'R' ed iiij^{ti} a^{o} vij^{o} ix s
. Item De eodem pro uno termino Anni ~~viij~~ octavi iiij s vj d
Item de Rector' Aschynden pro A^{o} decimo v s
Item De Rector' chillery pro termino michaelis anni undecimi iiij s
Item De M Jonnys pro eodem termino xx d
Item De Doctor' Bukmothe et Magistro Jonnys pro ij^{bus} terminis viij d
~~Item De~~
~~Item De~~
Summa iij li xviij d

Allocaciones liberorum ten'

. In primis de Colligio animarum pro diversis Arr' ut patet in rotula facta 6° anno R ed' iiij^{ti} iiij li vij s iij d
. Item De Eodem pro Anno vij^{o} pro ten' Johannis Spronte v s
. Item De Eodem pro Anno viij^{o} pro eodem ten' eiusdem spronte v s
. Item De Eodem pro gardino retro dict' ten' pro Anno vij^{o} viij s x d ob
. Item De Eodem pro eodem gardino retro dictum ten' pro Anno 8vo R Ed iiij^{ti} viij s x d ob
. Item De Abbatissa de Godstow pro diversis Arr' in rotula supradicta xvij s
. Item De Eadem pro Anno vij^{o} pro Shopa ex opposito magne porte sancte frideswide xx d

. Item De Eadem pro gardino quondam Maister xiiij d
. Item De Eadem pro anno vij° pro shopa ex opposito magne porte sancte frideswide xx d
. Item De Eadem pro gardino quondam Thome Maister pro A° viij° R' Ed' iiij^ti xiiij d
. Item De Abbate de Osnay pro diversis Arr' in rotula predicta xl s
. Item De Eodem pro Anno vij° vj s viij d
. Item De Eodem pro una shopa iuxta Johannem Spicer pro Anno 8° R' ed. iiij^ti vj s viij d
. Item De Abbatissa de godstow pro shopa ex opposito magne porte sancte frideswide xx d
. Item De eadem pro gardino quond' Thome Maister xiiij d
. Item De Abbate de Osney pro shopa iuxta Johannem Spicer vj s viij d
. Item De Collig' animarum pro ten' quondam Johannis Spronte v s
. Item De Eodem pro gardino retro dictum ten' viij s x s ob
. Item De Abbatissa de godstowe pro shopa ex opposito magne porte sancte frideswide pro A° 10° xx d
. Item De Eadem pro gardino quondam Thome maister xiiij d
. Item De Abbate de osney pro shopa iuxta Johannem Spicer vj s viij d
. Item De Collig' animarum pro ten' quondam Johannis Spronte v s
. Item De Eodem pro gardino quondam retro dictum ten' viij s x s ob
. Item De uxore Whitfeld' xij d
Item De Johanne Reede pro Anno decimo viij d
Item De Albis Monachis pro Anno decimo iiij s
Item De eijsdem pro anno undecimo iiij s
Item De abbatissa de godstowe pro shopa ex opposito magne porte sancte frideswide xx d
Item De eadem pro gardino quondam Thome maister xiiij d
Item De abbate de Osney pro shopa iuxta Johannem spicer vj s viij d
Item De Collig' animarum pro ten' quondam Rogeri Skybbow viij s
Item De Eodem pro ten' quondam Johannis Spronte v s

Item De eodem pro gardino quondam retro dictum ten' viij s x s ob

Item De Johanne Jannyns `pro defalcacione prati retri osney pro A^{o} 11°' iiij s iiij d

Summa xiiij li iiij s vij d ob

Allocaciones in partibus remotis

. In primis De Novocastro xxj li xv s xj d

. Item De eodem pro Anno tricesimo nono v li xv s vj d

. Item De eodem pro Annis 2° et 3° R' ed' iiij^{ti} vij li xvj d

. Item De eodem pro annis Magistrorum Banbrige et Thorlby iij li viij s x d

. Item De eodem pro anno Magistri Hull' iiij li ij s ij d

. Item de Eodem pro Anno 6° xxxviij s iiij d

. Item De eodem pro Anno 7° xxj s vj d

Item De eodem pro Anno 8° xix s iiij d

Item De Thoma Brown' de pecunijs de Holdernesse iij s iiij d

Item De Holdernesse xij s vj d

Item De Holdernesse pro Anno 7° iij li xx d

Item De Holdernesse pro Anno 8° viij s iiij d

Item De Johanne pownde pro `a^{o}' 3° xxviij s ob

Item De Eodem pro Anno 6° lv s

Item De eodem pro Anno 8° R' ed iiij^{ti} xlvj s iiij d

Item De Holdernesse viij s iiij d

Item De Johanne pownde pro Anno nono R' ed iiij^{ti} vij li xv s

Item De eodem pro Anno decimo viij li

Item De Terris in Holdernesse pro A^{o} decimo iij li xx d

Item De Novocastro pro Anno nono xx d

Item De Eodem pro Anno decimo iiij li xvij s ij d

Item De Johanne pownde pro Anno undecimo vj li xviij d

Item De domino Thoma tyrell' milite pro A^{o} 11° xx s

Item de Novocastro pro Anno undecimo xxiij s

Item de Dikson pro Anno undecimo liij s iiij d

~~Item De~~

~~Item De~~

~~Item De~~

Summa lxxxx li xiij s iiij d ob

Summa omnium Allocatorum clxix li iiij s viij d ob

Expense facte per M Bakster

Reparaciones Aularum	
In primis In Aula Enea	iij li xiij s viij d
Item In Aula Edwardi	vj s vj d
Item In Aula universitatis in Alto vico	xv s ij d
Summa iiij li xv s viij d[8]	
Reparaciones laicorum ten'	
In primis \`In´ Orto edwardi wodward	iiij s vj d
Item In ten' super quadrivium	iiij s viij d
Item In domo dudley	xiij s ix d ob
Item In domo Willelmi Barbur'	ij s vij d
Item In domo Thorpe	ij s ix d
Item In domo Thome Talyour	v s ij d
Item In domo Spendyng	v s viij d
Item In domo Willelmi Catryke	xlj s j d ob
Item In domo Turnour	vj d
Item In domo Janyn Cooke	viij s iij d
Item In domo Mortimar	xx d
Item In domo Thome spencer	ij s j d
Item In domo fflecher'	vj s x d
Item In domo Wattes	iij s iiij d
Summa v li ij s xj d	
Expense facte infra Colligium	
In primis In Reparacionibus infra Collig'	xxxiij li xiij s j d
Item In Aula et Capella	xxxj s xj d
Item In Stauro	xxv s j d
Item In diminutis expensis	xij s iij d
Summa xxxvij li ij s iiij d	
Soluciones facte servientibus	
In primis Pincerne	xxvj s viij d
Item Coco	xx s
Item Barbitonsori	vij s iiij d
Item lotrici	v s iiij d
Summa lix s iiij d	
Resoluciones	
In primis priori sancte frideswide	xviij s viij d
Item Abbatisse de godstowe	x s

[8] [ADMC] The correct total is £4 14s 4d.

Item Abbati de Osney	xxij s ij d
Summa l s x d	

Soluciones ffacte socijs

In primis Magistro loci	xxxiij s iiij d
Item M Gregford	xxvj s viij d
Item M Marshall'	xxvj s viij d
Item M Mulcastre	xxvj s viij d
Item M Medleham	xxvj s viij d
Item ~~M~~ Eidem pro stipendio	xl s
Item M Witton	xxvj s viij d
Item M Baxter	xxvj s viij d
Item Eidem pro stipendio	xxx s
Item Eidem pro Officio Procuratoris	x s
Item M Hynemarssh'	xxvj s viij d
Item Domino Hyton'	xx s
Item Eidem pro stipendio	xxxiij s iiij d
Summa xvj li xiij s iiij d[9]	

Alie soluciones

In primis Edwardo Worwarde	vij s viij d
Item Dikson'	v s viij d
Item M pavy	iiij d
Item Thome Lawe	ij s
Item pro Renovacione Caucionum	xxxviij s viij d
Item In Equitacionibus	xx s vj d
Summa iij li xiiij s vj d	

Pro communis

In primis In communis sociorum	xvj li ix s v d ob
Item pro Batillis domus	xvj s iij d ob q^a
Item In Jurnellis	xij s v d
Item In Contribucionibus	xj s viij d ob
Item pro ffesto sancte Trinitatis	vij s iiij d

[9] [ADMC] The correct total is £17 3s 4d.

Item pro ffesto sancti cuthberti xj s xj d

Summa xix li xiij s j d ob q^{a}

Summa omnium Expensarum lxxxxij li xij s ob q^{a}

Summa remanens in Cista lvj s iiij d

Summa Omnium Allocatorum et Expens' cclxiiij li xiij s j d q^{a}

⟨Allocatis huius compoto allocandis et computatis computandis collegium debet computanti ~~x s viij d~~ q^{a}[10]. Acta sunt Hec coram nobis M Thoma Stephyn huius universitatis commissario generali xxviij° die Maij Anno infrascripto⟩

[*At foot of roll, and inverted*] A° xj Ed 4^{ti}

[*Very clear and well-preserved roll; 3 membranes. There appear to be 3 minor errors of addition, all in group totals – presumably in these cases the group totals are correct and a slip has occured in the figure entered against an item. The totals all balance – provided 10s 8¼d is taken as the figure of the total deficit, despite its apparent deletion; see footnote below.*]

[10] [ADMC] Deletion on original exactly as shown. But since 10s 8¼d is required as the correct figure, presumably this is not a deletion, but either a total entered on top of a deletion (which does not seem to the case on the MS), or a deletion made in error and supposed to be corrected by the cross-strokes (In next year's roll, 10s 8d is repaid to Baxter).

ARREARS ROLL FOR 11 EDWARD IV (ROLL UC:BU1/F/81)

1470–1471

BURSAR: SIMON BAXTER

Memorandum quod hec subsequentia debita ex[tracta sunt e Rotulo][1] Magistri Simonis Baxter procuratoris siv[e Bursarsij Colle]gij seu Magne Aule universitatis oxon' reddito per eundum Anno Regni Regis Edwardi quarti undecimo ut clarius evidet in rotula inde confecta.

In primis de Ten' super quadrivium pro Anno ix^{o}	xlvj s viij d
Item de aulo tutonico pro eodem tenemento	xx d
Item de tenemento quod tenuit Antonius tutonicus apud quadrivium in manibus Collegij	xlvj s viij d
Item de T Dudlay	iij s ix d
Item de Eodem pro Anno Magistri Hulle	viij s iii d
Item de Brystow pro a^{o} tercio Regis Edwardi quarti	xiij s iiij d
Item de eodem pro tempore Magistri Baynbrig'	xiij s iiij d
Item de Thoma Talyour pro A^{o} xxxviij^{o} \`et A^{o} 3°´ r ed iiij^{ti}	v s x d
Item de Johanne Hall'	xj s iiij d
Item de Willelmo Stokys	xx d
Item de Johanne Morelay	xvj s x d
Item de Roberto ffuller' pro quodam gardino	xx d
Item de Johanne Coke	iiij s ij d
Item de Ricardo Wer' Carpentario	xxx s ij d
Item de Wappys	xxxiiij s ij d
Item de Wryche	iij s iiij d
Item de Thoma Mancipyll' pro Allrychyte	ij s
Item de Pedyngtone	viij s iiij d
Item de Trygrane pro A^{o} iij^{o} Regis Edwardi quarti	ij s ij d
Item de Pedyngton' et Trygran' pro A^{o} M^{i} Hull'	iiij s iiij d
Item de eijsdem pro A^{o} M^{i} Myddyllham	iiij s iiij d
Item de eijsdem pro A^{o} viij^{o} R' Ed quarti	iiij s iiij d

[1] [ADMC] The roll is damaged here, and words in square brackets are taken from Smith Vol. VIII p. 203; the roll was probably already damaged in his time, since the words were underlined or underwritten with dots.

Item de eijsdem pro A° vij° R' Ed quarti iiij s iiij d
Item de M° Gyllote pro yrlaund' v s
Item de Johanne Goware ij s ij d
Item de Baly Mason' pro annis 38 39 et primo R ed quarti xiij s iiij d
Item de Barton pro terris in Bellomonte pro annis primo et secundo R' ed' quarti iiij s
Item de uxore Whitfeld' pro Annis 5to et 6to R' ed' quarti iij s
Item de eadem pro A° 7mo R' ed iiij^{ti} ij s
Item de eadem pro A° 8 R' ed iiij^{ti} ij s
Item de Johanne Jannyns xiij s x d
Item de Johanne Chandelar' xxvj s viij d
Item de Palmer x d
Item de lampray pro annis M' Baynbryg' et Thorleby ix s iiij d
Item de eodem pro tempore M^{i} Hull' x s
Item de eodem pro A° 7mo R' ed iiij^{ti} iij s iiij d
Item de Roberto Beste x s
Item de Ricardo Cooke xij d
Item de Ricardo Brown pro Aula drowda pro A° 7° R' Ed iiij^{ti} iiij s
Item de ten' quondam Ric' Wod' et alijs tenementis iam in manibus Collegij A° 7° iij li xviij s viij d
Item de ten' quondam Thome Talyour in manibus collegij A° 8 R' Ed' iiij^{ti} xl s
Item de tenemento quod tenuit Scogan' in manibus collegij pro A° 8 R' ed' iiij^{ti} ix s
Item de Johanne Mancypyll' pro \`a°' 38 et de Johanne Herte et Willelmo Atkynns In arrario pro bonis Wappys xxvij s iiij d

Summa xxvj li xvij d

In primis De M W Sutton' iiij li iij s iiij d
Item pro parva universitatis in alto vico in manibus collegij pro Anno vij° R' ed iiij^{ti} xl s
Item de Mancipio Aule enee pro Aula edwardi pro annis xxxix R' Henrici sexti et primo R' ed quarti xvj s viij d
Item de M' Baynbryg' pro camera M^{i} ffurth in aula universitatis in vico scolarum xx d
Item pro parva Aula universitatis in vico scolarum in manibus collegij A° 7° liij s iiij d
Item de War' mancipio pro Aula Edwardi pro A° 7° iiij s

Item de eodem pro eadem aula pro A^{o} 8 R' ed. iiij^{ti} xvj s

Item de eodem pro ij^{bus} terminis pro A^{o} 9 viij s

Summa xj li iij s

In primis de M Carver de Aula Hampton' iij s viij d

Item de Clyfton' Collegij Regine iij s viij d

Item de M' Cutter vj s viij d

Item de M Lyonell' vj s viij d

Item de M' Johanne Paynter iij s iiij d

Item de M' quondam Aule beate marie vj s viij d

Item de M' Wrytter Aule cervine vj s viij d

Item de M Baynbryg' vj s viij d

Item de M' Russell' vj s viij d

Item de Whyte xx d

Summa lij s iiij d

In primis de Magistro fflemmyng' iiij s

Item de M' Daniell' xij s

Item de M' Batson' vj s viij d

Item de M' Pray vj s viij d

Item de Abbate de Ensham pro ij^{bus} terminis Re [*sic*] Ed iiij^{ti} A^{o} 7 ix s

Item de eodem pro uno termino Anni 8 iiij s vj d

Summa xlij s x d

In primis de Colligio animarum pro diversis arr' ut patet in rotula facta 6to A^{o} R ed' iiij^{ti} iiij li vij s iij d

Item de eodem pro annis 7 et 8 pro ten' Johannis Spronte x s

Item de eodem pro gardino retro dictum ten' pro annis 7 et 8° R ed iiij^{ti} xvij s ix d ob

Item de Abbatissa de Godstow pro diversis Arr' in rotula predicta xvij s

Item de eadem pro A^{o} 7° pro shopa ex opposito magne porte sancte ffrideswyde xx d

Item de eadem pro gardino quondam Thome Mayster xiiij d

Item de eadem pro A^{o} ~~7°~~ 8 pro shopa predicta xx d

Item de eadem pro gardino predict' pro A^{o} 8 R' Ed' iiij^{ti} xiiij d

Item de Abbate de Osnay pro diversis Arr' in rotula predict' xl s

Item de eodem pro A^{o} 7° R' ed iiij^{ti} vj s viij d

Item de eodem pro una shopa iuxta Johannem Spycer pro a° 8 R' ed. iiij[ti] vj s viij d

Item de Abbatissa de Godstow pro shopa ex opposito ut supra xx d

Item de eadem pro gardino quondam Thome Mayster xiiij d

Item de Abbate de Osney pro shopa iuxta Johannem Spycer vj s viij d

Item de Collegio animarum pro ten' quondam Johannis Spronte v s

Item de eodem pro gardino retro dictum ten' viij s x s ob

Item de Abbatissa de Godstow pro shopa ex opposito ut supra pro A° 10 x d

Item de eadem pro gardino quondam Thome Mayster xiiij d

Item de Abbate de Osnay pro shopa iuxta Johannem Spycer vj s viij d

Item de Collegio animarum pro ten' quondam Johannis Sprounte v s

Item de eodem pro gardino retro dictum ten' viij s x s ob

Item de uxore Whytfeld' xij d

Item de Abbatissa de Godstow pro shopa ex opposito ut supra xx d

Item de eadem pro gardino quondam Thome Mayster xiiij d

Item de Abbate de Osney pro shopa iuxta Johannem Spycer vj s viij d

Item de Collegio animarum pro ten' quondam Johannis Sprounte v s

Item de eodem pro gardino retro dictum ten' viij s x s ob

Item de Johanne Jannyns pro defalcacione prati retri osney iiij s iiij d

Summa xiij li xvj s v d ob

In primis de novo castro xvj li xv s xj d

Item de eodem pro A° xxix° v li xv s vj d

Item de eodem pro annis 2° et 3° R' ed' iiij[ti] vij li xvj d

Item de eodem pro Annis Magistrorum Baynbryg' et Thorleby iij li viij s x d

Item de eodem pro A° M[i] Hull' iiij li ij s ij d

Item de Eodem pro A° 6° xxxviij s iiij d

Item de eodem pro A° 7° xxj s vj d

Summa xlv li iiij s

[*Smith wrote here: Summa totius rotuli c li ob*]

[*A narrow roll of a single membrane, 5 inches wide. Clear and well-preserved, except for the heading. The roll lists all the items marked with a marginal dot in the Allowances of the main account in* **F/80**, *and no others. Presumably they are the arrears to be written off. However, in the section of Arrears in* **F/82**, *they are lumped together as the first item in each section, and are then omitted from the Allowances.*]